HISTORY OF
THE SECOND WORLD WAR
UNITED KINGDOM MILITARY SERIES
Edited by Sir James Butler

The authors of the Military Histories have been given full access to official documents. They and the editors are alone responsible for the statements made and the views expressed.

1. Lieut.-General Sir William Slim, G.O.C.-in-Chief, 14th Army

THE WAR AGAINST JAPAN

VOLUME IV

The Reconquest of Burma

BY

MAJOR-GENERAL S. WOODBURN KIRBY

C.B., C.M.G., C.I.E., O.B.E., M.C.

WITH

BRIGADIER M. R. ROBERTS, D.S.O.
COLONEL G. T. WARDS, C.M.G., O.B.E.
AIR VICE-MARSHAL N. L. DESOER, C.B.E.

The Naval & Military Press Ltd

LONDON: 1965
HER MAJESTY'S STATIONERY OFFICE

Published by

The Naval & Military Press Ltd

Unit 5 Riverside, Brambleside
Bellbrook Industrial Estate
Uckfield, East Sussex
TN22 1QQ England

Tel: +44 (0)1825 749494

www.naval-military-press.com
www.nmarchive.com

CONTENTS

                                                        Page

INTRODUCTION xxiii

CHAPTER I. PLANNING FOR THE 1944–45   1
    CAMPAIGN . . . .

CHAPTER II. THE ADMINISTRATIVE
    BACKGROUND (August 1944) . .   15

CHAPTER III. ARMY AND AIR FORCE
    REORGANIZATION (June–December 1944)   25

CHAPTER IV. 'CAPITAL' ANTICIPATED
    (August–October 1944)   39

CHAPTER V. JAPANESE PLANS (July–October
    1944)   53

CHAPTER VI. THE PACIFIC (August–October 1944)
    The Approach to the Philippines   63

CHAPTER VII. THE PACIFIC (October–December
    1944) The Battle for Leyte   73

CHAPTER VIII. THE PACIFIC (December 1944–
    March 1945) The Reoccupation of Luzon . . .   89

CHAPTER IX. PLANNING FOR THE ADVANCE
    INTO BURMA (August–November 1944) . .   101

CHAPTER X. REORGANIZATION IN
    SOUTH-EAST ASIA (November–December 1944)   113

CHAPTER XI. EVENTS IN CHINA AND THEIR
    EFFECT ON S.E.A.C. (November–December
    1944)   121

CHAPTER XII. THE ARAKAN FRONT
    (October 1944–January 1945) . . .   135

CHAPTER XIII. THE NORTHERN AND
    SALWEEN FRONTS (October–December 1944) .   143

CHAPTER XIV. THE CENTRAL FRONT
    (October–December 1944) 14th Army Crosses the
    Chindwin   149

CHAPTER XV. THE CENTRAL FRONT
(December 1944) Slim Changes his Plan .   .   163

CHAPTER XVI. THE CENTRAL FRONT
(December 1944–January 1945) The Advance to the
Irrawaddy   171

CHAPTER XVII. THE NORTHERN AND
SALWEEN FRONTS (December 1944–January
1945)   191

CHAPTER XVIII. HIGH LEVEL AND
ADMINISTRATIVE PLANS (December 1944–
January 1945)   199

CHAPTER XIX. THE ARAKAN FRONT
(January–February 1945) and EVENTS IN THE
INDIAN OCEAN (August 1944–February 1945)   211

CHAPTER XX. JAPAN RECONSIDERS HER
STRATEGY (January 1945)   .   .   .   225

CHAPTER XXI. THE PACIFIC (February–March
1945) The Capture of Iwojima   .   .   .   235

CHAPTER XXII. STRATEGIC AND
ADMINISTRATIVE PLANNING (February
1945)   241

CHAPTER XXIII. THE CENTRAL FRONT
(February–March 1945) The Crossing of the
Irrawaddy and the Capture of Meiktila   .   .   253

CHAPTER XXIV. THE NORTHERN FRONT
(February–March 1945)   275

CHAPTER XXV. THE CENTRAL FRONT
(5th–15th March 1945) The Battles of Meiktila and
Mandalay   283

CHAPTER XXVI. THE CENTRAL FRONT
(16th–31st March) The Battles of Meiktila and
Mandalay   297

CHAPTER XXVII. THE END OF N.C.A.C.
(March 1945)   315

CHAPTER XXVIII. PLANNING FOR THE
CAPTURE OF RANGOON (March–April 1945)   321

CHAPTER XXIX. THE ARAKAN FRONT
(February–April 1945) The Coast and Bay of Bengal
Cleared, 'Dracula' Mounted 341

CHAPTER XXX. THE CENTRAL FRONT
(1st–12th April 1945) The Capture of Pywabwe and
the Advance towards Yenangyaung . . . 355

CHAPTER XXXI. THE CENTRAL FRONT
(April–May 1945) The Battle of the Irrawaddy . 369

CHAPTER XXXII. THE CENTRAL FRONT
(April–May 1945) The Battle of the Rangoon Road
and the Reoccupation of Rangoon 381

CHAPTER XXXIII. AIR WARFARE IN
SOUTH-EAST ASIA (August 1944–May 1945) . 401

CHAPTER XXXIV. RETROSPECT . . . 415

INDEX . . 525

APPENDICES

Page

APPENDIX 1. The Chain of Command, South-East Asia, 20th June 1944 437

APPENDIX 2. Allied Oil Pipelines Completed, under Construction and Projected, August 1944 . . . 438

APPENDIX 3. The Principles of Joint Land/Air Action Defined by the Supreme Commander, South-East Asia, 17th June 1944 439

APPENDIX 4. Outline Order of Battle of Air Command, South-East Asia, 12th December 1944 . . . 441

APPENDIX 5. The Organization of Eastern Air Command, August 1944 and 12th December 1944 . . . 446

APPENDIX 6. Distances by Air from Air Bases in Assam, Eastern Bengal and Arakan to Principal Points in Central and Southern Burma 447

APPENDIX 7. The Distribution of the Japanese Army and Army Air Forces in August 1944, Showing Changes up to 31st January 1945 448

APPENDIX 8. Skeleton Order of Battle of *Burma Area Army*, 15th November 1944 452

APPENDIX 9. Japanese Merchant Navy Gains and Losses of Vessels over 500 tons, December 1941–August 1945 . 455

APPENDIX 10. Japanese Naval Order of Battle, 25th October 1944 457

APPENDIX 11. Proposed Maintenance and Forward Stocking Programme for 'Capital', including R.A.F. Requirements, August 1944 458

APPENDIX 12. Revised Chain of Command, South-East Asia, Resulting from Changes Introduced between 12th November and 4th December 1944 . . . 459

APPENDIX 13. The Assessment by 14th Army of Aircraft Required and the Airlift Available from 16th December 1944 to 15th May 1945, as Calculated on 11th December 1944 460

APPENDIX 14. The Cost of the Monsoon Campaign 461

APPENDIX 15. The Redeployment of Transport Squadrons of C.C.T.F. in support of 14th Army and XV Corps, December 1944–May 1945 462

APPENDIX 16. The Build-up of the Inland Water Transport Service on the Chindwin in 1945 . . . 464

APPENDIX 17. Composition of the Japanese *3rd Air Army*, November 1944–April 1945 470

APPENDIX 18. Outline Orders of Battle, Land Forces S.E.A.C., September 1944–May 1945 . . . 472

APPENDIX 19. Maintenance by Air of 14th Army during Phases 2 and 3 of 'Extended Capital', January–March 1945 496

APPENDIX 20. Deception Scheme 'Cloak', 25th January 1945 501

APPENDIX 21. Grouping of 14th Army for the Advance to Rangoon, March 1945 506

APPENDIX 22. Air Deliveries to 14th Army and XV Corps, January–May 1945 508

APPENDIX 23. Maintenance of 14th Army during Phase 4 of 'Extended Capital', April–May 1945 . . . 513

APPENDIX 24. 14th Army's Estimate of the Supply Position from March to May 1945, and Actual Deliveries in Tons a Day 517

APPENDIX 25. Tonnages Delivered to China Theatre, August 1944–June 1945 518

APPENDIX 26. The Supply of Petrol, Oil and Lubricants to 14th Army and 221 Group R.A.F., January–May 1945 519

APPENDIX 27. Code Names Used in the Text . 521

MAPS AND SKETCHES

MAPS

Facing page

1. Imphal—Shwebo .   .   15
2. Myitkyina—Lashio   39
3. Mandalay—Meiktila   55
4. Leyte .   88
5. Northern Luzon   100
6. North Arakan   .   134
7. South Arakan and Central Burma .   171
8. The Pacific (1944–45) .   .   .   252
9. The Irrawaddy Crossings (February 1945)   320
10. China (1944–45) .   340
11. Rangoon—Moulmein   414
12. The Indian Ocean (1944–45)   .   .   .   436
13. Burma and Malaya (1944–45)   .   *In pocket at end of volume*

SKETCHES

1. The Philippines .   .   .   *Facing page* 63
2. Palau Islands and Ulithi Atoll   .   .   66
3. The Battles of Leyte Gulf, Samar and Surigao Strait (October 1944)   84
4. Tiddim—Kalewa .   170
5. Kangaw   .   224
6. Iwojima   .   .   .   .   . *Page* 239
7. Army and Air Command Areas in Japan (February 1945) .   .   .   .   .   .   *Facing page* 240
8. The IV Corps Bridgehead at Nyaungu (13th–21st February 1945)   268
9. The Attack on Meiktila   272
10. Situation of 14th Army and Right Flank of N.C.A.C. on the 1st February 1945   274
11. Myitson—Mongmit   282
12. The Meiktila and Mandalay Battlefields superimposed over the Normandy Battlefield   284

13. Mandalay . . . . *Facing page* 302

14. 'Extended Capital' (19th December 1944–20th March 1945)   314

15. Dalet—An 354

16. The Defence of Meiktila (5th–30th March 1945) . . 360

17. Pyawbwe (1st–11th April 1945) . . . 368

18. Pegu (May 1945) 398

19. The Battles of the Irrawaddy and Rangoon Road . 400

20. The Economic Radius of Transport Aircraft from Air Bases   412

21. Diagrammatic Sketch of the India–Burma Lines of Communication (April 1945) 522

PHOTOGRAPHS

Most of the photographs in this volume are Crown copyright and are reproduced by the courtesy of the Imperial War Museum and the Ministries concerned. For permission to reproduce Nos. 4, 5, 43 and 44 the authors are indebted to the Japanese War History Office, Tokyo, for Nos. 65 and 66 to Mr. F. S. V. Donnison, for No. 7 to Harlip Ltd., New Bond Street, London S.W.1, for No. 21 to Gale & Polden, Aldershot and for No. 22 to J. Russell & Sons, Queen's Gate, London S.W.7.

1. Lieut.-General Sir William Slim, G.O.C.-in-Chief, 14th Army . . . . *Frontispiece*

2. Lieut.-General Sir Oliver Leese, Bt., C.-in-C. A.L.F.S.E.A., and Major-General G. E. Stratemeyer, U.S.A.A.F., Eastern Air Command . . .

3. Admiral Sir Arthur Power, R.N., C.-in-C., East Indies Fleet . . . .

4. Lieut.-General H. Kimura, C.-in-C., *Burma Area Army* . . . .

5. Lieut.-General S. Katamura, Commander *15th Army* . . . .

6. Air Marshal W. A. Coryton, Commander R.A.F., Burma . . . .

7. Air Marshal Sir Guy Garrod, Acting C.-in-C., Allied Air Forces . . . . .

8. Major-General H. C. Davidson, 10th U.S.A.A.F., Lieut.-General D. I. Sultan, Commanding General, India–Burma Theatre, and Lieut.-General A. C. Wedemeyer, Commanding General, China Theatre . . . . . .

9. Major-General F. J. Loftus-Tottenham, 81st (W.A.) Division . . . . .

10. The Tiddim Road during the 1944 monsoon

11. Elephants clearing the track in the Kabaw Valley .

12. River fleet assembling on the Mayu River near Buthidaung . . . . . .

13. Kaladan: close support by Hurricane fighter-bombers at Paletwa . . . .

Following page 48

14. Major-General H. C. Stockwell, 82nd (W.A.) Division . . . . . .
15. Major-General G. N. Wood, 25th Indian Division .
16. Rear-Admiral B. C. S. Martin, R.N., in command of naval operations, Arakan . . .
17. Tank Landing Craft (L.C.T.) loading at Akyab .
18. Vehicle beach, Myebon . . .
19. Transferring from ship to assault craft
20. The Arakan Yomas, near Taungup Pass . .

Following page 136

21. Major-General D. F. W. Warren, 5th Indian Division (killed in an air accident February 1945) .
22. Air Vice-Marshal S. F. Vincent, 221 Group R.A.F.
23. Admiral Lord Louis Mountbatten addressing troops . . . .
24. Lieut.-General Sir Montagu Stopford, XXXIII Corps, Lieut.-General Sir William Slim, 14th Army, and Major-General C. C. Fowkes, 11th (E.A.) Division, at Tamu . . .
25. Manipur River bridge, the cable ferry
26. Ropeway across the flooded Beltang Lui
27. The Chocolate Staircase, Tiddim . .
28. The Stockades area, Tiddim–Kalemyo Road
29. Laying 'Bithess' on the Kabaw Valley Road .
30. Ramped Cargo Lighter (post-war photograph taken at Singapore) . . .
31. The Kalewa boat factory .
32. Bailey pontoon bridge at Kalewa
33. L.5 aircraft on Kalewa airstrip . . .
34. DUKWs crossing the Chindwin near Shwegyin
35. The Catwalk, Kalewa–Shwegyin Road .
36. The Yeu Road near Pyingaing . . .

Following page 190

37. On the way to the Kabo Weir, Sipadon Chaung .
38. On the way to Gangaw, Myittha River
39. Kangaw beach . . . . .
40. Landing craft striking a mine off Kyaukpyu (Ramree) . . . . . .
41. Landing craft on the way to Ruywa .
42. 36th Division's advance on Indaw, Pinbaw
43. Lieut.-General M. Honda, *33rd Army* .
44. Lieut.-General S. Miyazaki, *54th Division*
45. 25-pdr. gun in action at Myitson . .
46. Mules crossing the Nammeik Chaung at Myitson
47. Kyaukmyaung ferry . . . .
48. Typical scenery, Shwebo plain

Following page 208

49. The Myittha valley near Tilin   .

50. Scenery near Pakokku   .   .

51. An attack on Monywa   .   .   .   .

52. A human anti-tank mine: a Japanese soldier, shot
   by a patrol in a foxhole while waiting to detonate a
   250-lb. bomb by hand under a tank   .   .   .

53. Major-General C. G. G. Nicholson, 2nd Division

54. Major-General G. C. Evans, 7th Indian Division

55. Nyaungu from Myitche beach   .

56. Medium tank on a Bailey raft   .

57. Meiktila. Where do we go from here?

58. Devastation in Meiktila   .   .   .

59. Major-General T. W. Rees, 19th Indian Division .

60. First 'close-up' of Mandalay Hill   .   .   .

61. 6-inch howitzer bombarding Fort Dufferin at
   point-blank range   .   .   .   .   .

62. The result—breaches in the North Wall   .   .

63. Mandalay Hill from Fort Dufferin (Major-General
   T. W. Rees in foreground)   .   .   .

64. North-west corner of Fort Dufferin   .   .   .

Following page 286

65. Mount Popa from the north-west. Summit not
   visible, crater in saddle   .   .   .   .   .

66. Looking west from the summit of Mount Popa. Lip
   of crater right foreground, Pyinma Chaung in the
   distance   .   .   .   .   .   .

67. Chauk oilfield   .   .   .   .   .

68. Yenangyaung. Burnt storage tanks and camouflage
   of one on fire .   .   .   .   .   .

69. Paddy fields near Prome .   .   .   .

70. Motors and a Stuart tank bogged near Prome

71. Remains of Yamethin railway station   .

72. Jeep train on the Myingyan–Meiktila railway   .

73. Transport crossing an extemporised bridge over the
   Pyu River

74. Japanese prisoners taken at Penwegon   .   .

75. Major-General E. C. R. Mansergh, 5th Indian
   Division   .   .   .   .   .   .

76. Major-General H. M. Chambers, 26th Indian
   Division   .   .   .   .   .   .

77. Gurkha paratroops dropping to attack Elephant
   Point   .   .   .   .

78. Japanese machine-gun post at Elephant Point   .

79. Landing Craft on the Rangoon River   .   .

80. Vice-Admiral H. C. T. Walker, 2nd in Command,
   East Indies Fleet   .   .   .   .   .

Following page 382

81. Myitnge bridges destroyed by the R.A.F. . .
82. Bridge at Natmauk (probably destroyed by Japanese) . . . .
83. Japanese supply train set on fire by the R.A.F. near Pegu . . . .
84. Bridge on Bangkok railway after attack by R.A.F. Liberators . . . . . .
85. The air base at Imphal . . . . .
86. Dakota Transport Aircraft . . . .
87. Mitchell Medium Bomber . . . .
88. Liberator Heavy Bomber . . . .
89. Hurricane Fighter-Bomber . . . .
90. Spitfire Fighter . . . . . .
91. Mosquito Light Bomber . . . .
92. Thunderbolt Fighter-Bomber . . . .

Following page 416

PUBLISHED SOURCES

SOUTH-EAST ASIA AND CHINA

Vice-Admiral the Earl Mountbatten of Burma, Report to the Combined Chiefs of Staff by the Supreme Allied Commander, South-East Asia, 1943–1945 (H.M.S.O., 1951).

Despatch by Admiral Sir Arthur Power on Naval Operations in the Ramree Island Area, 19th January to 22nd January 1945.
(Supplement to *The London Gazette* of 23rd April 1948, No. 38269).

Despatch by Admiral Sir Arthur Power on Carrier-Borne Aircraft Attacks on Oil Refineries in the Palembang–Sumatra Area, January 1945.
(Supplement to *The London Gazette* of 3rd April 1951, No. 39191).

Despatch by General Sir George Giffard on Operations in Assam and Burma, 23rd June 1944 to 12th November 1944.
(Supplement to *The London Gazette* of 30th March 1951, No. 39187).

Despatch by Lieut.-General Sir Oliver Leese on Operations in Burma from 12th November 1944 to 15th August 1945.
(Second Supplement to *The London Gazette* of 6th April 1951, No. 39195).

Despatch by Air Chief Marshal Sir Keith Park on Air Operations in South-East Asia from 1st June 1944 to the Reoccupation of Rangoon, 2nd May 1945.
(Third Supplement to *The London Gazette* of 6th April 1951, No. 39196).

SLIM, *Defeat into Victory* (Cassell, 1956).

ROMANUS and SUNDERLAND, *United States Army in World War II: The China–Burma–India Theater, Stilwell's Command Problems* (Washington, 1956) and *Time Runs Out in C.B.I.* (Washington, 1959).

CRAVEN and CATE, *The Army Air Forces in World War II, Volume V, The Pacific—Matterhorn to Nagasaki (June 1944 to August 1945)* (Chicago, 1953).

THE PACIFIC

MORISON, *History of United States Naval Operations in World War II:*
Volume XII, Leyte, June 1944–January 1945 (Boston, 1955).
Volume XIII: The Liberation of the Philippines, Luzon, Mindinao, The Visayas, 1944–1945 (Boston, 1959).
Volume XIV: Victory in the Pacific, 1945 (Boston, 1960).

CRESWELL, *Sea Warfare, 1939–1945* (Longmans, Green & Co., 1950).

VAN WOODWARD, *The Battle for Leyte Gulf* (Four Square Books, 1958).

CANNON, *United States Army in World War II: Leyte, The Return to the Philippines* (Washington, 1954).

The War Reports of General George C. Marshall, General H. H. Arnold and Admiral Ernest J. King (Philadelphia and New York, 1947).

WILLOUGHBY and CHAMBERLAIN, *MacArthur, 1941–1951* (Heinemann, 1956).

CRAVEN and CATE, *The Army Air Forces in World War II: Volume V, The Pacific—Matterhorn to Nagasaki (June 1944 to August 1945)* (Chicago, 1953).

GLOSSARY OF TERMS
USED IN THE TEXT

Air commando: A composite American force of fighter-bombers, troop carriers, light aircraft and gliders for independent support of specific land operations.

Aviation
battalion: An American airfield construction unit.

Bithess: Hessian treated with bitumen which, laid over levelled soil in long strips with a slight overlap, produced a waterproof surface.

Chaung: Burmese word for a water course.

Combat Cargo
Group: Four squadrons of transport aircraft (American).

Combat road: An American term for a road made to support tactical operations.

Corduroy road: A road made across soft ground by laying tree trunks or logs transversely side by side.

DUKW: An amphibious vehicle.

Force 136: The S.E.A.C. branch of Special Operations Executive.

Jedburgh team: A Force 136 team consisting of two British officers with a Burmese military or civilian officer, whose task was to organize and act as staff for Levies or resistance groups.

Jeep train: Railway trucks drawn by a jeep fitted with flanged wheels.

Special group: A Force 136 team normally composed of two British officers, one British other rank, two wireless operators and fifteen Burmese other ranks, whose main task was the raising of guerrilla forces.

Tank farm: A collection of storage tanks for petrol, oil and lubricants.

LIST OF ABBREVIATIONS
USED IN THE TEXT

Air O.P.	Air observation post (an army light aircraft used to spot for the artillery).
A.F.O.	Anti-Fascist Organization (in Burma).
A.G.R.E.	Army Group Royal Engineers.
A.L.F.S.E.A.	Allied Land Forces South-East Asia.
A. & M.T.	(Formation provided with) animal and motor transport.
B.N.A.	Burma National Army (Japanese-sponsored Burmese military organization).
C.A.A.T.O.	Combined Army Air Transport Organization.
C.A.G.R.E.	Commander Army Group Royal Engineers.
C.B.I.	China–Burma–India (Theatre).
C.C.A.O.(B)	Chief Civil Affairs Officer (Burma).
C.C.T.F.	Combat Cargo Task Force.
C.R.E.	Commander Royal Engineers.
D.C.E.	Deputy Chief Engineer.
F.A.M.O	Forward Airfield Maintenance Organization.
F.B.E.	Folding Boat Equipment (engineer river-crossing equipment).
F.M.A.	Field Maintenance Area.
G.P.T. (or G.T.)	General Purpose Transport.
G.R.E.F.	General Reserve Engineer Force.
I.E.	Indian Engineers.
I.E.M.E.	Indian Electrical Mechanical Engineers.
I.M.B.	Independent Mixed Brigade (a Japanese formation equivalent to a British brigade group).
I.N.A.	Indian National Army (a Japanese-sponsored organization recruited from Indian nationals in Japanese-occupied territory).
I.W.T.	Inland Water Transport.
L.C.A.	Assault landing craft.
L.C.G.	Gun landing craft.
L.C.I.	Infantry landing craft.
L.C.M.	Mechanized landing craft.
L.C.P.	Personnel landing craft.
L.C.S.	Support landing craft.
L.C.T.	Tank landing craft.
L.S.I.	Infantry landing ship.
L.S.T.	Tank landing ship.
L. of C.	Line of Communication
N.C.A.C.	Northern Combat Area Command.
P.I.A.T.	Projectile, Infantry Anti-tank.
P.O.L.	Petrol, Oil and Lubricants.

R.A.M.O.	Rear Airfield Maintenance Organization.
R.C.L.	Ramped Cargo Lighter.
S.A.C.S.E.A.	Supreme Allied Commander South-East Asia.
S.E.A.C.	South-East Asia Command.
S.O.G.	Small Operations Group (this controlled Combined Operations Pilotage Parties, Special Boats Section and the Sea Reconnaissance Unit).
S.P.	Self-propelled artillery (guns on tank mountings).
S.R.U.	Sea Reconnaissance Unit.
U.S.A.A.F.	United States Army Air Force.
V.C.P.	Visual Control Post (this accompanied forward army units to direct aircraft in the air on to targets by ground to air radio-telephone).

INTRODUCTION

ALTHOUGH this fourth and penultimate volume of the *History of the War Against Japan* covers the operations of all the Allied forces in South-East Asia and the Pacific from August 1944 to May 1945, it is primarily the story of one British/Indian Army—14th Army— and its commander—Lieut.-General Sir William Slim (now Field-Marshal the Viscount Slim). Slim had always felt, as he states in his book *Defeat into Victory*, that it would be necessary to defeat the Japanese armies in battle before the Allied armies could, with any assurance, break into central Burma and meet the enemy on his own ground. The Japanese High Command in Burma had played into the hands of the Allies by their attempt to capture Imphal in 1944. This ended in their defeat and made the reconquest of Burma possible.

The extent of the defeat of the Japanese *15th Army* is described in detail in Volume III. This volume takes up the story of the relentless advance into Burma by 14th Army, supported by 221 Group R.A.F., which, despite the severity of the monsoon, was undertaken without delay to ensure that the Japanese were given no time to reorganize and re-equip their battered forces. This advance from the Imphal plain across the Chindwin and the Irrawaddy almost to the gates of Rangoon, a distance of some 600 miles, which led to the reoccupation of Burma, is of itself an epic story. The volume shows how by flexibility in planning, by foresight, by superb administrative improvisation and by the utmost use of air supply, made possible only by the possession of complete air superiority, all the enormous difficulties imposed by jungle-covered mountains and broad rivers and the climate, as well as those imposed by the enemy, were overcome.

To enable the reader to understand how the many physical obstacles to an advance across the grain of the country into Burma with ever-lengthening lines of communication were overcome, considerable space has been devoted to administrative matters. The volume tells how by working air crews and their aircraft at a much higher rate than had up to that time been thought possible, by setting up a boat building industry on the banks of the Chindwin, by flying in engines and parts for river craft and bringing in by road and air locomotives and stores for the railways, the problem of maintaining an army so many hundreds of miles from its base was solved.

The final Japanese efforts at Meiktila to save their armies from utter destruction, although they failed, delayed 14th Army's advance sufficiently to make the race to reach Rangoon overland before the monsoon such a close-run matter that it eventually became necessary to launch an amphibious attack on the city as an administrative insurance, a decision which was justified by events but threatened to delay by several weeks the operations planned for the reoccupation of Malaya.

Although it was 14th Army which carried out the pursuit and the final destruction of the Japanese in Burma, a vital part was played by XV Corps which, supported by 224 Group R.A.F., secured the air bases at Akyab and Ramree essential for the maintenance of 14th Army as it advanced into southern Burma. The southward advance by the American-trained Chinese divisions and 36th British Division from Myitkyina not only covered 14th Army's left flank but made it possible for the Ledo Road to be connected to the old Burma Road and for a petrol pipeline to be operated eventually from Calcutta to Kunming and for heavy military stores and equipment to reach the Chinese armies by road. These operations have therefore been dealt with in sufficient detail to enable the reader to grasp their significance.

The Supreme Commander faced many difficulties in dealing with Allies whose objects differed in many ways from his own, and in conducting a campaign where the necessary resources were either not forthcoming from Europe owing to the delay in the defeat of Germany, or were being withdrawn to meet the wishes of an Ally. The embarrassment caused to Mountbatten by the demands for the withdrawal of the Chinese/American formations from the Northern front while 14th Army's operations were in progress, the failure of the Chinese Yunnan armies to carry out their part in the 1945 offensive and the repeated requests by Chiang Kai-shek and his American Chief of Staff, Wedemeyer, for the withdrawal of American transport aircraft from S.E.A.C. for use in China which, if acceded to, would have seriously prejudiced 14th Army's operations are described in some detail. It is shown how by perseverance and tact the Supreme Commander dealt successfully with the problems without losing the goodwill of either of his Allies. This provides many lessons for those who may be faced with inter-Allied co-operation in any future war.

The volume also covers, as in previous volumes, the American offensive in the Pacific, which resulted between August 1944 and March 1945 in the occupation of all the vital strategical areas in the Philippines and of Iwojima, thus bringing the Americans close enough to Japan to consider invading her territory. It does not, however, deal with the operations for the capture of Okinawa which began in April 1945, for these fit far better into the final volume.

We are indebted to Admiral of the Fleet Earl Mountbatten of Burma, Field Marshal Viscount Slim, Lieut.-General Sir Oliver Leese and many other officers, too numerous to mention by name, who have been good enough to read our drafts and send us their comments. We are grateful to Colonel S. Nishiura, War History Office,

Defence Agency, Tokyo, for information from Japanese sources and for research carried out in Japan on our behalf. We have had the advantage of using the Admiralty Staff History of the War Against Japan written by Major G. S. Goldingham R.M., the narratives written by Brigadier J. A. Blood and Brigadier M. Henry of the Cabinet Office Historical Section and the narratives prepared by Squadron-Leader W. M. Gould and Mr. D. Craik of the Air Historical Branch, Air Ministry.

Our thanks are due to the Cabinet Office Mapping Section under Colonel T. M. M. Penney for the excellent maps and sketches with which the volume is illustrated, to Miss M. M. Baird for her invaluable and careful research work and for the secretarial assistance given by Miss A. E. Davidson.

The quotation from *Allenby, Soldier and Statesman* is reproduced by kind permission of George Harrap & Company Ltd.

S.W.K.
M.R.R.
G.T.W.
N.L.D.

" . . . *while coolness in disaster is the supreme proof of a commander's courage, energy in pursuit is the surest test of his strength of will.*"

(Field Marshal Viscount Wavell, *Allenby, Soldier and Statesman*, Harrap 1946)

CHAPTER I

PLANNING FOR
THE 1944–45 CAMPAIGN

See Maps 6, 8 and 13

THE Battles of Imphal and Kohima described in Volume III were to prove to be the decisive battles of the war in South-East Asia Command (S.E.A.C.). They were entering their final phase when, on the 3rd June 1944, the Supreme Commander, Admiral the Lord Louis Mountbatten, received from the Combined Chiefs of Staff the directive which enabled him to begin planning for the 1944–45 campaign. In it he was directed:

'to develop, maintain, broaden and protect the air link to China in order to provide maximum and timely flow of P.O.L. [petrol, oil and lubricants] and stores to China in support of Pacific operations: so far as is consistent with the above to press advantages against the enemy by exerting maximum effort ground and air particularly during the current monsoon season; and in pressing such advantages to be prepared to exploit the development of overland communications to China. All these operations must be dictated by the forces at present available or firmly allocated to S.E.A.C.'

On the 9th June Mountbatten, in his turn, issued directives to his Naval Commander-in-Chief, Admiral Sir James Somerville, to 11th Army Group, General Sir George Giffard, to Northern Combat Area Command (N.C.A.C.), Lieut.-General J. W. Stilwell, U.S. Army, and to his Air Commander-in-Chief, Air Chief Marshal Sir Richard Peirse. These were to become operative on the 20th June when N.C.A.C. came under the direct command of Supreme Headquarters.[1]

Giffard's tasks were: in Arakan to maintain an active defence during the monsoon of the positions covering Maungdaw, and to prepare to capture Akyab by means of a land advance beginning as early as possible in the next dry season;[2] on the Central front, in order of priority, to re-establish communications on the Dimapur–Kohima–Imphal road not later than mid-July, to clear the Japanese

---

[1] For the issue of the directive see Volume III, Chapter XVII. For the reorganization of command in S.E.A.C. see Volume III, Chapter XVIII. For the chain of command in S.E.A.C. on the 20th June 1944 see Appendix 1.
[2] See Map 13 in end pocket.

forces from the Dimapur–Kohima–Imphal–Yuwa–Tamanthi area and to prepare to exploit across the Chindwin in the Yuwa–Tamanthi area after the monsoon. On the Northern front Stilwell was by October to seize and secure the Mogaung–Myitkyina area, construct, maintain and protect the road and pipelines from Assam to that area and establish and protect an oilhead and air ferry staging base within it.[1]

By the end of June, 14th Army (Lieut.-General W. J. Slim) had reopened the road to Imphal and was engaged in operations to destroy the two Japanese divisions north and east of Imphal,[2] and N.C.A.C. (Stilwell) had captured Mogaung and was investing Myitkyina. In co-operation with Slim, Giffard had by this time already begun to plan for his third task—exploitation across the Chindwin—as soon as the monsoon had ended. On the 2nd July, when he met Mountbatten at Sylhet, Slim said that a full-scale offensive could begin on the 1st November provided that he could be assured that he could have at his disposal on that date the forces he had had for the Battle of Imphal, and that his British units and Special Force,[3] which were seriously under strength, could be reinforced. Mountbatten gave the assurance Slim required but asked him for the early release of 50th Parachute (P.) Brigade for training. He also undertook to find as many reinforcements as possible to bring British units in 14th Army and Special Force up to strength. Slim immediately set up a tactical headquarters at Imphal and on the 11th, after consulting his corps commanders, sent Giffard his proposals for regrouping and resting his formations and, now certain that he would be in a position to resume the offensive in November, began to work on plans for the capture of Mandalay and Rangoon.[4]

On the 14th July, Giffard sent Mountbatten his proposals for carrying out that part of his directive of the 9th June which had not yet been completed. The Japanese, he said, were unlikely to be able to undertake any serious offensive action before the 1st January 1945 and, in order to retain the initiative, it was essential that the Allies begin their offensive before that date. The capture of Akyab would require at least four divisions. Since some of these could be employed more profitably on the Central front, he advocated the adoption of a defensive policy in Arakan and the use of the formations thus saved to add weight to the 14th Army offensive across the Chindwin. This

---

[1] The Arakan front extended from the Bay of Bengal to the Arakan Yomas, the Central front from the Chin Hills to the Naga Hills and the Northern front from Kamaing in the Mogaung valley to Myitkyina. See Map 13 in end pocket. In June 1944, 14th Army was deployed with XV Corps on the Arakan front and IV and XXXIII Corps on the Central front. The Northern front was held by five Chinese divisions and ancillary troops.

[2] See Volume III, Chapter XXIII.

[3] Special Force was the name given to the long-range penetration formations (the Chindits).

[4] See Volume III, page 365.

offensive should take the form of an advance in strength to cut the enemy's communications at some point between the Yeu–Shwebo area and Katha.

Two tank brigades and nine infantry divisions would be ready to begin operations in November.[1] By the 1st January, 50th (P.) Brigade and, provided adequate British reinforcements were made available, either two all-British or four mixed long-range penetration (L.R.P.) brigades would be ready for action. He would therefore have ample forces but, as some of them would have to be transported and initially supplied by air, he would need additional transport aircraft and the use of more air bases. To develop an adequate line of communications and organize a system of air supply, he would have to build roads and forward airfields and would therefore also need more engineering resources and general purpose transport (G.P.T.) companies. He asked for early decisions on broad policy covering the action to be taken in Arakan, the organization of an air-transported force, the provision of transport aircraft, G.P.T. companies and engineering resources, and the allotment of airfields east of the Brahmaputra for use by 3rd Tactical Air Force.[2]

On the same day that Giffard submitted his proposal the S.E.A.C. War Staff produced for Mountbatten's consideration three alternative plans which they considered would enable him to comply with his new directive. Two of these covered offensives into northern Burma by 14th Army, the N.C.A.C. forces and the Yunnan armies; the third covered an amphibious operation to establish a base at Rangoon and exploit northwards. Stilwell also submitted a plan of his own based on an advance from Myitkyina by way of Lashio to cut the Japanese lines of communication in the vicinity of Meiktila. Mountbatten considered these various plans at a series of conferences with his three Commanders-in-Chief, Lieut.-General D. I. Sultan, U.S. Army, who represented Stilwell (Commanding-General, China–Burma–India Theatre), and Major-General G. E. Stratemeyer, U.S. Army Air Force (Commanding-General, Eastern Air Command). He eventually decided to forward for consideration by the Chiefs of Staff two alternative plans for a post-monsoon offensive.

On the 23rd July, Mountbatten told them that the first part of his directive (i.e. to develop, broaden and protect the air link to China) had already been provided for, and preliminary examination had suggested that the best way to implement the remainder was by a further direct advance into northern Burma. He had, however, been asked in June to submit plans for the capture of Rangoon, and it appeared that such an operation might achieve the object of the

---

[1] This allowed for the fact that one division was already allotted to N.C.A.C., one was in G.H.Q., India, reserve, and two were resting.
[2] He calculated that four combat cargo groups and four airfields would be necessary.

directive as effectively as an advance into northern Burma, though less directly.

The first of the two plans (which was eventually given the code name of 'Capital') was for an advance to the general line Pakokku–Mandalay–Lashio in order to gain control of the centres in Burma from which communications led to the north, and thus prevent any large-scale enemy infiltration across the trace of the proposed road and pipelines to China. The operation would be launched in mid-November from the positions which should have been reached by that time, i.e. 14th Army from the line of the Chindwin as far south as Yuwa, the N.C.A.C. forces from a point on the railway some thirty-five miles south-west of Mogaung and on the Bhamo road some forty-five miles south of Myitkyina, and the Chinese Yunnan armies from the general line Tengchung–Lameng. It would be carried out in four phases, long-range penetration forces being used in the first three. In the first, to take place between mid-November and the end of January, 14th Army was to capture the Kalemyo–Kalewa area and establish bridgeheads across the Chindwin, and the N.C.A.C. forces were to advance southwards through Bhamo and gain the general line Sikaw–Namhkam, while the Yunnan armies captured Hsenwi. In the second, to take place during February and the first half of March, 14th Army was to occupy the Yeu area, and the N.C.A.C. forces, assisted by the Yunnan armies, were to capture Mogok, Mongmit and Lashio. In the third, beginning in the second half of March, 14th Army was to capture Mandalay and Pakokku, while the N.C.A.C. forces and the Yunnan armies consolidated the Maymyo–Hsipaw–Lashio area. The fourth phase was to be exploitation southwards towards Rangoon. Meanwhile vigorous minor offensive operations should contain the majority of the enemy forces in Arakan and south Burma.[1] The Strategic Air Force would be used to delay the arrival of reinforcements from outside Burma.

'Capital', Mountbatten continued, undoubtedly complied with his directive and had a good chance of success. It was the most direct way into Burma and if the Yunnan armies advanced, thereby clearing the old Burma Road to its junction with the trace of the new road by February 1945, a through road to China could be opened by March for the intermittent delivery of motor vehicles and artillery. The first 4-inch pipeline would reach Kunming by July 1945 and an all-weather road would be completed by January 1946. The operation could be carried out with the forces in and tentatively allotted to S.E.A.C., but would require a combat cargo group of four squadrons

---

[1] The object in Arakan was to secure, with the minimum force, the existing forward positions in the Maungdaw–Tunnels area, and prevent enemy penetration into the Kaladan valley which could bring them within striking distance of airfields south of Chittagong and threaten communications with Arakan. See Map 6, facing page 134.

and an air commando over and above the two combat cargo groups and No. 1 Air Commando already at his disposal.

The alternative plan (which was eventually given the code name of 'Dracula') was for the capture of Rangoon by an amphibious and airborne operation, with exploitation sufficiently far northwards to secure the Pegu area. The occupation of that area would cut the main Japanese lines of communication into Burma, with the exception of the road of limited capacity through Chiengrai and Kengtung. It would be carried out in January 1945 in co-operation with a vigorous offensive southwards by the forces on the Northern front as in 'Capital', and by 14th Army, both west and east of the Chindwin and in Arakan, to contain enemy forces in those areas.

Though less direct than 'Capital', 'Dracula' might, Mountbatten thought, prove the best solution if it forced the Japanese to withdraw from the north. It did not, however, comply with his directive in that it would require, apart from naval forces, the provision from sources outside S.E.A.C. of at least two infantry divisions and a parachute brigade, as well as large numbers of transport aircraft, gliders with pilots and British reinforcements.

Both plans committed S.E.A.C. to the reconquest of the whole of Burma. 'Capital' involved an advance from the north with all its inherent administrative difficulties and the postponement for a year of an airborne and amphibious attack on Rangoon. 'Dracula', on the other hand, began the right way round for the reoccupation of Burma.

Mountbatten went on to say that Stilwell believed that it was unsound to take the pressure off in northern Burma and go somewhere else on a venture of which the outcome could not be calculated, and that an operation on the lines of 'Capital', which would secure the road to China as early as possible, was required by the directive. Moreover, 'Dracula', which involved an unacceptable delay in securing overland communications with China, was not within the resources available to S.E.A.C. and involved risks unnecessary in the light of the current military situation in Burma.

'Since I am not', Mountbatten ended, 'in a position to judge whether either plan would be timely in relation to the Pacific advance, I am unable to say whether ['Dracula'] would sufficiently comply with my directive to be acceptable. Nor do I know whether the additional resources can be made available. I therefore request the Combined Chiefs of Staff to give me directions as to which operation I am to prepare for; the latest date by which I must receive these directions is by 1st September if the programme of the offensive is to be adhered to and the Japanese are to be prevented from seizing the initiative after the monsoon.'

.   .   .   .   .

By early August, 14th Army had driven the Japanese from the Imphal plain, had occupied Tamu in the Kabaw Valley and had cleared the Tiddim road to a point some fifty miles south of Imphal. Headquarters IV Corps and four infantry divisions had begun to leave the forward area for rest and reorganization, and XXXIII Corps, with 5th Division on the Tiddim road and 11th East African (E.A.) Division in the Kabaw Valley, was pursuing the defeated Japanese formations to the Chindwin.[1] The first two of the specific tasks for the Central front, set out in the Supreme Commander's directive of the 9th June, had been completed and preparations were in hand for the third. On the Northern front Stilwell's forces had captured Myitkyina on the 3rd August and were in a position to begin the task of securing and developing the Mogaung–Myitkyina area as ordered. In Arakan no major operations could take place until October or later.

On the 29th July Giffard had issued an instruction to Slim and Stratemeyer to prepare, by the 24th August, detailed plans for an offensive–defensive in Arakan, and for an advance on the Central front as outlined in the plan ('Capital') which Mountbatten had submitted to the Chiefs of Staff. At a conference on the 1st August he told them that they were to assume that 'Capital' was to be launched during December, that their plans were to be based on existing resources, that a decision whether 'Capital' or 'Dracula' was to be carried out would not be reached before September and that, pending such a decision, they were to examine to what extent preparations for 'Capital' would also meet the needs of 'Dracula' and to what extent the two operations would conflict with each other.

During July the Chiefs of Staff had warned Mountbatten that they would require him to come to London for consultation as soon as the situation in S.E.A.C. permitted. Since Stilwell, who had said that he wished to exercise his right as Deputy Supreme Commander and act for Mountbatten during his absence, could not be spared from his command of the Northern front till the end of the month, the visit was arranged to take place early in August. Stilwell reached Supreme Headquarters on the 1st,[2] and on the 2nd the Supreme Commander left by air, arriving in London on the 4th.

Between the 4th and 9th August Mountbatten had long discussions with the Prime Minister and Chiefs of Staff on 'Capital' and 'Dracula'. Mr. Churchill, who was convinced that excellent strategical opportunities were being thrown away with the abandonment of 'Culverin' (an operation to capture northern Sumatra as a stepping-stone to

---

[1] See Volume III, Chapter XXIV.
[2] Stilwell was promoted to General on the 1st. See Volume III, page 394.

Singapore),[1] viewed with gloom any operation which would bog the armies down in northern Burma. He was prepared to support 'Dracula' as second best, but was unwilling to agree to an advance northwards after the capture of Rangoon. It might, he thought, be better to march to the east rather than stop and mop up Burma.

The Chiefs of Staff thought that the main consideration in the existing situation in north Burma was that the Allied forces could not remain quiescent and that, if they did not retain the initiative, the Japanese had the necessary strength to push forward once again and render the situation precarious. But, while realizing that the Allies were committed to further operations in north Burma, they feared that these would inevitably expand and might involve a gradual reconquest of Burma from the north. This, they said, would be 'a slow and costly process which we are most unwilling to contemplate'. They therefore desired to keep operations in northern Burma down to the minimum necessary to hold the enemy in check while 'Dracula' was carried out. They considered, however, that the weight of the assault on Rangoon proposed by Mountbatten was too light.[2]

In order to reach a reasonable decision on the alternative plans they felt it was necessary to consider their scope and timing. 'Capital' could begin in November 1944 and, in three successive phases, end in the capture of the Mandalay area by March or April 1945. 'Dracula' could not be mounted before March 1945 since the required resources could not be freed from the European theatre in time to launch it earlier, and the operation could not be launched in safety after March because of the approach of the monsoon. The resources from Europe could, however, be provided in time only if the European war ended by the 1st October 1944, or if the defeat of Germany had progressed far enough by that date to warrant the withdrawal of the required forces. The problem to be solved therefore was whether the operations against the Japanese in northern Burma could be carried out between November 1944 and March 1945 without committing to them any of the resources needed for 'Dracula'. In these circumstances they considered the correct solution would be to decide in principle to carry out 'Dracula' in March 1945 and in the meanwhile to carry on with preparations for the first phase of 'Capital'. If, on the 1st September, it was found that forces from Europe could be freed, then the decision to carry out 'Dracula' could be confirmed and operations in northern Burma limited to the first phase of 'Capital'. If, on the other hand, it was found that forces from Europe could not be released in time, then the whole of 'Capital' should be authorized and 'Dracula' carried out as soon as possible after the monsoon of 1945,

---

[1] See Volume II, Chapter XXVI.
[2] Mountbatten agreed that 'Dracula' had been planned on too light a scale, but explained that he had tried to avoid making excessive demands.

thus completing the reconquest of Burma during the winter of 1945–46.

On the 9th August, after further prolonged discussions, the Prime Minister and Chiefs of Staff reached a conclusion on the role British forces should play in the Far East. The necessary steps, they decided, had to be taken to contain the Japanese in northern Burma; proposals to prepare for 'Dracula' should be presented to the American Chiefs of Staff, and intensive efforts should be made, in co-operation with them, to launch the operation at the earliest possible moment whether Germany surrendered or not. Arrangements should be made forthwith to move four British/Indian,[1] and two British divisions to the Far East as soon as they could be spared from Europe and the Middle East. If organized German resistance collapsed early, the situation would be reviewed and a decision taken between 'Dracula' and some other amphibious operation such as 'Culverin'. Plans should be drawn up for the recapture of Malaya in readiness for the time when the necessary forces were available, and, finally, an offer to provide the greatest possible naval assistance in the Pacific should be made to the American Chiefs of Staff, it being impressed on them that Great Britain desired to take a share with them in the operations against Formosa and the mainland of Japan.[2] These decisions marked the end of the long argument between the Prime Minister and the Chiefs of Staff on British Far Eastern strategy which had first arisen when the Combined Chiefs of Staff had decided at the Sextant Conference in Cairo in December 1943 that the main theatre of the war against Japan would be in the Central and South-West Pacific.[3]

On the 12th the Chiefs of Staff sent a telegram to the Joint Staff Mission in Washington and instructed them to communicate its contents to the American Chiefs of Staff. They pointed out that since the Sextant Conference the American advance to Japan in the Pacific had been greatly accelerated, the Japanese had, they thought, strongly reinforced Burma and the likelihood of aggressive action by the Japanese fleet in the Bay of Bengal had become remote. The Allies now had overwhelming air superiority in South-East Asia, the capture of Myitkyina ruled out any purely defensive policy in northern Burma and the progress of the war against Germany had rendered possible the partial or total collapse of that country, thus possibly freeing forces from Europe in the coming months. The directive given Mountbatten in June had committed him to a long-drawn-out struggle in the jungles and swamps of Burma against an enemy possessing superior lines of communication. In S.E.A.C. during the first six months of 1944 some 40,000 men had been killed or wounded

---

[1] The 4th, 6th, 8th and 10th Indian Divisions were in the Middle East.
[2] See Map 8, facing page 252.
[3] See Ehrman, *Grand Strategy*, Volume V (H.M.S.O., 1956), Chapters XI and XII.

or were missing, but wastage from sickness and disease had amounted to about 282,000. Mountbatten, they said, had now prepared two plans, the first of which was to continue to engage the Japanese in northern Burma. This plan they felt bound to reject since it would merely lead to a continuation of the present unsatisfactory state of affairs. The second plan, the capture of Rangoon, was now made practicable by the large measure of air superiority which the Allies enjoyed in South-East Asia and by the Japanese inability to dispute the sea lines of communication in the Bay of Bengal. The capture of Rangoon and Pegu would at one stroke sever the enemy's main line of communication to the interior of Burma and provide the opportunity to destroy the Japanese forces, thus ending once and for all the military commitments in Burma. Until such an operation could be launched the Japanese would have to be held by offensive action south of Myitkyina, but the bulk of the forces necessary for this was already available. The Chiefs of Staff asked the Combined Chiefs of Staff to approve the plan and agree that every effort should be made to find from British and American sources the balance of the forces required.

The Chiefs of Staff went on to say that a strong British fleet was being built up in the Bay of Bengal and, since the bulk of it would not be needed for South-East Asia, it would be available to play its full part in the main operations against Japan. If for any reasons the Americans were not able to accept the support of this fleet in the main operations, the Chiefs of Staff would be prepared to discuss an alternative such as the formation of a British Empire task force to operate in the South-West Pacific under General D. MacArthur's command. They ended by proposing that Lieut.-General A. C. Wedemeyer, U.S. Army,[1] who had accompanied Mountbatten to London, should go to Washington at once to explain the proposed operations in detail.

Mountbatten, fully aware of the Chiefs of Staff's preference for 'Dracula', had meanwhile told Stilwell and his three Commanders-in-Chief that he had been asked to give his views on the operations which should be carried out in northern Burma up to March 1945 if 'Dracula' were ordered to be launched that month. He himself thought that the object of operations in northern Burma should be to secure the Mogaung–Myitkyina staging base and prevent Japanese operations from locking up troops required for 'Dracula'. After the monsoon the Japanese might undertake a limited offensive in Arakan and either attempt to repeat the 1944 Imphal offensive or launch a major offensive against the Mogaung–Myitkyina area. He felt satisfied that any threat to Arakan could be met, that a repetition of the Imphal offensive was unlikely, and that the most probable Japanese

---

[1] Wedemeyer was Mountbatten's Deputy Chief of Staff.

action was an offensive against Mogaung and Myitkyina. If, however, the Japanese were to attempt another offensive towards Imphal there would, he considered, be sufficient forces deployed in the area to meet it provided that they were withdrawn from their forward monsoon positions back to the Imphal plain, and such a withdrawal would not prejudice the security of the Mogaung–Myitkyina area provided 'Dracula' was carried out in March 1945. Before any Allied offensive east of the Chindwin could affect a decision by the Japanese to attack the Mogaung–Myitkyina area it must threaten their main line of communication to the north; such an offensive would involve such large Allied forces that it would not be possible to launch 'Dracula' in March 1945. He asked whether, in the commanders' opinion, any Allied offensive action west of the Chindwin would in any way affect or reduce the scope of a Japanese offensive of that type or whether, if the Northern front were reinforced by one division, the area could be held until March against any probable enemy build-up.

The Commanders-in-Chief and Stilwell were unanimous in their replies. The Japanese, they said, had been decisively defeated and had lost heavily in men and material. The 14th Army, which had been ordered to pursue them to the Chindwin and secure Kalemyo, was making excellent progress, and it would be unsound and unwise to limit the extent or scope of its pursuit. It was essential to retain the initiative and keep the Japanese on the run; failure to do so would allow them time to rest and reorganize and to plan to take the offensive. Pressure by 14th Army and N.C.A.C. could be maintained without using more troops than would be required by a defensive strategy and, provided it was continuously applied, all the Japanese could do would be to undertake a limited offensive in Arakan, which could easily be dealt with. Neither operations west of the Chindwin nor the reinforcement of the Northern front by one division would be of any value. The security of the Mogaung–Myitkyina staging base rested entirely on the maintenance of pressure on the enemy forces within the limit of the existing resources, thus preventing them from undertaking any offensive operations. The maintenance of such pressure would eventually result in the release of the maximum forces for 'Dracula', provided planned rehabilitation proceeded, but additional resources of all types would have to be found if 'Dracula' were to be launched in March.

Having received these replies Mountbatten told the Chiefs of Staff that he was in full agreement with a report prepared by the Joint Planning Staff in London which stated that, to safeguard the Allied position in northern Burma, operations in that area must include a threat to Mandalay. This would mean attaining the objectives set out for the first two phases of 'Capital' and involve most of the formations needed for the full operation. If 'Dracula' were to be launched in March 1945 the time relationship between the two operations would make it impossible to extricate any forces from 'Capital' in time for them to take part in 'Dracula'. The additional resources required for 'Dracula' from overseas would thus have to reach S.E.A.C. between the 15th October and the 15th January.[1] On the 17th August Mountbatten cabled Giffard that the Chiefs of Staff wished the first two phases of 'Capital' carried out as soon as possible, and 'Dracula' launched in mid-March 1945 with resources being made available from Europe. Giffard was thus able to inform Slim of the Chiefs of Staff's wishes before the 14th Army Planning Staffs had completed their appreciation and before Mountbatten arrived back at his headquarters in Kandy in Ceylon on the 24th August.

On the 1st September the American Chiefs of Staff informed their British colleagues that in their opinion 'Capital' should be carried out with the object of gaining the general line Kalewa–Shwebo–Mogok–Lashio with exploitation towards Pakokku and Mandalay. Should German resistance collapse or the situation in Europe develop in such a way that forces could be allotted to mount 'Dracula' in mid-March 1945, then that operation could take place provided the objectives of 'Capital' were maintained and its first two phases were not jeopardized by preparations for 'Dracula'.

On the 5th September the Prime Minister and the Chiefs of Staff sailed in the *Queen Mary* to attend the Octagon Conference in Quebec. During the voyage the extremely difficult question of freeing forces from northern France and Italy and of transporting them to the Far East in time for 'Dracula' was discussed. As the situation in Europe precluded any definite conclusions being reached, they decided to argue at Octagon in favour of 'Dracula' against 'Capital', admit that the ability to carry out 'Dracula' was affected by the situation in Europe and other circumstances, and make it clear that only if the problem of mounting 'Dracula' were to prove insoluble would 'Capital' be carried through.

On the 13th Mountbatten cabled the Chiefs of Staff that after further discussions with his Commanders-in-Chief he was most anxious to carry out both 'Capital' and 'Dracula', though if the latter were to be mounted in March 1945 India base would have to exceed its estimated capabilities by, in some cases, as much as 100 per cent. The defeat inflicted on the Japanese *15th Army* had produced a situation which was steadily being exploited, and was inevitably leading to the first phase of 'Capital' to an extent which would make

---

[1] The forces required from outside S.E.A.C. amounted to:
Naval forces—8 L.S.I., 48 L.S.T.
Land forces—One airborne division, five infantry divisions, one tank brigade, one Special Service (Commando) brigade and 35,000 base troops.
Air forces—750 transport aircraft and 600 gliders.

it unreasonable to cancel the second phase. To stop pursuing a beaten enemy would not only be misunderstood by the Americans, but would be most damaging to the excellent morale of 14th Army just as the difficult period of partial demobilization began in the United Kingdom. Although the Japanese forces in northern Burma were, except on the Yunnan front, beaten and in poor shape, reinforcements were coming in and the enemy might offer fairly stiff opposition in southern Burma. Were it not for this factor he would unhesitatingly offer to undertake 'Dracula' with whatever he could spare in March and take the risk rather than wait to make sure of it in November 1945, by which time Burma and the rest of the occupied territories might be on the point of being recovered as a result of final American victory in the Pacific. Even so, he was so anxious to avoid finding himself immobilized in northern Burma that, if all the additional forces required for 'Dracula' from overseas could not be sent, he would welcome the opportunity of investigating the degree of risk involved in mounting the operation in March with reduced forces.

At Octagon the Combined Chiefs of Staff agreed that the object of the Allies was to force the unconditional surrender of Japan by limiting her ability and will to resist by establishing sea and air blockades, conducting intensive air bombardments and destroying Japanese air and naval strength. If necessary, Japan was to be invaded and objectives in her industrial area seized. The Americans agreed to the request that a British naval task force should participate in the main operations against Japan in the Pacific, provided that such a force was balanced and self-supporting and that the method of employing it was decided from time to time in accordance with the circumstances.

With regard to operations in South-East Asia, the Americans stated that, over and above the two combat cargo groups and one air commando already allotted to the theatre, they had decided to provide one additional combat cargo group and one air commando for the C.B.I. Theatre in order to ensure that Mountbatten had adequate resources to clear and secure the land line of communications to China. The remaining combat cargo group of the four which had been provisionally allotted to South-East Asia in 1943 was now required for the operations to recapture the Philippine Islands.[1] It was accepted, however, that the ability to carry out 'Dracula' would depend very largely on the provision of transport aircraft, and that their provision would in turn depend on the end of the war in Europe, when there would be available some 2,200 American aircraft of this type.

The Combined Chiefs of Staff also approved the text of a directive to be sent to the Supreme Commander, South-East Asia, for 'Capital' and 'Dracula'. This read:

---

[1] For this allotment see Volume III, Chapter XI.

'1. Your object is the recapture of all Burma at the earliest date. Operations to achieve this object must not, however, prejudice the security of the existing air supply route to China, including the air staging post at Myitkyina and the opening of overland communications.

2. The following are approved operations:

(a) The stages of Operation "Capital" necessary to the security of the air route, and the attainment of overland communications with China.

(b) Operation "Dracula".
   The Combined Chiefs of Staff attach the greatest importance to the vigorous prosecution of Operation "Capital" and to the execution of Operation "Dracula" before the monsoon in 1945, with a target date of the 15th March.

3. If "Dracula" has to be postponed until after the monsoon of 1945, you will continue to exploit Operation "Capital" as far as may be possible without prejudice to preparations for the execution of Operation "Dracula" in November 1945.'

The directive was approved in turn by the Prime Minister and President and sent to Mountbatten on the 16th September.

Two days later Mountbatten asked the Chiefs of Staff to give him as soon as possible another directive authorizing him to make preparations for the reoccupation of Malaya, Sumatra and any other territories which might have to be occupied, so that the operational background should exist to support the demands he would have to make in advance for their rehabilitation.

Map 1

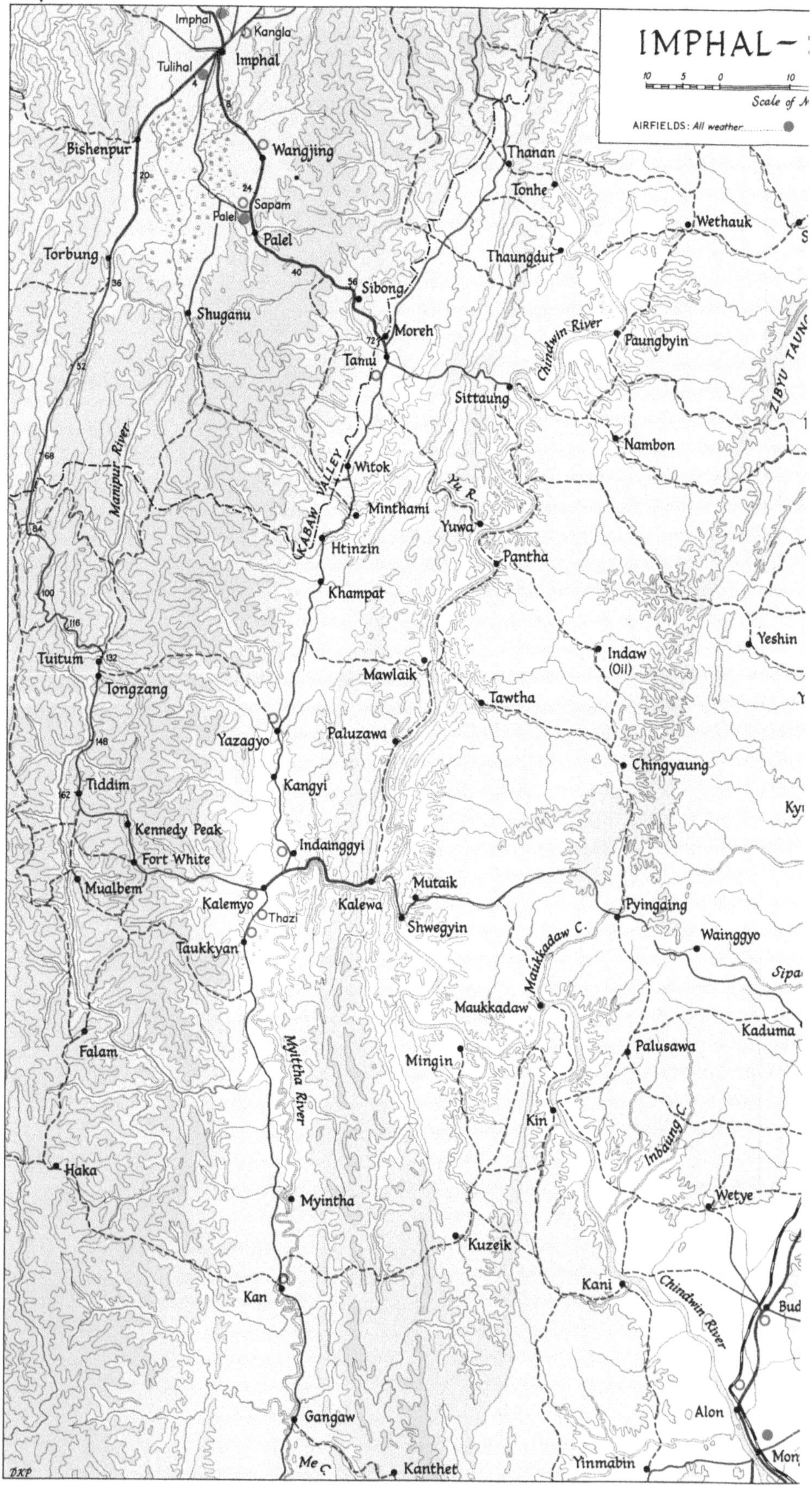

Imphal
Kangla
Tulihal
Imphal
4
8
Bishenpur
Wangjing
Thanan
Tonhe
20
24
Sapam
Wethauk
Palel
Palel
Torbung
40
Thaungdut
36
Sibong
56
Shuganu
Moreh
Chindwin River
Paungbyin
72
Tamu
52
Sittaung
ZIBYU TAUN
Witok
Nambon
68
Minthami
Yu R.
84
Yuwa
Htinzin
Pantha
100
Khampat
116
Indaw
(Oil)
Yeshin
Tuitum
132
Mawlaik
Tongzang
Tawtha
148
Yazagyo
Paluzawa
Tiddim
162
Chingyaung
Kangyi
Ky
Kennedy Peak
Fort White
Indainggyi
Mualbem
Mutaik
Kalemyo
Kalewa
Pyingaing
Thazi
Shwegyin
Winggyo
Taukkyan
Sipa
Maukkadaw C.
Maukkadaw
Kaduma
Falam
Myittha River
Mingin
Palusawa
Kin
Inbaung C.
Haka
Wetye
Myintha
Kuzeik
Kani
Chindwin River
Kan
Bud
Gangaw
Alon
Me C.
Kanthet
Yinmabin
Mon
DXP

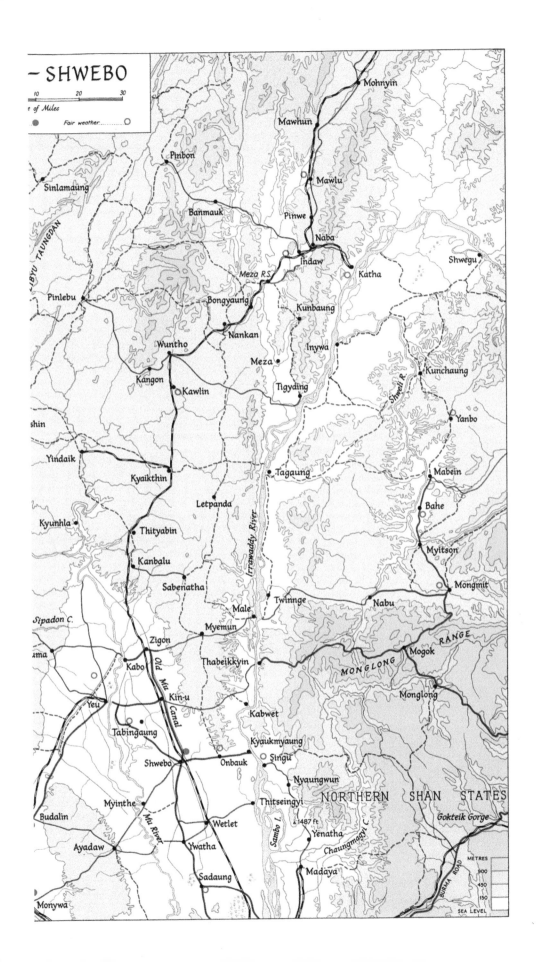

— SHWEBO

10 20 30

e of Miles

Fair weather............

Mohnyin

Mawhun

Pinbon

Mawlu

Sinlamaung

Banmauk

Pinwe

Naba

Shwegu

Indaw

Meza R.S.

Katha

Pinlebu

Bongyaung

Kunbaung

Nankan

Wuntho

Inywa

Kunchaung

Meza

Kangon

Kawlin

Tigyding

Yanbo

shin

Tagaung

Mabein

Yindaik

Kyaikthin

Bahe

Letpanda

Myitson

Kyunhla

Thityabin

Kanbalu

Mongmit

Sabenatha

Sipadon C.

Male

Twinnge

Nabu

Myemun

Zigon

RANGE

Kabo

Thabeikkyin

Mogok

ma

Kin-u

MONGLONG

Old Mu Canal

Monglong

Yeu

Kabwet

Tabingaung

Kyaukmyaung

Shwebo

Onbauk

Singu

Nyaungwun

Myinthe

Thitseingyi

NORTHERN SHAN STATES

Budalin

Mu River

Wetlet

▲ 1487 ft

Gokteik Gorge

Ayadaw

Ywatha

Yenatha

BURMA ROAD

METRES

Sadaung

Madaya

900

450

150

Monywa

SEA LEVEL

Irrawaddy River

Shweli R.

Sambo I.

Chaungmagyi C.

CHAPTER II

THE ADMINISTRATIVE
BACKGROUND
(August 1944)

See Maps 1, 6, 12 and 13 and Sketch 21

IN addition to the tasks of ensuring the internal security of India and defending the North-West Frontier, the responsibility for administering the country as a base for the supply and maintenance of S.E.A.C. lay with the Commander-in-Chief in India (General Sir Claude Auchinleck) assisted by his Principal Administrative Officer (Lieut.-General Sir Wilfred Lindsell). This involved the import, manufacture and storage of military equipment of all kinds, the provision of foodstuffs, the maintenance of rail and road communications within India as far east as Chittagong and the railheads at Dohazari, Dimapur and Ledo so that supplies could be sent forward to the fighting formations.[1] It also involved the provision of port facilities from which amphibious operations could be launched, the training and despatch of reinforcements to units and formations of the three services within S.E.A.C. and the establishment and maintenance of base hospitals for the sick and wounded.

The raising of an army of some 2·67 million men and the maintenance by India of 2·45 million of these,[2] coupled with the loss of her sources of supply in Burma and the Far East and the drastic reduction in her imports owing to shipping shortages, had placed a great strain on India's internal economy.[3] The shortage of coastal shipping, the fact that goods normally imported through east coast ports now arrived from the west and had to be transported overland, and the ever-growing demands of the armed forces had thrown a far greater load on the Indian railways than they were designed to carry. This extra load had to be met at a time when it was difficult to obtain

---

[1] See Sketch 21, facing page 522.
[2] This total was made up as follows:

Troops allotted to S.E.A.C.		1,050,000
Defence of India		300,000
Training formations and establishments		520,000
Staffs of arsenals and depots etc.		480,000
Indian state forces		100,000
	Total	2,450,000
Troops in European theatres		220,000
	Grand Total	2,670,000

[3] See Volume III, Chapters II and XXI.

replacements and some of the railway workshops had been switched to the manufacture or maintenance of military stores and equipment. The expansion of the armed forces increased the demand for consumer goods at a time when their production had been considerably reduced, and for foodstuffs, some of which were scarce. The resulting shortages and the inability of the overloaded railways to deal adequately with internal distribution led to foodstuffs being hoarded and to local famines. This in turn engendered a steep rise in prices and inflation.

Although drastic steps had been taken to improve India's economy, and to provide additional locomotives and trucks to enable the railways to meet the load they had to carry, the danger still remained that, as a result of economic difficulties, India's value as a base would be reduced in 1944. A major requirement towards ensuring her stability was a steady flow of imported wheat and great efforts had been made during the first half of 1944, despite the shortage of shipping.[1] Aware that the shipments delivered or on their way were not sufficient either to guard against famine or to maintain the level of India's war production, the Chiefs of Staff recommended in August that the despatch of 300,000 tons of wheat during the last quarter of the year should be regarded as a military essential. Drought, however, endangered the crops in Australia and shipments to India did not begin until December.

During 1943 plans had been made to establish a base in India capable of maintaining a force of 20 divisions and 154 R.A.F. and 30 Fleet Air Arm squadrons on behalf of S.E.A.C., in addition to the forces required for internal security of India and the defence of the North-West Frontier.[2] Work was begun in April and May 1943 on three major projects: the construction of two transit depots and four reserve bases, each to hold thirty days' supplies for the forces it was to maintain;[3] the expansion of the ports of Bombay, Cochin, Madras, Vizagapatam and Calcutta to enable them to embark, despatch and maintain large forces for amphibious operations; and the improvement of the capacity of the lines of communication to Assam to a maximum of 220,000 tons a month (7,333 tons a day) by the 1st January 1946,[4] with a corresponding increase in the capacity of the lines of communication to eastern Bengal and of the port of Chittagong.[5]

When planning for the reoccupation of Burma began in July 1944,[6]

---

[1] See Volume III, Chapter XXI.
[2] See Volume III, Chapter II.
[3] The four reserve bases were: No. 1 at Lahore and No. 2 at Benares for maintenance of the forces in India; No. 3 at Panagarh (98 miles west of Calcutta) and No. 4 at Avadi (20 miles west of Madras) for the maintenance of forces overseas. The two transit depots were at Calcutta and Vizagapatam. See Map 12, facing page 436.
[4] See Map 12, facing page 436. These figures included only dry stores and packed P.O.L. Bulk oil was to be sent forward by pipeline from Calcutta and Chittagong.
[5] See Volume III, Appendix 1 and Chapters II and XXII.
[6] See Chapter 1.

it was reckoned that India base would be some sixty to seventy-five per cent completed by the end of the year and would be able to meet in full all operational demands by May/June 1945. The various projects put in hand in the autumn of 1943 for the improvement of the capacity of the lines of communication to Assam and eastern Bengal had produced very satisfactory results.[1] Thanks to the relief afforded to the rail and river system by the construction of oil pipelines and the introduction of American railway troops to operate the railway between Parbatipur and Tinsukia, the overall rail and river capacity of the Assam lines of communications for dry stores and packed P.O.L. had reached 6,470 tons a day by August 1944.[2] The relaying of the railway over the hill section between Badarpur and Lumding, the doubling of the line between Lumding and Dimapur and the increased capacity of the Amingaon–Pandu ferry were expected to raise the capacity to 9,400 by 1945, thus exceeding the original target by some 2,000 tons a day twelve months earlier than laid down by the Chiefs of Staff.[3]

The lines of communication to eastern Bengal had similarly been improved by increasing the capacity of the Tistamukh–Bahadurabad rail ferry and its approaches, and by developing the port facilities at Chittagong. By August 1944 these lines of communication, including the river and rail routes as well as the direct sea route, could deliver at Chittagong some 5,150 tons a day of dry stores and packed P.O.L. (excluding stores required for the civil population) as well as some 1,100 tons of bulk P.O.L.[4]

The Assam Access Road from the broad-gauge railhead at Siliguri to Jogighopa on the Brahmaputra with a theoretical capacity of 180 vehicles a day was completed by August 1944. Vehicles could then be driven from Siliguri by way of the Jogighopa–Goalpara ferry and the all-weather Assam trunk road to Dimapur and Ledo without taking up capacity on the metre-gauge Assam railway. Work had begun in July 1944 to extend the Assam Access Road from Siliguri to the Grand Trunk Road north-west of Calcutta by repairing the old Ganges–Darjeeling road.[5] Work had, however, to be abandoned when a river near Siliguri changed its course, swept away long stretches of embankment and made it impossible for the road to be completed in time to be of use.

It had been planned in 1943 to deliver the requirements of P.O.L. in eastern Bengal and Assam, and in China by way of the Ledo Road,

---

[1] See Volume III, Appendix 5 for the projects.
[2] See Sketch 21, facing page 522.
[3] These figures included 1,100 tons a day by way of the Tistamukh ferry and the railway through eastern Bengal and over the hill section to Lumding.
[4] The average figure for dry stores and packed P.O.L. during March, April and May 1944 was only 2,800 tons a day. See Volume III, Chapter XXII.
[5] See Map 12, facing page 436.

partly by sending them forward in tank wagons or containers by rail to the railheads and by river to the river ports and partly in bulk through pipelines.[1] By August 1944 a British 4-inch pipeline, which was eventually to be extended along the Imphal Road to Tamu and Kalewa, was in operation from Chandranathpur (near Badarpur) to Dimapur.[2] This pipeline was fed temporarily by rail tank wagons from Chittagong, but its extension back to the port was under construction and would not be complete till February 1945. An American 6-inch pipeline was in operation from Calcutta to a tank farm at Tinsukia. By the installation of booster pumps and a branch pipeline, petrol, delivered by rail tank wagons at Parbatipur, could be pumped to Dhubri on the Brahmaputra for onward transport by barge to the river ports which were connected by pipelines to the airfields in north-eastern Assam as well as to Tinsukia and Digboi. A second American 6-inch pipeline, originally to run from Calcutta to Tinsukia, was now to follow the alignment of the British 4-inch line from Chittagong to Dimapur and thence by way of Tinsukia and the Ledo Road to Myitkyina and eventually to Kunming. This route was not only shorter but would enable airfields along it to be supplied, and tanker tonnage would be saved, since it could be fed direct from ocean-going tankers using a specially constructed berth near Chittagong port connected by a submarine pipeline to the shore. Work on it was not, however, expected to begin till mid-October and it would therefore not be in operation to Myitkyina until June 1945. Two 4-inch pipelines were under construction from Tinsukia along the alignment of the Ledo Road to Myitkyina, and it was estimated that one would be in operation in November 1944.[3] In September it was decided to extend one of these by way of Bhamo and Wanting to Kunming, and to terminate the other at Bhamo.[4] Early in 1945 it was decided to terminate the 6-inch pipeline at Myitkyina instead of extending it to Kunming.

In October 1944 Lieut.-General R. A. Wheeler (Principal Administrative Officer in S.E.A.C.) gave Lindsell (P.A.O. in India) the estimated requirements for dry stores and packed and bulk P.O.L. for both Assam and eastern Bengal for 1945. His figures were based on the assumption that full-scale operations for the reconquest of Burma would be continued, that the maximum aid by the air ferry route and, when opened, the Ledo Road would be furnished to China and that the build-up for 'Dracula' would proceed. Allowing fifteen per cent for unforeseen contingencies, the requirements for the Assam lines of communication for delivery at points on the river and railway

---

[1] For details see Volume III, Appendices 1 and 5, and Chapters II and XXII.
[2] See Sketch 21, facing page 522.
[3] These pipelines came into operation on the 2nd October and the 19th November.
[4] For details of the pipelines in operation and under construction see Appendix 2.

east of Pandu and Lumding were 10,580 tons a day by the 1st January 1945, dropping gradually to 9,885 tons by the end of the year; and for the Arakan lines of communication for delivery south of Chittagong and Dohazari, 6,625 tons, dropping to 5,335 over the same period.[1]

Early in November Lindsell replied that the capacity of the Assam lines of communication for military traffic east of Pandu, including traffic from eastern Bengal joining at Lumding, would reach 10,924 tons a day by the end of 1944, rising when the second American pipeline was in operation to 12,125 tons a day in July 1945, and that on the eastern Bengal–Arakan line of communications the tonnage would remain constant at 7,450 from the end of 1944. It was therefore evident that both these lines of communication would give ample capacity in excess of estimated requirements, and that there would be a wide margin of safety to meet contingencies such as serious interruptions during the monsoon. S.E.A.C. could therefore rest assured that all its requirements of supplies and P.O.L. could be delivered at Chittagong and the railheads at Dohazari, Dimapur and Ledo. To get them forward to the fighting formations was a problem which administrative staffs within S.E.A.C. would have to solve.

Communications to Arakan from Chittagong and Dohazari were by sea and land, supplemented in places by inland water transport (I.W.T.). The land line consisted of a one-way all-weather road with passing places from the railhead at Dohazari to Bawli by way of Chiringa, Ramu and Tumbru (at the head of the Naf River), with branches to Ultakhali and Cox's Bazar. Work on improving the Dohazari–Tumbru section of this road to a two-way all-weather standard had begun in June and was by August partly finished. From Bawli the road on to Maungdaw was two-way fair-weather, but most of the traffic for Maungdaw went by barge from Tumbru down the Naf River.[2] The sea line of communication was from Chittagong to Ultakhali, Cox's Bazar and Maungdaw by coastal vessels, sometimes towing barges. This route could be used as far as Cox's Bazar even in the monsoon, as there was sheltered water between the mainland and the off-shore islands.

---

[1] The breakdown of these figures in long tons was:

Nature of Stores	Assam East of Lumding		Arakan South of Chittagong	
	1/1/45	1/1/46	1/1/45	1/1/46
Dry stores and packed P.O.L.	7,360	5,860	5,175	3,885
Bulk P.O.L.	3,220	4,025	1,450	1,450
Total	10,580	9,885	6,625	5,335

[2] See Map 6, facing page 134.

These lines of communication were considered adequate to meet the requirements of XV Corps at a maximum strength of four divisions and a tank brigade, as well as the needs of the new airfields south of Chittagong required by Eastern Air Command for 'Dracula'. To relieve the strain on the road and to save motor transport, it was decided in October to develop an advanced base at Maungdaw, supplied direct by sea from Chittagong.

On the Central front forward of the railhead at Dimapur, 14th Army depended for its maintenance during 'Capital' on the Imphal Road as far as the plain. Beyond this point there were two alternatives: air supply from the group of airfields on the plain to forward airstrips built as necessary to keep pace with the advance, or an extension of the Imphal Road to Kalewa which, after the Chindwin River had been bridged, could be extended to Yeu.[1] Since the tonnage which could be delivered by air was at this time comparatively small compared with the army's requirements and neither tanks nor medium artillery could be moved by this means, the Imphal Road and its extension to Kalewa remained the main line of communication for 14th Army's advance. The extension of the Imphal Road to Kalewa could run either from Imphal by way of the Tiddim road and Fort White or through Tamu down the Kabaw Valley. The former was longer and offered considerable engineering difficulties, for it traversed a thickly forested mountain area with peaks of up to 8,000 feet in places.[2] There was not sufficient time to make it into an adequate line of communication for an advance in strength into Burma. The latter was therefore selected, despite the fact that it was more exposed to enemy interference and passed through highly malarious areas.

Since the Chindwin was navigable throughout the monsoon, the establishment before the 1945 monsoon of an I.W.T. service between Sittaung and Kalewa to relieve the Kabaw Valley road was considered. To make this a practical proposition, however, the thirty-six miles of road between Tamu and Sittaung had to be brought to an all-weather standard, which involved bridging the Yu River and cutting through some fourteen miles of rock in the hill section. Moreover, road transport would have to be provided to carry the I.W.T. craft from Dimapur to Sittaung. Since there was a considerable shortage of engineering resources and it appeared that road transport would barely suffice to meet the operational demands in the early phases of 'Capital', it was decided to concentrate solely on the construction of an all-weather two-way road down the Kabaw Valley to Kalewa which could carry the full load required by the army. This

---

[1] Air supply could be arranged from airfields farther west but, as the advance progressed, the long turnround would quickly render their use uneconomical.

[2] See Map 1, facing page 15.

decision did not, however, preclude, as a longer term project, the establishment of an I.W.T. service from Kalewa down river to Monywa and beyond for use in the later stages of 'Capital'.

Since the road from Dimapur to Kalewa would be liable to interruption during the monsoon, it had to be capable of carrying a much greater tonnage during the dry weather than that required for the day-to-day maintenance of the army, so that forward stocks could be accumulated. Its repair after the Battles of Kohima and Imphal and its extension to Kalewa as soon as possible after the monsoon thus became one of the primary administrative tasks. On the 1st July, shortly after the Imphal Road had been reopened, the Line of Communication (L. of C.) Road Transport organization (Colonel R. J. Holmes) began once again to operate as far forward as Imphal, employing a round-the-clock free running system with twenty G.P.T. companies and four bulk petrol companies.[1]

On the 1st August, 14th Army's advanced echelon, with its headquarters at Dimapur, resumed administrative control over all depots on the Imphal plain, and the L. of C. Road Transport organization began to operate as far forward as Palel. During August and September, owing to the monsoon weather, the poor state of the road after the battle, the shortage of labour and the density of operational traffic, the average turnround was considerably longer than before the road had been closed by the Japanese advance on Kohima.[2] Conditions gradually improved and, although the new organization began to operate as far as Tamu on the 1st October, the tonnage carried forward from Dimapur rose from 44,000 tons in July to 79,000 in October.[3]

It was estimated that, with a lift of 75,000 tons a month, a force of five divisions with corps and L. of C. troops and labour could be maintained from Imphal, though one division might have to be supplied by air. This lift, however, left little margin for the stocking of the forward depots during the dry weather. A further increase in the capacity of the road could, however, be expected since, by December, the number of G.P.T. companies would have been increased to twenty-five and there would be a greater number of 5-ton and 10-ton vehicles in the L. of C. Road Transport organization, even though by that time the organization would probably be operating as far as Indainggyi at the southern end of the Kabaw Valley.

Maintenance of the forces on the Northern front depended on the

---

[1] These companies consisted of one equipped with ninety-nine 10-ton, four with ninety-nine 5-ton, and fifteen with one hundred and thirty-two 3-ton vehicles. Each petrol company had fifty tankers.

[2] The turnround was 40 as against 26½ hours.

[3] During these four months deliveries increased at points between Kohima and Imphal by 5,500 tons, at Imphal by 10,500 tons and at Palel by 13,500 tons a month; deliveries at Tamu during October amounted to 6,000 tons. In the same period the vehicle mileage increased from 3 to 5.4 million miles a month.

Ledo Road and on air supply. The construction of a two-way all-weather road from Ledo down the Hukawng Valley to Myitkyina had begun early in 1943; when extended to join with the old Burma Road, it was to form a road link some 1,775 miles in length from Siliguri in northern Bengal to Kunming in China.[1] It was to be capable of maintaining those engaged in constructing and protecting it, and of delivering some 65,000 tons of supplies a month to China by the end of 1945.[2]

During 1944, however, it had become increasingly evident that the road would not reach Kunming until the end of 1945, by which time, as a result of the acceleration of their advance across the Pacific, American forces would either have occupied Formosa or have by-passed it and be operating well to the north. Enough stores could not therefore be delivered along it to re-equip the American-sponsored Chinese armies in time for them to co-operate with the U.S. Pacific forces; Major-General C. L. Chennault's 14th U.S.A.A.F. in China, however, would be able to co-operate, provided that it received adequate supplies from the airlift to China. In these circumstances it appeared that the carriage of large quantities of stores to China by road would not only be unnecessary but also uneconomical, since the vehicles using it would consume considerable quantities of petrol which would otherwise be available for 14th U.S.A.A.F.

In August 1944, the American Chiefs of Staff came to the conclusion that the C.B.I. Theatre should give priority to maintaining and increasing deliveries to China by air, to the construction of oil pipelines to China and to the delivery by way of the Ledo Road of only the stores required for building the pipelines and such artillery and vehicles as were required to re-equip the Chinese armies, thus considerably reducing the tonnage it would have to carry. Stilwell was told therefore that the road from Myitkyina through Bhamo to its junction with the old Burma Road at Wanting was to be two-way fair-weather standard only.[3]

At the beginning of August 1944 the Ledo Road had reached Shadazup, but its progress thereafter was so severely hampered by the monsoon that by the end of October it had been carried forward only the nine miles from there to Warazup. Road-building machinery had, however, been assembled at the head of the Mogaung valley so that work could begin as soon as the ground had dried out sufficiently. Since it was essential that a road should reach Mogaung and Myit-kyina as soon as possible, it was decided that the existing fair-weather road from Kamaing through Mogaung to Myitkyina should be improved and used as a combat road. For technical reasons the

---

[1] See Map 13 in end pocket.
[2] See Volume II and Appendix 1, Volume III.
[3] The length of the road from Ledo to Wanting was 483 miles.

extension of the Ledo Road forward of Warazup was to follow a different alignment, skirting the foothills east of the Mogaung River, passing north of Mogaung and thence east-south-east to join the Myitkyina–Bhamo road some eight miles north of Kazu.

As the weather improved, the combat road made rapid progress: it reached the Mogaung area early in November and was expected to be in use as far as Myitkyina by the middle of the month. The Ledo Road also made good progress and was expected to reach the Mogaung area early in January 1945 and Myitkyina–Bhamo two months later. Until the combat road was completed to Mogaung, 36th Indian Division, operating in the railway corridor, was without its own artillery and transport and was supplied entirely by air.[1] The Chinese divisions were based on Myitkyina which had an all-weather airfield. Between the capture of this airfield on the 17th May and the end of October, some 14,000 aircraft delivered on it over 40,000 tons of cargo, which included troops, light artillery, ammunition, food, heavy engineering stores and equipment.

---

[1] Five convoys totalling 315 vehicles with guns left Ledo between the 5th and 17th November and, travelling by way of Mogaung and Sahmaw, joined the division in the Mohnyin area before the end of the month.

CHAPTER III

ARMY AND AIR FORCE
REORGANIZATION

(June–December 1944)

See Maps 1, 10 and 13 and Sketch 21

TO fit the army to fight the Japanese in jungle country, the organization of the basic infantry formation in India—the division—had been adjusted several times, and by early 1944 there were no fewer than five different types in S.E.A.C.: the Indian light division, the Indian standard (A. & M.T.) division with either the higher or lower scale of motor transport, 36th Indian Division of two brigades each of four battalions organized for amphibious operations, and 2nd British Division, also organized for an amphibious role.[1] Having come to the conclusion that recent operations had shown that divisions designed for specialist roles were uneconomic and wasteful of S.E.A.C.'s limited resources, Giffard suggested to Mountbatten in May 1944 that all infantry divisions should be standardized. Provided it had an adequate period of training before being asked to carry out any particular operation, a standard division, he said, could perform all the tasks it was likely to be called upon to undertake, including air-transported and amphibious operations. For amphibious operations special units, such as beach groups, could be added to the standard division as necessary. Mountbatten accepted this proposal with the proviso that the reorganization did not interfere with the availability of formations for current operations.

By the end of May, at a conference between senior officers representing General Headquarters, India, 11th Army Group, 14th Army and IV, XV and XXXIII Corps, an organization for a standard infantry division capable of jungle fighting, of being transported by air and of undertaking amphibious operations was drawn up. Such a division was to consist of three brigades of three battalions each (to be increased to four as units became available), a reconnaissance battalion, a divisional headquarters battalion and a machine-gun battalion. The artillery was to consist of two field regiments, one mountain regiment and one anti-tank regiment. The engineers and signals were to remain as in A. & M.T. divisions. The scale of

---

[1] See Volume II, Chapter XIV and Volume III, Chapter III.

mechanical transport was to be reduced throughout the division and, in addition to unit first-line mules (which remained as in the existing A. & M.T. divisions), animal transport companies were to be provided on the scale of three for each division.[1] The reorganization of divisions allotted to S.E.A.C. was to take place as and when possible in the forward or rest areas, the extra units to bring them up to strength being added as they became available.

During the period of active operations in the first half of 1944, the wastage of British manpower in S.E.A.C. through battle casualties and sickness had increased to such an extent that the finding of replacements had become a serious problem. By the end of June most British infantry battalions were some eighteen per cent under strength, since the pool of British infantry replacements in India (calculated at four months' wastage at six per cent a month) which the War Office had to maintain was too small to meet the demands placed on it. The 11th Army Group proposed that the pool should be increased to five months' wastage, but this was impossible as the War Office was unable to maintain the pool even at its original strength owing to the demands of the war in Europe. In an attempt to improve the position Auchinleck had already agreed to reduce the forces required for the defence of the North-West Frontier and for internal security in India to well below what had formerly been considered the absolute minimum, and had combed out all the physically fit (A.1) men from garrison units and sedentary employment within India Command. In consequence there was no further source on which he could draw to meet the growing deficit in S.E.A.C.

At the end of June 1944 the British infantry units allotted to 14th Army were 3,500 men under strength and Special Force was short of 3,100 men. It was estimated that by the 1st November this deficiency would have increased to 11,000 and 7,300 respectively, making a total of 18,300 against which the replacements in sight totalled only 7,100, leaving an overall deficit of 11,200 men in infantry units alone. With the numbers at their disposal Mountbatten and Auchinleck found that it would be impossible to maintain the British infantry units allotted to Indian divisions as well as the British 2nd and predominantly British 36th Division and Special Force; they would therefore have to break up existing units and formations in order to

---

[1] The infantry battalion was to be simplified. The Bren carrier platoon was to be abolished and replaced by a battalion headquarters platoon organized as a rifle platoon. The strength of the rifle section was to be increased. The allotment of weapons was revised and limited to four 2-inch and six 3-inch mortars, the light machine-gun, the Sten gun, the rifle and bayonet and, as stocks became available, the new rifle grenade in replacement of the anti-tank rifle and the P.I.A.T. The transport was reduced to twelve jeeps and trailers, forty-one unit mules and fifty-four first-line R.I.A.S.C. mules.

find sufficient men to keep the formations engaged in operations up to strength. They decided that the best results would arise from giving priority to the deficiencies in the British infantry units forming part of Indian divisions in 14th Army and those in 36th Division which were in or were about to go into action. Since this would take all the available replacements they came to the conclusion that they would have to withdraw 2nd British Division into G.H.Q., India, reserve and, unless the War Office could provide additional reinforcements over and above the pool, reduce Special Force in size.

Since Mountbatten was most anxious to retain 2nd Division as a fighting formation, Auchinleck suggested in July the disbandment of three British light anti-aircraft regiments, and the anti-aircraft element of seven anti-aircraft/anti-tank regiments. This with a general reduction in artillery transport and certain readjustments in artillery organizations would release some 3,500 British of all ranks. Mountbatten agreed and decided to draft 2,500 men to bring 2nd Division up to strength for operations after the monsoon, and to use the balance of 1,000 towards the large deficiencies in Special Force. So that four brigades of Special Force could be reconstituted in time for operations, Mountbatten asked the Chiefs of Staff for 3,000 British reinforcements. None, however, were forthcoming. Plans were therefore made to break up 3rd West African (W.A.) Brigade and form three full-strength mixed British/Gurkha/West African brigades (23rd, 77th and 111th), 14th and 16th Brigades being reconstituted as and when reinforcements became available.[1]

The manpower problem worsened in September when the War Office decided that from the end of the year the qualifying period of service in the Far East for repatriation to the United Kingdom under the 'Python' scheme would be reduced from five to three years and eight months service. This meant an increase in the overall deficit for all arms in India Command of a further 5,700 men. In the second half of October, Mountbatten reported to the Chiefs of Staff that the overall shortage of British manpower in India Command and S.E.A.C. was about 30,000 men (including 11,000 infantry). He said that 10,000 men were urgently needed by 14th Army and requested that the deficiency should be made good within four months.

.   .   .   .   .

---

[1] Special Force originally consisted of twenty-four battalions (seventeen British, of which three were formed from artillery units, four Gurkha and three West African). Under this reorganization six British battalions (including the three from the artillery) were disbanded or dispersed; the three new mixed brigades absorbed five British, four Gurkha and three West African battalions, and the remaining six British battalions were left in 14th and 16th Brigade in cadre form. The reorganized Special Force consisted therefore of eighteen battalions, of which six were cadres only.

It had been decided in March 1944 that 44th Indian Armoured Division should be disbanded, but its headquarters and divisional troops took control (as 21st Indian Division) of the line of communication to Imphal and so remained in being. They were now to form the nucleus of an Indian airborne division consisting of 50th (P.) Brigade, a parachute brigade provided by the War Office from overseas and an air landing brigade found from within India Command or S.E.A.C.[1] The airborne division had not been formed by June and thus when the plans for 'Capital' and 'Dracula' were taking shape, both of which appeared to require airborne formations, the question of forming it was revived.

Since Auchinleck reported that the formation of such a division would interfere with the reorganization of the infantry divisions, and Giffard considered that airborne operations could be carried out equally well by a standard infantry formation reinforced by a parachute brigade, India Command and S.E.A.C. agreed that the formation of an Indian airborne division was undesirable. The Chief of the Imperial General Staff on the other hand believed that specialist formations were necessary in the initial stages of a major airborne operation. As it seemed that 26th Infantry Brigade (the only unallotted brigade available) would be needed to bring 36th Division up to full strength and a complete airborne division was not required until 1945, Mountbatten proposed at the end of August that its formation should be postponed. The War Office, however, considered that parachute formations would be required for both 'Capital' and 'Dracula' as well as for post-'Dracula' operations, and recommended that 44th Indian Airborne Division should be formed and begin its training without further delay. A decision was therefore made early in September to form the division as soon as its component units could be made available and training facilities provided. At the end of the month, when 26th Infantry Brigade was allotted to 36th Division operating on the Northern front, Mountbatten asked Giffard if he could find a brigade for inclusion in the airborne division from within his resources. Giffard replied that the only solution was to convert one L.R.P. brigade into an air landing brigade. To this Mountbatten agreed, and 14th (L.R.P.) Brigade was reconstituted during October with one Indian and two British battalions, converted into 14th Indian Air Landing Brigade and placed under command of 44th Airborne Division to begin training on the 1st November.[2] Auchinleck still hoped, however, that the second parachute brigade could be provided from the Middle East, but by November it became evident that the War Office was unable to make such a formation available.

---

[1] See Volume III, pages 316–17.
[2] The two British battalions were 2nd Black Watch and 2nd King's Own.

The original 'Capital' plan envisaged two brigades of Special Force being used in November,[1] but it was soon evident that no brigade would be ready for operations before 1945. In October Slim gave Special Force certain tasks for the later stages of 'Capital', but the change of plan in mid-December made these unnecessary; other tasks were suggested, but these depended on there being sufficient transport aircraft available.

At the end of December the Allied Land Forces Commander (Leese) paid a visit to Special Force and found himself 'not altogether happy with the state of [its] units'. This, in conjunction with the shortage of British manpower, the difficulties of finding a suitable operation for the force and the lack of transport aircraft to fly it in and maintain it even if a suitable operation could be found, brought him to the conclusion that the time had come to use its assets more profitably. He therefore proposed that 3rd (W.A.) Brigade should be reconstituted and returned to 81st (W.A.) Division and that, to ensure the readiness of 44th Indian Airborne Division for operations by October 1945, 77th Brigade should be formed into its second parachute brigade and that 14th Brigade (already part of the airborne division) should be brought up to strength by men drafted from Special Force.

On the 9th January Mountbatten asked the Prime Minister and Chiefs of Staff to agree to the break-up of Special Force. He explained that the force had been created for certain specific tasks and these had been fulfilled. With the Allied air forces masters of the sky and the army in S.E.A.C. having proved its superiority over the enemy, all that was now needed to speed the destruction of the Japanese forces were airborne troops and transport aircraft. He therefore wished to use the experience and training of the units of Special Force within the Indian airborne division. Later in the month Auchinleck sent the War Office a list of additional reasons why Special Force should be broken up. The force, he said, was organized and trained for one role and in that role it had sustained high wastage rates, which in many cases had reached ninety per cent in six months. Infantry in normal formations with proper artillery support were now defeating the enemy and yet sustaining far fewer casualties. Moreover, all the available British manpower was needed to complete and maintain units already in action and the shortage of reinforcements, made worse by the revision of the 'Python' repatriation scheme, was hampering the formation of the airborne division.

On the 5th February 1945 the War Office agreed to the disbandment of Special Force. The 77th Brigade was to become 77th Indian Parachute Brigade and with 50th Indian Parachute Brigade join

---

[1] See page 4.

44th Indian Airborne Division.[1] The 23rd and 111th Brigades were to be disbanded and 16th Brigade become a reserve brigade. The 3rd (W.A.) Brigade was reconstituted and rejoined its own division, and the remaining battalions were placed at the disposal of S.E.A.C.[2]

When S.E.A.C. was formed a large number of clandestine and para-military British and American organizations were in existence in India. Some of these were offshoots of world-wide intelligence organizations controlled from London and Washington, and others were of local origin. They included the Inter-Service Liaison Department (I.S.L.D.), controlled from London, whose task was to collect secret intelligence from and undertake counter-espionage in enemy-held territories; Special Operations Executive (S.O.E.), known in S.E.A.C. as Force 136, also controlled from London, whose main tasks were subversion, the preparation of resistance movements and sabotage by secret agents using raiding parties operating from bases established in enemy territory; the American equivalent of I.S.L.D. and Force 136 known as the Office of Strategic Services (O.S.S.); G.S.I.(Z), known as 'Z' Force, which dealt with internal security in India and the collection of information by patrols in enemy territory up to a distance of some sixty miles ahead of the fighting formations; Small Operations Group (S.O.G.), which included the Combined Operations Pilotage Parties (C.O.P.P.) and Special Boats Section (S.B.S.) which were commando-type parties for specific tasks such as maritime sabotage, attacks on isolated ports and beach intelligence; and finally the Political Warfare (P.W.) Section and its American counterpart, the Office of War Information (O.W.I.). These many organizations were functioning separately and each had little knowledge of the activities of the others, with the result that there was overlapping, waste of effort and confusion.

To co-ordinate their activities, Mountbatten formed a branch at his headquarters (known as 'P' Division) under Captain G. A. Garnons-Williams, R.N. and an American deputy. There were also at Supreme Headquarters 'D' Division, which had taken over and expanded the greater part of the Military Intelligence Directorate from General Headquarters, India, and was responsible for strategic

---

[1] The 50th Parachute Brigade consisted of one Indian and two Gurkha battalions. It and 77th Brigade were to be reformed with one British, one Gurkha and one Indian battalion each, which meant that they had to be given two British battalions from Special Force and an Indian battalion found from within S.E.A.C.

[2] The distribution in detail was: two British battalions to 44th Airborne Division for use in the two parachute brigades on reconstitution, one British battalion as divisional headquarters battalion of 36th Division, two British and three Gurkha battalions as reserves to replace war-weary battalions, one Gurkha battalion to replace the Indian battalion which was required to bring the parachute brigades up to strength, three British battalions in cadre form to 16th Brigade, one British battalion to A.L.F.S.E.A. for provost duties.

deception, and 'E' Group which, under the dual control of S.E.A.C. and India Command, was responsible for organizing rescue work and the escape of prisoners-of-war, if necessary in co-operation with the clandestine organizations. The 14th Army had its own intelligence groups; these included the Burma Intelligence Corps, whose main task was to furnish Burmese interpreters and guides for forward patrols, and 'V' Force, which provided intelligence from the area which lay closely behind the enemy's forward positions.[1]

In May 1944 the co-ordination of the tactical activities of the clandestine and para-military organizations with operations in the field was discussed at Supreme Headquarters. It was agreed that the strategic functions of such organizations were outside the responsibility of formation commanders, but that they should have operational control of these organizations when they fulfilled a tactical function. To ensure that the local activities in Burma of the various organizations were co-ordinated and that there was a proper distinction between their broad strategic functions (controlled by the Supreme Commander through 'P' Division) and their tactical activities, it was agreed that liaison officers from 'P' Division should be attached to 14th Army.

For the 1943–44 campaign 'V' Force had been organized into two zones, Assam and Arakan, the former covering the Central and Northern fronts and the latter the Arakan front.[2] The Assam zone had six groups, officered by volunteers from the army, the police and civilians with local knowledge. Each group consisted of a nucleus of platoons of Assam Rifles and men enrolled from the district in which it was to operate; the Arakan zone had three groups similarly formed around the nucleus of platoons of the Tripura Rifles.[3] To fit the force for the drive into Burma it was reorganized in August 1944 into three groups: the Assam and the Lushai groups for employment on the Central front, and the Arakan group for use on the Arakan front; the Assam Rifles in the case of the first two, and the Tripura Rifles in the last, supplying escorts for the operational headquarters within the groups. At the same time the original No. 1 Ledo group was placed under command of N.C.A.C. It was intended that, as the Allied armies advanced into Burma, the force should continue to operate by enrolling local inhabitants from liberated areas and disbanding those enrolled from areas no longer in the active zone. Its tasks remained as before those of obtaining local intelligence, particularly in areas

---

[1] For the formation of 'V' Force see Volume II, page 192.
[2] See Volume III, page 136 fn.
[3] The Assam zone consisted of No. 1 Ledo, No. 2 Kohima, No. 3 Imphal, No. 4 Chin Hills, No. 5 Aijal and No. 6 Tripura. The Arakan zone consisted of No. 7 Arakan, No. 8 Lungleh (acting as the link between the two zones) and No. 9 Kaladan.

beyond the normal patrol limits of the forward troops, and of acting as a link between the army and the local inhabitants.

Despite the existence of the various organizations for gathering intelligence, Slim found it necessary during the Battles of Imphal and Kohima to complain that he was without essential information of Japanese activities in rear of their forward areas and on their lines of communication.[1] He proposed that 'Z' Force should be expanded so that a network of some twenty patrols could be established in Burma to cover the whole area west of the Irrawaddy from Mogaung in the north to Henzada and Gwa in the south.[2] At the end of September he told Supreme Headquarters that he was forced to begin the autumn campaign blind, as he had no real intelligence of the enemy's dispositions along his whole front; only two 'Z' Force patrols appeared to have been formed and they had not yet gone into Burma, and no 'P' Division representative had yet been attached to his headquarters. He was told in reply that an officer of 'P' Division was being sent forthwith and would stop off at Advanced Headquarters A.L.F.S.E.A. to investigate the reasons for the scarcity of information reaching 14th Army from the organizations concerned, since the statement that there was no intelligence coverage of Burma was not confirmed by an analysis of the clandestine intelligence reports received.[3]

The intelligence situation on 14th Army front did not, however, improve and on the 27th December Slim told A.L.F.S.E.A. (which had now replaced 11th Army Group) that co-ordinated control of the clandestine and para-military organizations appeared to be entirely lacking and that their operational efficiency was extremely low. As a result of Slim's complaints a meeting was convened on the 4th January 1945 at Advanced Headquarters A.L.F.S.E.A. to examine his criticisms of the intelligence organizations, to consider the possibility of reducing the number of different British clandestine and para-military forces in the battle area and to decide on the best machinery for their co-ordination. After considerable discussion the meeting recommended that Force 136 and 'Z' Force should be amalgamated, that Force 136 should have the responsibility as its first priority for the collection of operational intelligence in the battle area and that all such intelligence should be reported direct to

---

[1] For example, the Japanese moved *151st Regiment* (less one battalion) from central Burma to the Bishenpur front without 14th Army receiving any information that the move was in progress. It was only when the regiment was identified by the forward troops in battle that it became known that the move had taken place. See Volume III, pages 345 and 354 fns.

[2] See Map 13 in end pocket.

[3] 'P' Division said that 521 reports had been received in the first half of 1944, and that in the previous six weeks some nineteen immediate operational reports had been sent to Headquarters 11th Army Group.

A.L.F.S.E.A., who would become responsible for screening and disseminating it; concurrently all intelligence reports would be passed back to the I.S.L.D. headquarters in Delhi. A.L.F.S.E.A. was at the same time to obtain the views of commanders in the field on the relative value they attached to the various clandestine and para-military services. These recommendations were approved by Mountbatten on the 7th January, who directed that staff officers of 'P' Division should be attached to the advanced headquarters of A.L.F.S.E.A. and certain other subordinate commands.[1]

By the end of 1943 Force 136 had begun to send agents into Burma to try to contact an anti-Japanese organization reported to be in existence in the south. Agents with wireless sets were established during 1944 in Arakan and some contacts were made with the Communistic Anti-Fascist Organization (A.F.O.) which, under the leadership of Thakin Soe in Rangoon, was attempting to organize a resistance movement. The A.F.O., through its executive council, had control over the Burma National Army (B.N.A.) which, under the command of Aung San, had been raised by the Japanese and given its title in August 1943 at the time Japan granted independence to Burma.[2]

On the 1st January 1945 a wireless message was received from an agent that the B.N.A., numbering some 8,000, was preparing to fight the Japanese and that reception committees for intelligence teams could be formed throughout the country. Force 136 thereupon began preparations to send into Burma as many wireless teams as possible to collect and send back operational intelligence and prepare the way for the eventual reception of Jedburgh teams, which would organize and raise guerrillas.[3] This plan to operate with the A.F.O. and the B.N.A. was given the code name of 'Nation'.

Force 136 had also been active on the Northern front. In the spring of 1943 it established a headquarters in the Kachin Hills between Myitkyina and Bhamo which enabled constant touch to be maintained with the Kachins. The headquarters was of considerable help to Wingate during the first Chindit incursion into Burma,[4] and gave constant information on the Japanese lines of communication which was particularly useful to 10th U.S.A.A.F. In September 1944 this

---

[1] Upon investigation the complete amalgamation of Force 136 and 'Z' Force was found to be impracticable, but operational integration was achieved with the formation by the beginning of April of a joint planning and operations section at Force 136 Headquarters in Calcutta.

[2] For the history and organization of the A.F.O. and B.N.A. see Donnison, *British Military Administration in the Far East, 1943–46* (H.M.S.O., 1956), Chapter XIX.

[3] A Jedburgh team consisted of two British officers and a wireless operator; such a team was not expected to be able to defend itself and had to rely on locally-raised guerrillas for its security.

[4] See Volume II.

area was handed over to the American Detachment 101 of the O.S.S., but before the British headquarters was closed it helped them to raise a force of some 2,000 Kachin Levies.

It was evident that as they advanced into Burma both 14th Army and N.C.A.C. would need close tactical air support from forward airfields and be dependent to a considerable extent on air supply for their maintenance, particularly during the 1945 monsoon. This would require the closest co-operation between army and air force commanders and their staffs and so, on the 26th June, Mountbatten defined certain principles for joint land/air action and appointed an inter-Service committee (under the chairmanship of Air-Vice Marshal J. Whitworth-Jones) to examine and report on the methods by which they could be applied on the 14th Army front.[1]

On the 15th August the committee made its report. It pointed out that the existing air defence arrangements consisted of an R.A.F. organization from Cox's Bazar in the south to Imphal in the north, extended by a similar American organization up to and including Ledo, together with a close air defence organization around Calcutta.[2] It was behind this shield that the Allied air forces had built up an air striking force and, in the 1943–44 campaign, taken the offensive which, by June 1944, had forced the Japanese air force to use the airfields in central and northern Burma for staging purposes and fighter defence activities only, and to base its main strength at Rangoon and in Siam.

During the 1943–44 campaign the air organization had had to perform two mutually incompatible tasks—defending the vital base areas and providing support for land forces. The former required the air commander to be in immediate contact with his machinery of operational control and command, whereas the latter called for close contact between the respective land and air commanders and the exercise of command through joint land/air headquarters. To mitigate the difficulties produced by the changing situation, Eastern Air Command (Stratemeyer) had moved to Calcutta and taken over responsibility for the air defence of that area, 3rd Tactical Air Force (Air Marshal Sir John Baldwin) had been formed and its headquarters placed alongside 14th Army Headquarters at Comilla, and the composite groups forming 3rd Tactical Air Force (221 and 224 Groups R.A.F. and Northern Air Sector Force, U.S.A.A.F.) had been located as far forward as airfields, equipment, communications and their defensive commitments permitted.[3]

---

[1] At this time 14th Army was responsible for the Arakan and Central fronts. For the principles see Appendix 3.
[2] See Sketch 21, facing page 522.
[3] See Volume III, Appendix 12.

The measures taken during the 1943–44 campaign provided a foundation for the changeover from the defensive to the offensive, but did not meet all the requirements. Under the existing organization, land commanders found themselves, at the height of operations, dealing with more than one air commander, while composite group commanders similarly found themselves, owing to the organization of the land forces, dealing with more than one land commander. Moreover, the group commanders had defensive as well as offensive commitments and the static character of their organization militated against the formation of joint land/air headquarters. Now that the Allies were turning to the offensive with the object of reoccupying Burma, it was necessary to adjust the organization of the land and air forces to fit in with the new strategy.

The committee recommended that, as soon as the plans for the 1944–45 campaigns were confirmed, 221 and 224 Groups R.A.F. should be reorganized as mobile groups, each with a main headquarters designed to combine with the headquarters of the appropriate army formation conducting offensive operations on the front it was to support. When reorganized, both groups should be relieved of responsibility for the air defence of their base areas, this responsibility being assumed by a base defence organization capable of moving forward to cover fresh base areas as they were established. Since successful offensive operations in Burma demanded the most careful co-ordination between the British/Indian forces operating under the command of 14th Army and the Chinese/American forces operating under the command of the Commanding General N.C.A.C., the committee recommended that a land commander of Allied forces in Burma should be appointed who would control and co-ordinate all land operations through an integrated British/American staff.[1]

The committee also reviewed the problems of air supply presented by the operations in the first half of 1944 and those likely to arise during the forthcoming offensive. They expressed the opinion that the scale of air supply achieved had almost revolutionized the system of supply and maintenance of land and air forces, and that the broad principles of employment and control of supply aircraft now needed to be clearly defined. They considered that special staff sections dealing with air supply should be established at Headquarters Air Command, S.E.A.C., Eastern Air Command and 3rd Tactical Air Force, and that joint land and air plans should then be made to

---

[1] When, in June 1944, N.C.A.C. passed directly under command of Headquarters S.E.A.C. (see Volume III, Chapter XVIII) Northern Air Sector Force, U.S.A.A.F., was abolished and 10th U.S.A.A.F. was re-formed and made responsible for air support on the Northern front, coming directly under the Commanding General, N.C.A.C. instead of forming part of 3rd Tactical Air Force. The last recommendation of the committee envisaged the formation of a joint headquarters between Eastern Air Command and an Allied land commander.

establish and organize air bases to handle mixed goods. It would be the joint responsibility of the air and land force commanders concerned to decide on the location of airfields tactically and technically suited to the functions of an air supply base; it would be for the army to provide at each of these suitable accommodation to hold, and units to load, mixed goods in the right proportions to meet the supplies required for the campaign. All transport aircraft used for supply or for the carriage of troops should be controlled by a single commander provided with a combined air force and army staff. This commander should be made responsible for the execution of all orders issued for air supply and troop transport, and would act as adviser to both army and air force commanders on all air supply projects. In order to ensure proper routing and the security of transport aircraft, their tactical control while in the air should be exercised by the air officer commanding the group through whose area they had to fly.

The recommendations of the committee, other than that dealing with the appointment of a land commander of Allied forces,[1] were accepted, and the necessary changes in the air force and army organizations were authorized by Supreme Headquarters. The 3rd Tactical Air Force was disbanded on the 4th December 1944. On the same day Headquarters R.A.F. Bengal/Burma was formed in Calcutta to combine the functions of the original Air Headquarters Bengal and the administrative responsibilities previously undertaken by 3rd Tactical Air Force.[2] The new organization, which was responsible for the base areas in Bengal, was gradually to extend its responsibilities eastwards as the offensive progressed into Burma. Its commander (Air Marshal W. A. Coryton) was also to be the deputy air commander Eastern Air Command so that both the British and Americans retained full administrative responsibility for their own units within Eastern Air Command. Headquarters 221 Group R.A.F. (Air Vice-Marshal S. F. Vincent), which was to be responsible for close support on the Central front, was to be located alongside Headquarters 14th Army. Similarly Headquarters 224 Group (Air Vice-Marshal the Earl of Bandon), providing close support for the Arakan front, was to be located alongside XV Corps. In order to make the tactical squadrons in close support of the army more mobile, wing headquarters were to be established on certain major airfields to take over the administrative functions previously undertaken by the squadrons themselves, and mobile servicing echelons were formed to refuel and rearm close support squadrons on forward airfields and airstrips.

A major reorganization of air supply and transport also took place. On the Northern front these were already controlled by 10th

---

[1] This was already under consideration; see Chapter X.
[2] Air Headquarters Bengal had been disbanded when 3rd Tactical Air Force was formed on the 12th December 1943.

U.S.A.A.F. (Major-General H. C. Davidson, U.S.A.A.F.). In September a new integrated British/American air headquarters, known as the Combat Cargo Task Force (C.C.T.F.), commanded by Brigadier-General F. W. Evans, U.S.A.A.F., with an R.A.F. deputy, was set up under Eastern Air Command to control all air transport and supply on the Arakan and Central fronts.[1] The Combined Army Air Transport Organization (C.A.A.T.O.), under command of Brigadier J. A. Dawson, was also established in October alongside Headquarters C.C.T.F. Its function was to receive and collate the daily requisitions for airlifts from army formations, assess their urgency and allot the tasks to the air force, according to the number of transport aircraft available from day to day.[2]

The C.A.A.T.O. also took command of the Rear Airfield Maintenance Organization (R.A.M.O.), formed to replace the existing air supply companies and to undertake at base airfields the loading and despatch of supplies by air to army formations in forward areas. Each R.A.M.O. comprised a small headquarters and a variable number of service units according to the quantity and range of stores to be handled. The essential components were air despatch companies R.A.S.C./R.I.A.S.C. (formerly called air supply companies), labour, transport and provost units. Other service units were attached as required. R.A.M.O.s were to hold stores at the base airfields or obtain them from local depots, pack them for supply-dropping when necessary and load them into the aircraft under the supervision of the R.A.F. staging post and the air crew. Each R.A.M.O. had to provide a twenty-four hour service for seven days a week in order to deal with last-minute changes in the composition of loads or changes from landing to dropping.

The large airfield expansion programme in Bengal and Assam, begun in 1942, had been more or less completed by the autumn of 1944. To support and supply the offensive into Burma and the air ferry to China there were eight groups of airfields.[3] Two groups were in the Calcutta area: the first (near Kharagpur, west of Calcutta) consisting of the five all-weather airfields which provided the main base for the B.29s of 20th Bomber Command U.S.A.A.F. (Major-General C. E. LeMay),[4] and the second in and around Calcutta consisting of twelve all-weather airfields suitable for heavy bombers, for use by the Strategic Air Force and the fighter squadrons responsible for the defence of the city. In eastern Bengal there were three

---

[1] The units assigned to the C.C.T.F. in December were 1st U.S. Air Commando Group, 1st and 4th U.S. Combat Cargo Groups, and 177 (Transport) Wing R.A.F. For the order of battle of Air Command S.E.A. on the 12th December 1944 see Appendix 4.

[2] For the organization of Eastern Air Command in August 1944 and the changes introduced in December 1944 see Appendix 5.

[3] See Sketch 21, facing page 522.

[4] The 20th Bomber Command had forward airfields in the Chengtu area in central China. See Map 10, facing page 340.

groups: the first, in the Silchar area, comprised two all-weather (Sylhet and Kumbhirgram) and two fair-weather (Lalaghat and Hailakandi) airfields which were used by transport squadrons and the light and fighter bombers of 221 Group R.A.F.; the second included five all-weather airfields at Agartala, Comilla, Feni, Chittagong and Hathazari, each with their fair-weather satellites, which were for use by both medium bombers and transport squadrons;[1] and the third, in the Chittagong–Cox's Bazar area, comprised four all-weather airfields (Chittagong, Chiringa, Dohazari and Cox's Bazar) and a number of fair-weather airstrips allotted to the tactical squadrons of 224 Group R.A.F. operating in support of XV Corps on the Arakan front.[2]

In Assam there were two groups. The first consisted of the all-weather airfields at Dimapur, Imphal, Tulihal and Palel and the fair-weather airfields at Kangla, Wangjing and Sapam on the Imphal plain (only the first of which could be used by transport aircraft even in dry weather) and Tamu.[3] These were used by the tactical squadrons of 221 Group R.A.F. in support of the Central front, and by transport squadrons.[4] The second was a group of nine all-weather airfields between Tezpur and Dinjan in north-east Assam, used by the American Air Transport Command operating the air ferry to China.[5] Finally, 10th U.S.A.A.F., responsible for the close support and air supply of the forces on the Northern front, was based on five airfields sited alongside the road from Ledo to Myitkyina (Ledo, Shingbwiyang, Tingkawk Sakan near Shadazup, Warazup and Myitkyina West). American engineers were building, as quickly as weather conditions allowed, a group of four new all-weather airfields in the Mogaung–Myitkyina area for use partly by 10th U.S.A.A.F. and partly by Air Transport Command as a staging base on the air ferry route to China.[6]

---

[1] The distances in miles from Chittagong to important centres in Burma are given in Appendix 6.

[2] Since Chittagong airfield was used by 224 Group R.A.F. as well as by medium bombers and air transport squadrons of 3rd Tactical Air Force, it appears in two groups.

[3] For Kangla, Wangjing and Sapam see Map 1, facing page 15.

[4] For the distances in miles from Imphal to important centres in Burma see Appendix 6.

[5] This group included Dinjan, Sookerating, Mohanbari, Chabua, Moran, Jorhat, Dergaon, Misamari and Tezpur. See Sketch 21, facing page 522.

[6] These four new airfields were Sahmaw, Namponmao, Myitkyina North and Myitkyina East.

Map 2

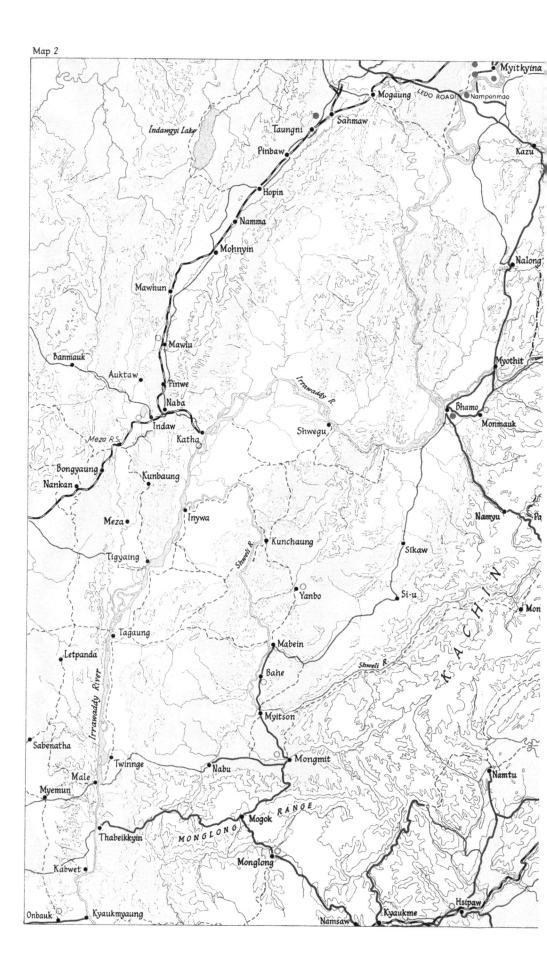

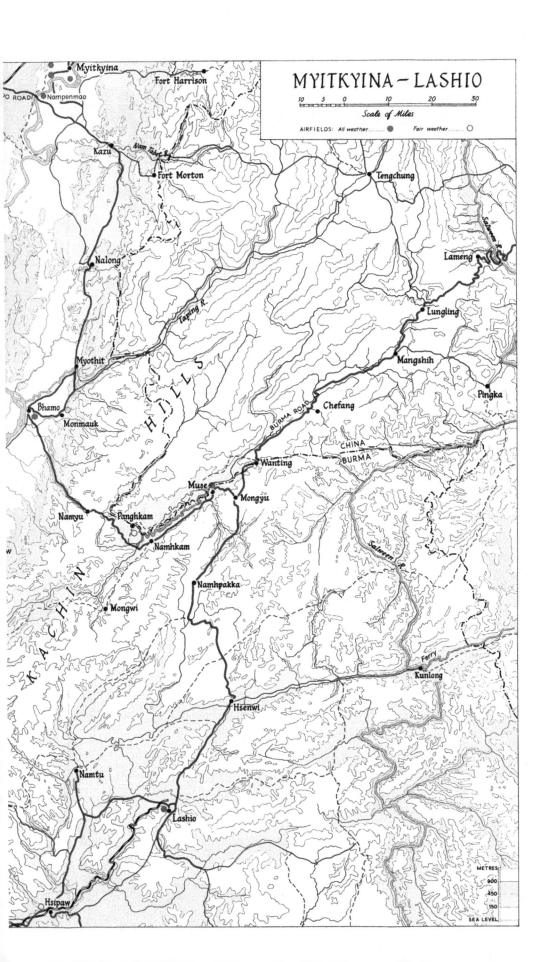

MYITKYINA — LASHIO

Scale of Miles

AIRFIELDS: All weather......... ●   Fair weather......... ○

Myitkyina
Fort Harrison
Namponmao
O ROAD
Kazu
Nam Tabe R.
Fort Morton
Tengchung
Nalong
Lameng
Taping R.
Lungling
Myothit
Mangshih
H I L L S
Pingka
Bhamo
Monmauk
Chefang
BURMA ROAD
Wanting
CHINA
BURMA
Muse
Mongyu
Namyu
Panghkam
Namhkam
K A C H I N
Namhpakka
Mongwi
Salween R.
Ferry
Kunlong
Hsenwi
Namtu
Lashio
Hsipaw

METRES
900
450
150
SEA LEVEL

CHAPTER IV

'CAPITAL' ANTICIPATED

(August–October 1944)

See Maps 1, 2, 6 and 13 and Sketches 4 and 21

BY the end of the first week of August 1944, S.E.A.C. land forces had consolidated the general line Maungdaw–the Tunnels–Taung Bazar–Mowdok,[1] cleared the Imphal plain and captured Myitkyina.[2] They were now deployed, facing east and south, on a 500-mile arc from Maungdaw on the Arakan coast, through Tamu on the Central front, to Myitkyina on the Northern front. The offensive by the Chinese Yunnan armies across the Salween in May had been brought to a halt and they were deployed facing west on a 60-mile front from Tengchung to Pingka.[3]

In Arakan, the situation had been static since June when both sides had taken up monsoon positions. There, XV Corps (Lieut.-General A. F. P. Christison) had 25th Indian Division (Major-General H. L. Davies) based on Maungdaw with one brigade holding forward positions covering the Tunnels, and 26th Indian Division (Major-General C. E. N. Lomax) based on Ukhia with a brigade forward in the Taung–Goppe–Bawli area. A detachment was watching the Japanese in Mowdok under orders of 81st (W.A.) Division (Major-General C. G. Woolner) which, less one brigade, was in corps reserve at Chiringa. The 82nd (W.A.) Division (Major-General C. McI. S. Bruce), the corps' fourth division, which had recently arrived in India, was at Ranchi undergoing intensive training.

On the Central front, XXXIII Corps (Lieut.-General M. G. N. Stopford) was steadily pushing south along the Tiddim and Tamu roads towards Kalemyo in anticipation of the first phase of operation 'Capital', then under discussion in London between the Supreme Commander and the Chiefs of Staff.[4] On the Tiddim road, the leading troops of 5th Indian Division (Major-General G. C. Evans) had reached MS 49 south of Imphal and were in patrol contact with the Lushai Brigade operating from the hills to the south-west against the Japanese lines of communication. On the Tamu Road, 11th (E.A.) Division (Major-General C. C. Fowkes) was taking over operational

---

[1] See Map 6, facing page 134.
[2] See Volume III, Chapters XIX, XXV, and XXIX.
[3] See Map 2, facing page 39, and Volume III, pages 394–97.
[4] See Chapter I and Map 1, facing page 15.

control from 23rd Indian Division, covered by 5th Brigade of 2nd Division (under command), which had occupied Tamu on the 4th August. On completion of the relief, the East African division was to drive south down the Kabaw Valley and east to the Chindwin at Sittaung.[1] The three divisions and the armoured brigade which were to remain in the Imphal–Kohima area under XXXIII Corps were moving into rest and training camps.[2]

On the Northern front, Myitkyina had been captured on the 3rd August and Stilwell had issued orders that the New Chinese First and Sixth Armies were to go into training camps in the Mogaung–Kamaing and Myitkyina areas respectively.[3] The Myitkyina area was covered by a regiment of 30th Chinese Division in the vicinity of Kazu. The Japanese had, however, completely evacuated the area and there was not even patrol contact, a situation which continued until the general advance began in mid-October. The Mogaung–Kamaing area was covered by 72nd Brigade (Brigadier A. R. Aslett) of 36th Indian Division (Major-General F. W. Festing), which had recently arrived by air at Myitkyina. From there it had moved to Mogaung and on the 9th August had cleared Taungni in the railway corridor.[4]

Since it was known that the Japanese were holding Pinbaw, which was uncomfortably close to the training areas allotted to the Chinese armies near Mogaung and constituted a threat to Stilwell's right flank, Festing was ordered to occupy the village as soon as his second brigade (29th) joined him. As none of 36th Division's artillery had arrived, three Chinese batteries under an American officer were put under command. On the 18th August the artillery was augmented by six 3·7-inch howitzers of 366th Light Battery, successfully dropped by parachute near the tactical headquarters of 29th Brigade (Brigadier H. C. Stockwell), which was preparing to attack Pinbaw.

On the 25th, after three days' bombardment by forty-five medium bombers and forty-two fighters of 10th U.S.A.A.F, the attack was launched and by the evening of the 27th all resistance had ceased. Stilwell had intended to make no further advance down the railway corridor until the general advance, timed for mid-October, but when

---

[1] The East Africans were chosen for this task in the notoriously malarial Kabaw Valley because of their believed high resistance to malaria. Anti-malaria measures to assist them included spraying D.D.T. from the air on occupied areas.
[2] The 2nd British Division at Maram (twenty-five miles south of Kohima), 7th Indian Division at Kohima, 20th Indian Division ten miles south of Imphal, and 254th Armoured Brigade at Kanglatongbi (fifteen miles north of Imphal). Formations which had moved out were Headquarters IV Corps, 17th and 23rd Indian Divisions, 23rd (L.R.P.) Brigade and 3 Commando Brigade.
[3] For the composition of New Chinese First and Sixth Armies see Appendix 18.
[4] See Map 2, facing page 39, and Volume III, Chapter XXIX. The 36th Division took over all animals left behind by Special Force and it had in addition about seventy jeeps.

it became evident that after the loss of Pinbaw the Japanese had made a considerable withdrawal Festing obtained permission to move forward and regain contact. By the 13th September, Namma (twenty miles south-west of Pinbaw) was occupied and contact made with the enemy four miles further south. This marked the limit of the advance for the time being, and 36th Division concentrated in the Pinbaw–Hopin area with its forward troops some six miles to the south.

The 15th Battalion I.E., working in co-operation with American engineers, was repairing the railway south of Mogaung to take 'jeep trains' and become the divisional line of communication, but 36th Division had advanced faster than repairs could be effected; it was therefore being entirely supplied by air by 10th U.S.A.A.F., which was also engaged in building up reserve stocks for the October offensive. At the same time the road and pipeline from Ledo to Myitkyina were being pushed forward as fast as monsoon conditions permitted, and Myitkyina itself was being developed as the main staging post for Air Transport Command on the route to China.[1] Farther to the east the Chinese Yunnan armies, with which Stilwell had hoped to make contact so that the trace for the proposed road and pipeline by way of Bhamo and Wanting into China could be covered, were engaged in besieging Tengchung, Lameng and Pingka and bringing pressure to bear on the Japanese who still held the vital Lungling area on the Burma Road.[2]

It was only on the Central front, where XXXIII Corps continued to move steadily forward, that mobile operations were carried on throughout the monsoon. By the end of July exploitation of the Battle of Imphal had been completed: the Japanese had been driven from the last of their strongholds overlooking the Imphal plain, the remnants of *15th* and *31st Divisions* were withdrawing in considerable disorder to the Chindwin and *1st Indian National Army (I.N.A.) Division* had disintegrated. Only *33rd Division* and the *Yamamoto Detachment* on the Tiddim and Tamu roads had retained their cohesion, mainly because they both had comparatively good lines of communication along which they had been reasonably well supplied and considerably reinforced.[3]

Air support of XXXIII Corps was the responsibility of 221 Group R.A.F., which, after receiving a reinforcement of two squadrons of Thunderbolt fighter-bombers in September, consisted of eleven

---

[1] See pages 18 and 23.
[2] See Chapter V, and Volume III, Chapter XXVIII.
[3] See Map 1, facing page 15. During the Imphal offensive reinforcements to these formations amounted to nine battalions—*33rd Division*: *II/154th Battalion, 151st Regiment* (less one battalion) and *I/67th Battalion*; the *Yamamoto Detachment*: *II/51st Battalion, I/60th Battalion, 61st Regiment* (less one battalion) and *I/213th Battalion*.

squadrons. The two Thunderbolt squadrons and a Mosquito light bomber squadron were based on Kumbhirgram and the rest were on the Imphal plain at Imphal, Palel and Tulihal airfields.[1] Air transport for the whole of 14th Army was controlled by 3rd Tactical Air Force and was provided by four squadrons of Dakotas; their major task was the air supply of the forward divisions of XXXIII Corps, but a certain amount of supply-dropping had to be done to the small force in the Mowdok area in Arakan and isolated posts in the Lushai, Naga and Chin Hills.[2]

After a conference with Giffard, Slim issued his orders for the pursuit to the Chindwin on the 6th August. The XXXIII Corps was instructed to pursue the enemy along the Tiddim–Kalemyo–Kalewa, the Tamu–Indainggyi–Kalewa and the Tamu–Sittaung roads.[3] Air supply would be available for a maximum of five brigades. Sittaung was to be occupied at once to prevent the enemy using the Chindwin River, Kalewa was to be seized at the first opportunity and a bridge-head was to be established east of the river.

The following day Stopford ordered the elimination of all enemy west of the Chindwin from Tamanthi to Kalewa and the capture of the important crossings over the Myittha and Chindwin Rivers at Kalemyo and Kalewa.[4] The 5th Indian Division (Evans), in conjunction with the Lushai Brigade, was to destroy the enemy forces on the Tiddim road and exploit to Kalemyo and Kalewa, one brigade being left uncommitted at the disposal of the corps, though it could be moved forward behind the division at Evans' discretion. The 11th (E.A.) Division (Fowkes) was to secure Sittaung and establish patrol bases to cover the track between it and Tamu, at the same time sending one brigade to advance south down the Kabaw Valley on Kalemyo and later to Kalewa. Since motor transport could not operate in the Kabaw Valley at that time of the year, supplies had to be delivered by air direct to the troops, even although low cloud would often make supply drops impossible. Casualties were to be held in forward areas since aircraft could not land and motor transport could not get forward. As it was probable that field artillery would be immobilized by mud, the divisional artillery was to be augmented by porter-borne 3·7-inch howitzers.[5] A battery of 1st Medium Regiment was, however, to be allotted for defensive tasks in the Tamu–Moreh area.

The mopping up of the area north of the Tamu–Sittaung road was entrusted to a column from 100th Brigade of 20th Indian Division,

---

[1] See Sketch 21, facing page 522.
[2] See Map 13 in end pocket.
[3] The decision to press the pursuit along the Tiddim road was a change of policy. The original intention had been to stop the pursuit at MS 70. See Volume III, Chapter XXIV.
[4] For Tamanthi see Map 13 in end pocket.
[5] Sixteen 3·7-inch howitzers were handed over by 17th Division before it left the Imphal plain.

known as Tarcol, which consisted of two Indian infantry battalions and an engineer detachment under Lieut.-Colonel G. L. Tarver. It remained in action until well into September, rounding up stragglers, destroying ammunition dumps and finding large numbers of bogged and abandoned enemy guns and vehicles which, since they were useless, were left where they lay.

By the 10th, 11th (E.A.) Division was ready to carry out the task allotted to it and Fowkes took over operational control in the Kabaw Valley. The 5th Brigade was ordered to rejoin 2nd Division in its rest area around Kohima and 268th Brigade was withdrawn to Imphal.[1] Of the reorganized 'V' Force, Assam Zone was allotted to XXXIII Corps, Lushai Zone to the Lushai Brigade and Arakan Zone to XV Corps.[2]

On the 12th August, 25th (E.A.) Brigade (Brigadier N. C. Hendricks), supported by 302nd (E.A.) Field Artillery Regiment less a battery, advanced east from Tamu along the Sittaung track, and 26th (E.A.) Brigade (Brigadier V. K. H. Channer) moved south down the Kabaw Valley. The 21st (E.A.) Brigade (Brigadier J. F. Macnab) was to be in corps reserve at Palel until it had completed its concentration and was then to move forward to Moreh. The 26th Brigade reached Htinzin unopposed on the 27th, but unusually bad weather then brought its advance temporarily to a standstill.[3] On the Sittaung track, Japanese rearguards in the mountains held up the advance of 25th Brigade for several days and it was not till the 4th September that it reached Sittaung. The enemy force which had been opposing it withdrew southwards without attempting to hold the ruins of the village; like Tamu and Moreh, it was found to be a shambles of corpses, abandoned vehicles and equipment which provided identifications of *15th* and *31st Divisions* and an independent engineer regiment. River patrols were immediately organized to prevent the Japanese using the now three-quarter mile wide waterway, but they found little to do.[4]

It is now known that both *15th* and *31st Divisions* had crossed the Chindwin at Sittaung, covered by a rearguard from the *Yamamoto Detachment*,[5] and that the remainder of the detachment (*213th*

---

[1] Its motorized battalions all returned to India. Brigade Headquarters remained and took command of various unbrigaded units.

[2] See page 31.

[3] By this time all armour and most of the wheeled transport had been withdrawn from the Kabaw Valley.

[4] The Japanese had intended to send a fleet of river craft up river to deliver supplies and bring back sick and wounded, but the effectiveness of the R.A.F. attacks forced them to abandon the idea.

[5] The rearguard consisted of *61st Regiment* less one battalion; after the crossing it rejoined *15th Division* at Yeu.

Regiment less one battalion) had withdrawn to Mawlaik and reverted to
33rd Division (Lieut.-General N. Tanaka). This division had been
ordered to withdraw to and hold the general line Mawlaik–Kalewa–
Gangaw, linking up with *15th Division* which was to hold the passes of
the Zibyu Taungdan west of Pinlebu and cover the left flank and
communications of *53rd Division* in the Indaw area which was
opposing the southward advance of 36th Division along the railway
corridor.

Meanwhile, Imphal Force, consisting of Headquarters 268th
Brigade (Brigadier G. M. Dyer) with five infantry battalions and its
own supply and medical detachments, had been organized and
ordered to take over the 150-mile river front from Sittaung northwards to Tamanthi, thus relieving both 25th (E.A.) Brigade and the
Tarcol detachment.[1] The former on reaching Moreh was to become
Fowkes' reserve and be ready to move south to the Yazagyo area as
soon as the Kabaw Valley road became passable; the latter was to
rejoin 20th Division.

At the beginning of September a slight improvement in the
weather enabled 26th (E.A.) Brigade to resume its advance, and its
advanced guard, on an air and porter supply basis, neared Yazagyo
before it began to meet opposition. Behind it, 21st (E.A.) Brigade had
moved forward to the vicinity of Htinzin and begun work on improving the track to enable divisional headquarters and the divisional
troops to move to Yazagyo on the 14th. A sudden deterioration in the
weather then took place which made all movement impossible.
Heavy rain continued for ten days with the result that 21st and 26th
Brigades found themselves completely cut off from the divisional
administrative area at Moreh. Although supplies were being dropped
fairly regularly, the sick and wounded could not be evacuated and
their accommodation and care became a serious problem. To make
matters worse, atmospherics and the blanketing effect of wet forest
made wireless unreliable and it was often difficult to learn the requirements of the two brigades. So bad were the conditions that Brigadier
J. S. Lethbridge and Brigadier G. N. Wood (B.G.S. of 14th Army and
XXXIII Corps), who were trying to reach the forward areas, could
get no farther than Tamu; beyond this point they would have had to
be parachuted in and could not have got back.

In anticipation of the early arrival of 25th Brigade in the forward
area, Fowkes had ordered 21st Brigade to move on Mawlaik. Despite
the appalling conditions both forward brigades were able to make
some progress, and by the end of September 26th Brigade, some five

---

[1] The battalions of Imphal Force were 1st Assam, 4/3rd Madras and 1st Chamar
Regiments, and the Mahindra Dal and Kalibahadur Regiments of the Nepalese Army.
In addition it had under command a 'V' Force operational headquarters and six platoons
of Assam Rifles.

miles south of Yazagyo, and 21st Brigade, in the hills eight miles north-west of Mawlaik, were both in contact with the enemy. Sickness and exhaustion had taken a heavy toll, and it was clear that no further progress could be made until tanks and artillery could be brought forward to support attacks on the prepared positions now being met, and the reserve brigade was available in the forward area.

The weather began to improve early in October but the track down the Kabaw Valley was still a sea of mud six to eighteen inches deep. Although the divisional engineers rebuilt the bridges washed away by the heavy rains of the latter part of September and, with the help of the infantry, constructed miles of corduroy road along which jeeps and six-wheel drive light lorries could bump, conditions were so bad that an advance of five miles in twenty-four hours for a convoy was considered to be outstanding, and guns had frequently to be winched forward from tree to tree. A light tank squadron of 254th Indian Tank Brigade (placed under command of the division on the 6th October) took some three weeks to reach Yazagyo from Tamu, despite almost superhuman efforts. The situation in the forward areas in the Kabaw Valley consequently remained static until late October when 25th (E.A.) Brigade with supporting arms at last got forward. The R.A.F., however, taking full advantage of the improved conditions, intensified their attacks on Japanese communications and supply dumps, and targets indicated by the forward troops.

Although operating under conditions which before 1944 would have been considered impossible, 5th Division was able to keep up a steady, though slow, advance on the Tiddim road. During periods of continuous heavy rain everything came to a standstill, but when the rain slackened for a few days the water drained off quickly, the smaller mountain streams became fordable and transport, guns and tanks were able, though with difficulty, to get forward along the main road. Despite strenuous opposition by small but well-handled Japanese rearguards, the advance averaged some two miles a day. This progress was made possible by the herculean efforts of the divisional engineers; in some places they had to cover the steep slopes which the road traversed with huge tarpaulins to prevent mudslides from obliterating it.

By the 22nd August, 9th Brigade (Brigadier J. A. Salomons), which had been leading the advance since the last week in July, had reached MS 83 and had established contact with the Lushai Brigade (Brigadier P. C. Marindin) which was now under command of 5th Division. From this point 161st Brigade (Brigadier D. F. W. Warren) was to pass through 9th Brigade and take up the advance.[1] Although the spell of exceptionally bad weather at the end of August increased the difficulties, 161st Brigade, making use of several good tracks through the mountains leading to MS 90, 100 and 109, was able to outflank Japanese positions astride the road and maintain the rate of advance.[2] By the end of the month the brigade had reached MS 96 and was in process of outflanking the enemy position at MS 100, which had been the scene of much fighting in the spring.

The division was now approaching the Manipur River, a formidable obstacle at that time of the year. The possibility of seizing the bridge before it could be destroyed was negligible; a frontal assault could succeed only with overwhelming artillery support, but guns and ammunition could not be got forward in time along the road, which was continually slipping and deep in mud. Evans therefore decided to send 123rd Brigade (Brigadier E. J. Denholm-Young) by motor transport from Torbung through Imphal and Palel to Shuganu. From there, completely self-contained and using pack and porter transport, it was to advance along mountain tracks on Tongzang with the object of taking the Japanese positions covering the Manipur River bridge in rear.[3] It was to establish a firm base on the high ground overlooking the track running east from Tongzang, destroy the enemy believed to be in the Tongzang–Tuitum area covering the Manipur River crossing, and subsequently exploit southwards to Tiddim. Meanwhile 161st Brigade, with the co-operation of the Lushai Brigade which was operating from the west against the Japanese line of communication, was to move forward to within frontal striking distance of the bridge. It was calculated that 123rd and 161st Brigades could be in position to attack the bridge from the front and rear by the 15th September, but the order to attack was to be given by divisional headquarters.

The 123rd Brigade had reached the track junction east of the river twenty miles north of Tuitum by the 11th without the enemy, it was hoped, being aware of its presence. If there were to be any chance of seizing the bridge intact by a concerted attack from both banks, its movements from this point had to be co-ordinated with those of 161st Brigade on the main Tiddim road west of the river. Evans therefore ordered 123rd Brigade to stand fast until he gave permission for it to

---

[1] The following figures give some idea of the cost of a monsoon campaign. The 9th Brigade had advanced fifty-six miles in twenty-six days. Its battle casualties were ninety-four but its losses from sickness were 507, including a large number of cases of the serious scrub typhus. The brigade had inflicted eighty-three known casualties on the enemy and taken eighteen prisoners, but had found 293 dead Japanese on the roadside and in abandoned hospitals. Captured enemy material included eleven tanks and fifteen guns.

[2] These tracks had been used during 17th Division's withdrawal to the Imphal plain in March 1944. See Volume III, Chapter XIII.

[3] A standard daily air drop was arranged and the brigade was reorganized to make it completely Indian, partly to simplify the ration supply and partly because the British battalion in the brigade was much under strength (see pages 26–27).

move on. The 161st Brigade was held up throughout the 12th by a well-entrenched Japanese rearguard at MS 119, where the old pack track dropped steeply to the river and the road turned east to drop more gently to the bridge. On the 13th the Japanese rearguard gave way and, as soon as this happened, Evans told 123rd Brigade to resume its advance. Next day 3/2nd Punjab of this brigade, after losing amongst others its commander wounded and two officers killed in an ambush, secured the dominant hill at the western bend in the river overlooking the bridge, which was seen to have been destroyed.

Almost simultaneously patrols of 1/1st Punjab (161st Brigade), accompanied by engineer reconnaissance parties, reached the north end of the destroyed bridge to find themselves confronted by a deep, raging, 8-knot torrent some one hundred yards wide and full of whirlpools. About seventy yards downstream from the bridge, rocks and sunken debris formed rapids in which nothing could live, so that any man or boat starting to cross at the bridge faced certain destruction if swept more than seventy yards downstream. The only hope in the circumstances was to get a line across, and it was decided to attempt this by firing one attached to an unfused 3-inch mortar bomb. But someone had to be on the far bank to secure it. With great gallantry Captain Zia-ud-Din (1/1st Punjab) swam across, but all attempts to fire a line to him failed and he had eventually to swim back.[1] While these efforts were being made, 123rd Brigade seized the Tuitum ridge on the 15th, thereby cutting the road to Tongzang, which was found to be held in strength. Next day the engineers, seizing a temporarily favourable moment, got a few men across the river in an F.B.E. (folding boat equipment) boat fitted with a powerful outboard engine. An improved method of attaching a line to an unfused mortar bomb proved successful and an F.B.E. boat cable ferry was established. After making only a few trips it was swamped and all its occupants were swept away and drowned. Meanwhile those who had reached the south bank in the short-lived ferry became aware that there were enemy in a bunkered position a few hundred yards from them on the lower slope of the Tuitum ridge. Fortunately the Japanese did not open fire, presumably because they knew that the ridge behind them had been occupied and, hoping to escape that night, were unwilling to disclose their presence unless it was essential. They attempted to get away after dark but many of them were killed.

Two cable ferries were established on the 19th with F.B.E. rafts instead of boats. During the next two days the headquarters and infantry of 161st Brigade were got across the river, but it was impossible to ferry even mountain artillery across since the rafts, though

---

[1] No one else succeeded in swimming the river. Of those who tried, several were drowned and one was rescued with difficulty.

normally adequate, could be loaded to only a fraction of their capacity without being swamped. In consequence, between the 19th and the 21st, 123rd Brigade, attacking Tongzang supported by one 4-gun mountain battery, could make no impression on the defences from where the Japanese kept up a galling harassing fire on the ferry with 105-mm. guns. On the 22nd, however, 1/17th Dogras cut the road south of Tongzang and this, together with raids made by 7/14th Punjab of the Lushai Brigade on the road in the gorge near MS 148, was effective, and the Japanese, abandoning guns, vehicles and equipment, took to the hills and withdrew towards Tiddim.[1]

That day the river rose nearly three feet, the current increased to about 16 knots in midstream and, after several men had been drowned, the ferries were temporarily closed. At the same time the road back to Imphal began to disintegrate, and it became clear that any hope of bridging the river would have to be abandoned. Next day Stopford told Warren, the new divisional commander,[2] that it would be impossible to maintain the road after the 2nd October, that anything not across the river by then would have to return to Imphal and that thereafter the division would be completely maintained by supply-dropping until a suitable landing-ground could be secured. For the advance on Tiddim the supporting arms for 5th Division were to consist of a half squadron of the Carabiniers (medium tanks), 28th Field Regiment with one battery of 4th Field Regiment, 24th Mountain Regiment less two batteries, and all three field companies of engineers.

From this moment the divisional engineers concentrated their efforts on constructing heavier rafts, up to one of 6-pontoon size capable of carrying medium tanks. By these means they achieved the gigantic task of ferrying about a thousand vehicles (including six medium tanks) and many hundreds of animals across this wide and deep river, which was liable to rise as much as three feet in two hours with a 2-knot increase in the current for each foot of rise.[3]

Since from the 2nd October 5th Division was to be without land communications to the rear in an area where it was impossible to establish airstrips until Tiddim had been captured, and it was expected that the Japanese would fight determinedly to hold it, all supplies had to be dropped and all sick and wounded had to be

---

[1] The Tongzang area was held by *215th Regiment*. It withdrew through *214th Regiment* holding Tiddim and Kennedy Peak to the Kalemyo area. The *II/213th Battalion* was also in the area.

[2] On the 23rd September Brigadier Warren of 161st Brigade was promoted to command the division in place of Major-General Evans who had contracted typhoid, and Brigadier R. G. C. Poole succeeded to the command of 161st Brigade.

[3] Forward of the river there were eventually 13,000 men, 996 four-wheel drive vehicles, six Lee and two bridging tanks and one bulldozer. This force required a daily supply drop of 62 tons which included 3,000 gallons of petrol. Only thirty-six per cent of the transport was still battleworthy by the time the division reached Kalemyo.

2. Lieut.-General Sir Oliver Leese, Bt., C.-in-C. A.L.F.S.E.A., and Major-General G. E. Stratemeyer, U.S.A.A.F., Eastern Air Command

3. Admiral Sir Arthur Power, R.N., C.-in-C., East Indies Fleet

4. Lieut.-General H. Kimura,
C.-in-C., *Burma Area Army*

5. Lieut.-General S. Katamura,
Commander *15th Army*

6. Air Marshall W. A. Coryton,
Commander R.A.F., Burma

7. Air Marshal Sir Guy Garrod, Acting
C.-in-C., Allied Air Forces

8. Major-General H. C. Davidson, 10th U.S.A.A.F., Lieut.-General D. I. Sultan, Commanding General, India–Burma Theatre, and Lieut.-General A. C. Wedemeyer, Commanding General, China Theatre

9. Major-General F. J. Loftus-Tottenham, 81st (W.A.) Division

10. The Tiddim Road during the 1944
monsoon

11. Elephants clearing the track in the Kabaw Valley

12. River fleet assembling on the Mayu River near Buthidaung

13. Kaladan: close support by Hurricane
fighter-bombers at Paletwa

carried with the division. The retention of the sick presented a very serious medical problem, for the incidence of scrub typhus in the division had risen from 199 in July to 728 in September. To save the life of a patient suffering from this disease, careful and highly skilled nursing was necessary in its early stages. Such a service could be provided only if trained nursing sisters accompanied the division but, with the unpleasant recollections of what had happened in Arakan in February 1944 when a main dressing station had been overrun,[1] the medical authorities were averse to the idea. There was, however, no alternative and early in October volunteers were called for. The only difficulty then was to select the most suitable nurses from the very large numbers who came forward, well aware of the hardships and risks entailed and the tremendous fortitude which would be required.

Warren planned to advance on Kalemyo in two phases. In the first, 123rd Brigade was to advance on Tiddim and Kennedy Peak, while 161st Brigade held a firm base at Tongzang and 9th Brigade held the bridge area until all the administrative units and vehicles accompanying the division had crossed the river and concentrated in the base area. As soon as 123rd Brigade reached MS 150, where the road left the gorge south of Tongzang and began the climb to Tiddim, the battalion of the Lushai Brigade operating west of the road was to move south to cover the right of the advance on Fort White and beyond, while the rest of the brigade captured Falam and Haka and sent forward reconnaissance patrols into the Myittha valley. The second phase was to be an advance by 9th Brigade to Kalemyo while 123rd Brigade consolidated in the Tiddim–Kennedy Peak area, which was to become the division's base. The 161st Brigade was then to establish itself at Fort White and be prepared to support the advance of 9th Brigade on Kalemyo.

The 123rd Brigade began its advance on Tiddim on the 24th September on a two-battalion front and on the 29th, meeting with little opposition, reached the Beltang Lui, a stream at the foot of the climb up to Tiddim (known to the troops as the Chocolate Staircase),[2] Haupi and the northern spur of the 8,000-foot high Sialum Vum. It was everywhere in close contact with the Japanese entrenched in well-sited positions.[3] Divisional headquarters and 161st Brigade were at Tongzang, the tail of the division (9th Brigade) was still on the wrong side of the Manipur River at MS 124, and the Lushai Brigade was making its way to Falam and across the Manipur River, near Mualbem, to raid the road south of Kennedy Peak.

---

[1] See Volume III, page 142.
[2] The road was so named since the spoil from the cuttings in the rich brown earth gave it, as it zigzagged up the steep slope, some resemblance to a chocolate-brown staircase.
[3] See Sketch 4, facing page 170.

It soon became evident that the forward troops were in contact with a force determined to stand and fight, for the Japanese holding the area were found to be well clothed and equipped, apparently physically fit, and well supported by artillery with an adequate supply of ammunition.[1] Moreover, their position was one of great natural strength and they had had time to dig and wire themselves in. The capture of Tiddim and Fort White was therefore likely to take time, as 5th Division, although outnumbering the enemy, was widely spread out and had only half of its normal allotment of artillery. Being entirely supplied by air drop it could not afford a lavish expenditure of ammunition and had therefore to rely almost entirely on the R.A.F. for support.

The 123rd Brigade spent the first few days of October infiltrating between the forward Japanese posts covering Tiddim and Kennedy Peak, in the course of which the Beltang Lui was crossed and a road-block established behind the Japanese holding the Chocolate Staircase. As the brigade was by now becoming dangerously dispersed and had nothing in reserve, Warren arranged that as soon as the Beltang Lui was bridged the tanks were to go through to link up with the forward troops in front of Tiddim. The 161st Brigade was to move up; one of its battalions (1/1st Punjab) was to carry out a wide enveloping movement through Dolluang, and the remainder to take over all commitments on the axis of the main road up to within two miles of Tiddim.

On the 6th October 123rd Brigade resumed its offensive, supported by powerful air attacks. The Japanese offered strong resistance at Dolluang and for ten days withstood every attack. On the 10th, 11th and 12th, 250 fighter-bomber sorties were flown and all-day cover given over the whole area from Tiddim to Vital Corner. After a day when no flying was possible anywhere, bad weather in the mountains forced the R.A.F. to turn its attention to the Kabaw Valley on the 14th. Nevertheless by the 16th continuous pressure, infiltration, the air attacks and steady bombardment by artillery took effect, and the Japanese evacuated Tiddim during the night. The capture of Tiddim was of great importance; its possession not only made it possible for the left flank of the Kennedy Peak and Fort White positions to be turned and their garrisons encircled, but in its neighbourhood lay the only ground suitable for the construction of a light airstrip from which the seriously sick and wounded, whose care was becoming a major administrative problem, could be evacuated.

---

[1] Tanaka had used his attached units (see fn. 3 page 41) to delay the Allied advance as far as the Manipur River while *33rd Division* rested, re-equipped and prepared defences in the Tiddim area.

The 14th Army and N.C.A.C. were now in a position, as soon as communications dried out, to make a concerted drive into northern Burma eastwards across the Chindwin and southwards on Indaw and Bhamo, a drive with which it was hoped the Chinese Yunnan armies would co-operate.

CHAPTER V

JAPANESE PLANS
(July–October 1944)

See Maps 1, 2, 3, 8, 10 and 13

THE loss of the battle of the Philippine Sea and of Saipan in the Marianas, coupled with the first bombing attack on Japan since the Doolittle raid of 1942, had brought about the fall of the Tojo Cabinet on the 18th July.[1] After a number of meetings held by a council of senior statesmen, General K. Koiso and Admiral M. Yonai were called upon to form a joint cabinet; this they did on the 22nd.[2] On the 31st July the first liaison conference between the new cabinet and *Imperial General Headquarters* was held, and four days later it was decided that a Supreme War Direction Council should be formed out of the liaison conference organization, which up to this time had been, in theory, responsible for the supreme direction of the war. Although the liaison conference was replaced by the new council, no real change was made and the army and navy remained, as before, supreme in their own spheres.[3]

On the 24th July, two days after the formation of the Koiso Cabinet, *Imperial General Headquarters* issued a new directive which covered the preparations to be made for future operations in all areas from Manchuria through the Pacific to the Southern Region. As a result of the losses suffered by the navy in the battle of the Philippine Sea and of the capture of the Marianas by American forces, the strategic position of Japan had completely changed. Not only were the vital communications between Japan and the Southern Region now in danger of being disrupted, but the homeland was within range of bomber aircraft based on the Marianas. The Americans, moreover, were in a position to invade the Philippines and perhaps even Japan herself. It was evident therefore that an attack by an enemy immensely strong on both sea and land, as well as in the air, would have to be met in the Philippines–Formosa–Japan area. The policy adopted was to make the most thorough preparations possible to defend the line from the Philippine Islands, through Formosa and the Ryukyu Islands, to Japan and the Kurile Islands

---

[1] See Map 8, facing page 252, and Volume III, Chapters XXVIII, XXXI and XXXII.
[2] Koiso had been Governor-General of Korea and was thus out of touch with the overall war situation as seen in Tokyo.
[3] See Volume I, Appendix 2.

with a view to gaining a decisive victory, while at the same time continuing the offensive in China (operation 'Ichi-Go') in order to prevent American bombers from attacking the homeland from Chinese airfields.[1] Preparations were therefore made for four separate operations: the defence of the Philippines ('SHO-1') and the defence of Formosa and the Ryukyu Islands ('SHO-2'), both to be ready by the end of August; the defence of the Japanese homeland ('SHO-3') and the defence of the north-east front ('SHO-4'), both to be ready by the end of October.

On the 19th August a meeting of the Supreme War Direction Council was held in Tokyo in the presence of the Emperor. Both the Chief of the Army and the Chief of the Naval General Staff expressed the opinion that the next battle would take place in the Philippines; the maximum strength should therefore be concentrated there in order to attain victory, and heavy losses would have to be accepted, provided that the American losses were more or less equal. The Council noted the orders already issued by *Imperial General Headquarters* to *Southern Army* on the action to be taken on the Pacific fronts, and agreed that the existing position in the Indian Ocean area should be maintained and that in China the utmost efforts should be made to prevent the launching of air raids on Japan. The Council also emphasized the importance of improving diplomatic relations with Soviet Russia, and the desirability of bringing about a termination of hostilities between that country and Germany.

A month later *Imperial General Headquarters* revised the agreement between the army and navy on the defence of strategic areas in the Southern Region. The land defence of Celebes, Borneo and the Andaman and Nicobar Islands, which had hitherto been the responsibility of the navy, was now to become a joint army/navy responsibility. This agreement was again revised the following month when the army was made entirely responsible for the land defence of these areas.[2]

The second phase of operation 'Ichi-Go' was divided into three distinct operations: the first to capture Changsha and Hengyang; the second to capture Kweilin and Liuchow; the third, and last, to occupy the southern portion of the Hankow–Canton railway and capture the airfields at Suichwan and Nanhsiung.[3] The first of these

---

[1] For operation 'Ichi-Go' see Volume III, Chapters XV and XXVIII.
[2] For the organization of Japanese forces in August 1944 see Appendix 7. Under the October revision of the agreement, *2nd Area Army* in Celebes, *37th Army* (previously known as the *Borneo Garrison Army*) and *29th Army* in Malaya were to take command of all naval and land units in their respective areas. The *94th Division* was formed in Malaya and placed under command of *29th Army*, and a *Singapore Defence Command* was created and placed under orders of *7th Area Army*.
[3] See Map 10, facing page 340, and Volume III, Chapter XV.

operations had been completed when Hengyang was captured by *11th Army* on the 8th August 1944.[1] The Japanese were by this time facing serious administrative difficulties, for the railway south of Hankow had been destroyed by the Chinese and, if it were repaired, would suffer from a shortage of rolling stock; the water level of the Yangtze River was at its lowest and large vessels could not be used; shipping was scarce owing to losses from Allied air attacks; and attempts to build a road parallel to the railway had not been successful. These difficulties had been largely responsible for the delay of some seven weeks in the capture of Hengyang, which had been reached on the 26th June.

To improve the system of command within *China Expeditionary Force*, considerable reorganization took place in July and August. In July, *34th Army* was formed in the Hankow area to take over responsibility for the security and administration of the Wuchang–Hankow area, and on the 26th August *6th Area Army* was formed, under the command of General Y. Okamura, to take control of *34th Army* at Hankow, *11th Army* in the Hengyang area and *23rd Army* at Canton. To free *11th Army* for its advance on Kweilin, *Headquarters 20th Army* was brought from Manchuria in September and made responsible for the Changsha–Hengyang area.[2]

Okamura's plan was to make a concentric attack on his objectives with *11th Army*, supported by *5th Air Army*,[3] moving south-west on Kweilin with six divisions, and *23rd Army* moving north-west on Liuchow with two divisions and two independent mixed brigades. For lines of communication *11th Army* was to use the many inland waterways and the railway where possible and *23rd Army* was to use the Hsi Chiang.

The *11th Army* began its advance on the 29th August. By the 8th September it had occupied Lingling and next day had reached the boundary of the Hunan and Kwangsi provinces, about two-thirds of the way from Hengyang to Kweilin, meeting with little opposition. There it paused to consolidate and to mop up Chinese formations which it had by-passed. The *23rd Army* began its advance about the 6th September and by the end of the month had captured the airfield at Tanchu, some 100 miles south-east of Liuchow.

·   ·   ·   ·   ·

---

[1] See Volume III, page 391.

[2] The composition of *6th Area Army* in September was—*34th Army*: *39th Division* and four independent infantry brigades; *20th Army*: *27th*, *64th*, *68th* and *116th Divisions* and some administrative units; *11th Army*: *3rd*, *13th*, *34th*, *37th*, *40th* and *58th Divisions*; *23rd Army*: *22nd* and *104th Divisions*, two independent infantry brigades and three independent mixed brigades.

[3] The *5th Air Army*, which consisted of nine air regiments and one independent air squadron with a strength of some 150 aircraft, including 64 fighters and 38 light bombers, was reinforced during September by one heavy bomber and two fighter squadrons.

Map 3

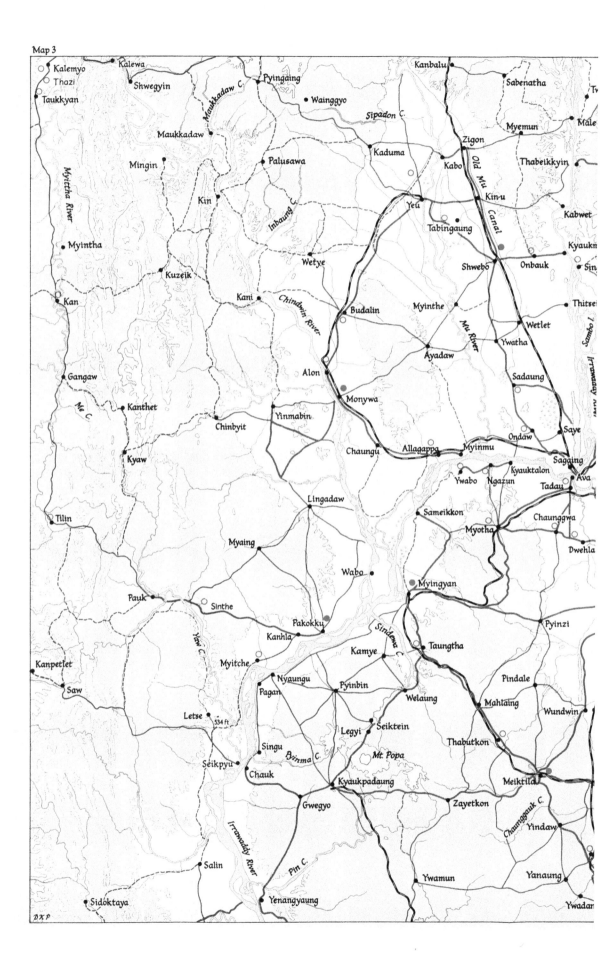

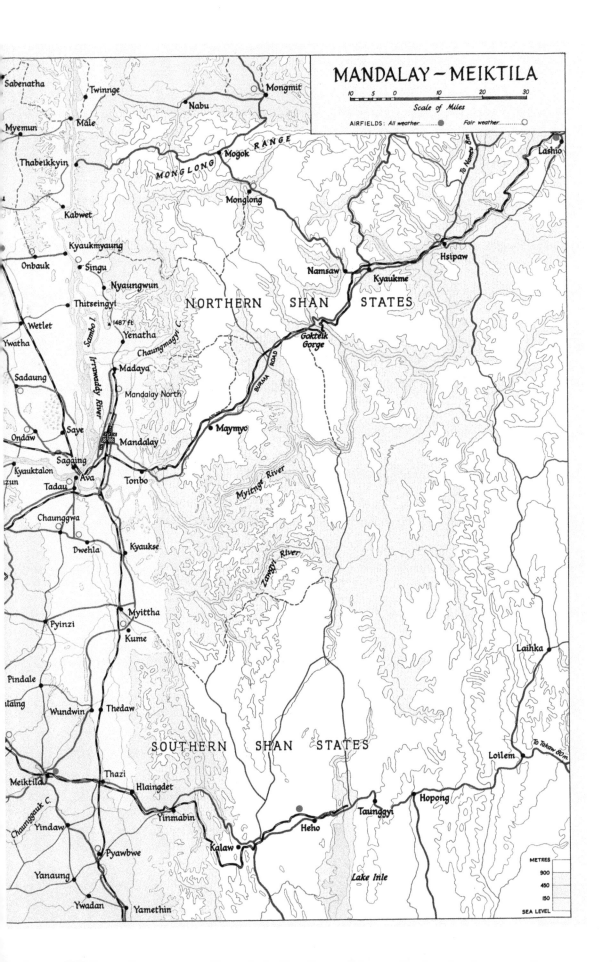

MANDALAY — MEIKTILA

10 5 0   10   20   30
Scale of Miles

AIRFIELDS: All weather.........●   Fair weather.........○

Sabenatha

Twinnge

Nabu

Mongmit

Male

Myemun

Thabeikkyin

MONGLONG   RANGE

Mogok

Monglong

Kabwet

Lashio

To Namtu 8 m.

Kyaukmyaung

Onbauk

Singu

Nyaungwun

NORTHERN   SHAN   STATES

Hsipaw

Thitseingyi

Namsaw

Kyaukme

Wetlet

▲ 1487 ft

Yenatha

Ywatha

Sambo I.

Chaungmagyi C.

Irrawaddy River

Madaya

Goktelk
Gorge

Sadaung

Mandalay North

BURMA ROAD

Ondaw

Saye

Maymyo

Mandalay

Sagaing

Ava

Tonbo

Kyauktalon

Tadau

Myitnge River

zun

Chaunggwa

Dwehla

Kyaukse

Zawgyi River

Myittha

Pyinzi

Kume

Laihka

Pindale

ataing

Wundwin

Thedaw

SOUTHERN   SHAN   STATES

Loilem

To Takaw 60 m.

Meiktila

Thazi

Hlaingdet

Hopong

Chaunggauk C.

Yindaw

Yinmabin

Taunggyi

Pyawbwe

Kalaw

Heho

Yanaung

Lake Inle

METRES

Ywadan

Yamethin

900

450

150

SEA LEVEL

Meanwhile in Burma, Lieut.-General M. Kawabe (*Burma Area Army*) had on the 9th July ordered *15th Army* (Lieut.-General R. Mutaguchi), then consisting of *15th, 31st* and *33rd Divisions* and *1st I.N.A. Division*, to abandon its Imphal offensive and withdraw into Burma. The withdrawal was to be carried out in two phases: the first to the Chindwin River during July and August, and the second to the general line Zibyu Taungdan–Mawlaik–Kalewa–Gangaw during September and October.[1] To keep the Burma Road closed and regain the initiative in that area, he directed *33rd Army* (Lieut.-General M. Honda), consisting of *18th, 53rd* and *56th Divisions*, to be prepared to take the offensive on the Salween front. To relieve Honda of responsibility for the Mogaung area, *53rd Division* was to be transferred to *15th Army* and, to compensate him for its loss, he was to be reinforced by *2nd Division* from south Burma and a regiment of *49th Division* on its arrival in Burma from Korea. At the same time Kawabe told Mutaguchi (*15th Army*) that as soon as *18th Division*, on its way from the area north of Mogaung to join *33rd Army*, had reached Indaw he could withdraw *53rd Division* from Mogaung if he thought it necessary.[2]

On the 12th July Kawabe ordered *28th Army* (Lieut.-General S. Sakurai) to send *2nd Division*, together with a large part of the army's motor transport, to *33rd Army*, and to hold with its remaining two divisions (*54th* and *55th*) the Irrawaddy delta and the strategic coastal area south of Tamandu (some 35 miles north-east of Kyaukpyu). The offshore islands of Ramree and Cheduba were to be held for as long as possible.[3] As the removal of *2nd Division* made it impossible for the army to hold the whole of Arakan as well as the Irrawaddy delta,[4] Sakurai ordered *55th Division* to withdraw in late July from north Arakan to the delta, leaving a detachment (*Sakura*) to screen the withdrawal and to delay for as long as possible any British advance north-west of the general line Myohaung–Akyab.[5] The *54th Division* was to be responsible from that line southwards to the Prome–Taungup road.

The situation on the Salween front early in July was that *56th Division* had brought the Chinese Yunnan offensive to a halt on the hills east of Lungling but its forward posts at Pingka, Lameng and Tengchung, each held by a battalion, were cut off and closely invested

---

[1] See Map 1, facing page 15, and Volume III, Chapter XXV.
[2] See Map 2, facing page 39.
[3] See Map 13 in end pocket.
[4] Including north Arakan, the area allotted to *28th Army* was nearly 400 miles from north to south and in the Irrawaddy delta sector was some 150 miles wide.
[5] The *Sakura Detachment* consisted of three infantry battalions, a reconnaissance regiment and a battalion of mountain artillery under command of Major-General T. Sakurai.

by superior Chinese forces.[1] Excluding these isolated garrisons, the division was disposed with three battalions in the Lungling area and the remainder in reserve in the Mangshih area.[2] Honda ordered *2nd Division*, on its arrival from south Burma, to concentrate at Namhkam and begin to put it and Bhamo into a state of defence. When *18th Division* reached Namhkam from Kamaing, *2nd Division* was to move forward to Mangshih, leaving one battalion and the divisional reconnaissance regiment to hold Bhamo. Honda planned to launch his offensive early in September eastwards from Lungling astride the Burma Road with *2nd Division* on the right, *56th Division* on the left, and *168th Regiment* of *49th Division* in reserve. Having driven the Chinese from their positions east of Lungling, the two divisions were then to regain touch with the beleaguered garrisons at Pingka, Lameng and Tengchung.

While preparations for the offensive were being carried out, the situation altered since the Chinese steadily increased their pressure on Tengchung and Lameng and attacked Lungling. By the end of August the garrison of Tengchung had been reduced by casualties to a third of its original strength of some 1,800 men and was hemmed in at the northern end of the walled town; the garrison of Lameng had been reduced to a quarter of its original strength of some 1,200 men and had been forced to withdraw within the walls of the town itself; and at Lungling, the pivotal point of the proposed offensive, the garrison, though reinforced by a battalion, had been forced out of its positions in the hills east of the town and was also confined within the town walls.

The Japanese offensive began at dawn on the 3rd September. The *2nd Division* was soon in difficulties south and south-east of Lungling, and *56th Division*, after early successes, was also held up. No progress was made in the ensuing days despite repeated attacks, and by the 7th there was complete stalemate. That day Lameng fell and on the 14th Tengchung also fell, the garrisons of both towns having fought to the last man. In the circumstances Honda decided to discontinue the offensive, and on the 15th September ordered *2nd Division* to hold Lungling and *168th Regiment* of *49th Division* to hold Mangshih, while *146th Regiment* of *56th Division* broke through to Pingka to rescue its garrison. Pingka was reached on the 22nd and *146th Regiment* with the remnants of the garrison (including 200 stretcher cases) got back to Mangshih on the 24th. By the end of the month, finding that neither the Allied forces on the Burma Road nor those at Myitkyina showed

---

[1] See Map 2, facing page 39, and Volume III, Chapter XXVIII.
[2] The *56th Division* at this time consisted of *113th* and *148th Infantry Regiments, I/146th Battalion, II/29 Battalion* (from *2nd Division*) and *I/119th Battalion* (from *53rd Division*). As a result of the severe fighting against vastly superior Chinese forces during May and June, the division was greatly under strength, its battalions being on an average only 300 strong.

any signs of taking the offensive, Honda redisposed his army with *56th Division* holding Lungling and the Burma Road and *18th Division* the Bhamo–Namhkam area, and on the 5th October offered to release *2nd Division* and *168th Regiment* of *49th Division* to *Burma Army Area*. During August and September *56th Division*'s casualties amounted to 3,150 killed and 200 wounded,[1] while *2nd Division*'s casualties amounted to some 1,600—a good indication of the severity of the fighting.

While the offensive on the Salween front was proceeding, *Imperial General Headquarters* had decided to make a number of changes in the higher command in Burma. On the 30th August, Lieut.-General H. Kimura replaced Kawabe as commander of *Burma Area Army*,[2] and Lieut.-General S. Katamura (hitherto the commander of *54th Division*) replaced Mutaguchi as commander of *15th Army*. At the same time Lieut.-General S. Tanaka was succeeded in command of *18th Division* by Lieut.-General E. Naka and became Chief of Staff *Burma Area Army*, and Major-General G. Yoshida succeeded Major-General M. Kunomura as Chief of Staff *15th Army*.

The failure of the campaign in north Burma, and the impossibility of replacing the heavy casualties incurred owing to the necessity of giving first priority in reinforcements to the Pacific, forced *Imperial General Headquarters* to consider a withdrawal from Burma altogether. The idea was, however, rejected as it was considered that such a withdrawal would endanger the security of the chain of defences from Burma through the Andamans to Sumatra which covered the western flank of *Southern Army's* area. They appreciated that an Allied attack on south Burma would have to be met although *Burma Area Army* (Kimura) was no longer strong enough to hold it and at the same time keep communications between India and China severed. In consequence a new directive was issued to Field-Marshal Count H. Terauchi (*Southern Army*) on the 19th September which required him to ensure the security of strategic areas of southern Burma at all costs and made the severance of communications to China of secondary importance. The order was passed to Kimura with instructions to regroup his forces to cover what he considered vital strategical areas in southern Burma, including the south-west coast, and to continue to interrupt India–China communications as long as he could do so without prejudice to his primary task.

It was clear to Kimura that the Yenangyaung oilfields and the vast rice-producing areas of the Irrawaddy delta were vital for the maintenance of his army and that to secure them he must be prepared

---

[1] The fight to the death at Lameng and Tengchung account for this extraordinarily high percentage of killed to wounded.

[2] Kimura, aged 66, was an ex-artillery officer who had been Vice-Minister of War in Tokyo from April 1941 to March 1943.

to hold, and if need be counter-attack to regain, the general line
Mandalay–Yenangyaung–Ramree Island.[1] He could carry out his
secondary task by undertaking the passive defence of the general line
Lashio–Mandalay with a comparatively small force which could fall
back, when forced to do so, to cover his right flank. He therefore
ordered *33rd Army* (Honda) with *18th* and *56th Divisions* and *168th
Regiment* of *49th Division* to retain control of the right sector from
Lashio to Mandalay exclusive; but, to guard against the danger of
Allied forces moving round the right flank of *15th Army* in order to
attack Mandalay from the north-east, it was to hold the Mongmit area
and be prepared to take offensive action there in addition to its
passive role of covering the Lashio–Mandalay road. The *15th Army*
(Katamura), with *15th, 31st, 33rd* and *53rd Divisions*, was to hold the
line of the Irrawaddy from Mandalay to Pakokku with three divisions
and retain one in reserve in the Meiktila area ready to co-operate
with the *Area Army* reserve. The *28th Army* (Sakurai), with *54th* and
55th Divisions, 72nd Independent Mixed Brigade (*I.M.B.*) and the *Katsu
Force*,[2] was to hold the general line Yenangyaung, the Arakan coast
and the Irrawaddy delta, including Bassein and Rangoon. Kimura
kept *2nd Division*, which was to move to Pyawbwe on the 28th October,
and *49th Division* (less *153rd* and *168th Regiments*) at Taunggyi as his
reserve, since from this area with its good road and rail communications a counter-offensive could be launched to support either *15th* or
28th Army according to whether the main Allied offensive was made
across the Irrawaddy or in Arakan.[3]

During November 1944, Katamura (*15th Army*) came to the conclusion after a personal reconnaissance that 14th Army would make
its main crossing of the Irrawaddy between Kyauktalon and Myinmu
and subsidiary crossings at Singu to the north and between Myingyan
and Pakokku to the south. He expected the Allies also to make an
attempt to drive a wedge between his army and *33rd Army* by infiltrating east of the Irrawaddy into the Monglong Range, and he took into
account the possibility of Allied airborne operations against Maymyo
and Meiktila. He estimated that, by December, the strength of his
four divisions would amount to some 21,400 men and that he would
have in addition one *I.N.A.* regiment.[4]

For the defence of the Irawaddy River line, he decided to build
main defensive positions on the hills north of Madaya, around Mandalay, at Myinmu and Myingyan and in the delta north-west of

---

[1] See Map 3, facing page 55.
[2] The *Katsu Force* consisted of *153rd Infantry Regiment* (less one battalion) from *49th
Division.*
[3] For the order of battle of *Burma Area Army* in November see Appendix 8.
[4] The estimated strength of the four divisions was: *31st*, 7,000; *33rd*, 5,400; *15th*, 4,500;
and *53rd*, 4,500. These figures include artillery units which had less than half their normal
number of guns, and represent approximately forty per cent of normal divisional strength,
except in the case of *31st Division.*

Myingyan, and arranged for covering positions to be prepared north and west of Sagaing and near Monywa. The *15th Division* was to occupy positions in depth on the general line Mongmit–Singu, in touch with *18th Division* of *33rd Army* at Mongmit, and prepare a lay-back position in the hills north-east of Madaya. The *31st Division* was to hold a bridgehead in the angle of the river at Sagaing and the high ground south of Kyauktalon and opposite Myinmu. The *33rd Division* was to occupy Sameikkon, the high ground around Myingyan and the confluence to its north-west, and Pakokku, with forward posts near Gangaw and Monywa. An *I.N.A.* regiment was to occupy both banks of the Irrawaddy in the Nyaungu area.[1] The *53rd Division* was to concentrate in the Meiktila–Kyaukse area, prepare positions against a possible airborne attack at Meiktila and be ready to move either to the Singu or Kyauktalon front. The main bodies of *31st* and *33rd Divisions*, the whole of *2nd* and *53rd Divisions* and elements of *18th* and *49th Divisions*, supported by *14th Tank Regiment* and army artillery units, would be made available for a counter-stroke in the Kyauk-talon–Myinmu area, and *15th* and *53rd Divisions*, supported by *14th Tank Regiment*, for an alternative counter-stroke in the Singu area.

Katamura, whose army was being gradually forced back by the steady pressure of 14th Army, decided to begin his withdrawal across the Irrawaddy on the 1st December. The *53rd Division* was to move first into army reserve. The *15th Division* was to withdraw towards Shwebo and then, retaining a bridgehead on the west bank, cross the Irrawaddy at Kyaukmyaung and occupy its allotted positions on the east bank of the river. The *31st Division* was to remain in the Kanbalu–Shwebo area to cover the withdrawal of *53rd* and *15th Divisions* and then, retaining a bridgehead at Sagaing, cross the Irrawaddy and take up its position in the Kyauktalon–Myinmu area. The *33rd Division* was to impose the maximum delay on the advance of 14th Army before falling back to its allotted positions at the confluence of the Irrawaddy and the Chindwin near Myingyan in touch with *28th Army*.

Sakurai (*28th Army*) decided to use *72nd Independent Mixed Brigade* to defend the Yenangyaung oilfields, to hold the Arakan coast from Taungup northwards with *54th Division* covered by the *Sakura Detachment* and to make *55th Division* (less the *Sakura Detachment*) responsible for the Rangoon–Bassein–Gwa–Prome area.[2] He divided his army area into three: a holding area comprising the area west of the Kaladan River basin, Akyab, the coastal islands and the

---

[1] At the request of *15th Army* the responsibility for the Nyaungu area was passed to *28th Army*. Command passed on the 14th February 1945, a most unfortunate date for the Japanese as it was on that day that IV Corps began its crossing of the Irrawaddy at Nyaungu. See Chapter XXIII.

[2] See Map 13 in end pocket.

southern end of the Irrawaddy delta, in which action was to be primarily defensive; a counter-attack area, comprising the coastal strip from Myebon to Pagoda Point and the Arakan Yomas; and the decisive battle area, which was to comprise the Irrawaddy River basin.

Sketch 1

THE PHILIPPINES
JAPANESE AND AMERICAN FLEET MOVEMENTS
leading to the
Battles of Leyte Gulf and Cape Engano
October 1944

120°   130°E

CHINA

Amoy

Swatow

Pescadores

FORMOSA

Hongkong

LUZON STRAIT

20°N   20°N

AMERICAN
Fast Carrier Task Group (T.F. 38) ....
Task Groups ....
Detached Forces ....
Submarines ....
JAPANESE
Northern Force (OZAWA) ....
Centre Force (KURITA) ....
Southern Force (NISHIMURA) ....
2nd Striking Force (SHIMA) ....

TAMA
11·10pm 25th
Midt. 25-26th
6pm 25th   ZUIHO
ZUIKAKU   1am 24th
Midt. 24-25th   CHIYODA
10am   CHITOSE
Detached cruiser force
2·30 pm   7pm
10·30am 24th   6·30 am   4·30pm
Detached Squadron   2·15am   Midt. 25-26th
11·15 am Battleship force and T.G. 38·2 detached to San Bernardino Strait
Midt. 24-25th   8·20am
5·50 am   1st Striking force flown off
2·40am 25th
Halsey forms battleship force

Northern Force (OZAWA)

Cape Engaño

LUZON

Lingayen Gulf

Task Group 38·3 (Sherman)
8am 24th   PRINCETON 6pm 24th

Midt. 24-25th R/V of Task Groups

Manila

Corregidor

Task Group 38·2 (Bogan)

2nd Striking Force (SHIMA)

CHINA SEA

8am 24th

MINDORO

San Bernardino Strait

Mindoro Str.
6pm 23rd
Palawan Passage
8am 24th
Departed 2am 24th

MUSASHI

Task Group 38·4 (Davison)

SAMAR

PANAY   LEYTE
Leyte Gulf   8am 24th
NEGROS   CEBU   Surigao Strait

10°   10°

MAYA
ATAGO
6·30am 23rd

PALAWAN

Bombed 9·18 am 24th

SULU SEA

Southern Force (NISHIMURA) Departed Brunei Bay 3pm 22nd

MINDANAO

Davao

6pm 22nd

Centre Force (KURITA) 8am 22nd

NORTH BORNEO

Tawitawi
Sulu Archipelago

Brunei Bay

CELEBES SEA

Talaud I's

Tarakan

Morotai

Halmahera

M.J.G.   120°   130°E

CHAPTER VI

THE PACIFIC

(August–October 1944)

The Approach to the Philippines

See Maps 4 and 8 and Sketches 1, 2 and 3

STRATEGY in the Pacific was still governed in August 1944 by the American Chiefs of Staff's directive of the 12th March.[1] After the capture of the Marianas,[2] the Central Pacific Forces (Admiral C. Nimitz) were to occupy the Palau Islands. Preparatory to a further advance to Formosa, either directly or by way of Luzon, the South-West Pacific Forces (General D. MacArthur), whose advance had reached the western extremity of New Guinea,[3] were to land at Mindanao, supported by the Pacific Fleet, with the object of establishing air bases from which Japanese forces in the Philippines could be reduced and contained. For some time, however, the lines of advance after the seizure of Mindanao and the Palaus had been undetermined. General MacArthur was insistent that the United States were in honour bound to liberate the Philippines before going farther and that it was good strategy to do so. Admiral E. J. King, Chief of Naval Operations, and, with less conviction, Admiral Nimitz believed that the better strategy was to by-pass the Philippines or, at least, Luzon and take Formosa and a part of the China coast in order to cut Japanese communications to the south. On the 8th September the American Chiefs of Staff directed MacArthur to occupy Leyte by the 20th December, six weeks after the planned date of the landing on Mindanao,[4] but left in abeyance the decision whether to go from there to Luzon or Formosa. Whichever alternative they selected, American forces would be astride the Japanese sea line of communication between the homeland and the Southern Region. From 1942 onwards American submarines had been taking such a toll of the shipping on this route that supplies reaching the homeland of essential articles such as rubber, tin, rice and, above all, oil, without which Japan could not continue the war, were constantly decreasing.[5] Possession of the

---

[1] See Map 8, facing page 252, and Volume III, pages 110–12.
[2] See Volume III, Chapter XXXI.
[3] See Volume III, Chapter XXX.
[4] See Sketch 1, facing page 63.
[5] See Appendix 9 for Japanese merchant shipping losses.

Philippines or Formosa would cut Japan off from this source of supply altogether.

Before his landing on Mindanao on the 15th November, MacArthur planned to occupy Morotai Island (which was less than ten miles from the northern promontory of the Halmaheras) on the 15th September and the Talaud Islands a month later, establishing airfields on both so that he could always operate within range of his land-based fighters. Nimitz decided to make his assault on the Palaus on the same day as the landing on Morotai, and then on the 5th October to seize Yap Island and Ulithi Atoll, the former to secure an additional airfield for the neutralization of Truk and the western Carolines, and the latter for development as a major fleet base.

A timetable for these operations was drawn up and presented to the Combined Chiefs of Staff at the Octagon Conference, which took place at Quebec between the 11th and 16th September. But meanwhile, in order to neutralize enemy bases from which aircraft could interfere with the coming operations, the fast carriers of the U.S. 3rd Fleet under Vice-Admiral W. F. Halsey had made a series of strikes on Yap, the Palaus and Mindanao. The lack of opposition encountered prompted Halsey to shift his attacks to the central Philippines, where again he was surprised by the apparent weakness of the defence. It seemed to him that the Japanese had few serviceable aircraft left in the Philippines and, although the invasion convoys for the capture of Morotai and the Palaus were already at sea and nearing their objectives, he suggested to Nimitz on the 13th September that MacArthur could by-pass Mindanao and seize Leyte without any intermediate operations. Nimitz and MacArthur agreed and the Combined Chiefs of Staff at Quebec were asked to sanction the revised plan. Within an hour and a half of receiving it they gave their approval, and instructed MacArthur to attack Leyte instead of Mindanao on the 20th October and to by-pass the Talaud Islands. To assist him in his task XXIV U.S. Corps, then partly loading at Hawaii and partly at sea for the assault on Yap, was placed under his command; as soon as the Palaus had been occupied, Nimitz was to seize Ulithi and send all his escort carriers, fire support ships and transports to co-operate with the 7th Amphibious Force in the capture of Leyte.

When early in 1944 they withdrew their defensive perimeter, the Japanese had concentrated some 30,000 men in Halmahera and had begun to develop it as an air base to guard the southern approaches to the Philippines. They had also begun to build an airstrip in the southern plain of Morotai, the only part of the island of military value, but had stopped work on it and reduced the garrison to some 500 men, most of whom were Formosan. MacArthur's object was to seize the southern plain and hold it against possible counter-attack from Halmahera. In view of the strength of the garrison in Halmahera he considered that the landing should be made by a reinforced division with a regimental combat team in reserve (about 28,000 troops). Prior to D-day a carrier group of the U.S. 3rd Fleet, which was operating fifty miles north of Morotai, struck airfields in Celebes, while 5th U.S.A.A.F. from New Guinea made sure that there would be no interference from Halmahera.

On the morning of the 15th September, 31st U.S. Division (from the Sarmi sector of New Guinea) began landing on the beaches in the south of the island, covered by fire from American and Australian cruisers and destroyers of the 7th Fleet and given close air support from six escort carriers. The landings were unopposed and the southern plain was soon secured. It had been hoped to make use of the unfinished airstrip, but the ground proved to be too boggy. A new airfield was therefore built, and by the 4th October fighters of 5th U.S.A.A.F. were able to fly in and the escort carriers were dispensed with. Shortly afterwards medium bombers began operating from Morotai, and on the 19th October (a day before the landing on Leyte) heavy bombers were using the new airfield.

Halsey's assault on the Palaus took place simultaneously with the landings on Morotai.[1] The group of islands (470 miles to the east of Mindanao) is fringed by coral reefs and extends some eighty miles in a north and south direction. The largest island—Babelthuap—lies in the centre, and north of it there is the Kossoi Passage, a wide strait ten miles long and enclosed by reefs. In the south are Pelelieu and Angaur Islands. After the 5th Fleet's carrier raid on the Palaus in March 1944, *Imperial General Headquarters*, in expectation of invasion, had sent reinforcements to the Palaus and in April *14th Division* had arrived from north China to augment the naval garrison. Lieut.-General S. Inoue, the divisional commander, had concentrated the greater part of the garrison on Babelthuap.

Halsey planned to take only the two southern islands and to clear the Kossoi Passage of mines, previously laid by the Americans, so that it could be used as an anchorage and sea-plane base. After the usual overture of bombing and bombardment by battleships and cruisers, 1st U.S. Marine Division was landed on the morning of the 15th September on the beaches opposite the airfield in the south of Pelelieu. Escort carriers of the 3rd Amphibious Force gave close air support. A beachhead was secured against stiff opposition and by the end of the second day the airfield, the main objective, had been occupied but not consolidated. On a coral ridge in the north-west of the island the Japanese had dug mutually supporting strong points commanding the airfield which were practically impervious to aerial bombing or

---

[1] See Sketch 2, facing page 66.

naval gunfire. Progress along the ridge was slow and costly, but by the 1st October sufficient of it had been secured to enable the airfield to be used. By the 7th an airstrip, 6,000 feet long and suitable for bombers, had been completed. The Japanese, however, clung to the northern end of the ridge and some six more weeks of bitter fighting lay ahead before all organized resistance on the island came to an end.

The 81st U.S. Division, which had been held for the first twenty-four hours as a floating reserve for Peleliu, began landing on Angaur Island, six miles south of Peleliu, on the morning of the 17th September. Opposition was less severe and by noon on the 20th the island had been overrun except for a small pocket of resistance in the north-west corner. Army engineers at once began work on the airfield which, by the 21st, was in use by Liberators. As soon as it became clear that the entire division was no longer needed on Angaur, a regimental combat team was sent to Ulithi. The Japanese had, however, abandoned the atoll early in September and it was secured on the 23rd without opposition. The port was quickly developed and during October it took the place of Eniwetok, in the Marshalls, as the main fleet base

With the capture of the Palaus and Morotai, Nimitz's line of advance from the Gilberts, by way of the Marshalls, across the central Pacific through the Marianas had converged with MacArthur's from southern Papua up the long coast of New Guinea. The Central and South-West Pacific Forces were now combined for the attack on Leyte. The Japanese were not unprepared. After the fall of the Marianas in July and the heavy losses suffered by the navy in the battle of the Philippine Sea, they had fallen back on an inner line of defence extending from the Kuriles and the Japanese home islands through Formosa and the Philippines to the Netherlands East Indies. The line had been divided into four sectors and a plan of operations ('SHO')drawn up for the defence of each, the plan for the defence of the Philippines, which *Imperial General Headquarters* believed was the point most likely to be attacked, being called 'SHO-1'.[1]

The Japanese knew that a successful defence of the Philippines was essential for, if these islands were lost, their communications to the source of raw materials, and particularly oil, in the Netherlands East Indies would be cut. In such circumstances the fleet, if kept in home waters, would be without fuel and, if in southern waters, without ammunition. They therefore decided to take full advantage of the fact that the American invasion fleets with only carrier-borne air support would have for the first time to expose themselves to attack by a strong land-based air force at short range, and make an all-out effort to repel an invasion force before it could land. The essence of their

---

[1] See page 54.

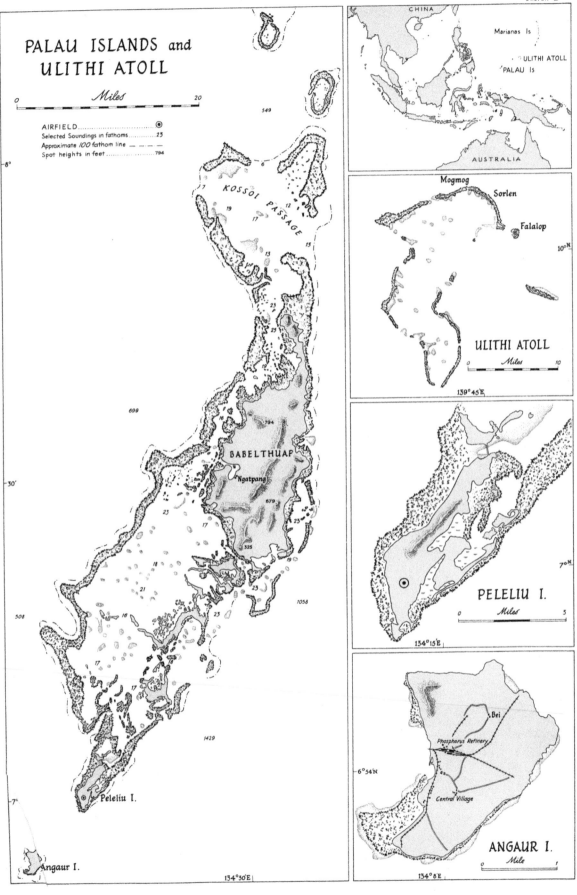

PALAU ISLANDS and
ULITHI ATOLL

Miles

0   20

AIRFIELD...⊙
Selected Soundings in fathoms.............*23*
Approximate *100* fathom line — — — —
Spot heights in feet..........................*794*

KOSSOI PASSAGE

BABELTHUAP

Ngatpang

Peleliu I.

Angaur I.

134°30'E

Sketch 2

CHINA

Marianas Is

ULITHI ATOLL

PALAU Is

AUSTRALIA

Mogmog

Sorlen

Falalop

10°N

ULITHI ATOLL

Miles

0   10

139°45'E

PELELIU I.

7°N

Miles

0   3

134°15'E

ANGAUR I.

Bei

Phosphorus Refinery

Central Village

6°54'N

Mile

0   1

134°6'E

plan was therefore to concentrate as strong a force of land-based aircraft as possible to attack and neutralize the American carrier forces as they approached the Philippines, and to use the whole strength of the combined fleet under this air umbrella to destroy the invasion fleet.

The basic strategy of the naval plans for 'SHO–1' was dictated by the weakness of the Japanese carrier force, most of whose aircraft had been lost during the battle of the Philippine Sea.[1] Although new carrier groups were being trained in Japan, it seemed unlikely that they would be ready in time. Admiral S. Toyoda (Commander-in-Chief, *Combined Fleet*), feeling that, if the Philippines were lost, his fleet was doomed, decided to use its still powerful gunnery strength to destroy the enemy invasion forces, relying on the land-based air force to give it protection. His plan was for the *1st Striking Force* (the battleships and cruisers which constituted the main strength of the *Combined Fleet* and were at Singapore in order to be near their oil supply) to come north and attack the invasion forces as they approached the beaches, while the *Northern Force*, consisting mainly of aircraft carriers, came from the Inland Sea in Japan, where it had gone to train new pilots, and decoyed the American fast carriers away from the scene of action. The shore-based *1st* and *2nd Air Fleets*, assisted by *4th Air Army*, were to engage raiding carrier aircraft in the initial stages, but once the invasion had started were to conserve their strength for strikes on the invasion forces.[2]

The American landings on Morotai and in the Palaus on the 15th September, coupled with the widespread bombing of the Philippines, confirmed the belief that the Americans would attack in the near future somewhere in the Philippines, and Field-Marshal Terauchi (*Southern Army*), in whose area the Philippines lay, realizing how long it would take to concentrate and deploy formations and units in that area, recommended to *Imperial General Headquarters* that 'SHO–1' should begin immediately.[3] Although *Imperial General Headquarters* did not agree, they told *Southern Army* to complete preparations for the operation by the 31st October at the latest, and ordered *1st Division* from Shanghai and *30th Fighter Group* from Japan to the Philippines and *23rd Division*, then in Manchuria, to concentrate ready to be moved south at short notice.

Southern Army had made *14th Area Army*, supported by *4th Air Army*, responsible for the land defence of the Philippines. Owing to the shortage of shipping, the dangers of moving reinforcements by sea and the weakness of *14th Area Army* which precluded it from properly

---

[1] See Volume III, Chapter XXXI.
[2] The *1st Air Fleet* was in the Philippines, but *2nd Air Fleet* was to train in Japan until 'SHO –1' was ordered to begin.
[3] See page 54.

defending more than a portion of the Philippines, Terauchi had ordered that priority should be given to the defence of Luzon, and that operations in the central and southern groups of islands should be considered as of secondary importance, although all areas of strategic importance required by the navy and air force were to be defended. The *14th Area Army* consisted of nine infantry divisions, one armoured division and three independent mixed brigades (I.M.B.s) of which one infantry and the armoured division were still in Shanghai and Manchuria respectively.[1] In view of the importance attached to the defence of the Philippines, Lieut.-General T. Yamashita, the conqueror of Malaya in 1942, was brought from Manchuria and on the 6th October assumed command of *14th Area Army*. He undertook the defence of Luzon himself with three infantry divisions and two independent mixed brigades, made *35th Army* (Lieut.-General S. Suzuki), with four infantry divisions and one independent mixed brigade, responsible for the defence of the central and southern islands and kept the armoured and two infantry divisions in reserve.[2] Suzuki gave *16th Division* (Lieut.-General S. Makino) the task of defending Leyte; *30th Division* was to defend Davao, *100th Division* northern and central Mindanao and *102nd Division* Panay, Negros and Cebu.

The *4th Air Army* consisted on the 17th October of *2nd* and *4th Air Divisions* (eight air regiments) and *30th Fighter Group* (ten air regiments) in the Philippines and *7th Air Division* (four air regiments) in Celebes. It was planned that, when 'SHO-1' was ordered, *4th Air Army* was to be reinforced in three waves by thirteen air regiments drawn from Japan, China, Formosa, Indo-China and Malaya to bring its total strength up to some thirty-four regiments.

By the beginning of October the long-drawn-out argument between Admiral King and General MacArthur on whether Formosa or Luzon was to be the next objective after the capture of Leyte was settled. On the 3rd the American Chiefs of Staff issued a directive, which proved to be the last one of importance in the Pacific theatre. In it MacArthur was ordered to invade Luzon with a target date of the 20th December 1944 and to provide support for the subsequent occupation of the Ryukyu Islands by forces under command of Admiral Nimitz. Nimitz was to provide cover and support for the Luzon operation. He was then to capture an island in the Bonins

---

[1] See Appendix 7.

[2] The detailed dispositions of *14th Area Army* were: for the defence of Luzon, *8th*, *103rd* and *105th Infantry Divisions* and *55th* and *58th I.M.B.s*; for the defence of the central and southern islands, *35th Army*, consisting of *16th*, *30th*, *100th* and *102nd Infantry Divisions* and *54th I.M.B.*; and in area reserve, *1st* and *26th Infantry Divisions* and *2nd Armoured Division*, of which only *26th Division* was in the Philippines at the end of October.

with a target date of the 20th January 1945 and one in the
Ryukyus with a target date of the 1st March. Although it was stated
that a directive for an invasion of Formosa would follow, it was
never issued for the operation required more troops than were likely to
be available before the defeat of Germany. Thereafter the strategic
conception in the Pacific remained the capture of Luzon, followed
by the seizure of an island in the Bonins to provide emergency landing facilities for the bombers based in the Marianas and a base for
fighter escorts for the bombing of Japan, and one in the Ryukyus which
could be developed into a naval and air base for the invasion of Japan
contemplated for the autumn of 1945.

The Philippine archipelago is divided into three main groups:
Luzon and adjacent islands in the north, the Visayan islands in the
centre,[1] and Mindanao and the Sulu Archipelago in the south. The
two largest islands in the eastern Visayas, Leyte and Samar, are
separated by the narrow San Juanico Strait and between them form
the arms of Leyte Gulf. Leyte has an approximate length of 115 miles
from north to south and a width which varies from 15 to 45 miles. The
greater part of the island is rugged and mountainous, except for a
stretch of flat land running north from Ormoc in the west, and a
broad fertile valley in the north-east which narrows and fades out
halfway down the east coast. The principal Japanese airfields were
one each at Tacloban near the entrance to the San Juanico Strait and
at Dulag eleven miles to the south, and three at Burauen farther
inland. It was on the beaches near Tacloban and Dulag that
MacArthur planned to land.[2]

Early in October 1944 his invasion fleets began to assemble at
Hollandia, which had become the main base in New Guinea, and at
Manus in the Admiralty Islands.[3] His naval forces were the U.S.
7th Fleet (under command of Vice-Admiral T. C. Kinkaid),[4] reinforced by the U.S. 3rd Amphibious Force from the central Pacific.
The U.S. 3rd Fleet under Halsey (consisting for the most part of
the four fast carrier groups, under command of Vice-Admiral M.
A. Mitscher) was to cover and support MacArthur's forces but
remain under Nimitz's orders.[5] The 6th U.S. Army (X and XXIV
Corps), commanded by Lieut.-General W. Krueger, provided the
land forces and 5th U.S.A.A.F. the supporting air force. Australian
troops who, until the capture of Hollandia, had borne the brunt of

---

[1] These include Samar, Leyte, Bohal, Cebu, Negros, Panay and Masbate. See Sketch 3,
facing page 84.
[2] See Map 4, facing page 88.
[3] See Map 8, facing page 252.
[4] It included two cruisers (H.M.A.S. *Australia* and *Shropshire*) and two destroyers
(H.M.A.S. *Warramunga* and *Arunta*) of the Royal Australian Navy and a fast minelayer
(H.M.S. *Ariadne*) of the Royal Navy.
[5] The four fast carrier groups were commanded by Vice-Admiral J. S. McCain and
Rear-Admirals R. E. Davison, F. C. Sherman and G. F. Bogan.

the fighting in New Guinea, were to play no part in the liberation of the Philippines, and on the 1st October 1st Australian Corps (Lieut.-General Sir Leslie Morshead) took over from the Americans the responsibility for operations against the large Japanese forces cut off in New Guinea, New Britain and the Solomons.

To reduce Japanese air strength and prevent reinforcement from the north before the invasion, the fifteen fast carriers of the 3rd Fleet made a series of heavy strikes on Japanese bases. On the 10th October they struck Okinawa in the Ryukyus. The following day, two task groups carried out a fighter sweep over northern Luzon and on the 12th and 13th all four groups concentrated their attacks on Formosa. The attacks provoked the strongest Japanese response hitherto experienced: every available aircraft was sent against the American carriers in the hope of inflicting a crushing blow. Although few managed to reach their target, a group of aircraft succeeded at dusk on the 13th in breaking through the fighter screen some eighty miles south of Formosa, torpedoed the Australian heavy cruiser *Canberra* and damaged three carriers. The cruiser was taken in tow. In the hope of preventing further attacks Halsey resumed his strikes on the Formosan airfields the following day, but enemy aircraft again broke through and torpedoed another heavy cruiser, the *Houston*. The damaged ships were given an escort of cruisers and destroyers and while they retired slowly south-eastward the Japanese redoubled their attacks. The unlucky *Houston* was hit by another torpedo on the 16th but remained afloat; no other ship was damaged. Once again the 3rd Fleet carriers had shown their ability to operate against land-based aircraft with comparative impunity. Between the 10th and the 17th October they lost twenty-six aircraft and had only two cruisers put out of action.

In his attacks on the Formosan airfields, Halsey was assisted by 20th Bomber Command from China. On the 14th, 130 B.29 bombers from Chengtu, each carrying seven tons of high explosive and incendiary bombs, launched a daylight attack on aircraft depots and airfields on the island. A second attack, though on a smaller scale, was made on the 16th. During these attacks only two bombers were lost, though several had to make emergency landings in China. The 20th Bomber Command claimed that they had destroyed about 100 Japanese aircraft on the ground and severely damaged maintenance installations.

The naval section of *Imperial General Headquarters* announced on the 15th October that, in the air battles of the 13th and 14th in the vicinity of Formosa, Japanese aircraft had sunk two American battleships and eleven carriers and had damaged many others, against a loss of 320 aircraft. The plan agreed for the decisive battle for the Philippines—'SHO-1'—was for the navy and air force to fight the battle whenever and wherever the Americans attempted to land, the army being fully committed only when Luzon itself was attacked, but on receipt of the news of the destruction of the American carriers *Imperial General Headquarters* altered it. Toyoda immediately ordered the land-based aircraft to undertake 'S H O–1', and *2nd Air Fleet* (some 350 operational aircraft), together with 150 carrier aircraft of Vice-Admiral J. Ozawa's *3rd* and *4th Carrier Squadrons* under command, was moved to Formosa. The *5th Fleet* (Vice-Admiral K. Shima), consisting of the *16th Cruiser Squadron* (one heavy and one light cruiser and one destroyer), and the *21st Cruiser Squadron* (two heavy cruisers, one light cruiser and seven destroyers), was ordered to sail from the Inland Sea and seek out and destroy the damaged American ships. At the same time the army section of *Imperial General Headquarters* ordered *Southern Army* to fight the decisive battle on Leyte instead of Luzon. Terauchi thereupon told *14th Area Army* to deploy its maximum strength to hold that island. Yamashita protested vehemently and only when the order was repeated on the 22nd October, two days after the American landing on Leyte, did he give way and order *35th Army* to concentrate for the defence of Leyte.

The Commander-in-Chief, *Combined Fleet*, had, however, taken no steps to investigate and confirm the accuracy of the pilots' reports of huge losses inflicted on the American fleet in the Formosan air battles, an oversight which was to have far-reaching results. The naval section of *Imperial General Headquarters* soon realized that the reports were wildly inaccurate and hurriedly ordered the *5th Fleet* to reverse course and make for the Ryukyu Islands.[1] The army section was not, however, told that the reports were inaccurate and therefore had no reason to alter its revised orders to *Southern Army*. Consequently Yamashita remained committed to the course, which he had so strongly opposed, of fighting the main battle on Leyte although naval support had been withdrawn and the Americans were firmly established on the island.

While the battle off Formosa between carrier-borne and land-based aircraft was in progress, Kinkaid's invasion forces were approaching Leyte Gulf in the wake of a typhoon. On the 17th and 18th October, despite heavy seas, troops were landed on two islands at the mouth of the gulf. These were secured with little difficulty and mine-sweepers began clearing an entrance channel. The bombardment and fire support groups under command of Rear-Admiral J. B. Oldendorf followed the sweepers into the gulf and took up their firing positions opposite the beaches on the 18th. Escorted by cruisers and destroyers, the transports entered the gulf on the night of the 19th/20th. At about 2 a.m. on the 20th a detachment broke off to land part of 21st

---

[1] Admiral Shima had already located a strong force of American carriers and had anticipated this order.

Regiment on Panaon Island off the south-eastern tip of Leyte, and at 10 a.m., after two days of bombardment by Oldendorf's battleships, cruisers and destroyers and bombing by aircraft from eighteen escort carriers, X Corps (1st Cavalry Division and 24th Infantry Division) was landed south of Tacloban and XXIV Corps (96th and 7th Infantry Divisions) near Dulag.[1] The weather by then had cleared and the assault troops were put ashore without difficulty. Meeting with very little resistance they quickly secured the beaches. By the 21st the two corps had begun to expand their beachheads and had occupied Dulag and Tacloban airfields which they began to prepare for use by 5th U.S.A.A.F.

---

[1] During the landings Japanese aircraft made sporadic attacks on the supporting fleets. On the 20th an American cruiser was damaged by a torpedo. On the 21st a bomber crashed into the foremast of H.M.A.S. *Australia*, causing considerable damage; escorted by the destroyer *Warramunga*, she returned to Manus.

CHAPTER VII

THE PACIFIC

(October–December 1944)

The Battle for Leyte

See Maps 4 and 8 and Sketches 1 and 3

WHEN the American invasion fleet was sighted approaching Leyte Gulf on the 17th October Admiral Toyoda alerted the *Combined Fleet,* and ordered the *1st Striking Force* to move as quickly as possible to Brunei Bay in north Borneo and the *5th Fleet* (Shima) to move from the Ryukyus to the Pescadores.[1] On the 18th, when *Imperial General Headquarters* ordered 'SHO–1' to be carried out, Toyoda ordered the *Combined Fleet* to carry out the pre-arranged plan, placed the *5th Fleet* under orders of the *South-West Area Fleet,* and ordered *2nd Air Fleet* from Formosa to reinforce *1st Air Fleet* on Luzon, whose strength had by this time been reduced to about 100 serviceable aircraft. He intended that a general air offensive by both air fleets, in co-operation with *4th Air Army,* was to be launched on the 24th, the day before the surface fleets were to penetrate into Leyte Gulf.

The *1st Striking Force* left Singapore on the 18th under Vice-Admiral T. Kurita and arrived on the 20th at Brunei Bay, where it refuelled.[2] Kurita, with the major part of his force (hereafter called the *Centre Force*), consisting of five battleships, ten heavy cruisers, two light cruisers and fifteen destroyers, sailed again at 8 a.m. on the 22nd and, skirting the west coast of Palawan, headed eastward through the central Philippines for San Bernardino Strait. The rest of his force (the *Southern Force*), consisting of two of the older battleships, one heavy cruiser and four destroyers under Vice-Admiral S. Nishimura, left at 3 p.m. the same day and made for Surigao Strait by way of the Sulu Sea.

On the 21st, Toyoda ordered the *South-West Area Fleet* to send the *5th Fleet* (Shima), less the *16th Cruiser Squadron* and the three destroyers of the *21st Squadron,* which had reached the Pescadores the previous day, south through the Surigao Strait to attack the American fleet in Leyte Gulf, co-ordinating its movements with the

---

[1] See Sketch 1, facing page 63.
[2] For the Japanese naval order of battle on the 25th October 1944 see Appendix 10.

73

Centre Force.[1] Kurita's force, coming from the north, and Nishimura's, coming from the south, were both to enter Leyte Gulf at first light (4.30 a.m.) on the 25th and engage the invasion force from two directions, while Shima's force (hereafter known as the *2nd Striking Force*) followed to take advantage of the confusion thus caused. But, since wireless silence had to be maintained, the *2nd Striking Force* was unable to contact Kurita and so remained unaware of Nishimura's approach route or the time of his advance. Meanwhile the *Northern Force* (Ozawa), consisting of four carriers with the remnants of their half-trained air groups (about one hundred and six aircraft) and two hermaphrodite battleship-carriers with no aircraft on board,[2] screened by three light cruisers and eight destroyers, had left the Inland Sea in Japan on the 20th and was heading south into the Philippine Sea to lure the U.S. 3rd Fleet northwards out of the way.

The first report of the approaching Japanese forces came from two American submarines which sighted the *Centre Force* as it was entering Palawan Passage at 1 a.m. on the 23rd October. Both attacked at about 6.30 a.m., sinking the heavy cruisers *Atago* (Kurita's flagship) and *Maya*, and damaging a third heavy cruiser (*Takao*) so badly that she had to return to Singapore for repairs.[3] Kurita and his staff were picked out of the water by a destroyer and transfered to the battleship *Yamato*.

On receipt of the report, Halsey brought the three fast carrier groups (Sherman's, Bogan's and Davison's), which were operating about 300 miles east of Luzon, nearer the coast, and at daybreak on the 24th sent out searches to the west and south. Soon after 8 a.m. a reconnaissance aircraft from Bogan's group sighted the *Centre Force* rounding the southern cape of Mindoro. An hour later aircraft from Davison's group sighted Nishimura's *Southern Force* in the Sulu Sea. It was attacked with bombs and torpedoes, and the battleship *Fuso* and a destroyer were damaged. Halsey thereupon ordered the three carrier groups to concentrate off San Bernardino Strait and attack the *Centre Force*, and recalled the fourth carrier (McCain's) group which was on its way to Ulithi to refuel.

Before this order could be carried out the Japanese attacked Sherman's group with some two hundred naval aircraft of *2nd Air Fleet* from bases on Luzon. Most of the aircraft were intercepted and sixty-seven were shot down. At 9.35 a.m., however, a lone bomber dived out of the clouds and hit the American light carrier *Princeton* with a

---

[1] The *16th Cruiser Squadron* was to provide escorts for the transports moving army reinforcements to Leyte, and the *21st Cruiser Squadron* for transports moving *2nd Air Division* to Negros.

[2] These were battleships converted for use as aircraft carriers with a flying deck aft.

[3] One of these American submarines ran aground during the action and had to be abandoned.

550-pound bomb which pierced the flight deck and exploded among the loaded aircraft below. Fires spread rapidly, a magazine blew up and that afternoon the ship had to be abandoned and sunk. The *Northern Force* had also sighted the American carriers that morning and at 11.45 a.m. had sent seventy-six aircraft to attack. Some were intercepted by fighters and suffered loss; the few that broke through attacked Sherman's group but achieved no success and then flew on to land on Luzon. Others failed to locate their target and returned to the carriers. At the end of the action Ozawa was left with only thirty aircraft in his whole force.

Throughout the 24th, aircraft from the American fleet carriers struck at the *Centre Force* in the Sibuyan Sea.[1] Having no air cover, the force had to rely on its guns for defence, with the result that only eighteen of the several hundred American aircraft sent out were shot down. The American pilots reported many ships, including battleships, sunk and others seriously damaged, and indicated that the speed and fighting power of the whole force was seriously reduced. However, in case Kurita persisted in his attempt to break out through San Bernardino Strait, Halsey shortly after 3 p.m. signalled to the 3rd Fleet that Task Force 34 would be formed 'to engage decisively at long range', and named the battleships and heavy cruisers which were to form the force.

The reports of Halsey's pilots were greatly exaggerated. In the air attacks the 18-inch gun battleship *Musashi* took no fewer than nineteen torpedoes but remained afloat until 7.35 that evening when she rolled over and sank. Her sister ship, the *Yamato*, and two other battleships were damaged but their fighting capacity remained unimpaired. The heavy cruiser *Myoko* had two of her propeller shafts damaged and had to return to Brunei. During the last strike Kurita reversed course and retired to the westward to avoid further attacks, informing Toyoda that he had done so, but shortly after 5 p.m. turned again and headed at 25 knots for San Bernardino Strait.

While the air battle in the Sibuyan Sea was being fought, Halsey was anxiously waiting for news of the Japanese carrier force. It was obvious that the Japanese Navy was making a supreme effort and he felt sure that the carriers must be committed somewhere. If Halsey was anxious to find the carriers, Ozawa was just as anxious to be found. His unsuccessful air strike on the morning of the 24th had failed to draw attention to the presence of his force. He therefore detached his two battleship-carriers with a light cruiser and four destroyers under Rear-Admiral C. Matsuda at 2.30 p.m. with orders to proceed south and attack the Americans.[2] At about 3.40 p.m. Halsey's aircraft sighted Matsuda's force and an hour later Ozawa's

---

[1] See Sketch 3, facing page 84.
[2] See Sketch 1, facing page 63.

main body. Believing from the over-optimistic reports of his pilots that Kurita's *Centre Force* had been so severely damaged in the Sibuyan Sea that it could no longer be considered a serious menace to the 7th Fleet, Halsey ordered Mitscher to concentrate three carrier groups at an agreed rendezvous and steam north to attack Ozawa at daybreak, and the fourth (McCain's), now returning from Ulithi, to fuel at sea and then join the others. It is not for this history to enumerate all the many reasons for Halsey's decision or to pass judgement. The fact remains that by midnight on the 24th/25th the three fast carrier groups with their attendant battleships—sixty-five ships strong—had met and were steaming north to engage Ozawa's seventeen ships, which could by then muster only some thirty aircraft between them. Not a single ship was left to guard the exit from San Bernardino Strait. Halsey had swallowed Ozawa's bait, hook, line and sinker.

While Kurita's *Centre Force* was fighting its way towards San Bernardino Strait, Nishimura's *Southern Force* was heading for Leyte Gulf with orders to arrive there at first light on the 25th simultaneously with Kurita. On the evening of the 24th Nishimura heard from Kurita that he had been delayed by enemy air attack in the Sibuyan Sea and that he would enter Leyte Gulf at about 11 a.m. on the 25th. Nevertheless Nishimura decided to press on, although he knew that he could expect no help from the *Centre Force* in the gulf from 4 a.m., when he expected to get there, until 11 a.m.

Halsey's aircraft, it will be recalled, had sighted and attacked the *Southern Force* in the Sulu Sea shortly after 9 a.m. on the 24th but had not seen it again during daylight. The same day the *2nd Striking Force*, which had left the Pescadores on the 22nd, was seen by an army bomber from Morotai just before noon. Kinkaid rightly concluded that both these forces intended to break through into Leyte Gulf by way of Surigao Strait and at 12.15 p.m. warned all ships to be ready for a night encounter. Throwing a screen of escort destroyers and light craft around the transports in the gulf, he stationed his thirty-nine motor torpedo-boats (M.T.B.s) in the Surigao Strait and Mindanao Sea.[1] He ordered Oldendorf to form a night patrol and augmented his group with the Close Support Group of cruisers and destroyers.[2] By dark, six of the older battleships, four heavy cruisers, four light cruisers and twenty-eight destroyers were steaming slowly backwards and forwards across the northern entrance to the Surigao Strait—more than enough to take care of Nishimura's two battleships, one

---

[1] See Sketch 3, facing page 84.
[2] This group included H.M.A.S. *Shropshire* and *Arunta*.

heavy cruiser and four destroyers and Shima's two heavy cruisers, one light cruiser and four destroyers.

Nishimura was sighted, reported and attacked by the M.T.B.s in the Mindanao Sea at about 11 p.m. on the 24th and for the next three hours successive sections of M.T.B.s engaged the Japanese as they made their way into and up the strait. They scored no hits, but their reports were valuable in keeping Oldendorf in touch with Nishimura's progress. Shortly after 2 a.m. on the 25th the M.T.B.s were told to keep clear and Oldendorf ordered three flotillas of destroyers to make a succession of co-ordinated attacks with guns and torpedoes. These attacks were most successful. Between 3 and 4 a.m. the battleship *Fuso* blew up and broke in two, two destroyers were sunk and a third was disabled and forced to retire. Nishimura's flagship, the battleship *Yamashiro*, had taken four torpedoes and the heavy cruiser *Mogami* had been hard hit and set on fire, but both ships with the remaining destroyer stood on to meet the concentrated fire of the American battleships and cruisers. These opened fire at about 4 a.m., using radar control, but twenty minutes later Oldendorf ordered the cease fire in order to allow destroyers retiring from the last attack to get clear. Although the Americans did not know it until later, the *Yamashiro* had gone down before fire could be reopened, taking the gallant Nishimura and practically all her ship's company with her, and the surviving ships were steaming south out of range.

Shima, meanwhile, had been following Nishimura forty miles astern. As he entered the strait at about 3.30 a.m. one of his cruisers, the *Abukuma*, was hit by a torpedo from an M.T.B. and with her speed reduced to ten knots dropped out of the line. Half an hour later he passed what he thought were the *Fuso* and *Yamashiro* on fire, but what in fact were halves of the burning *Fuso*. The night was very dark and made darker by the dense cloud of smoke to the northward made by the American destroyers. Although Shima knew neither what was ahead of him, nor what had happened to Nishimura, he stood on. He must, however, have suspected the worst, for at 4.15 a.m. he turned and retired with his whole force, informing all the 'SHO' forces that he was doing so. Shortly afterwards his flagship, the *Nachi*, collided with the damaged *Mogami* struggling down the strait, but both ships were able to continue at reduced speed.

Oldendorf did not begin his pursuit until 4.30 a.m. By that time it was too late. His light forces sank the destroyer damaged earlier that morning, but were recalled at 7.20 a.m. when he learnt that Kurita's *Centre Force* was engaging the escort carriers off Samar. The pursuit was taken up by aircraft from these carriers. They sighted Shima's force, now consisting of two heavy cruisers and four destroyers with the *Mogami* following astern, and at about 9 a.m. attacked the laggard, leaving her dead on the water, to be sunk later by one of her own destroyers. The damaged *Abukuma* was also sunk by army bombers from New Guinea during the morning. Shima's remaining ships made good their escape. The sole surviving destroyer of Nishimura's *Southern Force* informed Toyoda and Kurita at 10.18 a.m. that all Nishimura's ships, except herself, had been sunk.

Kurita, with the *Centre Force* now reduced to four battleships, six heavy cruisers, two light cruisers and eleven destroyers, but still powerful, made the narrow passage of San Bernardino Strait during the hours of darkness and emerged unchallenged into the Philippine Sea at 1.35 a.m. on the 25th. At that time Halsey's 3rd Fleet was away to the north following the trail laid for it by Ozawa, Kinkaid's battleships and cruisers under Oldendorf were waiting for Nishimura outside Surigao Strait and the escort carriers of the 7th Fleet were to the southward in the eastern approaches to Leyte Gulf, in support of the army ashore. The escort carriers, under the overall command of Rear-Admiral T. L. Sprague, were disposed in three groups: the northern under command of Rear-Admiral C. A. F. Sprague of six carriers, the centre under command of Rear-Admiral F. B. Stump of six carriers, and the southern of four carriers commanded by T. L. Sprague himself. Each group had a screen of three destroyers and the groups were some thirty to fifty miles apart.

On the night of the 24th/25th, Kinkaid was not unduly worried about the safety of Sprague's three groups of escort carriers. He had intercepted Halsey's signal made to the 3rd Fleet during the afternoon of the 24th on the subject of the formation of Task Force 34 and, when he heard that evening that Halsey was taking the three fast carrier groups to the north, had assumed that Task Force 34 had been formed and had been left to guard San Bernardino Strait. To make certain, however, he sent Halsey a signal at about 4 a.m. asking him if it were in fact guarding the strait. Halsey did not receive the message until three and a half hours later, and when Kinkaid received his reply just after 7 a.m. Kurita's guns had made it superfluous.

The escort carriers had just flown off a strike to pursue the Japanese ships escaping from Surigao Strait and also dawn patrols for their own protection and that of shipping in the gulf, when at 6.45 a.m. on the 25th look-outs in the northern group reported anti-aircraft fire to the northward. Soon afterwards the pilot of an aircraft on anti-submarine patrol reported that he was being fired on by battleships and cruisers, and in a few moments the unmistakable masts of Japanese capital ships began looming up over the horizon. C. A. F. Sprague at once turned into the wind and increased to 17½ knots (the maximum speed of his carriers) and ordered all ships to fly off every available aircraft and to make smoke. He then broadcast his position and the enemy's with an urgent appeal for help from all who could give it.

On leaving San Bernardino Strait Kurita had turned southward and headed at 20 knots down the east coast of Samar for Leyte Gulf. On sighting the escort carriers he altered course to east by south to get to windward, increased to full speed, and ordered 'general attack'. Meanwhile, under cover of his smoke screen, Sprague had hauled round to the south and south-west and had ordered his three destroyers and four smaller escort destroyers to attack with torpedoes. The attacks were pressed home with great gallantry, the destroyers closing to within 6,000 yards of the Japanese ships, hitting a heavy cruiser and forcing them to turn away. The smaller ships, however, paid the price of their temerity and three American destroyers were sunk. The Japanese made one destroyer counter-attack but their torpedoes were fired at long range and missed. The most effective contribution to the battle was made by American aircraft which struck incessantly at the Japanese ships. After the first half-hour Sprague's escort carriers were unable to turn into the wind because of the pursuing Japanese ships and, to refuel and rearm, their aircraft had to land either on the carriers of Stump's centre group or at the recently captured Tacloban airfield. Stump was not so hampered and his aircraft were able to strike at Kurita's ships again and again. There were not enough torpedoes to go round and some of the bombs with which the aircraft were armed were not suitable for attacking ships, but they went in with everything they had and sometimes with nothing but their machine-guns. The Japanese heavy cruisers (*Chokai* and *Chikuma*) were crippled and had to be sunk. Meanwhile C. A. F. Sprague's escort carriers, coming under heavy fire from the Japanese ships, were hard hit and the *Gambier Bay* sunk. Suddenly at 9.25 a.m., when it looked as if the end were near, the pursuing Japanese ships were seen to turn and retire to the northward. By 9.40 a.m. all firing had ceased. The battle was over.

The reason for this was that at 9.11 a.m. Kurita had issued an order that the engagement was to be broken off and the fleet to retire to the north. It was his intention to re-form his fleet, which had during the action become widely scattered, and then resume his course to Leyte Gulf. While re-forming, the *Centre Force* was harassed by aircraft from the American escort carriers but at about 11.45 a.m. Kurita resumed a direct course towards Leyte Gulf, and at 12.5 p.m. told *Headquarters Combined Fleet* that, despite enemy attacks, he was determined to penetrate into the gulf.

Kurita was, however, by this time considerably shaken: his flagship had been sunk under him on the 23rd, he had been under heavy air attack without any protective air cover throughout the 24th and again since dawn on the 25th, and his way to Leyte Gulf now appeared to be blocked by strong enemy forces. The aircraft that he had sent to reconnoitre Leyte Gulf had failed to return. He had intercepted messages sent in clear from which it seemed that a strong American force was moving towards him from the north and another was concentrating to the south near Leyte Gulf. Furthermore, he had intercepted a message to the effect that American aircraft had been ordered to land and refuel at Tacloban airfield; this gave him the impression that hordes of aircraft were waiting to attack him when he entered the gulf, where he would have no room for manoeuvre. Between noon and 12.35 p.m. he was shadowed by American aircraft and at 12.35 one of his own reconnaissance aircraft reported that there were thirty-five transports in Leyte Gulf. Kurita must have realized that, by continuing his advance towards the gulf without air cover, he might well be exposing his ships to an even heavier scale of air attack for very little return.[1] Whatever his reason, he decided at 12.36 p.m. to abandon the attempt to penetrate Leyte Gulf and told *Headquarters Combined Fleet* that he was proceeding north to search for an enemy task force (which was, from his interpretation of intercepted messages, heading towards him); this force he intended to engage decisively and then pass back through San Bernardino Strait.

Kurita's was not the only force which attacked the escort carriers that day. Concluding that orthodox methods could not provide adequate support for the navy in view of Japanese inferiority in the air, Vice-Admiral T. Onishi (the commander of the naval land-based aircraft in the Philippines) had on the 20th October organized from volunteers a special air force known as the *Kamikaze Special Attack Force*, consisting initially of thirteen pilots.[2] This special force was to adopt a new technique, the pilot deliberately aiming his aircraft in a steep dive to crash with himself and his bomb load on the ship selected as the target. On the 25th Onishi ordered the new force into action. There had been isolated suicide attacks before, some by damaged aircraft and some premeditated, but this was the first time that the *Kamikaze* aircraft had been organized and directed.[3] The southern group of escort carriers was the first to be struck. It was in the process of recovering aircraft returning from other missions when at 7.30 a.m. it was attacked by six *Kamikaze* aircraft. Two carriers were

---

[1] Since the landing had already taken place it was also probable that the transports were empty and might well retire southwards before he could arrive at the mouth of the gulf.

[2] The choice of the name *Kamikaze* for the suicide aircraft is of interest. During the thirteenth century Kublai Khan organized a Mongol armada to invade Kyushu, one of the main islands of Japan. The success of the invasion appeared to be assured when a typhoon suddenly blew up off the Japanese coast and dispersed the Mongol ships. The Japanese considered this fortuitous storm as proof of divine help and credited the salvation of their country to *Kami Kaze*—two Japanese words which mean Divine Wind.

[3] According to the Japanese, the first suicide air attacks were made on the American light cruisers *Franklin* and *Reno* by single aircraft on the 13th and 14th October.

hit but both survived, despite the fact that one of them was also hit by a torpedo from a submarine. Then no sooner had the hard-pressed northern group had its unexpected deliverance from the assault of Kurita's ships than it too was attacked by *Kamikaze* aircraft. Three ships were hit and the *St. Lo* was sunk. As the escort carriers made their way southward to safety the southern group was again attacked by *Kamikaze* aircraft; one ship was struck but survived. This was the last attack made on the escort carriers in the battle. From then on the *Kamikazes* transferred their attention to shipping in Leyte Gulf.

When Kurita emerged from San Bernardino Strait, Halsey's three fast carrier groups under Mitscher's command were chasing north after Ozawa whom he had last seen at about 4.35 p.m. on the 24th.[1] The next contacts were at 2.5 and 2.35 a.m. on the 25th when reconnaissance aircraft sighted first Matsuda and then Ozawa. Ozawa was steaming a south-easterly course about 205 miles east by north of Cape Engano and was then some 210 miles to the northward. Mitscher ordered dawn strikes to be flown off, and at 2.40 a.m. formed Task Force 34 (consisting of six battleships, seven cruisers and seventeen destroyers) and stationed it ten miles ahead of the carriers ready to engage if the two forces met. The next time the Japanese were sighted was at 7.10 a.m. The two enemy forces, now united, were steaming north-east at 20 knots and the distance between the two carrier forces had narrowed to some 150 miles. Mitscher had not waited for this report and his strike aircraft were already in the air, orbiting about sixty miles north of his carriers. The aircraft were at once directed at the enemy, and shortly after 8 a.m. they struck. The few remaining Japanese fighters were quickly shot down and, with only anti-aircraft fire to contend with, the American aircraft continued to strike at the enemy throughout the day. Six strikes in all were launched, and all four Japanese carriers (the *Zuikaku*, *Zuiho*, *Chitose* and *Chiyoda*) and a destroyer were sunk. Another destroyer, which had stayed behind to pick up survivors from the carriers, was also sunk that evening by light forces sent ahead by Mitscher, and a light cruiser (the *Tama*), damaged by the air attacks, was sunk by an American submarine which formed part of a group disposed to intercept the retreat. The remnants, the two battleship-carriers, two light cruisers and six destroyers, made the best of their way to Japan.

While the second strike was returning Halsey received a plain-language message at 8.22 a.m. from Kinkaid telling him of the surprise off Samar, followed by pleas for assistance. At 8.48 a.m. he instructed his fourth (McCain's) group, then fuelling about two

[1] See pages 75–76, and Sketch 1, facing page 63.

hundred and thirty miles to the eastward, to proceed at best possible speed to strike at Kurita, but he did not tell Mitscher to detach Task Force 34 to block Kurita's escape. At 10 a.m. Halsey received a message from Nimitz at Pearl Harbour asking him where Task Force 34 was, and another from Kinkaid asking him to send the battleships. His heavy ships were then about forty-two miles from Ozawa's *Northern Force*, which was already crippled by air strikes, and in a short while could have engaged it with their 16-inch guns. For a time Halsey hesitated, but so great became the pressure to help the 7th Fleet that, reluctantly, at 11.15 a.m. he ordered Mitscher to send one (Bogan's) group, together with the major part of Task Force 34, southward to help Kinkaid, and went himself in his flagship, the *New Jersey*.

By steering west at 30 knots, McCain's group was able to launch a strike of one hundred aircraft by 10.30 a.m. at Kurita's *Centre Force* at extreme range and another smaller strike about two hours later. Bombs had to be used instead of torpedoes on each occasion, for the range was too great to allow the aircraft with the heavier load to return with certainty to their ships, and the strikes did nothing to add to the damage already inflicted by the escort carriers.

Halsey did not arrive until the next morning. At 4.22 p.m. on the 25th, after the battleships had fuelled the destroyers, he went ahead at 28 knots with the two fastest battleships, five light cruisers and eight destroyers, not wishing to be tied down to the slower battleships. He arrived off San Bernardino Strait at 1 a.m. on the 26th, too late to catch Kurita, who had entered the strait at 9.30 p.m. the previous evening.[1] The only ship of Kurita's force he encountered was a destroyer which had been unable to catch up; she was sunk by gunfire at 1.10 a.m.

Bogan and McCain's groups made rendezvous at 5 a.m. on the 26th and together they launched strikes on the escaping Japanese ships. A light cruiser (the *Noshiro*) was sunk by a bomb, but no other serious damage was done to Kurita's force either by carrier-borne aircraft or by a force of forty-seven Liberators sent out from Morotai. The remainder of Kurita's *Centre Force*, which included four battleships, was able to make its escape to Brunei Bay before proceeding to Japan.

The battle for Leyte Gulf was the last action fought by surface ships in the Second World War, perhaps the last in any war. Japanese losses were not as heavy as they might have been, but nevertheless they were devastating. They had lost three battleships, four carriers, six heavy cruisers, three light cruisers and eight destroyers. Against this the Americans had lost only one light carrier, two escort carriers

---

[1] See Sketch 1, facing page 63.

and three destroyers. Although six of the nine Japanese battleships survived, the loss of supporting forces and especially of the carrier forces was so great that never again were Japanese surface forces able to offer any serious challenge to the American fleet. From now on the Japanese had to rely almost entirely on shore-based aircraft to resist the American advance. Here, too, losses had been so heavy and the reserve of trained pilots was so scanty that they had to rely on the *Kamikaze* aircraft with their new technique which required little training and against which there could be little effective defence.

As soon as he heard that the Americans had landed on Leyte, Suzuki (*35th Army*) instructed *16th Division* to keep control of the airfields at all costs, and ordered that Leyte should be reinforced by four battalions.[1] On the 22nd, having been told by Yamashita that he was to fight the decisive battle on Leyte and that his army was to be reinforced by two divisions and an independent mixed brigade from Luzon,[2] he ordered more reinforcements to Leyte from Davao and Cebu to bring his strength to the equivalent of four strong divisions.[3] He thought at the time that the Americans had landed only two divisions and that, if the decisive naval and air battles planned to take place on the 24th and 25th were successful, he would have a good opportunity of destroying the invading forces as soon as his reinforcing formations had reached the island. He therefore planned to concentrate his army in the Carigara plain, covered by *16th Division* which was to hold the general line Burauen–Dagami and the hills west of Tacloban.[4]

Owing to the belated Japanese decision to fight the decisive battle on Leyte, the 6th U.S. Army was able to advance rapidly against light opposition and, by the 2nd November, had reached the general line Carigara–Jaro–Dagami–Burauen–Abuyog, with an advanced detachment in Baybay, and had occupied all five Japanese airfields, scattering *16th Division*, which had been thrown into confusion by the unexpected landing at Tacloban. Krueger intended that X Corps moving round the northern, and XXIV Corps round the southern, end of the central range should launch a concentric attack on Ormoc, the main Japanese base and port of entry for reinforcing formations.

The Americans were, however, seriously hampered by their inability, owing to the nature of the soil and the torrential rains, to make the captured airfields quickly serviceable. This prevented 5th

---

[1] Two each from *30th* and *102nd Divisions* in Davao and Cebu respectively.
[2] The *1st* and *26th Divisions* and *68th I.M.B.*
[3] The *102nd Division* and the greater part of the infantry of *30th Division*.
[4] See Map 4, facing page 88.

U.S.A.A.F. from giving adequate close air support to 6th Army and from stopping the Japanese bringing reinforcements to Ormoc.[1] Kinkaid was therefore forced on the 26th October to appeal to Halsey to fill the gap. Three of the fast carrier groups stayed in the vicinity of the Philippines, one group bombing Manila and the others standing off Leyte to protect shipping in the gulf. On the 30th they had to return to Ulithi to rearm and replenish supplies, but not before three carriers had been damaged by *Kamikaze* aircraft. The Japanese had meanwhile begun to reinforce *4th Air Army* in Luzon, as planned, by aircraft brought from Formosa and elsewhere. As a result, they were able to regain control of the air over Leyte as soon as the fast carriers were withdrawn. On the 1st November Kinkaid was forced once again to ask Halsey for help. Halsey decided that his best course would be to attack the Japanese aircraft at their bases; accordingly on the 5th and 6th November three groups of carriers attacked airfields on Luzon and, meeting with only light opposition, destroyed or damaged many enemy aircraft for the loss of twenty-five. They also sank the heavy cruiser *Nachi*. The *Lexington* was, however, damaged by a *Kamikaze* and the cruiser *Reno* was torpedoed by a submarine, but both managed to reach Ulithi. The immediate effect of the attack on Luzon was a sharp reduction in enemy air activity over Leyte.

Meanwhile the Japanese were managing to bring reinforcements into Leyte through Ormoc, but in doing so suffered severe losses in transport and naval escorts. The four battalions ordered up from Davao and Cebu arrived safely between the 26th and 28th October, though the convoy and its escort were attacked after the troops had disembarked, a light cruiser (*Kinu*) and two destroyers being sunk. The main body of *1st Division* and some 2,000 men of *26th Division* from Luzon were landed at Ormoc on the 1st and 2nd November with the loss of only one transport. The convoy carrying the remainder of *1st Division* and some 10,000 men of *26th Division* left Manila on the 8th November. As it entered Ormoc Bay on the 9th it was subjected to a low-level attack by 5th U.S.A.A.F. Although all the transports suffered considerable superficial damage they reached port, and the troops, but not their equipment, were landed. Unable to risk staying at Ormoc during daylight the transports then put to sea but, on the 10th, 5th U.S.A.A.F. sank all but one. The same day another convoy, carrying the remainder of *26th Division*, was seen by reconnaissance aircraft as it left Manila Bay, and MacArthur asked Halsey to attack it as it made its way south. Halsey ordered the carriers, which were then steaming eastwards to a refuelling

---

[1] Tacloban was able to operate only a limited number of aircraft and Dulag could operate none till the middle of November. The three airfields near Burauen could not be brought up to an adequate standard and the new airfield near Tanauen to replace them could not be completed till the 25th December.

rendezvous some 400 miles west of Saipan, to reverse course and make all speed to the west.[1] At 6 a.m. on the 11th, when the carriers were some 200 miles off San Bernardino Strait, a reconnaissance aircraft found the convoy entering Ormoc Bay. Three-quarters of an hour later it was attacked by 347 carrier-borne aircraft. All the transports and four of the escorting destroyers were sunk for the loss of nine aircraft.

At a conference at Tacloban on the 11th November the American commanders at Leyte came to the conclusion that the Japanese would defend Leyte to the last, despite their losses in the naval battle and the devastating strikes on the convoys at Ormoc. They considered that, if a repetition of the long-drawn-out battle for Guadalcanal were to be avoided, the fast carriers would have to give further support at least until the state of the airfields on the island enabled 5th U.S.A.A.F. to be built up to the necessary strength. The fast carriers therefore began a new series of attacks on Luzon, this time concentrating on shipping rather than on the airfields. On the 13th and 14th carrier aircraft sank the light cruiser *Kiso*, four destroyers, a submarine chaser and several transports, and destroyed a number of enemy aircraft, for the loss of twenty-five. The attack was repeated on the 19th and although little shipping was seen many enemy aircraft were claimed for the loss of thirteen. The third and final attack took place on the 25th November during which the heavy cruiser *Kumano*, damaged in the battle of Leyte Gulf, was sunk. The Japanese on this occasion counter-attacked and four carriers were hit and damaged by *Kamikaze* aircraft, two so seriously that they had to be withdrawn for extensive repairs. After this attack the fast carriers were released, having been in continuous action off the Philippines for eighty-four days.

Despite the efforts of the fast carriers and 5th U.S.A.A.F. the Japanese were still able to bring reinforcements to Leyte. On the 17th November the main body of *102nd Division* was landed at Ormoc without loss; on the 9th December *68th I.M.B.* was disembarked at San Isidro and *77th Infantry Regiment* (less one battalion) reached Palompon; two days later *5th Infantry Regiment* was also disembarked at Palompon. Altogether the Japanese succeeded in reinforcing the original garrison of about 15,000 by some 45,000 men and landing 10,000 tons of stores, but the cost was high, particularly in naval and merchant shipping which they could ill afford to lose.[2] Even with these reinforcements, *35th Army* was greatly outnumbered by 6th U.S. Army whose strength by the 2nd December had been built up to some 183,000.

---

[1] For Saipan see Map 8, facing page 252.
[2] In their attempts to reinforce Leyte the Japanese lost one light cruiser, eight destroyers, six escort craft and seventeen transports.

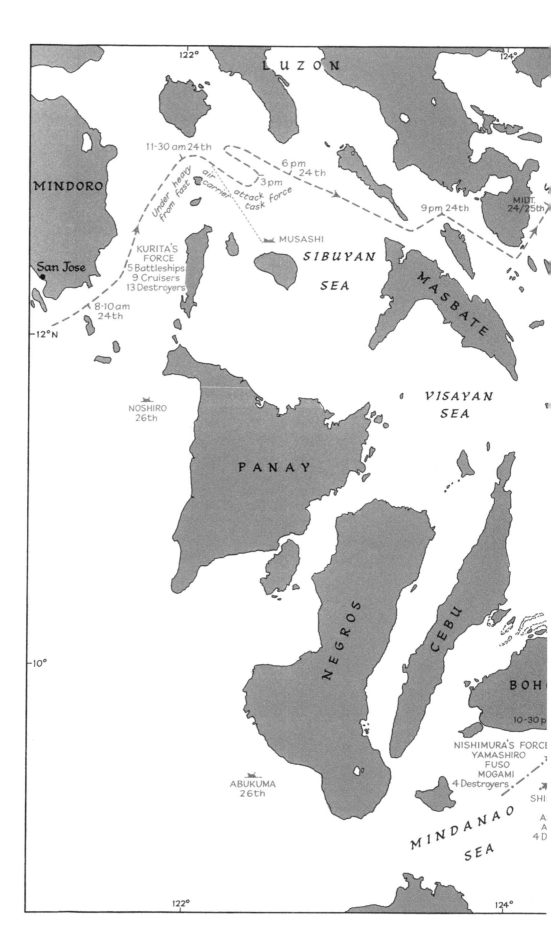

LUZON

122°

124°

11-30 am 24th

6 pm
24th

3pm

*Under heavy
from fast*

*air
carrier*

*attack
task*

force

MUSASHI

9pm 24th

MIDT.
24/25th

MINDORO

SIBUYAN

SEA

M A S B A T E

San Jose

KURITA'S
FORCE
5 Battleships
9 Cruisers
13 Destroyers

8-10 am
24th

−12°N

NOSHIRO
26th

VISAYAN
SEA

PANAY

−10°

N E G R O S

C E B U

B O H

10-30 p

NISHIMURA'S FORCE
YAMASHIRO
FUSO
MOGAMI
4 Destroyers

ABUKUMA
26th

SHI

A
A
4 D

M I N D A N A O

SEA

122°

124°

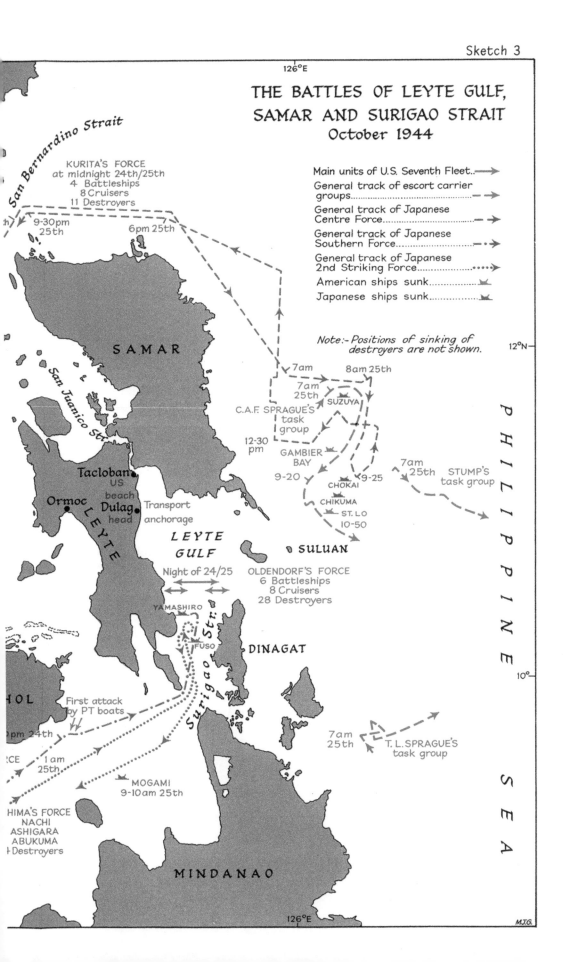

THE BATTLES OF LEYTE GULF, SAMAR AND SURIGAO STRAIT
October 1944

San Bernardino Strait

KURITA'S FORCE
at midnight 24th/25th
4 Battleships
8 Cruisers
11 Destroyers

9-30pm
25th

6pm 25th

Main units of U.S. Seventh Fleet..	⟶
General track of escort carrier groups................................	
General track of Japanese Centre Force............................	
General track of Japanese Southern Force........................	
General track of Japanese 2nd Striking Force....................	
American ships sunk................	
Japanese ships sunk................	

Note:- Positions of sinking of destroyers are not shown.

12°N

SAMAR

San Juanico Str.

7am

8am 25th

7am
25th

SUZUYA

C.A.F. SPRAGUE'S
task
group

12-30
pm

GAMBIER
BAY

7am
25th   STUMP'S
task group

9-20

9-25

CHOKAI

Tacloban
US
beach
head

Ormoc   Dulag

Transport
anchorage

CHIKUMA

ST. LO
10-50

LEYTE
GULF

SULUAN

PHILIPPINE

Night of 24/25

OLDENDORF'S FORCE
6 Battleships
8 Cruisers
28 Destroyers

YAMASHIRO

Surigao Str.

FUSO   DINAGAT

10°

First attack
by PT boats

pm 24th

1am
25th

7am
25th   T. L. SPRAGUE'S
task group

MOGAMI
9-10am 25th

HIMA'S FORCE
NACHI
ASHIGARA
ABUKUMA
Destroyers

SEA

MINDANAO

126°E

126°E

MJG.

By the 1st November Suzuki knew that he was opposed by two American corps each of two divisions and realized that he could not carry out his original plan. He therefore ordered *1st Division* and the advanced echelon of *26th Division*, as soon as they arrived at Carigara and Jaro respectively, to hold the American X Corps in the north, and sent the rest of his reinforcing units to help *16th Division* oppose the advance of the American XXIV Corps in the south. The result was an encounter battle early in November west of Carigara, and by the 15th the American advance had been brought to a complete halt near Limon and to the west of Jaro.

As a result of the naval defeat, the heavy losses in aircraft and the shortage of transports and naval escort vessels, Yamashita came to the conclusion during the first week in November that there was little hope of holding Leyte and that, if operations on the island were continued, the defence of Luzon would be weakened. He therefore suggested to *Southern Army* that the attempts to reinforce Leyte should be abandoned, but, after hearing Yamashita's views at a conference on the 9th and 10th, Terauchi decided to adhere to his plan.

On the 12th, considering that it was essential to prevent the Americans from building up their air strength on Leyte, Yamashita ordered *35th Army* to use *26th Division* on the Burauen front with a view to launching a counter-attack with *16th Division* to gain control of at least some of the airfields. This order, which completely upset Suzuki's plan, which was to concentrate his army and fight the main battle in the north, forced him to divide his forces into two groups. He ordered *26th Division* to move along the Albuera–Burauen track and *102nd Division*, as soon as it reached Ormoc, to move to the Mount Pina area to protect the right of *1st Division*, which was grimly holding on at Limon.

The *4th Air Army*, which had been reinforced from Japan by *2nd Raiding Group*,[1] decided on the 22nd November to use it to destroy aircraft on the ground and inflict damage on the Leyte airfields. Yamashita decided that the ground and air efforts should be co-ordinated and, on the 23rd, reached an agreement with *4th Air Army* that an air offensive would be launched from the 23rd to the 27th November.[2]

On the 27th November three aircraft carrying specially trained demolition detachments, which were to have landed at Tacloban and Dulag, crashed without reaching their objectives. At dawn on the 6th December a unit of *16th Division* (150 strong) reached north Burauen airfield, but the advance of *26th Division* along the tortuous mountain track had been seriously delayed, and only one of its battalions was

[1] Forty aircraft and some 250 paratroopers.
[2] The *4th Air Army* was not under command of *14th Area Army*. Co-operation was through mutual agreement.

able to reach the Burauen area. Through a mistake in co-ordination, a parachute drop did not take place till the evening of the 6th and the paratroops failed to contact the ground troops. Thus, although the Japanese succeeded in occupying two of the airfields for a short time,[1] they caused only temporary inconvenience; the American units on the spot were able to deal with the piecemeal attacks and little damage was done.

Meanwhile, with X Corps held up by strong Japanese opposition near Limon and XXIV Corps delayed in its advance north from Baybay by the difficulty of the country which everywhere favoured the defence, Krueger decided to make a fresh landing on the west coast south of Ormoc so that a wedge could be driven between the two wings of his opponents. On the morning of the 7th, 77th U.S. Division was landed some four miles south of Ormoc without meeting with any opposition. The convoy and its escorts, however, were attacked after the troops had been landed and during their return to Leyte Gulf; two destroyers were sunk and two severely damaged by *Kamikaze* aircraft. As he had no reserves immediately available in the Ormoc area, Suzuki ordered *16th* and *26th Divisions* to postpone their offensive and to oppose this fresh landing. It was too late, and 77th Division, meeting negligible opposition, entered Ormoc on the 10th December.

With the capture of Ormoc, the end of the campaign for Leyte was in sight. With his main base on the island in American hands, Yamashita told Suzuki that no more reinforcements would be sent to Leyte, that troops already there would have to be self-supporting and that he was to continue to resist in the central and southern Philippines as best he could. The Japanese resistance now quickly collapsed. On the 20th, X Corps and 77th Division met at Cananga. Part of these formations then turned west and on the 25th December, with the help of a force moved by sea from Ormoc, captured Palompon, the only port of any importance left to the Japanese. All organized resistance then ceased.

The defence of the Philippines, which was vital to the Japanese, presented them with a very difficult problem. The *Combined Fleet* had had to be divided into two portions: the battleships and the majority of the cruisers were located at Singapore near the sources of oil fuel, the carriers being based on Japan so that they could re-equip with aircraft and train new pilots. The oil fuel position was so precarious that the carriers could make one sortie only, and the fleet at Singapore, once committed to action, could not refuel and be ready for

---

[1] Neither airfield was operational. See page 84 fn.

action again for about a month. The Japanese could not therefore risk the use of the *Combined Fleet* until they were certain where the Americans would strike, and then had to concentrate it for action at the decisive point from widely separated bases. Nevertheless they had one advantage: the Americans had to expose their fleet and the invasion forces to air attack by shore-based aircraft at short range with only the protection that could be provided by their carrier aircraft.

Toyoda's plan to destroy the invasion forces by using the guns of the fleet, which would be protected and aided by the shore-based aircraft, while the carriers decoyed the American fleet away from the decisive point was sound. But success depended on an adequate number of shore-based aircraft being concentrated and ready for action in Formosa and the Philippines before the Americans showed their hand. The Japanese were extremely short of aircraft and trained air crews, and the Philippines, having been until a few months previously mainly an administrative area with a small garrison, did not have enough air bases. The speed of the American advance gave the Japanese insufficient time to recover from their losses in the Marianas and in the battle of the Philippine Sea or to prepare the Philippines to resist invasion. When the Americans struck in October, the air forces allotted for the defence of the islands were neither ready nor in position, with the result that the Americans were ashore on Leyte before the shore-based aircraft were ready to strike or to support the *Combined Fleet*.

The Japanese could not spare sufficient army formations to defend the whole of the Philippines, which *Imperial General Headquarters* expected to be the American objective. Assuming that the navy and air force would be able to prevent the Americans from establishing air bases in the central Philippines within close range of Luzon, they decided to concentrate their strength for the defence of Luzon and such areas as were required for operational purposes by the navy, and particularly by the air forces. The American air attacks on Formosa early in October, however, led the Japanese into a premature attempt to destroy the American fleet and into a last-moment change of plan based on unconfirmed reports of huge American losses. The decision to fight the decisive battle on Leyte which caused the hasty change of plan finally destroyed, as Yamashita had warned his superiors, any hopes the Japanese had of successfully defending the Philippines.

Map 4

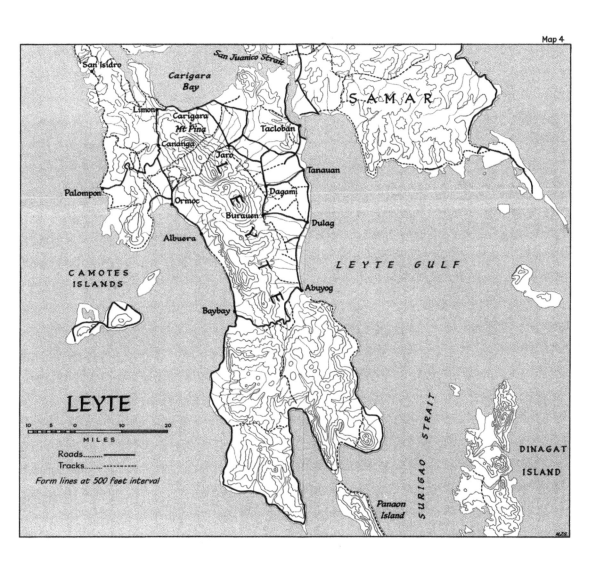

San Isidro

Carigara
Bay

San Juanico Strait

S A M A R

Limon

Carigara
Mt Pina
Canonga

Tacloban

Jaro

Tanauan

Palompon

Ormoc

Dagami

Burauen

Albuera

Dulag

CAMOTES
ISLANDS

L E Y T E   G U L F

Abuyog

Baybay

LEYTE

```
10    5    0         10         20
|—————————————|———————————|
          MILES
```

Roads.........━━━━━
Tracks........----------

Form lines at 500 feet interval

S U R I G A O   S T R A I T

DINAGAT

ISLAND

Panaon
Island

CHAPTER VIII

THE PACIFIC

(December 1944–March 1945)

The Reoccupation of Luzon

See Maps 5 and 8 and Sketches 1 and 7

WHILE the struggle for Leyte was taking place, the Americans were building up the air base in the Marianas from which long-range B.29 bombers could attack the Japanese homeland.[1] Work on the construction of five airfields (one at Saipan, two on Guam and two on Tinian) had begun shortly after the occupation of the islands in June 1944, but progressed only slowly. The advanced headquarters of 21st Bomber Command was established at Saipan in August and by the end of October, when the first airstrip on the island was completed, 73rd Wing was flown in. The 313th Wing began to arrive at Tinian at the end of December and 314th Wing at Guam at the end of January 1945.[2]

On the 10th October the American Chiefs of Staff directed that the long-range bombers should first be used to destroy the Japanese aircraft industry by attacking it from 30,000 feet with 500-lb. high explosive bombs. They specified that the targets were to be industrial plants in the Tokyo–Yokohama area, at Nagoya, and in the Kobe–Osaka area.[3] Tokyo was to be the first objective, the main target selected being a large aircraft factory in its north-western suburbs. Early on the 24th November, 111 B.29s took off to make the first attack on the city since the Doolittle carrier-borne raid of April 1942.[4] Twenty-four bombers attacked the aircraft factory and the remainder the dock area, but cloud partly obscured the target area, making accurate bombing difficult, and little damage was done. Despite being intercepted by some 125 fighters, the force lost only one bomber rammed by a fighter, and one at sea during the return flight.

---

[1] See Map 8, facing page 252.
[2] The 20th Bomber Command at Chengtu and 21st Bomber Command at Saipan were part of 20th U.S.A.A.F. which had its headquarters in Washington. Initially both commands were to have two wings, each of 112 B.29 bombers. In practice one wing (58th) was sent with 20th Bomber Command to India and China and three wings (73rd, 313th and 314th) to the Marianas. The 58th Wing was transferred to the Marianas at the end of March (see page 133).
[3] See Sketch 7, facing page 240.
[4] See Volume II, page 225.

On the 27th November the attack was repeated with sixty-two aircraft but the target was once again obscured, and the aircraft factory escaped unscathed though some damage was inflicted on the docks.

To ensure that there was no interference with the build-up of 21st Bomber Command in the Marianas, Nimitz had set out from August 1944 to neutralize the Japanese airfields in the Bonin Islands and in particular those at Iwojima, which by October had been attacked forty-eight times by 7th U.S.A.A.F. The Japanese were nevertheless still able to use its airfields as staging points, and on the 2nd November attacked the Saipan airfield with nine, and on the 7th with ten, bombers, losing three in each raid but causing little damage. On the 27th the Japanese sent in two bombers at high level and followed up later in the day with a low-level attack by twelve fighters. This time they succeeded without loss to themselves in destroying four and damaging thirteen B.29s which, since the base was incomplete, were packed closely together. These attacks made it more than ever necessary that Iwojima be neutralized, and 7th U.S.A.A.F. was ordered to make it its main target. Plans were therefore made to step up the attacks, but on the 7th December, before they could be put into effect, the Japanese again struck, destroying three B.29s and damaging twenty-three others. The following day Iwojima was attacked by B.24s, B.29s (specially diverted for the task) and fighters, and was in addition bombarded by a cruiser force. Thereafter it was attacked daily and, in order to make it difficult for the Japanese to repair the runways, often by night.[1] Despite this, the Japanese were able to carry out repairs and no runway was out of action for a complete day. On the 25th December the Japanese again attacked Saipan, destroying one and damaging fourteen B.29s; this, however, turned out to be their last major attack despite the failure by the Americans to put the Iwojima airfields out of action. Although there were raids by single Japanese aircraft up to the 2nd January 1945, when the last enemy bomb fell on the Marianas, there were no further losses of aircraft.

Meanwhile 21st Bomber Command had been continuing its attacks on Japan. On the 3rd December seventy-six B.29s raided Tokyo but, although the weather was clear, the main target (the aircraft factory) suffered little damage and six bombers were lost. Thereafter attacks were made by sixty to ninety bombers at intervals of four to five days.[2] With one exception the results were very disappointing, partly because weather conditions were invariably bad and the target obscured by

---

[1] During December 7th U.S.A.A.F. flew seventy-nine missions and between the 8th December and 15th February there was no day on which there was not at least one strike on the island. Naval vessels also bombarded it on the 24th and 27th December and on the 5th and 24th January.

[2] One, with 72 B.29s, was made to coincide with the landings on Luzon. See page 95.

low cloud, and partly because the bomber crews were insufficiently trained and the necessary degree of maintenance skill had not been reached.[1] The one exception was an attack made in good weather on the 19th January by sixty-two B.29s on an aircraft factory twelve miles west of Kobe when, without loss, many direct hits were made on the factory buildings.[2] By the end of January it had become evident that the attempts to destroy the Japanese aircraft industry by high altitude attacks had failed, for of the nine most important factories listed for attack only one had been severely damaged.

Nimitz and MacArthur had by the end of October completed their plans for the operations detailed in the directive of the 3rd.[3] To provide air cover for the invasion convoys during their approach to Luzon and over the northern part of the island, MacArthur decided to seize Mindoro on the 8th December, establish airfields near San José at its southern end for use by 5th U.S.A.A.F., and make his landing on Luzon in the Lingayen Gulf area on the 20th.[4] He had also agreed with Nimitz that, after taking part in the invasion of Luzon, the U.S. 3rd Fleet and the fast carrier force would make an incursion into the China Sea. Nimitz decided that his objective in the Bonin Islands was to be Iwojima, which would be invaded on the 20th January, while the objective in the Ryukyu Islands was to be Okinawa, which would be attacked on the 1st March.

To seize Mindoro (some 262 air miles from Leyte Gulf) meant taking a considerable risk, for not only was the island within close range of Japanese airfields on Luzon, but it was also beyond the normal range of land-based fighters from the Leyte airfields. Moreover, during their passage the invasion convoys would have to pass within close range of the Japanese airfields on Negros and Panay, and might therefore have to face a heavy scale of air attack at a time when the only air cover that could be provided would be given by 5th U.S.A.A.F. for the short period that the convoy was within range of Leyte and Morotai and by the escort carriers which accompanied the naval covering force. The difficulties experienced by 5th U.S.A.A.F in establishing adequate airfields on Leyte and the increasing danger from air attacks on shipping by *Kamikaze* aircraft, coupled with the need to provide shipping for the Ormoc landing,[5] caused MacArthur

---

[1] Between December 1944 and the end of February 1945 an average of twenty-one per cent of the B.29s failed to reach their target due to mechanical failures which necessitated their return to base.

[2] From air photographs it was estimated that thirty-eight per cent of the roofed area of the factory was damaged. It was ascertained after the war that every building of importance had been hit and that production had been reduced by ninety per cent.

[3] See pages 68–69.

[4] See Sketch 1, facing page 63.

[5] See page 87.

to postpone the Mindoro operation till the 15th December and consequently the invasion of Luzon till the 9th January 1945. At the same time the attack on Iwojima was postponed till the 19th February and that on Okinawa till the 1st April.

To reduce the scale of air attack on the convoys during their approach to Mindoro, the fast carrier force was to keep an umbrella of fighters over the airfields in north Luzon and around Manila Bay. Several convoys carrying some 18,000 men left Leyte Gulf on the 12th December, protected by a covering force of six escort carriers, three battleships, three light cruisers and eighteen destroyers. The next day, as they rounded the southern end of Negros, *Kamikaze* aircraft severely damaged the flagship (the light cruiser *Nashville*) and the destroyer *Haraden*. On the 14th an all-out Japanese attempt to attack the convoys from the airfields in the central Philippines failed, since they had been routed well out into the Sulu Sea and the Japanese, believing their destination to be either Negros or Panay, searched the wrong area. The attacks by the fast carriers on the Luzon airfields on the 12th, 13th and 14th prevented their use and thus the convoys reached their destination without loss. The landing was made early on the 15th in perfect weather, against little opposition, and by noon San José was occupied and the four abandoned enemy airstrips secured.[1] Although, during the build-up, enemy aircraft constantly attacked the convoys and the follow-up supply convoys, sinking and damaging a number of ships, the construction of the airstrips was not hindered. One was completed on the 20th December and a second on the 28th, and aircraft of 5th U.S.A.A.F. were flown in.

Realizing that Mindoro in American hands would greatly increase the difficulty of defending Luzon, the Japanese considered a counter-offensive to recapture the island, but Yamashita, already short of troops, was unable to spare any from Luzon.[2] It was therefore decided that a naval force should be sent to destroy American shipping off the island and to bombard the beaches and the San José area. Since the new aircraft carrier *Unryu* had been sunk by an American submarine while sailing south from Japan on the 19th, Toyoda (Commander-in-Chief of the *Combined Fleet*) had to despatch from Camranh Bay the only available force (one heavy and one light cruiser and five destroyers) without any air cover. This force was spotted on the 26th December when about 180 miles to the west of Mindoro, and was attacked by aircraft from the newly completed airstrip that evening. Nevertheless it stood on and, despite attacks from aircraft and motor torpedo-boats, bombarded the anchorage and beach area for some forty minutes after dark. Having destroyed some thirty aircraft on the

[1] The Japanese garrison on the island was only about a hundred men.
[2] A raiding party of one hundred men was sent to delay the build-up of the San José air base, but it was completely ineffective.

ground and set one transport on fire, it withdrew, losing one destroyer. From the 28th enemy air activity was confined to attacks on supply convoys for Mindoro; these were repeatedly attacked until the 4th January when the Japanese turned their attention to the approaching Luzon invasion fleet. During this period the Americans lost four merchant ships and two landing craft and had two destroyers and five merchant ships severely damaged, mainly by *Kamikaze* attacks. Mindoro was, however, securely held, and from its airstrips air protection could be given to the large convoys carrying the forces for the attack on Luzon as they made their way north to Lingayen Gulf.

It was clear from the experience of the Leyte campaign that *Kamikaze* attacks constituted a very serious danger to shipping of all kinds.[1] The first counter-measure taken was to reorganize the fast carrier force into three instead of four groups so that the anti-aircraft protection and the effectiveness of the screen could be increased. The carriers also embarked a greater proportion of fighters at the expense of bombers. Additional light anti-aircraft weapons were fitted to all ships and a new proximity anti-aircraft fuse was issued. Finally, when within range of enemy land-based aircraft, picket destroyers, fitted with radar, were stationed some sixty miles outwards from a task force.

After reorganization, the fast carrier force carried out the planned day and night attacks on the Luzon airfields during the 14th to 16th December. In some 1,670 sorties (the majority by fighters) and at a cost of sixty-five aircraft, a considerable number of Japanese aircraft were destroyed, thus preventing the Japanese from launching an attack from Luzon on the Mindoro convoys.[2] No enemy aircraft penetrated the carrier force's defensive screen during the operation. However, what the Japanese were on this occasion unable to do the weather did: on its way to a refuelling rendezvous, the 3rd Fleet ran very unexpectedly into a newly-formed tight typhoon, the centre of which passed over part of the fleet. Three destroyers, which were short of fuel, were forced on to their beam ends and capsized, and six other ships were seriously damaged. Before the fleet could run clear of the storm, 800 officers and men and 146 aircraft were lost and so great was the damage that the fleet had to return to Ulithi for repair and refit.

The naval plan for the invasion of Luzon followed the now familiar pattern. Halsey's 3rd Fleet and the fast carrier force were to launch

---

[1] The United States Government kept the news of *Kamikaze* attacks secret until the 12th April 1945.
[2] The Americans claimed 208 aircraft destroyed on the ground and 62 in aerial combat.

air strikes on airfields in Formosa, the Pescadores, the Ryukyu Islands and Luzon from the 3rd to the 9th January 1945 and then, if circumstances permitted, make an incursion into the China Sea. B.29s of 20th Bomber Command from China were to strengthen the air attack on Formosa by attacking harbour installations and shipping. Kinkaid's 7th Fleet was to embark and transport the troops and support the landing. As before, Kinkaid made Oldendorf responsible for the approach to Lingayen Gulf, for minesweeping and for the preliminary bombardment until he himself arrived with the two amphibious forces (Vice-Admirals D. C. Barbey and T. Wilkinson) and assumed command.

The I and XIV Corps of 6th U.S. Army (Krueger) were each to land two divisions at the head of Lingayen Gulf; both corps were to be brought up to a strength of three divisions as soon as possible.[1] The assembly of these formations from widely separated points throughout the Pacific, some of which were 3,000 miles from Lingayen Gulf, and their marshalling at the right time and place was no mean achievement and needed very careful planning.[2] Leyte Gulf was selected as the assembly area from where the two amphibious forces were to sail for Luzon.

Oldendorf's command consisted of 164 ships, including six battleships, six cruisers and nineteen destroyers, an escort carrier group of seventeen carriers and twenty destroyers, ten destroyer transports (carrying underwater demolition teams) and eighty-six miscellaneous ships, including minesweepers and gunboats. He sailed on the 3rd January from Leyte Gulf, passed through Surigao Strait into the Sulu Sea and turned north to pass west of Mindoro on his passage to Lingayen Gulf. The Japanese, using all their aircraft as *Kamikazes*, attacked that evening and damaged a tanker; the attacks were repeated the next day and the escort carrier *Ommaney Bay* was sunk. On the 5th, when the force was abeam of the main Luzon airfields, the Japanese were more successful since bad weather had temporarily put the Mindoro airfields out of action and the force was left entirely dependent on its own air defence. Seven ships were damaged, including the cruiser *Louisville* and the Australian cruiser *Australia* and destroyer *Arunta*. On the 6th, just as minesweeping operations in the gulf began, the *Kamikazes* attacked again. A minesweeper was sunk and eleven ships damaged, including the battleships *New Mexico* and *California* and, for the second time, the cruisers *Louisville* and *Australia*.[3]

---

[1] The I Corps consisted of 6th and 43rd Divisions (later reinforced by 32nd Division), and XIV Corps of 37th and 40th Divisions (later reinforced by 1st Cavalry Division).

[2] Formations and units were embarked at sixteen different points, including Bougainville, New Britain, Milne Bay, Finschhafen, Lae, Hollandia and Biak.

[3] The *New Mexico* had aboard as observers Admiral Sir Bruce Fraser, Commander-in-Chief, British Pacific Fleet, and Lieut.-General H. Lumsden (the Prime Minister's Personal Liaison Officer with MacArthur's headquarters). The latter was killed.

Oldendorf, thoroughly perturbed by the losses and damage suffered, asked that Halsey should do his best to put all the Luzon airfields out of action since he feared that, if on arrival the amphibious forces received similar treatment, losses, especially before the troops could be landed, would be heavy. On the 7th two minesweepers were sunk and on the 8th the unlucky *Australia* received further serious damage from two more *Kamikaze* attacks, but survived. On the 9th the minesweeping and the demolition of underwater obstacles were completed and the amphibious forces arrived, having had only two escort carriers and a landing ship damaged and one troopship hit, fortunately without any of the troops being injured.[1] At 9.30 a.m., under cover of a bombardment, XIV Corps began to land almost unopposed at the southern end of the gulf, and I Corps, landing at its south-eastern end, met with only slight opposition; these landings were made in almost the same area where the Japanese had themselves landed four years before.[2]

The 3rd Fleet and the fast carrier force had meanwhile left Ulithi on the 30th December and on the 3rd and 4th January had attacked Okinawa, Formosa and Luzon. After refuelling on the 5th, Halsey concentrated during the 6th and 7th on attacking the northern Luzon airfields and on the 8th and 9th returned to complete his task on Formosa.[3] During the week the carrier aircraft flew some 3,000 sorties, dropping 700 tons of bombs on enemy airfields and installations and losing eighty-six aircraft. Though the value of many of the strikes was reduced by bad weather, they did prevent aircraft from Formosa from reinforcing Luzon and so reduced the scale of the *Kamikaze* attacks on Oldendorf's and Kinkaid's convoys.

Having completed his mission in support of the Luzon landings on the 9th, Halsey led his fleet through the Luzon Strait into the South China Sea where no American surface ship had ventured since early 1942. On the 11th he formed a separate force of battleships and cruisers which, supported by air strikes, was to bombard Camranh Bay where he expected to find ships of the *Combined Fleet*, including the battleships *Ise* and *Hyuga*, survivors of the battle for Leyte Gulf.[4] On the 12th, when fifty miles from the coast, air strikes launched from all three carrier groups swept 420 miles of the coast of Indo-China. The surprise was complete. Although no enemy capital ships were found in Camranh Bay, there were many merchant ships in the area. A convoy of fifteen ships was severely handled, nine fully laden

---

[1] During the approach Oldendorf's and Barbey's forces intercepted and sank two Japanese destroyers: the *Momi* and *Hinoki*.

[2] There were further losses from *Kamikaze* attacks on the 10th, 11th and 12th both in the gulf and among empty returning convoys. During these attacks eight ships, including two destroyers, were damaged.

[3] B.29s of 20th Bomber Command from China also attacked Formosa on the 9th January.

[4] Both these ships were actually at Singapore.

tankers and the escort—the light cruiser *Kashii*—being sunk. In all, forty-four ships of some 132,000 tons were sunk, including fifteen naval vessels and twelve oil tankers, at a cost of twenty-three aircraft.

At sunset the fleet set course to the north-east and, despite bad weather, topped up with fuel and altered course to the northwards to launch strikes against Formosa. During the early hours of the 15th, Halsey sent aircraft to search the Pescadores, Amoy, Swatow and Hong Kong,[1] as well as Hainan in the hope of finding the missing battleships, but without success. Soon after sunrise he launched strikes against airfields on the China coast as well as against harbours and airfields in Formosa, sinking two destroyers and a transport. In the evening he closed the China coast and on the 16th launched a strike on Hong Kong which met with very heavy anti-aircraft fire. The weather continued to be stormy and, after refuelling with some difficulty on the 19th in the lee of Luzon, Halsey led his fleet on the 20th back through the Luzon Strait, shooting down on the way fifteen enemy aircraft.[2] On the 21st he once again struck at Formosa and the Pescadores, sinking ten merchant ships (including five tankers) and damaging a destroyer. Only three enemy aircraft were encountered over Formosa and of these two were shot down, but at sea *Kamikazes* from Formosa and Luzon delivered a damaging counter-attack. Two fleet carriers, the *Langley* and *Ticonderoga* (the latter twice) and the picket destroyer *Maddox* were hit and damaged. The 3rd Fleet then headed north to make strikes against the Ryukyus, mainly to get photographic intelligence and, after refuelling, returned to Ulithi on the 25th.

There, at midnight on the 26th, Vice-Admiral R. A. Spruance hoisted his flag in command and the fleet once again became the 5th Fleet. Spruance had no small responsibility in succeeding to the command of a fleet with such a reputation. During the five months in which the 3rd Fleet had been commanded by Halsey, it claimed to have destroyed some 7,000 aircraft, 90 warships of all types and about 600 merchant ships.

Owing to the reduction in the strength of *14th Area Army* resulting from the abortive attempt to hold Leyte and the severe losses suffered by the army and navy air force formations, Yamashita realized that he could defend neither the whole of Luzon nor even the vital central plain against the superior ground, air and naval forces which the Americans could bring against him. He therefore decided on a policy of delaying the invasion forces as much as possible without holding the beaches or becoming too involved, and then withdrawing into

----

[1] See Sketch 1, facing page 63.
[2] These were engaged on evacuating airmen from Luzon to Formosa.

selected mountain strongholds from which he could undertake a protracted defence and harass the Americans. He selected three such strongholds: the area north of the line from Lingayen to Baler Bay with Baguio as its headquarters, the Cabusilian Mountains west of and dominating Clark Field, and the mountainous area between Manila and the east coast of the island.[1]

Towards the end of December he began to prepare strongly defended and self-sufficient bases in the three areas, and arranged that *4th Air Army* and the remaining naval air units should as their primary task concentrate on the destruction of the invasion convoys. He allotted four infantry divisions, an independent mixed brigade and an armoured division to the northern area, an airborne group to the Clark Field area with orders to fall back to the Cabusilian Mountains, and two divisions to the Manila area with the responsibility for all operations in central and southern Luzon and the defence of the third stronghold east of Manila.[2] In addition to the military garrison there were some 25,000 naval ratings under command of Vice-Admiral D. Okochi (Commander *South-West Area Fleet*); these were mostly in the vicinity of Manila, which Yamashita decided should be an open town.

At the beginning of January there were about 120 army and 130 naval aircraft in Luzon. Since their task had been defined as the destruction of the invasion convoys, the aircraft were not used to oppose the carrier-borne preliminary attacks on the island. From the 4th the remaining aircraft, employing *Kamikaze* tactics, continually attacked the invasion convoys with the results already described. By the 12th there were no serviceable aircraft left except for four kept for liaison purposes. The remaining airmen of *4th Air Army* were converted into infantry and *2nd Air Fleet* was disbanded, the remnants being sent back to join *1st Air Fleet* in Formosa. Nevertheless twenty-seven aircraft were made serviceable after the 12th and were used in *Kamikaze* raids on the 15th, 21st and 25th.[3] The *14th Area Army* was thereafter left to fight without air support.

On the night of the 9th/10th January, while the build-up on the Lingayen beaches east of Lingayen and each side of San Fabian was continuing, a fleet of some seventy small suicide craft from Port Sual attacked Wilkinson's group of transports (which had carried XIV

---

[1] See Map 5, facing page 100.

[2] The garrison of Luzon consisted of *8th, 10th, 19th, 23rd, 103rd* and *105th Infantry Divisions, 58th I.M.B., 2nd Armoured Division* and an airborne group. All these formations were well below strength and only partly equipped. The total combatant strength, excluding naval personnel, amounted to some 90,000 men. The total strength, including administrative and naval personnel, was at least double this figure.

[3] One of the attacks on the fast carrier force on the 21st was carried out by some of these aircraft.

Corps.)[1] The craft were spotted but nevertheless succeeded in sinking two landing craft and damaging eight other ships; no further similar attacks were, however, made in the gulf.

The XIV Corps on the right had been ordered to advance as rapidly as possible towards Clark Field with Manila as its objective; I Corps was to swing left, advance to the general line San José–Pozorrubio and there contain the Japanese. As its advance threatened to outflank the defences of the northern strongholds, I Corps met with increasing opposition and on the 16th a Japanese counter-attack very nearly reached the beaches before being thrown back. The XIV Corps met with little opposition but its advance was slow, for the Japanese had ripped up the railway lines and destroyed all the bridges and culverts along the roads and the corps was extremely short of bridging material and transport. It was not till the 29th that it reached the outskirts of Clark Field and occupied San Fernando. The 32nd Infantry and 1st Cavalry Divisions were landed at Lingayen Gulf on the 27th, and were sent to reinforce I and XIV Corps respectively.

To prevent the Japanese from making a prolonged resistance in the Bataan peninsula as American troops had done in 1942, MacArthur landed part of XI U.S. Corps in the vicinity of San Antonio and Subic Bay on the 29th, with orders to cut off the peninsula and make contact with XIV Corps at San Fernando.[2]

On the 30th January Krueger ordered XIV Corps to take Clark Field and advance aggressively southwards, and I Corps to capture San José. Clark Field was captured on the 1st February, the Japanese defenders retiring westwards into the Cabusilian Mountains. The same day 1st Cavalry Division led a rapid advance by XIV Corps on Manila. To outflank the Manila defences and speed up its capture, 11th Airborne Division (part of 8th U.S. Army) was landed without opposition at Nasugbu on the 31st with orders to advance rapidly to capture Tagaytay and then move northwards on Manila between Manila Bay and Laguna Bay. On the 3rd February the leading troops of 1st Cavalry Division, closely followed by 37th Division, reached the outskirts of Manila. By the 4th the northern portion of the town was secured and the many internees and prisoners-of-war held in that area liberated, but no further progress could be made. The airborne division had also advanced on Manila from the south-west and, assisted by a parachute drop of four battalions at Tagaytay on the

---

[1] These craft were fast plywood boats 18½ feet in length, carrying two 260-lb. depth charges, one light machine-gun with a few hand grenades and a crew of two or three men. Their tactics were to approach their target, if possible unseen, from astern and, when nearly alongside and so close that guns could not be brought to bear, to drop their depth charges with a shallow setting.

[2] This force consisted of 38th Division and 34th Regimental Combat Team. It made contact with XIV Corps at San Fernando on the 5th February.

3rd, reached the vicinity of Nichols Field on the 4th. There it was held up by fierce opposition. By the evening of the 4th it was clear that MacArthur's hope of securing Manila quickly was not to be fulfilled.

Despite Yamashita's orders that Manila was to be an open town, Rear-Admiral S. Iwabachi (*31st Special Naval Base Force*), who had been left in command of naval forces some 16,000 strong in the Manila area when Okochi moved to join Yamashita at Baguio, insisted on defending it. He assumed command of the three battalions left in Manila to backload stores and maintain law and order when the army withdrew to the stronghold east of the city, organized its defences and those of the islands at the mouth of Manila Bay and on the 1st February ordered the destruction of the wharves and port installations. When American troops reached the northern and south-western outskirts of the city, Philippino guerrillas within it cut telephone lines and demolished bridges, with the result that all cohesion inside the city was lost. When he learned in the middle of February that his orders were not being obeyed, Yamashita ordered the commander of the eastern stronghold to withdraw all army units from the city, but it was by then too late since it was surrounded on all sides.

On the 12th, 11th Airborne Division captured Nichols Field and thereafter, as Iwabachi refused to surrender, the struggle for Manila developed into a desperate house-to-house combat; it was not until the 4th March that resistance ceased, by which time the city was a shambles. Meanwhile, to clear the entrance to Manila Bay, a regimental combat team had been landed on the 15th February at Mariveles at the southern end of the Bataan peninsula and, meeting with very little resistance, had soon driven the Japanese into the mountains where they were no longer a threat. After preliminary heavy bombing and naval bombardment, the island of Corregidor which guarded the entrance to Manila Bay was subjected on the 16th to a combined parachute and amphibious assault. The defenders, numbering some 4,500, put up a fanatical resistance in the maze of tunnels and caves, and resistance on the island did not cease until the 26th. The first ship entered the harbour at Manila on the 15th March, which by the end of the month was capable of handling 50,000 tons of shipping. The Americans now controlled all the strategic points of importance in the Philippines, but they still had to mop up the large number of Japanese troops who, without air or naval support, held the remainder of the Visayan group of islands, Mindanao, and the three strongholds established by Yamashita on Luzon.

Map 5

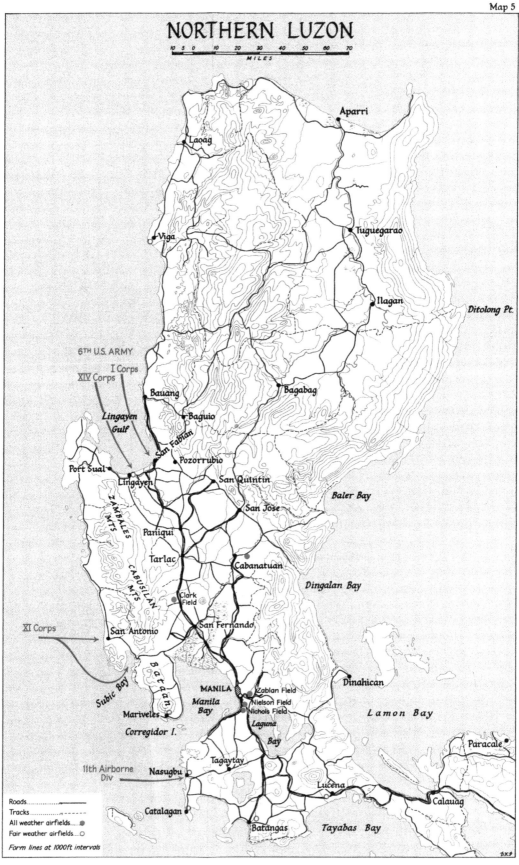

NORTHERN LUZON

10 5 0   10   20   30   40   50   60   70
MILES

Aparri

Laoag

Viga

Tuguegarao

Ilagan

Ditolong Pt.

6TH U.S. ARMY

I Corps

XIV Corps

Bauang

Bagabag

Baguio

Lingayen
Gulf

San Fabian

Port Sual

Pozorrubio

Lingayen

San Quintin

Baler Bay

ZAMBALES
MTS

San Jose

Paniqui

Tarlac

Cabanatuan

Dingalan Bay

CABUSILAN
MTS

Clark
Field

XI Corps

San Antonio

San Fernando

Dinahican

Subic Bay

Bataan

MANILA

Zablan Field

Nielson Field

Nichols Field

Manila
Bay

Lamon Bay

Mariveles

Laguna
Bay

Corregidor I.

Paracale

11th Airborne
Div

Nasugbu

Tagaytay

Lucena

Calauag

Roads.............
Tracks.............
All weather airfields.....●
Fair weather airfields.....○

Catalagan

Batangas

Tayabas Bay

Form lines at 1000ft intervals

CHAPTER IX
PLANNING FOR THE ADVANCE
INTO BURMA
(August–November 1944)

See Maps 1, 6, 12 and 13 and Sketch 21

ON the 24th August 1944, 14th Army and 3rd Tactical Air Force submitted their joint appreciation and first outline plan for 'Capital' together with their views on 'Dracula' to 11th Army Group.[1] On the 14th September Giffard passed it to S.E.A.C. Headquarters with his comments. The appreciation was based on the army's object being the capture of Mandalay and Pakokku and, in conjunction with the N.C.A.C. and the Chinese Yunnan armies, consolidation on the general line Pakokku–Mandalay–Maymyo–Lashio.[2] In accordance with its terms of reference, 14th Army proposed to achieve the object in four phases: the first, the seizure of Kalemyo and Kalewa by a co-ordinated advance down the Kabaw Valley and the Tiddim road and an airborne operation in the Kalemyo and Kalewa area; the second, an airborne assault in the Yeu–Shwebo area followed by a rapid build-up with air-transported formations and fighter aircraft, in conjunction with an advance from Kalewa by land to open the road to Yeu so that tanks and artillery could be brought forward for the assault on Mandalay; the third, the capture of Mandalay and Pakokku; and the fourth, consolidation and exploitation.

The most worthwhile objective for an enemy offensive on 14th Army's front appeared to be Chittagong with its air bases and pipeline terminals. Since its loss or neutralization would have disastrous consequences, Giffard considered it necessary to allot four divisions to the Arakan front, one of which would be in reserve; these would include the two West African divisions, of which one had only two brigades and the other had not been in action. Excluding the Lushai Brigade, 268th Brigade and Special Force, all of which had localized or specialized tasks, the total force available was thirteen infantry divisions, two armoured brigades, 3 Commando Brigade and 50th (P.) Brigade. Of these, four divisions had to be allotted to the Arakan front and one (36th) was with N.C.A.C. Three divisions, two armoured

---
[1] See page 6.
[2] See Map 13 in end pocket.

brigades and the parachute brigade were required for 'Dracula', and two divisions had to be held in reserve for rehabilitation. This left only four divisions for 'Capital' which, in view of the strength it was known that the Japanese could concentrate in the Mandalay–Shwebo area, was considered to be quite inadequate. The first two phases of 'Capital' could not therefore be carried out unless the forces for 'Dracula' were provided from outside S.E.A.C.

The broad concept envisaged airborne operations for both 'Capital' and 'Dracula', which meant that 50th (P.) Brigade would have to be used in each operation since it was the only parachute formation in the theatre and the arrival of a second parachute brigade from the Middle East was by no means certain.[1] If the operations already in hand for the capture of Kalewa did not succeed and an airborne operation had to be launched in that area, the brigade would have to undertake three separate operations within a very limited period, and this would be beyond its capabilities.[2] As the parachute brigade could not be fully ready for action before February, the second phase of 'Capital', the assault on the Yeu–Shwebo area, could not be carried out until then. There would thus be insufficient time to extricate it from the Yeu area, transport it to the Arakan airfields and reorganize and retrain it for 'Dracula' by mid-March 1945. For these reasons 14th Army and 11th Army Group considered that both Kalewa and Yeu would have to be taken if possible without the use of airborne troops.

An examination of the general administrative factors involved in the two operations showed that, if 'Dracula' were to be mounted in mid-March 1945, engineering resources would have to be allotted without delay to the construction of the necessary base in the Chittagong area. If this were done, however, the remaining resources would be insufficient for the construction of an all-weather road from Tamu down the Kabaw Valley into upper Burma. The maintenance of the troops taking part in 'Capital' would therefore have to depend on fair-weather roads forward of Tamu, on such river traffic as could be developed on the Chindwin and on air supply. The maintenance problem could be solved on this basis until the monsoon, but it would then become acute unless the forces landed at Rangoon could join up with those advancing south from the Mandalay and Pakokku area before the stocks placed east of the Chindwin during the dry season became exhausted.

The conclusion reached was that 'Capital' was a feasible operation provided its administrative problems could be satisfactorily solved,

---

[1] Two battalions of 50th (P.) Brigade had been used in the Battle of Imphal in a normal infantry role (see Volume III), and had not been withdrawn for reorganization until the end of July 1944. For this reason only one of the three parachute battalions could be ready in time for Phase I of 'Capital'.

[2] The three operations were the capture of Kalewa, the capture of the Yeu–Shwebo area and 'Dracula'.

but that a full-scale 'Capital' and 'Dracula' could not be mounted unless extra divisions, engineering resources and aircraft came from outside S.E.A.C. If these could not be provided, 'Dracula' should be used as a cover plan, since the Japanese would probably be very sensitive to any threat to the south Burma coast.

The main factors affecting the administrative planning for 'Capital' were the shortness of time before the monsoon, which might begin any time after the 15th May; the length of the line of communication from Dimapur to Shwebo, which would reduce delivery at roadhead to about a quarter of a ton per vehicle, and its vulnerability to enemy action and the weather; the availability of transport vehicles and air-craft, airfields and engineering resources; and finally the danger of the intensely malarious Kabaw and Chindwin valleys.

The 14th Army planners proposed that, in order to keep down intermediate consumption of supplies and reduce casualties from malaria, the number of troops on the lines of communication should be reduced to a minimum. This postulated the movement of casualties and reinforcements by air so as to obviate the need for large hospitals and reception camps in the Kabaw Valley. As a safeguard in the event of interruptions of land communications and to achieve a reduction in demands for air supply during the monsoon, when flying conditions would be poor, reserve stocks should be built up in the Kalewa area and across the Chindwin. To reduce flying time, forward air bases should be developed on the Imphal plain and forward airfields constructed in both the Kalewa–Kalemyo and the Yeu–Shwebo areas. Finally, all available engineering resources should be concentrated on the building of roads, airfields and depots along the main line of communication only.

To enable the army to capture the Kalemyo–Kalewa area and to establish a bridgehead over the Chindwin at Kalewa, the line of communication from Imphal to Kalewa had to run down the Kabaw Valley.[1] The existing fair-weather track down the valley was under water and would probably not have dried out sufficiently for the movement of wheeled vehicles and armour much before the 1st December. The engineers would therefore have to build a new fair-weather road from Tamu to Kalewa as early as possible, construct and maintain fair-weather airstrips in the Kabaw Valley and around Kalemyo, make a start on providing depot accommodation at Indainggyi and bring forward bridging material to span the Chind-win at Kalewa.[2] Since all engineer resources would be absorbed by these tasks, the building of a road to Sittaung and the development of the Chindwin as a water line of communication from that point to Kalewa would not be feasible. In addition to these tasks, the engineers

---

[1] Engineer resources were insufficient for both the Kabaw Valley and the Tiddim roads.
[2] See Map 1, facing page 15.

would have to restore the Palel–Tamu road to a two-way all-weather standard by the end of October; they would, as soon as weather conditions permitted the use of machinery, also have to begin constructing a bithess surfaced all-weather road in the Kabaw Valley from Tamu to Kalewa on a new trace sited to avoid flooding and linked with the fair-weather road at intervals.[1] The fair-weather airfield at Tamu would have to be restored at once, tactical airfields provided as necessary in the Kabaw Valley and two fair-weather airfields built in the Kalemyo–Kalewa area. The material for bridging the Chindwin with a Class 30 Bailey pontoon bridge and a Class 9 folding boat bridge, amounting to some six hundred vehicle loads, had to be concentrated between Imphal and Tamu by mid-December so that it could be moved forward, as soon as road conditions allowed, to Indainggyi, where a depot to hold 30,000 tons of stores would have to be built as soon as possible.

In the second phase the essentials were the construction (or repair) and maintenance of forward airfields in the Yeu–Shwebo area, the improvement of the Kalewa–Yeu road to take the armour and artillery which would have to be brought forward to join the airborne or air-transported formations, the forward move of fighter squadrons and the transport required for forward stocking. After the forward concentration had been completed, traffic on the road would be reduced to what was required for operational purposes and engineering maintenance, and air supply would be used for the maintenance of the forward troops and for essential airfield construction material. Additional engineering tasks would be the support of the assault crossings of the Chindwin, the establishment of ferries, the subsequent bridging of the river at Kalewa, the improvement of the road to Yeu to an all-weather standard and the provision of water points along it, the construction of four fair-weather and four all-weather airfields in the Yeu–Shwebo area, the provision of a depot near Shwebo to hold some 60,000 tons of stores, and the movement forward of the heavy rafting material required for the crossing of the Irrawaddy in the third phase.

To ensure that there would be adequate engineer resources to undertake these formidable tasks, 14th Army had reviewed all engineering projects in its area. Some were cancelled (such as that of bringing the Chittagong–Sylhet road up to an all-weather standard) and the scope of others (such as specifications for all accommodation projects including hospitals, reinforcement camps and airfields) reduced on the assumption that the rapid completion of 'Capital' would make them unnecessary or cut their period of usefulness.

The movement programme of the tonnages required for daily

---

[1] For bithess see glossary and photograph No. 29.

maintenance and for forward stocking was a complex problem and throughout involved considerable air supply commitments. The main difficulties arose from the shortage of G.P.T. companies, the restricted capacity of base airfields, and the necessity to reduce the haul for transport aircraft to the minimum. It was decided to extend the radius of the L. of C. Road Transport organization, already operating from Dimapur to Palel,[1] as far as Indainggyi (a total distance of 281 miles) and to introduce forward of that point a new transport echelon (Army Transport Columns) which would deliver to divisional areas at Shwebo, Yeu, Mandalay and Pakokku. Twenty-two G.P.T. companies could be expected as reinforcements (five by the 1st November, five a month from January to March and the balance in April), and these would be used first to strengthen the L. of C. Road Transport and then to create the Army Transport Columns. Since the road forward of Tamu would not be up to an all-weather standard for some time, all transport vehicles would have to be of the 4- or 6-wheel drive type, with a reserve large enough to make good a wastage rate as high as ten to twelve per cent. The completion of the oil pipeline from Dimapur to the Imphal plain with a daily delivery of 350 tons by the 1st March 1945 would thereafter considerably reduce the load on the L. of C. Road Transport organization.

To enable the stockpile at Shwebo (hereafter known as the Central Burma Stockpile) to be built up, some 63,000 tons of supplies (including R.A.F. stocks) would have to be carried forward. The shortage of motor transport made it necessary to ferry these supplies forward by stages as the advance progressed, and special dumps for this purpose were to be made at Palel and Indainggyi. From Indainggyi, supplies would be ferried forward to Shwebo as soon as the road to it was open. Even so, it was estimated that, including the R.A.F. portion which was to be moved by air, not more than 45,000 tons could be placed at Shwebo by the 15th May; the remaining 18,000 tons would therefore have to be moved by air during the monsoon.

After having allowed for 150 aircraft being permanently allotted to the Northern front, the planners assumed for the purposes of calculation that there would be 94 transport aircraft available to 14th Army for 'Capital' in September, 214 in October, 234 in November and December and 350 from January onwards.[2] They estimated that the army's permanent maintenance requirements, which varied according to the size of the forces to be maintained and the distance of the

---

[1] See page 21.
[2] September: 1st Combat Cargo Group (100), four R.A.F. squadrons (80), three U.S.A.A.F. squadrons (48), No. 1 Air Commando (16)=244 − 150=94.
October: 94+one R.C.A.F. squadron (20), and 2nd Combat Cargo Group (100)=214.
November and December: 214+one R.C.A.F. squadron (20)=234.
January: 234+3rd Combat Cargo Group (100) and No. 2 Air Commando (16)=350.

advanced formations from the air supply bases, would range from 57 aircraft in September 1944 to 322 between mid-March and mid-May 1945, and that, allowing for training the parachute brigade and its fly-in for both phases (if necessary), the maximum number required at any time would be 342. The main base airfields were to be Tulihal and Kangla on the Imphal plain (with Imphal airfield in reserve), Comilla, Agartala and Chittagong (Hathazari). Three R.A.M.O.s were to be deployed at Imphal and one at each of the other three base airfields, and two F.A.M.O.s were to be held ready for use at the Kalemyo and Yeu–Shwebo airfields as required. The Feni group of airfields was to be kept in reserve, but all the material required for the construction of the airfields in central Burma was to be concentrated there ready to be flown in when wanted.[1] On these assumptions an outline movement programme for maintenance and stocking of the line of communication was then worked out.[2]

To conserve morale, it was proposed that leave should remain open to all ranks throughout the operation subject to no more than five per cent of each unit being absent at any one time and there being a minimum present strength of eighty per cent, all those on leave being flown in and out through Imphal. So that reinforcements would arrive fresh and ready for action, reinforcement camps were to be established in the Comilla area and all reinforcements flown forward to the airstrip nearest to their formations or units. All casualties would be evacuated by ambulance or light aircraft to the nearest Dakota airstrip and flown back from it to hospitals at Imphal or in India.

After a careful examination of 14th Army's appreciation and the comments on it by 11th Army Group, and after a series of conferences with his Commanders-in-Chief, Mountbatten told the Chiefs of Staff on the 1st October that he now regarded 'Capital' and 'Dracula' as two phases of one operation for the clearance of Burma. The basic factor in the 'Capital'–'Dracula' co-ordinated plan was the early junction of the forces from the north with those from the south so that the 'Capital' forces would have a sound line of communication through Rangoon for their maintenance during the monsoon. If this junction were not made and the 'Capital' forces were to remain in central Burma, they would have to rely on the Central Burma Stockpile as long as it lasted, on air supply and on the relatively small amounts which could be got forward along the tenuous land line of

---

[1] See Sketch 21, facing page 522.
[2] See Appendix 11. It should be noted that the movement plan made no allowance for the forward movement of river craft required for the river line of communication from Kalewa to Monywa in the later phases of 'Capital'. An allowance for this purpose could not be made owing to the general shortage of transport.

communication. Experience had shown that air supply was liable to interruption during the monsoon and that, owing to the greater distances involved, conditions in 1945 would be even more difficult than those in 1944. It was therefore evident that the consequences would be most serious if adequate resources were not placed at his disposal to enable him to launch 'Dracula' in mid-March 1945—a fact which had not been fully appreciated when the outline plan had been discussed in London in August.

Further investigation had shown, Mountbatten continued, that the statement he had made in London to the effect that, if 'Dracula' were postponed in the spring, it could be carried out in November 1945 could no longer be upheld. The ground on which the airstrips required for the airborne and air-transported forces would have to be built would not dry out in time to mount the operation in November, and the earliest date would now be the 1st January 1946. A postponement would therefore not only prejudice the attainment of the object given in his directive—to open up land communication with China—but would lose the opportunity which existed of routing the Japanese armies while they were on the run. Next day he told them that the 'Capital'–'Dracula' plan needed considerable additional air resources, most of which should reach S.E.A.C. by the 1st January 1945.[1]

On the 2nd October Mountbatten issued directives to 11th Army Group and N.C.A.C. which were to become effective from midnight on the 4th/5th October. In these he said that S.E.A.C.'s broad mission was to destroy or expel all the Japanese forces in Burma as soon as possible. Operations to achieve this object were not, however, to prejudice the security of the existing air supply route, including the air staging post at Myitkyina, or the opening of the road to China. The 11th Army Group was given the task of conducting offensive operations to destroy the enemy west of the general line Maungdaw–Yeu–Thabeikkyin and the boundary with N.C.A.C. by mid-February, of providing the necessary ground forces for the defence of India and Ceylon and possibly for the development of the Cocos Islands as a base, and of carrying out 'Dracula' for which a separate directive would be issued.[2] The army group's specific tasks were: in Arakan, to conduct defensive–offensive operations to secure the Arakan line of communication and the vital Chittagong–Ramu–Bawli Bazar air operational area, and to contain the maximum enemy forces;[3] and on the Central front, to capture Kalemyo

---

[1] The air requirements over and above those already in the theatre were 826 C.47 transport aircraft, of which 190 had been promised but not assigned (making a total of 1,386), 1,596 gliders, of which 1,012 had been promised or assigned, eight fighter squadrons, two special duty squadrons, one B.25 bomber group and 1,000 glider pilots.

[2] See Map 12, facing page 436.

[3] See Map 6, facing page 134.

and Kalewa and secure a bridgehead across the Chindwin at Kalewa by mid-December 1944, capture the Yeu–Shwebo area by combined airborne and land operations by mid-February 1945 and be prepared to exploit in anticipation of the later phases of 'Capital'.

The N.C.A.C. was given the main task of expelling or destroying the enemy east of its boundary with 14th Army,[1] and of occupying the area north of and including Indaw, Kunchaung, Sikaw and Namhkam by mid-December 1944, and as far south as the general line Thabeikkyin–Mogok–Mongmit–Lashio by mid-February 1945. It was also to protect the air and overland routes to China and, within the confines of the command boundaries, to be responsible for the security of Assam and the occupied portion of upper Burma.

Meanwhile, in London, the Chiefs of Staff had been investigating the withdrawal of formations from Europe for use in South-East Asia, and the transportation to India of all the resources required for the mounting of 'Dracula' in mid-March 1945. By early October it was clear that the trend of operations in Italy would not justify the withdrawal of formations from that theatre, and the stronger German resistance made it unlikely that the war in Europe would be brought to an end, as had been hoped, in 1944. The Chiefs of Staff were therefore with great reluctance forced to the conclusion that they would be departing from first principles should they jeopardize operations for the defeat of Germany for the sake of 'Dracula'. They proposed that 'Dracula' should be postponed and that Mountbatten should be told to exploit 'Capital' throughout 1945 as far as was possible without prejudicing preparations for the execution of 'Dracula' at the earliest moment after the end of the 1945 monsoon. On the 5th October, the Prime Minister warned Mountbatten that 'Dracula' would have to be deferred to November 1945. The American Chiefs of Staff agreed with this, and the postponement was officially confirmed on the 11th October. The same day the Chiefs of Staff told Mountbatten that both they and the Prime Minister were surprised at his statement that, if 'Dracula' were postponed beyond March 1945, it could not be mounted before January 1946. They asked him to meet the Prime Minister and the C.I.G.S. at Cairo on the 16th October to discuss the whole problem.[2]

On the 13th and 14th October Mountbatten conferred with his

---

[1] The boundary between N.C.A.C. and 14th Army was the road and track from Indaw to Tigyaing on the Irrawaddy, the river as far south as Thabeikkyin and thence the Mogok–Hsipaw–Loilem–Loikaw road. (See Maps 1, 2, 3, facing pages 15, 39 and 55, and Map 13 in end pocket).

[2] The Prime Minister and the C.I.G.S., who were at the Tolstoy Conference in Moscow proposed to stop at Cairo on their way back to London.

Commanders-in-Chief to determine the earliest date on which 'Dracula' could be mounted after the monsoon, to discuss the effect of its postponement on 'Capital' and to decide what operations, if any, other than 'Capital' should be undertaken in 1945. They agreed, for the reasons already given to the Chiefs of Staff, that it would not be possible to mount 'Dracula' before the end of December 1945 at the earliest, but that, although the postponement of 'Dracula' would ease the air transport position and allow an extra division to be allotted to 11th Army Group as a reserve for 'Capital', it would enable the Japanese to concentrate all their forces to hold the Pakokku–Mandalay–Lashio area or to prevent exploitation south from it.

When operations other than 'Capital' came to be discussed, Giffard pointed out that, as engineering resources and administrative units allotted to 'Capital' were already barely adequate, it had become imperative to find some way of freeing forces from Arakan where greatly superior Allied forces, kept there to ensure the security of the airfields required for 'Dracula', were being tied down by a much smaller enemy force. He advocated an operation to turn the enemy out of Arakan, release two or three of the divisions in that area as well as considerable administrative and engineering resources, and end a wasteful commitment. All agreed that offensive action in Arakan should be undertaken as soon as possible.

The Supreme Commander decided that detailed planning for 'Dracula' should be kept up to date on the assumption that the operation would be mounted as soon as practicable after the 1945 monsoon and that operations should be undertaken before the monsoon for the capture of either Cheduba Island, or Fort Cornwallis in the Andamans, or the Hastings Harbour–Victoria Point area on the Kra Isthumus. The G.H.Q. India reserve, which Auchinleck was prepared to release, and any divisions which would become available when Arakan was cleared up, could be used.

On the 15th October Mountbatten left for Cairo, but it was not till the 20th that he met the Prime Minister and the C.I.G.S., who had been delayed in Moscow. He told them that 'Dracula' could not possibly be mounted before the end of December 1945, and that he had given orders that 'Capital' should not be taken beyond the second phase until he had been able to reconsider the position. He explained that he had done this as it seemed to be pointless to push farther south in central Burma, driving the Japanese closer to Rangoon and so putting them in a better position to oppose 'Dracula'. It had always been his intention, he said, if 'Dracula' had been carried out in March 1945, to undertake further operations after the monsoon; now that 'Dracula' had been postponed, he had been considering operations which could be put in its place so that time which would otherwise be wasted could be usefully employed, and had reached certain tentative conclusions. The Prime Minister and the C.I.G.S. agreed that it was essential that operations, other than 'Capital', should be undertaken by S.E.A.C. before the beginning of the 1945 monsoon, and invited Mountbatten to put forward definite proposals together with a statement of the resources required to enable them to be carried out.

On the 29th October Mountbatten submitted his proposals, which were to carry out the first two phases of 'Capital' as planned, further exploitation depending on the situation as it developed and on the resources available ;[1] to launch an offensive early in January 1945 to clear north Arakan ('Romulus') and capture Akyab ('Talon') in order to release two or more divisions and administrative resources tied up on that front ;[2] to launch an amphibious operation in March 1945 with two divisions to establish a forward naval and air base on the Kra Isthmus before the monsoon ;[3] to launch a post-monsoon 'Dracula'; and finally to mount an amphibious operation down the coast of Malaya irrespective of the monsoon as soon as the necessary resources reached the Far East. These operations, he said, were the minimum required to retain the general initiative then enjoyed in South-East Asia and to make a timely and effective contribution to the overall offensive against Japan.

On the 17th November the Chiefs of Staff gave their approval in principle to 'Romulus' and 'Talon'. They agreed that an operation for the capture of a suitable base on the Kra Isthmus would have strategic value, but they were uneasy lest a prolongation of the war in Europe might have the effect of making it a 'dangerous and hampering commitment'. They reminded Mountbatten that the earliest possible clearance of Burma must remain his first objective. The situation in Europe was not developing rapidly enough for them to guarantee that all the forces required for 'Dracula' in December 1945 could be released in time; if they could not be released there was a danger that the two divisions which would be the only means of making good a deficit for a post-monsoon 'Dracula' might have already been committed to the Kra Isthmus. In such an event he would find himself stuck both in Burma and on the Kra peninsula and forced to hold the latter for several months to no good purpose. In the circumstances they felt that, before they could approve the Kra Isthmus operation, they ought to have an appreciation and plan

---

[1] Those required for 'Capital' were 1,200 skilled engineers, twelve G.P.T. companies and certain small but vital administrative units.

[2] For this operation Mountbatten asked for twenty-two landing craft and 200 DUKWs to reach Calcutta by the 15th December.

[3] For this operation Mountbatten required one fleet carrier and twelve assault carriers, an amphibious group, a beach group, three road construction companies and six artisan works companies.

together with an estimate of the possible Japanese build-up against it. They also asked for an appreciation and plan for the capture of the Andaman Islands. In preparing these appreciations, Mountbatten could count on receiving in India an assault group consisting of ninety-two landing craft.

CHAPTER X

REORGANIZATION
IN SOUTH-EAST ASIA
(November–December 1944)

See Maps 2, 10 and 13

SINCE the formation of his command in South-East Asia in November 1943, Mountbatten had found that its organization was made unsatisfactory by the multiple appointments held by General Stilwell and by the tendency of the Americans to use the C.B.I. Headquarters as an operational headquarters distinct from S.E.A.C. instead of as a solely administrative one within S.E.A.C.[1] In May 1944 he had sent his Chief of Staff (Lieut.-General Sir Henry Pownall) to London to discuss the matter with the Chiefs of Staff. Stilwell's refusal to serve under the command of 11th Army Group, and his insistence after the capture of Kamaing in June 1944 that N.C.A.C. should be placed under the direct operational command of Supreme Headquarters, further complicated the position and made the chain of command lopsided.[2] Mountbatten had therefore asked the Chiefs of Staff in July to replace 11th Army Group and its commander (Giffard) by an Allied land forces headquarters and a new Commander-in-Chief who was acceptable to the Americans and who could direct operations on both the 14th Army and Northern fronts.[3] The Chiefs of Staff, while agreeing that some form of reorganization was both necessary and advisable, were unable to come to any agreement with the American Chiefs of Staff, who were themselves involved in trying to persuade the Generalissimo to accept Stilwell as Commander-in-Chief of the Chinese armies in China in order to halt the dangerous Japanese offensive aimed at capturing the American airfields which had been established in south-eastern China.[4]

When Mountbatten visited London in August he was asked, on the assumption that the appointment of an Allied land forces Commander-in-Chief would eventually be approved by the Combined

---

[1] Stilwell's appointments were Deputy Supreme Commander, Commanding General, C.B.I. Theatre and Chief of Staff to Generalissimo Chiang Kai-shek, and in addition he took command of N.C.A.C. See Volume III, pages 45–46 and 257–61.

[2] For Kamaing see Map 13 in end pocket.

[3] See Volume III, Chapter XVIII.

[4] See Volume III, Chapter XXVIII.

Chiefs of Staff and accepted by the Generalissimo, to put forward proposals for the reorganization of command in preparation for the forthcoming offensive into Burma. He replied on the 8th September that he assumed that the 1944–45 operations would be undertaken by XV Corps on the Arakan front, 14th Army (with IV and XXXIII Corps under command) on the Central front, and the Chinese/ American forces on the Northern front together with the Chinese Yunnan armies when they had crossed over the agreed operational boundary. He proposed that all operations should be placed under the command of an Allied land Commander-in-Chief whose head-quarters would be called H.Q. Allied Land Forces, South-East Asia (A.L.F.S.E.A.). The Commander-in-Chief should be a British officer with experience of active command, the staff being Anglo-American. The main headquarters should be at Kandy in close touch with Supreme Headquarters so that the new Commander-in-Chief could carry out his function of tendering advice on land operations through-out the theatre and keep in touch with broad future planning. An advanced H.Q. A.L.F.S.E.A. should, however, be in Calcutta, in close touch with Eastern Air Command, from where the Com-mander-in-Chief could co-ordinate the planning and mounting of 'Capital' and 'Dracula'. To control 'Capital', Headquarters 14th Army would be moved to Imphal and there form a joint land/air headquarters with 221 Group R.A.F. To avoid 14th Army Head-quarters having to carry the responsibility for a great deal of local administrative work throughout the extensive line of communication area, a Line of Communication Command would be established and placed under control of A.L.F.S.E.A. with headquarters in either Comilla or Calcutta. The formation of such an L. of C. Command (which had been first suggested by Giffard) was, however, required in any event and was not dependent on the setting up of A.L.F.S.E.A.[1] Finally, all general administrative tasks hitherto the responsibility of 14th Army would be undertaken partly by A.L.F.S.E.A. and partly by the new L. of C. Command.

When 'Capital' and 'Dracula' were approved in September, Giffard, who knew he was to be relieved, suggested to Mountbatten that the officer appointed in his place should reach India as soon as possible so that he could become acquainted with the theatre before the operations began. In urging the Chiefs of Staff to expedite the arrival of the new Commander-in-Chief, A.L.F.S.E.A., Mountbatten impressed on them the need to ensure that he would be acceptable to both the American Chiefs of Staff and the Generalissimo. On the 27th September Mountbatten was told that Lieut.-General Sir Oliver Leese's selection for the appointment had been approved and that he

---

[1] Approval for the formation of the Line of Communication Command was given by the Chiefs of Staff on the 5th October; it came into existence on the 15th November.

would be sent to India as soon as he could be relieved of the command of 8th Army in Italy. The Chiefs of Staff did not, however, propose to obtain the agreement of either the Americans or Chinese to the appointment. This brought an immediate warning from Mountbatten that, unless such an agreement were reached, Stilwell might not agree to N.C.A.C. coming under the control of any British officer other than himself. There for the moment the matter rested.

The delay was caused by the growing difference between Washington and Chungking on Stilwell's position in China. On the 6th July 1944 the President had told the Generalissimo that drastic measures would have to be taken in China to halt the Japanese offensive southwards from Hankow, and he had suggested that the power to co-ordinate all the Allied and military resources in China (including the Communist forces in the north-west) should be placed in Stilwell's hands.[1] Two days later the Generalissimo had signified his agreement to the idea that Stilwell should be given, under him, the command of all Chinese and American troops in China, but had deferred action by explaining that it was not advisable to carry out such a change immediately. At the same time he had asked that an influential person with full powers and farsighted political vision and ability should be sent to Chungking to represent the President. This representative could work with him, improve his relationship with Stilwell and enhance the co-operation between the two countries. To meet this request the President had appointed Major-General P. J. Hurley to be his personal representative in Chungking and had promoted Stilwell to full General in order to give him additional prestige in Chinese eyes.[2]

The political situation in China at this period was very unsettled: the Japanese held the north-east and key points in central China; the Chinese Communist armies controlled the north-west and were not prepared to accept orders from Chungking; and, although Chiang Kai-shek theoretically controlled the whole of the south not occupied by the Japanese, some of the Generals (War Lords) in the south-east were contemplating a revolt against the Nationalist Government with the object of forcing the Generalissimo's resignation. It was clear that, unless some success was achieved in improving the political relations between the Nationalist Government and the Chinese Communists in control in north-west China, there was every likelihood that there would be civil war in China as soon as the Japanese were defeated. The events between August and October

---

[1] See Map 10, facing page 340.
[2] See Volume III, Chapter XXVIII. General Hurley arrived in Chungking on the 6th September.

resulting in Stilwell's recall must be viewed in the light of this situation.

While the negotiations to settle the terms under which Stilwell was to take command of the Chinese armies were making only slow progress, the military situation was rapidly deteriorating. By the middle of September the Japanese, moving south-west from Hengyang and north-west from Canton, had captured Lingling and were threatening the two largest American air bases in south-east China—Kweilin and Liuchow. On the Yunnan front, it appeared that the new Japanese offensive might drive the Yunnan armies back from Lungling towards the Salween.[1] The Generalissimo, however, apparently relying on the American advance in the Pacific bringing the war with the Japanese to an end, appeared to be more interested in retaining the forces under his personal control intact for use in the probable civil war in China than in defeating the Japanese offensive in southeast China. When it seemed that the Yunnan armies, which had been starved of reinforcements since their offensive in May, might be driven back and Kunming menaced, Chiang Kai-shek threatened to withdraw them across the Salween unless Stilwell attacked from Myitkyina towards Bhamo within a week.

The President was at the Octagon Conference in Quebec when he was acquainted with a report sent by Stilwell on the 15th September that Kweilin was being evacuated and that Liuchow would have to be abandoned as soon as the Japanese approached it. Moreover, if the Generalissimo's threat to withdraw the Yunnan armies across the Salween were carried out, it would ruin the possibility of quickly driving a road through to Kunming.[2] The President reacted immediately. On the 19th he sent a strongly worded message to Chiang Kai-shek in which he said that he and the Prime Minister had just decided to press vigorous operations to open the land line of communications to China, on the assumption that the Yunnan armies continued unremitting pressure from the Salween area. If the Yunnan armies were not reinforced or were withdrawn, the chance of opening land communications to China would be lost and the security of the air route over the Hump jeopardized, which was exactly what the Japanese had been trying to achieve by their operations in south-east China. He made it clear that the Generalissimo would have to be prepared to accept the consequences and assume personal responsibility if this occurred. He went on to point out that Stilwell had not yet been placed in command of all the forces in China, and that the Allies were faced with the loss of a vital area in south-east China

---

[1] See Chapter V and Map 2, facing page 39.
[2] It should be noted that by the 15th September the Japanese *33rd Army*, having failed to break the Chinese resistance near Lungling, had called off their offensive. See Chapter V.

which would result in the Kunming air terminal coming under the menace of constant attack, with possible catastrophic consequences. He urged the Generalissimo to take drastic action to forestall the threatened disaster to China and himself.

This telegram was sent to Stilwell to be delivered to the Generalissimo, as had been the custom heretofore, instead of being passed through Hurley. Angered that Stilwell should have presented this telegram himself Chiang Kai-shek asked on the 25th September for him to be recalled, saying that he had lost confidence in him. He had come, he said, to this decision with deep regret, but it had been manifest to him that Stilwell 'had no intention of co-operating with me but believed that he was in fact being appointed to command me.'[1] He was, however, still prepared to accept a qualified American officer in his place as Field Commander of the forces in China.

The President expressed his surprise at the Generalissimo's reversal of his agreement to Stilwell's appointment and said that, since the situation in China had so deteriorated, he no longer felt inclined to assume the responsibility involved in placing an American officer in command of the ground forces in China. He would relieve Stilwell of his appointment as Chief of Staff and of his responsibility for Lend-Lease matters, but, since the maintenance of the Hump tonnage was of such tremendous importance to the stability of the Chinese Government, he proposed that Stilwell should continue to have direct command, under the Generalissimo, of Chinese forces in Burma and the Yunnan armies, though the control of the air ferry route would be placed in the hands of General Sultan.

The Generalissimo would not accept this and again requested the President to recall Stilwell on whom he unjustifiably placed the responsibility for the Allied failure to carry out an amphibious operation in the Bay of Bengal.[2] On the 18th October the President issued instructions for Stilwell to be relieved of his appointments and recalled to America and told the Generalissimo that, although he was no longer prepared to place an American officer in command of the Chinese forces in China, he would furnish a qualified officer to serve as the Generalissimo's Chief of Staff. Among others, he offered to send General Wedemeyer (Mountbatten's Deputy Chief of Staff). Stilwell left India for the United States on the 27th October, and the way was now clear for a complete reoganization of command in the Far East.

With the departure of Stilwell from the Far East the American Chiefs of Staff decided to divide the C.B.I. Theatre into two, the India–

---

[1] Romanus and Sunderland, *U.S. Army in World War II, The China–Burma–India Theater, Stilwell's Command Problems*, page 453.
[2] See Volume II, Chapter XVII and Volume III, page 55.

Burma portion coming under command of General Sultan and the China portion under command of General Wedemeyer, who would also be Chief of Staff to Chiang Kai-shek. Since Sultan would also be placed in active command of N.C.A.C., they proposed to appoint General Wheeler as Deputy Supreme Commander, though he would still retain his existing staff assignment of Principal Administrative Officer at Supreme Headquarters. They suggested to Chiang Kai-shek that the co-ordination of the Yunnan armies and N.C.A.C. should be effected by Wedemeyer, in his capacity as Chief of Staff, in consultation with Sultan and Mountbatten. By the 8th November, all these proposals had been accepted and agreement had been reached that Sultan and the Chinese/American troops in N.C.A.C. would operate under the Commander-in-Chief, Allied Land Forces.

On the 12th November,[1] Leese became Commander-in-Chief, A.L.F.S.E.A. and took command of all formations and units which had formed 11th Army Group, the American, Chinese and British (36th Division) forces operating under command of N.C.A.C., and any part of the Yunnan armies which had crossed the border from China into Burma. His main headquarters were to be at Kandy alongside Headquarters S.E.A.C. and his advanced headquarters at Barrackpore on the outskirts of Calcutta, close to Eastern Air Command. At the same time Wheeler became Deputy Supreme Allied Commander, Major-General H. H. Fuller, U.S. Army, took Wedemeyer's place as Deputy Chief of Staff to Mountbatten, and Sultan took command of N.C.A.C. in addition to the American Burma–India Theatre. On the 15th, XV Corps ceased to form part of 14th Army and came directly under command of A.L.F.S.E.A. The L. of C. Command (Major-General G. W. Symes) came into being the same day with headquarters at Comilla.[2]

Other changes took place during the second half of 1944. On the 23rd August, Admiral Somerville relinquished command of the Eastern Fleet on appointment to Washington, and was replaced by Admiral Sir Bruce Fraser. On the 22nd November the Eastern Fleet ceased to exist. Fraser hoisted his flag as Commander-in-Chief, British Pacific Fleet, and his second-in-command, Vice-Admiral Sir Arthur Power, became Commander-in-Chief, East Indies Fleet. Air Chief Marshal Peirse, whose term of office as Allied Air Commander-in-Chief expired on the 27th November, was to have been succeeded by Air Chief Marshal Sir Trafford Leigh-Mallory. On his way out to

---

[1] For the organization of command in S.E.A.C. from the 12th November 1944 see Appendix 12.
[2] The L. of C. Command comprised 202 L. of C. Area (Gauhati) with five sub-areas covering most of Assam, Manipur State and Fort Hertz, and 404 L. of C. Area (Chittagong) with five sub-areas covering eastern Bengal and Assam south of Shillong. The boundary between the command and 14th Army and XV Corps was approximately the political boundary between India and Burma.

Ceylon Leigh-Mallory was killed in an air crash, and Air Marshal Sir Guy Garrod, who had been deputy to Peirse, was appointed Acting Allied Air Commander-in-Chief until Air Chief Marshal Sir Keith Park assumed command on the 24th February 1945. On the 20th December Lieut.-General Pownall, who had been suffering from bad health, relinquished his appointment as Chief of Staff, S.E.A.C., and was replaced by Lieut.-General F. A. M. Browning.

CHAPTER XI

EVENTS IN CHINA AND THEIR EFFECT ON S.E.A.C.

(November–December 1944)

See Maps 1, 2, 8, 10 and 13 and Sketches 7 and 21

GENERAL WEDEMEYER assumed his new appointment as Chief of Staff to Generalissimo Chiang Kai-shek on the 31st October 1944, and his arrival in Chungking coincided with the resumption by the Japanese of their 'Ichi-Go' offensive towards Kweilin and Liuchow.[1] At the end of September the Commander-in-Chief, *China Expeditionary Force* had ordered *6th Area Army* (Okamura) to resume operations. Heavy rains, however, made any advance impracticable, and it was not till late October that Okamura issued his orders. He attached more importance to the complete destruction of the Chinese armies than to the capture of the cities, more especially as it was thought that the Americans had already evacuated the airfields at Kweilin and Liuchow. He therefore ordered *11th Army* to advance on the 3rd November, occupy Kweilin and then move to the area west of Liuchow, and *23rd Army* to occupy Liuchow with a detachment and then use its main body in co-operation with *11th Army* to destroy the main Chinese armies in the area.[2]

Despite considerable opposition from four Chinese divisions well supported by American aircraft, *23rd Army* had succeeded in capturing Wushuan by the 4th November and on the 7th began its advance towards Liuchow. Meanwhile, *11th Army* decided, contrary to the policy laid down by *6th Area Army*, to occupy Kweilin and Liuchow simultaneously, the former with three divisions (*37th, 40th* and *58th*) and the latter with two (*3rd* and *13th*). When Okamura heard of this new plan, he feared that co-ordination between the two armies would break down and that the Chinese armies would be able to escape destruction. He therefore told *11th Army* to send its main body deep behind Liuchow and make no attempt to occupy the town. Communications within China were, however, so poor that once the operation had been launched there was no possibility of making an

---

[1] See pages 54–55 and Map 10, facing page 340.
[2] For the composition of *11th* and *23rd Armies* see page 55 fn 2.

alteration, and both objectives were occupied on the 10th November.[1] On the 9th, realizing that his orders had not been carried out, Okamura ordered the divisions attacking Liuchow to be temporarily transferred to *23rd Army* and *11th Army* to direct as large a force as possible to Ishan on the Kweichow–Kwangsi railway and then pursue the Chinese armies into Kweichow province.[2] By the 2nd December *13th* and *3rd Divisions* had crossed the provincial border and had occupied Tuhshan and Pachai respectively.

Meanwhile *China Expeditionary Force* told *6th Area Army* that the Liuchow–Laipin–Nanning–Suilu road should be occupied as it was intended to pass two divisions (*22nd* from *23rd Army* and *37th* from *11th Army*) along it to reinforce the Japanese garrison in Indo-China.[3] Shortly after the capture of Liuchow, *23rd Army* was therefore ordered to seize Nanning and detail *22nd Division* to garrison the town and protect the Laipin–Nanning road. The town was occupied on the 24th November and *22nd Division* then moved into position.

Early in December *11th Army* reported that, owing to shortage of supplies and lack of reserves, its pursuit into Kweichow had reached its limit. The *6th Area Army* thereupon designated Tuhshan (the terminus of the railway) as the end of the pursuit, and ordered *11th Army* to hold key positions in Kwangsi province, in particular the Kweichow railway and the Liuchow–Nanning road. The army was also to take over command of *22nd Division* from *23rd Army* and, in co-operation with *21st Division* from Indo-China, open the road from Nanning to the border. The *23rd Army*, less *22nd Division*, was then to concentrate and return to its garrison duties in the Canton area. On the 10th December the leading troops of *22nd Division* and *21st Division* met at Suilu, and preparations were begun for the move of the reinforcing formations into Indo-China.

The second phase of the 'Ichi-Go' offensive had now been brought to its conclusion and the immediate object—the destruction of American airfields in the Hunan and Kwangsi provinces—accomplished. The offensive had not struck the Chinese a fatal blow, and the Japanese thought that the only practical advantage they had gained was the temporary dislocation of the American air forces and the control of a large zone extending down the east of China from which American air activities could be watched. They failed to appreciate that their incursion into Kweichow province would result in the Allies moving Chinese formations from N.C.A.C. to China, thus to some extent relieving the pressure on their hard-pressed *Burma Area Army*.[4]

---

[1] The *104th Division* from *23rd Army* captured the airfield at Liuchow on the 9th and *13th Division* of *11th Army* captured the city on the following day.

[2] The *104th Division* of *23rd Army* garrisoned Liuchow and *3rd* and *13th Divisions* were ordered to Ishan.

[3] See page 229.

[4] See page 124 et seq. and Chapter XXII.

They estimated that the Chinese, who had suffered considerable losses, would now be forced to concentrate on reorganizing and training their armies and would not be able to launch a counter-attack for some considerable time. They themselves would therefore be free to deal with any attempt on the part of the American Pacific forces to land on the China coast.

There was a distinct difference between the position and tasks given by Washington to Stilwell and those which were to be assigned to Wedemeyer. Stilwell, who was appointed Commanding General, C.B.I. Theatre and Chief of Staff to the Supreme Commander, China Theatre, had the tasks of increasing the effectiveness of American assistance to the Chinese Government for the prosecution of the war and of improving the efficiency of the Chinese armies. Wedemeyer was appointed Commanding General of the American forces in the China Theatre and authorized to accept the position of Chief of Staff to the Generalissimo, no mention being made of the Generalissimo's role as Supreme Commander, China Theatre. Wedemeyer was not therefore limited, as Stilwell had been, to assisting the Generalissimo in the conduct of combined Sino/American operations in China, but was free to advise him on any topic, with the authority of his own position as Commanding General of all American forces in China.

Wedemeyer, who had had no previous experience of command, arrived in Chungking to find the Chinese leaders quarrelling among themselves, a state of affairs verging on civil war, the national economy in danger of collapse as a result of rapidly growing inflation, the Chinese armies in the south-east facing defeat and a threat to both Chungking and Kunming growing. There were, however, bright spots in this otherwise sombre picture, for all danger to the air traffic over the Hump had disappeared, the tonnage carried by Air Transport Command had vastly increased and, with the opening of the Myitkyina staging base, would further increase,[1] and a road from India to China was shortly to be opened, along which vehicles and artillery could be sent to equip the Chinese armies and materials quickly delivered for the construction of the projected pipelines from Bhamo to Kunming.[2]

By mid-November Wedemeyer had completed his first appreciation of the Japanese intentions in China. He formed the opinion that they did not necessarily mean to end the war in China by bringing military pressure to bear on the Generalissimo's régime, but were intent on preparing a continental inner defence zone in eastern China to compensate for the loss of the island barrier in the Pacific, within

---

[1] For tonnage carried by air to China see Appendix 25.
[2] See Appendix 2 and Sketch 21, facing page 522.

which they could interpose a barrier of fighter aircraft to prevent 14th U.S.A.A.F. from attacking their shipping off the China coast. Nevertheless, their rapid advance in south-east China had created a threat to Kunming, the loss of which would, he felt, mean the end of the Allied effort to save China. He came to the conclusion that his first task was to prepare for the defence of Kunming and Chungking. It is now known, however, that *Imperial General Headquarters* did not have any intention of making an attempt to take Kunming or to create a defence zone in eastern China.

Between the 16th and 24th November Wedemeyer, whose personal relationship with Chiang Kai-shek was satisfactory from the beginning, presented him with a plan ('Alpha') for the concentration by the 31st December of the most reliable Chinese armies on the several possible Japanese lines of approach to Kunming.[1] The greatest strength was to be placed in the vital Tuhshan area in Kweichow province from which both Kunming and Chungking could be threatened, and a strong central reserve was to be created. Since he had formed the opinion that the poor showing of the Chinese armies was partly due to the fact that they were controlled directly from Chungking by the Generalissimo, who was out of touch with events in the field, he proposed that, to ensure co-ordination between the Chinese armies engaged in the defence of Kunming, a Chinese field commander with a Sino/American staff should be placed in charge of all Chinese armies included in the plan. To increase the fighting potential of the Chinese formations, he asked Chiang Kai-shek to bring them up to strength as soon as possible, and to reorganize the transport and supply services on American lines with American aid. The Japanese move along the Kweichow railway towards Tuhshan, which began in the second half of November, gave the impression that a move towards Kunming or Chungking or both had actually begun. Although the Generalissimo himself did not appear to be disturbed by this possible threat, Wedemeyer felt that immediate steps to bolster the defences of the two cities had become imperative and obtained the Generalissimo's consent to the withdrawal of the American-trained 22nd and 38th Chinese Divisions from the Northern front in Burma.

To provide additional airlift to enable him in an emergency to concentrate the Chinese armies speedily, Wedemeyer had, earlier in November, asked the American Chiefs of Staff for the use of the two heavy bombardment groups of the Strategic Air Force (part of Eastern Air Command). They granted Wedemeyer's request, but

---

[1] See Map 10, facing page 340.

failed to inform either the British Chiefs of Staff or Mountbatten of the request and their reply. On the 20th November Wedemeyer told Mountbatten that a serious situation was developing rapidly in China which would require additional airlift to facilitate the redisposition and supply of Chinese forces. He pointed out that the first phase of 'Capital' had been successfully completed without the aid of airborne operations, and it seemed likely that the second phase might also be carried out without such assistance. He therefore asked Mountbatten to investigate and report, as a matter of urgency, whether two combat cargo squadrons (fifty aircraft) could be relieved for use in China from the 25th November till the 15th January. On the 22nd Mountbatten reported to the Chiefs of Staff that there was already an overall deficiency of transport aircraft for 'Capital' and that the need to husband resources had been further emphasized by a report from General Sir Adrian Carton de Wiart that the Generalissimo was contemplating moving part of the Yunnan armies away from the Salween front owing to the situation in China.[1] He therefore considered that the removal of any transport aircraft to China would greatly prejudice the success of 'Capital'. Nevertheless, he was prepared to meet Wedemeyer's requirements by releasing one heavy bombardment group (forty-eight B.24 aircraft) provided it was returned in time to take its place for the attack on Akyab in January.[2] The Chiefs of Staff agreed with Mountbatten's views, and on the 26th he informed Wedemeyer that 7th Heavy Bombardment Group was being held in readiness to move to China at short notice. On being told of this decision Stratemeyer (Eastern Air Command) suggested that, as heavy bombers were not entirely suitable for use as transport aircraft, the release of two combat cargo squadrons would provide a far more satisfactory method of meeting Wedemeyer's requirements. From discussions which he had held with Headquarters 14th Army it seemed possible, he said, that, subject to further examination, the plan for 'Capital' could be modified and two such squadrons could be released without prejudicing the success of the operations.

Meanwhile, Carton de Wiart had warned Mountbatten that the Generalissimo was contemplating the withdrawal, once Bhamo had been captured, of two or three of the Chinese divisions which at that time were employed under the command of N.C.A.C. in operations on the Northern front. Mountbatten immediately asked Carton de Wiart to tell the Generalissimo that such a withdrawal would drastically restrict the Burma campaign to his own disadvantage and put an end to any hopes of an amphibious operation. He then told the Chiefs of Staff that the loss of these divisions at that time would

---

[1] General Carton de Wiart was the Prime Minister's and Mountbatten's personal representative in Chungking. See Volume III, Chapter IV.
[2] See Chapter IX and Map 13 in end pocket.

weaken the N.C.A.C. share of 'Capital' and jeopardize the whole of the operation, and that the replacement of the divisions in N.C.A.C. would destroy any chance of carrying out a pre-monsoon operation. He concluded, 'I am quite clear that their removal would endanger the accomplishment of my directive and undermine the whole policy of aid to China which had governed Allied strategy in South-East Asia.' On the 30th November Wedemeyer told the American Chiefs of Staff, Mountbatten and Sultan that the situation in China had continued to deteriorate, since the Japanese had crossed the border of Kweichow province and had occupied Nantan on the 28th. As the Chinese were unable to provide trained, equipped and properly led formations from within China, it was now imperative that 22nd and 38th Chinese Divisions should be withdrawn from Burma and transported by air to positions selected for the defence of Kunming. He recommended that, since the principal object of operations in Burma would be nullified if the terminal of supply in China were lost, Mountbatten should be told to conduct 'Capital' and 'Romulus' only 'in such a manner and to a degree that will not militate against the measures required to ensure the defences of the Kunming area.'

On the 2nd December the Chiefs of Staff sent Mountbatten the text of the instructions which the American Chiefs of Staff proposed to send Wedemeyer. It read:

> '1. [American] Chiefs of Staff... approve your recommendation to transfer two divisions ... to China specifically 22nd and 38th if you consider other available divisions are not satisfactory.
> 2. You should, however, work out a selection of units to be moved to China which fulfils your requirements while at the same time causing least interference with Mountbatten's operations in north Burma.
> 3. Call on Sultan for any U.S. air forces including A.T.C. [Air Transport Command] and other United States resources required for the transport and support of the two divisions and to meet other requirements arising out of the present emergency in China. Should you and Sultan be unable to agree on any details, radio the facts to us.
> 4. The United States Chiefs of Staff do not propose to question the Generalissimo's decision to use his own forces to defend China in the critical situation depicted in your message. The Combined Chiefs of Staff are informing Admiral Mountbatten that they concur with the instructions to you and Sultan contained in this message.'

The Chiefs of Staff told Mountbatten that they had no option but to agree to the withdrawal of two Chinese divisions from the Northern front, although they hoped that it would be possible for Wedemeyer to avoid selecting 22nd and 38th Divisions. Since they were unable to agree to the third paragraph without first having full knowledge of its implications on the current operations, they asked for an estimate in the fullest possible detail of the number of aircraft required from S.E.A.C. resources and Air Transport Command over and above 7th Heavy Bombardment Group already allotted, and the effect of any diversion from S.E.A.C. resources on 'Capital' and 'Romulus'.

On the same day they told the Americans that they were deeply concerned over Wedemeyer being given what amounted to a blank cheque on all American air forces in South-East Asia, since it placed Mountbatten in constant danger of having the transport aircraft needed for 'Capital' suddenly withdrawn. The American Chiefs of Staff replied that the retention of transport aircraft to assist S.E.A.C.'s future operations was not justified when their transfer appeared imperatively necessary to halt an approaching catastrophe in China. They reminded the Chiefs of Staff that it had been agreed, when the British and American air forces in India had been integrated in December 1943, that they had the right to re-assign units from 10th to 14th U.S.A.A.F.[1] Moreover, Air Transport Command and 20th Bomber Command were not under control of the Supreme Commander. They therefore proposed to issue the directive as originally drafted, but were prepared to direct Wedemeyer to limit his demands for transport aircraft to those not then actively employed or urgently required for supply of S.E.A.C.'s forces engaged with the enemy, unless no other means of meeting his emergency could be found. The Chiefs of Staff accepted this, but said that, if Wedemeyer still felt compelled to call for aircraft whose release would affect S.E.A.C. operations, Mountbatten should report the facts to the Combined Chiefs of Staff who would then decide what should be done.

On the 4th, Mountbatten pointed out that the directive not only authorized Wedemeyer to deal direct with Sultan (who was Mountbatten's subordinate) but also in the case of disagreement allowed Sultan to refer the matter to the American Chiefs of Staff. He was not prepared to agree that Sultan's views alone should be taken as representing the views of the command, and claimed that he himself must be given a voice in matters which so vitally affected his operations. Apprised of Mountbatten's views, Wedemeyer told the American Chiefs of Staff that, while he agreed that Mountbatten should have a voice in matters which affected his own operations, he himself must have a voice in matters which likewise affected operations in China. He suggested, therefore, that whenever he

---

[1] See Volume III, page 46.

communicated with Sultan or Stratemeyer on matters appertaining to S.E.A.C. he should send copies of the telegrams to Mountbatten and Wheeler, and, conversely, that he should be sent copies of Mountbatten's communications with Sultan and Stratemeyer which dealt with firm plans and recommendations appertaining to air or ground forces tentatively earmarked by the Combined Chiefs of Staff for employment in China.

While the terms of the instructions to Wedemeyer were being argued over, Mountbatten had been discussing with Sultan how best to meet Wedemeyer's demands for two Chinese divisions without completely wrecking operations on the Northern front, and had urged Wedemeyer to accept 14th and 50th Divisions, neither of which was actively engaged at the time. On the 3rd December, Wedemeyer said that the Generalissimo would agree to the immediate transfer of 14th Division, to be followed by either the 22nd or 38th, but at the same time indicated that it might be necessary to ask for other divisions to be transferred later to the Kunming area. He also told the American Chiefs of Staff that he was moving some 60,000 troops by air from Sian (where they had been watching the Chinese Communist forces).

Two days later Wedemeyer asked Sultan for two combat cargo squadrons in order to accelerate the move of forces within China. Before making any recommendations to the American Chiefs of Staff, Sultan discussed this demand with Mountbatten. He said that he interpreted the instructions to Wedemeyer to mean that any aircraft in his (Sultan's) command which was not actively employed, nor urgently required for the supply of forces already committed to battle, could be called on. He felt, however, that it was essential, before releasing aircraft, that he should obtain Mountbatten's agreement. He pointed out that two R.A.F. transport squadrons (forty aircraft) were engaged in purely training activities in India for airborne operations; they could not be considered as urgently required for the supply of forces engaged with the enemy and there were now indications that airborne units would not after all be required for 'Capital'. Moreover, 4th Combat Cargo Group was already arriving in India and would be ready for operations by the 1st January 1945, and there was the possibility that, once the Chinese divisions had been removed from the Northern front, some of the transport aircraft then supporting that front might become available for re-allocation. In these circumstances he considered that the two combat cargo squadrons asked for by Wedemeyer could be safely released to China and be replaced in S.E.A.C. by the two R.A.F. squadrons.

Mountbatten replied that two air commando transport squadrons had already been temporarily released to move 14th Chinese Division to Kunming; the two R.A.F. squadrons had been withdrawn purely for rehabilitation and the opportunity taken to use them for training 50th (P.) Brigade. Full account had already been taken of the arrival of 4th Combat Cargo Group. The withdrawal of the R.A.F. squadrons from their temporary training duties would make any airborne operations in support of 'Capital' impossible and would postpone for an indefinite period the final readiness of 44th Indian Airborne Division.[1] Since, however, he realized the urgency of Wedemeyer's predicament, he was, in anticipation of the Combined Chiefs of Staff's approval, giving orders for two combat cargo squadrons to be released at once and their place in S.E.A.C. operations taken by the two R.A.F. squadrons; but, until he was able to ascertain the full effect of diversions from S.E.A.C.'s resources on 'Capital' and 'Romulus', he would not be able to consider any further requests for aircraft.

On the 10th and 11th December a conference was held at Advanced Headquarters A.L.F.S.E.A. in Calcutta to examine the air supply capabilities of the available air transport squadrons and the implications of any diversion of air resources on current operations. The demands from 14th Army for air supply showed increases on the original estimates of the 24th August, since both 19th and 7th Divisions would be on air supply from the second half of December and, as the Northern front was being weakened by the removal of Chinese divisions, an extra British/Indian division sent to replace them would require air supply after the middle of February. On the assumption that four combat cargo squadrons would be diverted to China before the 1st January 1945 and that only one of them would be returned by the 1st February, it was ascertained that there could be no further airborne training, which would preclude any airborne operations being mounted. Although there were adequate aircraft for maintenance and some forward stocking up to the 3rd March, there would thereafter be a considerable shortage and it would be possible to maintain only five instead of six divisions in the forward areas. This reduction in strength would, however, make it possible, despite an expected shortage of G.P.T. companies, to amass a total of forty-seven days' stocks by road and air between Indainggyi and Shwebo for the forces which were to remain in Burma during the monsoon.[2]

Mountbatten was now in a position to reply to the Chiefs of Staff's telegram of the 2nd December. On the 13th he told them that 14th and 22nd Chinese Divisions were being flown to Kunming from

---

[1] See pages 28–30.
[2] See Map 1, facing page 15. For details of 14th Army requirements and the available airlift from the 16th December 1944 to the 15th May 1945 see Appendix 13.

Myitkyina and Si-u respectively,[1] and that to complete the move by the 1st January (the date by which Wedemeyer required them) two air commando troop-carrier squadrons and at least thirty sorties a day by 10th U.S.A.F. were necessary. Two combat cargo squadrons had left for China on the 11th December, and 7th Heavy Bombardment Group had been placed at Wedemeyer's disposal. Since only eighteen of its aircraft had been called forward to China, the remaining thirty were being used for bombing operations and would be required for the capture of Akyab.

To comply with his directive he had to maintain pressure on the Japanese and the present momentum of the advance on both the Central and Northern fronts, but the withdrawal of the Chinese divisions and the halting of the Yunnan armies at Wanting would inevitably reduce the impetus of operations in north-east Burma.[2] He had not sufficient aircraft left to enable him to fly a reinforcing British/Indian division to the Northern front as well as to meet the demands of 'Capital'; two brigades of 19th Indian Division were therefore marching overland to Indaw, which would take at least five weeks, and the third brigade would go to Pinlebu.[3] The arrival of this division would enable Sultan to transfer 38th and 50th Chinese Divisions further east.

The two combat cargo squadrons (fifty aircraft) which had been sent to China on the 11th had been replaced by two R.A.F. squadrons (forty aircraft), but these had already been included in the estimate of aircraft needed for 'Capital'. Even if the troop-carrier aircraft of the two air commandos were returned to S.E.A.C. as soon as the fly-in of the Chinese divisions had been completed on the 1st January, the effect on 'Capital' of the diversions already made to China would be that its airborne operations could not be carried out, with a consequent reduction in the chances of surrounding and destroying the Japanese north of Mandalay. The diversions would, however, have no effect on the proposed land advance in north Arakan, but the loss of eighteen aircraft from 7th Bombardment Group would affect the amphibious assault on Akyab.

Despite the forward Japanese elements having been pushed back in the Tuhshan area, and indications that the enemy's intentions might well be less ambitious than at first thought, Wedemeyer had given a warning that he would eventually need 38th Chinese Division, and perhaps a fourth division, and six or seven transport squadrons. Since the issue of that warning he had made a demand for four combat cargo

---

[1] See Map 2, facing page 39.

[2] See Map 13 in end pocket. At the beginning of December, Wedemeyer told Mountbatten that the Generalissimo had decided that the Yunnan armies would not cross the China–Burma frontier and would halt at Wanting.

[3] See Map 1, facing page 15. The 19th Division made contact with 36th Division two days after the despatch of this telegram; see page 159.

squadrons to redispose and supply Chinese forces within China and to support the increased tactical offensive by the 14th U.S.A.A.F., and for a fifth, based in Burma and Assam, to give logistical support to these four.

The withdrawal of more Chinese divisions, and in particular the 38th, would, Mountbatten said, probably make the task of securing the trace of the Burma Road beyond the capacity of the remaining troops. Apart from the recent transfers of aircraft to China, one of his transport squadrons had, since July, been employed in maintaining the Yunnan armies on the Salween front and, for convenience, had been based temporarily in China while the fair-weather airfields in Burma were drying out. He was in the circumstances prepared to waive his claim for the return of this squadron.

The withdrawal of a total of five combat cargo squadrons would have a serious effect on 'Capital'. It would entail a halt on 14th Army front, and might even enforce the army's withdrawal west of the Chindwin so that adequate air supply could be given to the forces on the Northern front securing the road trace. There would be no transport aircraft for an emergency and the only source from which they might later be found would be from 10th U.S.A.A.F., if and when the Ledo Road could maintain formations operating on the Northern front. Despite this, Mountbatten said that he was prepared to release a third combat cargo squadron immediately, and a fourth on the 1st January provided it was returned or replaced from outside S.E.A.C. by the 1st February. Wedemeyer's demands for a fifth squadron to be based in Assam or Burma in order to maintain those transferred to China would, however, have to be met by Air Transport Command, which had the responsibility for logistical support of all American forces in China.

He asked the Chiefs of Staff to urge the Combined Chiefs to persuade the Generalissimo that the transfer of forces from S.E.A.C. should be restricted to 14th and 22nd Chinese Divisions (though plans for moving 38th Division would be prepared so that in emergency it could be moved at short notice); to limit the transfer of aircraft to China to the three combat cargo squadrons (over and above the one allotted to the Yunnan armies in July) on the understanding that they were replaced from outside S.E.A.C. by the 1st March; and to authorize the loan of a fourth combat cargo squadron from the 1st January only on the distinct understanding that it was returned or replaced from outside S.E.A.C. by the 1st February.

The long-range B.29 bombers of 20th Bomber Command, based on the group of airfields at Kharagpur near Calcutta and Chengtu in

China, had begun to attack Japan's steel industry in June 1944,[1] but the formidable administrative difficulties involved in lifting stocks of aviation petrol, bombs and ammunition to China made their attacks infrequent. The B.29s were also used at times to attack targets in South-East Asia and in the Pacific theatre. On the 10th August fifty-four bombers took off from Kharagpur to attack the Palembang oil-fields in Sumatra and lay mines in the river approaches to the town; staging in Ceylon, they accomplished this long round flight of 4,000 miles with the loss of only one aircraft, despite opposition from fighters and anti-aircraft fire.

Targets at Nagasaki were attacked on the 11th August and at Yamata on the 21st, with negligible effect.[2] The Japanese usually received warning from their Intelligence services in China of the date of an impending raid and the target selected,[3] and since the attackers had to fly over China their time of arrival could be calculated, air-raid precautions put into effect and fighters made airborne. The losses suffered by the B.29s, however, were less than a tenth of the strength employed, for the performance of the Japanese night fighters was poor and their numbers were insufficient for their task.

From October onwards 20th Bomber Command attacked whenever stocks at Chengtu permitted, but switched their targets from the steel industry to other factories in Kyushu and at Mukden in Manchuria.[4] Attacks were also made on Formosa to help the invasion of the Philippines.[5] On the 5th November fifty-three B.29s from Kharagpur were sent to attack the naval base at Singapore, another round flight of some 4,000 miles. The bombers reached the naval base at dawn on the 6th and scored direct hits on the graving dock and on workshops and buildings in its vicinity; they met with little opposition but two aircraft were lost during the return flight. The Japanese reacted to these attacks by making a series of night raids on the Chengtu airfields with a few bombers operating singly. The B.29s were, however, widely dispersed and the raids caused little damage.

Although early in December Wedemeyer had told the American Chiefs of Staff that it would be unwise to remove 20th Bomber Command from China, later in the month he asked for its removal on the grounds that the proportion (about fourteen per cent) of the airlift over the Hump required to maintain it at Chengtu would be more usefully employed in carrying equipment for the Chinese armies

---

[1] See Volume III, Chapter XXVIII.

[2] See Sketch 7, facing page 240.

[3] Most of this information was obtained from *5th Air Army* which monitored wireless traffic between the American airfields in China.

[4] Attacks were made on the 25th October, 11th and 21st November, 7th and 19th December 1944, and the 6th January 1945.

[5] See pages 70 and 95 fn. 3. See also Map 8, facing page 252.

and supplies for 14th U.S.A.A.F. The American Chiefs of Staff agreed, and in the middle of January 1945 ordered the withdrawal of its aircraft from Chengtu to Calcutta (Kharagpur) and the closure of the Chengtu airfields. The withdrawal was completed by the 27th February. The new air base under construction in the Marianas was to be 20th Bomber Command's eventual destination,[1] but, as this would not be ready to receive it until April, it was in the meantime to be used for limited operations within S.E.A.C.[2]

---

[1] See page 89.
[2] For its operations within S.E.A.C. see Chapter XXXIII.

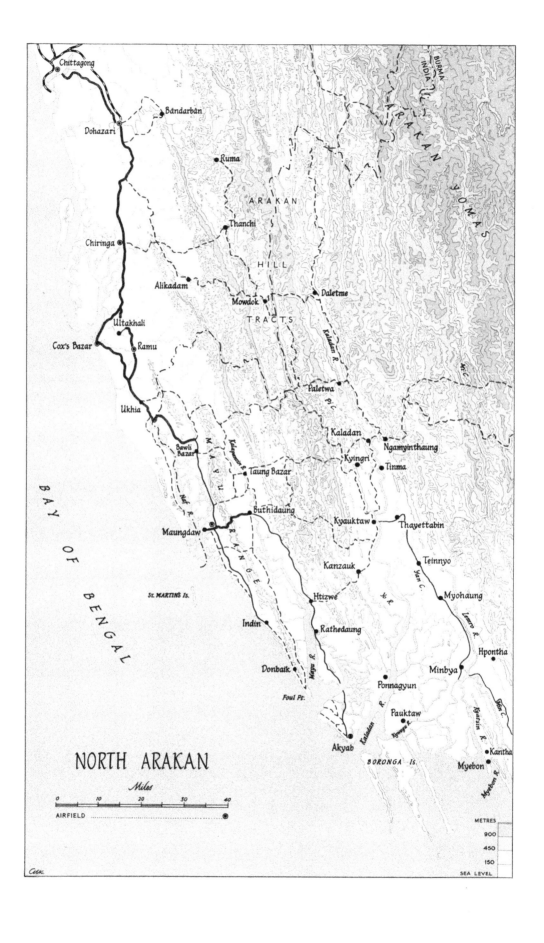

Chittagong

Bandarban

Dohazari

Ruma

ARAKAN

Thanchi

Chiringa

HILL

Alikadam

Mowdok

Daletme

Ultakhali

TRACTS

Cox's Bazar

Ramu

Kaladan R.

Ukhia

Paletwa

Kaladan

Ngamyinthaung

Bawli Bazar

Kyingri

Tinma

MAYU

Kalapanzin R.

Taung Bazar

Naf R.

Buthidaung

RANGE

Kyauktaw

Thayettabin

Maungdaw

Kanzauk

Teinnyo

ST. MARTINS IS.

Htizwe

Myohaung

Yan C.

Mayu R.

Indin

Rathedaung

Lemro R.

Hpontha

Donbaik

Minbya

Foul Pt.

Ponnagyun

Pauktaw

Kaladan R.

Akyab

Kantha

NORTH ARAKAN

BORONGA IS.

Myebon

Myebon R.

BAY OF BENGAL

Miles

| 0 | 10 | 20 | 30 | 40 |

AIRFIELD ·······················

CBH.

METRES	
900	
450	
150	
SEA LEVEL	

ARAKAN YOMAS

BURMA
INDIA

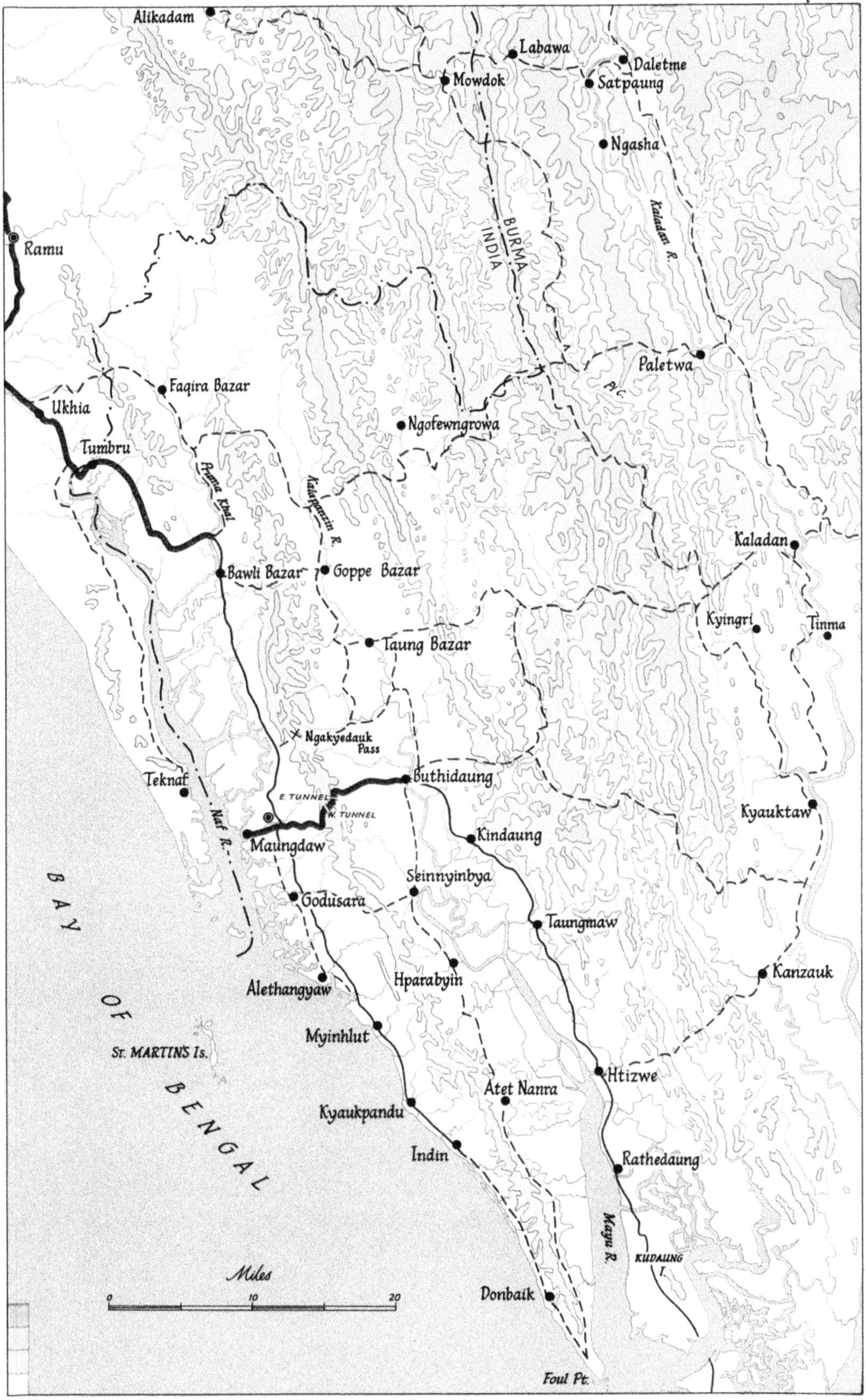

Map 6

Alikadam

Labawa

Mowdok • Daletme
• Satpaung

Ngasha

Kaladan R.

Ramu

Paletwa

Faqira Bazar

Ukhia

Ngofewngrowa

Tumbru

Pruma Khal

Kalarpanzin R.

Kaladan

Bawli Bazar • Goppe Bazar

Kyingri

Tinma

Taung Bazar

× Ngakyedauk
Pass

Teknaf

Buthidaung

E. TUNNEL

Kyauktaw

Naf R.

W. TUNNEL

Maungdaw

Kindaung

Seinnyinbya

Godusara

Taungmaw

Kanzauk

Alethangyaw

Hparabyin

B A Y

Myinhlut

St. MARTIN'S Is.

O F

Atet Nanra

Htizwe

Kyaukpandu

B E N G A L

Indin

Rathedaung

Mayu R.

KUDAUNG
I.

Miles

0   10   20

Donbaik

Foul Pt.

BURMA
INDIA

CHAPTER XII

THE ARAKAN FRONT
(October 1944–January 1945)

See Maps 6, 12 and 13

THE situation in Arakan had remained unchanged from mid-June to early September, but as the rains lessened the forward troops of XV Corps and the *Sakura Detachment* began to reoccupy points of tactical importance abandoned when they had become isolated by the rising flood waters in June.[1] This had led to fighting which, though localized and on a small scale, was often severe and caused comparatively heavy casualties to both sides, particularly as the *Sakura Detachment* acted aggressively to cover its own weakness and to delay the British advance by imposing caution. In mid-October XV Corps (Christison) had its forward posts on the general line Godusara–the Tunnels–Ngakyedauk–Taung and Goppe Bazars–Mowdok.[2] The 25th Indian Division (Major-General Wood), based on Maungdaw, held the right sector from the coast near Godusara to Ngakyedauk Pass.[3] The 26th Indian Division (Lomax) was in reserve in the Ukhia area, but had one brigade forward on the left of 25th Division with forward posts at Taung and Goppe Bazars and a detachment at Ngofewngrowa watching the track from the Kaladan to Ukhia. The 81st (W.A.) Division (Major-General F. J. Loftus-Tottenham), watching the left flank, was based on Chiringa with its forward troops in the Mowdok area.[4] The 82nd (W.A.) Division (Bruce) at Ranchi preparing to move to Chiringa, 50th Indian Tank Brigade (Brigadier G. H. N. Todd) at Ranchi,[5] 3 Commando Brigade (Brigadier G. R. Hardy) at Ramu and 22nd (E.A.) Brigade (Brigadier R. J. Johnstone) in Ceylon were earmarked to join the corps. Air support was provided by 224 Group R.A.F. (Bandon). The formation of a joint headquarters with XV Corps was being planned and, to increase the close air support which could be

---

[1] The *Sakura Detachment* (see pages 56 and 60) held the front from the coast across the Mayu Range and River to the Arakan Yomas with three infantry battalions (*II/112th, I/143rd* and *III/144th*), and the Kaladan Valley with *55th Reconnaissance Regiment*, later reinforced by one company of *II/143rd Battalion*.

[2] See Map 6, facing page 134. The XV Corps came directly under the command of A.L.F.S.E.A. on the 15th November (see page 118).

[3] Wood, promoted from Brigadier General Staff XXXIII Corps, succeeded Davies, who had been taken seriously ill, on the 14th October 1944.

[4] Loftus-Tottenham was promoted from the command of a brigade of 7th Indian Division to succeed Woolner on the 24th August 1944.

[5] See Map 12, facing page 436.

given to the land forces, it was arranged that 12th Bombardment Group, U.S.A.A.F. should be available when required to operate for limited periods under the command of 224 Group.[1] One R.A.F. transport squadron was allotted to provide air supply for the corps, and a squadron of L.5 light aircraft was allotted to Headquarters XV Corps for liaison duties and for the evacuation of casualties.

When it had become evident early in October that the bulk of *55th Division* had withdrawn from Arakan,[2] Giffard (11th Army Group) came to the conclusion that it was uneconomical to keep four divisions in Arakan in a defensive role. He had therefore told Christison to prepare plans for clearing the Japanese out of north Arakan, including Akyab, and, in recommending this course to Mountbatten, assessed that on its completion at least two divisions could be released for 'Capital' and 'Dracula'.[3] Christison's plan, which was explained at a Commander-in-Chief's conference on the 18th October,[4] envisaged an advance by 25th Division on the right, 82nd (W.A.) Division in the centre and 81st (W.A.) Division on the left to the general line Donbaik–Rathedaung–Myohaung, where he expected the Japanese to offer determined resistance. While this was being overcome, 3 Commando Brigade, followed up by 26th Division, would make an amphibious assault on the Myebon Peninsula, and the Japanese sea communications to Akyab would be cut by the Arakan Coastal Forces (Captain J. Ryland, R.I.N.).[5] Finally Akyab would be assaulted from the mainland across the creeks and estuaries with the support of the Strategic Air Force and the Eastern Fleet. This plan was approved in principle, and on the 25th October Christison gave his divisional commanders its outline and issued a warning order for the relief of the forward brigade of 26th Division in the Kalapanzin valley by a brigade of 82nd (W.A.) Division as soon as it could be brought forward.

On the 8th November, in a directive to his three Commanders-in-Chief, Mountbatten confirmed the change of operational policy in Arakan and ordered an offensive to be launched as soon as possible to clear north Arakan ('Romulus'), and to capture Akyab ('Talon') by the end of January. Thereafter XV Corps was to release 3 Commando Brigade at once, followed by certain engineer and administrative units and finally by two infantry divisions, one before, and one as soon as possible after, the 1st March 1945. Joint force commanders

---

[1] For order of battle of 224 Group R.A.F. and 12th Bombardment Group U.S.A.A.F. see Appendix 4.

[2] See page 56.

[3] See page 109.

[4] At this conference Slim asked for airfields to be established south of Akyab for the support of 'Capital'.

[5] The Arakan Coastal Forces consisted of 55th and 56th (R.I.N.), 49th (South Africa) and 59th (Burma) Flotillas, each of seven or eight motor launches, H.M.S. *Kedah* (a depot ship) and two small tankers.

14. Major-General H. C. Stockwell,
82nd (W.A.) Division

15. Major-General G. N. Wood,
25th Indian Division

16. Rear-Admiral B. C. S. Martin, R.N., in command of naval operations, Arakan

17. Tank Landing Craft (L.C.T.) loading at Akyab

18. Vehicle beach, Myebon

19. Transferring from ship to assault craft

20. The Arakan Yomas, near Taungup Pass

were to be appointed and a plan submitted by the 25th November 1944.[1]

While the plan was being prepared, the divisions which were to carry out 'Romulus' and 'Talon' moved into position and infiltrated forward to gain convenient starting places for the general advance. The 25th Division cleared the coastal plain in the Godusara area and, on the eastern side of the Mayu Range, established a strong outpost line astride the Maungdaw–Buthidaung road to cover the concentration of 82nd (W.A.) Division, less its brigade(2nd) in the Kalapanzin valley.[2] That brigade, with 81st (W.A.) Reconnaissance Regiment under command, began to probe the Japanese defences north of Buthidaung and sent patrols along the Taung Bazar–Kaladan (Soutcol) track to make contact with 81st (W.A.) Division in the Kaladan valley.[3]

To align itself with the division on the main front, 81st (W.A) Division had to make a considerable advance. Loftus-Tottenham began his move to the Kaladan valley in mid-October on a broad front in an attempt to envelop an enemy force known to be in the Satpaung area. The 5th Brigade reached Ngasha unopposed and, by the 16th, 6th Brigade had captured Labawa. Both brigades then converged on Satpaung but the enemy forces there eluded them. The division, supplied entirely by air, then turned south and by the 29th October 5th Brigade was back at Ngasha and 6th Brigade was in the Pi Chaung valley about six miles to its west. At this stage Christison ordered the division to establish a firm base in the Kaladan–Tinma–Kyingri area by the 1st December, clear the Soutcol track and prepare to exploit south to Kyauktaw, Myohaung and Kanzauk. With the possibility of meeting considerable resistance as he neared his objective and having only two brigades available, Loftus-Tottenham decided to move down the Kaladan River in depth and sent his reconnaissance regiment (less one squadron), supported by a detachment of artillery and mortars, to move down the Pi Chaung on Kyingri with orders to clear the Soutcol track and link up with its own squadron operating eastwards from the Kalapanzin. The 5th Brigade occupied Paletwa on the 14th November; 6th Brigade then took up the advance and reached Kaladan on the 30th. Four days later, against negligible opposition, it occupied Tinma and by the 11th December the division, less its reconnaissance regiment which had reached Kyingri on the 30th November, had concentrated in the Tinma area.

---

[1] Rear-Admiral B. C. S. Martin (Flag Officer Force 'W'), Christison and Bandon were nominated.

[2] During this operation Sepoy Bhandari Ram, 10th Baluch Regiment, won the Victoria Cross.

[3] This track was used by a column known as Soutcol to reach and withdraw from the Kaladan valley in the first Arakan campaign. See Volume II, Chapters XV and XIX.

Meanwhile, in view of the increasing Allied pressure on both the Mayu and Kaladan fronts, *28th Army* had during November ordered *54th Division* to form the *Matsu Detachment* (Major-General T. Koba) of three battalions, which with *55th Reconnaissance Regiment* under command was to defend the Kaladan, leaving the *Sakura Detachment* with the sole task of delaying the Allied advance on the Mayu front.[1] Koba, leaving one battalion (*I/111th*) in Akyab, moved two battalions to the Kaladan early in December and on the 15th attacked 81st (W.A.) Division in the Tinma area. Though a post was overrun and some guns lost, the attack, which fell mainly on one battalion of 5th Brigade, was repulsed and in a counter-attack next morning the guns were recovered intact.[2]

Meanwhile the Joint Force Commanders had issued their directive for operation 'Romulus' on the 23rd November. Their plan, which closely followed Christison's original proposal, required a brigade of 25th Division, supported by a naval force and supplied entirely by sea, to begin moving down the coastal plain two days before the general advance began on the 11th December.[3] The rest of 25th Division was to move down the Mayu Range and the west bank of the Mayu River, crossing it to seize Rathedaung; the whole division would then close in on Foul Point and mop up the Mayu peninsula. The 82nd (W.A.) Division was to move down the east side of the Mayu River to Htizwe, cross to the Kaladan valley by way of Kanzauk to relieve 81st (W.A.) Division between the 14th and 31st January and exploit towards Myohaung and Minbya, which were to be occupied by the 28th February. The left wing of 25th Division (53rd Brigade) was to be maintained by air, and 82nd Division, when south of Buthidaung, by boat down the Mayu River. The guns and equipment of 53rd Brigade were also to be carried by boat since there was a lack of tracks fit for wheels. The I.W.T. was therefore to collect all available river craft in the Maungdaw–Bawli area and transport them across the Mayu Range to Buthidaung as soon as it was taken.[4]

The assault on Akyab ('Talon') was to be carried out by 26th Division, 3 Commando Brigade and a regiment of 50th Indian Tank Brigade, supported by 'saturation' bombing by the R.A.F. and

---

[1] The *Matsu Detachment* consisted of *Headquarters 54th Infantry Group, 111th Regiment* (less *II/111th Battalion*), *III/154th Battalion* and an artillery battalion. Koba, who as a colonel had commanded the column which had driven 81st (W.A.) Division out of the Kaladan in March 1944 (see Volume III, Chapter X), was now in command of the infantry group of *54th Division.*

[2] During this fighting Havildar Umrao Singh, Royal Indian Artillery, won the Victoria Cross.

[3] The naval force (commanded by Captain E. W. Bush) consisted of the destroyers *Napier* and *Nepal*, the Arakan Coastal Forces, minesweepers, landing craft and pilotage parties.

[4] This type of movement is one of the disadvantages of operating against the 'grain' of the country which have been referred to previously in this history. This considerable and by no means easy move was, however, a minor affair in comparison with the build-up of the I.W.T. fleet on the Chindwin which began soon afterwards.

intensive bombardment by the Royal Navy on the 20th January. As soon as possible after the capture of Akyab, 3 Commando Brigade was to be released and, to secure Akyab against a Japanese counter-attack and assist the exploitation down the Kaladan valley, 26th Division was to make an amphibious assault on the Myebon Peninsula and occupy it by the end of February. The directive recommended that at first 22nd (E.A.) Brigade should be located at Chiringa in corps reserve with the primary duty of securing the mounting base for 'Dracula', arriving there not later than the 15th January.

The general advance began on the 14th December when 2nd (W.A.) Brigade (Brigadier E. W. D. Western) advanced astride the main road on Buthidaung, with 1st (W.A.) Brigade (Brigadier C. R. A. Swynnerton) on its right clearing the jungle-clad hills to the south. By the evening of the 15th, Buthidaung had been occupied against slight opposition and the advanced guards of both brigades were across the river. This enabled the task of bringing boats across the Mayu Range to begin next morning. In all, 640 craft had been collected, of which 400 were locally purchased country boats and dugouts; most of them had to be carried by lorry from Maungdaw through the Tunnels and, between the 16th and 20th December, two convoys of fifty vehicles making one trip a day delivered them at Buthidaung. There, 425th Field Company, I.E. (assisted at first by 63rd Field Company) assembled and launched them. The powered portion of the I.W.T. fleet consisted of eight rafts, each of two folding boats, twenty-five assault boats powered by 22 h.p. outboard motors, and forty-eight assault boats powered by 10 h.p. outboard motors.

The 74th Brigade (Brigadier J. E. Hirst), which had begun its advance according to plan on the 12th, had meanwhile reached Myinhlut and established the first stage of its sea supply line,[1] such opposition as it had encountered having been dispersed as soon as the artillery and the destroyers opened fire. By the 20th it was closing in on Indin. The 53rd Brigade (Brigadier A. G. O'C. Scott), moving down the east side of the Mayu Range, ran into resistance on the 18th near Seinnyinbya. When the brigade approached Hparabyin on the 20th opposition increased, and a considerable force of Japanese was found to be in a prepared position and obviously intending to give battle. East of the Mayu River the advance of 2nd (W.A.) Brigade had by the 20th reached Kindaung, where it too began to meet considerable opposition, particularly from enemy artillery, and was held

---

[1] The 74th Brigade was supplied by coastal vessels and landing craft from the advanced base at Maungdaw. As the brigade advanced and the distance from Maungdaw lengthened, a staging post was established on St. Martin's Island. Supplies were landed at suitable beaches from the landing craft and delivered forward by the fleet of some 400 motor vehicles which accompanied the brigade, or were transhipped from coastal vessels anchored offshore to DUKWs which, after reaching the shore, delivered forward as necessary.

up a few miles farther south. At this time 1st (W.A.) Brigade was in the Buthidaung area where the I.W.T. line of communication was being organized, and 4th (W.A.) Brigade (Brigadier A. H. G. Ricketts) was mopping up the Kalapanzin valley where small parties of enemy were still operating. Identifications at Hparabyin and Kindaung showed that the opposition was coming from the *Sakura Detachment*. In the Kaladan 81st (W.A.) Division had resumed its advance on the 18th, when, in order to outflank the Japanese who were occupying the general line Kyauktaw–Thayettabin, 6th Brigade moved from Tinma eastwards into the Yan Chaung valley with orders to turn south along it and advance on Myohaung.

Wood now appreciated that he would reach Foul Point long before the estimated date (the 14th January), and reported that he hoped to get there and clear the whole of the Mayu peninsula by the end of December. On the 21st at a conference with his Commanders-in-Chief, Mountbatten, believing that the advance of 81st (W.A.) Division was drawing forces from the Mayu to the Kaladan, ordered alternative plans to be prepared for the earlier capture of Akyab, provided that they did not interfere with the plans for a major assault in March which might have to be launched if the Japanese were to reinforce the garrison. Within a few days Joint Force Headquarters confirmed that the attack could be made with little risk of failure between the 20th and 27th January.

At this stage operations everywhere began to move very rapidly. On the 23rd December, 22nd (E.A.) Brigade arrived in the forward area and took over Ngakyedauk Pass, the Tunnels and the XV Corps forward maintenance centre at Buthidaung, thus releasing 4th (W.A.) Brigade and 51st Brigade to join their respective divisions in the drive to clear the Mayu peninsula and valley. The same day a battalion of 74th Brigade, which had moved rapidly down the beaches by forced marches, reached Donbaik, the scene of the heaviest fighting of the disastrous 1942–43 Arakan campaign.[1] It was thought that the Japanese might again try to hold this naturally strong position to delay the advance, but it was found to be deserted. In the centre at Hparabyin 53rd Brigade was ordered not to press the Japanese too hard, for 51st Brigade (from reserve) was moving in behind them to ensure their destruction. On the other side of the river 4th (W.A.) Brigade passed through 2nd (W.A.) Brigade at Kindaung and, after overcoming resistance near Taungmaw on the 24th, continued the advance towards Htizwe.

By this time there were further indications that enemy troops were moving from the Mayu to the Kaladan valley and an even earlier capture of Akyab seemed possible. The gradual movement towards

---

[1] See Volume II, Chapters XV and XIX.

the Kaladan was due to the fact that, considering the *Sakura Detachment* could not hold on for much longer, Sakurai had asked *28th Army* for permission to withdraw. This was granted and he was ordered to rejoin *55th Division* at Prome.[1] The withdrawal began on the 26th December and by the 31st the detachment had concentrated south of Myohaung, covered by the *Matsu Detachment*. On the 31st, Koba ordered *I/111th Battalion* to evacuate Akyab and withdraw to Ponnagyun, from where it was to move to rejoin him north of Myohaung.

On the 27th December 74th Brigade reached Foul Point, and the same day captured orders showed that there were two battalions of *111th Regiment* in the Kaladan valley in addition to one of the *154th*. Christison concluded that there could not be more than one battalion holding Akyab, and that it should be attacked without further delay. The Joint Force Commanders immediately set to work on the necessary plans, anticipating the receipt of orders from A.L.F.S.E.A. The 53rd Brigade crossed the Mayu River and occupied Rathedaung and Kudaung Island on the 31st without opposition; 51st Brigade, finding the enemy had withdrawn from Hparabyin, carried out a sweep of the Mayu peninsula from the Kyaukpandu–Atet Nanra track southwards to Foul Point to ensure that no enemy parties had been left behind to disrupt communications. The 82nd (W.A.) Division had meanwhile reached Htizwe and was preparing to begin its move to Thayettabin where 81st (W.A.) Division had run into stubborn opposition from the *Matsu Detachment*, the bulk of which Koba had moved there when he became aware of the thrust down the Yan Chaung.

On the 30th December the Joint Force Commanders directed the naval force, 25th Division and 3 Commando Brigade to attack Akyab on the 3rd January and secure the ground commanding the anchorages.[2] The 3 Commando Brigade, supported by a squadron of medium tanks and a regiment of medium artillery as well as by some light and heavy anti-aircraft guns, was to embark in assault craft on the Naf River and land on the northern beaches of Akyab island at 12.30 p.m. on the 3rd January. The 74th Brigade, moving in landing craft from Foul Point, was to follow up and, passing through the commando brigade, was to capture Akyab by the 5th.[3] Naval support was to be

---

[1] For Prome see Map 13 in end pocket.

[2] This ground included the northern tip of the Boronga Islands, the south-western tip of the Pauktaw peninsula and the islands in the mouth of the Kywegu River.

[3] The fact that the attack on Akyab was brought forward from the 20th to the 3rd January and was to be mounted from the Naf River and Foul Point instead of from Chittagong profoundly affected the maintenance plan. Because of the congestion at Chittagong it had been arranged that the maintenance of the force on arrival at Akyab would at first be by ship direct from Calcutta. Sailings from Calcutta could not be brought forward and thus no ship would reach Akyab before the 20th. To overcome this difficulty XV Corps opened an F.M.A. at Foul Point from which troops there and in Akyab could be supplied. The F.M.A. was stocked from Maungdaw by means of coastal craft taken from Chittagong and Maungdaw.

given by a Bombardment Force (Rear-Admiral A. D. Read) consisting of three cruisers (*Newcastle, Phoebe* and *Nigeria*) and the Arakan Coastal Forces. Air support was to be provided by 224 Group R.A.F. with some 200 aircraft.

On the 2nd January, an artillery air observation officer, seeing no sign of Japanese on the island, landed in a rice field and was assured by the inhabitants that they had gone. On receipt of this information Christison and Bandon also landed and were warmly welcomed by the local inhabitants. Orders were immediately issued for the landing to take place as planned, but without bombardment. An alarming meteorological report from S.E.A.C. Headquarters of an imminent storm caused Martin to consider turning back the assault craft carrying the commandos, but Christison insisted that the operation must continue. The storm did not in fact materialize. Akyab town was occupied on the 4th and patrols soon reported that all the ground commanding the anchorages was clear. Work on the repair of the airfield began at once, and a squadron of Spitfires was able to operate from it in time to disperse the first Japanese air attack a few days later. By this time all opposition in the Mayu peninsula had ceased and, in the Kaladan, 81st Division was holding a firm base in the hills south-east of Thayettabin facing Japanese forces, estimated to be a regimental group with artillery, in the Teinnyo–Myohaung area.

The landing at Akyab, though operationally an anti-climax, was of considerable training value and, as will be seen, the early occupation of the island came at a most opportune moment.

CHAPTER XIII

THE NORTHERN AND SALWEEN
FRONTS
(October–December 1944)

See Map 2

ON receipt of the Supreme Commander's directive of the 2nd October,[1] Stilwell decided that the advance on the Northern front should begin on the 16th October. At that time N.C.A.C consisted of the New Chinese First Army (30th and 38th Divisions), the New Chinese Sixth Army (14th, 22nd and 50th Divisions), 36th British Division and Mars Task Force.[2] Air support was provided by 10th U.S.A.A.F.[3] The 36th Division, the only formation in touch with the enemy, and the Chinese Sixth Army (less 14th Division) were west of the Irrawaddy,[4] the former in the railway corridor near Namma,[5] and the latter with 50th Division at Hopin and 22nd Division in the hills ten miles south-east of Mogaung.[6] The Chinese First Army was east of the Irrawaddy, with 38th Division on the Bhamo road some ten miles south of Myitkyina and 30th Division immediately east of the town. The 14th Chinese Division and Mars Force (which was in the process of being formed) were in command reserve.

It was believed at Headquarters N.C.A.C. that the Japanese in north Burma were disposed with *53rd Division* (less an infantry regiment) about 5,500 strong in the railway corridor with a light covering force between the railway and the Irrawaddy, and that east of the river they had an outpost position astride the road near Nalong and strong positions near the junction of the Taping River with the Irrawaddy immediately north of Bhamo. This was a reasonably accurate appreciation. The *53rd Division* (part of *15th Army*), less three battalions but with two independent infantry battalions under command, was in depth between Namma and Pinwe, where it was

---

[1] See pages 107–8.
[2] For order of battle of N.C.A.C. see Appendix 18.
[3] For order of battle of 10th U.S.A.A.F. see Appendix 4.
[4] The 36th Indian Division had been designated an Indian division since it had been formed in India. It was re-designated 36th British Division on the 1st September 1944.
[5] See page 41.
[6] See Map 2, facing page 39.

preparing a defensive position. The *33rd Army* (Honda), after the failure of its Lungling offensive, and the loss of Lameng and Teng-chung,[1] was disposed at the end of September with *56th Division* facing the Chinese Yunnan armies in the Lungling–Mangshih area, *168th Regiment (49th Division)* at Wanting, *18th Division* at Namhkam, and *2nd Division* at Muse in readiness to move to central Burma but finding a force of about two battalions for the defence of Bhamo.[2] The Nalong outpost position had been abandoned late in September, and the main defences of Bhamo were around the town and on the line of the Taping River.

Stilwell had planned to launch a three-pronged offensive south from Myitkyina: on the right, 36th British Division followed by 50th Chinese Division was to secure the Indaw–Katha area; in the centre, 22nd Chinese Division was to seize the abandoned airstrip (used by the Chindits in March 1944) at 'Broadway',[3] secure a bridgehead over the Irrawaddy at Shwegu and occupy Sikaw; and on the left, 38th Chinese Division was to secure Bhamo and Namhkam. The advance began punctually on the 16th October. The 36th Division (Festing) soon ran into opposition, which at first amounted to little more than sniping, but on the 25th the advanced guard of 29th Brigade was held up near Mawhun by well-prepared defensive positions blocking all roads down the valley, and did not succeed in breaking through along the railway until the evening. The Japanese withdrew next day but it was not till the 29th that the small pockets of resistance they had left behind were cleared and the advance was resumed. Mawlu was occupied on the 31st October. The Japanese had meanwhile begun to raid the division's already precarious supply route and Festing was forced to ask Sultan to tell 50th Chinese Division to comply with its orders and protect it.[4] When 148th Chinese Regiment reached Mawlu on the 9th November the advance was resumed, 72nd Brigade being directed on Naba junction at the southern end of the railway corridor and 2nd East Lancashire Regiment on Auktaw to protect the brigade's right flank. By the 12th the advance was held up north of Pinwe and widespread and confused fighting developed, with numerous enemy counter-attacks. The stubborn resistance and identifications of both *119th* and *151st Infantry Regiments* showed that the division was facing the main enemy defences covering Indaw and Katha.

Festing decided to launch a deliberate attack on the 22nd November

---

[1] See Chapter V.

[2] For *Burma Area Army's* plan for the defence of Burma in October 1944 see pages 58–59. For order of battle of *Burma Area Army* see Appendix 8.

[3] See Volume III, Chapter XII.

[4] General Sultan succeeded Stilwell in command of N.C.A.C. on the 24th October; see pages 117–118.

with 29th Brigade directed on Auktaw and 72nd Brigade directed on Pinwe. To enable him to do so, he obtained the agreement of Sixth Army that 50th Chinese Division would move forward to provide a firm base for his attack. It soon became clear, however, that Chinese co-operation was very doubtful.[1] Realizing that it would be dangerous to commit his two brigades on a broad front without a secure base and an effective reserve, Festing altered his plan and decided to attack Pinwe with 72nd Brigade, keeping 29th Brigade in reserve behind it and relying on 50th Division to cover his right flank from the enemy's forces known to be in Auktaw. Having obtained Sultan's agreement to this change of plan and his promise to order 50th Division to co-operate, Festing launched his attack on the 22nd. On the 29th the Japanese began to give way, and, on the 30th, 29th Brigade (which had relieved the 72nd on the 27th) found that they had abandoned the Pinwe position, leaving behind 100 unburied dead.[2] The action cost 36th Division some 400 casualties, mostly in 72nd Brigade. Indaw, Naba and Katha were occupied without opposition between the 9th and 13th December, and on the 16th contact was made with 19th Indian Division at Banmauk. Sultan then ordered Festing to advance astride the Irrawaddy as far south as Tigyaing as soon as his third brigade (26th) had arrived. From there the whole division was to operate east of the Irrawaddy to clear the crossings of the Shweli River south of Mabein and then take Mogok.

While 36th Division was fighting its way down the railway corridor, 22nd Chinese Division reached the Irrawaddy unopposed on the 3rd November, crossed the river north-west of Shwegu in rubber boats which, with outboard motors, had been dropped by air, and occupied the town on the 7th. From there it moved south-east to cut the Bhamo–Mabein road, leaving one regiment to hold Shwegu, and by the end of November 65th and 66th Chinese Regiments had reached Si-u. Since Sultan had been directed to release 22nd Division to follow 14th Chinese Division back to China,[3] he ordered 475th American Infantry Regiment (part of Mars Force) to relieve 22nd Division.[4] Two of its battalions reached Si-u on the 10th December just in time to meet and

---

[1] One of the reasons given by the commander of 50th Chinese Division for not falling in with Festing's plans was that he had to send a large draft and an escort for it to 22nd Division. The Chinese commanders frequently failed to co-operate or comply with orders received from N.C.A.C. owing to the receipt of secret instructions from the Generalissimo. Although no decision had been reached on which divisions were to return to China, the Chinese commanders had evidently been warned from Chungking that 22nd Division had been one of those selected.

[2] The withdrawal of *53rd Division* was in accordance with *Burma Area Army's* plan to withdraw across the Irrawaddy (see Chapter V). It was co-ordinated with that of *15th Division* which was falling back before the advance of 19th Division towards Pinlebu and Banmauk (see Chapter XIV).

[3] See page 128.

[4] The 22nd Chinese Division was to be flown to China from nearby airstrips.

repel small-scale Japanese attacks;[1] the third remained in the Shwegu area and made patrol contact with 36th Division near Katha. Sultan also ordered 50th Chinese Division to move east from Mawlu by way of Shwegu to link up with the Chinese First Army in the Namhkam area.

The advance of 38th Chinese Division east of the Irrawaddy and of 22nd Chinese Division on Shwegu had convinced Honda early in November that the Allies were contemplating an advance against Mongmit, which would not only drive a wedge between *15th* and *33rd Armies* but would leave the direct route to Mandalay wide open. He had therefore ordered *18th Division* to move to the Mongmit area in mid-November, leaving *55th Regiment* (less one battalion) at Namhkam. This regiment, under command of Colonel Yamazaki, together with one battalion from *56th Division* and one from *168th Regiment*, was to form the *Yamazaki Force* which was to be responsible for the defence of Namhkam under the direct control of *33rd Army*.

The 38th Chinese Division had meanwhile advanced on Bhamo and 113th Regiment had ocupied Myothit without opposition on the 28th October. When the crossings over the Taping River north of Bhamo were found to be strongly defended, 112th and 114th Regiments were ordered to turn east, cross the river upstream and then move south and envelop Bhamo. On the 10th November the two regiments reached the plain to the east of Bhamo and came up against a strong enemy outpost position at Monmauk (eight miles east of the town). The position was overrun on the 17th, and 114th Regiment advanced on Bhamo from the east while 112th Regiment moved south-east on to the Namhkam road. Profiting by the diversion, 113th Regiment had in the meantime crossed the Taping River and, leaving a detachment to watch the town from the north, moved across the line of advance of the other two regiments to its south in the hope of achieving surprise.

The Japanese garrison was well supplied with ammunition and food and was prepared to fight, if necessary, to the last.[2] Bhamo, with well spaced-out buildings and many pagodas with walls thick enough to be shellproof, gave the defenders good fields of fire and excellent cover and, though overwhelmingly outnumbered, they expected to be able to hold out for a month. By the 28th November 38th Division, supported by twenty-four guns and 10th U.S.A.A.F., had hemmed in the garrison against the Irrawaddy with 114th Regiment on the north-east and 113th Regiment (reinforced by a battalion of the 112th) on the south and east of the town.

---

[1] These attacks were made by elements of *18th Division* and were designed to assist the break-out of the Bhamo garrison which took place on the night of the 14th/15th December.
[2] The garrison consisted of *II/16th Battalion* and *2nd Divisional Reconnaissance Regiment* (equipped with tanks) supported by four field guns and a few mountain guns, with a total strength of some 1,200 men.

Sultan had meanwhile ordered 30th Chinese Division, which had been following up the 38th, to move to Namyu on the Bhamo–Namhkam road (some twenty miles south of Bhamo) to prevent the Japanese forces known to be in Namhkam from interfering with 38th Division's operations. The arrival of the leading troops of 30th Division at Namyu on the 1st December was timely, for on the 30th November Honda had ordered the *Yamazaki Force* to attack the rear of the Chinese investing Bhamo so as to help the garrison break out. After some days of patrol activity the Japanese attacked with three battalions on a narrow front on the 9th and succeeded in penetrating the Chinese positions, overrunning some artillery units. The Chinese quickly counter-attacked and heavy fighting followed. On the night of the 14th/15th December the Bhamo garrison, reduced to some 900 men (300 of whom were wounded), broke out in compliance with orders received on the 6th. Moving along the bed of the shrunken Irrawaddy and helped by the early morning mist, it succeeded in making its way through the encircling Chinese and reached Namkham without further loss on the 18th. On the 15th, as soon as he knew that the Bhamo garrison had escaped, Yamazaki disengaged in the Namyu area and withdrew to Namhkam.[1]

The arrival of the Chinese First Army on the Taping River at the end of October coincided with the launching of an offensive by XI Chinese Army Group of the Yunnan armies along the axis of the Burma Road towards Wanting.[2] On the 29th October two divisions of 71st Army, supported by 14th U.S.A.A.F. and a strong force of artillery, attacked Lungling frontally, while 200th Division (which had fought under Stilwell's command in the 1942 Burma campaign) moved round the south of the town to cut the road immediately to its west. The position of *56th Division* soon became critical and Lieut.-General S. Matsuyama, with Honda's approval, abandoned Lungling on the 3rd November and withdrew to Mangshih. The Chinese entered the town but made no attempt to follow up the retreating enemy. Only on strong representations from Wedemeyer did the Generalissimo give orders for the offensive to be resumed. The advance on Mangshih and Wanting then began on a broad front with 71st Army astride the road, 53rd Army on the right and 2nd and 6th Armies on the left. It was an unhurried advance, which suited the Japanese who, under orders to avoid battle, carried out a leisurely withdrawal, laying waste the country and carrying out extensive demolitions. The Chinese occupied Mangshih on the 20th November and Chefang on the 1st December. There the advance came to a

---

[1] The strength of the *Yamazaki Force* was some 3,000 men supported by nine guns. During these operations its losses were 150 killed and 300 wounded.
[2] The XI Chinese Army Group consisted of 2nd, 6th, 53rd and 71st Armies.

standstill and, despite more protests from Wedemeyer, was not resumed for a month.

With the capture of Indaw and Katha, the link-up of 36th British Division with 14th Army, and the occupation of Si-u, the right and centre wings of N.C.A.C. had completed their tasks in the first phase of 'Capital'.[1] Although Bhamo had been occupied, the Chinese First Army on the left was still a long way from its objective, Namhkam, the capture of which would threaten the communications of the Japanese opposing the advance of the Yunnan armies which were even farther from their objective, Hsenwi. The position on the 16th December was that 36th Division was in the Indaw–Katha area, 475th American Infantry Regiment of Mars Force was in Si-u, 50th Chinese Division was about to leave the Indaw area for Namhkam, 30th and 38th Chinese Divisions were in the Bhamo–Namyu area and the Yunnan armies were at Chefang. There was thus a wide gap between the N.C.A.C. and the Yunnan armies which had to be closed before the Ledo Road could be joined up with the old Burma Road and traffic could flow from India to China. With his force reduced by two divisions, Sultan had to pause to reconsider his plans and regroup his forces.

[1] See page 108.

CHAPTER XIV

CENTRAL FRONT
(October–December 1944)
14th Army Crosses The Chindwin

See Maps 1, 3, 12 and 13 and Sketch 4

MOUNTBATTEN'S directive of the 2nd October 1944 gave 11th Army Group the specific tasks on the Central front of securing a bridgehead across the Chindwin by mid-December and of capturing the Yeu–Shwebo area by combined airborne and land operations by mid-February 1945.[1] On the 11th, Giffard instructed 14th Army (Slim) to carry out these tasks and to exploit towards Mandalay and Monywa.[2] Kalewa was to be taken, if possible, without an airborne operation, for 50th (P.) Brigade would not be ready for action until the end of January. The airborne operation for the capture of the Yeu–Shwebo area was to take place not later than the middle of February. Administrative preparations were to consist of improving the Tamu–Kalewa–Yeu road to a standard capable of delivering 800 tons daily in dry weather and 300 tons in the monsoon, accelerating the laying of the pipeline to Imphal, establishing an I.W.T. organization on the Chindwin and building up forty-five days' reserve plus fifteen days' working stock forward of Kalewa before the 1945 monsoon.

Slim had already on the 6th August given XXXIII Corps the task of capturing Kalemyo and establishing a bridgehead across the Chindwin at Kalewa, and Stopford was well on the way to accomplishing it.[3] On the 1st October he had issued orders to XXXIII Corps for its advance eastwards from the Chindwin, and on the 2nd he gave Lieut.-General G. A. P. Scoones, whose headquarters were at Ranchi,[4] a directive to prepare plans for IV Corps to co-operate with the advance of XXXIII Corps from the Chindwin by capturing Yeu by an airborne operation and seizing or preparing airfields there in order to build up a force of two divisions transported by air. He placed 7th and 19th Indian Divisions and 50th (P.) Brigade (the last named

---

[1] See pages 107–8 and Map 1, facing page 15.
[2] For Mandalay see Map 3, facing page 55.
[3] See Chapter IV.
[4] For Ranchi see Map 12, facing page 436.

for planning purposes only) under Scoones's command. The object of this operation, which was to take place in early February, was to put into effect Slim's intention of bringing the Japanese to battle and destroying them in the Shwebo–Mandalay plain. By establishing itself in Yeu, IV Corps would form the back stop for the drive by XXXIII Corps from Kalewa eastwards which was expected to start in December. If the advance of XXXIII Corps turned out to be unexpectedly rapid, or the Japanese forces in north and central Burma disintegrated, IV Corps' airborne/air-transported operation was to be carried out south of Mandalay, which was then to be captured by the combined assault of XXXIII Corps from the west and IV Corps from the south.

The problem now facing Slim was how to concentrate XXXIII and IV Corps on the Chindwin by mid-December in readiness for the second phase of 'Capital'—the advance across the Chindwin into north Burma. Very little could be done till the monsoon rain ceased early in October, when the ground would begin to dry out and the engineers could start work on reconditioning the fair-weather road from Tamu to Kalemyo so as to enable XXXIII Corps to concentrate forward, and on the all-weather road and the forward airfields in the Kabaw Valley required for the maintenance of 14th Army. To enable the necessary preparations to be made, the southern end of the Kabaw Valley had first to be cleared and Kalemyo and Kalewa occupied as soon as possible. On the 18th October Headquarters XXXIII Corps moved from Imphal to Sibong, and a powerful force of armour and artillery was assembled at Tamu ready to move forward to Yazagyo.[1] The 2nd and 20th Divisions, due to move forward as soon as Kalemyo and Kalewa were captured, remained in their rest area near Kohima and at the southern end of the Imphal plain respectively.[2]

Meanwhile IV Corps Headquarters had once again become operational on the 4th October and had taken command of 7th Indian Division at Kohima. By the 11th, Scoones had established an advanced headquarters at Imphal. During the second half of October 19th Indian Division and 255th Indian Tank Brigade arrived from India and concentrated north of the Imphal plain, coming under command of IV Corps from the 19th. At the same time the engineer units for the construction of the fair-weather and all-weather roads from Tamu to Kalewa, for bridging the Chindwin at Kalewa and for the construction of forward airfields had begun to assemble in the

---

[1] This force consisted of 254th Tank Brigade (less a squadron), one regiment of medium and one of field artillery, an artillery survey unit and an air O.P. squadron. This last unit was to prove an invaluable aid in the flat-bottomed and jungle-covered valley.

[2] For Kohima see Map 13 in end pocket.

Palel area, ready to move forward into the Kabaw Valley under orders of XXXIII Corps, as opportunity offered.[1]

By this time the L. of C. Road Transport organization was operating as far forward as Moreh, and the airstrip at Tamu, on which repair work had begun late in September, was ready for use. On the 20th October two R.A.F. fighter-bomber and two American light aircraft squadrons were moved to it from Imphal to give increased air support for XXXIII Corps' advance and to enable sick and wounded to be evacuated from the light airstrip under construction at Khampat and the airstrips about to be built farther south. The monsoon rain ceased on the 19th October and fair-weather roads forward of Imphal began to dry out. By mid-November the engineers had brought the thirty-six miles of the Palel–Tamu road up to a two-way fair-weather standard fit to take medium tanks throughout, and work to make it all-weather had begun. In the Kabaw Valley, work went on night and day and by the 7th November the two-way fair-weather road (suitable for use by 3-ton vehicles) from Tamu had reached Yazagyo, fifty-five miles farther south. Thereafter its rate of construction was determined by the speed of 11th (E.A.) Division's advance.[2]

At the end of October the information regarding the Japanese forces opposing XXXIII Corps on the Central front was that *15th Division* was in the Wuntho area with detachments holding the passes over the Zibyu Taungdan, that *31st Division* was still west of the Irrawaddy in the Shwebo area, but of little fighting value, and that the withdrawal of *33rd Division* on Kalemyo had been covered by *61st Regiment* (less a battalion) in the Kabaw Valley and by *151st Regiment* (less a battalion), *II/154th* and *I/67th Battalions* on the Tiddim road.[3]

It was not till Tongzang was reached that contact was made with *215th Regiment* of *33rd Division* (Tanaka). This division had in fact been given the task of delaying XXXIII Corps for as long as possible to cover the withdrawal of *15th* and *31st Divisions* across the Chindwin, and to gain time for the backloading of the large quantity of stores

---

[1] The engineer force for road construction, which was named D.C.E. 145, consisted of three works C.R.E.s with G.R.E.F. troops. It was organized into three constructional groups, each consisting of two field companies, an engineer battalion, a platoon of a G.P.T. company, a mechanical engineering platoon, a detachment of the Elephant Company, R.I.A.S.C. and some Indian pioneer companies. Two of these groups leap-frogged each other on construction work and the third surfaced the road behind them. The bridging organization consisted of Headquarters 274th Army Group Engineers, Headquarters XXXIII Corps Troop Engineers, 67th, 76th and 361st Indian Field Companies, a field platoon of 322nd Indian Field Park Company, two bridging companies and a company of 10th Engineer Battalion, I.E. The organization for constructing forward airfields was 459th Forward Airfield Engineers. This unit was already employed on the reconstruction of the airstrip at Tamu.

[2] The road reached a point two miles south of Kangyi on the 18th and Indainggyi on the 28th November.

[3] These were all units which had been sent to reinforce *33rd Division* during the Imphal offensive; see Volume III, Chapter XXIII.

which had been collected at the southern end of the Kabaw Valley during the Imphal offensive. Tanaka had decided to stand and fight at Mawlaik on the Chindwin, Indainggyi in the Kabaw Valley and Tongzang and Kennedy Peak on the Tiddim road. He had used his attached units to cover the initial stages of his withdrawal while the three regiments of his division prepared these places for defence.[1] At the beginning of November, the Kennedy Peak–Fort White area was held by *214th Regiment* with *II/213th Battalion* under command, the Indainggyi area by *215th Regiment*, after its withdrawal from Tongzang, and the Mawlaik area by *213th Regiment* (less one battalion).

After the capture of Tiddim on the 16th October, 5th Indian Division (Warren) began to close in on Kennedy Peak and Fort White.[2] By the end of the month, 123rd Brigade had cleared the area south and south-east of Tiddim as far as Dimlo,[3] and one battalion (1/1st Punjab of 161st Brigade under command) had occupied Dolluang; 161st Brigade (less a battalion) had occupied Mualbem; 9th Brigade, which had been allotted the task of breaking through the enemy position at Kennedy Peak and capturing Fort White, had infiltrated a battalion (3/9th Jats) to a position behind the peak near MS 55 on the Fort White–Tiddim road where it was lying up hidden in the jungle; and much farther south the Lushai Brigade had occupied Falam and Haka without opposition. Kennedy Peak was now encircled.

On the 1st November, supported by artillery and concentrated air strikes by the R.A.F.,[4] 123rd Brigade closed in on Vital Corner. On the 3rd the Japanese on Kennedy Peak began to withdraw towards Fort White, but 3/9th Jats, emerging from its hideout, blocked their retreat and inflicted severe casualties on them. Unable to break through, the Japanese separated into small parties and moved eastwards by jungle paths, but many were intercepted and dispersed at Dolluang. The following day the advanced guard of 9th Brigade, supported by a troop of medium tanks, linked up with the Jats but its attempt to move towards Fort White was held up by enemy rearguards. Meanwhile 161st Brigade, moving east from Mualbem, had on the 5th cut the Kalemyo road two miles south-east of Fort White, and 1/1st Punjab, leaving detachments at Dolluang and Pimpi, had occupied the high ground overlooking the road near No. 3 Stockade. The Japanese were now surrounded but, to cover their withdrawal across country, they fought back viciously and it was not till the 8th

---

[1] By this time all the attached units were under orders to rejoin their divisions, with the exception of *61st Regiment* which had been ordered to Yeu to be in *15th Army* reserve.

[2] See Chapter IV and Sketch 4, facing page 170.

[3] For his actions during these operations Jemadar (acting Subadar) Ram Sarup Singh, 1st Punjab Regiment, was awarded a posthumous Victoria Cross.

[4] Four fighter-bomber squadrons flew 96 sorties on the 1st and 136 sorties on the 2nd November.

that 9th Brigade occupied Fort White. The 161st Brigade, fighting its way east along the Kalemyo road, gained contact with and resumed command of 1/1st Punjab. It then drove Japanese rearguards from a series of positions along the road, and reached the crossroads immediately west of Kalemyo on the 12th November.

The 11th (E.A.) Division (Fowkes) had meanwhile resumed its offensive down the Kabaw Valley. The 26th (E.A.) Brigade moving south from Yazagyo was, however, held up immediately north of Indainggyi, and 21st (E.A.) Brigade was unable to overcome opposition in the Mawlaik area, despite support by four medium bomber squadrons and all the fighter-bomber squadrons of 221 Group R.A.F. In view of the urgent need to clear the valley and to renew the momentum of the advance, Fowkes ordered his reserve, 25th (E.A.) Brigade, to by-pass Indainggyi on the west and move direct on Kalemyo, where it was to make contact with 5th Division, while 26th Brigade continued its efforts to take Indainggyi and sent a detachment to by-pass the village on the east with a view to blocking the Japanese line of retreat from Kalemyo to Kalewa in the Myittha River gorge. On the 10th November, finding that the Japanese had evacuated Mawlaik, 21st Brigade began to move south on the west bank of the Chindwin. By the 12th November, the day that 11th Army Group ceased to exist and was replaced by A.L.F.S.E.A. and Leese took over command from Giffard,[1] XXXIII Corps had isolated Kalemyo, the junction of all the motorable roads and tracks west of the Chindwin. Next day patrols of 25th Brigade met patrols of 5th Division west of Kalemyo, and on the 14th the Africans entered the town to find it deserted and in ruins. The same day 21st Brigade occupied Paluzawa on the Chindwin, and the Lushai Brigade, by occupying Myintha, blocked the track in the Myittha valley leading to the Irrawaddy at Pakokku.[2]

The task of mopping up the Kalemyo area had been allotted to 5th Division, which, after completing it, was to be flown out to rest and reorganize. The 11th (E.A.) Division was thus free to concentrate its whole strength for the capture of Kalewa and the establishment of a bridgehead on the eastern bank of the Chindwin. Fowkes ordered Hendricks (25th Brigade) to help 26th Brigade to take Indainggyi by sending a column to attack it from the south and with the remainder of his brigade to advance as quickly as possible to attack Kalewa from the west. Macnab (21st Brigade) was to assist Hendricks by sending one battalion from Paluzawa along the west bank of the river to attack Kalewa from the north, and with the rest of his brigade was to cross the river and move south to seize the east bank opposite Kalewa.

---

[1] See page 118.
[2] For Pakokku see Map 13 in end pocket.

The final attack on Indainggyi, supported by a heavy air attack, began on the 17th November, but it was not until the appearance of the column from 25th Brigade to the south of the town on the 19th that the Japanese, taken by surprise, withdrew. On the 20th a battalion, supported by tanks, forced the entrance to the Myittha River gorge, but the gorge itself was not finally cleared until the 26th. The 25th Brigade then met with opposition from an enemy rearguard some six miles west of Kalewa; its resistance, even with the help of heavy air strikes, was not overcome till the 29th November. The brigade was again held up three miles nearer the town but, with the battalion of 21st Brigade from Paluzawa threatening their line of retreat, the Japanese withdrew across the river and Kalewa was occupied on the 2nd December. The enemy still held the east bank of the river opposite the town, for 21st Brigade east of the river had encountered such difficult country that, although opposition was slight, it was by the 2nd still eight miles from its objective.[1] The 25th Brigade had therefore to prepare for an opposed crossing and, on the night of the 3rd/4th, a battalion crossed in assault boats only to find that the enemy had vanished. The same evening 26th Brigade began to cross after dark and, by the 6th, two brigades were holding a restricted bridgehead across the Chindwin opposite Kalewa.

The progress of operations for the capture of Kalemyo had by the 6th November made large-scale moves into the Kabaw Valley possible. On that day Slim ordered Scoones to send a brigade group, maintained by air from the Imphal air base, to cross the Chindwin not later than the 20th to capture Pinlebu, establish contact with 36th Division on the Northern front in the Indaw–Katha area, patrol the railway from Wuntho to Indaw and report on the practicability of moving large forces (including medium tanks) from the Chindwin to the Wuntho–Indaw area. The boundary between IV and XXXIII Corps was to be from Shuganu through Witok, Pantha and Indaw (Oil) to Yindaik on the Mu River. All engineer resources in IV Corps, including those of 7th Division, were to be employed in improving the roads from Tamu to Sittaung and Tonhe, and in preparing a report on the possibility of making the Tamu–Tonhe road fit for medium tanks.

Scoones ordered 19th Indian Division (Major-General T. W. Rees) to find the brigade group. Rees sent 62nd Brigade (Brigadier J. R. Morris) with orders to move to Sittaung with a battalion of 64th Brigade under command, cross the Chindwin, pass through the bridgehead held by 268th Brigade (Dyer) and then carry out the allotted tasks. The brigade reached Sittaung on the 15th November.

---

[1] In places ropes had to be used to enable men to scale or descend the steep escarpments which were encountered.

A few days later the rest of the division was ordered forward to the Chindwin: 98th Brigade (Brigadier C. I. Jerrard) to the Tonhe–Thanan area, where it was to establish a bridgehead and a ferry to it, and 64th Brigade (Brigadier G. A. Bain), less one battalion, to take over the Sittaung bridgehead from 268th Brigade. The 268th was then to concentrate east of the Chindwin south of the inter-corps boundary, act as a link between the two corps and protect the right flank of 62nd Brigade during the early stages of its advance towards Pinlebu.[1] The divisional engineers were to improve the Tamu–Tonhe road so that it could be used by medium tanks. By the 21st November divisional headquarters was established at Moreh and the division's move to its allotted areas was completed. The same day Head-quarters 14th Army, now freed of the command of XV Corps and of the administrative control of back areas, moved to Imphal and formed a joint headquarters with 221 Group R.A.F.[2]

Meanwhile Slim had instructed Scoones to examine with 221 Group R.A.F. and representatives of C.A.A.T.O. and C.C.T.F. whether the introduction of IV Corps into the Yeu–Shwebo area could be speeded up in any way. Their joint report of the 15th November made it clear that, with the aircraft and gliders available, no airborne operation was practicable before February 1945. This confirmed Slim's belief that the capture of Yeu might be quicker by land than by air, and therefore the sooner the whole of the leading division of IV Corps was across the Chindwin the better. Accordingly, on the 18th he ordered Scoones to concentrate IV Corps in the Yeu–Shwebo area as quickly as possible, either by moving the whole corps across country or by using 19th Division alone and later flying the rest of the corps into captured or newly-built airfields. The move of the whole corps by air, as previously ordered, was not, however, to be entirely ruled out and the final decision was to be left until reports were received from 19th Division on the practicability of the routes east of the Chindwin. To hasten the collection of this information, Slim authorized Scoones to commit the whole of 19th Division east of the river, but not 7th Division.

On the 16th November, 62nd Brigade, covered by a battalion of 268th Brigade already east of the river, crossed the 300-yards-wide Chindwin at Sittaung on locally made rafts towed by powered assault boats, and by the 18th had without opposition secured a bridgehead some fifteen miles deep from Nanbon to the Pinlebu track, eight miles south-east of Paungbyin. The 64th Brigade then moved into Sittaung and 98th Brigade occupied Thaungdut, where it established a

---

[1] The 268th Brigade was placed under command of IV Corps on the 11th November, when it ceased to be Imphal Force (see page 44). It shed two of its battalions but retained 4/3rd Madras, 1st Chamar and Mahindra Dal Regiments. These three battalions remained with it for the rest of the campaign.

[2] See page 114.

bridgehead in the deep bend of the river. The engineers soon had an F.B.E. ferry operating and later augmented it with a ramped cargo lighter (R.C.L.) which had been brought forward in sections by road to the Yu River and reassembled there. The successful arrival of this lighter proved the feasibility of moving I.W.T. craft to the Chindwin, and many more were brought up and put into use.[1]

The concentration of 14th Army on the Chindwin during November presented a most difficult problem, for the only track down the Kabaw Valley had largely disintegrated during the monsoon and forward airfields were scarce. Priority had to be given to the engineers repairing the track and constructing forward airfields, and to the convoys carrying the equipment to bridge the Chindwin at Kalewa which had to reach the Indainggyi area by the end of the month. The problem was eased by the capture of the enemy airfield at Taukkyan (near Kalemyo) on the 13th November in an undamaged state, from where 5th Division could be maintained by air-landed supplies, and by the opening of the Dakota airstrip at Yazagyo on the 16th.[2]

As soon as 19th Division of IV Corps was clear of Tamu, Stopford was able to begin moving the rest of his corps to the southern end of the Kabaw Valley. The forward move of 2nd Division began on the 14th November with the ferrying of 6th Brigade's animals in motor vehicles from the Kohima area to Moreh. The whole brigade reached the division's concentration area at Yazagyo by the 25th. On the 19th the bridging train left Palel and by the 24th had reached Kangyi (five miles south of Yazagyo). From there the bridging required to repair the road in the Myittha River gorge and the assault bridging needed at Kalewa were moved forward as wanted by 11th (E.A.) Division. On the 21st the main body of 6th Brigade moved by road transport to Yazagyo. The following day 32nd Brigade (Brigadier D. A. L. Mackenzie) of 20th Division, with a battalion of 100th Brigade under command, began to march from the Imphal plain by way of the track through Shuganu and Htinzin to Mawlaik, where it arrived at the end of the month. The two-way fair-weather road reached Indainggyi on the 28th November, and on the 5th December the bridging train moved there from Kangyi in readiness to construct the Bailey pontoon bridge across the Chindwin at Kalewa. On the 30th November 80th Brigade, moving by motor transport, reached Khampat (seven miles south of Htinzin) and next day went on to Kalemyo to relieve the last brigade of 5th Division and protect the right of 11th (E.A.) Division. Its place at Khampat was taken by

---

[1] For details see Appendix 16.
[2] The 11th (E.A.) Division remained, however, largely dependent on supply drops, though some ammunition and petrol were sent forward from Yazagyo by road.

Headquarters 20th Division and 100th Brigade, less a battalion. By the 7th December 2nd Division was at Yazagyo ready to take over from the East African division. The forward concentration of XXXIII Corps was now complete. Stopford, who had moved his headquarters to the south of Yazagyo on the 26th November, had meanwhile ordered the engineers to extend the airstrips at Yazagyo and Taukkyan to 2,000 yards in order to take fighters and C.46 transport aircraft, and to build new fighter airstrips at Kalemyo and Thazi, a pair of runways at Indainggale (one mile north of Indainggyi) suitable for use by transport aircraft, and an airstrip for light aircraft at Inbaung (five miles north of Indainggyi).[1]

On the 3rd December, Slim was told by Leese that, owing to the worsening situation in China and the Generalissimo's request for the return of two Chinese divisions from the Northern front to defend Kunming,[2] he was to press on with his present operations with a view to linking up with N.C.A.C. as soon as possible, and was to study as a matter of urgency the feasibility of moving 7th Division to the railway corridor.

At a conference on the 6th, Slim succeeded in persuading Leese that it was unnecessary to fly 7th Division (the leading brigade of which was already on its way to Thaungdut) to the railway corridor, since he had a plan in mind under which XXXIII Corps would carry out its advance to Shwebo and Monywa as originally planned and IV Corps would speed up its advance, 19th Division carrying out a wide enveloping movement to contact 36th Division in the Indaw–Naba area with its outer flank and then swinging south to meet XXXIII Corps in the Yeu–Shwebo area. This manœuvre, he hoped, would catch the main Japanese forces between the two corps and ensure their complete destruction.

On the 7th, Slim issued an operational instruction to Lieut.-General F. W. Messervy, who was to succeed Scoones in command of IV Corps on the 8th.[3] The information (which proved to be accurate) regarding the Japanese positions was that *15th Division*, with a combat strength of not more than five battalions, had withdrawn some of its forward detachments from the Zibyu Taungdan area, and there were indications that it was taking up new positions farther south; *33rd Division*, now equivalent in strength to little more than four battalions, had withdrawn east of the Chindwin and was expected to fight delaying actions astride the Yeu road; *31st Division*, now reduced to

---

[1] See Sketch 4, facing page 170.
[2] See Chapter XI.
[3] Scoones had been appointed General Officer Commanding-in-Chief, Central Command, India. Messervy was succeeded in command of 7th Division by Evans, who had previously commanded 5th Division.

the strength of about one regiment, was in army reserve, with part of the division believed to be in the Monywa area and part possibly in the Mu River valley moving towards Pinlebu; two battalions of *61st Regiment (4th Division)* were also believed to be in army reserve, possibly in the Sagaing area;[1] and the weak *53rd Division* was thought to be in the Meza area with forward positions covering Indaw and Katha and, under pressure, might possibly withdraw to Wuntho. To his original intention of concentrating 14th Army in the Shwebo–Mandalay plain and there bringing the enemy to battle and destroying him Slim added the rider that, in the process, direct assistance was to be given to the advance on the Northern front. The IV Corps task was therefore to advance as rapidly as possible to make contact with 36th Division in the Indaw–Wuntho area, capture Pinlebu, exploit to Wuntho in order to isolate and destroy any Japanese forces to the north of it, and relieve 36th Division for operations farther east. The corps was to concentrate in the Yeu–Shwebo area by the 15th February at the latest. 'You will realize,' the order ended, 'that the Japanese opposing you are neither in great strength nor in good shape. It is therefore legitimate for you to take certain risks, which in other circumstances would not be justified, in order to achieve a rapid advance to the area Indaw–Wuntho.'

The outstanding feature of the country between the Chindwin and the Irrawaddy is the precipitous and almost unbroken escarpment of the Zibyu Taungdan which faces west for nearly 200 miles, rising to over 2,000 feet, and overlooks a tangled mass of foothills and deep ravines. On the front of 19th Division's advance from the Chindwin to Pinlebu and Pinbon, only two usable tracks crossed it. There were also a few jungle paths passable only by lightly-armed men, some of which came to a dead end at the foot of the main escarpment. Of the two tracks, the northern, which ran from Tonhe by way of Sinlamaung to Pinbon, was motorable in fair weather for it had been extensively improved and used by the Japanese before the Battles of Imphal and Kohima; the southern, which ran from Paungbyin to Pinlebu, was a fair-weather motorable track for part of its length, but degenerated into a mule track over the escarpment. The information available to Rees on the Japanese dispositions, together with identifications obtained in patrol clashes of *67th* and *51st Regiments* of *15th Division* on the Pinbon and Pinlebu tracks respectively, showed that the two passes through which the tracks ran might be strongly held, and that enemy tanks might be encountered east of the escarpment.

The artillery of 19th Division was still at Tamu, and most of its men were engaged in improving the road and track to Tonhe to enable it to get forward to the Chindwin. At Tonhe the river was

---

[1] For Sagaing see Map 3, facing page 55.

400 yards wide, and the ferry, served by one ramped cargo lighter and a few F.B.E. rafts, had a very limited capacity. It would, therefore, be some days before the artillery and transport, other than essential unit fighting vehicles, could be assembled east of the river, and from there on would have to use the northern track. This meant that the brigade advancing on Pinlebu would be without artillery and its transport until Pinbon was taken and the track from there to Pinlebu along the eastern side of the escarpment was opened.[1]

If Indaw were to be reached quickly, the division clearly could not wait for its artillery. If, on the other hand, it advanced without its artillery and the Japanese were in strength on the passes it would almost certainly be held up. Air support was available, but experience had shown that air attack on well-concealed positions on steep ridges in thick jungle was ineffective. Moreover, the forward troops of a long column on a constricted road would be very vulnerable to counter-attack and, without artillery support, might be roughly handled before units in rear could get forward to help them. The risks involved were increased by the fact that the division was as yet untried in battle, and an early reverse might have considerable effect on its confidence in itself and its commander.

Against opposition in strength the advance was likely to be a formidable undertaking. Rees might have been excused had he asked Messervy whether he could postpone the advance until he could get his artillery forward, and Messervy might have been excused had he agreed. But both men were leaders who believed that great results could not be achieved without taking risks, and, having been directed by Slim, in whom they had complete confidence, to accept risks, it is hardly surprising to find that by the 8th December the leading troops of 62nd Brigade were fighting to clear the pass within sixteen miles of Pinlebu, and that those of 64th Brigade (which had crossed the Chindwin at Sittaung after 62nd Brigade and had then moved north along the Paungbyin–Sinlamaung track) had entered Sinlamaung, which they found to be unoccupied. On the 14th December 62nd Brigade seized Pinlebu, its small garrison escaping unscathed owing to the fact that the detachment sent to cut its line of retreat lost its way, and 64th Brigade had reached Pinbon.[2] Next day patrols from 64th Brigade made contact with those of 36th Division at Banmauk. There, a staff officer of 36th Division met Rees on the 16th and contact was established between the Central and Northern fronts.[3] While this rapid advance by the forward brigades of 19th Division had been going on, 98th Brigade had moved forward behind 64th Brigade to

---

[1] In the circumstances 62nd Brigade was instructed to operate as if it were a long-range penetration group.

[2] During the advance indications of recent occupation by *I/* and *III/67th Battalions* had been obtained on the Pinbon track and of *51st Regiment* on the Pinlebu track.

[3] See page 145.

Sinlamaung and the divisional artillery, now across the Chindwin, was on the move to join it. Rees had carried out the first portion of his task and would be ready to swing south as soon as he could concentrate his division.[1]

On the right of 19th Division, the leading troops of 268th Brigade occupied Indaw (Oil) on the 14th and sent patrols the next day towards Yeshin east of the Zibyu Taungdan. Farther south 32nd Brigade of 20th Division, which had crossed the Chindwin at Mawlaik, reached Tawtha by the 7th, occupied Chingyaung without opposition on the evening of the 16th and sent a battalion (4/10th Gurkhas) to block the Kalewa–Yeu road east of Pyingaing.

The two bridging companies had begun to move on the 6th December from Indainggyi to Kalewa and, although the road conditions along the Myittha River gorge road were so bad that the arrival of the bridging material was seriously delayed, a Class 30 Bailey pontoon bridge, 1,150 feet in length, was opened for traffic across the Chindwin by 3 p.m. on the 10th. The 11th (E.A.) Division had meanwhile broken out of its originally restricted bridgehead, only to meet with further Japanese opposition on the ridge immediately north of Shwegyin—the scene of Burcorps' last action during the retreat from Burma in 1942[2]—and it was not until the middle of the month that the Japanese withdrew both along the Yeu road and down the Chindwin. By the 16th, Tactical Headquarters 2nd Division and 6th Brigade had reached Mutaik, and the division began to relieve the African division which, having completed its task, was withdrawn to Imphal for rest and rehabilitation.

The policy of keeping relentless pressure on the Japanese *15th Army* to give it no opportunity to rest and recover had, despite the monsoon, succeeded, though at the cost of some 50,000 casualties (about fifty-five per cent of the average strength of XXXIII Corps), of which more than nine-tenths were due to sickness.[3] That the results were worth the cost will be seen from the succeeding chapters.

From early December a suspicion that the Japanese forces opposing 14th Army were withdrawing much farther than had been thought likely began slowly to turn into a certainty. By the middle of the month Slim and his staff had come to the conclusion that it was not after all going to be possible to destroy them in the Yeu–Shwebo area and that a change of plan was inevitable.

On the 14th December, as 14th Army deployed for the reconquest of Burma, the commanders who had made this possible—

---

[1] When the leading troops reached Sinlamaung it was found that the road from there to Pinbon could not take artillery and heavy transport without major repairs. These were carried out with the greatest urgency as Rees was determined there should be no delay in beginning his southward advance.

[2] See Volume II, Chapter XII.

[3] See Appendix 14.

Lieut.-General Slim and his three corps commanders, Lieut.-Generals Christison, Scoones and Stopford — were, with special permission of King George VI, knighted by the Viceroy of India (Field-Marshal Earl Wavell) at Imphal in the presence of the Supreme Commander, the Governor of Assam and a large number of officers and men of 14th Army.[1]

---

[1] Slim had been gazetted K.C.B. and his three corps commanders K.B.E. on the 28th September 1944 for their services at the Battles of Ngakyedauk Pass, Imphal and Kohima.

CHAPTER XV

THE CENTRAL FRONT
(December 1944)
Slim Changes His Plan

See Maps 1, 3 and 13 and Sketch 14

AS has already been shown, Slim had been planning to bring the Japanese armies to battle and destroy them in the Yeu–Shwebo area, but early in December he began to suspect that Kimura, the new Japanese Commander-in-Chief, did not intend to fight a major battle between the Chindwin and the Irrawaddy. By the middle of the month it appeared that *15th Division* had been withdrawn and that the bulk of its strength was in the Kyaikthin-Thabeikkyin area with only small rearguards farther north, and that *53rd Division*, opposing N.C.A.C., had broken contact and had fallen back across the Irrawaddy at Tigyaing to fill the gap between Thabeikkyin and the left flank of *18th Division* on the Shweli River near Myitson.[1] To the south the tired and depleted *33rd Division* was showing further signs of weakening, and there was no indication that the Japanese contemplated preparing anything more than delaying positions along the Shwegyin–Yeu road. The *31st Division* seemed, however, to be taking up positions across the Shwebo plain on both sides of this road, forming a screen extending from the left flank of *15th Division* near Wuntho to Monywa on the Chindwin. It looked therefore as if the remnants of *33rd Division* would withdraw through *31st Division*; the latter, owing to its widespread dispositions, would, however, not be able to do more than provide a screen for the withdrawal.

This picture of the Japanese dispositions, coupled with the lack of opposition to 19th Division's advance, as well as information from captured documents and local reports from the inhabitants of liberated Burmese villages, indicated that the enemy was contemplating a withdrawal to the south of Mandalay.[2] Reports by reconnaissance aircraft of the movement of troops and supplies from Monywa to Pakokku and thence across the Irrawaddy as well as signs that the bulk of *2nd* and *49th Divisions* was disposed south of Pyinmana and that the Japanese were apparently neither preparing defensive

---

[1] See Map 1, facing page 15.
[2] See Map 13 in end pocket.

163

positions nor locating a mobile reserve in the Mandalay area, all confirmed Slim's suspicions and led him to make a drastic change in his plans.

On the 16th December Lethbridge (Slim's Chief of Staff) sent a brief telegram to Advanced Headquarters A.L.F.S.E.A. saying that news received during the previous forty-eight hours had convinced Slim that the Japanese would probably withdraw southwards and not fight for a decision near Mandalay. The original plan for 'Capital' was therefore being scrapped and a new plan was being prepared which would be sent in as soon as possible.

On the 17th December Slim sent Leese a telegraphic summary of his revised plan, which he called 'Extended Capital', and followed it up on the 20th with a detailed appreciation and plan. His overall object, he said, remained as before—the destruction of all enemy forces in Burma. The Japanese, who were retreating everywhere, might be intending either to withdraw from Burma altogether, or to fall back to cover the south Burma ports, or to concentrate for a counter-offensive when his own forces were extended in pursuit. His immediate object therefore was to force them to give battle on ground favourable to 14th Army, if possible in central Burma where his lines of communication would be shorter than in southern Burma and thus provide him with the opportunity of destroying them. His ultimate object would, for administrative reasons, have to be the capture of a south Burma port between March and May.

His revised plan was based on the assumptions that 17th Indian Division would be made available to 14th Army, that only two Chinese divisions from N.C.A.C. (14th and 22nd) would be sent to China before the 1st March (which meant that even so N.C.A.C. would be able to do no more than secure the general line Mongmit–Lashio and thereafter cover the road trace to China or follow up an enemy withdrawal),[1] and that three combat cargo squadrons would be moved permanently to China and a fourth for the month of January only. Unless these aircraft were replaced from outside the theatre, 50th (P.) Brigade would not be fit for operations before the 1945 monsoon, no fly-in or move by air of formations would be possible and the air supply capabilities would be as given on the 11th December at the Calcutta conference.[2]

As it now appeared extremely unlikely that the enemy would attempt to do more than delay a direct advance on Mandalay, Slim could not attain his immediate object by concentrating 14th Army in the loop of the Irrawaddy as originally planned. He now had to place a force south of Mandalay as rapidly as possible so that the Japanese would have to fight in order to extricate themselves from

---

[1] See Map 3, facing page 55.
[2] See page 129 and Appendix 13.

central Burma. Speed was of the utmost importance, for the degree of opposition likely to be encountered in the eventual southward advance from Mandalay towards Rangoon would depend on the extent to which the Japanese could be forced to commit formations to battle in the area immediately south of Mandalay in order to extricate their forces remaining in or north of that area.

There were, however, neither airborne forces nor aircraft available to enable Slim to move a force to the south of Mandalay by air, nor was it possible to by-pass Mandalay to the east by way of N.C.A.C. as there were no north–south communications which could carry a large force with armour. A good route with suitable sites for airfields did exist along the Myittha valley to the Irrawaddy at Pakokku which could take a force including armour and bridging equipment without heavy engineering work. He proposed therefore to move a force along it as rapidly as possible with orders to cross the Irrawaddy near Pakokku and then advance to Meiktila and Thazi, which were the key points on the road and rail communications between Mandalay and Rangoon and constituted the main Japanese administrative area in central Burma.

He proposed to modify the second phase of 'Capital' and order XXXIII Corps (2nd, 19th and 20th Divisions, 268th Brigade and 254th Tank Brigade) to occupy the Shwebo–Monywa area and close up to the Irrawaddy, and IV Corps (7th and 17th Divisions, 28th (E.A.) Brigade and 255th Tank Brigade) to advance up the Myittha valley and seize a bridgehead near Pakokku. In the third phase XXXIII Corps would encircle Mandalay, while IV Corps seized Meiktila, forcing the Japanese to give battle and, he hoped, commit their general reserve (*2nd* and *49th Division*).[1] The fourth and fifth phases would cover the pursuit southwards by both corps, each reduced to two divisions and a tank brigade, the maximum which could be maintained until a south Burma port was captured: XXXIII Corps would advance on the Mandalay–Nyaunglebin axis with detachments operating in the Shan States, and IV Corps on the Myingyan–Henzada axis. In these phases he intended to make use of any favourable opportunity to seize a south Burma port by a rapid overland advance assisted, if possible, by a limited airborne operation mounted from central Burma, and by Special Force operating in rear of the enemy in the Pegu Yomas. A decision on the feasibility of these last two phases could, however, be made only after the result of the operations in the third phase was known. The 5th Indian Division, 11th (E.A.) Division and the Lushai Brigade were to constitute 14th Army reserve.[2] The target date for the occupation of Shwebo,

---

[1] See Sketch 14, facing page 314.
[2] The Lushai Brigade was to be withdrawn into reserve when IV Corps had passed through Gangaw on its way up the Myittha valley.

Monywa and Pakokku would be the 31st January and for Mandalay and Meiktila the 28th February; the pursuit to Henzada and Nyaunglebin would begin as soon as possible thereafter.

The plan, Slim continued, presented a number of major administrative problems. So that the army could be maintained in central Burma during the monsoon if a port were not captured, it was essential that an all-weather base should be constructed in the Shwebo–Mandalay–Meiktila–Myingyan–Monywa area.[1] This implied all-weather communications from Imphal into the dry belt of central Burma, all-weather airfields in either the Shwebo or Meiktila area capable of handling 700 tons a day throughout the monsoon as well as an assured airlift of this daily tonnage,[2] and a stockpile of forty-five days' reserves (50,000 tons) in central Burma by the beginning of the monsoon. Since the greatly increased scope and speed of the operations made it desirable that the greatest amount of engineering resources would be available to maintain the mobility of the army during its advance, the existing project for an all-weather road from the Kalewa bridgehead to Shwebo would have to be abandoned and, in its place, an I.W.T. service established on the Chindwin and the Irrawaddy capable of carrying 100 tons a day from Kalewa to Alon (near Monywa) by the 1st March, rising to 500 tons a day to Myingyan by the 1st May.

In addition to developing the I.W.T. service on the Chindwin, the engineers would be called on to complete the all-weather road down the Kabaw Valley to Kalewa by the 20th April and a two-way fair-weather road from Kalewa to Shwebo, capable of taking some jeep traffic during the monsoon. They would have to be prepared to ferry large forces and tanks across the Irrawaddy in both the Pakokku and Sagaing areas, and also to construct fair-weather airfields (or rehabilitate captured enemy airfields) every fifty miles on the line of advance for use by the tactical air forces and for the landing of supplies, and all-weather airfields in the Shwebo or Meiktila area capable of handling the required total of 700 tons a day. Finally, they would have to arrange to keep the maximum amount of Bailey bridging material on wheels in order to provide the army with mobility during the fourth and fifth phases of the operation.[3] To enable them to carry out these tasks, the engineers would require additional G.P.T. companies; these, Slim suggested, might be found by reducing work in rear areas such as that of preparing the new base area for launching 'Dracula'.

---

[1] See Map 3, facing page 55.

[2] This figure of 700 tons a day was that proposed by Eastern Air Command at the conference of the 11th December; see Appendix 13.

[3] This involved the replacement before the end of January 1945 of the Bailey pontoon bridge across the Chindwin by one with a high level centre span to allow the passage of boats.

During the fourth and fifth phases L. of C. Command would have to be prepared to take control of the army's lines of communication as far east as Monywa and Sagaing. The mobility of the army in these phases would depend on the ability of the air force to land or drop supplies close to formations, thus reducing the turnround of motor transport vehicles, and this would demand a bigger airlift over greater distances than was at the time available. It would therefore be necessary in these phases to reduce the turnround of aircraft and this, Slim thought, could be achieved by moving some or all of the air supply bases from Imphal and eastern Bengal to Arakan.[1] Although operations could not be carried beyond the third phase unless extra aircraft could be provided, Slim proposed that planning and operations should continue for the time being on the assumption that all the operations would be possible; the situation should be re-examined some time in March by which time a decision could be reached on the feasibility of the fourth and fifth phases.

He summed up the major administrative implications of the operations as the provision of additional aircraft to lift slightly increased tonnages over longer distances, and the provision of additional administrative, engineer and signal units and, in particular, G.P.T. companies. It would be desirable, though not absolutely essential, that aircraft were available to lift 17th Division to Pakokku, to fly in and maintain one reserve division in emergency, and to train the troops for, and to mount, an airborne operation by a parachute brigade and one air-transported division against a south Burma port during April 1945. If the additional resources required, particularly aircraft, were not available, operations would have to be limited to the capture and consolidation of the line Meiktila-Yenangyaung.

When forwarding the appreciation to Leese, Slim wrote:

'I am confident that, if these comparatively small extra resources can be provided, there is every prospect of attaining the object. The enemy is still disheartened and disorganized, and provided that we can maintain the pressure, we may well inflict a major defeat on him. If, however, he is given time to recover, we may be forced to employ considerably greater forces after the 1945 monsoon to achieve the same object.

'I believe that the prize before us is of a value quite out of proportion to the few extra resources required to achieve it. I therefore request that the most strenuous efforts should be made to obtain these resources for the Fourteenth Army in time to enable the operation which I have proposed to be carried out.'

---

[1] See page 136 fn. 4.

Meanwhile on the 18th December, the day after he had sent Leese the summary of his revised plan, Slim met his two corps commanders, Messervy and Stopford, at Headquarters IV Corps in Tamu. Having brought them up to date with the latest information on the Japanese dispositions and the situation on the Northern front,[1] he issued verbal orders (confirmed in writing next day) for a rapid advance in co-operation with N.C.A.C. with the object of destroying the enemy forces in central Burma, to be followed by an advance to the general line Henzada–Nyaunglebin and the seizure of any opportunity to capture a south Burma port. The IV Corps was to move by way of the Myittha valley to Pakokku and establish a bridgehead across the Irrawaddy; it was then to seize Meiktila and its group of airfields and later be prepared to advance south on the Myingyan–Henzada axis. The XXXIII Corps was to take Monywa, occupy the Yeu–Shwebo area, where it was to repair captured airfields or construct new ones, and then capture Mandalay; later it was to advance down the Mandalay–Rangoon road to Nyaunglebin. To ensure that the Japanese, who were already in contact with 19th Division of IV Corps, would be convinced that the whole of 14th Army was advancing east from the Chindwin, the utmost secrecy in respect of the southward advance of IV Corps was to be maintained and steps were to be taken to deceive the enemy in every possible way.[2] As 14th Army held the initiative and the Japanese forces opposing it had suffered heavy loss, the corps commanders were to take risks which would not in other circumstances be justified in order to achieve a rapid advance.

The two corps were to regroup under mutual arrangements, and without holding up the advance, by the 26th December, on which date XXXIII Corps was to take command of all formations already across, or in the process of crossing, the Chindwin, and IV Corps of all formations west of the river.[3] The 28th (E.A.) Brigade, 255th Tank Brigade and 11th Cavalry (P.A.V.O.), newly-arrived from India, were to come under command of IV Corps, which was later to be reinforced by 17th Indian Division brought forward from India. The boundary between N.C.A.C. and 14th Army was to be the Irrawaddy from Tigyaing to Thabeikkyin, thence the road and track to Mogok and the Burma Road to Hsipaw and then southwards to Loikaw, the places named being in 14th Army's area. When regrouping had been completed the inter-corps boundary was to be the Chindwin to Myingyan and thence along the road eastwards to Myittha on the railway south of Mandalay, all inclusive to IV Corps

---

[1] See Chapters XIII and XIV.

[2] For details of the deception measures employed see pages 173–74 and Appendix 20.

[3] This regrouping could be carried out easily for it required no large movement of troops and entailed only 19th Division and 268th Brigade passing *in situ* from the command of IV to XXXIII Corps, and the Lushai Brigade, also *in situ*, passing from XXXIII to IV Corps.

but XXXIII Corps could make use of the Chindwin for operations. The Kalemyo–Pakokku road was to be improved sufficiently to pass IV Corps through and would not thereafter be maintained; the Kalewa–Yeu–Shwebo road was to be brought to a fair-weather standard only. Each corps was allotted its own airlift for dropped and landed supplies.[1] They were to make every effort to construct a temporary airstrip capable of taking C.46 aircraft every fifty miles and were to make the utmost use of the Chindwin River as a line of communication.

---

[1] The allotment in long tons a day was:

	To 31st Dec.	1st-15th Jan.	16th-31st Jan.
IV Corps	20	155	325
XXXIII Corps	433	408	463
	453	563	788

Sketch 4

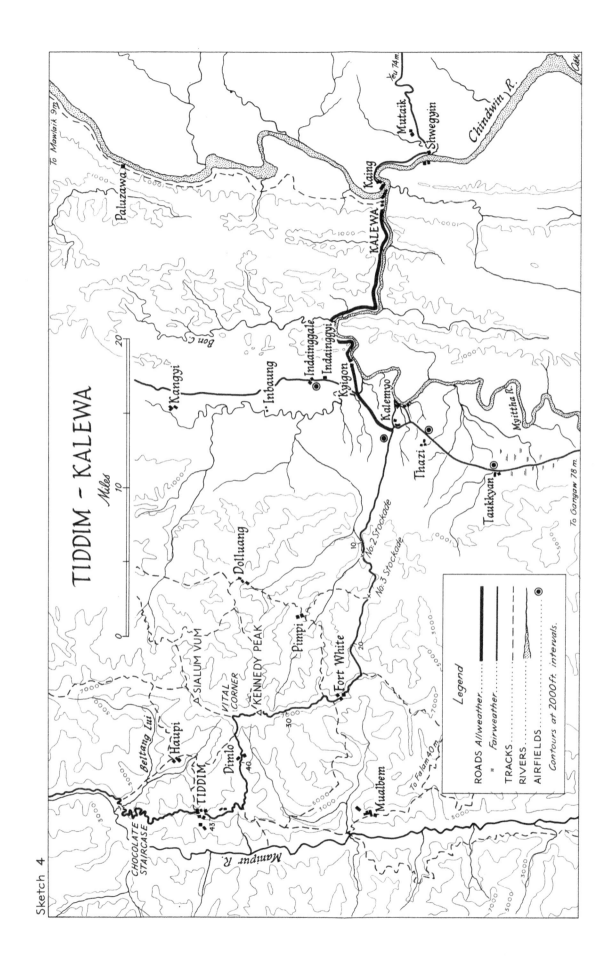

TIDDIM – KALEWA

Miles

Legend

| ROADS | Allweather.......... |
| | " Fairweather........ |
| TRACKS........................ |
| RIVERS......................... |
| AIRFIELDS...................... |

Contours at 2000 ft. intervals.

To Mawlaik 9 m.

Paluzawa

Bon C.

Kangyi

Inbaung

Indainggale

Indainggyi

Kyigon

KALEWA

Kaing

Mutaik

Shwegyin

Chindwin R.

Yu 74 m.

Creek

Kalemyo

Thazi

Myittha R.

Taukkyan

To Gangaw 78 m.

Dolluang

No.2 Stockade

No.3 Stockade

Pimpi

Fort White

SIALUM VUM

VITAL CORNER

KENNEDY PEAK

CHOCOLATE STAIRCASE

Beltang Lui

Haupi

TIDDIM

Dimlo

443

Mualbem

To Falam 40 m.

Manipur R.

CHAPTER XVI

THE CENTRAL FRONT

(December 1944–January 1945)

The Advance to the Irrawaddy

See Maps 1, 2, 3, 7 and 9 and Sketches 4, 10 and 14

O N the 19th December, when Slim's two corps commanders were preparing to put into effect his new orders for the advance to the Irrawaddy,[1] XXXIII Corps (Stopford) was deployed with the Lushai Brigade (Marindin) at Gangaw, 2nd Division (Major-General C. G. G. Nicholson) in the process of crossing the Chindwin at Kalewa with 6th Brigade half-way to Pyingaing (where there was known to be a considerable enemy force), and 20th Division (Major-General D. D. Gracey) with two of its brigades west of the Chindwin at Kalemyo and Khampat and 32nd Brigade across the river at Chingyaung with a battalion (4/10th Gurkhas) astride the Shwegyin–Yeu road eight miles east of Pyingaing.[2] The IV Corps (Messervy) had 268th Brigade (Dyer) in the vicinity of Yeshin in touch with XXXIII Corps in the Chingyaung area, and 19th Division (Rees) with its forward brigades on the general line Kangon–Wuntho–Nankan.[3] Contact between 19th Division and the right-hand N.C.A.C. division (36th), which was moving down the west bank of the Irrawaddy towards Tigyaing,[4] was being maintained by detachments at Kunbaung and Meza. The 7th Division at Kohima, with 114th Brigade forward at Tonhe, and 28th (E.A.) Brigade at Imphal were in IV Corps reserve. There was no contact with the enemy except at Gangaw, where the Lushai Brigade, which had no artillery support, had been unable to drive out a determined garrison, and east of Pyingaing where 4/10th Gurkhas had cut the Japanese line of communication to Yeu.

The general withdrawal of the Japanese *15th Army* was known to be continuing, *53rd Division* across the Irrawaddy at Tigyaing and *15th Division* towards Thabeikkyin, while considerable movement of troops and stores was reported to be taking place from Monywa to Pakokku.[5]

---

[1] See pages 168–69.
[2] See Map 1, facing page 15 and page 160.
[3] See pages 159–60.
[4] See page 145.
[5] See Map 3, facing page 55.

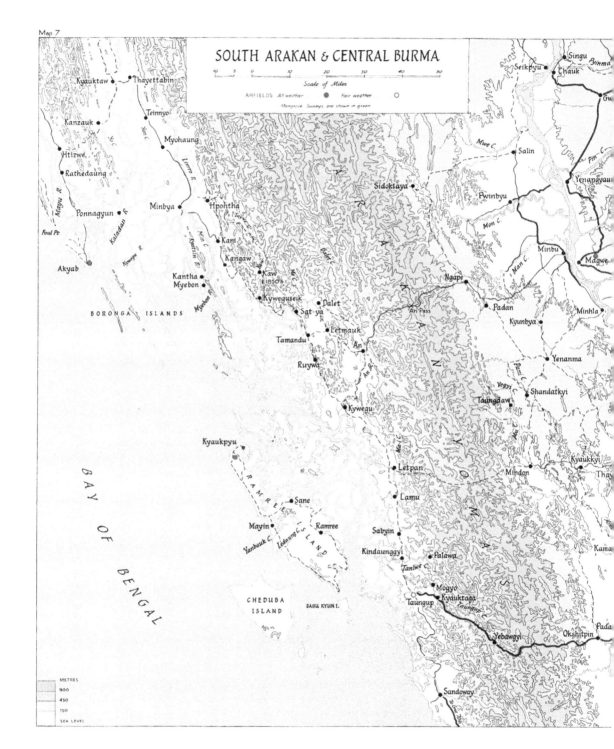

Map 7

SOUTH ARAKAN & CENTRAL BURMA

Scale of Miles

10   5   0   10   20   30   40   50

AIRFIELDS All weather ●   Fair weather ○

Mangrove Swamps are shown in green

BAY

OF

BENGAL

BORONGA ISLANDS

Foul Pt.

Akyab

Kyauktaw
Thayettabin
Kanzauk
Teinnyo
Htizwe
Rathedaung
Myohaung
Ponnagyun
Minbya
Hpohtha
Kani
Kangaw
Kantha
Myebon
Kaw
1850 ft.
Kyweguseik
Sgt·ya
Dalet
Letmauk
Tamandu
An
Ruywa
Kywegu

Kyaukpyu

Sane
Mayin
Ramree
Yanbauk C.

RAMREE ISLAND

Ledaung C.

CHEDUBA
ISLAND

SAGU KYUN I.

Sidoktaya
Pwinbyu
Mon C.
Ngape
An Pass
Padan
Kyunbya
Yenanma
Taungdaw
Shandatkyi

Letpan
Mindon
Lamu
Sabyin
Kindaunggyi
Palawa
Tanbwe C.
Mogyo
Kyauktaga
Taungup
Yebawgyi
Okshitpin

Sandoway

Seikpyu
Chauk
Singu
Byinma
Gw
Salin
Yenangyaung
Minbu
Magwe
Minhla
Kyaukkyi
Thay
Kama
Pada

METRES
900
450
150
SEA LEVEL

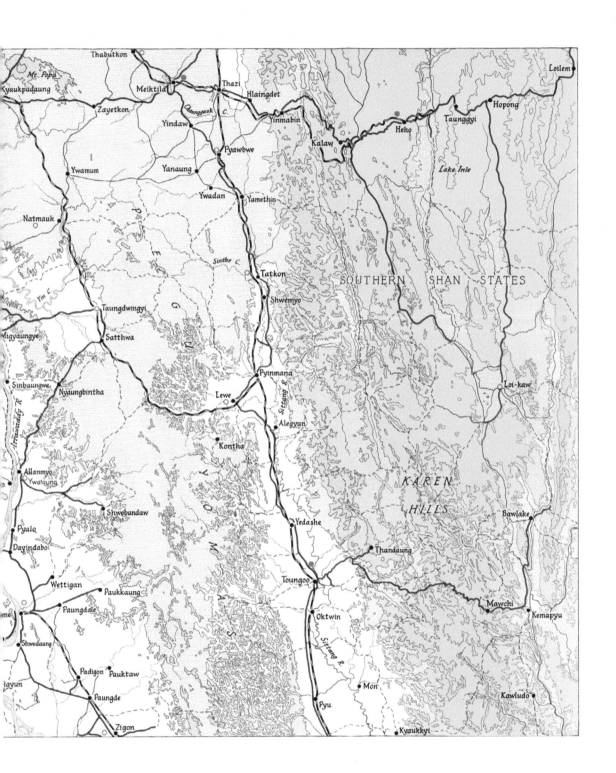

It was believed that the Japanese force at Pyingaing was *213th Regiment* from *33rd Division*. There was reliable information that a detachment from *31st Division* was moving westwards from Yeu towards it, and it was thought that the object of this move was to help the tired and depleted *33rd Division* to break contact.

Before describing the methods adopted by the corps commanders to carry out the tasks Slim had given them, it would be as well to take stock of the immediate administrative difficulties with which 14th Army had to contend during its advance to the Irrawaddy. The immediate task of IV Corps was to concentrate as quickly as possible at Pakokku, establish a bridgehead over the Irrawaddy and then bring the enemy to battle at Meiktila. The only available road from Kalemyo to Pakokku, some 230 miles long, was for the most part unmetalled, narrow and tortuous, with many steep hills, hairpin bends and bridges too weak to carry the necessary loads. The improvement of this road to take tanks on transporters and its maintenance while in constant use by the advancing formations and units posed the engineers a very difficult problem; one which could be solved only if they were given priority of movement and other traffic on the road was reduced to a minimum. Maintenance south of Taukkyan would therefore have to be entirely by air and, to make full use of the capacity of the available aircraft, landing grounds would have to be provided at suitable points along the road not more than fifty miles apart.[1] To avoid interference with the engineers, troops would have to march, ferrying by motor transport being resorted to only in emergency.

The immediate task of XXXIII Corps was to capture the weir at Kabo intact. This controlled the canal system throughout the Yeu–Shwebo plain which provided the only adequate source of water during the dry season. It was then to secure the Monywa–Yeu–Shwebo area and finally establish bridgeheads over the Irrawaddy for the attack on Mandalay.[2] This involved the corps in an advance on a broad front and meant that, once across the Chindwin, it would be dependent for its maintenance on supply-dropping (or supplies landed on temporary airstrips when possible) until the existing airfields at Budalin, Yeu, Shwebo and Onbauk were captured and brought into use. Furthermore, until the road from Kyigon to Yeu was open for the passage of heavy transport, the corps would have to operate temporarily without some of its administrative troops and most of its armour. The rapid improvement of the road to the required standard was therefore a matter of urgency. The engineers were faced with a problem of considerable magnitude, for the roads from Kyigon to Kalewa and from Shwegyin to Yeu had to be improved to take

---

[1] Kan and Tilin were selected as sites for airfields.
[2] See Sketch 14, facing page 314.

tank transporters and the road from Kaing to Shwegyin, some five miles in length, connecting the two had to be almost entirely reconstructed.[1] Until the road from Kaing to Shwegyin was in working order, all troops, guns and vehicles using this axis of advance would have to be ferried by DUKWs and I.W.T. craft from Kalewa to Shwegyin.[2]

By the time that Stopford and Messervy issued their orders implementing the new plan on the 20th and 21st December respectively, preliminary moves on verbal orders had already begun. Since the regrouping of the two corps was to come into effect on the 26th December, when all formations west of the Chindwin would pass to the command of IV Corps and those to the east of it or about to cross to the east to the command of XXXIII Corps, these orders were to take effect on that day.[3] The method of issue provides the background of the whole operation: those of XXXIII Corps were issued in the normal manner to headquarters of formations, but those of IV Corps, which was to move under a cloak of secrecy, were issued by name to only those officers who had to know the corps commander's intentions.

Messervy's intention was that either the Lushai Brigade (then facing Gangaw) or 28th (E.A.) Brigade should lead the advance so that the presence of 7th Division would remain unsuspected until it deployed to attack Pakokku and cross the Irrawaddy. The 255th Tank Brigade was to concentrate at Witok and remain there until called forward; it was then to move down the valley on transporters and the engineers were instructed to make the road fit for the passage of these vehicles by the 31st January.[4]

To preserve secrecy and ensure that the thrust towards Meiktila was a complete surprise, Slim had given instructions that there was to be wireless silence south of Kalemyo except for the link already working between XXXIII Corps and the Lushai Brigade, that intercommunication was to be by land line, air letter service and liaison officers in jeeps, and that, when Headquarters IV Corps moved to the

---

[1] For Kyigon and Kaing see Sketch 4, facing page 170. The existing road was narrow and winding with many weak bridges, including a timber catwalk built on piers on a cliff face overhanging the river, and steep gradients. It was impassable to two-wheel drive vehicles and even those with four-wheel drive had to be winched up the worst gradient. No new alignment was possible. The engineers had to traverse across the re-entrants to reduce the gradients, which involved much blasting. Seven new Bailey bridges had to be constructed, including one of 200 feet with a central pier to negotiate the catwalk. The reconstruction of the road in twenty-three days was an impressive feat.

[2] See Sketch 4, facing page 170. The road as far as Shwegyin was to be fit to take 3-ton vehicles and unloaded transporters by the 10th January. Between Shwegyin and Yeu the road was to be fit to take loaded transporters by the 18th to 22nd January, with the exception of the section eastwards from Pyingaing to the vicinity of Wainggyo which was to take only unloaded transporters.

[3] See page 168.

[4] See Map 1, facing page 15. The 17th Division, which was still in India at Ranchi, was to concentrate in January on the Imphal plain in readiness to be moved forward when required.

Myittha valley, a dummy headquarters was to remain in operation in the Tamu area to transmit all messages and orders by wireless between XXXIII Corps and those formations which had previously operated under the control of IV Corps; this station was to maintain a normal flow of messages and also transmit some 'slightly insecure' telephone conversations to 14th Army and XXXIII Corps. To supplement 14th Army's deception plans IV Corps prepared its own scheme ('Cloak'), designed to conceal the presence of the corps in the Myittha valley for as long as possible and then mislead the enemy as to its crossing place over the Irrawaddy and its objective.[1]

The deployment of XXXIII Corps, as well as that of 19th Division and 268th Brigade due to come under command on the 26th December, was well advanced and the new plan made little difference to its immediate task or dispositions except that Stopford resumed his advance on a three-division front. On the right, 20th Division was to capture Monywa and be ready to cross the Irrawaddy and attack Mandalay from the south;[2] in the centre, 2nd Division, in conjunction with 19th Division on its left, was to seize the Kabo Weir intact, and then secure the Yeu–Shwebo area with its airfields as quickly as possible preparatory to advancing south on Mandalay; and 19th Division was to continue its southward drive towards Shwebo astride the railway on a broad front and be prepared to establish a bridge-head across the Irrawaddy at Thabeikkyin for the passage of troops detailed to attack Mandalay from the north. The gap between 2nd and 19th Divisions was to be filled by 268th Brigade, which was to capture Kyunhla on the Mu River.[3] The 254th Tank Brigade which, less its detachments with 2nd and 20th Divisions, had not yet crossed the Chindwin, was to move to the Yeu–Shwebo area as soon as the road was capable of taking transporters.

The deployment of IV Corps on the other hand had not even begun, and the bulk of 7th Division was at Kohima. Messervy therefore made his first moves within a few hours of getting Slim's verbal instructions. The first need was to make the Myittha valley road fit to take the artillery required by the Lushai Brigade to support its attack on Gangaw, and subsequently to extend the road to enable 28th (E.A.) Brigade, 7th Division and 255th Tank Brigade to reach the forward concentration area at Kan.

On the 19th December 7th Divisional Engineers were moved in motor transport from Tonhe to Kalemyo. There they were joined by an Army Group Royal Engineers (A.G.R.E.), and began improving the road southwards. The 114th Brigade followed on foot. The 28th (E.A.) Brigade was ferried forward in stages, a battalion at a time

---

[1] See Appendix 20.
[2] See Map 3, facing page 55.
[3] See Map 1, facing page 15.

beginning on the 22nd, from the Imphal plain to Minthami and a few days later to the junction of the Myittha and Manipur Rivers where the engineers had established a ferry; from there it marched to Gangaw. At the same time 7th Division (Evans), less 114th Brigade and the divisional engineers, began to move from Kohima in motor transport behind the Africans to the ferry and thence on foot to Kan. The armour was concentrated at Witok, and the reconnaissance regiment (7/2nd Punjab) moved along the west bank of the Chindwin towards Kin with orders to gain and keep touch with the right of 20th Division, which was advancing down the east bank. These moves were delayed by a spell of heavy rain in the first week of January which flooded the Myittha valley, immobilized all motor transport and delayed the attack on Gangaw.

On the 10th, after Gangaw had been attacked for an hour and a half by four squadrons of B.25 medium bombers followed by one squadron of Thunderbolts and two squadrons of Hurricane fighter-bombers in a series of low-level strikes with bombs, cannons and rockets, the Lushai Brigade occupied the village without meeting opposition.[1] The 28th (E.A.) Brigade then passed through and occupied a position on the Me Chaung from its junction with the Myittha River to Kanthet to cover the concentration of 7th Division in the Kan–Gangaw area. By the 14th the concentration was complete, 7/2nd Punjab had reached Kuzeik and the Lushai Brigade had been withdrawn into army reserve, leaving the recently rejoined Chin Hills Battalion, and the Lushai Scouts and Chin Levies under command of 7th Division to operate in the hills on the flanks of the main advance.

While IV Corps was moving towards Pakokku, XXXIII Corps had been completing its deployment east of the Chindwin in preparation for its advance on Monywa and Shwebo. On the right, 20th Division (less 32nd Brigade already across the Chindwin north and east of Pyingaing) had crossed the river at Kalewa between the 24th and 26th December and moved to Maukkadaw. The 32nd Brigade had moved south to Palusawa, leaving 4/10th Gurkhas (under command of 2nd Division) closely engaged with the Japanese at Wainggyo. In the centre, 6th Brigade of 2nd Division, followed by 5th Brigade, had reached Pyingaing by the 24th and was preparing to attack the Japanese forces whose line of retreat had been cut by the Gurkhas at

---

[1] A procedure for joint land-air attacks on selected targets such as strongly defended enemy positions had been standardized during 1944. The technique adopted was to begin with a relatively heavy bombing attack. After this, fighter-bombers in low-level attacks with bombs, cannons and rockets dealt with the target area in sections, and finished with dummy attacks to keep the enemy pinned down as the ground forces made their final approach.

Wainggyo. The 4th Brigade had been kept back west of the river until 20th Division had crossed. By the 26th, 268th Brigade, in touch with 2nd Division on its right and 19th Division on its left, had established a base south of Yeshin and pushed patrols forward to Kyunhla, and 19th Division had reached the general line Thityabin–Letpanda.[1] It was on this date that both formations passed under command of XXXIII Corps.

When, however, 19th Division began to advance south from the Thityabin–Letpanda area it met with increasing resistance from enemy rearguards which fought resolutely, incurring comparatively severe losses and giving ground only when driven from their positions or to escape encirclement. The reason for this became evident when it was found that the rearguards were from *31st Division*; these were clearly holding prepared positions to enable *15th Division* to disengage and cross the Irrawaddy. The resistance was overcome on the 29th, Kanbalu and Sabanatha were occupied and by the 5th January the division had secured the Zigon–Male road.

The advance of 20th Division on Monywa was temporarily delayed when it was found that the country on the east bank of the Chindwin beyond Maukkadaw was trackless. Gracey therefore decided to cross the river, move down the west bank to within a few miles of Kin and then recross, leaving one battalion to continue down the west bank to make contact with 7/2nd Punjab of IV Corps. As soon as this move was completed the advance on Monywa began, led by 32nd Brigade (Mackenzie) with orders to clear Budalin on the way. The 100th Brigade (Brigadier C. H. B. Rodham), now at full strength with the return of 4/10th Gurkhas from Wainggyo, followed, while 80th Brigade (Brigadier S. Greeves), less its battalion moving down the west bank, remained in divisional reserve at Kin. On the 4th January 32nd Brigade ran into stiff opposition at Budalin.[2] An attempt to send a motorized column of infantry and carriers to seize Monywa by a *coup de main* had to be abandoned when its advanced guard was ambushed and most of its vehicles lost. On the 6th heavy rain set in which brought all motor transport to a standstill and prevented supplies being distributed from the dropping areas. Gracey ordered a standfast next day and placed the division on half rations. As a result Budalin (like Gangaw) was not cleared until the 10th. By this time the supply situation had returned to normal and the advance was resumed on a broad front, with 32nd Brigade directed on Monywa and the 100th on Ayadaw, while 80th Brigade moved up behind them. By the 14th January patrols were probing the defences of Monywa and

---

[1] During its advance from the Chindwin 19th Division, which had become widely dispersed laterally and in depth, had been maintained entirely by supply-drop. An airstrip was constructed at Kawlin and came into use on the 25th for air landing, since most of the division was by this date within the radius of its second-line motor transport from Kawlin.

[2] Identifications showed that the opposition was from *III/213th Battalion*.

Ayadaw, and 80th Brigade (less its battalion west of the river) had moved into Budalin.

On the 2nd Division front resistance in the Pyingaing area ceased on the 28th December, the retiring Japanese rearguards suffering severe losses from the Gurkha ambushes east of Wainggyo.[1] The 6th Brigade (Brigadier W. G. Smith) then pushed rapidly on to Kaduma from where, on the 31st, a detachment of 1st Royal Welch Fusiliers in armoured carriers with a half squadron of medium tanks and a company of engineers made a dash for the Kabo Weir, which they found intact. On the 1st January 2nd Reconnaissance Regiment seized Yeu airfield, but its main strip was so badly cratered that the engineers preferred to extend a dispersal strip rather than try to repair it. The 5th Brigade (Brigadier M. M. Alston-Roberts-West) now passed through and on the 2nd occupied Yeu, meeting with only sniping and sporadic shelling from the east bank of the Mu River where the Japanese had posts covering the destroyed bridge. During the next three days the Japanese rearguards were driven from the east bank after several sharp engagements, and a Bailey bridge was built across the river.[2] By the 5th, patrol contact with 19th Division was established at Kin-u and 268th Brigade took over the protection of the Kabo Weir.

That day Stopford ordered 2nd Division to advance from Yeu and take Shwebo. It was to be relieved there by 19th Division and was then to attack Mandalay from the north in co-operation with an advance by 20th Division from the west. The 19th Division was to occupy Kin-u, relieve 2nd Division at Shwebo, cross the Irrawaddy at Thabeikkyin and then advance on Mogok. It will be seen that this plan had to be considerably modified as a result of the speed of 19th Division's advance and the fact that 36th Division, the right-hand division on the Northern front, had been directed on Mogok.[3]

To comply with Stopford's orders, Nicholson sent 4th Brigade down the Yeu–Shwebo road to block the southern and western exits of Shwebo, while 5th Brigade advanced along the railway to attack the walled city from the north and 6th Brigade remained in reserve at Yeu. Rees sent 98th Brigade down the east bank of the Old Mu Canal to capture the airfield and the cantonment east of the city, and 64th Brigade to seize the airfield at Onbauk and then close the city's south-eastern exits; 62nd Brigade was to remain in reserve but send a

---

[1] The 4/10th Gurkhas picked up 110 Japanese dead during its operations. These identifications proved that *124th Regiment* of *31st Division* was in the area and not, as was thought, part of *33rd Division*. This regiment had in fact relieved *33rd Division* at Pyingaing in mid-December.

[2] From a captured document it was ascertained that a composite force had been formed to hold the Yeu bridgehead. This consisted of *I/124th Battalion*, a company and a half of *III/124th Battalion*, a mountain battery, two field guns and a platoon with an infantry gun from *58th Regiment*.

[3] See Chapter XVII.

battalion to capture Thabeikkyin. The spell of heavy rain which had delayed both IV Corps and 20th Division also delayed 2nd Division; the troops had to be put on half rations for a short time and it was not until the 8th January that the advance was resumed. The 98th Brigade co-ordinated its advance with 5th Brigade, but 64th and 62nd Brigades pushed ahead fast and, by-passing opposition, had by the 7th reached their respective objectives—Onbauk, where the airstrip was found to be of firm gravel and little damaged, and Thabeikkyin. During this advance *51st* and *60th Regiments* were identified, which indicated that the whole of *15th Division* had not yet crossed to the east of the Irrawaddy.

Rees had been told by Stopford that he could send patrols to and occupy Shwebo and Kyaukmyaung if they were found empty, so, at about 8 p.m. on the 7th, he gave Bain (64th Brigade) verbal orders to send his nearest battalion (5/10th Baluch) into Shwebo from the east. On the afternoon of the 8th, by which time the battalion was in position between the cantonment and the city and had patrols in both, he followed up his verbal order with a message telling Bain 'to put the troops of *31st Division* in Shwebo in the bag'. Bain thereupon told 1/6th Gurkhas to move at once to cut the road and railway south and south-east of the city and 5/10th Baluch to enter it next morning. Just as the Baluchis were about to move they were halted by Rees, who had been warned by Stopford that, as 5th Brigade (2nd Division) was to attack the city from the north on the 9th, 19th Division was to keep outside it and merely block its southern and eastern exits.

Having dispersed minor opposition, 5th Brigade reached the city's northern wall at 1 p.m. on the 9th. Supported by tanks, 7th Worcestershire Regiment advanced into it and by 4 p.m. had made contact with 5/10th Baluch. By nightfall the Worcesters with their accompanying tanks had reached the southern wall, encountering only occasional sniping, and the remainder of the brigade had occupied its northern half. Since at this time the nearest troops of 4th Brigade were still some five miles to the west, the south-west exits had remained open throughout the day and the Japanese garrison had been able to make good its escape.

On the 11th, while 2nd Division was mopping up the Shwebo area, 19th Division turned east. The 62nd Brigade (Morris), less its battalion at Thabeikkyin, drove a small Japanese detachment from Kyaukmyaung and established a post on the east bank of the Irrawaddy during the night. Meanwhile 98th Brigade (Jerrard) had taken over Thabeikkyin from the battalion of 62nd Brigade which had occupied it, and had begun operations against an enemy force which was found to be holding a bridgehead on the west bank of the Irrawaddy at Kabwet. On the 12th the build-up of the bridgeheads at Kyaukmyaung and Thabeikkyin began. The same day 64th

Brigade established the divisional firm base at Onbauk. In order to leave 98th Brigade free to establish a strong bridgehead at Thabeik-kyin, Rees sent the bulk of his divisional machine-gun battalion and his reconnaissance regiment to contain the Japanese force (*51st Regiment* of *15th Division*) at Kabwet until arrangements for its destruction could be made.

On the 12th Nicholson regrouped 2nd Division. To regain contact with the retreating enemy he formed a motorized column, concentrated 4th and 5th Brigades south and south-west of Shwebo and, on relief by 268th Brigade at Yeu, moved 6th Brigade forward to the north of Shwebo. Since west of the Irrawaddy neither 2nd nor 19th Division was in contact with the enemy, except at Kabwet, their regrouping was unmolested except for attacks by enemy aircraft which came into action in larger numbers than had been seen for some time. On the 13th, thirty aircraft raided Shwebo and twelve the airfield at Onbauk, where they destroyed four Dakotas on the ground. Daylight landings thereupon ceased and were not resumed till the 18th when fighter aircraft had been established at Tabingaung and air cover was available. The airfield was used, however, for night landings from the night of 14th/15th.

While in XXXIII Corps' sector 20th Division was closing in on Monywa, 2nd Division regrouping at Shwebo and 19th Division establishing bridgeheads at Thabeikkyin and Kyaukmyaung, IV Corps had secretly concentrated 7th Division in the Kan–Gangaw area, covered by 28th (E.A.) Brigade on the Me Chaung. By the 14th January the forward divisions of 14th Army were in a position to begin their final drive to the Irrawaddy and were planning the crossings which would place strong forces within striking distance of Meiktila and Mandalay.[1]

When 14th Army began the last stage of its advance to the Irrawaddy in mid-January, it was known that *215th Regiment* and a battalion of *153rd Regiment* were opposing the advance of 7th Division in the Myittha valley,[2] and that the rest of *33rd Division* was withdrawing astride the Chindwin towards Myingyan and Pakokku, while *31st Division* was in the Sagaing area and *53rd Division* about Mandalay with *15th Division* north of it in the Thabeikkyin–Kabwet area.[3] It was thought that elements of *2nd Division* were at Meiktila. Captured maps showed that a defended area existed eight miles north of Monywa and at Ayadaw and that another very extensive one stretched from Myinmu to the Sagaing hills, apparently designed for

---

[1] See Map 3, facing page 55.
[2] The *153rd Regiment* formed part of the *Katsu Force*. See page 59 and fn. 2.
[3] See Map 3, facing page 55.

a garrison of some ten battalions. There was also a defended area of about two square miles east of the Irrawaddy at Kabwet which was believed to contain *Headquarters 15th Division*.

On the 15th January Messervy issued verbal orders for IV Corps' advance to begin on the 19th. The 28th (E.A.) Brigade was to advance on Tilin followed by 114th Brigade, while 89th Brigade moved through the hills to Pauk by way of Kanthet to cut the road behind the Japanese should they decide to stand on the defile at the head of the Myittha valley between Tilin and Pauk. The Chin Levies were to operate in the hills on the right flank and both the Chin Hills Battalion and the Lushai Scouts on the left flank.[1] From Tilin 28th (E.A.) Brigade was to move south to Seikpyu and threaten a crossing of the Irrawaddy opposite Chauk and Yenangyaung, and 114th Brigade, passing through 89th Brigade, was to capture Pakokku in conjunction with 7/2nd Punjab advancing down the Chindwin valley. The 33rd Brigade was to remain at Kan to practise for the assault crossing of the Irrawaddy.[2]

On the 17th Slim gave Messervy a directive which carried the plan a stage further. Having captured Pakokku, the corps was to establish a bridgehead across the Irrawaddy and then seize Meiktila with its airfields.[3] If the destruction of the Japanese armies in Burma were to be achieved, speed, surprise and punch were essential to ensure that a striking force would reach Meiktila before the enemy could with-draw from the Mandalay area. As much as possible of 17th Division was therefore to move by road from the Imphal plain to the Kan–Pauk area in motor transport borrowed from 5th Indian and 11th (E.A.) Divisions, then in reserve in Assam. If necessary, Messervy was to arrange with the C.C.T.F. and 1st Air Commando to move some of the division's men and mules by air, and consider using gliders to assist his subsequent advance.

Messervy appreciated that, once across the Irrawaddy, he would enter the dry belt of Burma where the watering of animals would present such a problem that it would seriously impede his movements. On the other hand, the waterless plain between the Irrawaddy and Meiktila provided good going for tanks and motor transport. He therefore proposed that he should keep the motor transport offered on loan by Slim and put forward a suggestion, which was accepted, that 17th Division be reorganized with two brigades motorized and one transportable by air. Messervy had assessed his object as that of getting a force to Meiktila in time to cut off the Japanese withdrawing from Mandalay before the advance of XXXIII Corps

---

[1] The Chin Hills Battalion and the Lushai Scouts were left behind when the Lushai Brigade was withdrawn to India. The former had recently joined the brigade in relief of 7/14th Punjab.

[2] The airstrip at Kan was completed on the 16th January.

[3] See Sketch 14, facing page 314.

and, given this highly mechanized striking force, believed it could be done. On the 19th January he estimated that 7th Division must take Pauk by the 1st February, secure a bridgehead across the Irrawaddy (probably in the Nyaungu area) by the 15th and by the 19th expand it to a size capable of taking 17th Division and its armour. The concentration of 17th Division east of the Irrawaddy would have to be completed by the 22nd, and the drive on Meiktila begun the next day to get there by the 25th.[1] On the 20th January he issued the necessary operation instruction, in which he said that the reorganized 17th Division would begin to arrive at Pakokku on the 15th February. The 7th Division (Evans) was to seize Pauk by the 1st February and, not later than the 15th, establish a bridgehead over the Irrawaddy between Chauk and Pakokku suitable for the passage of 17th Division and its accompanying armour on its drive towards Meiktila. He allotted Evans a squadron of 16th Light Cavalry (armoured cars), a regimental group of 255th Tank Brigade and a medium battery, the last two following his advance but not to be used without reference to Headquarters IV Corps. Forward airfield engineers were to establish a corps airhead in the vicinity of Pauk.[2] When 17th Division had passed through the bridgehead, 7th Division was to advance to Seikpyu and the railway terminus at Kyaukpadaung and then send strong reconnaissance forces down the west bank of the Irrawaddy as far south as Yenangyaung. On the 20th detailed planning began for crossing the river and it was decided that the corps bridgehead should be at Nyaungu, from where motorable roads and tracks ran east, south-east and south. Since it was such an obvious place for a crossing, every form of deception was to be brought into play to disguise Messervy's intention.

The reorganization of 17th Division began on the 22nd January and, including training exercises, was completed by the 31st. The 48th and 63rd Brigades and most of the divisional troops dispensed with their animals and took over motor vehicles from 5th and 11th Divisions and from 99th Brigade, which then became an air-transported brigade with a small number of jeeps as its only land transport.[3] The divisional mountain artillery regiment and one field company were also reorganized so as to be air-transportable, giving up all their animals and vehicles except for a small number of jeeps.

Representatives from 14th Army, IV Corps, 17th Division, 221

---

[1] It will be seen that these timings were very closely adhered to.

[2] An airhead was established at an enlarged Japanese airstrip at Sinthe some fifteen miles east of Pauk.

[3] The 99th Brigade had joined the division at Ranchi when it was reorganized as a standard (instead of a light) division. The 5th Indian Division was later reorganized in the same way. In the meantime it was immobilized, a matter of little importance because it was rehabilitating and a high proportion of its men were on leave in India. Vehicles for its reorganization were provided by A.L.F.S.E.A.

Group R.A.F., the C.C.T.F. and Nos. 1 and 2 Air Commandos attended a conference on the 26th January at which IV Corps' plan was further developed. It was decided that the two air commandos would provide support for the corps with fifty Mustangs and seven Mitchell bombers, augmented from mid-February by fifty Thunderbolts;[1] 221 Group R.A.F. was thus freed to use its whole strength for tasks in support of 14th Army and XXXIII Corps. The 8th February was fixed as the target date for IV Corps' crossing of the Irrawaddy, and the 20th February for the advance on Meiktila by way of Welaung and Mahlaing by 17th Division (less 99th Brigade) and 255th Tank Brigade (less a regiment). As soon as a suitable airfield was available in the Meiktila area, 99th Brigade was to be flown in; gliders were to be used, if necessary, to bring forward airfield engineers, petrol and ammunition.

As had been hoped, 7th Division's advance continued undiscovered by the Japanese and no mention of it was made in the Allied Press. On the 22nd a small Japanese rearguard covering Tilin resisted for a short while and provided identifications of *I/214th Battalion*. The 89th Brigade, which had advanced without being detected, cut the road west of Pauk on the 25th and then turned east to secure the village and the crossings of the Yaw Chaung. The low ridge east of the chaung was secured on the 29th after some opposition and the Irrawaddy was at last in sight. By the end of the month 28th (E.A.) Brigade, with a field battery of 7th Division in support, had concentrated at Tilin in readiness to advance south to Seikpyu, 114th Brigade (less a battalion) had moved forward in rear of 89th Brigade in readiness to pass through it and take Pakokku,[2] 33rd Brigade had moved into Pauk and the airstrips at Kan and Tilin were in use. The 17th Division less 99th Brigade was under orders to leave Imphal for Kan on the 1st February, picking up 255th Tank Brigade (less its regiment with 7th Division) on the way.

By the middle of January the administrative situation in XXXIII Corps was far from satisfactory. Divisions were tending to outrun their communications and were short of petrol and ammunition. Many of its corps troops were still west of the Chindwin and some as far back as Imphal. This was due to several factors: the nature of the country and the speed of 19th Division's advance which meant it had to be maintained almost entirely by supply drop; the difficulties in getting the roads east of the Chindwin fit for heavy traffic which made 2nd and 20th Divisions dependent to a very great degree on air-

---

[1] These American squadrons were to receive instructions direct from Headquarters IV Corps and not through Headquarters 221 Group, R.A.F.

[2] A battalion of 114th Brigade (4/14th Punjab) had been sent to deal with a considerable enemy force confronting the Chin Levies in the hills north of Saw.

landed supplies; and the spell of bad weather, already referred to, which for a time prevented supplies being moved to the troops from forward airfields and dropping zones. 'Teething troubles' of the new C.C.T.F./C.A.A.T.O. organization sometimes prevented supplies being delivered in accordance with demands or in the right areas. There was in addition a general shortage of motor transport, which was aggravated by the heavy demands on it for the forward movement of R.A.F. units, and the airlift tonnage required by divisions and corps troops had been underestimated.[1] A fortnight was therefore needed to build up reserves and to concentrate the corps troops before any advance across the Irrawaddy could be contemplated. The Yeu airfield was brought into use on the 10th, Onbauk on the 12th, Shwebo on the 18th and Budalin on the 22nd January.[2] The Kaing–Shwegyin road was opened to 3-ton vehicles on the 7th and to tank transporters on the 15th January.[3] By the 18th the Shwegyin–Yeu road had been improved sufficiently to take heavy vehicles. Thus with the help of extra transport temporarily loaned by 14th Army and the fly-in of urgently required administrative troops,[4] the situation began to improve in the second half of the month. It was, however, evident that the forward concentration of the corps could not be completed much before the 7th February.

The operations of XXXIII Corps in the second half of January developed as planned with one significant modification. The knowledge that 36th Division on the Northern front had been given Mogok as its objective, that the Japanese had prepared extensive positions covering Sagaing and that they might have a striking force behind them awaiting an opportunity to deliver a counter-stroke induced Stopford on the 15th January to consider revising his original plans for 2nd and 19th Divisions. These had been for 2nd Division to attack Mandalay from the north and 19th Division to advance from Thabeikkyin on Mogok.[5] He now asked Nicholson and Rees to consider a plan whereby 2nd Division operated against the Sagaing position while 19th Division, in conjunction with an advance by 20th Division from the south-west, attacked the city from the north, leaving a brigade in the Singu area to protect its rear from interference by the Japanese opposing 36th Division. Next day Slim warned A.L.F.S.E.A. and XXXIII Corps that there were signs of a Japanese counter-offensive across the Irrawaddy with the Yeu–Shwebo area as its objective.

---

[1] The allotment had been fixed on the basis of 100 air-landed tons a day for a division and 50 a day for corps troops. Experience proved that the figures should have been 130 tons a day for both a division and corps troops.

[2] Onbauk was temporarily closed for daylight landings on the 13th. See page 179.

[3] See Sketch 4, facing page 170.

[4] The 14th Army, itself extremely short of transport, made 240 3-ton loads available and flew in two medical units and a reinforcement reception unit.

[5] See page 177.

Nicholson and Rees both said that they thought the new plan was feasible, and, after a conference with Slim at Yeu, Stopford confirmed it on the 17th. In his orders issued that day he said that no major offensive with armour could take place until 254th Tank Brigade had completed its forward concentration early in February. There would therefore be time before the offensive began to build up the administrative services; during this period 2nd Division could supply one and 19th Division two brigades by air, but all other formations (including 20th Division) were not to operate beyond the range of their own first- and second-line transport from the existing forward airheads.[1] His object was to capture Mandalay as soon as possible after the resumption of operations in February. Meanwhile forward troops were to maintain contact and the initiative. The 19th Division was to continue the development of the bridgeheads at Thabeikkyin and Kyaukmyaung, be prepared to hold them against powerful counter-attacks and be ready to advance in February on Mandalay from the north. The 2nd Division was to attack the Sagaing defences as soon as the armour came up,[2] threaten a crossing of the Irrawaddy north-west of Mandalay and be prepared to cross the Irrawaddy at a point to be selected later. The 20th Division was to capture Monywa, establish a brigade in the Myinmu area, where it was to threaten a major crossing, and be ready eventually to cross the river west of Myinmu early in February with the object of advancing on Kyaukse and isolating Mandalay from the south. The 150th Regiment R.A.C. (medium tanks), a troop of 7·2-inch howitzers and 268th Brigade were to remain in corps reserve.[3]

At the time this order was issued, the drive by 20th Division to the Irrawaddy was just gaining momentum. The 100th Brigade had by the 17th January surrounded Ayadaw and taken heavy toll of the garrison, which had had to fight its way out. The 32nd and 80th Brigades had by the 19th cut all the tracks leading out of Monywa and occupied the west bank of the river opposite the town. From the 18th Monywa had been subjected to heavy air attacks; these culminated on the 20th in an intensive attack lasting some ninety minutes by Thunderbolts and Mosquitos and a very effective rocket strike by Hurricanes. The 32nd Brigade then began to infiltrate into the town and by the 22nd it had been cleared. Meanwhile 4/10th

---

[1] See Appendix 19.

[2] At this time there was only one squadron of the Carabiniers forward with 2nd Division.

[3] The 20th Division was to be supported by a regiment of light tanks (7th Light Cavalry), headquarters and two squadrons of armoured cars (11th Cavalry), a troop of medium artillery and half the heavy anti-aircraft regiment (for use in long-range harassing fire); 2nd Division by a regiment of medium tanks (Carabiniers) and a troop of medium artillery; and 19th Division by a squadron of armoured cars (11th Cavalry), a battery of medium artillery and half the heavy anti-aircraft regiment. The supporting units came under command of their respective divisions as they arrived in the forward area.

Gurkhas, the leading battalion of 100th Brigade, had reached the Irrawaddy south of Myinmu, mopping up several enemy detachments on the way, and on the 22nd cornered a rearguard against the river. Many boatloads of Japanese trying to escape were sunk by small arms and mortar fire, and the astonishing spectacle was seen of a party of twenty-four Japanese soldiers apparently committing suicide by marching into the river in full equipment. Fire was not opened on them. Patrols fanned out east and west, making contact with a motorized column from 2nd Division at the Mu River bridge some ten miles to the north-east, and with 14/13th Frontier Force Rifles of the 4/10th's own brigade (100th) at Allagappa. From the 23rd to the end of the month the division systematically mopped up the northern bank of the Irrawaddy between the Chindwin and the Mu River, carried out reconnaissances and began training for the crossing, but for reasons of security not even patrols were for the time being allowed to cross the river.

The 2nd Division was out of contact with the enemy until the 21st when 4th Brigade, advancing south from Sadaung, was shelled. Ondaw was occupied without opposition on the 24th and contact made with patrols of the motorized column which was already in touch with 20th Division on the Mu River. On the 31st, 4th Brigade, with 2nd Dorsetshire Regiment of 6th Brigade under command and supported by a squadron of the Carabiniers, began its attacks on the Japanese positions covering Sagaing, the key points of which were the northern terminus of the Kyauktalon ferry, a fortified position on the Shwebo road some twelve miles north-west of Sagaing, and Saye. Despite heavy air and artillery bombardments, the first attack launched on the 31st failed to make progress. Meanwhile, on the left, units from 5th Brigade had met Japanese on the Irrawaddy near Thitseingyi on the 22nd. There was, however, no fighting and, to create the impression that preparations were being made for a crossing north-west of Mandalay, patrols were sent to collect boats as ostentatiously as possible.

Throughout the second half of January 19th Division was involved in almost continuous fighting to extend and consolidate its bridge-heads at Thabeikkyin (98th Brigade) and Kyaukmyaung (64th Brigade) and in destroying the Japanese bridgehead at Kabwet.[1] At Thabeikkyin and Kyaukmyaung there were minor actions and patrol clashes from the outset. It was not, however, until the 21st that the Japanese launched their first deliberate counter-attack at Kyauk-myaung, but by that time the bridgehead had been thoroughly con-solidated and the attack was thrown back.

By the 25th a striking force had been assembled by 98th Brigade to

---

[1] See pages 178–79.

destroy the Kabwet bridgehead.[1] Preceded by heavy air and artillery bombardment, the first attack was made on the 28th. Although the Mitchell bombers were off target, the low-level attacks by Thunderbolts, Hurricanes and Spitfires, thanks to good visibility and clearly defined targets, were most effective. By the 30th only one strongpoint, a massive walled pagoda, remained. This time, however, an infantry attack following a bombardment failed to make progress, but the Japanese had had enough. That night there was a tremendous explosion in the pagoda and dawn patrols found the position deserted.[2]

The 62nd Brigade relieved the 64th at Kyaukmyaung on the 27th and 28th and the infantry in the bridgehead was increased to five battalions.[3] No sooner had this relief been completed than an enemy counter-attack supported by artillery, including heavy field guns, nearly reached brigade headquarters before it was finally thrown back. The pursuit by part of the brigade reserve ended in hand-to-hand fighting far outside the bridgehead perimeter.

Throughout the retreat from Imphal and the Chindwin, intelligence reports received by Katamura (*15th Army*) on the Allied moves and dispositions were often incomplete, inaccurate and conflicting. As a result, he was unable to ascertain the whereabouts of 5th, 7th and 17th Divisions (in fact the whole of IV Corps) and came to the conclusion that 5th and 17th Divisions had suffered such severe casualties that they had been withdrawn from further operations. By mid-January all *15th Army* formations were more or less in their allotted positions along the Irrawaddy.[4] The construction of the proposed defences had, however, been much slower than expected; in most areas they were less than half finished and in some, such as Meiktila, Myingyan and Pakokku, they were scarcely begun.

By this time an Allied division, identified as 19th Indian, had established bridgeheads east of the Irrawaddy at Thabeikkyin and opposite Kyaukmyaung, despite local counter-attacks. The fact that each bridgehead was apparently held by about a brigade and that patrols were being pushed eastwards led Katamura to the conclusion that 14th Army's intention was that 19th Division, having crossed the Irrawaddy ahead of the rest of the army, which was approaching the

---

[1] This force consisted of 2nd Royal Berkshire Regiment, 11th Sikh Machine-Gun Battalion (less two companies), one company 1st Assam Regiment, one squadron 11th Cavalry (armoured cars), 1st Medium Regiment R.A., 240th Field Battery, one troop of anti-tank guns and a detachment of the Sea Reconnaissance Unit.

[2] This fighting cost 2nd Royal Berkshires, already seriously below strength, 100 officers and men.

[3] The 2nd Welch Regiment, 3/6th Rajputana Rifles and 4/6th Gurkhas (all from 62nd Brigade), 1/6th Gurkhas from 64th Brigade, 1st Assam Regiment (less one company) and a company of 15th Punjab Regiment.

[4] See pages 59–60.

river further west, would occupy the Monglong Range area in co-operation with the force, identified as 36th British Division, moving up the Shweli River towards Myitson.[1]

He decided, and *Burma Area Army* agreed, to exploit the possibility of driving in 19th Division's bridgeheads before they were firmly established. He therefore ordered *53rd Division*, which was in the process of withdrawing south from Mandalay to its allotted area near Kyaukse, to reverse its course, assemble at Madaya and take up a defensive position south of Kyaukmyaung, thus enabling *15th Division* to concentrate on the destruction of the two bridgeheads.[2] The divisions of *15th Army* were, however, so depleted that the strength of a regiment was now often down to that of a battalion. It therefore became necessary to use both *15th* and *53rd Divisions* for the counter-offensive against the bridgeheads. The *15th*, less *51st Regiment* holding Kabwet, was ordered to attack the bridgehead at Thabeikkyin, leaving a small detachment to aid the *53rd* in its attack on the Kyaukmyaung bridgehead. Katamura also ordered both *31st* and *33rd Divisions* to send forward strong fighting patrols to keep contact with 14th Army, delay its advance and interfere with its preparations for crossing the Irrawaddy, and *33rd Division* to send a regiment (*215th*) to Madaya as a reserve for the offensive against 19th Division's bridgeheads.

The attacks on the bridgeheads failed, as already described, and by the end of the month *15th Division* had lost about one-third of its already depleted strength, *53rd Division* had suffered severe casualties and *51st Regiment* had been forced to withdraw from Kabwet across the river. By this time the threat of a crossing in strength by 14th Army south-west of Mandalay had increased, and Katamura felt obliged to abandon any further offensive action north of the city and turn his attention to meeting this greater threat. He therefore ordered *15th Division* to continue its efforts to contain the Kyaukmyaung bridgehead, *53rd Division* to move to the Kyaukse area, a strong force from *31st Division* to concentrate in the vicinity of Mandalay, *33rd Division* to concentrate in the hills south of Myinmu and a composite force, mainly consisting of airfield and administrative units, to be organized for the defence of Meiktila. He suggested to *Burma Area Army* that he should be reinforced by *2nd Division*, that the Pakokku–Myingyan sector should be transferred to *28th Army* and that *33rd Army's* front should be contracted so that *18th Division* could be transferred to his army.

Meanwhile Kimura (*Burma Area Army*) had on the 17th January ordered *2nd Division* (less one regiment) then at Toungoo to move to Meiktila to deal with any airborne assault on the town and to be

---

[1] See Map 2, facing page 39.
[2] See Map 3, facing page 55.

readily available to take part in any counter-offensive which the army might have to undertake.[1] On the 28th January, however, an order was received from *Southern Army* to the effect that *2nd Division* and *5th Air Division* were to be transferred at once to Indo-China.[2] The withdrawal of *2nd Division* as well as airfield base units at Meiktila not only depleted the garrison of that town but completely upset the Japanese plans for the whole area.

At the end of January, as a result of the pending move of the bulk of *2nd Division* and Katamura's decision to abandon the offensive north of Mandalay, *53rd Division* was on its way, for the second time, to Kyaukse; *15th Division* was left on its own to contain the Kyauk-myaung and Thabeikkyin bridgeheads; *31st Division*, leaving two battalions in the Sagaing area, had withdrawn to the left bank of the Irrawaddy to positions running from Taukyit westwards to Kyigon;[3] *33rd Division* on its left had *213th Regiment* at and north of Myingyan, the *214th* (with a battalion of the *215th* under command) at Pakokku with a battalion forward at Kanhla, and the rest of *215th Regiment* (recently returned from Madaya) at Nabaung behind the junction of *31st* and *33rd Divisions*.[4] The *28th Army* was responsible for the area west of Pakokku and had *72nd I.M.B.* and the *Katsu Force* in the Yenangyaung oilfields area and an *I.N.A.* regiment in the Nyaungu–Pagan area.[5]

By the 1st February the forward troops of 14th Army were in sight of or on the Irrawaddy from Myitche (twenty-five miles north of Chauk) to Thabeikkyin (sixty miles north of Mandalay), but there were two Japanese-held enclaves at Pakokku and Sagaing which were about to be attacked by 7th and 2nd Divisions respectively. The commanders of 7th and 20th Divisions had begun their detailed planning for assault crossings, 19th Division had made its two bridgeheads north of Mandalay almost impregnable against any force the Japanese could send against them, and the motorized 17th Division, with its

---

[1] For Toungoo see Map 7, facing page 171.

[2] See page 229. The whole of *2nd Division* did not in fact go to Indo-China: *16th Regiment* and one artillery battalion remained in Burma. The regiment (less *II/16th Battalion*) became known as the *Aoba Force*. The *II/16th Battalion* was attached to *53rd Division*. Part of *4th Infantry Regiment* also stayed in Burma. The move of *5th Air Division* began early in February but was spread over several months; *4th Air Brigade*, with *64th Air Regiment* and elements of *8th* and *81st Air Regiments*, did not actually leave Burma until about the end of April, but was gradually forced to operate from airfields in Siam.

[3] See Map 9, facing page 320.

[4] On the 22nd January *215th Regiment* had been placed under the direct command of *15th Army*, withdrawn from the Myingyan area and sent to Madaya but, on arrival there, it had been immediately ordered to return and rejoin its own division. It reached its new area on the 31st. The average strength of its battalions at this time was one hundred men and the regiment had only three medium machine-guns, two battalion guns and one regimental gun.

[5] For the dispositions of the Japanese between Saw and Myitson as known to 14th Army on the 1st February 1945 see Sketch 10, facing page 274.

powerful armoured component, was on its way to its forward concentration area. Slim had achieved complete strategic initiative. Screened by the Irrawaddy and by the possession of air superiority, he could strike where and when he liked on the front of some 200 miles, and it is evident from the moves and counter-moves described in the preceding paragraphs that this fact was already causing uncertainty in the minds of the Japanese commanders.

21. Major-General D. F. W. Warren, 5th
Indian Division (killed in an air accident
February 1945)

22. Air Vice-Marshal S. F. Vincent,
221 Group R.A.F

23. Admiral Lord Louis Mountbatten addressing troops

24. Lieut.-General Sir Montagu Stopford, XXXIII Corps, Lieut.-General Sir William Slim, 14th Army, and Major-General C. C. Fowkes, 11th (E.A.) Division, at Tamu

25. Manipur River bridge, the cable ferry

26. Ropeway across the flooded Beltang Lui

27. The Chocolate Staircase, Tiddim

28. The Stockades area, Tiddim–Kalemyo Road

29. Laying 'Bithess' on the Kabaw Valley Road

30. Ramped Cargo Lighter (post-war photograph taken at Singapore)

31. The Kalewa boat factory

32. Bailey pontoon bridge at Kalewa

33. L.5 aircraft on Kalewa airstrip

34. DUKWs crossing the Chindwin near Shwegyin

35. The Catwalk, Kalewa–Shwegyin Road

36. The Yeu Road near Pyingaing

CHAPTER XVII

THE NORTHERN AND SALWEEN FRONTS

(December 1944–January 1945)

See Maps 2 and 3 and Sketch 11

IN the middle of December 1944, as a result of the move of 14th and 22nd Chinese Divisions from N.C.A.C. to China, Sultan had to regroup his forces and revise his plans.[1] The 22nd Division was to have played a major part in his operations as the pivot of a swing to the east from Si-u to cut the old Burma Road behind the Japanese *33rd Army*, which was opposing the advance of the Yunnan armies in the Wanting area.[2] The right flank of this swing was to have been covered by 36th British Division's southward advance along the east bank of the Irrawaddy and up the Shweli valley on Mongmit and Mogok, with Kyaukme as its final objective, while the Chinese First Army (30th and 38th Divisions) captured Namhkam and linked up with XI Chinese Army Group at Wanting.[3] It was then to have opened the road to China by driving the Japanese away from the junction of the old Burma Road with the Bhamo road, which by this time had been linked to the Ledo Road.

Sultan came to the conclusion that, by substituting Mars Force for 22nd Division and filling the gap between it and 36th Division with 50th Chinese Division, he could carry out his original intention; he would, however, be left with a very small reserve, but this was a reasonable risk in view of his immense superiority. His new plan therefore left 36th Division with its task unaltered, while 50th Division, which had been following it, came up on its left flank and was directed on Lashio. On its relief at Si-u by 50th Division, Mars Force was to move east across the mountains and middle reaches of the Shweli River, by way of Mongwi, to cut the old Burma Road south of Namhpakka. The Chinese First Army was to occupy the upper Shweli valley between Namhkam and Wanting, clearing both those places and then disposing itself so that traffic could begin to move to China along the Burma Road as soon as battle damage to the road had been repaired.

---

[1] See page 148.

[2] See Map 2, facing page 39.

[3] The XI Chinese Army Group consisted of four armies, with a numerical strength about equal to four British divisions. See page 147 fn. 2.

To assist the offensive on the Northern front, Force 136 introduced nine special groups behind the Japanese lines during December 1944 and January 1945.[1] Three of these operated in the Hsenwi–Lashio area until it was occupied by N.C.A.C. forces;[2] the Kachin Levies they had raised were then handed over to the Civil Affairs Organization. Three other groups operated in the Shan States between the Burma Road and the Thazi–Loilem road and another three east of the Salween River;[3] these six groups raised between them some 1,400 Shan and Lahu Levies, sent back intelligence of particular value to 10th U.S.A.A.F. and fought a number of minor actions on the enemy's lines of communication.

At the time that Sultan's new plan came into being, 36th Division was advancing south, with 29th Brigade moving down the Irrawaddy valley on Twinnge and 72nd Brigade moving up the Shweli valley on Myitson, followed by 26th Brigade in reserve; 50th Chinese Division had started on its way to Si-u, where the bulk of Mars Force had already relieved 22nd Chinese Division with a view to taking over its task; and 30th Chinese Division had been ordered to move at once on Namhkam with its flanks protected by regiments of 38th Chinese Division.[4] The 90th Regiment was to lead the advance; it made, however, no attempt to do so, and it was not till the beginning of January, when General Sun Li-jen (the army commander) was persuaded to supersede its commander, that it began to move.

By this time the forward brigades of 36th Division had reached Tagaung on the Irrawaddy and Kunchaung on the Shweli without meeting any opposition; 50th Chinese Division had relieved Mars Force at Si-u but the Chinese First Army had still not advanced south of Namyu, twenty miles north-west of Namhkam. Despite the obvious inferiority of the Japanese forces opposing them and requests by both Sultan and Wedemeyer that the Chinese commanders should resume the advance, XI Chinese Army Group had not moved for a month and had made no attempt to capture Wanting. The reluctance of the commanders of the Chinese Yunnan armies to advance may well have been due to the fact that once they crossed the border they came under command of S.E.A.C., while the commander of the Chinese First Army may possibly have been disinclined to commit himself until XI Chinese Army Group had moved and the advance of the right wing

---

[1] These special groups each consisted of two British officers, one British other rank, two wireless operators and some fifteen Burmese. Unlike the Jedburgh teams, they were expected to defend themselves.

[2] See Chapter XXIV.

[3] See Map 3, facing page 55.

[4] See Map 2, facing page 39.

of N.C.A.C. had brought it within striking distance of *33rd Army's* communications on the Kyaukme–Lashio road.

The main task of *33rd Army* (Honda) was to prevent the junction of N.C.A.C. and the Yunnan forces. To implement it Honda had *56th Division* in the Wanting area opposing the Yunnan armies, the *Yamazaki Force* at Namhkam opposing the advance of the Chinese First Army and *18th Division* (less one regiment) in the Mongmit area to cover his communications to Mandalay against forces known to be in the lower reaches of the Shweli River.[1] The *4th Regiment* (*2nd Division*) and *168th Regiment* (*49th Division*), each using the code name and call signs of their respective divisions to mislead Allied Intelligence, were in reserve, but were well back near Hsenwi in case Kimura needed them at short notice for *Burma Area Army* reserve.

At the beginning of January the Yunnan armies and First Army at last began to close in on Wanting from north and west. Part of XI Chinese Army Group by-passed the strong defences covering Wanting by moving west along the Shweli River with the intention of crossing it north of Mongyu and then striking south at that town, which lay at the junction of the old Burma Road with the Ledo Road. Owing to poor security the plan became known to Honda and he took steps to meet the threat by sending *168th Regiment* forward to Mongyu and placing it under command of Matsuyama (*56th Division*). He also moved *4th Regiment* forward to Namhpakka from where it could be moved quickly to support either the *Yamazaki Force* at Namhkam or *168th Regiment* at Mongyu, but kept it for the time being under his own command. At the same time Matsuyama ordered *148th Regiment* to move from its positions north-east of Wanting to the Shweli River west of the town, where he knew the Chinese were intending to cross. It attacked the Chinese as they crossed the river and drove them back in some disorder; as a consequence the Allied offensive again came to a halt which lasted for a week.

The Chinese commanders evidently failed to realize why their every move was being met and did nothing to improve their security. Their new plans thus soon became known to Honda who, realizing that an overwhelming force was closing on *56th Division* and its communications, decided that an early withdrawal was inevitable. To ensure co-ordination he now placed *4th Regiment* at Namhpakka and the *Yamazaki Force* at Namhkam under command of *56th Division*, and gave Matsuyama permission to withdraw as soon as his positions were no longer tenable but before there was a risk of any part of his forces being cut off and destroyed.

By the middle of January the Chinese First Army had surrounded

---

[1] For the composition of the *Yamazaki Force* see page 146.

Namhkam and the Japanese rearguard had to fight its way out. At the same time XI Chinese Army Group finally overwhelmed the Wanting defences and compelled Matsuyama to order withdrawal to the Namhpakka area. By the 18th January the Japanese forces on the old Burma Road (about 16,000 strong, excluding administrative personnel) were disposed between Mongyu and Namhpakka with Mars Force and First Army closing in on them from the west and XI Army Group stationary, but in overwhelming strength, to their north. This was in itself a critical position but, in addition, Honda was aware by this time of the increasing threat to his communications with Mandalay arising from 36th Division's advance in the Shweli River valley and the establishment of bridgeheads by 14th Army at Thabeikkyin and Kyaukmyaung.[1]

After an advance through difficult mountainous country, Mars Force reached the hills overlooking the Burma Road immediately south of Namhpakka on the 18th January and began to harass the Japanese communications between that village and Hsenwi, but made no attempt to place itself squarely astride the road and cut it. On the 20th January, finding Wanting deserted, First Army made contact with XI Army Group. The next few days were devoted to a ceremonial opening of the road and the gathering of a convoy and a large group of Press reporters, all ready to push through to Kunming as soon as the Japanese heavy field artillery shelling the road could be silenced.[2] The first 'official' convoy to Kunming by the old Burma Road left Wanting on the 28th January and arrived at Kunming on the 4th February with some 105 and 75-mm. guns and supplies, to be welcomed with a civic reception followed by a banquet.[3] As a result of the capture of Wanting, the Generalissimo on the 22nd January ordered the Yunnan armies to withdraw across the border into China and to take no further part in the fighting in Burma, thus ending the Salween campaign. Of that campaign it might be said that never had such a large army remained so inactive before so small an enemy force for so long; its ending, however, made little difference to the war in Burma. It now became the task of First Army to move south down the road towards Lashio to make contact with 50th Chinese Division and 36th British Division making for Hsipaw and Kyaukme respectively.

The presence of Mars Force in the hills overlooking the Burma

---

[1] See Chapter XVI.

[2] Although the 483-mile-long road from Ledo to Wanting was first used for through traffic to China in January and by pipeline construction gangs, it was not metalled throughout and finally completed till the 20th May 1945.

[3] In the meantime a B.B.C. world-wide broadcast had been made announcing the arrival of a convoy at Kunming on the 20th January. The confusion had arisen from the arrival of a few trucks under command of an American lieutenant; they had made their way with difficulty by a track through Tengchung which had been improved by large numbers of Chinese labourers and was never again used.

Road south of Namhpakka, a large supply-drop on the 24th January and the increasing pressure from the Chinese divisions from the north made Matsuyama (*56th Division*) decide that the position of his division and attached formations was critical.[1] That night he told Honda (*33rd Army*) that he proposed to destroy the bulk of his ammunition and withdraw towards Hsenwi. Honda did not consider the situation sufficiently serious to justify such drastic action, and ordered Matsuyama to hold on to his existing positions until all his casualties and ammunition had been evacuated. At the same time he sent a staff officer with a convoy of some forty vehicles loaded with petrol to Namhpakka to assist in the evacuation. Aware of the movement during the night, Mars Force opened fire on the road, but the convoy got through with the loss of only one vehicle. Thus encouraged, the Japanese beat off several attempts by the Chinese to block the road immediately north of Namhpakka and succeeded in the next few days in evacuating about 1,000 casualties and a considerable quantity of ammunition. The position of *56th Division* became, however, more parlous as each day passed and the Chief of Staff of *33rd Army*, when visiting Namhpakka on the 30th, gave Matsuyama permission to withdraw. The retirement began on the night of the 31st January/1st February and by the 4th February the division had disengaged, passing down the Burma Road within sight of Mars Force. By the 10th, it had regrouped with *113th Regiment* near Namtu, *146th Regiment* at Hsenwi and the rest of the division at Lashio. The *4th, 55th* and *168th Regiments* were then returned to their respective formations, *2nd, 18th* and *49th Divisions*.[2]

Further west, the advance of 36th Division and of 50th Chinese Division on its left met with no opposition until the 18th January, when 29th Brigade (Brigadier G. E. R. Bastin) found a small force of Japanese north of Twinnge;[3] though by-passed, the enemy fought stubbornly for several days. This delayed the left wheel of the brigade, whose task was to advance on Mongmit from the west while 72nd Brigade, moving south along the east bank of the Shweli River, approached it from the north. On the 19th, 72nd Brigade, moving south from Mabein, also began to encounter small but determined enemy rearguards whose task was obviously to delay its advance. Japanese patrols were also very active throughout the area: the most significant clash was when a patrol of 26th Brigade, working east to cover the left flank of 72nd Brigade and make contact with 50th Chinese Division in the Shweli River valley south of Si-u, killed several men of *114th Regiment* in a small but fierce action, thus

---

[1] The Japanese assumed that the supply-drop signified the landing of a large airborne force to reinforce Mars Force.

[2] The combatant strength of *56th Division* at this time was about 9,000, that of *4th Regiment* was 1,000, *55th Regiment* 1,300 and *168th Regiment* 1,500.

[3] Bastin took over command of 29th Brigade from Stockwell on the 9th January 1945.

obtaining the first definite confirmation of *18th Division's* presence in that area. On the 20th Festing told 72nd Brigade to secure a bridge-head across the Shweli at Myitson; 29th Brigade, after mopping up at Twinnge, was to co-operate by moving east on either Mongmit or Mogok as ordered by himself, the decision depending on the speed of 72nd Brigade's advance after crossing the river at Myitson.

Slowed up by active Japanese rearguards, 72nd Brigade reached Bahe on the 25th, where 26th Brigade (Brigadier M. B. Jennings) passed through and took up the advance. By the 31st its leading battalion (2nd Buffs) had reached the bend in the Shweli River north of Myitson. Patrols of other battalions of the brigade, operating wide on the flanks, had already been in action to the east with patrols of *113th Regiment* of *56th Division*, but it was believed that not more than one battalion of that division was in the area. Mounting resistance, however, indicated that the Japanese would oppose the crossing of the river which at Myitson formed a formidable obstacle 400 yards wide and four to five feet deep with a 3-knot current. Hopes rose, however, when on the night of the 31st patrols sent to an island one mile to the east of the ferry and the south bank beyond it found un-occupied enemy positions.[1] To take advantage of this unexpected situation an attempt at infiltration in strength was immediately made by 2nd Buffs, supported by a field company, but it quickly ran into difficulties since the Japanese had in the meantime reoccupied the positions and could call on powerful artillery support.[2] The company which landed on the south bank became isolated. An unsuccessful attempt was made to reinforce it but some boats were sunk by gun-fire and others were swept downstream. Eventually it was with difficulty withdrawn by night. The action caused the Buffs and engineer troops 114 casualties (including sixty-two killed and missing), a very high proportion of those engaged. Meanwhile 29th Brigade, moving east from Twinnge, had also begun to meet determined opposition. It was becoming quite evident to Festing that a considerable enemy force was barring the way to Mongmit from north and west and that on his left 50th Chinese Division, which was advancing from Si-u towards Lashio, though unopposed, was making little progress.

By the beginning of February N.C.A.C. was still some way from completing its task for the second phase of 'Capital'—the occupation of Mogok, Mongmit and Lashio.[3] In making his plans for the capture

---

[1] See Sketch 11, facing page 282.

[2] It seems possible that this was an example of the suspected Japanese ruse of leaving positions unoccupied but watched by carefully concealed observers who reported when patrols examined the positions. As soon as the patrols withdrew, the Japanese would occupy the defences in the hope—more often than not fulfilled—of surprising their unsuspecting opponents as they moved in.

[3] See page 108.

and consolidation of that area, Sultan's problem appeared to be rendered more difficult by the withdrawal of the Yunnan armies into China, which meant that N.C.A.C. would have to accept responsibility for the area from Lashio to the China border. This was not, however, as serious a matter as it might have been, for the massive pressure of 14th Army was already making it essential for the Japanese to concentrate the maximum force in central Burma. Nevertheless, Honda could feel satisfied that, although withdrawal was inevitable in the near future, he had, with greatly inferior forces, kept the N.C.A.C. and Yunnan forces apart for eight months.[1]

---

[1] Since the Yunnan armies crossed the Salween in May 1944, the overall numerical Chinese superiority had been in the ratio of about 8:1, and at times locally (e.g. at Lungling) it had been considerably greater.

CHAPTER XVIII

HIGH LEVEL AND ADMINISTRATIVE PLANS

(December 1944–January 1945)

See Maps 1, 7, 10 and 11 and Sketches 14, 20 and 21

BY the end of December 1944 the administrative plan for the maintenance of 14th Army in central Burma during the latter phases of the original 'Capital' was well advanced. The fair-weather road down the Kabaw Valley had reached Kalewa and a track was under construction connecting the new Bailey pontoon bridge to the Shwegyin–Yeu fair-weather road;[1] the L. of C. Transport Column was operating from Dimapur to Kalewa;[2] and an advanced depot at Indainggyi had been opened to maintain the troops in the Kalewa area and to hold part of the Central Burma Stockpile in readiness for forwarding by road to the Shwebo area. Work on the new all-weather bithess road ninety-five miles long from Tamu to Kalewa was progressing at the rate of about one mile a day, and the new airfields at the southern end of the Kabaw Valley were in action.

A beginning was being made in the build-up of an I.W.T. service on the Chindwin which was eventually to carry some 700 tons a day downstream to Myingyan, about 200 miles to the south. Prefabricated boats were to be sent forward in sections by rail and road or by air from Calcutta for reassembly at a suitable site on the banks of the Chindwin upstream from Kalewa, where timber was close at hand to build river craft. The necessary I.W.T. units for setting up a ship-yard, reassembling and building boats and for operating the service were also being brought forward. So that the Bailey equipment could be released for use in the forward areas and I.W.T. craft allowed a free passage on the river, the original Bailey pontoon bridge at Kalewa was to be replaced by a new pontoon bridge (known as the Falls bridge) which had a central span giving

---

[1] See Map 1, facing page 15.

[2] During December the L. of C. Transport Column had delivered 34,500 tons of stores to Imphal, 15,000 to Palel, 20,000 to Tamu, 6,500 to Indainggyi and some 300 tons to the Kalewa–Kalemyo area. The greater part of the tonnage carried down the Kabaw Valley was lifted from Palel. The vehicle mileage rose from 5·1 million miles in November to 6·33 in December. The number of 5- and 10-ton vehicles available had risen to twenty-eight per cent of the total fleet, thus greatly increasing the potential lift.

fifteen feet clearance above water level. Work on these projects and on the salvaging of sunken craft and the buoying of the channel was expected to begin about the 1st January 1945. The conception of the project showed great foresight in planning, and the creation of an I.W.T. fleet in the upper reaches of Burma's river system demanded a degree of extemporization seldom surpassed in the history of war.[1]

The receipt of Slim's plan for 'Extended Capital', in which the main battle was to be fought south of Mandalay instead of on the Shwebo plain,[2] and which offered a reasonable prospect of Rangoon being captured before the monsoon set in, posed both A.L.F.S.E.A. and S.E.A.C. new and difficult administrative problems. It was immediately evident that the tonnage which could be delivered by road from Dimapur through Imphal and Kalewa would decrease the farther 14th Army penetrated southwards and so lengthened the turnround; the greater therefore would be the army's dependence on air supply. But, as the economic range of transport aircraft was only some 250 miles, 14th Army would clearly soon pass beyond the economic limit of aircraft based on the Imphal plain and the eastern Bengal airfields.[3] Thus, if it were to be maintained in the Meiktila area and during its subsequent advance along the railway and river towards Rangoon, air bases would have to be moved further forward.

The economic range of aircraft based on Imphal extended to Myingyan and Mandalay, and that of aircraft based on the Chittagong group of airfields (Hathazari, Chittagong and Dohazari) extended as far as Magwe and Myingyan. To maintain 14th Army during the third phase of 'Extended Capital', the air bases at Agartala, Feni and Comilla would therefore have to be replaced by others in the Chittagong area. The occupation of Akyab on the 4th January fortunately meant that, when airfields had been built on the island, aircraft could operate economically as far south-east as the general line Henzada–Toungoo. To bring Rangoon within the economic range of transport aircraft, it would be necessary to have airfields on Ramree Island. Considering that the island should be occupied without delay, Leese ordered his administrative staff, in co-operation with Eastern Air Command, to prepare plans for the redeployment of the transport squadrons and supply bases, making full use of both Akyab and Ramree.

At the same time Leese told Mountbatten that with the transport aircraft at his disposal he could not maintain 14th Army beyond Shwebo. If, however, two of the combat cargo squadrons sent to

---

[1] For full details see Appendix 16.
[2] See Sketch 14, facing page 314.
[3] See Appendix 6 and Sketch 20, facing page 412.

China were returned by the 1st February and the third by the 15th February and if, to make up the loss in the forward stocking programme arising from the absence of three squadrons during January, an additional squadron were made available by the 1st March, he could maintain 14th Army up to the general line Chauk–Thazi–Mandalay; this would include Meiktila where Slim intended to fight his main battle in March.

At a meeting with Leese at Kandy on the 9th January, Mountbatten approved his proposal for a further advance down the Arakan coast and the construction of an all-weather airfield on Ramree Island; he accepted the need for additional transport aircraft and decided to send his new Chief of Staff (Browning) to London to impress on the Chiefs of Staff that the provision of the four squadrons (100 aircraft) by the given dates was a matter of overriding importance. The same day he told the Chiefs of Staff that the increased speed of operations in Burma made it imperative that the directive he had asked for after the Octagon Conference in September 1944 should be issued without delay.[1]

On the 11th Mountbatten informed the Chiefs of Staff of the adjusted 'Capital' plan,[2] explaining that the advance across the Irrawaddy would be possible only if two combat cargo squadrons were returned from China by the 1st February and one by mid-February, and if an additional squadron were provided by the 1st March. To assist 'Capital', 26th Division, now freed by the occupation of Akyab, would assault Ramree Island about the 19th January, and all-weather airfields would be built at Akyab and on Ramree Island, so that the utmost value could be got from the limited number of transport aircraft available for the supply of 14th Army and so that the tactical air forces could operate from forward all-weather bases. 'Given the return of my seventy-five aircraft from China,' he said, 'plus the additional twenty-five now asked for by the dates shown, I would feel confident of turning the present promising situation into a major victory.' Three days later he asked for forty more aircraft to enable him to fly food supplies into Burma for the civil population liberated as the army advanced.

On the 11th Mountbatten approved the redeployment plan for transport aircraft submitted by A.L.F.S.E.A. and Eastern Air Command. Of the eleven transport squadrons available at that time three were located on the Imphal plain, four at Agartala, three at Comilla and one (which was maintaining XV Corps) at Chittagong.[3] The plan proposed that all the squadrons at Agartala and two of the three at Comilla should move forward to the Chittagong area at the

---

[1] See page 13.
[2] See Chapter XV.
[3] See Appendix 15.

end of January.[1] When the airfields to be built at Akyab came into operation about the 15th April two squadrons would move there, and when the airfields on Ramree Island were ready about the 1st May three squadrons would be located there. The plan took no account of the four extra squadrons asked for from the Chiefs of Staff; these would, if received, be deployed as events demanded.

The move of the air bases from Agartala and Comilla, which were dependent on No. 4 Advanced Base Supply Depot at Mymensingh, to the Chittagong group of airfields, based on No. 5 Advanced Base Supply Depot at Chittagong, presented considerable administrative difficulties.[2] The intake to Chittagong by rail was already at its maximum and it would not therefore be possible to transfer stocks from Mymensingh. Stocks were generally low at Chittagong and the tonnage called forward in January was sufficient only for current maintenance in Arakan. Since the stock position could not be rectified overnight and the redeployment of aircraft would of necessity reduce the number of sorties which could be flown while the squadrons were changing their bases, a temporary shortfall of supplies to 14th Army would have to be accepted. On the completion of the move, however, the tonnage which could be delivered by air would be increased by fifteen per cent and, excluding any tonnage delivered from Imphal, should reach a figure of 870 tons a day thirty days after the move began.

The 14th Army, whose strength, including line of communication troops, would reach about 260,000 men by March 1945, was being maintained at the end of 1944 almost entirely over the Assam line of communication and the Imphal Road,[3] and the A.L.F.S.E.A. reserve stocks of all commodities had been sited accordingly. The redeployment plan and the southward advance of the army would, however, lead progressively to the switching of its maintenance from the northern (Assam) rail/road to a southern sea (Arakan coast) line of communication until it was entirely maintained from the south. But the reserve stocks had to be so located that, whether 14th Army succeeded in capturing Rangoon before the monsoon or was held up in central or lower Burma, it could still be maintained. It was therefore arranged that by the 15th April half the reserve stocks for 14th Army, including those for the Central Burma Stockpile, would be held along the Assam line of communication and half on the Arakan coast. The relief afforded to the Dimapur–Kalewa road would,

---

[1] For technical reasons one squadron would have to remain at Comilla to handle reinforcements to, and evacuate casualties from, 14th Army. The R.A.M.O. organizations at the Chittagong airfields were established in the second half of January and the squadrons moved in on the 1st February.

[2] See Sketch 21, facing page 522.

[3] At the end of March the strength of the British portion of A.L.F.S.E.A. had reached 971,828, i.e. 127,139 British, 581,548 Indians, 44,988 East Africans, 59,878 West Africans and 158,275 civilian labourers.

however, be largely offset by its having to carry all the heavy stores for building up the I.W.T. service on the Chindwin as well as those required for the rehabilitation of the Burma railways.

The redeployment made it essential that two new ports, one at Akyab and one at Kyaukpyu on Ramree Island, should be developed, through each of which three divisions of 14th Army in central Burma and those formations of XV Corps operating on the Arakan coast would eventually have to be maintained.[1] The full capacity of the port at Chittagong (2,500 tons a day) would, however, still be required throughout the whole period. But, as it would constitute a bottleneck until the ports at Akyab and Kyaukpyu were fully in operation, it was arranged that exports from Chittagong by coastal vessels to Ultakhali, Cox's Bazar and Maungdaw should be reduced to a minimum and that nothing should pass through Chittagong for the Assam line of communication except bulk petrol for the pipelines.

On the 20th January Mountbatten met Leese, Stratemeyer, Coryton and a representative of the Air Commander-in-Chief at Calcutta. After a full discussion of the situation he told Leese to make every endeavour to defeat the Japanese armies in Burma and to capture Rangoon before the monsoon. The 14th Army was to continue its current operations designed to bring this about, and XV Corps was to occupy Ramree and Cheduba Islands, establish a bridge-head at Taungup, carry out reconnaissances and be prepared to open up the Taungup–Prome road, provided that the progress of 14th Army's operations warranted this and that it could be done before the monsoon. The 81st (W.A.) Division and any other troops no longer required for the furtherance of XV Corps' operations were to be withdrawn to India during February. In the event of Rangoon not being captured before the monsoon, Headquarters XV Corps and three divisions would have to be withdrawn to India for training for a post-monsoon operation to wipe out enemy forces in Burma. To overcome the shortfall in supplies to 14th Army which had developed during the early part of January,[2] Mountbatten decided that transport aircraft would have to be worked above the sustained rate for an indefinite period, despite the fact that this was unsound and made no allowance for inevitable emergencies; a decision, however, which in no way affected the demand for additional transport aircraft.

---

[1] On this basis it was estimated that during February and March the port at Akyab would have to cope with the maintenance of 46,000 men, the construction stores required for two all-weather airfields and the tonnage necessary to build up a 20,000-ton reserve for 14th Army. A sea lift of 850 tons a day for February and March would be required which, as XV Corps was gradually withdrawn to India, would drop to 650 tons in April and 600 tons in May. The port of Kyaukpyu would have to maintain 36,000 men from February to May and handle the stores necessary to construct two all-weather airfields and to build up a stockpile of 22,000 tons; this represented a daily import of 450 tons in February and 650 from March to May.

[2] See pages 182–83.

The decision to work transport aircraft above the sustained rate could not, however, show results for some time, and by the 22nd January it became evident that the supplies being delivered to 14th Army were inadequate. To meet this situation, Air Headquarters, S.E.A.C. authorized Eastern Air Command to exceed the sustained rate to any extent found necessary, and ordered thirty-two Dakota aircraft to be diverted from airborne training and allotted to Eastern Air Command for transport duties. By these means it was hoped that the lift could be increased from 1,030 short tons a day to 1,480; this figure, based on sixty per cent being landed and forty per cent being dropped, should ensure that 14th Army's demands were met. After a careful examination of statistics, Air Headquarters decided on the 27th to increase the effective sustained rate for transport aircraft to 125 hours a month from the 1st February.[1] Meanwhile, to relieve 14th Army's administrative staff of the burden of responsibility for its ever-lengthening line of communications, the control of the L. of C. Transport Column operating on the Dimapur–Kalewa road was taken over by L. of C. Command on the 24th.

At the end of January 1945 Leese sent Mountbatten and Auchinleck his ideas on the future organization of the lines of communication stretching into Burma. Since he considered that L. of C. Command would not be able to exercise effective control in Burma as the advance proceeded, he proposed to establish new administrative districts progressively in Burma under his own command. He envisaged a gradual development in a number of phases: the first would be the establishment of 505 District for the administration of northern and part of central Burma, the second would be the transfer to General Headquarters, India, of 202 L. of C. Area (except for 256 L. of C. Sub-Area at Imphal which would pass to 505 District) and part of 404 L. of C. Area, including Silchar, the remainder of 404 L. of C. Area being raised to district status in view of the increasing importance of the southern line of communication along the Arakan coast. Further phases would include the eventual abolition of L. of C. Command and the establishment of a district in southern Burma. These proposals received Mountbatten's approval in principle.

While steps were being taken to arrange for the maintenance of 14th Army during its advance from the Chindwin to Rangoon, Slim had

---

[1] The sustained rate had up to that time been 100 hours a month for R.A.F. and 120 a month for U.S.A.A.F. transport aircraft. The decision to adjust this figure to a flat rate of 125 hours a month meant that the intensive rate (which could be maintained for about a month) would be approximately 185 hours, and the maximum rate (which could be sustained for ten days only) would be 250 hours a month. Each transport squadron could, working at the new sustained rates, fly approximately 3,000 hours a month.

asked Force 136 to consider the possibility of raising Levies in the Karen Hills with a view to assisting the army's advance during the final phase of 'Extended Capital'.[1] Towards the end of January the force presented an outline plan for raising and using Karen Levies (operation 'Character'). It was assumed that the road and railway from Pegu to Pyinmana were the main Japanese lines of communication from the south and that garrisons for their protection would be located along them, that the Toungoo–Bawlake–Loi-kaw road was likely to be used as a subsidiary line of communication both for reinforcements and for withdrawal, and that it was unlikely that the Japanese would operate offensively between these two in the Karen Hills. The objects would be to provide intelligence of enemy movements and dispositions on these lines of communication, attack them or specific targets when ordered to do so by 14th Army, undertake guerrilla action against enemy troops withdrawing in disorder through the Karen Hills and prevent the enemy from destroying specific installations.

The Karen district was for the purpose of the operation to be divided into three zones:[2] the northern included the Pyinmana–Loi-kaw–Bawlake–Yedashe area, the central lay to the south of the northern as far as the line Kawludo–Mon and the southern extended to the south of this line as far as Kamamaung–Mokpalin. In each of these zones a special group, consisting initially of three to five British officers, a British wireless operator, fourteen Burmese (including some engineers) together with interpreters and Karen liaison officers, was to be dropped by parachute. Each group was to be responsible for operations in its own area and was to raise static and mobile Levies, the former to guard villages and vital posts and the latter to undertake sabotage and guerrilla operations. Arms were to be dropped as required in each zone, and it was hoped that by May some 3,800 Levies would have been raised and equipped. This plan was approved and resources were placed at the disposal of Force 136, who were instructed to put it into effect towards the end of February.

Meanwhile Force 136's other main operation ('Nation') was getting under way.[3] Two all-Burmese teams were dropped on the 27th January near Toungoo and Tharrawaddy with orders to establish contact with the Anti-Fascist Organization, raise guerilla bands and report back any military intelligence that they could collect.[4] At the

---

[1] See Map 7, facing page 171.
[2] The Karen district was defined for the purposes of the plan as the area bounded by the Salween River on the east, the line Kamamaung–Mokpalin on the south, the Sittang River on the west and the line Pyinmana–Loi-kaw on the north (see Maps 7 and 11, facing pages 171 and 414).
[3] See page 33.
[4] For Tharrawaddy see Map 11, facing page 414.

same time plans were put in train for the establishment as and when convenient of six Jedburgh teams along the Japanese line of communication from Pyinmana to Pegu.[1]

Meanwhile, in London, in an effort to resolve the difficulties which had arisen over the removal of American resources from S.E.A.C. to China and to form a judgement on the conflicting claims of Mountbatten and Wedemeyer for these resources,[2] the Chiefs of Staff had late in December told their American colleagues that, whereas in China the threat to Kweiyang seemed to have receded,[3] in Burma there were signs that strong enemy opposition would be met when the Mandalay–Lashio line was reached. To enable a severe blow to be struck at the enemy in that area it was essential that there should be sufficient transport aircraft at Mountbatten's disposal to ensure the maintenance of strong forces there, particularly when the monsoon began. The transfer of the two divisions to China, already under way, would not have any serious effect on Mountbatten's plans and, even if a third division were to go, it would still be possible to carry out the first two phases of 'Capital'. The crux of the problem lay in the despatch of the combat cargo squadrons. Since it was doubtful whether a decision on a firm date for their return to S.E.A.C. could yet be taken, the Chiefs of Staff recommended that the whole position should be reviewed towards the end of January when the situation both in Burma and China should be clearer. Concerned at the suggestion that no date need yet be fixed for the return of his squadrons, Mountbatten told the Chiefs of Staff on the 1st January 1945 that the advance into central Burma was going so rapidly that 14th Army was about to enter the Mandalay plain and that exploitation south from Mandalay and Meiktila was already being examined. Since the advance depended almost entirely on air supply, it was essential that he should know at least four months in advance the number of squadrons on which he could count. The next day, considering that the situation in China had improved sufficiently to allow of an immediate decision on the return of the squadrons, the Chiefs of Staff asked the Americans to agree to their return by the 1st March.

The Chiefs of Staff had told Mountbatten on the 12th January that they considered Browning's visit to London unnecessary.[4] Mountbatten, however, determined to impress on them that the aircraft he had asked for would mean the difference between a great success and

---

[1] For Jedburgh teams see page 33 fn. 3.
[2] See Chapter XI.
[3] See Map 10, facing page 340.
[4] See page 201.

a possible disaster, decided not to stop him,[1] and Browning arrived in London on the 15th. After discussing with him Mountbatten's telegram of the 11th asking for the earlier return of the squadrons, the Chiefs of Staff told the Americans on the 18th that the situation in Burma had improved out of all recognition and that there were now excellent prospects of the Japanese being routed in the Mandalay area and a reasonable chance of Rangoon being reached. The failure to provide Mountbatten with the aircraft he required might well make the difference between rapid and complete victory and a stalemate which would prolong the campaign by many months. They considered therefore that, as there was now no threat to Kweiyang, Wedemeyer should be able, without harm to his own plans, to return during the first half of February the three combat cargo squadrons loaned to him. They were proposing themselves to find the fourth squadron which Mountbatten had asked for by sending an R.A.F. squadron to India from the Middle East theatre, replacing it by a newly-formed squadron from the United Kingdom.

On the 22nd, however, Wedemeyer announced that he was prepared to return two combat cargo squadrons to S.E.A.C. on the 1st February, but that he would have to keep the third permanently in China. To meet Mountbatten's demand for 140 aircraft, and taking into account the return of the two combat cargo squadrons (fifty aircraft) from China, the Chiefs of Staff then proposed that one R.A.F. squadron (twenty-five aircraft) should be sent to India from the Middle East theatre by the 15th February, that an R.A.F. transport squadron (thirty aircraft), formed to meet the Admiralty's requirements in the Pacific, should be diverted to S.E.A.C. by the 1st March and that the establishment of the eight existing R.A.F. transport squadrons already allotted to S.E.A.C. should be raised by five aircraft a squadron by the 1st March. This plan would give Mountbatten 145 aircraft. The American Chiefs of Staff agreed on the 25th to these proposals and approved Wedemeyer's decision to return two combat cargo squadrons and keep the third. 'It seems,' they said, '. . . that with complete development of the other logistical facilities and organization of the lines of communication and with maximum utilization of each available transport aircraft, S.A.C.S.E.A. will be able to support adequately his offensive in Burma.' The next day the Chiefs of Staff ordered Middle East to send an R.A.F. transport squadron to S.E.A.C. and told Mountbatten the steps they were taking to meet the balance of his requirements after the return of the two squadrons from China. The immediate problems of providing transport aircraft for the maintenance of 14th Army's advance into central Burma had been solved, and Mountbatten replied that the news had put new heart into them all.

---

[1] Mountbatten's Report, Section B, para. 380.

The other aspect of the problem raised by the transfer of troops and aircraft to China—that of the policy regarding the use of American resources assigned to S.E.A.C.—had been under constant discussion during December.[1] The directive Mountbatten had issued on the integration of the British and American air forces in S.E.A.C. in December 1943 had allowed for co-ordination of planning and operations by Eastern Air Command (which included 10th U.S.A.A.F.) and 14th U.S.A.A.F. to be arranged between the Deputy Supreme Commander, who at that time commanded all American air forces in India, Burma and China, and the Air Commander-in-Chief, S.E.A. Since then the situation had completely changed, for with the splitting of the C.B.I. Theatre American resources in China had been placed under a commander with no direct interest in operations in Burma, although these operations might be seriously affected by the diversion of forces from S.E.A.C. to meet the situation in China. Furthermore, owing to the Japanese offensive action in China, the diversions asked for were likely to be far larger and their effect on Burma far greater than had been envisaged when the American reservation on the right to reassign units from 10th to 14th U.S.A.A.F. had been accepted. The Chiefs of Staff held strongly to the view that the reservation had never been intended to apply to the move of major resources, though they were quite agreeable to the American Chiefs of Staff making minor adjustments between their forces in the two theatres. They therefore insisted that only the Combined Chiefs of Staff could approve the large-scale removal of resources affecting operations agreed to by them. The Americans held that their air units had been deployed specifically for the assistance of China and that the necessity for their rapid transfer, when required, had been recognized by the Combined Chiefs of Staff. They considered therefore that the transfer of American forces and resources between the India–Burma and the China Theatres was quite distinct from the general allocation of resources between the theatres, which was under the jurisdiction of the Combined Chiefs of Staff.

After much argument, a temporary solution was reached at the end of December 1944 when the British and American Chiefs of Staff agreed that, if Mountbatten reported that a proposed diversion of resources to China would materially hamper the execution of his approved operations, then a decision on the transfer would lie with the Combined Chiefs of Staff; if, however, an extreme emergency should arise in China, such a diversion could be made on the authority of the American Chiefs of Staff. In accepting this solution, the British made it clear that it would hold good only until they themselves could discuss the whole matter with the Americans.

This opportunity arose when the Prime Minister, the President and

[1] See pages 126–28.

37. On the way to the Kabo Weir, Sipadon Chaung

38. On the way to Gangaw, Myittha River

39. Kangaw beach

40. Landing craft striking a mine off Kyaukpyu (Ramree)

41. Landing craft on the way to Ruywa

42. 36th Division's advance on Indaw, Pinbaw

43. Lieut.-General M. Honda,
33rd Army

44. Lieut.-General S. Miyazaki,
54th Division

45. 25-pdr. gun in action at Myitson

46. Mules crossing the Nammeik Chaung at Myitson

47. Kyaukmyaung ferry

48. Typical scenery, Shwebo plain

the Combined Chiefs of Staff met at the Argonaut Conference at Malta at the end of January 1945. The following agreement was reached on the 1st February:

> 'The primary military object of the United States in the China and India–Burma Theatres is the continuance of aid to China on a scale that will permit the fullest utilisation of the area and resources of China for operations against the Japanese. United States resources are deployed in India–Burma to provide direct or indirect support for China. These forces and resources participate not only in operating the base and the line of communications for United States and Chinese forces in China, but also constitute a reserve immediately available to China without permanently increasing the requirements for transport of supplies to China.
>
> The United States Chiefs of Staff contemplate no change in their agreement to S.A.C.S.E.A.'s use of resources of the United States India–Burma Theatre in Burma when this use does not prevent the fulfilment of their primary object of rendering support to China including protection of the line of communications. Any transfer of forces engaged in approved operations in progress in Burma which is contemplated by the United States Chiefs of Staff and which, in the opinion of the British Chiefs of Staff, would jeopardise those operations, will be subject to discussion by the Combined Chiefs of Staff.'

The same day the Combined Chiefs of Staff drew up the new directive on future operations for which Mountbatten had asked in September 1944.[1] This read:

> '1. Your first object is to liberate Burma at the earliest date. . . .
> 2. Subject to the accomplishment of this object your next main task will be the liberation of Malaya and the opening of the Straits of Malacca. . . .
> 3. In view of your recent success in Burma and of the uncertainty of the date of the final defeat of Germany you must aim at the accomplishment of your first object with the forces at present at your disposal. This does not preclude the despatch of further reinforcements from the European theatre should circumstances make this possible.
> 4. You will prepare a programme of operations for the approval of the Combined Chiefs of Staff.
> 5. In transmitting the foregoing directive the C.C.S. direct your attention to the agreed policy in respect of the use in your theatre of United States resources deployed in the India–Burma theatre.'

This directive was sent to Mountbatten on the 3rd February 1945.

---

[1] See page 13.

CHAPTER XIX

THE ARAKAN FRONT
(January–February 1945)
and
EVENTS IN THE INDIAN OCEAN
(August 1944–February 1945)

See Maps 6, 7, 11, 12 and 13 and Sketches 5, 20 and 21

WHEN, on the 23rd August 1944, Admiral Fraser relieved Admiral Somerville,[1] the Eastern Fleet consisted of the battleships *Queen Elizabeth*, *Howe* and *Richelieu*,[2] the battle cruiser *Renown*, the fleet carriers *Illustrious*, *Victorious* and *Indomitable*, eleven cruisers and thirty-two destroyers. On the 24th August the *Victorious* and *Indomitable*, under command of Rear-Admiral C. Moody and supported by the *Howe*, two cruisers and five destroyers, carried out airstrikes on selected targets at Padang and other points on the south-west coast of Sumatra.[3] On the 18th September the two carriers, again supported by the *Howe* with two cruisers and seven destroyers, carried out airstrikes on selected targets near the northern tip of Sumatra as well as photographic reconnaissance of the Nicobar Islands and northern Sumatra. These operations were mainly designed to give battle training to the young and inexperienced pilots of the carrier aircraft, but the almost complete lack of any opposition detracted from their value. To coincide with the American assault on Leyte in October, Mountbatten was asked to use the Eastern Fleet to create a diversion in the Indian Ocean. He decided to attack the Nicobar Islands, and Fraser placed a force under command of Vice-Admiral Power to carry it out.[4] Between the 17th and 19th October targets on the islands were attacked from the air and bombarded from the sea, but again negligible opposition was encountered until the morning of the 19th when, in an air battle, seven out of a

---

[1] See page 118.
[2] The *Howe* replaced the *Valiant* which had to be sent to the United Kingdom for refit after damage resulting from the collapse of the floating dock at Trincomalee. The *Richelieu* (Free French) left for Casablanca for docking on the 14th September.
[3] See Map 12, facing page 436.
[4] The force consisted of a battle cruiser, two fleet carriers, three cruisers and eleven destroyers.

force of twelve Japanese fighters were shot down for the loss of three of the carrier aircraft. As a diversion the attacks had no effect, for the Japanese had already concentrated all their naval forces for the defence of the Philippines.[1]

On the 22nd November the Eastern Fleet ceased to exist. The part remaining in South-East Asia was renamed the East Indies Fleet, commanded by Admiral Power. It consisted of the battleship *Queen Elizabeth*, the battle cruiser *Renown*, eight cruisers, five escort carriers (including two ferry carriers), twenty-four destroyers and escort forces mustering some seventy ships. The other part formed the new British Pacific Fleet,[2] and Admiral Fraser took under his command the battleships *King George V* (Vice-Admiral Sir Bernard Rawlings, Flag Officer Commanding 1st Battle Squadron and Second in Command of the Fleet) and *Howe*, the fleet carriers *Indefatigable* (Rear-Admiral Sir Philip Vian, Flag Officer Commanding aircraft carriers), *Illustrious*, *Victorious* and *Indomitable*, five cruisers and three flotillas of destroyers.[3]

On the 2nd December Fraser left Ceylon in the *Howe* for Australia on his way to fly to Pearl Harbour to see Admiral Nimitz, leaving the rest of his fleet to follow at a date to be decided later. He arranged, however, that, before the ships of the British Pacific Fleet left the Indian Ocean, Power would use them to carry out a series of operations designed to interfere with Japanese oil supplies. Power selected as his targets the oil refineries at Pladjoe and Soengei Gerong near Palembang. As a rehearsal he ordered Vian with the fleet carriers *Indomitable* and *Illustrious*, four cruisers and eight destroyers to attack the refineries at Pangkalan Brandan, thirty miles north-west of Belawan Deli in northern Sumatra. Vian sailed from Trincomalee on the 17th December and, without being detected, reached the flying-off position early on the 20th.[4] Twenty-seven Avenger torpedo-bombers took off at 7.15 a.m. but, finding their target obscured by cloud, attacked the port at Belawan Deli instead. On the 4th January 1945 Vian, with the fleet carriers *Indomitable*, *Victorious* and *Indefatigable*, attacked Pangkalan Brandan and caused considerable damage.

On the 16th January Vian sailed from Ceylon with his four fleet carriers, the battleship *King George V*, three cruisers and ten destroyers to join Fraser and the *Howe*, already in Pacific waters. On its way to Australia the fleet launched its attack on the Palembang refineries. Pladjoe was attacked on the 24th by fifty Avengers escorted by eighty fighters. The attackers met with heavy anti-

---

[1] See Chapter VI.
[2] See pages 9 and 12.
[3] The cruisers were the *Swiftsure*, *Argonaut*, *Black Prince*, *Ceylon* and *Newfoundland*. These were later reinforced by the two New Zealand cruisers, *Gambia* and *Achilles*.
[4] See Map 13 in end pocket.

aircraft fire and a balloon barrage and had to contend with considerable fighter opposition, but nevertheless succeeded in causing damage which reduced production at the refinery by half. A second strike was launched on the 29th on Soengei Gerong; the bombing this time was more accurate and the damage caused stopped production at the refinery until the end of March. The two attacks were, however, costly; sixteen aircraft were lost through enemy action and twenty-five from other causes. Nine of the airmen who were shot down survived and were taken prisoner, but later were put to death by the Japanese. Immediately after the second attack a few Japanese torpedo-bombers managed to reach the fleet, but had no success, all being shot down by fighters or gunfire. The fleet then sailed for Australia, reaching Fremantle on the 4th February. Thus, after long delays, the British Pacific Fleet entered its operational area to work alongside the Americans.

In the Indian Ocean the general reconnaissance (maritime) squadrons maintained their extensive anti-submarine patrolling from bases as far apart as India (including Ceylon), southern Arabia and East Africa, and the 4th and 8th Submarine Flotillas continued to patrol off Sumatra and Java and in the restricted and shallow waters off the coast of Burma and in the Malacca Strait.[1] In September the 8th Flotilla was sent to Australia to join the American submarines operating in the Pacific. Although, as earlier in the year, it found few worthwhile surface targets, the remaining submarine force succeeded in sinking the German *U.859* off Penang on the 23rd September and *U.168* off the coast of Java on the 5th October, but subsequently suffered similar losses when the *Stratagem* was sunk by a Japanese destroyer on the 22nd November 1944 in the Malacca Strait and the *Porpoise* was lost off Penang on the 16th January 1945. A raid on the harbour at Phuket Island was made in October when two midget submarines sank one enemy merchant ship, damaged another and returned safely to their parent submarine.

Until August both Japanese and German submarines had been active and nine ships (57,732 tons) were sunk in the Indian Ocean. On the 12th August, however, after a week's intensive search by ships and aircraft, the German *U.198* was sunk by the frigate *Findhorn* and the R.I.N. sloop *Godavari*. During September the Japanese ordered their submarines to concentrate in the Pacific for the defence of the Philippines and, as a result of the mining of Penang harbour by Liberators of the Strategic Air Force,[2] the Germans, whose submarines

---

[1] For the action of the R.A.F. general reconnaissance squadrons and the submarine flotillas earlier in the year see Volume III, Chapter XXVI.
[2] See Volume III, Chapter XXVI.

were already becoming less efficient owing to the lack of spare parts
and the shortage of torpedoes, moved their base to Batavia. Enemy
submarine activity thereupon began to diminish and had practically
ceased by the end of October. Early in January 1945, all German
submarines were ordered to return to their home ports.[1]

With the end of the U-boat threat the role of 222 and 225 Groups
R.A.F. was changed. Their primary task was now mine-laying in the
Malacca Strait and in the Singora, Padang and Singapore areas, and
operations against enemy shipping in the Indian Ocean. They had
also to undertake photographic reconnaissance over the Andamans,
Nicobar Islands, northern Sumatra and parts of Malaya, for which
purpose Liberators and Mosquitos based in Ceylon were used. A
coastal wing was formed at Akyab to provide escort for convoys and
to make a force easily available to attack enemy shipping off the
Burma coast.

By the beginning of 1945 command of the Indian Ocean and the
Bay of Bengal had been regained, and all vessels other than troop-
ships were able to sail independently without escorts. This made it
possible for amphibious operations to be undertaken along the
Arakan coast and against Rangoon without the fear of heavy losses
and without the need for powerful naval covering forces.

The regaining of command of the Bay of Bengal and the capture of
Akyab three weeks earlier than had been expected was most opportune.[2] The original XV Corps plan had envisaged the use of 26th
Division (Lomax) for the capture of Akyab ('Talon') and for subsequent exploitation.[3] To clear north Arakan ('Romulus') the division
was to strike during February north-east towards Minbya and east
towards Myebon to cut off and destroy the Japanese operating in the
Kaladan. Thereafter, XV Corps was to release around the 1st March
at least half its strength for use in the drive to capture Rangoon.[4] The
rapid mopping-up of the Mayu peninsula and the decision to employ
25th Division for the capture of Akyab meant that 26th Division
would be available for other tasks for at least two months. The Joint
Force Commanders, headed by Christison, therefore prepared a plan
for the capture of Ramree Island by that division. This was ready by
the 2nd January, two days before Akyab was occupied. Thus, when it
became evident in the first week in January that in its drive on
Meiktila 14th Army would pass beyond the economic range of its air
supply bases at Imphal and Agartala, and that new bases would have

---

[1] In January 1945 the German submarine force consisted of ten U-boats. From August
to December 1944 some five submarines at a time were on patrol in the Indian Ocean.
[2] See page 142.
[3] See Map 7, facing page 171.
[4] See page 136.

to be established at Chittagong, Akyab and Ramree, Leese had a ready-made plan for the capture of Ramree Island, a plan which was accepted by Mountbatten on the 9th January.[1]

Before describing the Battle of the Arakan Beaches, it is of interest to consider what the actual Japanese dispositions were and why they had decided to abandon Akyab which they had so strenuously defended against all attacks since the autumn of 1942. Lieut.-General S. Miyazaki (*54th Division*) had in December been ordered to hold the An and Taungup passes in order to protect the rear of *15th Army* in the Irrawaddy valley where the Japanese expected the decisive battles of the 1945 campaign to be fought.[2] Miyazaki had decided to base his defences on two strongly defended areas at Kangaw and Taungup covering the An Pass and the Prome road respectively, Kangaw being the main one. He had made *154th Regimental Group* responsible for Kangaw and the *121st* for Taungup, and was prepared to use his reserves in either area for counterattack. He had ordered the *Matsu Detachment (111th Regimental Group)*, leaving a small detachment at Akyab to cover its communications with Kangaw, to act as a covering force in the Kaladan and impose as much delay as possible. When forced to withdraw it was to fall back on Kangaw. He had also placed detachments at Myebon and Ramree and on the line of communication at Tamandu and Kywegu.[3] From these dispositions it will be seen that Myebon and Ramree were held purely as outposts and that there was no intention of defending Akyab. For the task given him Miyazaki could scarcely have bettered them and their effectiveness will become clear as the story unfolds, but they did not prevent the Allies from achieving their object of establishing air bases at Akyab and Ramree.

On the 14th January, with Leese's approval, the Joint Force Commanders ordered 26th Division to assault Ramree on the 21st, and a Royal Marine detachment to occupy Cheduba Island. The 25th Division (Wood) and 3 Commando Brigade were to exploit 'Talon' and 'Romulus'. Exploitation began on the 8th January as soon as it was clear that Akyab and the ground covering the anchorages had been secured. The 53rd Brigade (Brigadier B. C. H. Gerty),[4] with 7/16th Punjab under command, which had occupied Ponnagyun that day, was to hold Akyab and establish firm bases east of the Kaladan River from which raids were to be made to cut the Minbya—

---

[1] See Sketch 20, facing page 412, and pages 200–201.
[2] Miyazaki had been commander of *31st Division Infantry Group* during the Battles of Imphal and Kohima and had commanded with distinction the rearguard covering the division's retreat.
[3] The strength of these detachments was: at Myebon approximately half a battalion, at Ramree one battalion (*II/121st*), at Tamandu two companies and at Kywegu a battalion less a company. Each detachment was self-contained with a proportion of artillery, engineers and ancillary services.
[4] Gerty succeeded Scott on the 19th December.

Myohaung road. The rest of the division, with 3 Commando Brigade under command, was to occupy the Myebon Peninsula and then strike east towards Kangaw where the coast road, the only line of communication to the Lemro valley by that time left to the *Matsu Detachment*, passed through a defile.[1] To free Wood for the Myebon operations, Headquarters XV Corps took 53rd Brigade, which was already involved in heavy fighting in its attempts to reach Minbya, under direct command.[2]

The initial assault on the Myebon Peninsula was to be made by 3 Commando Brigade on the 12th January. As soon as an adequate beachhead had been secured, 74th Brigade was to pass through, gain the line of the Kantha Chaung and then strike towards Kangaw. The naval forces, under command of Captain D. C. Hill, R.N., consisted of the destroyer *Napier*, the cruiser *Phoebe* (which, though she could not approach the shore, could give anti-aircraft covering fire and protection from seaward), the sloops *Narbada* and *Jumna*, four mine-sweepers and forty-nine landing craft and motor launches.[3] Four commando units, carried to the release point in the sloops and mine-sweepers and three large infantry landing craft (L.C.I.), were trans-ferred to assault craft early on the 12th. As the beaches were protected by anti-boat stakes some 600 yards from the shore, a combined opera-tions pilotage party (part of Small Operations Group) attached explosives to a number of these. Set off at zero hour, they made gaps for the landing craft to pass through. Under cover of a smokescreen laid by the R.A.F. and the fire of the supporting landing craft and the motor launches, the first wave quickly got ashore and overcame slight opposition near the beaches where the strong defences were not fully manned, but suffered casualties from land mines. Tanks, vehicles and stores could not, however, be landed on the muddy beaches, and it was not until the engineers had blasted an exit from a small beach on a nearby rocky promontory that they could get ashore. Thereafter, the commandos made steady progress: they occupied Myebon on the 13th and by the 15th were within a mile of the Kantha Chaung. From there 74th Brigade (Hirst) took up the advance and, against determined opposition from small forces in most difficult country, had by the 17th secured the whole peninsula, including the Kantha Chaung, and had begun to exploit.

The plans for the West Africans in the Kaladan, whose task was to destroy the *Matsu Detachment* as soon as its communications had been

---

[1] The loss of Akyab had deprived the Japanese of their main sea/river route to the Kaladan. The loss of Minbya or Myebon would cut the route to the Lemro River by the Myebon or Kyatsin Rivers. See Sketch 5, facing page 224.

[2] For his part in this fighting, which continued until the end of January, Lance-Naik Sher Shah, 7/16th Punjab, was awarded a posthumous Victoria Cross.

[3] Three L.C.I., five L.C.T., twelve L.C.M., eighteen L.C.A., four L.C.P., three L.C.S. and four motor launches.

effectively cut at Minbya and Kangaw, had meanwhile been changed. The original intention had been that 82nd (W.A.) Division would relieve 81st (W.A.) Division (Loftus-Tottenham) in the Thayettabin area beginning on the 14th January. With the fall of Akyab on the 4th, Christison ordered the relief to be hastened and, to ensure that there was co-ordination of effort in the Kaladan pending the arrival of the whole of 82nd (W.A.) Division there, he placed 4th (W.A.) Brigade (Brigadier H Gibbons), the leading brigade of 82nd Division, under command of the 81st.[1] Loftus-Tottenham had meantime planned to attack Myohaung on the 10th, but fearing that 25th Division would not have had time to cut the Japanese line of retreat by that date, Christison ordered him to defer his attack until the 15th. Three days later he again changed the plan and ordered 82nd Division, now commanded by Major-General Stockwell,[2] to move east from Htizwe as soon as possible and, instead of relieving 81st Division, cut the Japanese communications in the Lemro valley south of Myohaung and then assist in the capture of the town. Skilful delaying tactics on the part of the enemy and the difficult country with its many deep tidal chaungs made progress slow, and it was not until the 25th January that Myohaung, the ancient capital of Arakan, was occupied.

Christison's immediate object was to prevent all enemy forces still north of the general line Kangaw–Kantha (and in particular their guns and transport) from escaping; including the *Matsu Detachment*, he estimated them to be some 5,000 strong. In order to achieve this he decided to block both the coastal road which ran through the defile at Kangaw and the pack track which by-passed Kangaw and rejoined the road to An at Kyweguseik. If he could succeed in this he would cripple *54th Division* and complete his allotted task. By mid-January he had realized that, owing to the nature of the country, the small enemy force on the Myebon Peninsula could cause serious delay to a force many times its size and that, although the attack on Myohaung had been delayed, 74th Brigade, which had the task of cutting the communications to Myohaung, would be unlikely to reach the road in the Kangaw area in time.[3]

At a conference of the Joint Force Commanders on the 17th January, at which Mountbatten was present, Christison directed Wood (25th Division) to leave 74th Brigade to maintain pressure in

---

[1] The 4th Brigade reached Kanzauk on the 7th.

[2] Stockwell, formerly in command of 29th Brigade, succeeded Bruce who was evacuated sick on the 12th January.

[3] Documents captured at Myebon, confirmed by air reconnaissance, indicated that the Japanese had constructed a series of defences covering Kangaw from the north and stretching across the Min Chaung to the hills north-east of Kantha.

the Myebon–Kantha area and with the rest of his force launch an amphibious assault on Kangaw on the 22nd, sending a detachment as soon as possible to occupy Kyweguseik. To ensure that there was sufficient strength for the task in hand he told Wood that he was prepared to reinforce him with two battalions from 53rd Brigade. On the 24th, the day before the fall of Myohaung, Christison ordered 82nd (W.A.) Division to resume command of its 4th Brigade and, supplied by air, pursue the *Matsu Detachment*. It was to move down the Hpontha–Kani track on Kangaw and along the Taywe and Yaw Chaungs on Kyweguseik, a detachment west of the Lemro River making contact with 53rd Brigade at Minbya.[1] The 81st (W.A.) Division was to mop up the Myohaung area and then withdraw to Chiringa.[2]

While the Joint Force Commanders were preparing for the amphibious operations against Kangaw and Ramree, Leese was considering extending XV Corps' operations still further. His information about the Japanese dispositions in Arakan led him to believe that XV Corps could give direct assistance to the advance of 14th Army by containing *28th Army* on the Arakan coast. It was known that one regimental group of *54th Division* (the *Matsu Detachment*) was opposing the West Africans in the Kaladan and a second (*121st Regiment*) was disposed along the coast in the Taungup area with possibly a detachment on Ramree Island. The exact location of the remainder of the division was unknown. There were good reasons for believing that the *Sakura Detachment* of *55th Division* had withdrawn by way of Taungup to rejoin its division, that two regiments of that division were disposed along the coast between Gwa and Rangoon and that the bulk of the third regiment with divisional headquarters was in the Henzada area.[3] It was also known that the Japanese were making use of the track over the An Pass in addition to the Prome–Taungup road as a line of communication between the Arakan coast and the Irrawaddy valley. It seemed to Leese that, once Kangaw and Ramree had been taken and the *Matsu Detachment* destroyed, troops would be available to take Taungup and perhaps even to drive inland towards Prome, thereby containing *55th* as well as *54th Division*. On the 25th January, by which time the Kangaw and Ramree operations were developing satisfactorily, he warned Christison of a possible further extension of operations. Early in February he instructed XV Corps to

---

[1] To provide 82nd Division with first-line transport while moving along the Taywe Chaung, the I.W.T. country boat fleet which had operated on the Mayu River during the advance from Buthidaung was moved through the network of chaungs to Hpontha. In addition the division had its own porter transport.

[2] For Chiringa see Map 6, facing page 134.

[3] For Gwa, Henzada and Rangoon see Map 11, facing page 414.

clear central Arakan, establish a bridgehead at Taungup, if possible
open the Prome road and, as a matter of urgency, develop advanced
bases at Akyab and Kyaukpyu. The L. of C. Command was, however,
to assume responsibility for the general administration and development of both air bases on the 12th February, though the corps was to
remain responsible for the defence of Akyab and Ramree Island.[1]

The assault on Ramree Island was to be mounted from Chittagong
and the Naf River and launched on the 21st January.[2] Covered by
fire from the battleship *Queen Elizabeth*,[3] the cruiser *Phoebe*, the
destroyers *Rapid* and *Napier*, the sloop *Flamingo* and the R.I.N. sloop
Kistna, and by air strikes by Thunderbolts and Mitchells of 224
Group on the beaches and by some eighty-five Liberators of the
Strategic Air Force, 71st Brigade (Brigadier R. C. Cottrell-Hill)
landed unopposed west of Kyaukpyu at 9.42 a.m. on the 21st.[4] The
leading motor launch and a landing craft struck mines and were
blown up, causing some confusion. It was, however, short-lived and
the landing was delayed by only twelve minutes. By afternoon the
beachhead had been secured. Next day 4th Brigade (Brigadier
J. F. R. Forman) landed and took over the beachhead and occupied
Kyaukpyu. On the 23rd, 71st Brigade began to move south along the
west coast. Mayin was occupied on the 25th and the Yanbauk
Chaung was reached on the 26th against stiffening opposition from
the enemy garrison, which had been identified as *II/121st Battalion.* The
same day the Royal Marines landed on Cheduba Island to find it
deserted. On the 31st Lomax, finding that 71st Brigade was meeting
with determined opposition on the Yanbauk Chaung, ordered it to
swing north-east to Sane and then exploit southwards towards
Ramree town, leaving 4th Brigade to watch the Yanbauk Chaung,
harass the defenders and follow up with the utmost vigour should they
withdraw.

By the 1st February 71st Brigade had entered Sane and units of
36th (the reserve) Brigade had occupied Sagu Kyun Island and
relieved the Royal Marines on Cheduba Island. As a result of Leese's

---

[1] The L. of C. Command made 404 L. of C. Area responsible for both advanced bases
on the 12th February. The 451 L. of C. Sub-Area was placed in charge of Akyab and
453 Sub-Area of Kyaukpyu.

[2] See page 215 and Sketch 21, facing page 522. Captain Bush, R.N., Major-General
Lomax and Wing-Commander H. Smith were appointed Joint Assault Commanders.

[3] At the conference of the Joint Force Commanders at Akyab on the 17th January,
Mountbatten was told that the Japanese were placing guns in caves overlooking the
landing beaches on Ramree Island. He thereupon ordered the battleship *Queen Elizabeth*
and the escort carrier *Ameer* to be sent up from Trincomalee, escorted by the destroyers
Norman, *Pathfinder* and *Raider*, to take part in the preliminary bombardment. With aircraft
from the *Ameer* spotting for her, the *Queen Elizabeth* fired sixty-nine 15-inch rounds.

[4] The brigade was supported by one squadron of 146th Regiment R.A.C., 160th Field
Regiment (less one battery) and 12th F.F. Regiment M.G. Battalion (less two companies).

orders for the extension of operations in Arakan, Christison instructed Lomax on the 4th to destroy the enemy garrison on Ramree Island, clear the islands between it and the mainland with the help of the naval force, and raid the coast between Taungup and the An River in order to disrupt the Japanese line of communication to the north and find out their strength and dispositions in the Taungup area. He was also told that he need not garrison Cheduba Island and that 22nd (E.A.) Brigade would be sent to Kyaukpyu to come under his command and garrison Ramree Island.

On the 7th February, 71st Brigade, supported by tanks, reached the western exits of Ramree town, where it met with considerable opposition. The 4th Brigade, which had reached the Ledaung Chaung, was ordered to turn eastwards to assist it, and on the 9th the town was occupied. The naval forces and 26th Division then concentrated on blocking the escape routes from the chaungs on the eastern side of the island to the mainland. In an attempt to break the blockade the Japanese launched an air attack on the 11th, during which a destroyer was seriously damaged by a near miss, and sent a fleet of some forty small craft to rescue the remainder of the garrison. Resistance on the island ceased on the 17th but the blockade continued until the 22nd, taking a heavy toll of the craft and their occupants in the chaungs through the crocodile-infested mangrove swamps. Nevertheless, in spite of the fearful odds against them, some 500 men succeeded in withdrawing to the mainland, having carried out their allotted task with courage and determination.

For the attack on Kangaw, Wood planned that 3 Commando Brigade should seize a beachhead on the east bank of the Daingbon Chaung two miles south-west of Kangaw.[1] The 51st Brigade would then pass through, capture Kangaw and join hands with 74th Brigade, which would advance north-east from Kantha and cross the Min Chaung in assault boats. The Japanese would then be hemmed in between the two brigades and the West Africans advancing down the main road from the north and through the mountains on Kyweguseik. The distance from Myebon to Kangaw by way of the Myebon River was only eight miles but, as the route was commanded by Japanese artillery and surprise could not therefore be achieved, another line of approach had to be found. Wood decided that the assault convoys should approach by way of the Thegyan River and the narrow and tortuous Daingbon Chaung, a distance of some twenty-seven miles.

During the 21st the troops were ferried in assault landing craft (L.C.A.) to the R.I.N. sloop *Narbada*, the minesweepers and four

---

[1] See Sketch 5, facing page 224.

infantry landing craft (L.C.I.), while a bulldozer, vehicles and stores were loaded on a tank landing craft (L.C.T.) and twelve mechanized landing craft (L.C.M.). The whole fleet of over fifty vessels moved off in the evening and anchored for the night in the Thegyan River estuary. Next morning the troops were transferred to the assault craft, and the fleet, less the *Narbada*, sailed up the Daingbon Chaung in three convoys preceded by minesweepers, support landing craft (L.C.S.) and motor launches. The first convoy, consisting of twenty-two L.C.A.s and 'Z' craft carrying artillery,[1] left at 11.5 a.m. on the 22nd, followed closely by the second consisting of the L.C.M.s and at 11.45 by two L.C.I.s and the L.C.T.

The Daingbon Chaung had not been mined and the convoys, approaching in silence, were not seen. At 12.40 p.m. the *Narbada* from the Thegyan River and the R.I.N. sloop *Jumna* from the Myebon River bombarded the area north-west of Thames beach to neutralize enemy artillery believed to be there, while medium bombers of 224 Group R.A.F. laid a smoke screen. At the same time field guns on 'Z' craft and medium guns from the Myebon Peninsula shelled Point 170 which dominated the landing beaches. At 1.03 p.m. the first wave landed at Hove Beach and 1 Commando pushed on to Point 170, which it secured except for the extreme northern end. Before nightfall 5 Commando, following up, had consolidated and, at first light on the 23rd, 1 Commando cleared the northern end of the Point 170 feature. During the day 44 Commando occupied Milford unopposed and then Pinner. By evening 42 Commando had taken over Milford.

The Japanese reacted quickly. On the night of the 23rd/24th they attacked Pinner without success, and on the 24th their artillery became increasingly active and brought down accurate fire on Point 170. Administrative difficulties were great: the beaches were but steep, muddy gaps in the mangrove-fringed banks of the chaung and it was some time before any vehicles could be got ashore. Worse still, wheeled vehicles could not be used owing to the nature of the ground, so that everything had to be manhandled, and there was no fresh water.

Efforts to infiltrate towards Kangaw met with stiff resistance and reinforcements were therefore brought in. On the 26th, 51st Brigade (Brigadier R. A. Hutton) landed, and a troop of medium tanks of 19th Lancers was put ashore with great difficulty. The same day two battalions of 53rd Brigade, operating under corps orders, were sent forward to Myebon: 9th York and Lancaster by sea from Akyab and 7/16th Punjab by land from Minbya.

---

[1] The 'Z' craft were large but very manoeuvrable lighters with flat iron decks and end loading ramps which could mount a troop of 25-pounders on deck with adequate ammunition. They were invaluable in the Arakan creek fighting.

As soon as he became aware of the landing, Miyazaki ordered the *Matsu Detachment* to move as quickly as possible to Kangaw but, before it could arrive, 51st Brigade had established itself on Melrose overlooking the road. This did not entirely close it for, until Perth to the north-east of Kangaw was occupied, the Japanese could continue to use it by making a short diversion. The arrival of the *Matsu Detachment* was signified on the 31st January by a fierce attack on Point 170. This feature was the key to the whole position, since its loss would cut off 51st Brigade from the beaches and make an already difficult supply situation impossible. Attack and counter-attack, involving 1 and 42 R.M. Commandos, raged on Point 170 for some thirty-six hours, culminating on the 1st February in a desperate enemy attack on a troop of tanks near the foot of the hill, in which two tanks were put out of action by pole charges and a tank-hunting party of seventy Japanese engineers perished.[1]

This was the climax but not the end of the action at Kangaw. By this time 74th Brigade was moving in from the north-west and the West Africans were moving south down the road towards Kangaw and through the hills to Kyweguseik. By the 8th, although the position of 51st Brigade had scarcely changed, 74th Brigade had firmly established itself in the Kyauknwa–Shoukchron area, 2nd (W.A.) Brigade had reached Kani, where it was placed under Wood's command for the final advance on Kangaw, and 4th (W.A.) Brigade had reached Kaw.

Realizing that 26th Division, which by this time had occupied the greater part of Ramree Island,[2] might make a landing on the coast in the Tamandu area, Miyazaki ordered the *Matsu Detachment* to withdraw to Tamandu and *154th Regimental Group* to break off the action at Kangaw and withdraw to the area west and north of the Dalet Chaung. Resistance at Kangaw therefore diminished rapidly but, hampered by spring tides which flooded the approaches to Kangaw, it was not till the 18th February that 25th Division completed the mopping up of the area. Although their losses had been crippling, the Japanese, by their realization of the importance of Kangaw and their preparations to defend it, had avoided destruction and still retained control of the An Pass.

As a result of the fighting at Kangaw and Ramree, Christison had early in February a much clearer picture of the Japanese dispositions. He felt certain that *54th Division*, after its withdrawal to the south of

---

[1] Lieutenant G. A. Knowland, 1 Commando, won a posthumous Victoria Cross for his part in this fighting. The commando losses in this action were 66 killed, 15 missing and 259 wounded. When they finally withdrew, the Japanese left over 300 dead.

[2] See pages 219-20.

Kangaw, would be disposed in two groups: the northern, withdrawing to the Dalet Chaung–An area to cover the An Pass, consisting of *111th* and *154th Regiments* and *54th Reconnaissance Regiment,* all now greatly reduced in strength; and the southern, consisting of *121st Regiment,* in the Taungup area. To ensure that his plans would fit with those of 14th Army, Christison flew to see Slim who asked him to ensure that no large Japanese force could move into the Irrawaddy valley by way of the An Pass, which, according to reliable reports, was being used as a line of communication. To assist Slim and at the same time to ensure that there would be no interference with his own operations against Taungup, Christison decided that his first task was to destroy the Japanese northern group. Accordingly, on the 4th February he directed 82nd (W.A.) Division (less 2nd Brigade) to move south-eastwards from Kaw, cross the Dalet Chaung and advance directly on An, and 25th Division to land a brigade as soon as possible after the 15th February on the An River with orders to move up it through Kywegu to join hands with 82nd Division. On completion of this operation 82nd Division would advance southwards towards Taungup and 25th Division would be withdrawn to Akyab, less one brigade which would remain in the An area to prevent infiltration across the pass. Finding that the landing craft which could be spared from the Kangaw area were insufficient to support a landing so far south as the An River, Wood obtained Christison's agreement to a revised plan under which a brigade of 25th Division would establish a bridgehead on the 16th in the Ruywa area due west of An, through which 2nd (W.A.) Brigade, after its release from Kangaw, could be passed.

Between the 5th and 8th February, to draw attention away from Ruywa, interrupt the enemy line of communication to the north and destroy the Dalet Chaung ferry and the Japanese I.W.T. base at the mouth of the chaung, the Tamandu area was bombarded by the naval force and attacked night and day by 224 Group R.A.F. On the 15th, 53rd Brigade (Gerty) with its supporting arms was embarked at Myebon,[1] and the next day was landed unopposed at Ruywa. Cover was provided by artillery which had been landed on an offshore island under the protection of 44 R.M. Commando,[2] by bombardment from the *Narbada, Jumna* and *Flamingo* and by an airstrike. By the 17th all objectives had been secured and consolidated, and the next day the leading battalion of 2nd (W.A.) Brigade was landed.[3]

---

[1] The supporting arms consisted of 27th Field Regiment, one troop of 6th Medium Regiment, one anti-tank battery, one field company I.E. and a beach group.

[2] As soon as this task was completed 44 R.M. Commando returned to Akyab to rejoin 3 Commando Brigade.

[3] The remainder of 2nd (W.A.) Brigade was in contact with the enemy at Kangaw till the 18th (see page 222). As soon as it disengaged it was sent to Ruywa, where it arrived on the 22nd.

Led by 82nd Divisional Reconnaissance Battalion and followed up by 4th (W.A.) Brigade (less one battalion), 1st (W.A.) Brigade began to move on the 15th from Kaw by way of Point 1850 to the Dalet Chaung with orders to establish a firm base south of the chaung on the Dalet–Letmauk road.[1] The going was hard, since game tracks provided the only passable routes and the descent from the Point 1850 feature towards the chaung entailed cutting a track through thick bamboo forest. Progress was painfully slow and it was not until the 18th that 1st Brigade reached the Me Chaung, where it met with Japanese patrols.

By the 18th February XV Corps had occupied Kangaw and Ramree, had cut the enemy's coastal communications at Ruywa, and 22nd (E.A.) Brigade had arrived at Ramree Island, thus freeing 26th Division for operations on the mainland. At this moment, however, Leese warned Christison that air supply to XV Corps would be drastically reduced from the end of the month. Fresh plans had therefore to be made to speed up the destruction of the Japanese force in the Dalet area while adequate air supply was still available.

---

[1] One battalion of 4th (W.A.) Brigade was left to contain an enemy force north-west of Kyweguseik.

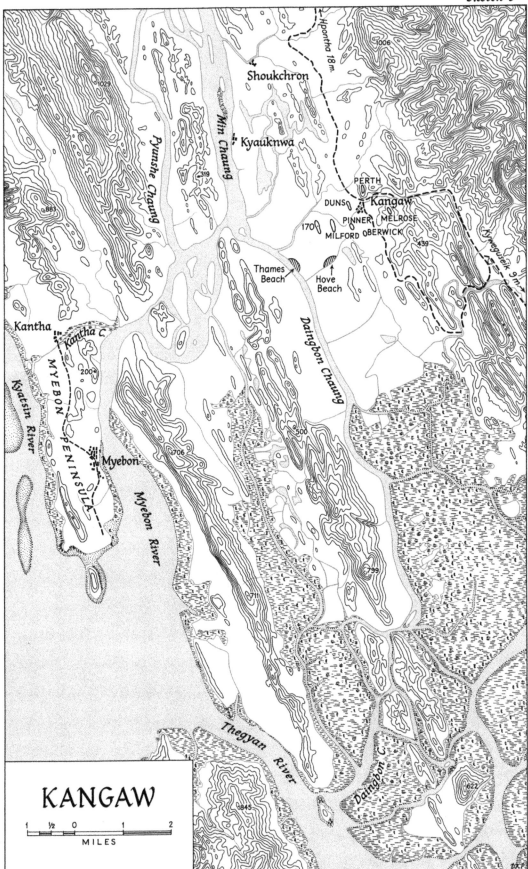

Sketch 5

KANGAW

MILES

CHAPTER XX

JAPAN RECONSIDERS HER
STRATEGY

(January 1945)

See Maps 8, 10 and 13 and Sketches 1 and 7

BY the middle of January 1945 events forced *Imperial General Headquarters* to reconsider their general strategy. The outlook was exceedingly gloomy. In western Europe the Allies had successfully established a Second Front and had driven the German armies back to their frontier, while in eastern Europe the Russian winter offensive had almost exhausted Hitler's last strategic reserves. With the almost inevitable collapse of Germany, the attitude of Soviet Russia towards Japan was becoming a matter of growing concern. In the Pacific the plan for the defence of the Philippines ('S H O –I') had failed.[1] The Americans had severely mauled the Japanese fleet at the battle of Leyte Gulf, had destroyed the greater part of the air formations disposed for the defence of the Philippines, and by the capture of Morotai, Mindoro and Leyte and their landing on Luzon —an island which could not be properly defended with the forces available to *14th Area Army*—had virtually obtained strategic control of the Philippines.[2] These islands had now become a liability rather than an asset, and the Southern Region was almost isolated. This, coupled with the severe losses of merchant ships, especially tankers, had resulted in the flow of oil and other vital raw materials to the homeland dwindling to a trickle, with a subsequent considerable reduction in the ability of Japanese industry to meet the requirements of the fighting forces. In Japan the growing scale of the American air offensive was beginning to affect the morale of the civil population and to reduce her industrial capacity still further.

Imperial General Headquarters realized that there was a possibility that the Soviet Union would renounce the Soviet–Japanese Neutrality Pact at short notice. They concluded that American strategy in the Pacific would be to isolate Japan from the Asian continent as well as from the Southern Region, coupled with efforts to demoralize the Japanese people and destroy their industrial capacity by air-raids, and finally to invade the homeland. To achieve these aims there

---

[1] See Map 8, facing page 252, and Chapter VIII.
[2] See Sketch 1, facing page 63.

appeared to be two choices open to the Americans : either they could continue their ever-growing offensive by advancing by way of China to the Ryukyu Islands, or they could establish bases in the Ryukyu and Bonin Islands, using Formosa as a stepping stone. In either case they would be well placed to mount amphibious operations against Japan. Feeling that the Americans would be very anxious to end the war as quickly as possible after the defeat of Germany, and influenced by intelligence reports which indicated that an attack on Iwojima was being planned for February, *Imperial General Headquarters* concluded that they would take the shortest route towards Japan and adopt the second of the alternatives. Nevertheless they considered that their plans should be such that either alternative could be met.

There was no hope of turning the tide of war in the Philippines. It was thought, however, that final victory would go to those who would accept increasing hardship and that in this respect the Japanese would prove superior to their enemy who, if the war dragged on, might advocate a compromise peace. *Imperial General Headquarters* therefore began to prepare for a last ditch stand in Japan. They decided to rely on diplomacy to maintain the *status quo* with the Soviet Union and to make every effort to prepare Japan and Korea to withstand heavy air-raids and invasion. Formosa and the Ryukyu Islands were to be held to deny their use as air and sea bases from which the homeland could be attacked, and their armies in China were to prevent the Americans from securing bases in the lower reaches of the Yangtze and in the Canton area. The *Southern Army* was to concentrate on holding strategic zones in French Indo-China, Siam, Malaya and Sumatra.

During the early stages of the war the bulk of the Japanese army had been sent overseas to operate at strategic points in Asia or in the Pacific. The situation early in 1945 made it essential that army and air formations should be brought back for the defence of Japan, but the tide of war had turned so quickly that it was now impossible to withdraw many of the formations located in the southern and central Pacific. It was estimated that, in addition to the formations already in Japan, some forty new divisions, twenty independent mixed brigades and other ancillary units would be required for the defence of the homeland. To provide for these and to meet as far as was possible the need for improving the country's air defence, some one and a half million reservists (of whom there were theoretically some four and a half million fit for active service) would have to be called up. Although on paper it appeared that there was adequate manpower to meet the new requirements, in practice this was not the case for the Japanese Government had made little attempt during the course of the war to draw up any co-ordinated military/civil mobilization plan, with the result that about half the pool of reservists, including most of the skilled men required for drafting to the technical units of the new formations, had been taken into the food and munition industries. To provide the required number of men for the new formations, *Imperial General Headquarters* realized that they would have to withdraw trained officers and technical personnel, as well as stores and munitions, from Manchuria.

In the circumstances they decided to give priority to the expansion of fighter and anti-aircraft formations and to increased production of weapons for them. A well-equipped and trained land force for home defence was to be organized, even if it had to be limited in size, backed by a mainly civilian force which would inevitably be poorly armed. As a corollary to these measures, the self-sufficiency of the forces overseas, particularly those in Manchuria and China, was to be increased as far as possible so that they could operate without assistance from the homeland.

Towards the end of January *Imperial General Headquarters* began to issue instructions to give effect to these plans. In Manchuria *Kwantung Army* had been progressively weakened since August 1943 by the despatch of formations to the central and southern Pacific, with the result that by the beginning of 1945 its strength had been reduced from seventeen to ten divisions,[1] and, as it also suffered from a shortage of officers, technical units, arms and equipment, it had become an unbalanced force of comparatively low fighting efficiency. Nevertheless, *Imperial General Headquarters* moved yet another first-line division (*71st*) to reinforce Formosa, which they considered might be invaded, and recalled selected officers and men as well as arms and equipment to provide a nucleus for the new formations in Japan. To offset this and give *Kwantung Army* at least a semblance of strength, eight new divisions (*121st–128th*) and four new independent mixed brigades (*77th–80th*) were to be formed in Manchuria.

In Korea *17th Area Army* was to be formed early in February and made responsible for the defence of the country and in particular of the main north–south railway. The existing garrison of three depot divisions was to be increased by the formation of two new first-line divisions (*79th* and *96th*) in Korea, using local recruits.

In Japan, to replace the original three commands (*Eastern, Central* and *Western*), five new area army headquarters (*11th, 12th, 13th, 15th* and *16th*), together with five military district headquarters (*North-Eastern, Eastern, East Coast, Central* and *Western*), were created,

---

[1] Compare Appendix 12, Volume III, with Appendix 7 of this volume. Between August 1943 and August 1944 *1st Division* had been sent to Japan, *9th, 24th* and *28th* to the Ryukyu Islands, *14th* and *29th* to the central Pacific, *10th* to Formosa, *8th* and *2nd Armoured* to the Philippines and *27th* to China. This left six of the original divisions in Manchuria. The *Kwantung Army* had, however, been brought up to a strength of ten divisions by the arrival of four newly-formed divisions (*107th, 108th, 111th* and *112th*). In the latter part of 1944 *12th Division* had been ordered to Formosa and *23rd* to the Philippines, and had been replaced by the newly-formed *119th* and *120th* Divisions.

the former assuming responsibility for operations and the latter for administration.[1] At the same time, with depot divisions as a nucleus, a beginning was made in the formation of the first group of eighteen new first-line divisions.[2]

The *China Expeditionary Force* was ordered to abandon any long-range operations contemplated against Chungking and to prepare to meet an American invasion along the southern and eastern Chinese coasts, with special emphasis on the lower regions of the Yangtze River and the retention of control of areas in which the Americans could establish air bases within range of Japan and Manchuria.[3] Orders were also issued for the force to be reorganized and expanded by the end of 1945 to twenty fully and twenty partially equipped divisions, six divisions for internal security duties, seventeen independent mixed brigades and fifty line of communication battalions.[4] Since there was a distinct possibility that the Americans might make a landing somewhere on the China coast in the early months of 1945 and since the difficulty of moving formations by sea was steadily increasing, sufficient troops to form three new divisions were hurriedly assembled in Japan and sent to China. By the end of March 1945, *131st, 132nd* and *133rd Divisions*, as well as twelve independent mixed brigades and the necessary army troops, had been formed in China, and *Headquarters 6th Army* had been moved from Manchuria to Shanghai to command the formations allotted for the defence of the lower regions of the Yangtze River.

The *10th Area Army* was also formed in February to co-ordinate the defence of Formosa and the Ryukyu Islands. It was to take command of *32nd Army* (*24th, 28th* and *62nd Divisions*), which had hitherto been responsible for the defence of the Ryukyu Islands, and *40th Army*, newly created to command the formations in Formosa. To rebuild the strength in Formosa, reduced by the transfer of *10th Division* and an independent mixed brigade to the Philippines early in 1944, *40th Army* (*12th, 50th* and *66th Divisions*) was to be reinforced by *9th Division* from Okinawa as well as by *71st Division* from Man-

---

[1] See Sketch 7, facing page 240. The *11th Area Army* (*North-Eastern District*) with headquarters at Sendai and *12th Area Army* (*Eastern District*) with headquarters at Tokyo to replace *Eastern Command*; *13th Area Army* (*East Coast District*) with headquarters at Nagoya and *15th Area Army* (*Central District*) with headquarters at Osaka to replace *Central Command*; and *16th Area Army* (*Western District*) with headquarters at Fukuoka to replace *Western Command*. The *5th Area Army*, already responsible for Hokkaido, Sakhalin and the Kurile Islands, was also provided with a newly-formed (*Northern*) administrative district headquarters.

[2] Owing to the shortage of manpower and materials, the new divisions for the defence of Japan had to be raised in three groups: the first of eighteen divisions in February and March, the second of eight divisions in May and the third of sixteen divisions in June. Of the first group, thirteen (*140th, 142nd–146th* and *151st–157th*) were to be allotted to Honshu (the main island), one each to Hokkaido, Sakhalin and the Kurile Islands (*88th, 89th* and *147th*) and the remaining two (*150th* and *160th*) to Korea.

[3] See Map 10, facing page 340.

[4] At the time this order was issued *China Expeditionary Force* consisted of twenty-five infantry and one armoured divisions, ten I.M.B.s and eleven independent infantry brigades.

churia, while five independent mixed brigades were to be formed locally.[1] The commander of *10th Area Army* was instructed to hold Okinawa at all costs since it contained vital bases for air operations over the east China Sea, and, should the enemy attempt to land on the east coast of China, to assist *China Expeditionary Force* by destroying enemy convoys at sea by air attack.

Although the strategic value of *Southern Army* had greatly diminished after the loss of Leyte and the army was virtually cut off, it was still in a position to assist in delaying the expected invasion of Japan. Field-Marshal Count Terauchi was to hold strategically important areas in Luzon, French Indo-China, Siam, Malaya and Sumatra vital for the security of the Southern Region, and was to limit his other activities to maintaining control of areas containing essential natural resources or those which the Allies appeared most anxious to capture.[2] Since the Allies now controlled the sea communications in the Pacific and *Southern Army* could no longer rely on receiving supplies or reinforcements from Japan, he was to reorganize and develop internal transportation facilities so as to become as far as possible self-sufficient. He was to pay special attention to the security of French Indo-China, which was considered to be strategically the most important area in the Southern Region since it now lay open to invasion by American forces from the Philippines. Nevertheless, he was to send back to Japan men and materials required for the defence of the homeland, particularly air units and oil fuel.[3]

The *Southern Army*, whose headquarters had been moved from Manila to Saigon in November 1944, had in December formed *Headquarters 38th Army* in Saigon to command the garrison in French Indo-China, which then consisted of *21st Division* and two independent mixed brigades. An arrangement had already been made for the transfer of two divisions (*22nd* and *37th*) from China to French Indo-China during January and February 1945.[4] Terauchi ordered *Burma Area Army* to send *2nd Division* to reinforce *38th Army*, and ordered *4th Division* from Sumatra to be transferred to *39th Army* in Siam and *46th Division* from Celebes to *29th Army* at Singapore.

The Vichy French Indo-China Government, which had not been displaced by the Japanese when they entered the country before the outbreak of war in 1941, had co-operated with them during its early stages. However, after the defeats inflicted on the Japanese forces in

---

[1] It had been intended that *84th Division* should be sent from Japan to replace *9th Division* in Okinawa but, as experience had shown that outlying islands were very difficult to defend, *Imperial General Headquarters* decided that the defence of the homeland took priority over that of Okinawa and the move was cancelled.

[2] See Map 8, facing page 252.

[3] Despite every effort to carry out this order and to penetrate the Allied blockade, only about half the ships despatched got through.

[4] See page 122.

the central and south-west Pacific and on the Italian/German forces in north Africa, the attitude of the local government had turned to one of indifference. By February 1945 *Imperial General Headquarters* felt that, should the Americans make a landing on the French Indo-China coast, the French authorities might support them. On the 28th February, therefore, they ordered *Southern Army* to assume military control of the country in case of emergency. At 6 p.m. on the 9th March the Japanese Ambassador to French Indo-China presented a demand to the Governor-General that, in the event of invasion, the country would put itself under the control of the Japanese army and act in accordance with its instructions. If this were not accepted unconditionally within the next two hours, the Japanese army would consider this as a refusal on the part of the French Indo-China Government to carry out joint defence and would act accordingly.

At 10.15 p.m. (some two and a quarter hours after the given deadline) the French asked for more time in which to give a final answer, requesting the Japanese to refrain from military action until then. With the approval of *Southern Army* the commander of *38th Army* immediately ordered his formations to take control of the country. In the northern area there was resistance at Hanoi and Langson, but the former was occupied by the evening of the 10th and the latter by the 14th.[1] In the central area there was resistance at Hue, which was also overcome on the 10th, but in the south the Japanese occupied the Saigon area unopposed. The control of the country was completely in Japanese hands by the 14th March, but some French Indo-China army formations, numbering between twenty and thirty thousand men, escaped into China and other troops retreated into the mountains along the Siamese border. Japanese intelligence reports indicated that most of the local inhabitants were pleased that military action had been taken against the French authorities, since they felt that they now had the opportunity to achieve their independence. Annam and Cambodia did, in fact, declare their independence of the French shortly after the Japanese had taken control of the country.

The problem of the air defence of Japan had not been given serious consideration during the early stages of the war since it was thought that the forward defences in South-East Asia and the Pacific would protect it from invasion and ensure immunity from air attacks other than small-scale raids. Only four air regiments with about one hundred obsolete aircraft constructed in 1937 and some anti-aircraft units equipped with 75-mm. guns had therefore been allotted to the defence of Japan. After the Doolittle raid on Tokyo on the 18th April 1942 the air defence of Japan had been reorganized, *1st Air*

---

[1] See Map 13 in end pocket.

Army being formed with three (*17th, 18th* and *19th*) air brigades which were placed under the tactical control of *Eastern, Central* and *Western Commands* respectively, and steps were taken to produce 120-mm. anti-aircraft guns and to improve the radar installations. It was not, however, found possible at the time to replace the obsolete aircraft. At the same time the Imperial Navy formed three (*302nd, 332nd* and *352nd*) fighter groups and allotted them to the Yokohama, Kure (near Hiroshima) and Sasebo (near Nagasaki) naval districts.

During 1943 the Japanese learnt that the Americans were producing a high performance long-range bomber and that long runways were being built at Kharagpur near Calcutta and at Chengtu in China. Since this clearly indicated an intention to attack Japan, its air defences were further strengthened, production of more heavily armed high-altitude fighters was begun, that of 120-mm. anti-aircraft guns was speeded up and the training of pilots in high-altitude night flying was introduced. Progress, particularly in the training of pilots, was slow, since fuel was extremely limited and there was a dearth of suitable equipment and instruments for night flying.

After the reverses suffered in the Pacific in 1944 which brought the Americans nearer to Japan, the air defences were once again reorganized. The three air brigades became three air divisions (*10th, 11th* and *12th*), the number of air regiments in each was increased and two night-fighter squadrons were raised. At the same time a naval fighter group was placed under control of each of the three commands so that the army and navy interceptor forces could be co-ordinated, and additional 120-mm. anti-aircraft guns were brought into use.[1]

The American air attacks launched from China which began in June 1944 did comparatively little damage but quickly showed up the weakness of the air defences.[2] There were insufficient aircraft fit for night operations and none of them was equipped with radar. Their performance, speed and fire-power were inferior to those of the B.29s and their operations were seriously restricted by the shortage of airfields. As a result, the losses inflicted on the American attackers were negligible. When 21st Bomber Command began operating from the Marianas in November 1944 and attacks were made on the aircraft industry around Tokyo, Nagoya and Osaka,[3] the weakness of

---

[1] As a result of this reorganization the air defences of Japan consisted of:

	Aircraft	Anti-Aircraft Guns
Eastern Command (10th Air Division and 302nd Naval Fighter Group)	400	300
Central Command (11th Air Division and 332nd Naval Fighter Group)	200	150
Western Command (12th Air Division and 352nd Naval Fighter Group)	150	150
TOTAL:	750	600

[2] See pages 131–32 and Volume III, page 393.
[3] See pages 89–91.

the air defences became even more marked.[1] The Japanese military leaders now realized that they had neither the equipment nor the technical skill to defeat attacks by B.29 aircraft and therefore that Japan would be compelled to endure serious losses and damage to her industrial centres and cities without being able to offer any real resistance. Above all, they feared that the Americans would use incendiary bombs to which the Japanese type of residential buildings would be extremely vulnerable. In the hope of warding off attack they ordered the American bases in the Marianas to be attacked, but it soon became clear that the number of aircraft available for the task was too small to be effective.

After reviewing their general strategy in January 1945 *Imperial General Headquarters* decided that the air defences of Japan and the approaches to it would have to be further reorganized and strengthened, and that the action of naval and army units would have to be more closely co-ordinated. They entrusted the air defence of the homeland to *1st Air Army*, which consisted of *10th, 11th* and *12th Air Divisions* (some 400 fighter and forty-five reconnaissance aircraft), and to the naval air defence units (some 160 aircraft); the three air divisions were, however, placed under the operational command of *12th, 15th* and *16th Area Armies* respectively.[2] To meet the expected Allied advance towards the east China Sea, they began preparations, which were to be completed by the end of March, for an air operation ('Ten-Go') with the object of destroying approaching enemy convoys. The air forces allotted to 'Ten-Go' were *3rd, 5th* and *10th Air Fleets* and *6th Air Army* operating from Japan, *1st Air Fleet* and *8th Air Division* operating from Formosa and part of *5th Air Army* operating from China. The naval air forces were to attack the enemy task forces, and the army air forces the enemy transport convoys, though each would assist the other as necessary. Both air forces were instructed, however, to indoctrinate their pilots in the *Kamikaze* spirit and make every effort to increase the number and strength of such special attack units. The *10th Air Fleet* was to consist entirely of special attack (*Kamikaze*) units and was to be brought up to a strength of 700 aircraft by the end of March and 2,000 by the end of April. About half of *6th Air Army* (with a strength of some 700 aircraft) was also to consist of special attack aircraft, the remainder being fighter, bomber and reconnaissance aircraft used in their normal role.

To provide sufficient air units for the air defences of Japan and the approaches to it on reorganization, *Imperial General Headquarters* de-

---

[1] Efforts were then made to increase the climbing rate and ceiling of the fighter aircraft by stripping them of armour. By dint of hard training some pilots became capable of engaging the B.29s at 30,000 feet, but the fire-power of their aircraft was found to be inadequate. An attempt was then made to fit heavier weapons to several types, but this proved a failure as their performance was adversely affected.

[2] See Sketch 7, facing page 240.

cided, despite the danger of losses at sea, to bring back air formations from the Southern Region, for they considered that the situation in that area had so deteriorated that air support could no longer be of much assistance. They therefore ordered *Southern Army* to send back six air regiments from *2nd Air Division* in the Philippines, two air regiments and a heavy bomber squadron from *7th Air Division* in Celebes and one heavy bomber squadron from *9th Air Division* in Sumatra, as well as the transport brigade of *1st Airborne Group* and *30th Fighter Group* from the Philippines. The reduced *2nd* and *7th Air Divisions* were to be placed under command of *3rd Air Army*, while the airmen of *4th Air Division* and *1st Airborne Group*, which were now bereft of all their aircraft, were to be posted to *14th Area Army* as infantry reinforcements.[1] On the industrial front every effort was to be made and priority given to increasing the output of aircraft despite the interruption caused by enemy air attacks on aircraft factories. By these means it was estimated that by the end of March 1945 air formations equipped with some 3,100 naval and 2,100 army aircraft would be available to meet the expected American offensive towards Japan.

---

[1] See page 97.

CHAPTER XXI

THE PACIFIC
(February–March 1945)
The Capture of Iwojima

See Map 8 and Sketch 6

THE island of Iwojima in the Bonin Islands is only some four and a half miles long and two and a quarter miles broad. It lies at the southern end of a chain of islands extending due south for some 700 miles from the coast of Japan near the entrance to Tokyo bay, and is almost exactly half-way on the direct air route between Tokyo and the Marianas.[1] Except for Mount Suribachi, the extinct volcano at its southern end which rises to a height of 556 feet, its surface is comparatively flat.[2] It was therefore of great value to the Japanese as a staging point on their air route to the central and southern Pacific and as a convenient outpost for the defence of the homeland. During the early years of the war they had built airfields on it and, after the loss of the Marshall Islands in February 1944, had begun to prepare it for defence. When the Marianas were lost in July 1944 and the Americans began later in the year to use them as a base from which to bomb Japan, the importance of Iwojima was greatly enhanced, for it was evident that the Americans would require it as a staging point on their bombing route from the Marianas and as an advanced air base should they contemplate an invasion of Japan.

The *109th Division* (Lieut.-General T. Kuribayashi) was sent early in 1944 to garrison the island and put it in a state of defence. When the 'SHO' operations were being planned later in the year,[3] the preparation of the defences was speeded up. There were already two airfields in the centre of the island capable of operating light bombers and work was begun on a third in the north. Recognizing that, if the island were attacked, the beaches could not be held in face of the overwhelming naval and air strength which the Americans could bring to bear, Kuribayashi decided to turn the higher ground around Mount Suribachi at its southern end and on the plateau around Motoyama into fortresses which could be defended to the death, and

---

[1] See Map 8, facing page 252.
[2] See Sketch 6, page 239.
[3] See Chapter VI.

to cover the only two possible landing beaches by fire. Despite constant American air attacks,[1] strong, mutually supporting defensive positions in depth were built across the island between Nos. 1 and 2 Airfields and between No. 2 Airfield and Motoyama, connected by an intricate network of tunnels and supported by artillery and mortars sited in caves or concrete emplacements and tanks dug in hull-down. Defences of a similar type were built around Mount Suribachi. The beaches, in addition to being covered by artillery, mortar and machine-gun fire, were heavily mined. By the end of January 1945 the garrison had been brought up to a strength of some 21,000 men.[2]

Nimitz entrusted the Iwojima operation to Admiral Spruance (5th Fleet). Spruance placed Rear-Admiral R. K. Turner in command of the Joint Expeditionary Force and gave the task of capturing the island to 5th U.S. Amphibious Corps (3rd, 4th and 5th Marine Divisions). He arranged for the landing to be covered by the fast carrier force (Mitscher),[3] and by an amphibious support force (Rear-Admiral W. H. P. Blandy), the latter being an innovation designed to ensure that all the preliminaries to the actual assault were placed under one commander.[4] The 5th Fleet was to be maintained by a seagoing logistics group designed to provide it at sea with fuel, replacement aircraft, ammunition, spare parts, dry stores and clothing.

Since it was known that the Japanese had been actively preparing Iwojima for defence for a long period, Spruance decided that a considerable amount of 'softening up' would be necessary. He therefore arranged that 7th U.S.A.A.F. should attack the island's defences with B.24s from the Marianas night and day from the 31st January to the 15th February,[5] and that there should be a three-day naval bombardment from the 16th to the 18th February. To create a diversion and protect the amphibious support force from air attack while operating off the island, he ordered the full strength of the fast carrier force to be used to attack airfields and other targets in the Tokyo area of Japan for the first time on the 16th and 17th.

---

[1] See page 90.

[2] *Headquarters 109th Division, 2nd Mixed Brigade* and *145th Infantry Regiment* (totalling nine battalions), *26th Tank Regiment*, two independent machine-gun battalions, five independent anti-tank battalions, one heavy and two medium mortar battalions, and naval units with a strength of some 6,000 men.

[3] The fast carrier force had been reinforced and reorganized into five groups, one of which was a night flying group. It now consisted of eleven fleet and six light carriers, eight battleships, six heavy and nine light cruisers and 117 destroyers.

[4] The amphibious support force included an air support control unit, a support carrier group of twelve escort carriers, a minesweeping group, underwater demolition teams, three groups of L.C.I.(G) consisting of gunboats, mortar boats and rocket support boats and, until D-day, a gun-fire and covering force of six battleships, one light and four heavy cruisers and sixteen destroyers. Spruance, flying his flag in the cruiser *Indianapolis* and accompanied by two more battleships, took command of the gun-fire and covering force on D-day.

[5] The 7th U.S.A.A.F. dropped some 1,100 tons of bombs and 1,100 drums of napalm during the sixteen days. In addition twenty-one B.29s attacked pin-point targets on Mount Suribachi with 84 tons of bombs on the 12th February.

Thanks to careful routing and thick weather, the fast carrier force reached its flying-off position only sixty nautical miles from the Japanese coastline at dawn on the 16th February without being detected. Five fighter sweeps over Honshu were made early that morning, only one of which met with opposition. Later in the day bombers successfully attacked aircraft factories north-west of Tokyo, but the operations were hampered throughout the day by poor weather. Night fighters covered the Tokyo airfields at dusk but the Japanese made no counter-attacks. Next day both fighter sweeps and bomber attacks were launched but, as the weather grew steadily worse, Mitscher cancelled further operations before noon, recovered all airborne aircraft and withdrew his fleet towards the position west of Iwojima from where he was to give direct support to the landings on the 18th. During the attacks on Honshu some 2,750 sorties were flown and 88 aircraft were lost. The task force claimed to have shot down some 340 and destroyed 190 enemy aircraft on the ground. The Japanese admit that considerable damage was done to factories and grounded aircraft and that one 10,000-ton merchant ship was sunk in Tokyo bay. The fact that the homeland had been raided by carrier-borne aircraft caused considerable alarm and tended to confirm *Imperial General Headquarters'* worst fears.[1] Since their home defence air force was in the process of reorganization and training, the Japanese could not make any large-scale counter-attacks, but *6th Air Army* was ordered, as and when possible, to attack the American fleet to help the defenders of Iwojima.

The amphibious support force arrived off Iwojima at 6 a.m. on the 16th February. Minesweeping was immediately begun but, as visibility was poor, the island was bombarded only during the intervals when spotting aircraft could observe the fall of shot. The Japanese made no reply. Next day the weather improved and the heavy ships were ordered to close the beaches for destructive bombardment. This resulted in some of the defence batteries disclosing their positions. When later in the day the underwater demolition teams, covered by the L.C.I.(G.) flotillas, closed the shore, the Japanese, evidently assuming that the main landing was imminent, reacted strongly, thus disclosing the presence of more batteries which were immediately attacked by the heavy ships.[2] The bombardment of the first two days had blasted away much of the camouflage and revealed more of the island's defences. Thus when the heavy ships closed in on the third and last day of the preliminary bombardment to within 2,500 yards or less they were able to shatter many of the blockhouses and pillboxes.

---

[1] See page 232.
[2] On the 17th, in addition to the naval bombardment, forty-two B.24s dropped 832 260-lb. fragmentation bombs on selected defences.

At 6 a.m. on D-day, the 19th, Turner arrived with the main body of the expeditionary force. Shortly after dawn seven battleships, seven cruisers and the destroyers opened up the most concentrated pre-landing bombardment of the war in the Pacific. At 8 a.m. it was interrupted for some twenty-five minutes to allow aircraft of the fast carrier force to blast the beaches, airfields and the known defence positions with bombs, rockets and napalm. The naval bombardment was resumed at 8.25 a.m. and twenty-five minutes later lifted to form a moving barrage on the interior of the island.[1] The beaches were then attacked again for some seven minutes by the carrier aircraft and at 9 a.m. the first wave of assault craft carrying the Marines landed on the beaches on the south-eastern side of the island.

Despite the severity of the bombardments, the defensive works had been so well constructed and concealed that many of them had suffered little damage. No sooner had the first landing been made than the garrison, which had sheltered deep underground, came to life, and the Marines found themselves under heavy fire and virtually pinned to the beaches. To make matters worse the weather, suddenly deteriorated; rising surf and strong currents increased the difficulty of landing men, tanks and stores and for a time there was near chaos on the beaches. Progress ashore was slow and casualties heavy,[2] but, under cover of supporting fire by the guns of the fleet and accurate air attacks from the fast carrier force and the escort carriers, infantry attacked with flame-throwers and grenades and engineers with explosives blew in cave entrances and destroyed pillboxes. By the evening of the 19th the Marines had gained a beachhead some 1,000 yards in depth up to the edge of No. 1 Airfield, and had reached the west coast and the foot of Mount Surabachi.

During the next ten days the Marines slowly overcame the tough Japanese resistance. On the 23rd February Mount Suribachi was scaled, No. 1 Airfield secured and the edge of No. 2 Airfield reached. By the 1st March No. 2 Airfield and Motoyama were occupied, by the 16th the remaining Japanese defenders were hemmed into two pockets in the north and north-east of the island and by the 26th March all resistance had ceased. The battle for the island had been the costliest of any action to date in the Pacific. The Japanese garrison of about 21,000 died almost to a man, only about 200 prisoners being taken. The Americans suffered some 26,000 casualties, of which about 6,800 were killed.

The 5th Fleet did not go entirely unscathed while the struggle on the island was going on. On the night of the 20th/21st February come twenty Japanese aircraft attacked the fast carrier force without

---

[1] During this pre-landing bombardment 31,000 shells were fired, of which nearly 4,000 were of 12–16-inch calibre.

[2] On the first day they amounted to about 2,500.

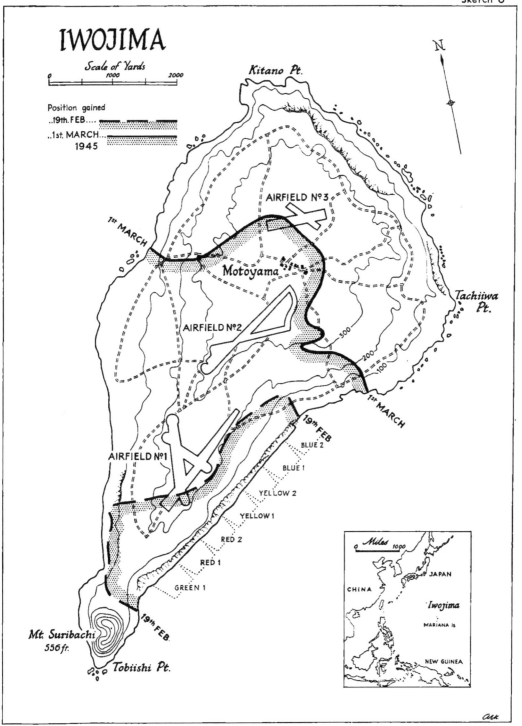

IWOJIMA

Scale of Yards

1000   2000

Position gained

..19th. FEB....

..1st. MARCH...

1945

N

Kitano Pt.

AIRFIELD Nº 3

1st MARCH

Motoyama

Tachiiwa
Pt.

AIRFIELD Nº2

500

200
100

1st MARCH

19th FEB

AIRFIELD Nº1

BLUE 2

BLUE 1

YELLOW 2

YELLOW 1

RED 2

RED 1

GREEN 1

19th FEB

Mt. Suribachi
556 ft.

Tobiishi Pt.

Miles   1000

JAPAN

CHINA

Iwojima

MARIANA Is

NEW GUINEA

success but next afternoon six *Kamikazes* attacked the fleet carrier *Saratoga* and within three minutes five of them had hit their target. Two hours later five more attacked, of which four were shot down and only one succeeded in reaching its target. The ship remained afloat, but the damage was so severe that she had to return to the west coast of America for extensive repairs. The same evening two *Kamikazes* attacked the escort carrier *Bismarck Sea* which was operating to the east of Iwojima. One of them crashed on the ship and caused such damage that within a few hours she sank. The fast carrier force replied by launching more attacks on Japan on the 25th February but bad weather intervened and the strikes were largely ineffective. Mitscher thereupon withdrew to his base at Ulithi and, on his way there, bombed Okinawa on the 1st March.

Although the enormous American armada lay for weeks in the open sea off Iwojima and was therefore highly vulnerable to attack by submarines, the Japanese navy made no major attack and thus missed a great opportunity. Two midget submarines were sunk on the 26th and 27th February and one, after having been kept submerged by destroyers for some forty-eight hours, was forced to return to its base. Two more left Japan on the 1st March but soon returned without having achieved success. One large submarine was sunk on the 26th.

The American air force quickly made use of Iwojima. No. 1 Airfield was brought into use on the 6th March and P.51s of 7th U.S.A.A.F. began to operate from it on the 8th, thus enabling the escort carriers to be withdrawn to safety on the 10th. By the 16th No. 2 Airfield was in use and by the 23rd March one night and two day fighter groups were operating from the island and work had been begun to convert it into an advanced air base with three airfields.[1] From early April therefore B.29s could be escorted by fighters when attacking Japan, and, before long, damaged bombers had a haven to which they could return within a few hours' flying time from their targets. Iwojima, which had previously been a threat to the success of the B.29 bombing attacks on Japan, had now become an asset of inestimable value and was to save countless lives.[2]

---

[1] It was finally decided to construct only two airfields capable of operating long-range bomber aircraft. The first runway suitable for B.29s was completed on the 7th July.

[2] By the end of the war some 2,400 B.29s had made emergency landings on Iwojima. The air crews involved totalled some 25,000 men.

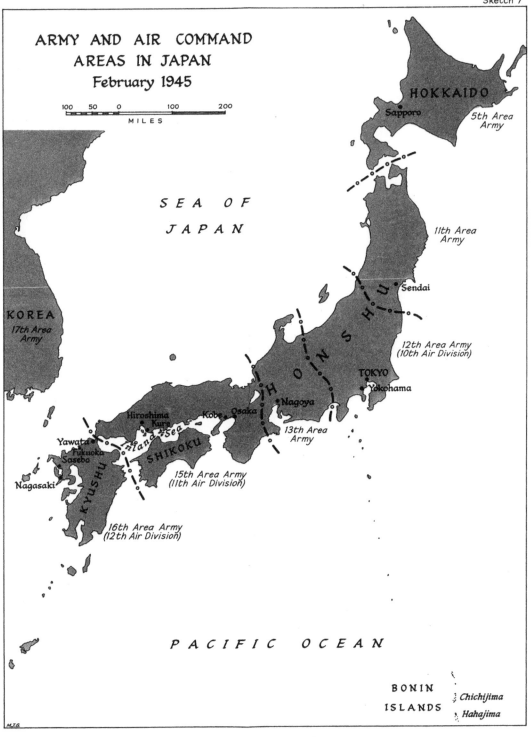

ARMY AND AIR COMMAND
AREAS IN JAPAN
February 1945

100 50 0   100   200
MILES

SEA OF
JAPAN

HOKKAIDO

Sapporo

5th Area
Army

11th Area
Army

Sendai

12th Area Army
(10th Air Division)

KOREA
17th Area
Army

TOKYO

Yokohama

Nagoya

Hiroshima
Kure

Kobe   Osaka

HONSHU

13th Area
Army

Yawata
Fukuoka
Sasebo

Inland Sea

SHIKOKU

15th Area Army
(11th Air Division)

KYUSHU

Nagasaki

16th Area Army
(12th Air Division)

PACIFIC OCEAN

BONIN

ISLANDS

Chichijima

Hahajima

M.J.G.

CHAPTER XXII

STRATEGIC AND ADMINISTRATIVE PLANNING

(February 1945)

See Maps 3, 11 and 13 and Sketch 20

ON the 5th February, two days after the receipt of his new directive from the Combined Chiefs of Staff,[1] Mountbatten issued an operation instruction to his Commanders-in-Chief in which he stated that his intention was to continue with the offensive in Burma to the limit of the resources available in order to secure the port of Rangoon before the monsoon. He gave A.L.F.S.E.A. the specific tasks of securing the Ledo–Burma Road, opening up the Taungup–Prome road as a fair-weather supply road, developing airfields as might be necessary to enable air resources to be deployed for the air support and maintenance of the land forces in their advance towards Rangoon, and finally capturing Rangoon by the 1st June and destroying the main Japanese forces in Burma, excluding Tenasserim.[2] He placed all the 'Dracula' and 'Dracula' mounting base resources at A.L.F.S.E.A.'s disposal and directed that nothing was to be held back for post-monsoon operations. He also said that, as the completion of the overall task might depend on the provision of engineering and administrative resources beyond those under the control of his Commanders-in-Chief, they were to notify him at the earliest possible moment of any additional requirements. The effect of these instructions was immediately to involve A.L.F.S.E.A. in planning for the fourth phase of 'Extended Capital', which was to take place after the expected capture of Meiktila and Mandalay in March.

As soon as he knew that the 'Dracula' resources had been placed at his disposal, Leese asked for an examination to be made at Supreme Headquarters of an amphibious operation which would assist in the capture of Rangoon before the monsoon. The Joint Planning Staff reported on the 11th February that such an operation would best take the form of an assault by a glider-borne brigade to secure the Elephant Point area at the mouth of the Rangoon River and a follow-up

---

[1] See page 209.
[2] See Map 13 in end pocket.

by two amphibious brigades to carry out the exploitation, the operation being mounted between the 20th April and the 5th May.[1]

Meanwhile Slim had also been considering his future plans and had sent Leese an abridged copy of 14th Army/221 Group planning paper No. 10 on the 7th February giving his appreciation and outline plan for the fourth phase of 'Capital', together with a summary of its administrative implications. Two days later the complete bulky and detailed document was sent to A.L.F.S.E.A. with a covering letter which stated that, as the full administrative implications could not be gauged at 14th Army Headquarters, it was for A.L.F.S.E.A. and Eastern Air Command to say whether the administrative bill could be met. The outline plan was based on the assumption that 14th Army would by early March have occupied the Mandalay–Meiktila–Thazi area, with IV Corps (two divisions) in the Meiktila–Thazi area and XXXIII Corps (three divisions) in the Mandalay–Maymyo–Kyaukse area, and that an advanced army base would have been established at Myingyan with forward maintenance areas at Kyaukse and Pagan.[2] One division would be in army reserve.

Slim pointed out that, although for administrative reasons it was imperative that Rangoon should be captured before the monsoon, the destruction of the Japanese divisions driven east from Meiktila and Mandalay during the third phase was the biggest prize to be gained in the fourth. Since these divisions would be quite capable of staging a counter-attack against the flank and rear of the forces detailed to advance southwards along the railway axis towards Rangoon, and against the vital airfields and administrative installations in the Meiktila–Mandalay area, it was essential that, in any plan adopted, the strongest force which could be provided should be allotted the task of destroying them. Once the Japanese divisions had been destroyed, Rangoon could be occupied without difficulty. He therefore proposed that XXXIII Corps (consisting of 2nd, 19th and 20th Divisions, 268th Brigade, 254th Tank Brigade less a regiment, and 11th Cavalry) should be directed to destroy the Japanese forces in the Kyaukme–Takaw–Thazi–Mandalay area and capture Loilem and Takaw, which would entail an advance due eastwards in the Shan States, while IV Corps (consisting of 17th Division, 255th Tank Brigade and 16th Cavalry), reinforced by a second division (5th) by mid-March, should be directed south on to Rangoon moving down the railway axis, and 7th Division with 28th (E.A.) Brigade and a regiment of 254th Tank Brigade should move down the Irrawaddy axis and capture Yenangyaung, Magwe and Prome. Every means of increasing the speed of the advance was to be exploited, and the supporting air forces were to be based as far forward as possible

---

[1] See Map 11, facing page 414.
[2] See Map 3, facing page 55.

since they provided the most potent means of impeding and slowing up the Japanese withdrawal. Provided that the Meiktila–Mandalay area was occupied by the 1st March he hoped to reach Rangoon between the 10th and 15th April. It will be noted that Slim had originally intended to send IV Corps down the Irrawaddy valley and XXXIII Corps down the road and railway to Rangoon.[1] The change now introduced in the role of IV Corps ensured the most economical use of its quick-moving motorized divisions and enabled Messervy to plan the advance on Rangoon as the immediate exploitation of the capture of his objective—Meiktila.[2]

Slim said that his object from the administrative point of view was to maintain the forces he needed for carrying out his plan and to provide them with the necessary mobility, while maintaining sufficient flexibility to meet unforeseen contingencies and to exploit any opportunities which might arise. He realized that his plan would strain his administrative resources to the utmost and that the principal consideration would be that of the airlift, especially as XXXIII Corps' thrust to the east would involve a much longer turnround for transport aircraft. He was, however, prepared to accept a reduction in the size of XXXIII Corps if the whole of it could not be maintained so far from the air bases.

He proposed that 425 tons of supplies a day should be delivered by road and I.W.T. to Monywa and Myingyan by the end of April and throughout the monsoon, and that a stockpile of forty-five days' supplies should be built up in that area. He hoped that some 300 tons a day (dropping to 100 tons during the monsoon) would be delivered along the Taungup–Prome road which was to be opened up by XV Corps. To maintain his six divisions, the necessary corps and army troops and 221 Group R.A.F., to provide for moves of formations, units and reinforcements, and to augment the Central Burma Stockpile by 200 tons a day, he estimated that the airlift would have to deliver 2,245 tons a day during the first half of March, 2,520 tons during the second half of the month and an average of 2,540 during April, figures greatly in excess of the forecast of available airlift from the 1st March onwards. He would also require twenty-three G.P.T. companies, against which only fifteen and a half would be available by the 1st March. The plan would therefore be administratively feasible only if the airlift could be considerably increased and seven and a half additional G.P.T. companies were put at his disposal by the 1st March.

At a meeting at Supreme Headquarters on the 14th February, Major-General I. S. O. Playfair (Major-General, General Staff A.L.F.S.E.A.) explained Slim's plan and said that it could not be carried out if any administrative resources were used for mounting

---

[1] See page 165.
[2] See Chapter XVI.

an operation such as the one suggested by the Joint Planning Staff on the Elephant Point area, which under the proposed timetable would be of no assistance to 14th Army in capturing Rangoon. He did not, however, necessarily rule out a smaller operation which could be mounted from Arakan and reach the critical area much sooner, and which might lend assistance to 14th Army's attack on Rangoon. Since it now seemed that the city could be captured by 14th Army, Mountbatten decided that the plan for an amphibious attack on it prepared by the Joint Planning Staff should not be proceeded with, but that an amphibious force should be formed and plans prepared so that it could exploit any success gained by 14th Army by means of a thrust down the Malayan peninsula or alternatively, if 14th Army operations did not turn out as planned, by launching an amphibious attack on Rangoon.

Slim's plan, which made heavy demands on transport aircraft and motor vehicles, had been accepted in principle by A.L.F.S.E.A. but not as yet by Eastern Air Command. Mountbatten gave orders for it to be examined with particular reference to the airfield deployment programme and the provision of the administrative facilities involved; a committee under the chairmanship of Major-General R. F. S. Denning was set up and ordered to report by the 20th.

The Denning Committee reported that, as it stood, the plan proposed by 14th Army could not be supported logistically since the available aircraft could not at sustained rates lift more than about 1,400 tons a day to the operational areas envisaged. The committee therefore proposed that the plan should be modified to reduce the airlift by at least 500 tons a day to bring it within the carrying capacity of the available transport aircraft flying at twenty-five per cent above the sustained rate. This would probably necessitate a considerable reduction in the scope of the operations eastwards into the Shan States. With regard to the approved airfield deployment programme,[1] the committee recommended that at Akyab resources should be concentrated on the preparation of fair-weather airstrips with one all-weather airstrip as an insurance, provided that its construction did not conflict with the use of the fair-weather strips. On Ramree Island one all-weather airfield should be built, work on the fair-weather strips being abandoned. Every effort should be made to ensure that air supply bases at Akyab and on Ramree Island could operate as early and intensively as possible. The committee also recommended that the development of the all-weather road from Tamu to Kalewa and the establishment of an I.W.T. service on the Chindwin should continue; that the size of the Central Burma Stockpile should be reduced from forty-five to thirty days' supplies; and that the project to develop the Taungup–Prome road as a supply route should be abandoned.

---

[1] See pages 201–2.

In co-operation with Eastern Air Command, A.L.F.S.E.A. had meanwhile carried out its own examination of the plan, and on the 19th Leese had warned Slim that in the form presented it was not administratively feasible, for it entailed the greatest number of formations advancing on axes which took them farthest from their air bases, thus reducing the tonnage that the available aircraft could deliver to far below that required; the concept of the operations would therefore have to be considerably modified.

As by this time it was evident that 14th Army's advance was going fast, it was becoming necessary not only to step up the tonnage which could be carried by the airlift but also to accelerate the opening of the new air base at Akyab since the date originally planned, the 15th April,[1] would be far too late. In view of help given by the Royal Navy and an arrangement made at New Delhi on the 8th February whereby the I.W.T. fleet in Arakan was to receive some 2,400 deadweight tons of additional barges with suitable powered craft to match by the 1st March,[2] Leese decided to withdraw all air supply (130 tons a day) from XV Corps from the end of February and use it for the maintenance of 14th Army. He ordered his Major-General i/c Administration (E. M. Bastyan) not only to examine the possibility of getting the air base at Akyab into operation by the 15th March with two squadrons, and by the 31st March with four squadrons, but also to examine how far the maintenance of current XV Corps and air force operations would prejudice the speedy development of the air bases at Akyab and Ramree. At the same time he told Bastyan that he was prepared to accept a curtailment in XV Corps' operations only if it was absolutely necessary to achieve the object. He was, however, prepared to agree to a reduction in the scale of reserves to be held at Akyab from thirty to fifteen days.

Bastyan held a meeting with all concerned on the 20th February. The 25th Division, operating in the Dalet–An area, was then being maintained from Akyab, and it seemed as if the maintenance of 82nd (W.A.) Division, when it came off air supply on the 1st March, would have to fall on Kyaukpyu. The 26th Division and 22nd (E.A.) Brigade, whether on Ramree Island or operating on the Arakan coast, would continue to be maintained from Kyaukpyu. It was evident that these commitments were prejudicing the development of the air bases at Akyab and Kyaukpyu, which were already behind schedule.[3]

---

[1] See page 202.

[2] On the 8th March some 600 I.W.T. craft, employing some 6,000 men, were operating between Chittagong and Kyaukpyu. Of these, about 200 were in south Arakan. The craft included coasters, creek steamers, paddle steamers, tugs, powered lighters, 'Z' craft, oil barges, harbour launches, Burley boats, flats, port lighters, Higgins barges, waterboats, fire-fighting vessels and hospital carriers.

[3] The schedule was for Akyab to be ready by the 15th April and Kyaukpyu by the 1st May. See page 202. The administration of both air bases had been taken over by L. of C. Command on the 12th February and was thus A.L.F.S.E.A.'s responsibility (see page 219 and fn. 1).

Chittagong, where the air base was already supplying some fifty-five per cent of 14th Army's requirements,[1] was also congested and would become more so when the advanced base at Maungdaw was closed on the 1st March and by the fact that four American air squadrons were unexpectedly operating from Cox's Bazar.[2] The meeting recommended that, if the Akyab air base development were to be accelerated as required, 25th Division would have to be withdrawn from operations to Akyab for onward despatch to Madras,[3] steps would have to be taken to maintain 82nd (W.A.) Division by sea without involving Kyaukpyu and the American air squadrons would have to be removed from Cox's Bazar by the 1st March. Furthermore, if the air base at Kyaukpyu were to be ready on time there should, if possible, be no further operations involving 26th Division. If Leese were prepared to accept these conditions, then air supply from Akyab to 14th Army could begin with two squadrons on the 20th March increasing to four on the 1st April, and Kyaukpyu would be ready on time.

It was so important that 14th Army, which was conducting the main offensive, should not be hampered by lack of supplies that Leese accepted these recommendations and, though it meant that the scope of operations in Arakan would be drastically reduced, he told XV Corps that the withdrawal of its formations was to continue as originally planned.[4] At the same time, to free Akyab, and to a lesser extent Kyaukpyu, from the burden of maintaining XV Corps and thus accelerate their development as air bases, the maintenance of 82nd (W.A.) Division, as well as elements of 25th Division until they were all withdrawn from the mainland, was to be direct by sea from Chittagong to Ruywa or to the F.M.A. at Tamandu as soon as it was opened (about the 10th March). The 22nd (E.A.) Brigade and 4th Indian Brigade were to be maintained from Kyaukpyu until they were landed on the Arakan coast, when maintenance would be by sea from Chittagong to a convenient F.M.A. to be opened wherever necessary; ammunition and P.O.L. would, however, continue to be supplied by Kyaukpyu.

So that Slim could be given data on which to revise his plan for the final phase of 'Extended Capital', A.L.F.S.E.A. and Eastern Air

---

[1] See Appendix 21.
[2] These squadrons were part of 1st Air Commando Group.
[3] One brigade at a time on the 1st, 15th and 31st March.
[4] The withdrawal of formations as originally planned and as actually took place was: 81st (W.A.) Division, originally Chittagong to Madras in March after concentration at Chiringa in February, actually 5th to 24th March; 3 Commando Brigade, originally on completion of 'Romulus', actually from Akyab to Madras 14th to 18th March; 25th Division, originally in March on relief by 82nd (W.A.) Division, actually 2nd to 5th April; 26th Division, originally during April and May, actually one brigade from Ramree to Madras between 28th March and 1st April, but was sent back to Kyaukpyu to rejoin the division for 'Dracula' (see Chapter XXVIII).

Command had meanwhile been drawing up a fresh army/air administrative plan, based on the Denning Report and on their own examination of the problems involved, taking into account the decisions reached on accelerating the completion of the Akyab and Kyaukpyu air bases. This plan assumed that aircraft would be operating at 160 hours a month (some thirty per cent above the sustained rate) until the monsoon and at the sustained rate during it, that supplies reaching 14th Army from the Imphal and Chittagong air bases would be landed in the Myingyan area which was within the economic range of 250 miles from both, and that supplies from Akyab could be landed at suitable airheads established by the leading formations of 14th Army during their drive south within the economic range of 250 miles.[1]

On the 23rd February Mountbatten, who had been touring the Northern and Central fronts, met his Commanders-in-Chief at Calcutta. Park (Air Commander-in-Chief Designate, who took over from Garrod on the 24th), Wheeler (Deputy S.A.C. and P.A.O.), Fuller (Deputy Chief of Staff), Sultan and Stratemeyer were also in attendance. Leese reported that the 14th Army offensive was going well and that he expected the battle for Mandalay would be over in two or three weeks; his object would then be to drive into the centre of the Japanese armies, striking towards Loilem, and, while keeping as large an enemy force as possible engaged in central Burma, to move one corps southwards towards Rangoon.

The new army/air plan was then examined, and it was realized that, as the revised figures for deliveries were the highest possible, Slim would have to reduce his requirements. Leese said, however, that he was satisfied that the plan was sound and, when put into effect, would meet the requirements for current and proposed operations in Burma. Mountbatten thereupon directed Park and Leese to put it into effect at once, and reaffirmed that the object of the current operations was to occupy Rangoon before the monsoon.

In order to indicate the maintenance capacity likely to be available until May, Leese gave 14th Army the relevant details of the army/air plan on the 25th February. It was based, he said, on fourteen transport squadrons being available by the 1st March, increasing to fifteen by the 20th but decreasing to fourteen on the 15th May; on fair-weather airfields at Akyab being available to operate four squadrons from the 1st April until the monsoon and on all-weather airfields being available at both Akyab and Ramree to operate three squadrons from each throughout the monsoon; on the completion of an all-weather road from Tamu to Kalewa and its maintenance throughout the monsoon; and on the operation of an I.W.T. service on the Chindwin from Kalewa to Myingyan throughout the monsoon with a

---

[1] See Sketch 20, facing page 412.

capacity which would gradually increase from 400 tons a day and reach 700 tons a day by the 15th May.

On this basis the air transport capabilities of the C.C.T.F., as shown in the table below,[1] would meet requirements with certain limitations.

Calculations were based on all deliveries being landed in Burma within a radius of 250–280 miles from the despatching air bases. If the distances had to be increased up to 300 miles the tonnages shown for the 280-mile radius would have to be reduced by ten per cent, and if up to 350 miles by twenty per cent; deliveries beyond a 350-mile radius would be uneconomical and could be made only in extreme cases of operational necessity. Should supply-dropping be required, the maximum that could be dropped would be 500 tons a day,[2] which would mean an overall reduction in the total airlift of 75 tons.

To ensure that the largest number of transport aircraft operating from the Imphal and Chittagong air bases were employed at the most economical radius, it was essential to make it possible for them to deliver at Myingyan by improving the facilities for delivery by road and rail forward of the airhead. A.L.F.S.E.A. therefore proposed to rehabilitate the railway from Myingyan to Thazi and thence as far south as possible, to repair the principal roads from Myingyan to Thazi and thence to the east and south, to increase the I.W.T. facilities south of Myingyan without any reduction in the I.W.T. lift from Kalewa to Myingyan and, finally, to provide 14th Army with five 3-ton G.P.T. companies or their equivalent.

In the absence of a guarantee that Rangoon would be captured before the monsoon, tonnage would have to be allotted to establish a stockpile of at least fifteen days' supplies in the Myingyan area. Of this, 200 tons a day would be delivered by the airlift, 169 tons a day

[1]

Air Bases	1st–20th March*		20th–31st March*		1st–30th April		1st–15th May		After 15th May	
	Miles radius†		Miles radius†		Miles radius†		Miles radius†		Miles radius†	
	250	280	250	280	250	280	250	280	250	280
Imphal	480	420	305	261	114	100	114	100	85	75
Chittagong	1,352	1,198	1,400	1,280	1,442	1,280	1,520	1,340	962	850
Akyab	—	—	182	160	365	320	441	388	258	227
Ramree	—	—	—	—	—	—	—	—	258	227
TOTAL	1,832	1,618	1,887	1,701	1,921	1,700	2,075	1,828	1,563	1,379

Notes:
Aircraft would fly 160 hours a month from 1st March to 15th June and thereafter at 125.
* Average delivery for March, 1860 and 1,660 long tons.
† See Sketch 20, facing page 412.

[2] This figure was determined by the loading capabilities.

by the L. of C. Transport Column and the balance by I.W.T.[1] Leese suggested that, to reduce the overall maintenance lift, two R.A.F. wings (908 and 910) might be located in the Kalewa area, where they could be maintained by road.

To co-ordinate operations on his three fronts, Leese issued an operation instruction on the 27th February to N.C.A.C., 14th Army and XV Corps. He said that the battle for Mandalay was approaching its climax and large enemy forces were now concentrated in that area. The battle would therefore be slow and probably grim, but its outcome was certain. His object was to destroy the Japanese forces in the Mandalay area, which would necessitate a concerted effort by 14th Army and N.C.A.C. Sultan was therefore to seize the Kyaukme–Lashio area and then turn south-west to co-operate in the battle for the Mandalay area. Slim was to destroy the Japanese armies in the Mandalay area and capture Rangoon before the monsoon. In Arakan the withdrawal of XV Corps formations was to continue as planned; Christison, with the resources at his disposal but without air supply, was to destroy the enemy forces in the An area and operate towards Prome as far as resources permitted from a bridgehead in the Taungup area.

Slim had been warned that it would not be possible to maintain a corps in the mountainous country east of the Mandalay–Rangoon road and that his plan for the destruction of the Japanese forces in that area and to cover the left flank of his drive on Rangoon would have to be modified. However, Force 136 operations in being or being planned would, in fact, to some extent protect that flank.

In addition to the nine special groups dropped into Burma on the Northern front at the beginning of 1945,[2] the force had inserted three other special groups east of the Irrawaddy on the Central front. One of these was dropped near Maymyo to watch enemy movements along the Burma Road; it passed back excellent intelligence until caught up by 14th Army's advance. The second was dropped at the edge of the Shan plateau east of Yamethin, but was soon ambushed and destroyed. The third was dropped near Pyinmana but failed to gain the confidence of the local inhabitants, and by the time it was reached by 14th Army it had achieved nothing.[3]

Operation 'Character' (the raising of Karen Levies) began later in February. The three groups designated to organize the northern,

---

[1] It should be noted that, despite 14th Army's proposal to build up the Central Burma Stockpile to forty-five days' reserve, the Denning Committee proposed that this should be reduced to thirty days and in the revised army/air plan A.L.F.S.E.A. reduced it to fifteen days' reserves.

[2] See page 192.

[3] See Map 11, facing page 414.

central and southern zones of the Karen district were dropped by parachute between the 21st and 25th in the vicinity of Papun at the south-eastern corner of the central area.[1] When the first party arrived the local population was undecided whether they would support the operation, fearing a renewal of Japanese reprisals.[2] The arrival of the remaining parties, together with supplies of rifles, Bren guns and Sten guns turned the scale, and by the end of the month some 250 static and 150 mobile Levies had been recruited. Recruitment in the Papun area exceeded expectations and it seemed that the numbers of Levies which could be recruited would depend only on the speed at which it was possible to fly in arms and equipment without attention being drawn to the dropping areas. Early in March the parties for the northern and southern zones set off for their respective areas, but, because of delays, a fourth group was dropped in the northern zone towards the end of March and the original northern group took over part of the central zone. Recruitment and training of the Levies went on at great speed so that they would be ready to operate when ordered to do so by 14th Army.

The beginning of the plan to co-operate with the Burma National Army (B.N.A.) and Anti-Fascist Organization (A.F.O.) (operation 'Nation') brought to the fore a number of political problems since, by its very nature, it involved dealings with organizations which, though anti-Japanese, were probably equally anti-British and likely to demand immediate independence for Burma after the eviction of the Japanese.[3] The arming of members of the A.F.O. and their use as guerrillas might also produce a number of long-term political disadvantages. On the advice of the Chief Civil Affairs Officer, Burma— Major-General C. F. B. Pearce (C.C.A.O.(B))—Leese decided in the middle of February that no member of the A.F.O. was to be armed by any military force. Force 136 objected to this ruling and urged most strongly that, while there should be no arming of the A.F.O. as an organization, a limited number of individuals claiming membership of the A.F.O. should be armed as necessary, subject to a suitable

---

[1] See page 205.

[2] During the retreat from Burma in 1942 some 1,500 Karen Levies were raised by officers of the Oriental Mission (which later became Force 136) to cover the flank of the withdrawing Burma Army, but were later ordered to disperse and hide their arms and await the return of British forces. Major H. P. Seagrim (Burma Rifles, attached Force 136) remained, however, in hiding in the Papun area. Two other officers were dropped in that area in October and December 1943 with a wireless transmitter, and contact was established with Seagrim. Useful information was passed back to India together with an estimate that some 5,000 Levies could be recruited, but with the warning that they should not be armed until a British offensive was imminent. The two officers were ambushed and killed in February 1944 and the Japanese began reprisals in the Karen Hills. To save further reprisals Seagrim gave himself up, was imprisoned and eventually shot in September 1944.

[3] For a detailed account of the A.F.O. and nationalism in Burma see Donnison, *British Military Administration in the Far East, 1943–46* (H.M.S.O., 1956), Chapter XIX.

system of control being instituted which would facilitate the recovery of the bulk of the arms distributed. Force 136 also pointed out that refusing help to the A.F.O. was likely to cause more trouble than giving it.

On the 27th February Mountbatten, to whom these conflicting views had been submitted, told Leese that he reserved all political decisions for himself and that, in reaching them, he took into account the views expressed by the Governor of Burma (then resident in India); he said that the advice Leese had received from the C.C.A.O.(B) did not fit into 'the broad policy for Burma which I have decided on'. He ruled that political considerations were not to limit the activities of Force 136 and ordered Leese to instruct the force to proceed immediately with its planned operations. Mountbatten's point of view is clear from the following extract from his report:

'. . . If I now discouraged the only Resistance movement in Burma (apart from the hill tribes), I would not only be losing what military assistance the guerrillas might provide; but I would be increasing our operational difficulties by throwing away a chance of fighting over territory in which elements of the local population were actively engaged in fighting on our side. . . . I might find myself . . . in the predicament of having to suppress the B.D.A. [B.N.A.] by force, and to divert to this task troops who should be fighting the Japanese. Moreover, I considered that armed intervention on our part, to prevent the Burmese from fighting the common enemy and helping to liberate their own country, could not fail to have unfavourable repercussions in the United Kingdom, in the United States, and in other parts of the world.'[1]

In accordance with Mountbatten's ruling, Leese issued a directive on the 8th March dealing with procedure for arming and negotiating with the civil population in Burma. The directive stated that the Supreme Commander had laid down that no arms were to be supplied to the A.F.O. or other political bodies in Burma as organizations but, subject to his previous approval, permission could be given for the arming of such limited numbers of the A.F.O. or any other political organization in Burma as might be necessary for approved Intelligence or any other para-military operations. All proposals for the issue of such arms would be submitted through Headquarters A.L.F.S.E.A. to the Supreme Commander for a ruling. Great care was to be taken to keep accurate records of weapons issued, and the directive made it clear that the force concerned in the issue of arms would be responsible, when the time came, for their recovery.

---

[1] Mountbatten's Report, Section B, para. 490.

The receipt of a new directive for S.E.A.C. on the 3rd February had enabled an investigation to be carried out on the course that future strategy in the theatre should take. Thus, at the conference at Calcutta on the 23rd,[1] Mountbatten and his Commanders-in-Chief were able to consider proposals put forward by the Joint Planning Staff. They agreed that the correct strategy would be to advance on Singapore by way of the Kra Isthmus, capturing as a first step Phuket Island which would provide a convenient forward air base and naval anchorage.[2] Leese said he was prepared to undertake the capture of the island (operation 'Roger') if he had at his disposal two divisions and a commando brigade. Mountbatten ruled that this strategy was to be adopted whether or not Rangoon was captured before the monsoon, and directed that planning for 'Roger' should begin on the 2nd March so that the operation could be launched on the 1st June.

On the 26th February he told the Chiefs of Staff that, subject to the fall of Rangoon, his main objective would be Singapore. He indicated that he planned to secure the Phuket Island area early in June and the Port Swettenham—Port Dickson area in October, and that he hoped to reach Singapore between December 1945 and March 1946. Although 'Dracula' in its original form was not now likely to be carried out, it was essential that, as an approved plan, it should not be cancelled since the resources allotted for it would be required for the operations down the Kra Isthmus. He requested, moreover, that, if possible, the tempo of their delivery should be increased.

In order to provide a force for the Phuket Island operation, Mountbatten asked Auchinleck to form a new corps headquarters in India. At the end of February Auchinleck raised XXXIV Indian Corps (Davies)[3], making use of some of the units of the disbanded Special Force,[4] and 23rd Indian Division (the India Command reserve division). He agreed to assign the new corps to S.E.A.C. on the understanding that his reserve was replaced as soon as a division was withdrawn from Burma. Davies established his headquarters at Poona, took under command 23rd Division, 81st (W.A.) Division and 3 Commando Brigade. He was instructed to have plans for the capture of Phuket Island ready by the 1st April.

---

[1] See page 247.
[2] See Map 13 in end pocket.
[3] Davies, who had formerly commanded 25th Division, was replaced in command of the corps by Lieut.-General O. L. Roberts on the 12th March.
[4] See pages 29–30.

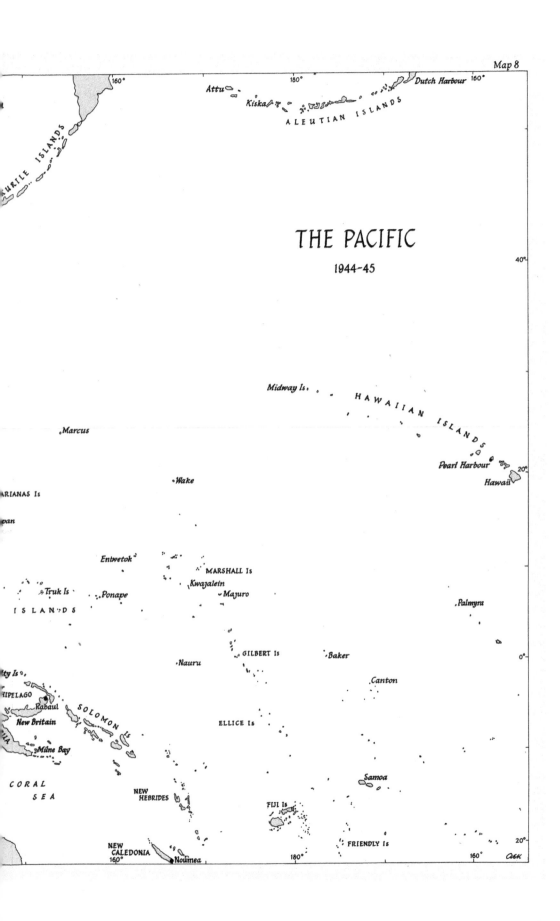

Map 8

THE PACIFIC

1944–45

Attu
Kiska
Dutch Harbour
A L E U T I A N   I S L A N D S

KURILE ISLANDS

40°

Midway Is
H A W A I I A N   I S L A N D S
Marcus

Pearl Harbour
Hawaii
20°

Wake

RIANAS Is

pan

Eniwetok
MARSHALL Is
Kwajalein
Truk Is
Ponape
Majuro
Palmyra

I S L A N D S

GILBERT Is
Nauru
Baker
0°

Canton

ty Is
HIPELAGO
Rabaul
SOLOMON Is
New Britain
ELLICE Is

Milne Bay
Samoa

CORAL
SEA
NEW
HEBRIDES
FIJI Is
NEW
CALEDONIA
160°
Nouméa
180°
FRIENDLY Is
160°
20°

CHAPTER XXIII

THE CENTRAL FRONT
(February–March 1945)
The Crossing of the Irrawaddy and the
Capture of Meiktila

See Maps 1, 2, 3 and 9 and Sketches 8, 9, 10 and 21

AFTER 14th Army's rapid advance in January from the Chindwin to the Irrawaddy, during which Pauk and the Monywa–Yeu–Shwebo area were occupied and bridgeheads established across the river at Thabeikkyin and Kyaukmyaung,[1] there had to be a pause in operations. This was necessary to enable airfields to be developed and new airheads established in the forward areas,[2] the R.A.F. to be redeployed, armour, supplies of food, ammunition and bridging material to be brought forward, the army's administrative tail to be closed up, the redeployment of the air bases in eastern Bengal to be completed,[3] and plans to be made for the crossings.

As 14th Army advanced towards the Irrawaddy during January, 221 Group R.A.F. had gradually moved its wings forward in close support. Towards the end of January it was arranged that two Thunderbolt (P.47) and two Mustang (P.51) squadrons of Nos. 1 and 2 Air Commandos, based in Arakan, would provide close support for IV Corps,[4] and the air commandos accordingly set up a joint headquarters with Messervy. By the beginning of February all but one of the short-range squadrons of 221 Group had been moved forward. Headquarters 906 Wing was located with four squadrons at Tabingaung and three at Onbauk; Headquarters 907 Wing with two squadrons at Sinthe and one at Imphal; and Headquarters 909 Wing with two squadrons at Kalemyo and one each at its satellites at

---

[1] See Map 3, facing page 55. For the situation of 14th Army on the 1st February 1945 and the enemy dispositions as known on that date see Sketch 10, facing page 274.

[2] At the beginning of February, IV Corps was being maintained from airheads established on airstrips at Kan and Tilin, but preparations were being made to open airheads at Sinthe and, when occupied, Myitche. The XXXIII Corps was being supplied from airheads at Budalin and Shwebo pending the opening of forward airstrips nearer the Irrawaddy at Allagappa and Ondaw. See Appendix 19.

[3] See Chapter XVIII and Appendix 15.

[4] See page 182.

Thazi and Taukkyan.[1] So that they should not add to the air supply commitment in the forward areas, the long-range Mosquitos, Beaufighters and Thunderbolts of 908 and 910 Wings (each of three squadrons) were kept back for the time being at Kumbhirgram and Wangjing respectively.[2] The forward deployment of the short-range squadrons enabled air cover to be extended over enemy airfields in central Burma, and ensured that close support for the army would be readily available during the crossings of the Irrawaddy and the thrusts on Meiktila and Mandalay. The long-range squadrons had, however, to fly some four to five hundred miles to reach enemy airfields and rail and road communications in south-east Burma. To give 14th Army additional support, 905 Wing of 224 Group R.A.F. (four Thunderbolt squadrons), based in Arakan but working from airfields in the forward areas, was to operate as required from day to day under 221 Group, and, on the assumption that the assault on Mandalay would require air support in excess of that which could be given by 221 Group, 12th Bombardment Group U.S.A.A.F. from the Strategic Air Force (four B.25 Mitchell medium bomber squadrons) was placed under its operational command. At the same time it was arranged that up to half of the heavy bombers of the Strategic Air Force, i.e. five Liberator squadrons, would be available to the group as required for attacks on selected targets in the battle area and, in particular, to take all possible action to destroy enemy forces attempting to reinforce Mandalay or withdraw from it towards the Meiktila area. To ensure close co-operation, the R.A.F. provided Visual Control Posts (V.C.P.s) to move with the forward troops to assist in the identification of targets and to control from the ground aircraft engaged in close support of the army formations to which they were attached.[3]

On the 9th February Combined 14th Army/221 Group Headquarters moved forward from Indainggyi to Monywa,[4] and the same day, after a conference between Leese and Slim, the outline plan for the fourth phase of 'Extended Capital', given in 14th Army/221 Group planning paper No. 10 of the 7th,[5] was confirmed, subject to A.L.F.S.E.A.'s ability to meet the increased demands for airlift and

---

[1] 221 Group had been reinforced by six squadrons since the 12th December and the number of squadrons in the wings had been adjusted to conform with the tactical situation.

[2] See Sketch 21, facing page 522.

[3] The V.C.P. was usually carried in a jeep but in thick country light pack sets were carried by wireless operators. The team with a V.C.P. consisted of an R.A.F. officer with flying experience and two wireless operators trained in radio telephony so that communication could be established with the aircraft. In the early stages of 14th Army's advance there were only three V.C.P.s, one with IV Corps and two with XXXIII Corps, but by the time Mandalay and Meiktila were captured there were fifteen in operation in 14th Army. During the advance on Rangoon they proved invaluable.

[4] On the 22nd February this headquarters was joined by the rear headquarters of 221 Group R.A.F. from Imphal.

[5] See pages 242–43.

motor transport. The 5th Division, then in army reserve in the vicinity of Dimapur, was to be reorganized on similar lines to 17th Division by the 1st March,[1] and moved forward later in the month to join IV Corps and take part in the battle south of Mandalay.

While waiting for the army to close up to the Irrawaddy and for the administrative services to be reorganized and made ready for the further advance, Slim's corps commanders were perfecting their plans for the crossing of the river by IV and XXXIII Corps and for the attack on Mandalay by 19th Division, which was already holding two bridgeheads on the east bank. Slim's strategic object was to deceive the Japanese into believing that the whole of 14th Army was moving on Mandalay and that the force in the Myittha valley was a comparatively small diversionary one. If this could be achieved, there was a strong possibility that the consolidation of IV Corps' bridgehead by 7th Division and the concentration within it of 17th Division would not be hindered by any counter-attack in strength and would be completed so quickly that the thrust on Meiktila would catch the Japanese unprepared and unable to meet it.

Slim planned to begin the battle for the Irrawaddy with a thrust by 19th Division to break out of the Kyaukmyaung bridgehead and seize Singu, from where a good fair-weather road led to Mandalay. This was to be followed by a crossing in the Myinmu area by 20th Division with as great a show of force as possible and an aggressive build-up of a bridgehead. These two operations would, Slim hoped, attract all available enemy reserves since they would give the Japanese a clear indication that 14th Army was beginning an enveloping attack in great strength against Mandalay, as in fact would be the case, though it would not be the main thrust. Twenty-four hours after 20th Division had begun its move, 7th Division was to cross as unostentatiously as possible near Nyaungu and, as soon as a large enough bridgehead had been secured, the Meiktila striking force (17th Division less one infantry brigade, but with a tank brigade less one regiment under command) was to cross the river and make for Meiktila with all possible speed by way of Taungtha.[2] There was to be no attempt to keep the road behind it open; its third (air transported) brigade was to be flown in as soon as an airstrip near Meiktila could be secured. The 7th Division was later to reopen the road to allow the administrative tail to go through to Meiktila. Until sufficient river-crossing material became available for it to force a crossing

---

[1] See pages 180–81.
[2] The striking force in detail consisted of 17th Indian Division less 99th Brigade, 255th Tank Brigade less 116th R.A.C., 16th Light Cavalry (armoured cars) less one squadron, and 59th Self-Propelled (S.P.) Battery. The tank brigade had two lorried infantry battalions—4/4th Bombay Grenadiers and 6/7th Rajput Regiment. The whole force was mounted in wheeled or tracked vehicles.

near Ava, 2nd Division was to continue its efforts to mop up the Sagaing area.

Messervy (IV Corps) gave Evans (7th Division) the task of establishing a corps bridgehead at Nyaungu by the 15th February, after first capturing Pakokku. The exact date was to be fixed later. To ensure a sufficiently rapid build-up on the far bank to get 17th Division off on its drive on Meiktila before the enemy realized that his lifeline was threatened, a short turnround was essential since there was a dearth of river craft. Nyaungu was an obvious place for such a crossing as at that point the river narrowed to about half a mile, there were no sandbanks to negotiate, it was a direct crossing and, from the village, roads and tracks ran east to Mandalay and Meiktila and south to the railway at Kyaukpadaung and the Yenangyaung oilfields. Though the corps crossing place was to be Nyaungu, this did not necessarily mean that the initial assault crossing was to be made there. In fact, reconnaissance showed it to be impossible for, on the northern bank of the river opposite Nyaungu, there was an 800-yards-wide sandy beach, impassable for wheels until track was laid and, as there was no cover, this could not be done until Nyaungu was secured.[1] The assault crossing had, however, to be made close enough to it to enable the bridgehead to be quickly extended to include the village.

To ensure quick success the enemy had to be misled as to the exact crossing point and thus, in addition to the army and corps deception plans,[2] a very good divisional one was necessary. Evans planned to deceive the Japanese by presenting them with three alternatives and choosing a fourth. The first alternative was an advance on Pakokku by 114th Brigade, followed if possible by a crossing. The second was a simulated crossing by 28th (E.A.) Brigade on the right flank at Seikpyu towards Chauk in conjunction with a deception parachute landing, and, to draw further attention to this flank, Evans arranged for a column (Westcol) to emerge from the hills west of Yenangyaung and make for the river as if to cover the Africans' flank.[3] The third was a subsidiary crossing at Pagan, six miles south-west of Nyaungu, by a battalion of 89th Brigade in country boats, to take place just before the main crossing. Nobody was to appear interested in the real crossing area, the north bank of the river eastwards for 15,000 yards from Myitche, in which the actual crossing points were to be selected after secret reconnaissance. Any movement in that area had to be made in the half light or darkness because the south bank consisted of

---

[1] See Sketch 8, facing page 268.
[2] See pages 173–74 and Appendix 20.
[3] Westcol had been formed when 7th Division turned east at Tilin and the Lushai Scouts, no longer needed on that flank, joined the Chin Hills Battalion to cover the corps' western flank.

an almost continuous cliff about a hundred feet high, which completely overlooked the north bank.

By the 3rd February the plan for 7th Division's assault crossing was ready for the final co-ordinating conference, and Evans estimated that it was time to start 28th (E.A.) Brigade (Brigadier W. A. Dimoline) off on its mission to Seikpyu. It was accompanied by a battery of artillery, a troop of armoured cars and a deception unit and, to give an impression of strength, its vehicles all carried the 11th (E.A.) Divisional sign and moved at wide intervals, trailing bushes to make continuous dust clouds. On the 5th, 114th Brigade (Brigadier H. W. Dinwiddie) began its move on Pakokku. Its first objective, the hill overlooking the road junction at Kanhla through which all vehicles and materials for the assault crossing had to pass to reach the assembly positions on the river bank, was to be attacked by 4/5th Royal Gurkhas. The 2nd South Lancashire Regiment, which was to be placed under command of 33rd Brigade (Brigadier R. G. Collingwood) to lead the assault at the main crossing, was to move across country, clear the river bank and carry out the necessary detailed reconnaisances.[1] The 89th Brigade (Brigadier W. A. Crowther), less 1/11th Sikhs which was detailed to carry out the subsidiary crossing at Pagan, was to hold the divisional firm base at Pauk, where the assault force, less the South Lancashires, was to assemble and carry out final dry-shod rehearsals.[2] Meanwhile 17th Division (Major-General D. T. Cowan) moved forward to Kan where it was near enough to get to the river quickly and far enough in rear not to be discovered.

The supply and road situation had improved so much by the 7th February that the date for the general advance to begin hinged solely on the readiness of 7th Division to start to cross the Irrawaddy. Its preliminary moves had already begun. The 28th (E.A.) Brigade had reached Seikpyu unopposed and so successful was it in simulating a major crossing that it was counter-attacked and driven back to Letse, thereby drawing away from the main battlefield the only formidable striking force the Japanese had in the area.[3] The leading battalion of 114th Brigade (4/5th Royal Gurkhas) found the Japanese dug in on the hill dominating the Kanhla road junction and, though an immediate attack by the leading company nearly reached the top of the

---

[1] The 2nd South Lancashire was selected in view of its experience in amphibious operations gained in Madagascar in 1942. See Volume II, Chapter VIII.

[2] The assault force consisted of Headquarters 33rd Brigade, 2nd South Lancashire, 4/15th Punjab, 4/1st Gurkhas, 1st Burma Regiment, one company 13th F.F. Rifles M.G. Battalion, one troop 24th Anti-Tank Regiment, one battery 3-in. mortars, observation and reconnaissance parties of divisional and corps artillery, and nine tanks of 116th R.A.C. In support were one bridging company and two field park companies for erecting landing bays and rafts and operating assault boats and outboard motors, one beach signal group, the necessary provost and medical units and an infantry company as a working party. The R.A.F. provided one V.C.P.

[3] This was *153rd Regiment*, less one battalion (the *Katsu Force*); see page 59 fn. 2.

hill in hand-to-hand fighting, it was not until the 10th that, with the assistance of tanks, it was finally cleared. By this time 4/14th Punjab, which had rejoined its brigade after dealing with a Japanese detachment in the hills north of Saw,[1] had by-passed Kanhla. Leaving the South Lancashires to move to the river bank, the brigade then pushed eastwards, linked up with 7/2nd Punjab (the divisional reconnaissance regiment which had moved down the west bank of the Chindwin to keep touch with 20th Division)[2] and closed on Pakokku; the village was found resolutely defended by *214th Regiment* whose rearguard had caused the delay at Kanhla. The 1/11th Sikhs had meanwhile found Myitche clear and had moved south-west to collect country boats and find a place from which it could cross to Pagan.

The capture of Kanhla on the 10th was the signal for Slim to order 14th Army's general advance to begin. As darkness fell, the assault force of 7th Division began to pass through the village on its way to its assembly positions. Far to the north, Rees, who had regrouped 19th Division and got medium and light tanks across the Irrawaddy into the Kyaukmyaung bridgehead,[3] which had been expanded towards Singu, ordered 64th Brigade (Brigadier J. G. Flewett)[4] to take Singu on the 11th. Fifty miles upstream from Pakokku, Gracey, who had been awaiting the signal to go, ordered 20th Division to cross on the night of the 12th/13th. By this time 2nd Division (Nicholson) had established itself from the mouth of the Mu River through Ondaw to Saye, with 268th Brigade on its left linking up with 19th Division. It had beaten off a Japanese counter-attack in the Mu River area and was meeting determined resistance at Saye. Nicholson had already issued orders on the 7th for an assault crossing of the Irrawaddy to be made by 5th Brigade in the area immediately east of the mouth of the Mu River, on or after the 14th February.

The operations of 14th Army were planned in such a way that Mandalay, actually XXXIII Corps' objective, was made to appear the sole army objective. This had the effect of focusing Japanese attention on XXXIII Corps' advance and away from IV Corps' main thrust towards Meiktila. In the north 19th Division, which had begun to break out of its bridgehead at Kyaukmyaung by capturing Singu on the 11th February, now prepared to carry out the exhortation in the closing sentence of an order of the day issued by Rees, 'Your task now is, on to Mandalay.' By the 20th February the Japanese had stopped trying to contain the division's bridgeheads, and Rees had sent 98th

---

[1] See page 182 fn. 2.
[2] See page 175.
[3] One squadron 150th R.A.C. (medium tanks) from corps reserve and one squadron of 7th Light Cavalry (light tanks) from 20th Division had been allotted to 19th Division.
[4] Flewett succeeded Bain on the 8th February.

Brigade (Jerrard) from Thabeikkyin on a sweep south to link up with the rest of the division in the Kyaukmyaung–Singu area. On the 22nd the division regrouped for its drive south on Mandalay and next day Rees issued his orders. The 62nd Brigade (Morris) was to advance south with its right on the Irrawaddy, and the 64th, with all the armour, was to advance astride the main track to Nyaungwun and seize the high ground to its north-east; 98th Brigade was to remain in divisional reserve at Singu.[1]

The advance of 62nd Brigade met little resistance, but its progress was considerably hindered by the many deep chaungs, lakes and marshes which barred the way. The 64th Brigade, on the other hand, had to fight its way through the hills to Nyaungwun.[2] The battalion, moving along the bare rocky heights on the east of the track, suffered intensely from thirst and heat, and 7th Light Cavalry operating along the road had two tanks destroyed and two disabled by anti-tank weapons concealed in the thick jungle through which the track ran along the foot of the hills. Nevertheless on the 2nd March Nyaung-wun, the lake area to the west and the hills to the east were secure, and Rees ordered 98th Brigade to pass between the two forward brigades and make with all speed for the Chaungmagyi Chaung, believed to be held in strength, and establish a bridgehead across it. The task of 62nd Brigade on the right was to clear the twelve-mile-long Sambo Island and link up with the 98th at the mouth of the Chaungmagyi Chaung, and that of 64th Brigade was to fight its way down the main road, clearing the enemy off the hills on each side of it. It was hoped that the Japanese holding the hills around Point 1487 would be cut off by the advance of 98th Brigade.

The bold southward thrust of this brigade through the narrow gap between the hills and the eastern arm of the Irrawaddy which formed Sambo Island seems to have taken the Japanese by surprise, and by the evening of the 4th a bridgehead had been established across the Chaungmagyi Chaung near its junction with the Irrawaddy. Meanwhile 62nd Brigade, having cleared Sambo Island, moved east into the area behind 98th Brigade and thus effectively cut the retreat of the Japanese who were opposing 64th Brigade to the north. By the 5th March 19th Division's forward troops were deployed along the Chaungmagyi Chaung, with patrols moving out to intercept the remnants of the Japanese force withdrawing from the hills to the north before the advance of 64th Brigade. On this day Rees formed a motorized column known as Stiletto Force to cross the chaung as soon as the engineers could bridge it, and then strike south-east to the

---

[1] Identifications made it appear that at this time 19th Division was opposed by *15th Division* plus *I/119th Battalion of 53rd Division*, a battalion or elements of *58th Regiment* of *31st Division* and *53rd Engineer Regiment*. There was also identification of *128th Regiment* but it was not thought that any unit of that regiment was in the area.

[2] See Map 3, facing page 55.

road at Madaya to threaten the rear of the Japanese force believed to be holding the south bank of the Chaungmagyi Chaung.

Under Gracey's plan for 20th Division's crossing, which was to begin some thirty-six hours before that of 7th Division of IV Corps, 100th Brigade (Rodham) was to establish a bridgehead about six miles wide and four miles deep with its left on the river bank opposite Myinmu. The 32nd Brigade (Mackenzie) was to establish a subsidiary bridgehead in the Kyigon area with one battalion, and subsequently extend it to link up with the Myinmu bridgehead on its left.[1] The 80th Brigade (Greeves) was concurrently to maintain activity in the angle between the Chindwin and Irrawaddy to give the impression of a crossing there, and eventually pass through the Myinmu bridgehead and make for Kyaukse, the divisional objective. A strong artillery group of four field regiments, one medium and one heavy anti-aircraft regiment and one troop of 7·2-inch howitzers was so sited that it could be switched to any part of the divisional front.[2] A Sea Reconnaissance Unit was to report at the last moment whether the landing beaches were clear. The 7th Light Cavalry (less one squadron), an engineer company and a Mobile Balloon Flight of the corps artillery remained in the divisional commander's hand for use as required. With the boats and rafts available,[3] it was not expected that the whole division could get across in under ten days.

The 2nd Border Regiment began to cross from Satpangon as soon as it was dark on the 12th February, and by 2.30 a.m. on the 13th was across, meeting with opposition only from small reconnoitring patrols. The 14/13th F.F. Rifles followed at 4 a.m. By this time the Borders had pushed inland and eastwards and were in contact with an enemy force whose artillery opened up on the crossing, though with little effect: a company of infantry, which crossed at 9.30 a.m. to occupy the beach defences, suffered no loss. By nightfall on the 13th the bridgehead was 2,500 yards wide and 1,000 yards deep.

The subsidiary crossing by 32nd Brigade, with 1st Northamptonshire Regiment leading, met with trouble from the outset, for in rough water and a rising river many boats were swept downstream and others overturned. When the first flight finally landed at Kyigon it ran into enemy fighting patrols almost at once, as did a company of 9/14th Punjab Regiment which was landed a few miles upstream to

---

[1] See Map 9, facing page 320.

[2] The 9th, 10th, 18th (S.P.) and 114th Field Regiments, 1st Medium Regiment and 101st Heavy Anti-Aircraft Regiment.

[3] Ninety-three ranger boats, fifty-nine assault boats, thirty-five outboard motors, eight light tank rafts, three motor vehicle rafts, six propulsion units and nine DUKWs. By no means all the boats were serviceable as they had had to be carried overland by bad tracks from the Chindwin.

form a link with the Myinmu bridgehead. Enemy mortars and artillery, which soon opened harassing fire on the beaches, became so accurate that all idea of daylight crossings had to be given up and it was not until the morning of the 14th that the Northamptons were across, but without their transport. In the Myinmu bridgehead 100th Brigade completed its crossing during daylight on the 13th. That night the first Japanese counter-attack was made, and 80th Brigade in reserve on the near bank reported that enemy patrols were still active on the many islands of the Chindwin–Irrawaddy confluence.

For the next few days there was bitter fighting since the Japanese did their utmost to prevent 32nd Brigade from linking up with 100th Brigade. The brunt of the fighting fell on 14/13th F.F. Rifles in the right sector of the Myinmu bridgehead until the 18th,[1] when, supported by two squadrons of 7th Light Cavalry, 4/10th Gurkhas took Talingon and consolidated, after which the tanks were withdrawn. For the next five days this tiny village was the centre of what was described by the divisional commander as the fiercest fight of the whole operation. From the 19th to the 25th the Japanese (identified as *I/*and *III/16th Battalions*) kept up their attacks, supported by tanks and artillery. Although it was known that enemy tanks were in the area, extensive air reconnaissance had failed to locate them, until on the 19th two Hurricanes of 20 Squadron R.A.F., flying low over the area, noticed a suspicious heap of foliage in the open. They attacked and their fire blew away the branches, disclosing a Japanese tank. Other similarly camouflaged tanks were seen and the whole squadron was brought into action. In some thirty sorties the squadron destroyed thirteen tanks with rockets and cannons; this was a serious blow to the Japanese who had by this time expended the greater part of their limited resources in armour, but it was fortunate for the defenders of Talingon. Though fighting in well-dug and wired positions, the Gurkhas suffered 177 casualties and at the end of the action 504 enemy dead, one gun and eighteen machine-guns were found on the battlefield in addition to large quantities of small arms and equipment.

At Kyigon Japanese fighting patrols reached and attacked the beach but, after dealing with these, 32nd Brigade steadily extended its bridgehead eastwards, and by the 21st was complete on the south bank, except for its transport which had not yet crossed the river as it could not operate there until tracks had been made. By this time all three battalions of *215th Regiment* had been identified but all, according to prisoners-of-war, were much under strength. The enemy seemed by now to have realized that the Myinmu bridgehead was the main threat and infantry attacks on 32nd Brigade ceased on the 21st,

---

[1] Jemadar Parkash Singh, 14/13th Frontier Forces Rifles, was posthumously awarded the Victoria Cross for his part in this action, which cost his battalion 143 casualties.

though accurate harassing shelling continued. On this same day 80th Brigade (Greeves) crossed into the Myinmu bridgehead and on the following two days 1st Devonshire Regiment took over Talingon and cleared the Kanlan area. By the 28th the two bridgeheads had made patrol contact, but the two battalions of 32nd Brigade in the Kyigon area were still without their transport and more or less immobilized. While 80th Brigade cleared a way from the Myinmu bridgehead westwards to get the transport through to 32nd Brigade, 100th Brigade pushed east to link up with 2nd Division which had begun its crossing at Ngazun on the 24th February. On the 5th March 20th Divisional artillery crossed the river, the Kyigon bridgehead was closed down and 32nd Brigade moved to the Kanlan area, suffering many casualties on the way from almost continuous artillery harassing fire. The division was now ready to break out of its bridgehead.

By the end of February identifications of no fewer than thirteen Japanese battalions belonging to four different divisions (*2nd, 31st, 33rd and 53rd*) had been obtained in the attacks against 20th Division's Myinmu bridgehead, and the possibility of a very large concentration in the area could not be ignored. It had always been Slim's intention that, as soon as 5th Division's reorganization had been completed, it should be moved forward to join IV Corps at Meiktila. He now decided, in view of the possibility of a Japanese counter-attack from Sagaing towards the Chindwin, to concentrate it (less 9th Brigade) east of the Chindwin at once. On the 3rd March he ordered it to begin its move to Monywa, led by 161st Brigade which was already under orders to join IV Corps. By locating his reserve at Monywa, he was in a position either to use it to meet the possible enemy counter-attack or to move it quickly to join IV Corps as originally intended. The 9th Brigade was to be sent forward to Palel in readiness to be flown to Meiktila to reinforce IV Corps when required.

Owing to the shortage of assault boats and rafts, 2nd Division's crossing could not take place until 20th Division had more or less completed its crossing. Thus, except for an attack on Saye, which was taken with trifling loss on 20th February, there was little activity in its sector until the 23rd when 268th Brigade began to take over the Sagaing salient from 4th Brigade. Next day 5th Brigade began to cross, while 4th and 6th Brigades concentrated to follow it as soon as a bridgehead had been established. Two crossings had been planned —one by 7th Worcestershire Regiment from Tadaing about half a mile east of the mouth of the Mu River, and the other by 1st Queen's Own Cameron Highlanders from Myittha opposite Ngazun, some two miles further east. The Worcesters' crossing soon became disorganized and was abandoned, but the Cameron Highlanders pressed home their assault in spite of fifty-two casualties, and finished their crossing in daylight on the morning of the 25th covered by smoke screens and artillery concentrations. Although accurate enemy artillery and mortar fire prevented the recovery of several craft and some of the four available DUKWs which had been stranded, a two-battalion bridgehead had been established by the Cameron Highlanders and 2nd Dorsetshire Regiment about 3,000 yards west of Ngazun by the evening of the 25th. The next day the Carabiniers began to cross but, as a result of strenuous use since the Irrawaddy crossings began, the tank rafts were beginning to break down, and by the early morning of the 27th only a half squadron was across. However, enemy opposition was light and by then an adequate bridgehead had been established at Ngazun. On the 27th, 6th Brigade passed through and pushed south to deepen the bridgehead while 4th Brigade crossed into it and began to push west to make contact with 20th Division. By the evening of the 1st March the bridgehead was four and a half miles wide and two and a half deep, its left including Ngazun with its ferry and the road running south from it. On the 2nd March (the day that 4th Brigade contacted 100th Brigade of 20th Division) the divisional artillery completed its concentration in the bridgehead. The fighting to expand the bridgehead was chiefly characterized by fanatical attacks on tanks by individual Japanese soldiers in the thick scrub country south of Ngazun. The Carabiniers lost three tanks and had twelve casualties among tank crews from grenade, submachine-gun and even sword attacks by Japanese who succeeded in jumping on to moving tanks with open turrets. By 5th March the whole division was across the river and was preparing to strike eastwards at Ava.

The stroke which was to deal the Japanese army in Burma a mortal blow was IV Corps' thrust to Meiktila. This began in the early hours of the 14th February, when the leading troops of 7th Division crossed the Irrawaddy near Nyaungu. The speed and secrecy with which two divisions and an armoured brigade were concentrated across the river and a powerful column sent to strike at the astonished defenders of Meiktila was largely due to the fact that the enemy's attention had been focused on the crossings already made by XXXIII Corps to the north and the south-west of Mandalay, the very name of which drew to itself the attention of Allies and Japanese alike. The very obvious advances to envelop this historic city provided Slim with the perfect cover for the thrust which isolated the Japanese *15th* and *33rd Armies* from their base and eventually resulted in *Burma Area Army* losing control.

The crossing of the Irrawaddy in the Nyaungu area was the longest opposed river crossing attempted in any theatre in the Second World War. At the point selected for the initial crossing, four miles upstream from Nyaungu, the river was over 2,000 yards wide, but observation over the take-off bank was sufficiently good to make it necessary for all preparations to be undertaken under cover of darkness. Even without any opposition it was therefore a formidable undertaking. A Sea Reconnaissance Unit and a Special Boats Section, which had arrived in the area on the 11th, were to report whether any of the beaches appeared to be occupied. A company of the South Lancashires was to make a silent crossing by rowing from 'C' Beach at 3.45 a.m. on the 14th February, and occupy the ground on the cliff-top on the far bank between 'B.3' and 'B.4' beaches.[1] The rest of the battalion was to cross in powered assault craft at 5.30 a.m., by which time the Special Boats Section would have marked the sandbanks with screened lights. The remainder of 33rd Brigade and nine tanks were to follow as soon as possible.

By the night of the crossing the river had risen and there was a steady 3-knot current running which, combined with a strong wind, made the water 'lumpy'. Nevertheless, the silent crossing went according to plan and by 5 a.m. the company making it was in position on the cliff-top east of 'B.4' beach. Unfortunately two Japanese swimming in the river were encountered and shot by the Sea Reconnaissance Unit; this alerted the enemy and when the rest of the South Lancashires, who had been delayed by a breakdown in their embarkation arrangements, approached their landing beaches after daylight they came under fire from machine-guns at the water's edge. Two company commanders and one of the engineers in charge of the boats were killed, and several wireless sets were knocked out. The commanding officer's boat was sunk near the shore, and he escaped capture by swimming back across the river. Casualties mounted as many boats were swept down river past the machine-guns on the beaches. Under covering fire from tanks and artillery and from aircraft called up by the Visual Control Post, the boats made their way back to the near bank and at 8 a.m. the situation was much as it had been at 5 a.m., except that the company of South Lancashires above 'B.4' beach was now isolated and in danger of being overwhelmed. Collingwood ordered 4/15th Punjab to cross as soon as possible and arranged for all available tanks, artillery, and aircraft to cover it. By 9.30 the engineers succeeded in assembling at 'B' beach the boats which had got back, and the second attempt began. An eye witness describing the scene wrote:

'At 9.45 the leading company moved off under heavy covering fire. In view of the desperate possibilities that lay ahead the

[1] See Sketch 8, facing page 268.

parade-like calm of the embarkation was beyond all praise. With maddening sluggishness the boats nosed their way across the water. Two boats grounded on a submerged and treacherous sandbank, but the men, quite undaunted, waded shoulder deep in the swift current to the beaches. At last all the boats grounded and the men swarmed up the cliffs and nullahs to their objectives on the high ground. More and more boats followed, heavily laden with troops, until boats were going both ways in an almost continuous stream while the air and artillery curtain of fire moved gradually downstream and then back again behind the cliffs and beaches.'

By 1 p.m. the crossing had become a procession and by nightfall the original programme had almost been achieved, for three battalions were across. No crossings were made during the night so as to avoid any risk of damage to the craft, which were in short supply and irreplaceable.

Meanwhile the subsidiary crossing at Pagan had also met opposition. A patrol of 1/11th Sikhs, which had been hiding near Pagan with a wireless set, had reported the town unoccupied, but, just as the battalion was about to begin its crossing in country boats manned by local boatmen, the patrol gave warning that a Japanese column was marching in. The crossing went on but, when it came under fire, the boatmen panicked and the boats were swept downstream. Before the second attempt could be made, a small boat with a white flag put out from the far shore. In it were two *I.N.A.* officers, who said that the Japanese had gone north towards Nyaungu and left Pagan to be held by a company of *I.N.A.*, which wished to surrender. A platoon of Sikhs crossed in the only three boats now left, anxiously watched by their comrades for there was the possibility of treachery, but the garrison of Pagan marched down to the beach and laid down its arms.[1] By nightfall on the 14th the whole of the battalion was across and the right flank of the main crossing was secure.

At first light on the 15th the crossing of the main body of 7th Division was resumed. By this time the engineers had assembled tank rafts and landing bays, and all day a steady stream of tanks, men, animals, supplies and ammunition poured into the beaches. Workshops on both banks were set up by the I.E.M.E., who, by working day and night, succeeded in keeping sufficient power craft in operation. The Japanese in the area had meanwhile withdrawn into catacombs at Nyaungu. There they refused to surrender and, since it was certain death to try and enter, the entrances were blown in with high explosives. The number of Japanese who perished in the catacombs was never discovered. By the 16th Nyaungu was clear and contact had been made with the Sikhs in Pagan, which meant that the divisional

---

[1] Altogether 250 *I.N.A.* surrendered, 160 at Pagan and 90 at Nyaungu.

bridgehead was some 6,000 yards wide and 4,000 yards deep, with 89th Brigade holding the west and south-west face and the 33rd the east and south-east. On the left flank all was well, for 114th Brigade was mopping up at Pakokku. On the right flank, however, 28th (E.A.) Brigade was withdrawing on Letse pursued by a strong Japanese column.

On the 17th, although 7th Division had not finished crossing and the bridgehead was not yet big enough to hold the whole of the Meiktila striking force, Messervy ordered it to begin to move across the river at the corps crossing place at Nyaungu, opened that day, and, if necessary, concentrate part of the force outside the bridgehead but within the patrol area.[1] The 48th Brigade began to cross at once and, although the Japanese air force attacked 114th Brigade at Pakokku and 7th Division's beaches a few miles upstream, it was not molested. Next day (18th) enemy aircraft attacked 63rd Brigade as it followed 48th Brigade across the river, but there was little damage and few casualties and the attack was not repeated. The inevitable counter-attack was launched during the next few days by *II/153rd Battalion* of the *Katsu Force* on the west sector of the bridgehead held by 89th Brigade, and was easily thrown back. It did not therefore interfere with the column (Tomcol) which Cowan sent out to reconnoitre the tracks to Taungtha and cover the break-out of his main body from the bridgehead.[2]

A most unpromising start had thus in three days developed into complete success. The reasons are clear. The IV Corps thrust had struck the junction between *15th* and *28th Armies*, and the elaborate deception measures had not only succeeded in focusing the enemy's attention on the threat to Mandalay, but had made him believe that the threat from the Myittha valley was a diversionary one and would develop west of the Irrawaddy. The defence of the Pagan–Nyaungu area had been left mainly to the *I.N.A.* and the only immediately available formation (the *Katsu Force*) was used to counter-attack the East Africans. Nevertheless, the main credit must go to Messervy and his formation commanders who seized every opportunity, took risks and allowed nothing to interfere with the rapid achievement of their respective objects.

Having cleared the way for the Meiktila striking force, the task of

---

[1] The IV Corps vehicle ferry at Nyaungu began to function on the 15th February, from which date 7th Division's ferries farther upstream gradually closed down. During the next five weeks it transported over 10,000 vehicles including tanks and guns, mainly belonging to 17th and 5th Divisions. There were no accidents but one Bailey raft and a motor boat were sunk by Japanese aircraft. The ferry was equipped with sixteen Class 9 F.B.E. rafts, seven Class 18 pontoon rafts and six Class 40/70 Bailey rafts (for medium tanks and transporters).

[2] Tomcol consisted of one squadron 16th Light Cavalry, one company lorried infantry, reconnaissance troops of 5th (Probyn's) and 9th (Royal Deccan) Horse and a signal detachment.

7th Division was to extend its bridgehead south to Chauk and contain the Japanese forces in the oilfield area, capture Myingyan, which was required as the main river port and forward base for 14th Army,[1] and recapture Taungtha so as to reopen the road to Meiktila after 17th Division and its armour had passed on its way.

In the middle of February, when IV Corps began its drive on Meiktila, the information about the Japanese forces opposing 14th Army indicated that *15th* and *53rd Divisions* had given up any idea of a counter-attack towards Shwebo and were withdrawing south on Mandalay;[2] that, except for *58th Regiment, 31st Division* had withdrawn across the Irrawaddy and was holding the southern bank from opposite Myinmu to Sagaing; and that *33rd Division* had *214th Regiment* at Pakokku, the *213th* at Myingyan and the *215th* at Taungtha. The Yenangyaung–Chauk oilfields were believed to be the responsibility of *28th Army* which had *153rd Regiment* of *49th Division* (the *Katsu Force*) and another regiment, thought to be the *61st* of *4th Division*, in the area.[3]

When issuing his orders on the 12th, Cowan's immediate concern was the presence of the enemy regiment believed to be at Taungtha and to have prepared a position covering the junction of the six roads and tracks at Pyinbin, with anti-tank ditches and concrete blocks at most defiles. His ultimate intention was to capture Meiktila and then Thazi with a view to destroying all Japanese forces moving south from Mandalay. The first phase was for 48th Brigade (Brigadier R. C. O. Hedley) supported by a squadron of tanks, the S.P. battery and, if needed, by airstrikes, to secure the Pyinbin road junction, establish a firm base there and send patrols to occupy Welaung and Seiktein while the rest of the Meiktila force moved up to Pyinbin. In the next phase 48th Brigade was to capture or seal off Taungtha while the rest of the force, led by 255th Tank Brigade (Brigadier C. E. Pert), by-passed it to the south and captured Mahlaing, where 63rd Brigade (Brigadier G. W. S. Burton) was to establish a firm base. The armour was then to seize Thabutkon airfield, required for the fly-in of 99th Brigade, and 48th Brigade was to abandon Taungtha and rejoin the rest of the division as quickly as possible at Mahlaing. Orders for the assault on Meiktila were to be issued after the force had concentrated in the Mahlaing–Thabutkon area.

On the 19th, the reconnaissance column (Tomcol) reported Pyinbin clear but the next day met strong resistance at Oyin to its south-east. Cowan moved at once, and, by evening of the 21st, 48th

---

[1] See Chapter XXII, Appendix 16 and Map 9, facing page 320.
[2] On the 30th January *53rd Division* had been ordered to Myotha, thirty miles southwest of Mandalay.
[3] The two battalions of *61st Regiment*, which had taken part in the final stages of the Battle of Imphal (see Volume III, pages 354–55), had been renumbered *542nd* and *543rd Battalions* and incorporated in *72nd I.M.B.* (see Appendix 8).

Brigade arrived in the Pyinbin area. Japanese patrols were active but there was no real opposition until the tank brigade attacked Oyin. The fight was short and fierce with seventy casualties, mostly in 6/7th Rajputs, and a tank destroyed.[1] Seventy-two Japanese dead provided identification of two companies of *II/16th Battalion (2nd Division)*. To the north at Kamye, 48th Brigade ambushed a Japanese column from which there were identifications of a company of *215th Regiment* and *214th Regimental Gun Company*. These diverse identifications made it seem possible that heavy opposition might soon be met, but the tank brigade overran Welaung on the 23rd. Next day, four miles south of Taungtha, a Japanese rearguard fought resolutely, apparently to cover the evacuation of a hospital since many of the 180 dead found seemed to be hospital patients who had committed suicide.[2] That day (24th) 48th Brigade took Taungtha from the west, and 255th Tank Brigade, 63rd Brigade and divisional headquarters swept past it towards Meiktila. Thabutkon airfield was occupied at 2 p.m. on the 26th, and by nightfall bulldozers had filled in the craters and slit trenches obstructing the 1,600-yard runway, thus enabling the fly-in of 99th Brigade (Tarver) to begin. By the evening of the 27th, fifty-three Dakotas of 1st U.S. Air Commando Group had safely landed part of the brigade. Although the airfield was under sporadic small-arms fire during the next few days, the Dakotas continued to use it and by the 2nd March the fly-in of the brigade was completed without loss.

By nightfall on the 27th, 9th Border Regiment of 63rd Brigade with 5th Horse (medium tanks) was within six miles of Meiktila after destroying two roadblocks and killing fifty Japanese. Meanwhile 48th Brigade had broken off the action at Taungtha, during which fairly severe casualties were incurred by both sides, and had caught up the division. On the 28th it took the lead. Its advanced guard (1/7th Gurkhas and a troop of tanks), brushing aside slight opposition, was in position that night one and three quarter miles north of Meiktila on the east bank of the north lake.[3] Meanwhile 255th Indian Tank Brigade, now reinforced by 16th Light Cavalry (armoured cars) and with a battery of S.P. guns under command,[4] made a wide detour to the north, going for the airfield east of the town. Everything was set for the assault next day.

---

[1] This was the first case seen of a Japanese sitting in a hole in the ground detonating a high-explosive charge and blowing the tank (and himself) up; see Photograph 52, following page 286.

[2] Identifications included all three regiments of *33rd Division* and *II/16th Battalion* of *2nd Division*.

[3] See Sketch 9, facing page 272.

[4] The 16th was less one squadron which was with 7th Indian Division.

Pakokku 12 m.

Myitche

OUT

Veh   Inf

Signals
Signals

Inf

R E and Tks

C

Signals

A

B

R   I   V   E   R

Z (Sandbank)

Int   Veh   Tks
(7 Div only)

1 2 3 4

A   Tks Veh Inf

B

I R R A W A D D Y

Regulating H.Q.

S Lan R

4/15 P

Nyaungu

33 Bde

33

17 DIV
(less Tks)

2 I BURMA

ROUTE 10
Myingyan 42 m.

Site of
Div H.Q. ×

Assembly
Route
12

4/I G.R.

255 Tk Bde

ROUTE 11
Byinbin 13 m.

89   KOSB

7 Div Bridgehead

17 DIV
Reserve Assembly

Pagan

ROUTE 12
Kyaukpadaung 27 m.

1/11 Sikh

89 Bde
from D + 2

4/8 G.R.

The IV Corps Bridgehead at Nyaungu
February 13-21 1945

1/11
Sikh

Miles
0   1   2

IV Corps (less 7 Div) .... RED
7 Division .... BROWN
Traffic Control Posts ....
Beaches ....
A B C
1 2 3 4

1/11
Sikh

Note: After establishment of 7 Div Bridgehead
their installations on the north bank ceased to
function and the Corps routes were used

Chauk 19 m.

O.S.K.

By this time the Japanese had reoccupied Taungtha and the Meiktila striking force was entirely dependent on air supply for all its needs. The 7th Division had, however, begun operations to clear the Nyaungu–Myingyan–Taungtha–Welaung area to open road communications, but it had in addition the task of protecting IV Corps' right flank against counter-attack from the Chauk and Saw areas where the Japanese forces in the area were believed to be of considerable strength. The 114th Brigade (Dinwiddie), which had completed the clearance of Pakokku on the 21st, was ordered by Evans to send 4/14th Punjab to help 28th (E.A.) Brigade at Letse,[1] where it had dug itself in after being driven back from Seikpyu, and take over the left sector of the Nyaungu bridgehead to release 33rd Brigade for operations to clear Myingyan and Taungtha. The 89th Brigade (Crowther), holding the right sector, had meanwhile steadily increased pressure towards Chauk to prevent any forces from the oilfield area moving towards Meiktila.[2]

By the 28th February the operations of 4/14th Punjab and a squadron of tanks against the flank and communications of the enemy force attacking the East Africans at Letse had restored the situation on the right flank. By this time orders had been received for 28th (E.A.) Brigade to be withdrawn to India, under arrangements to be made by 7th Division as soon as the situation in the bridgehead–Myingyan–Taungtha area permitted. The 89th Brigade in a series of hard-fought actions (in one of which, near Monatkon, 2nd K.O.S.B. lost one-third of its officer strength) had driven the Japanese from strong positions along the chaung which ran from the Kyaukpadaung road to the Irrawaddy at Monatkon.[3] The Japanese had then withdrawn to Singu and the Pyinma Chaung, which formed the northern boundary of the Chauk oilfield. The Nyaungu bridgehead static defences had by this time been reorganized to enable them to be held by one battalion, and a mobile column of all arms (Puffcol) had been formed to seek out and destroy any enemy on the tracks leading south-east to Kyaukpadaung, Mount Popa and Seiktein.[4]

On the left, 33rd Brigade, advancing on Myingyan with one battalion on the Pyinbin track and one on the road bordering the river, ran into stiff opposition two miles west of Letpanchibaw, and a column sent north from Pyinbin to help clear the position was

---

[1] Brigadier T. H. S. Galletly succeeded Dimoline in command of 28th (E.A.) Brigade on the 21st February.

[2] The 7th Division had 116th R.A.C. (medium tanks) under command, of which one squadron was allotted to 33rd Brigade and one to 28th (E.A.) Brigade. The commander of the divisional artillery had one section of medium guns and one of heavy (7·2-inch) howitzers so placed that they could at short notice support any of the brigades.

[3] See Map 9, facing page 320.

[4] Puffcol, commanded by Lieut.-Colonel L. H. O. Pugh, R.A., consisted of one squadron, 16th Cavalry (armoured cars) less one troop, two companies 2nd South Lancashire Regiment in lorries, one platoon medium machine-guns and one battery mountain artillery (mechanized).

ambushed and suffered considerable loss. Collingwood sent forward his tanks and was about to make a deliberate attack when, before dawn on the 28th, the Japanese abandoned their position and the advance on Myingyan was resumed. Contact was regained along the Sindewa Chaung on the morning of the 2nd March. From there progress became very difficult, since the country was intersected by sheer-sided tank-proof ravines and there was considerable opposition, including accurate artillery harassing fire.[1] Collingwood decided to attack Myingyan and Taungtha simultaneously, the former with two battalions and the latter with one, and by the evening of the 5th March his brigade was deployed with 4/15th Punjab and 4/1st Gurkhas three miles south-west of Myingyan and 1st Burma Regiment a similar distance west of Taungtha.

By the end of February 63rd Brigade had moved forward from Thabutkon to an assembly position west of Meiktila near Antu, where the divisional artillery was also concentrating, and 99th Brigade was concentrated at Thabutkon.[2] Cowan was now poised to strike, and at 7 a.m. on the 1st March he issued orders verbally for the general attack on Meiktila to begin. The 63rd Brigade from the west was to seize the gap between the north and south lakes, 48th Brigade from the north was to secure the north shore of the south lake and 255th Indian Tank Brigade (less its detachments with the infantry brigades but with two lorried infantry battalions under command) was to make a wide detour to the north and seize the airfield on the east edge of the town and then push on to the east shore of the south lake. Each brigade had a strong column of all arms watching its rear and, in addition, a battalion from 99th Brigade at Thabutkon had been sent to help block the roads from Mandalay from where counter-attack was expected to be heaviest.

On the 2nd March 63rd Brigade, advancing through an area of scattered buildings and dense thickets, cleared the western section of the town in two attacks, each made by tanks escorted by a battalion. The 48th Brigade attack, led by 1/7th Gurkhas, had to pass through the heart of the town to reach its objective. Mines, accurate artillery and mortar fire and fortified buildings made progress slow, and, despite the assistance of an airstrike at 3.45 p.m., the forward troops had only got as far as the railway by 5.30 p.m. when 4/12th Frontier Force Regiment, which had passed through the Gurkhas, dug in and the tanks withdrew for the night. In the eastern sector 255th Indian

[1] Naik Gian Singh, 4/15th Punjab Regiment, won the Victoria Cross during this action.
[2] See Sketch 9, facing page 272.
[3] Slim and Messervy had been flown to Meiktila to confer with Cowan, and see whether he required any assistance. They followed this attack on foot, and left feeling that the operations were in safe hands.

Tank Brigade mopped up the cantonment area east of the south lake, secured the airfield and sent patrols up to twelve miles south and east of the town without meeting any further opposition. Patrols operating up the Mandalay road, however, found the satellite airstrip at Thedaw occupied by a well-concealed and dug-in force.

On the 3rd, 48th Brigade, using two squadrons of 9th Royal Horse with 1st West Yorkshire in support, completed clearing the north sector of the town,[1] and the remnants of the garrison, breaking out eastwards, were intercepted and almost annihilated by the lorried infantry of 255th Tank Brigade. That evening Cowan reported to Messervy, whose headquarters had moved forward from Kan to Myitche the previous day, that Meiktila was clear except for stragglers and that a final clean-up would be made the next day.[2] During the 4th, while mopping up was being carried out and the satellite airfield on the Mandalay road captured, the whole force concentrated for the defence of Meiktila; the airfield was taken into use instead of Thabutkon, and patrols penetrated as far as Thazi and Pyawbwe, both of which were found to be held. By the evening of the 4th Meiktila had been consolidated and its garrison had been destroyed or dispersed for the loss of half a dozen tanks and 200 killed and wounded.

The garrison of Meiktila consisted of two airfield battalions, a reinforcement battalion of three extemporized infantry companies and a number of administrative units. It so happened that, at the moment 17th Division's attack developed, *168th Infantry Regiment*, on its way from Lashio to rejoin its own (*49th*) division in *Burma Army Area* reserve, was approaching Meiktila; it was thus drawn into the battle and, having no anti-tank weapons, suffered severely, the regimental commander, Colonel Yoshida, being among the dead. The *Burma Area Army* had been dealt a crippling blow, but the fight to retain Meiktila was to be long and bitter since the Japanese concentrated every unit and formation they could to break 14th Army's stranglehold on their main line of communications, a stranglehold which threatened the destruction of all their forces in north Burma.

It is of interest at this point to consider how the Japanese, bereft of the initiative and partly disorganized, reacted to Slim's strategy and to what extent his deception plans affected their actions. Katamura (*15th Army*) had decided towards the end of January to abandon his counter-offensive north of Mandalay in favour of one to throw back

---

[1] Lieut. W. B. Weston, The Green Howards attached 1st West Yorkshire, was posthumously awarded the Victoria Cross for his part in this action.

[2] The 17th Division reported that at Meiktila on the 3rd March 800 Japanese dead were counted and thirty-six prisoners taken. Eleven guns were captured, bringing the total taken since leaving Nyaungu to thirty-eight, as well as two aircraft and thirty-six aero engines.

14th Army's expected main thrust south-west of Mandalay, and had asked *Burma Area Army* for reinforcements.[1] Kimura agreed with Katamura's plan and, having decided to send him reinforcements from *28th* and *33rd Armies*, summoned Honda (*33rd Army*) to a conference which was held at *Burma Area Army's* advanced headquarters at Kalaw on the 13th February. Honda, who had already been forced to abandon his mission of keeping closed the communications between India and China and was withdrawing to the general line Lashio–Mongmit, suggested that *18th Division*, then at Myitson,[2] should be ordered to leave one regiment at Mongmit to delay the advance of 36th British Division and move at once to Mandalay, and that eventually the whole of either *18th* or *56th Division* should reinforce *15th Army*. Kimura accepted the proposal regarding the immediate move of *18th Division*.

No sooner had this decision been taken, however, than a completely new and more dangerous situation arose as a result of 14th Army's successful crossings of the Irrawaddy at Myinmu and Nyaungu. In the circumstances *Burma Area Army* convened another conference at Meiktila, conducted by Tanaka, Chief of Staff of *Burma Area Army*.[3] The situation as presented by the area army chief Intelligence officer to the conference was extremely gloomy. He expected that seven Allied infantry divisions and two armoured brigades would be used on the Irrawaddy front: two north of and including Mandalay, either three or four between Sagaing and the Chindwin and either one or two and both the armoured brigades west of Myingyan. Some officers expressed anxiety lest a powerful thrust might be made from Nyaungu towards Meiktila, but the majority opinion was that, if made, the thrust would be on the scale of a Chindit operation, with which the forces on the spot would be quite able to deal. This view was confirmed when a message was received that a force accompanied by 200 vehicles was advancing on Meiktila.[4]

The ultimate British object was expected to be a drive southwards down both the Irrawaddy valley and the railway, which, it was estimated, could reach Rangoon by the end of April; in conjunction with this drive an amphibious landing would be made somewhere in the Irrawaddy delta to coincide with the arrival of the advance down the railway in the Toungoo area. The conference agreed that the best means of countering the British plans would be to launch an offensive

---

[1] See page 187.

[2] See Map 2, facing page 39.

[3] The Japanese records are uncertain about the exact date of this conference but suggest that it took place on the 23rd February. (On this date the advanced guard of IV Corps was within forty-five miles of Meiktila and moving fast.)

[4] The Japanese records say that the figure of 200 in this message was wrongly transmitted and should have been 2,000.

Sketch 9

THE ATTACK ON MEIKTILA

British Advance ....
Enemy outer defences ....
Enemy defended Localities ....

MILES
0   1   2   3

from Mahlaing 17m.
& Taungtha 51m.

Taungtha 51m.
Myingyan 55m.

Div Arty
harbour
½ Mar.

Antu

Kyaukpyugon

from Kyaukpodaung

Myingan   48m.

63 Bde.
Road Block
28/2 2/3 March

63 Bde on foot

Oknebok

Inpetlet

North Lake

MEIKTILA

1st MARCH

2nd

2nd

2nd

South
Lake

356

355

354

Pauwbwe 24m.

Khanda

2nd

2nd

1st MARCH

1st MARCH

Strong
Position

255 Tk. Bde. Plus Two Inf. Bns.

Kyigon   340

Magyigyauk

341

A I R F I E L D

Airfield
in operation
5th March

Tamongan

Nyaungbintha

Kinlu

Thazi 17m.

Thazi 7m.

Myindawgon
Lake

Myindawgon

48 Bde.

Pindale 16m.

Nyaunggon

342

Shawbyugan

Gwedaukkon

Okshitkon

345

A I R S T R I P

344

48 Bde
Road Block
3rd March

Thedaw

Mandalay 85m.
Wundwin 15m.

N

south-west of Mandalay, as contemplated earlier by *15th Army*,[1] to be delivered on the 10th March from Sagaing towards Myinmu concurrently with a secondary offensive from Myingyan northwards directed on the river bank opposite Myinmu.[2] The *33rd Army*, now reduced to *56th Division* and a regiment of the *18th* was to hold the Monglong Range in order to cover *15th Army's* right flank. On the left, *28th Army*, with *72nd I.M.B.* and the *Katsu Force* reinforced by the *Kanjo Force* (*112th Regiment*, less one battalion, and a battalion of artillery) under command,[3] was to attack with the maximum possible strength northwards from Yenangyaung along the west bank of the river towards Pakokku.

The loss of Meiktila within a few days of this decision made it impossible for the plan to be carried out, since it became urgently necessary to concentrate all Japanese forces not already committed in an effort to regain the town and thereby reopen their main line of of communication to Rangoon.

On the 5th March the trap had closed on the Japanese *15th* and *33rd Armies*. To the south, IV Corps had seized Meiktila, was preparing it for defence, mopping up the area to its west and pushing strong fighting patrols east to the railway. To the north, 19th Division of XXXIII Corps was about to drive south on Mandalay and southeast to cut the road at Maymyo and link up with 36th Division of N.C.A.C. near Kyaukme. To the west of Mandalay, 2nd and 20th Divisions of XXXIII Corps had crossed the Irrawaddy and were about to drive east to attack the city from the south, mop up all forces in the area between it and Meiktila and interfere with any attempt by either *15th* or *33rd Army* to break its way through or past Meiktila. It is a tribute to the Japanese that nobody in 14th Army had any doubt that, rather than break off the fight and withdraw, they would launch a counter-offensive with every unit they could assemble.

---

[1] See page 187.

[2] For this offensive *15th Army* was to have at its disposal *15th, 31st, 33rd* and *53rd Divisions*, *18th Division* (less one regiment) and a composite regiment from *2nd Division* (the *Aoba Force*).

[3] The *Kanjo Force* had been formed from *55th Division* earlier in the month and ordered to move to the Irrawaddy front and come under command of *15th Army*. It arrived in the Mount Popa area on the 22nd February. It was then passed back to *28th Army* and placed under command of General T. Yamamato (*72nd I.M.B.*). Yamamato had commanded the Japanese force in the Kabaw Valley and on the Shenam Pass during the Battle of Imphal (see Volume III).

Situation of 14th Army and right flank of N.C.A.C. on the 1st February 1945

Enemy dispositions are as known to 14th Army

Miles

0   50   100

14ᵗʰ Army

Kalemyo

Myittha R.

Kan

IV

33 BDE

Gangaw

7

Mawle

LUSHAI SCOUTS

114 BDE

Tilin

4/14 P

28 (EA)

Pauk

Saw ?

Letse

Seikpyu

Chauk ?

Kyaukpadaung

Chindwin R.

7/2 P

89 BDE

Myaing

33 DIV + one Bn
49 DIV

Pakokku

Myitche

Nyaungu

Yaw C.

Irrawaddy R.

Bahe

36

72 BDE

26 BDE

Shweli R.

Myitson

ELEMENTS OF 18 & 56 DIVS

Mongmit

Mogok

N.C.A.C.

Approx Army Boundary

29 BDE

Twinnge

Thabeikkyin
98 BDE

15 DIV

268 BDE

XXXIII

Yeu

62 & 64 BDE

19

Kyaukmyaung

254 TK

Shwebo

6 BDE

2

5 BDE

53 DIV

Madaya

3 DG

2 RECCE

Monywa

20

32 BDE

100 BDE

Mu R.

Myinmu

4 BDE

Saye

MANDALAY

Maymyo

Myitnge R.

80 BDE

Ava

31 DIV

Kyaukse

Myingyan

Taungtha

Wundwin

Meiktila

Kalaw

CHAPTER XXIV

THE NORTHERN FRONT

(February–March 1945)

See Maps 2, 3, 10 and 13 and Sketch 11

WHILE 14th Army was closing in on Meiktila and Mandalay during February and the first few days of March, activity on the Northern front had been confined to patrol engagements, except on the extreme right where 36th Division was operating. The Chinese Yunnan armies were withdrawing across the border into China. The 30th Chinese Division (and later the 38th) somewhat discreetly followed up the rearguards of *56th Division* and occupied Hsenwi on the 19th February without opposition, Mars Force was withdrawn into a rest area at the end of the first week of February and, after a tardy advance, 50th Chinese Division, reinforced by 1st Chinese Regiment, which had been given the task of cutting the retreat of *56th Division* near Hsipaw, came to rest near Namtu in the third week of February, thirty-five miles short of its objective.[1] As a result of these dilatory tactics on the part of the Chinese First Army, possibly under instructions from the Generalissimo given without Sultan's knowledge, the only major operations on the Northern front were those undertaken by 36th British Division.

The division's task was to move along the east bank of the Irrawaddy and up the Shweli valley on Mongmit and Mogok, with Kyaukme as its final objective.[2] It was opposed by the Japanese *18th Division* whose object was to ensure that any Allied forces in the lower reaches of the Shweli River could not strike at Mandalay from the north-east or cut the communications of *56th Division* withdrawing from Namhpakka. The first attempt by 26th Brigade (Jennings) of 36th Division to cross the Shweli by way of the island one mile east of Myitson, which had begun so promisingly on the 1st February, had run into difficulties,[3] and, although Festing was quick to order a withdrawal, the two companies of 2nd Buffs and their supporting engineers which had reached the far bank suffered 114 casualties before they got clear. It was obvious that, however good the island might be as a bridgehead site, a second assault on it would be foolhardy. Failing the island, it was desirable that any bridgehead

---

[1] See Map 2, facing page 39.
[2] See page 191.
[3] See page 196.

should include Myitson, where an existing ferry joined the roads coming from the north to that leading towards Mongmit. The village lay in the angle between the Shweli, where it turns north, and the Nammeik Chaung, which joins it from the south.[1] It could therefore be attacked either from the north across the 400-yards-wide, unfordable and fast flowing river or across the 200-yards-wide chaung. It was discovered without arousing suspicion that the chaung was fordable when a reconnaissance party watched an enemy patrol wade across it chest-deep close to Myitson. It was evident that an assault column could make a crossing there in the dark with the help of life-lines, provided that surprise could be ensured.

By the 6th February a new plan had been made which was to be put into effect by 26th Brigade. So that the brigade could reach the crossing point undetected, and to avoid the possibility of bringing down one of the heavy and accurate artillery concentrations that any large move in the Myitson area evoked, it had to be ferried across to the west bank of the Shweli some six miles to the north and then move southwards to reach the selected crossing place. The 72nd Brigade was ordered to send a battalion (9th Gloucesters) to cover the exposed western flank and protect the line of communication, which had to be west of the Shweli until a firm bridgehead had been established at Myitson and a direct ferry into it put into operation.

During the night of the 8th/9th February, 1/19th Hyderabad Regiment got across the Nammeik Chaung close to Myitson but, despite achieving initial surprise, suffered forty-five casualties; it was followed up next day by 2/8th Punjab Regiment. By the evening of the 10th a two-battalion bridgehead had been consolidated and casualties had risen to 146. The 2nd Buffs then crossed and began to expand the bridgehead southwards, while 2/8th Punjab worked its way along the south bank of the Shweli to the line of the The Chaung. By the 12th the bridgehead was about a mile square and the brigade had incurred 340 casualties, but the heaviest fighting was yet to come for, though the Japanese drew back that day, it was only for the purpose of reorganizing for a counter-attack. Opposition to the crossing of the Nammeik Chaung might have been heavier had not 72nd Brigade kept up harassing operations in the area of the first attempted crossing (by way of the island east of Myitson) to pin down the enemy forces, or had the Japanese got information of the moves west of the Shweli and the Nammeik Chaung. Meanwhile 29th Brigade (Bastin) was making only slow progress from Twingge along the Male–Mongmit road.

It will be realized that 36th Division was now widely dispersed with 26th and 72nd Brigades separated by the unbridged Shweli River, the former being in close contact with a considerable Japanese force,

---

[1] See Sketch 11, facing page 282.

and 29th Brigade some twenty-five miles away on the other side of a 3,000-foot mountain range. It was therefore somewhat disturbing when on the 12th the Kachin Levies,[1] operating in the mountains between the Irrawaddy and the Shweli Rivers, reported that a column of some 400 Japanese was approaching the exposed flank of the communications to the Nammeik bridgehead. This report was soon confirmed, for next day the communications were cut and the Gloucesters met with stiff resistance when they set about clearing the area.

By the 15th February a ferry was in operation across the Shweli at Myitson, and all administrative troops and Headquarters 26th Brigade were moved from the west bank either to the east bank or into the bridgehead itself. The ferry, however, could operate only at night owing to the accuracy of the Japanese artillery fire and, even then, the evacuation of casualties was sometimes interrupted by harassing fire. By this time it was clear that an attack on the bridge-head from the south and south-east was imminent, and Festing, wishing to have the whole of 26th and 72nd Brigades to meet it, flew to see Bastin to urge him to speed up 29th Brigade's advance. Such an advance would not only threaten the flank of any force attacking Myitson from the south, but would also, by cutting across the escape route of the enemy column operating on the west bank of the Shweli River and the Nammeik Chaung, force it to withdraw, thereby saving the two brigades at Myitson from having to find detachments to secure their right flank.

Unusual though it was for the Japanese to make deliberate attacks of this nature by day, the expected counter-attack began at 7.30 a.m. on the 17th February with a bombardment, during which some 2,000 shells of all calibres fell in the small bridgehead, followed by an infantry attack supported by flame-throwers. Attacks, the brunt of which fell on 2/8th Punjab on the east side of the perimeter, went on all day regardless of losses. In spite of well-dug trenches and wire, the Punjabis had 125 casualties out of a total of 153 incurred by the brigade. The Japanese losses must have been considerable for, despite the fact that they had the whole night of the 17th/18th February to remove their dead and wounded, they left 132 bodies on the battlefield. During the next three days there were sporadic attacks on the bridgehead, but the Japanese were now obviously thinning out, since patrols ranging south and south-east met with little opposition except from snipers. On the 21st even the long-range shelling of the Myitson ferry ceased, and it was able to operate for the first time in daylight.[2]

---

[1] Kachin Levies had covered the flanks of the forces operating on the Northern front during the whole advance from Myitkyina.

[2] The *18th Division* began to withdraw to Mandalay on the 19th February, leaving one regiment (*114th*) to defend Mongmit. See page 272.

On the 22nd, after an air and artillery bombardment, the island one mile upstream of Myitson was occupied and a small enemy detachment on the south bank dispersed. Work to bridge the river began at once, and Festing ordered the advance on Mongmit to begin on the 25th.

Festing believed that the Japanese would have a force of about 2,000 to defend Mongmit. His plan was that 29th Brigade on the right should advance as quickly as possible along the Male–Mongmit road while 72nd Brigade in the centre moved up the east bank of the Nammeik Chaung to join it; both brigades were then to close in on Mongmit from the west while 26th Brigade, advancing along the main road from Myitson, attacked from the north. When the advance began on the 25th February, it was found that enemy parties had infiltrated back on to the hills astride the main road around Point 1154. These were driven off without much difficulty, but it soon became evident that the Japanese had left a small rearguard on each line of approach to Mongmit with orders to harass and delay the advance without getting seriously engaged. The only determined opposition occurred on the 7th March when the advanced guard of 26th Brigade was held up for a day in a mountain defile near Point 1633. The same day 72nd Brigade, advancing from the west, took the lead from 29th Brigade and reached the town just after the leading troops of 26th Brigade.[1] It then took up positions beyond it to cover the regrouping of the division for its advance on Mogok and the construction of an airfield. Meanwhile 38th Chinese Division, having taken some six weeks to cover the sixty-seven miles from Namhpakka, occupied Lashio unopposed on the 6th March.

While the N.C.A.C. forces on the Northern front were advancing towards Mongmit, Hsenwi and Lashio, the future of the Chinese divisions and Mars Force was under discussion between Wedemeyer, Mountbatten and the British and American Chiefs of Staff. With a view to taking the offensive in China during 1945, Wedemeyer had recommended to the Generalissimo as early as January that all the remaining Chinese divisions under command of N.C.A.C. should be returned to China.[2] He did not suggest hasty action, since the formations were in action on the Northern front, but proposed that he should ask for them to leave Burma in time to arrive in east China by about the 1st May,[3] so that the offensive could begin about the 1st August.

---

[1] The 72nd Brigade had been reinforced by 1/1st Gurkhas, which had joined the division from India.

[2] Two divisions (14th and 22nd) had already been returned; see Chapter XI.

[3] Romanus and Sunderland, *Time Runs out in C.B.I.*, page 225.

Sultan told Mountbatten on the 21st February that Wedemeyer wanted one regiment of Mars Force (475th) to move to China as soon as possible, and the rest of the force to be ready to move by the 1st April. This request was put forward officially by Sultan at Mountbatten's conference with his Commanders-in-Chief at Calcutta on the 23rd February,[1] with the addition that an aviation battalion should be sent with 475th Regiment.

Mountbatten told the Chiefs of Staff on the 26th that he had to view Wedemeyer's request in relation to its effects on current operations in Burma and on the protection of the Burma Road. He had already given up two good Chinese divisions and some air units, with the result that operations had been slowed down, but he was relying on the continued assistance of all the remaining American and Chinese forces assigned to S.E.A.C. for the rapid capture of Rangoon. If any more formations had to be given up, his whole strategic programme would be thrown out of gear, since the removal of Mars Force would deprive N.C.A.C. of a reserve, reduce the offensive value of the remaining Chinese formations, and delay the pursuit towards Loilem of the Japanese forces cleared from the Mandalay area by XXXIII Corps.[2] He had been given to understand that Wedemeyer wanted Mars Force in order to break it up and use its components to provide nuclei for schools and liaison groups in an effort to rebuild the Chinese army. Since he was anxious not to hamper Wedemeyer in any way, he was prepared to provide cadres for this purpose, subject to their not exceeding the strength of one battalion.[3] He was also willing to allow an aviation battalion to go at once but considered that, as all transport aircraft allotted to S.E.A.C. were already working well above sustained rates in support of operations, Wedemeyer should arrange to move these units to China in his own aircraft and motor transport. He asked for a firm assurance that, under the policy agreed at the Argonaut Conference in January 1945 regarding the allocation of resources between the India–Burma and China Theatres,[4] no forces beyond those he had now offered would be moved from Burma until Rangoon had been captured.

The protection of the Burma Road, Mountbatten continued, was, according to the policy agreed at Argonaut, the primary object of the American/Chinese forces in Burma, but he had been given to understand by Sultan that the American policy was that no Chinese troops would eventually remain in Burma. He had always understood, however, that, although British/Indian formations retained the responsibility for the overall security of Burma, N.C.A.C. would provide the

---

[1] See page 247.
[2] See Map 3, facing page 55.
[3] Later on Mountbatten agreed that it would be better to release one complete battalion rather than individuals from many units.
[4] See page 209.

force for the actual security of the Burma Road. If he were to carry out the tasks given him for 1945, he could not spare British/Indian formations to protect the road and therefore either the Generalissimo, in consultation with Sultan and Leese, would have to leave sufficient Chinese troops to patrol it until relieved by formations from Europe, or the risk of leaving it unprotected would have to be accepted. He was visiting Chungking on the 7th March and proposed to ask the Generalissimo to choose one or other of these alternatives, unless the Combined Chiefs themselves decided on the course to be followed.

On the 28th February Sultan told Mountbatten that, to allow time for training the divisions which were already in China, moving the formations from N.C.A.C. and allowing them a reasonable period of rest and rehabilitation, Wedemeyer felt that it was essential that Mars Force should be released as soon as possible, one Chinese division on the 1st May, a second on the 15th May and the third and last on the 1st June, corps and army troops being phased between the 15th April and the 15th June to ensure that there was a balanced force both in N.C.A.C. and in the China Theatre during the period. Since Mars Force was required to provide the training cadres, Wedemeyer had now submitted an official request to Washington for one battalion of 475th Regiment to be moved to China at once, the rest of the regiment beginning to move on the 10th March (in transport aircraft found from the China Theatre), and the remainder of Mars Force during April (in aircraft provided from outside the China Theatre). Sultan indicated that the Chinese, while agreeing that the security of the Hsipaw–Lashio area was essential and that some move to the south would be necessary to achieve it, did not wish any Chinese formation operating on the Northern front to be committed to any serious advance beyond that area since, if they were so committed, it might not be possible to withdraw them in accordance with the proposed timetable. In any event, with the 148 aircraft then supporting N.C.A.C., Sultan could not undertake any considerable advance south of these two towns. In forwarding this information to the Chiefs of Staff, Mountbatten asked them to give him their decision before his visit to Chungking.

By this time it was clear to both Leese and Sultan that, if N.C.A.C. were to carry out the tasks given it in A.L.F.S.E.A.'s operation instruction of the 27th February,[1] no reduction in its strength was possible. With this in view, Leese told Mountbatten on the 1st March that, if N.C.A.C. could not carry out its allotted tasks, he could not guarantee the success of 14th Army's operations. He hoped that the N.C.A.C. forces would remain under his command until the operations then taking place in Burma were completed, and pointed out

---

[1] See page 249.

that the chances of reaching Rangoon before the monsoon would be negligible if any transport aircraft were removed from the theatre.

On the 6th March the Combined Chiefs of Staff told Mountbatten to avoid discussing the move of Chinese forces from N.C.A.C. and the responsibility for the protection of the road with the Generalissimo, as these matters were *sub judice*. During a meeting on the 9th between the two leaders at Chungking, Chiang Kai-shek explained that he hoped to raise and equip thirteen armies, each of three divisions.[1] Of these, fifteen divisions would be used to recapture Hunan and Kwangsi provinces, and the five divisions from N.C.A.C. would provide the experienced spearheads.[2] He therefore wished the present advance of the N.C.A.C. forces to be stopped at Lashio and advised Mountbatten to halt his advance at Mandalay. Mountbatten explained why he could not possibly accept this advice and suggested that the withdrawal of Chinese troops from Burma should be phased according to the measure of success achieved in the current operations. If all went well, it might be possible for the troops to be released sooner than the Generalissimo planned. Wedemeyer's staff explained that China's most pressing need was for the whole of 475th Regiment so that the reorganization and training of the Chinese army could begin at once. Although on purely military grounds Leese advised against its release, Mountbatten, anxious to give every possible help to the China Theatre, was prepared to take the risk of releasing it, and told Sultan on the 11th March that he could move it to China as soon as convenient in transport aircraft from China Theatre.

---

[1] The thirty-nine divisions included the five from N.C.A.C. and eleven from the Yunnan armies.
[2] See Map 10, facing page 340.

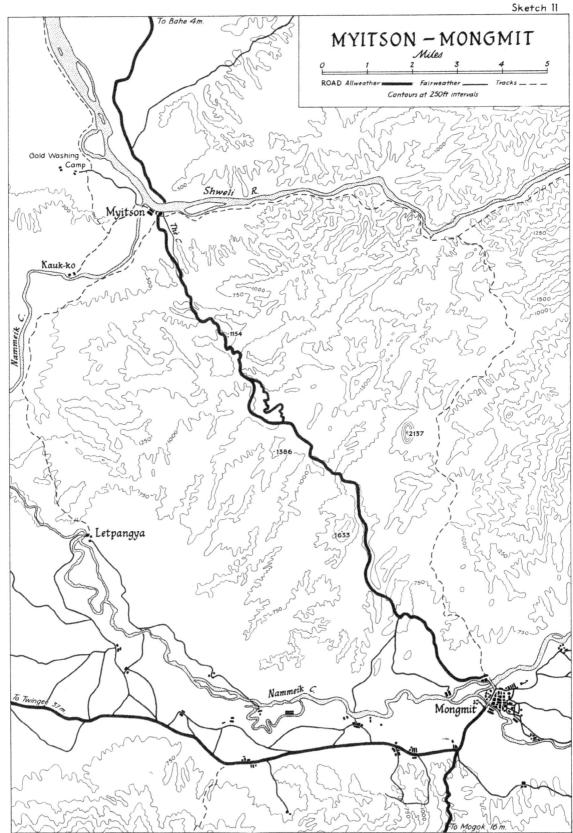

MYITSON — MONGMIT

Miles

0   1   2   3   4   5

ROAD *Allweather* ▬▬▬   *Fairweather* ———   *Tracks* — — —

Contours at 250ft intervals

To Bahe 4m.

Gold Washing Camp

Shweli R.

Myitson

Kauk-ko

Nammeik C.

Thi C.

•1154

•1386

•2137

1633

Letpangya

Nammeik C.

To Twingee 37m.

Mongmit

To Mogok 16m.

CHAPTER XXV

THE CENTRAL FRONT

(5th–15th March 1945)
The Battles of Meiktila and Mandalay

See Maps 3 and 9 and Sketches 12, 13 and 16

BY the 5th March, 14th Army had crossed the Irrawaddy in four places on a 120-mile front, and had seized Meiktila by a bold thrust which had taken the Japanese by surprise. On the right, Messervy (IV Corps) had 7th Division, based on the bridgehead at Nyaungu, with the threefold task of capturing Myingyan and Taungtha so that the road to Meiktila could be reopened, maintaining pressure on the enemy in the Chauk–Kyaukpadaung area and securing the right flank west of the Irrawaddy on the general line Saw–Letse; and 17th Division and 255th Tank Brigade, supplied entirely by air, holding Meiktila and preparing to meet the expected counter-offensive. On the left, Stopford (XXXIII Corps) had 2nd and 20th Divisions ready to strike east from their bridgehead in the Ngazun–Myinmu area to the Myitnge River to isolate and attack Mandalay from the south; 268th Brigade containing the Japanese bridgehead near Sagaing; and 19th Division, with a bridgehead across the Chaungmagyi Chaung, the last serious obstacle in its path, poised to attack Mandalay from the north.[1] Slim's reserve, 5th Division, less its air-transportable brigade which was waiting at Jorhat in readiness to be flown to Meiktila, was moving forward by road to Monywa, from where it could either meet a Japanese counter-stroke which might possibly be directed towards that area, or join IV Corps as planned.[2]

The battlefield on which the operations dealt with in this chapter were to take place was roughly a triangular area of some 8,000 square miles, with its base on a line from Saw to Madaya and its apex at Thazi.[3] In this large area two corps battles were being fought, each on a wide front but both closely co-ordinated by 14th Army, with the object of destroying the Japanese armies in central Burma. Success depended on IV Corps being able to hold Meiktila and block the rail and road communications to the south, while XXXIII Corps

---

[1] See Map 3, facing page 55.
[2] See Chapter XXIII.
[3] See Sketch 12, facing page 284.

destroyed the Japanese forces in the Mandalay area for whom there could be little possibility of escape as long as IV Corps remained astride their line of retreat to the south. If this were achieved, there was little the Japanese would be able to do to prevent 14th Army from driving south to secure a seaport, preferably Rangoon, through which it could be maintained in south Burma during the monsoon.

On the 5th March Slim had at his disposal six strong, well-equipped divisions, of which one was in reserve, and two independent brigades, supported by two tank brigades and an air force enjoying complete command of the air. The Japanese *15th Army* facing him had on that date the equivalent of six divisions, of which one was in reserve,[1] and an *I.N.A.* division (on which little reliance could be placed), supported by a weak tank regiment and a negligible air force, but it was possible that it could be reinforced quickly by formations drawn from *28th* and *33rd Armies*, provided the situation on the fronts held by these armies permitted. Three of the enemy divisions (*15th, 31st* and *33rd*) had in 1944 suffered crippling losses, and most of the others were considerably under strength.

Slim not only held the initiative but the morale of his troops had never been higher. There were, however, no signs of any deterioration in the morale of the enemy, and it could be expected that every Japanese soldier would still be prepared to die rather than surrender. It was therefore evident that the forthcoming battle would be grim and might be long drawn-out, and time was of great importance. In the circumstances, and as the threat of a Japanese counter-thrust north of the Irrawaddy could now be discounted, Slim placed 5th Division under Messervy's command on the 9th March.[2] This left him temporarily without a reserve, but the decisive stage in the battles for Mandalay and Meiktila had been reached and he was confident that its intervention on the battlefield would ensure success.

The second phase of the battle for Meiktila, of which the operations of 7th Division (Evans) from the Nyaungu bridgehead formed part, began on the 6th March. The situation in 7th Division's sector was that, west of the Irrawaddy, its right flank was protected by Westcol at Saw, while the pressure on 28th (E.A.) Brigade (Galletly), which had dug itself in at Letse, had been eased by the operations of 4/14th Punjab and tanks sent to its assistance.[3] In the Chauk sector 89th

---

[1] The *15th, 31st, 33rd* and *53rd Divisions, 72nd I.M.B., 16th Regiment* of *2nd Division* (the *Aoba Force*), *153rd Regiment* of *49th Division* (the *Katsu Force*), *112th Regiment* of *55th Division* (the *Kanjo Force*), and in reserve *49th Division* (less a regiment).

[2] Divisional headquarters and the two brigades moving to Monywa by road were to take orders from Messervy on arrival there. The air-transportable 9th Brigade was ordered to move from Jorhat on the 10th and 11th March to Palel from where it was to be flown into Meiktila on the 15th, 16th and 17th March.

[3] See page 269.

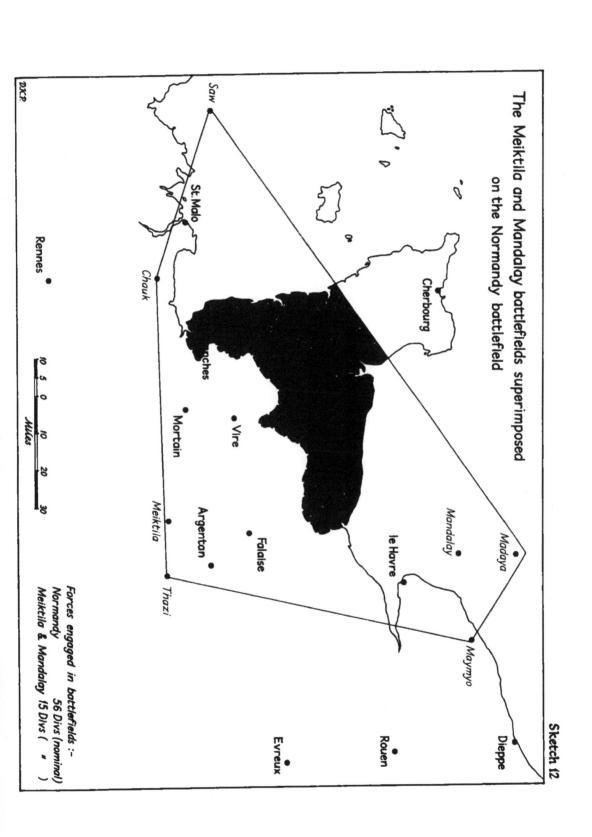

The Meiktila and Mandalay battlefields superimposed
on the Normandy battlefield

Sketch 12

D.X.P.

Saw

St.Malo

Chauk

Rennes

Cherbourg

Mortain

Vire

Mandalay

le Havre

Madaya

Maymyo

Meiktila

Argentan

Falaise

Thazi

Rouen

Evreux

Dieppe

10 5 0 10 20 30
Miles

Forces engaged in battlefields :-
Normandy   56 Divs (nominal)
Meiktila & Mandalay 15 Divs (")

Brigade, deployed north of the Pyinma Chaung, had orders not to attempt to cross it for the time being, but to harass the Japanese from points of vantage in the hope that they would be exasperated into attacking and so lay themselves open to severe losses. In the bridge-head 114th Brigade (less 4/14th Punjab) had a mobile column (Puffcol) operating offensively towards the Mount Popa and Kyauk-padaung area, which left Dinwiddie with one and a half battalions to hold vital points covering the bridgehead and provide a mobile re-serve to support Puffcol.[1] On the left, 33rd Brigade was preparing to attack Taungtha with 1st Burma Regiment, and Myingyan with 4/15th Punjab and 4/1st Gurkhas. The river was kept under close observation by units of the Small Operations Group.

Until the 15th March there was little change in the situation, although there was incessant fighting and the Japanese became steadily more aggressive. At Letse the enemy tried unsuccessfully to surround 28th (E.A.) Brigade; this led to a series of attacks and counter-attacks, the latter by 4/14th Punjab which was acting as a floater battalion outside the defended area. In the Chauk sector 89th Brigade obtained identifications of *188th Battalion* and of *1/61st Battalion (4th Division)*, which gave rise to the belief that *61st Regiment* as well as *72nd I.M.B.* was in the Chauk area.[2] In the Nyaungu bridgehead 114th Brigade spent an uneventful ten days searching for enemy parties reported to be in the vicinity. In the 33rd Brigade sector, 1st Burma Regiment entered Taungtha without difficulty, but was unable to dislodge the enemy from Points 1788 and 676 which between them dominated the town and road.[3] The sudden appear-ance of Japanese near Welaung caused Collingwood to withdraw 4/1st Gurkhas from Myingyan into reserve at Kamye, where it could protect the administrative echelons of both 17th Division and 255th Tank Brigade, which were waiting to go through to Meiktila as soon as the road was opened, and at the same time be well placed to reinforce the attack on Taungtha or Myingyan. On the 11th March Collingwood sent the Gurkhas back to the Myingyan area to cover the right of 4/15th Punjab while it attacked Saka.[4] The action was successful, the enemy leaving 114 dead and two guns on the battlefield as well as numerous documents which revealed the Japanese dispositions in the Myingyan, Taungtha and Mount Popa areas. The 4/1st Gurkhas then moved back towards Taungtha and on the 14th, supported by two squadrons of 116th R.A.C. and 139th Field Regiment, captured Point 676. Next day a company of

---

[1] For composition of Puffcol see page 269 fn. 4.

[2] The *1/61st Battalion* had been renumbered *542nd Battalion* and incorporated in *72nd I.M.B.* (see page 267 fn. 3). Battlefield identifications nevertheless continued to be those of *61st Regiment*.

[3] See Map 9, facing page 320.

[4] There was a strong position at Saka covering Myingyan.

1st Burma Regiment succeeded in reaching the summit of Point 1788 but a fierce counter-attack while it was consolidating drove it off again, so the road to Meiktila remained closed.

Meanwhile 161st Brigade of 5th Division, followed by 123rd Brigade, had arrived at Monywa where, in accordance with Slim's order of the 9th, they came under Messervy's command. Realizing that without assistance Evans could not accomplish his threefold task,[1] particularly as he was under orders if possible to relieve the East Africans by the 1st April, Messervy on the 14th ordered 161st Brigade forward to relieve 33rd Brigade and told Evans, on its arrival, to speed up the capture of Taungtha and Myingyan.[2] The reinforcement of 7th Division was timely, for on the 15th a document was found on a Japanese body left behind after an attack on 89th Brigade which proved to be an order for an offensive northwards, under command of Major-General Yamamoto, to capture Sinthe, Myitche and Nyaungu.

At Meiktila, mopping up and consolidation had been completed by the evening of the 5th March. Although 17th Division was surrounded and liable to be counter-attacked by numerically superior forces, Cowan's policy was to retain the initiative by using a very small number of troops for static defence and sending out columns in all directions to strike at Japanese communications and enemy forces which had cut his own land communication with Taungtha and the Nyaungu bridgehead. He disposed his force in six harbours round the south lake, in each of which there was a 'keep' garrisoned by an infantry company with machine-guns and mortars.[3] The 99th Brigade (Tarver) was made responsible for the defence of Meiktila, the airfield and F.A.M.O. dump, with orders to hold it as a secure base from which the remainder of the division could operate in a mobile role. Tarver was also responsible for the keeps, but not for the formation harbours. Garrisons for the three company keeps on the north side of the lake were supplied by 99th Brigade, and for the other three by 48th Brigade, 63rd Brigade and the divisional headquarters defence battalion. This meant that Tarver had two battalions in hand for the defence of the airfield and F.A.M.O. and to provide a local reserve; these he disposed in the Kyigon and airfield areas. This arrangement remained in force, subject to inter-unit and brigade reliefs, until the end of the battle.

The offensive sweeps began on the 6th March when five columns

---

[1] See page 283.
[2] In his order of the 14th March Messervy had intended to keep 161st Brigade directly under his own control, but on the 16th cancelled this and placed it under command of 7th Division.
[3] See Sketch 16, facing page 360.

49. The Myittha valley near Tilin

50. Scenery near Pakokku

51. An attack on Monywa

52. A human anti-tank mine: a Japanese soldier, shot by a patrol in a foxhole while waiting to detonate a 250-lb. bomb by hand under a tank

53. Major-General C. G. G. Nicholson,
2nd Division

54. Major-General G. C. Evans,
7th Indian Division

55. Nyaungu from Myitche beach

56. Medium tank on a Bailey raft

57. Meiktila. Where do we go from here?

58. Devastation in Meiktila

59. Major-General T. W. Rees,
19th Indian Division

60. First 'close-up' of Mandalay Hill

61. 6-inch howitzer bombarding Fort Dufferin at point-blank range

62. The result—breaches in the North Wall

63. Mandalay Hill from Fort Dufferin (Major-General T. W. Rees in foreground).

64. North-west corner of Fort Dufferin

moved out, one each on the roads to Mahlaing, Zayetkon, Pyawbwe, Thazi and Wundwin. Four of the columns reached their objectives, Mahlaing, Zayetkon, Pyawbwe and Thazi, almost unopposed, but the fifth operating on the Wundwin road found the enemy holding a position near the airstrip at Thedaw.[1] The guns were quickly brought into action and the infantry, leaving their lorries, mounted the tanks, which then moved round to attack the Japanese right flank. The enemy artillery was, however, superior and, since there was a risk of unacceptable losses in armour, the advance was halted while an air-strike was called up by the V.C.P. and directed on the target by artillery fire. When the tanks and infantry went in again, the Japanese left their positions and tried to get away through the scrub to the east, but they were intercepted by the tanks which took a heavy toll; 110 dead were counted and six guns of various types were captured. The column was then replaced by a larger one consisting of a battalion of infantry, a regiment of tanks and one of artillery and a squadron of armoured cars. Having established a base at Ywadan, it struck out towards Wundwin and the railway. For the next three days it kept the railway cut, mopped up many small enemy parties and, at Thedaw railway station, destroyed a new tank and a number of lorries and blew up an ammunition dump. The column was then re-called, since by the 8th it was apparent that considerable enemy forces were moving west past Wundwin and that Japanese patrols were infiltrating to the road between Ywadan and Meiktila.

A second series of raids began with the despatch of similar columns by 63rd Brigade towards Pyawbwe and by 48th Brigade towards Mahlaing. The former met enemy forces in strength at Yindaw, ten miles to the south, and, during actions on the 9th and 10th, 9th Border Regiment suffered 141 casualties and lost one of its supporting tanks; it remained in the area till the 13th when it was withdrawn to Meiktila. The 48th met the Japanese ten miles north-west of Meiktila on the 8th. There were sharp actions that day when three enemy guns were destroyed, and again on the 10th and 11th, when roadblocks were encountered between MS 5 and 6 covered by a considerable force of artillery near Mindawgan Lake. On the 11th, however, the Japanese abandoned their positions, and, as at Ywadan, the tanks took a heavy toll as they withdrew. The dead were not counted, but it was estimated that the Japanese losses during this series of raids amounted to some 300 killed and six more guns.

A third series of raids went out on the 13th and 14th. One on the Pyawbwe road met the Japanese at Kandaung, some seven miles from Meiktila, on the 14th and, after an action lasting all day, overran the

---

[1] The column on the Wundwin road consisted of a squadron of 5th (Probyn's) Horse, a company of 6/15th Punjab, a battery of 24th Mountain Regiment, a detachment of 16th Cavalry (armoured cars) and a V.C.P.

enemy position to find eighty-four dead, while a sweep round the north of Meiktila by 5th (Probyn's) Horse to locate and destroy enemy artillery successfully accounted for another eight guns. It was evident, however, that the Japanese were closing in on the town, particularly so when fighting patrols from 63rd Brigade found them holding Antu (from where 17th Divisional artillery had supported the attack on Meiktila during the first three days of March). To use a boxing metaphor, Cowan had been keeping his opponents at a distance with a series of straight lefts while they were making every effort to get inside his guard. On two occasions the columns ranging around Meiktila met with disaster: on the Pindale road an infantry column was ambushed on the 9th, losing thirty killed, two armoured carriers, six trucks, all its weapons and much equipment, while near Mindawgan Lake a Gurkha company was overwhelmed on the 13th and lost its transport and mortars.

The immediate task given to XXXIII Corps was to capture Mandalay and destroy all enemy forces defending it.[1] Stopford had already given 19th Division (Rees) its orders, and it was ready to cross the Chaungmagyi Chaung on the 5th and begin an enveloping thrust to destroy the Japanese forces believed to be holding Madaya, to be followed by speedy exploitation by armour and lorried infantry towards Mandalay.[2] Rees therefore needed no further instructions. The operations of 20th and 2nd Divisions had, however, to be co-ordinated and, on the 5th, Stopford told both divisional commanders that his intention was to seize the general line Singaingmyo–Ava as quickly as possible with the object of capturing Mandalay in co-operation with 19th Division, and of preventing either the reinforcement of the enemy forces in the Mandalay area or their withdrawal to the east or south.[3] The 20th Division (Gracey) on the right was to raid Myotha, disrupt enemy communications and, after the occupation of the Singaingmyo–Ava line, be prepared to exploit either south-east to Kyaukse or north-east so as to close the eastern exits from Mandalay; 2nd Division (Nicholson) on the left was to close the southern escape routes from Mandalay between the Myitnge bridge and Ava.

On the day these orders were issued 19th Division had 98th Brigade on the north bank of the Chaungmagyi Chaung, with Stiletto Force standing by ready to strike south as soon as the engineers reported the

---

[1] The further task of exploiting south-east into the mountains towards Loilem and Takaw given in Slim's planning paper of the 7th February (see page 242) had been cancelled by an army instruction of the 2nd March and was to become purely a deception scheme (see 'Conclave', page 367).

[2] See pages 259–60.

[3] See Map 9, facing page 320.

tank crossing ready.[1] Rees had ordered 62nd Brigade, then concentrating north of the chaung, to relieve 98th Brigade which was to see Stiletto Force across the chaung and then follow it up to Madaya and Mandalay. The 64th Brigade, then debouching from the hills in the Point 1487 area, was to mop up the area between the hills and the chaung and come into divisional reserve, while 62nd Brigade got ready to move on an all-pack basis to Maymyo.

Stiletto Force began its advance at 8 p.m. on the 5th. By midday on the 6th it had by-passed Madaya and was making for Mandalay, while 98th Brigade was closing in on Madaya where, according to Japanese prisoners-of-war, it should have met *67th Regiment* which had been ordered to hold the town on its withdrawal from Point 1487[2]. The Madaya field works were found undefended but, while the leading battalion (2nd Royal Berkshire) was consolidating, it was counter-attacked by about a hundred Japanese of whom about one-third were killed and a few taken prisoner. During the 7th, while the rest of 98th Brigade moved up to Madaya, Stiletto Force advanced to within a few miles of Kabaing.[3] The force passed through the village unopposed that night and at 6.15 a.m. on the 8th burst into the northern outskirts of Mandalay, scattering small parties of surprised Japanese and seizing the northern slopes of the pagoda-crowned Mandalay Hill. The 8/12th F.F. Regiment, following up, had a brush at Kabaing with some enemy parties (which had presumably arrived there after Stiletto Force had passed through) and did not reach the northern outskirts of the city till 2 p.m. The extent of the surprise achieved can be judged from the fact that there was no enemy reaction until late in the evening, when artillery fire opened on Mandalay Hill.

During the 8th, Rees received fresh orders from Stopford: he was to send a brigade group to cut the Mandalay–Maymyo road, isolate Mandalay from the north and east, cut the escape routes between Tonbo and the Myitnge River and, having established a firm base there, close the southern exits of the city. These four tasks were too much even for a commander of Rees's energy and drive, and the last of them was later given to 2nd Division.[4]

During the night of the 8th/9th March, 98th Brigade (Jerrard) began its assault on the city. Brought up from Madaya to Kabaing in lorries, 4/4th Gurkhas, after a long and difficult night march, stormed

---

[1] See Map 3, facing page 55, and page 259. Stiletto Force (Lieut.-Colonel S. Gardiner) consisted of 1/15th Punjab (carried in lorries), C Squadron 7th Light Cavalry, 239th Field Battery, R.A., a machine-gun company, a troop of anti-tank artillery and a detachment of Indian engineers.

[2] The prisoners had little information on the whereabouts of the other two regiments of *15th Division* which had been in position north of Point 1487, except that the bulk of *60th Regiment* had withdrawn down the east bank of the Irrawaddy. They gave the strength of *67th Regiment* when in the Point 1487 area as about 800.

[3] See Sketch 13, facing page 302.

[4] See page 299.

Mandalay Hill from the east and by dawn had secured the northern and higher of its two peaks.[1] Meanwhile 8/12th F.F. Regiment had infiltrated forward towards the north face of Fort Dufferin in the hope that the enemy could be caught unawares and one of the entrances rushed. The Japanese, however, having reached their chosen battleground, were alert and ready to strike back. The Gurkhas on Mandalay Hill were twice counter-attacked during the 9th, and met with fierce resistance when they began to mop up snipers lurking among the rocks and trees and in the deep caves and bunkers on the hillsides.[2] The 8/12th had meanwhile reached the northern wall of the fort to find the moat full of water, the two bridges wired though not mined, the immensely strong walls of the fort completely undamaged by bombing, and any attempt to approach the moat in daylight subjected to small-arms fire.

Fort Dufferin was a walled enclosure one mile square, which contained government offices and houses and the Mandalay railway station[3]. It was surrounded by a forty-foot wide moat bridged in five places. The wall, some twenty-three feet high, was constructed of brick banked up on the inner side by an earthen ramp and buttressed every 300 feet. It was some thirty feet thick at the base, narrowing to about twelve feet at the top, along which there was a walk protected by a crenellated brickwork superstructure several feet thick. The gates in the centre of each wall were set at an angle to the bridge leading to them and defiladed by massive buttresses. It was a fortress of great strength.

Rees had sent 64th Brigade (Flewett) to carry out Stopford's instruction to isolate Mandalay from the east. By the time its leading troops reached a village some three miles east of the city on the 9th, the Japanese had opened the sluice gates of the Mandalay Canal, flooding the whole area. Finding his task done for him in this unexpected manner, Flewett withdrew to the main road three miles to the north of the city, leaving fighting patrols to watch any usable tracks through the flooded area. With his reserve thus strengthened, Rees sent his divisional headquarters battalion (1/15th Punjab) to reinforce Jerrard (98th Brigade), who had planned that 8/12th F.F. Regiment should break into the fort on the 10th under cover of an intensive artillery bombardment after the wall had been breached near the north gate by a medium gun firing at point-blank range. The Gurkhas were to complete the mopping-up of Mandalay Hill.

---

[1] This attack was made possible at such short notice by the presence of an officer of the Gurkhas who had been in Mandalay in peacetime and knew the Mandalay Hill area very well. He was thus able to lead the battalion to its forming-up position on the eastern slopes.

[2] The Gurkhas were assisted in this task by tanks of 150th R.A.C. from the road along the foot of the hill, escorted by a company of 2nd Royal Berkshires.

[3] The fort, built by King Mindon when he established his capital in Mandalay in 1858, was renamed after the Earl of Dufferin who was Viceroy of India when north Burma was annexed in 1886.

On hearing that he was being reinforced, Jerrard decided to begin clearing the city and gave the Berkshires (less their company with the Gurkhas) and a squadron of 7th Light Cavalry (light tanks) the task of clearing it west of the fort as far as its southern face, and placed 1/15th Punjab in brigade reserve.

The Berkshires began their advance into the city at 9.30 a.m. on the 10th, but soon became involved in street fighting and made only slow progress. The medium gun opened fire on the north wall at 10 a.m. and by 1 p.m. had opened a breach, which an air observation post reported usable since the rubble had formed a ramp on the inside. Under cover of a heavy artillery concentration, the assault company of the 8/12th and a detachment of engineers reached the bridge and began to dismantle the wire. In spite of close support by medium tanks and a smokescreen put down by mortars, the attackers began to suffer heavy casualties from small-arms fire as soon as the artillery concentration lifted. By 4 p.m. the attackers had lost a third of their number and Rees, who was watching the attack, told Jerrard to abandon the attempt. During the day the Gurkhas cleared the Racecourse and the west face of Mandalay Hill and reached the north-eastern corner of the fort, but failed either to dislodge the enemy from the southern extremity of the hill or to complete the mopping-up of the northern half. On the right, the Berkshires could get no farther than half-way down the western wall, and 1/15th Punjab, sent forward to pass through and clear the city as far as the southern wall, was brought to a standstill after a gain of only about one hundred yards. There it was ordered to dig in, and the Berkshires were withdrawn into brigade reserve.

By the evening of the 10th Rees had 98th Brigade in close contact with Fort Dufferin on its north and west sides and had secured the northern and part of the western quarter of the city, with 64th Brigade in reserve on its northern outskirts. He had heard that the leading battalion of 62nd Brigade had secured Maymyo cantonment and that the rest of the brigade was moving up to join it. It was now clear that the only opposition to the quick capture of the city lay in Fort Dufferin and that, in the hands of fighters of the calibre of the Japanese, it was likely to prove a most formidable task.

During the next four days repeated attempts by 98th Brigade to break into the fort failed. Progress was, however, made to the west of the fort, where the forward troops cleared the city to a point about a mile beyond its south-west corner, and to the east where the bridge half-way down the eastern wall was reached. Although completely surrounded, the Japanese at the southern end of Mandalay Hill fought to the death and it was not till the 13th that mopping-up was completed. Towards the end it became a matter of engineers, escorted by infantry, blowing in bunkers; although it was evident that the occupants of many had run out of ammunition, they faced burial alive rather than surrender. Air support was provided as required during these operations but, owing to the close quarters at which fighting was going on, it proved difficult and not always effective. On one occasion, west of the fort, troops who had been pulled back to allow a heavy air strike to take place found themselves unable to regain their vacated positions; these had been occupied by the enemy who, realizing what the withdrawal portended, had infiltrated forward into the area of comparative safety.

On the 14th Rees decided that 64th Brigade was to relieve 98th Brigade the next day and become responsible for operations against the fort. That night 98th Brigade made a last and nearly successful effort to break into the fort; two platoons of 8/12th F.F. Regiment got across the moat in assault boats but, as they could not force their way into the breach to hold it while the rest of the battalion broke in, the attack was called off. After the relief 64th Brigade was to have five battalions and two squadrons of tanks with which to renew the attack on the fort, which left 98th Brigade with two battalions supported by a field regiment to seal the escape routes south-east of the city.[1] Although 2nd Division was on its way to attack Mandalay from the south, its leading troops had not yet reached Ava or the Myitnge River.[2] There was thus a wide gap to the south of the city and, since Ava, like Mandalay, contained a formidable fort, it was quite possible that there might be a prolonged delay before the gap was closed. While his division was regrouping, Rees therefore began to consider new methods of capturing Fort Dufferin, whose garrison clearly intended to fight to the last man, and whether he could bring 62nd Brigade in from Maymyo to complete the encirclement of the city.

On the 5th March Stopford had ordered 20th and 2nd Divisions to undertake a co-ordinated advance to the general line Singaingmyo–Ava.[3] Gracey (20th Division) on the right planned to hold the Myinmu bridgehead with 100th Brigade while his other two brigades concentrated forward at Gyo to bring them in line with 2nd Division. From Gyo he intended to move with 80th Brigade on the right directed on Kyaukse and 32nd Brigade on the left on Singaingmyo, from where it was to turn south and attack Kyaukse from the north in

---

[1] The 64th Brigade group consisted of two of its own battalions, 2nd Worcesters and 1/6th Gurkhas; 2nd Royal Berkshires and 8/12th F.F. Regiment from 98th Brigade; 1/15th Punjab from divisional headquarters; one squadron 150th R.A.C. and one from 7th Light Cavalry; 134th (Medium), 115th (Field) and 33rd Anti-Tank (Mortar) Regiments; and 65th Field Company, I.E. The 98th Brigade group had its own 4/4th Gurkhas; 5/10th Baluch from 64th Brigade; 4th Indian Field Regiment; one platoon Indian Engineers; and one company 11th Sikh Machine-Gun Battalion.

[2] See page 293.

[3] See page 288 and Map 9, facing page 320.

conjunction with 80th Brigade's attack from the west. The raid on Myotha was to be launched from Gyo by a column from 100th Brigade. Nicholson, too, decided to advance on a two-brigade front. The 6th Brigade on the right was to move by the Myintha–Myinthi track and thence along the railway to Sizon, where it was to turn north and capture the Myitnge rail and road bridge, while 5th Brigade on the left was to move along the river bank, capture the fort at Ava and secure the southern end of the Ava bridge. The 268th Brigade in the Sagaing area north of the river was to co-operate by seizing the northern end of the Ava bridge. The 4th Brigade in reserve was to move to Myintha and gain touch with 20th Division at Gyo.

The 20th Division's advance was faster than expected. Gyo was occupied on the 10th, a day ahead of schedule, the only opposition met being from isolated parties of Japanese infantry, often accompanied by artillery, who avoided action if possible but fought fiercely when cornered. The Myotha raiding column moved off from Gyo on the 11th and reached its objective the same day, having been able to bring to action only one of several enemy parties seen. By the evening of the 14th, 80th Brigade had occupied Dwehla, 32nd Brigade was within five miles of Singaingmyo, while 100th Brigade, following up, had moved to Myotha, sent one battalion to block the road to Myingyan and another to deal with parties of Japanese reported by the Burmese to be north of the town. Both forward brigades spent the 15th establishing bridgeheads across the Panlaung River in face of minor infantry opposition but considerable artillery fire.

The advance of 2nd Division received an early check when on the first day the leading battalion of 6th Brigade (1st Royal Berkshires) came up against opposition in a well-concealed position near Myintha and lost twenty men and two of its supporting tanks. The 6th and 5th Brigades reached the Myotha–Kyauktalon road on the 10th and 11th respectively. When the advance was resumed next day there was more delay when 5th Brigade encountered a large number of refugees who said they were some of a thousand convicts released by the Japanese from the Mandalay gaol. On the 13th the tanks with 5th Brigade's advanced guard ran into a minefield in a chaung some two and a half miles west of Tadau and, in the action which followed, the infantry unfortunately found themselves the target of their supporting aircraft owing to a misunderstanding about the bomb line. On the 14th, 6th Brigade cut the road running south from Ava and seized intact the railway bridge across the Panlaung River. The 4th Brigade in reserve had meanwhile moved unopposed to Myinthi.

The 15th March saw the end of the co-ordinated advance of 20th and 2nd Divisions, for on that date the whole pattern of the battles for Mandalay and Meiktila changed. It had become evident that the Japanese *18th Division* withdrawing from the Northern front had by-passed Mandalay and was operating in IV Corps' area, and that there was a steady exodus from Mandalay to the crossings of the Myitnge River. This, combined with the decreasing opposition met by the Chinese divisions of N.C.A.C. advancing towards Lashio and Namtu, by 36th Division advancing towards Mongmit and by 62nd Brigade advancing on Maymyo,[1] showed that the Japanese were losing interest in the Mandalay area and the Burma Road. The in-creasing pressure at Meiktila and on the bridgehead and administra-tive base in the Nyaungu area indicated that their main, if not sole, object was now the destruction of the forces in Meiktila. Success there would enable *15th Army* to withdraw from Mandalay and from the Irrawaddy area in good order; quick counter-action was there-fore necessary.

To prevent the Japanese interposing a large force between his corps and the left of IV Corps, Stopford ordered Gracey (20th Division) to form a strong column to push south towards Meiktila, while 2nd Division turned north and north-east to link up with 19th Division on the Myitnge River and to take Ava, thus making contact with 268th Brigade. Gracey acted quickly. He arranged to reinforce his reserve brigade (100th) with the equivalent of a tank regiment, two squadrons of armoured cars and an artillery regiment and told Rodham, its commander, that he was to clear the whole area south-wards to Wundwin,[2] make physical contact with 17th Division and then strike at Kyaukse from the south.

The complete change in the pattern of the battle in the middle of March was not of course solely attributable to the moves of 14th Army. Slim's strategy had forced the Japanese to change their plans, and it is necessary at this juncture to examine the changes they made in their desperate attempt to save their armies from disaster.

Shortly after the conference of the 23rd February,[3] Katamura (*15th Army*) became aware of the growing threat to Meiktila and de-cided, in view of its vital importance as a supply and communication centre, that it would have to be securely held. Accordingly he pro-posed to cancel the general offensive then under preparation, reduce the number of troops left on the Irrawaddy to a minimum and pre-pare to defend Meiktila. His plan was for *15th Division* to withdraw to the hills north of Madaya, *53rd Division* to hold Taungtha and delay the Allied advance towards Meiktila, and *18th Division* (Naka),

---

[1] See Chapter XXIV.
[2] The area to be cleared averaged twenty miles in width and forty in depth.
[3] See pages 272–73.

already under orders to join his army from Mongmit,[1] to move to Kume and be prepared to take the offensive westwards by the 10th March. *Burma Area Army*, apparently out of touch with the situation on the Irrawaddy front, was not at first prepared to approve this change of plan but, after learning of the loss of Thabutkon, approved it on the 27th and at the same time ordered *49th Division* (less its regiment already in the Yenangyaung area) to move on Meiktila. With his plan approved, Katamura immediately told Naka to speed up his move to Kume by every means at his disposal. Events, however, had moved too swiftly to enable the revised plan to be put into force.

With the fall of Meiktila on the 3rd March Katamura had to abandon this plan also and replace it by an all-out effort to recapture the town, and so, on arrival at Kume on the 4th, Naka found orders awaiting him to destroy the Allied force which had seized Meiktila, the methods to be adopted and the control of the operations being left to his discretion. He was told that *119th Regiment* (less one battalion) from *53rd Division* had been ordered to move to Pindale to cover his concentration, and that two battalions of *214th Regiment* of *33rd Division* (the *Sakuma Force*) were covering the Mahlaing road north-west of Meiktila. Both these formations were to come under his command, together with an artillery group (the *Naganuma Group*) and the remnants of *14th Tank Regiment* (nine tanks).[2] Since *Burma Area Army* had already ordered *49th Division* to move on Meiktila from the south and *15th Army* had ensured that the force in the town was trapped by blocking its communications to the west, Naka was to co-operate with *49th Division* to destroy it.

Naka, who had already sent *55th Regiment* to Wundwin, decided to attack Meiktila from the north and west with the intention of splitting the defence by seizing the causeway over the channel between the two lakes.[3] He ordered *214th Regiment*, then in the vicinity of Antu, to move to the south-west of the town, establish contact with *49th Division* and attack in conjunction with it. At the same time he deployed *56th Regiment* and *18th Mountain Artillery Regiment* on the Mahlaing road, and ordered the rest of his force to concentrate in the vicinity of Mindawgan Lake, north of Meiktila. The deployment was completed, though with difficulty, on the 12th, by which time it was evident that resistance by *15th Army* was breaking down all along the Irrawaddy front, and that unless Meiktila was reoccupied without delay the situation could not be restored. Naka felt that he could not afford to wait for the arrival of *49th Division*, with which he was

---

[1] See page 272.
[2] The *Naganuma Group* consisted of nine 105-mm. guns, two 149-mm. howitzers, fifteen field guns, six regimental guns and thirteen anti-tank guns.
[3] See Sketch 16, facing page 360.

out of touch because of a breakdown in signal communications, and decided to make his effort to seize the causeway forthwith. The attack made no progress, but during it he became aware of the steady stream of aircraft to and from the main airfield east of the town and decided on the 16th to switch the axis of his attack towards the airfield. To the south, *49th Division* had reached the Kandaung area on the 14th after severe fighting, and that night made an unsuccessful attempt to capture the main airfield.[1]

By the middle of March Kimura *(Burma Area Army)* realized that Katamura, already engaged in a desperate defensive battle from Mandalay to Myingyan, could not be expected to control the offensive against Meiktila as well, and that, if *15th Army's* resistance collapsed before 14th Army's stranglehold on Meiktila had been broken, disaster was inevitable. On the 14th March, therefore, he ordered Honda *(33rd Army)* to move with his headquarters to Kalaw, take control of the battle and co-ordinate the forces attacking Meiktila.

By the middle of March, IV Corps, reinforced by 5th Division, was tightening its grip on the Japanese communications to Rangoon, and XXXIII Corps was striking south to Wundwin with 20th Division to contact IV Corps and harass the enemy forces attacking Meiktila from the north, while its other two divisions were closing in on Mandalay. The headquarters of the Japanese *33rd Army* had taken control of the counter-offensive to destroy 14th Army's forces in the Meiktila area.

Slim was moving 14th Army into the kill, while Kimura was concentrating all his available strength to keep open an escape route to the south.

---

[1] The extent of the breakdown of communications is shown by the fact that Naka had no knowledge of *49th Division*'s attack on the airfield on the night of the 14th/15th.

CHAPTER XXVI

THE CENTRAL FRONT
(16th–31st March 1945)
The Battles of Meiktila and Mandalay

See Maps 3, 7 and 9 and Sketches 13 and 16

BY the middle of March it had become evident that the Japanese were making an all-out effort to recapture Meiktila and thus keep open a route for their withdrawal to the south.[1] Slim had committed his reserve,[2] and was content to leave his two corps commanders to complete the destruction of the Japanese in the Meiktila–Mandalay area, but on the 17th he called them to a conference to discuss future operations. The following day he issued an instruction covering operations up to the capture of Rangoon. Alterations in the availability of the airlift and the delay in the capture of Myingyan made an amendment necessary, and a new instruction was issued on the 23rd.[3]

Slim defined his intention as the completion of the destruction of the Japanese forces in central Burma, to be followed by the capture of Rangoon as soon as possible and at all costs before the monsoon; Yenangyaung and the airfields at Magwe and Prome were to be seized, and the Myingyan–Mandalay–Maymyo–Meiktila–Chauk area and the road and railway from Meiktila to Rangoon secured.[4] Messervy's task was to secure Taungtha, contain the enemy in the Kyaukpadaung–Chauk–Seikpyu area, capture Pyawbwe about the 1st April, cut the enemy communications at Thazi, attack the enemy in the Meiktila area at every opportunity and finally concentrate his corps in the Meiktila–Thazi–Pyawbwe area ready to strike south to Rangoon. Stopford was to secure the Mandalay–Maymyo–Kyaukse area and destroy all Japanese forces as far south as Wundwin, concentrate 20th Division in the Wundwin area ready to advance southwest to the Irrawaddy, move 2nd Division to the Myingyan–Nyaungu area and send the 19th, a brigade at a time, to Meiktila and Thazi. He was then to advance down the Irrawaddy, capturing in turn

---

[1] See page 294.
[2] See page 284.
[3] It was the practice at Headquarters 14th Army to issue completely fresh orders rather than amendments to existing orders. For full details of the order of the 23rd March see pages 324–26.
[4] See Map 3, facing page 55. For Magwe and Prome see Map 11, facing page 414.

Seikpyu and Chauk, Yenangyaung, Magwe and Prome, and then push on to Rangoon.

On the Japanese side, Kimura's decision of the 14th March to place Honda (*33rd Army*) in charge of the counter-stroke to recapture Meiktila necessitated a reorganization and regrouping of *15th* and *33rd Armies*, which was to take effect from the 18th. Honda was given *18th Division* (less *114th Regiment* but with *119th Regiment* and the *Sakuma Force* (Colonel T. Sakuma) under command) already in action north and west of Meiktila, *53rd Division* (less *119th Regiment*) at Taungtha, and *49th Division* (less *153rd Regiment*) already advancing on Meiktila from the south. Katamura (*15th Army*), with *15th Division* in the Mandalay area, *31st Division* in the Kyaukse area and *33rd Division* (less *214th Regiment* but with *16th Regiment* of *2nd Division* (the *Aoba Force*) under command) in the Myingyan area, was ordered to hold Mandalay and contain 14th Army north of Meiktila while *33rd Army* recaptured the town. Kimura left *56th Division*, with *114th Regiment* under command, to cover the right flank of both armies and hold the Shan plateau. He had already ordered *28th Army* (Sakurai) to concentrate as large a force as possible in the Yenangyaung area and attack northwards to drive in the Nyaungu bridgehead,[1] an operation which, if successful, would have destroyed all hopes of an early reopening of land communication to Meiktila by IV Corps.

On arrival at Kalaw on the 17th March, Honda received an extremely gloomy report from his Chief of Operations Staff, who had spent the previous three weeks with *15th Army*. The divisions of *15th Army*, he said, were down to a third of their normal strength and had lost so many guns that their artillery was practically ineffective. There was little hope of the army being able to contain the Allied forces opposing it, and there were signs that the forward troops were losing confidence in the High Command. The formations attacking Meiktila were fighting with inferior equipment and supplies against an enemy well maintained by air and with apparently unlimited mobile forces, consisting mainly of tanks. In his opinion, the only hope of success lay in attacking airfields and supply lines and in regrouping the reconstituted *33rd Army* to do this. The outcome of the battle for Meiktila, his report concluded, would decide the fate of the Japanese forces in Burma.

While Messervy and Stopford were preparing their plans to put Slim's instructions into effect and Honda was getting ready to implement his instructions from Kimura, the battles of Meiktila and Mandalay continued with unabated fury.

---

[1] See page 273.

At Mandalay Rees had ordered 64th Brigade (Flewett) to make a silent break-in to Fort Dufferin on the night of the 17th/18th March,[1] and 62nd Brigade (Morris) to move west from Maymyo and take over from 98th Brigade (Jerrard) south-east of Mandalay. On relief Jerrard was to move west to make contact with 2nd Division south of the city and complete its encirclement. Meanwhile 221 Group R.A.F. had begun an attempt to make more breaches in the north wall of the fort. Mitchell medium bombers armed with 2,000-lb. bombs attacked it on the 15th March from an altitude of 6,000 feet. Although several bombs dropped within the fort, the wall itself was not breached, and it was clear that heavy bombs dropped from a safe altitude could have no effect unless there happened to be a direct hit on the wall itself. On the 16th low-flying Thunderbolt fighter-bombers, attacking from south to north, tried to breach the north wall from the inside with 500-lb. bombs. Although the wall was hit, no breach was made owing to the massive earth embankment and because bombs frequently ricocheted and exploded in the vicinity of Mandalay Hill. The direction of the attack was altered on the 17th to north to south so that bombs would strike the exposed brickwork on the outside of the fort. This gave better results, and a number of gaps were made in the upper part of the wall. No clear breaches were made and the rubble which had fallen outwards made additional obstacles for assaulting troops to scale. This failure to breach the wall did not greatly matter for, in the intervals between air attacks, medium artillery had carried out further destructive shoots at point-blank range and had opened up a number of usable breaches in the north and east walls.

Flewett's plan for 64th Brigade's silent attack was for 1/15th Punjab at the north-west corner and 8/12th F.F. Regiment at the north-east corner to infiltrate into the fort through the breaches already made in the walls. To avoid noise, the troops were to wear rubber-soled shoes and neither wear nor carry steel helmets. Each battalion was to have a platoon of engineers with assault boats and scaling ladders,[2] a detachment of six man-pack flame-throwers and a company of machine-guns. Having entered the fort, the battalions were to exploit towards each other and secure its northern half. As soon as the engineers had cleared a bridge and a gate, tanks were to move into the fort. The remaining three battalions were to send fighting patrols to block all exits on the west, south and east faces of the fort and, if possible, infiltrate into it; the rest of each battalion was to stand by to act under divisional orders should the main attack succeed.

The attack began at 10 p.m. on the 17th, and an hour later a company in the north-east corner and a platoon in the north-west corner

---

[1] See Sketch 13, facing page 302.
[2] Fifteen 5-man and two 2-man boats.

had paddled themselves across the moat. So far not a shot had been fired but, as the leading troops on the north-east scrambled up towards the breaches, they glimpsed Japanese silhouetted against the skyline hurrying to man them, and it was not long before the boats came under aimed fire. At midnight an assault boat was sunk, and reports began to trickle back that the attackers were finding immense difficulty in clambering over the rubble in the breaches. In the extreme north-west corner near the railway bridge there was silence until 3 a.m. on the 18th, when the platoon came under murderous fire from automatics which its flame-throwers could not reach, and it was driven back. The time was fast approaching when a withdrawal would have to be ordered since, if the attack were to fail, no one could survive after daybreak on the narrow ledge between the moat and the wall. At 3.30 a.m. Rees reluctantly gave the order for the operation to be abandoned. Elsewhere around the fort no Japanese had attempted to leave, nor had any British or Indian patrol succeeded in getting in.

While these further attempts were being made to break into Fort Dufferin, the leading battalions of 62nd Brigade from Maymyo had reached Tonbo. The battalion of 98th Brigade already there then set off to seize the road and railway bridges over the Myitnge River, but, late on the 17th, it was held up some two miles from its objective by enemy positions which covered all approaches to both bridges. A prisoner who belonged to *II/51st Battalion (15th Division)*, taken there that day, said that his unit was now only one hundred strong, and that Fort Dufferin was held by the remnants of *60th Regiment* which had been ordered to fight to the last as relief was impossible. Realizing that resistance in Mandalay was about to collapse, Rees ordered all units attached to 64th Brigade to return to their own formations, and 62nd Brigade to take over from 98th Brigade the task of closing the south-eastern as well as the eastern exits from the city. The whole of the 98th was then to move westwards to take over the task formerly allotted to 2nd Division in an attempt to seal the southern exits quickly before there was any possibility of a break-out by the remnants of the garrison of Mandalay. This regrouping was completed on the 19th.

On the 18th the R.A.F. continued their attacks on the north wall without much success. On the 19th they were called off, and every available 6-inch howitzer was brought into action at ranges of 300 to 500 yards. By evening there were seventeen more breaches in the north and east walls. About 12.40 p.m. on the 20th March, as the dust and smoke cleared after a heavy air attack on the fort, six Burmans carrying a white flag and a Union Jack were seen to emerge from its east gate and make their way towards the gun positions of 134th Medium Regiment which had been battering the wall from a range of

500 yards. They reported that there were no Japanese left in the fort. Morris at once ordered 62nd Brigade to move into the fort and at 1.30 p.m. a gunner of the medium regiment, a detachment of which went in with the infantry, nailed a Union Jack to the fort flagstaff. Kipling himself, who immortalized Mandalay, could not have thought of a more suitable ending to the battle.

The defence of Mandalay had been entrusted to *15th Division* which was, after its retreat from Thabeikkyin and Singu, about 3,000 strong. After continuous fighting in the city the division was driven into its southern suburbs by the 17th March, and *60th Regiment* holding the fort was more or less encircled. Katamura (*15th Army*) had intended to defend Mandalay to the end but, in view of the situation at Meiktila and the advance of two Allied divisions towards the Myitnge River and Kyaukse, he came to the conclusion about the middle of the month that to continue his attempt to defend Mandalay would in no way assist the overall position of his army. He therefore ordered the division to withdraw across the Myitnge River. On the night of the 19th/20th March the remnants of *60th Regiment* withdrew from the fort and took up a rearguard position in the Government Farms area to the south of the city; the units of the division which were still in the area passed through the position that night. The following night *60th Regiment* withdrew south with the intention of crossing the river at Myitnge.

While the Allied commanders were making their formal entry into Mandalay, the mopping-up of the Japanese attempting to withdraw to the south began. The 5th Brigade of 2nd Division had taken the fort at Ava without difficulty on the 18th and had then gone on to link up with 268th Brigade, which had secured the northern end of the broken Ava Bridge after mopping up the Sagaing area.[1] At the same time 6th Brigade secured the Myitnge bridge, damaged but repairable. On the 21st, 4th Brigade, passing through 6th Brigade, occupied the town and made contact with 98th Brigade of 19th Division two miles to the east of it, and 5th Brigade, having handed over the Ava area to 268th Brigade, moved east and aligned itself on the left of 4th Brigade. The last gap in the cordon along the Myitnge river now appeared to be closed and Rees told 62nd Brigade to sweep south towards it. Many parties of Japanese were met and all, large and small, fought to the death when cornered.[2] About 500 Japanese

---

[1] See Map 9, facing page 320.
[2] It is a tragic coincidence that on the 23rd March 1945 the 4th Marquis of Dufferin and Ava, working with a Field Broadcasting Unit, was killed in an ambush between Ava, from which the 1st Marquis took the second part of his title, and Fort Dufferin, to which the 1st Marquis gave his name when Earl of Dufferin (see page 290 fn. 3).

were killed and only two taken prisoner; sixty-six loaded lorries, a workshop unit, eleven serviceable guns complete with tractors and trucks were taken and eight damaged or burnt-out tanks found. Nevertheless, the remnants of *15th Division* managed to cross the river at a number of points between Myitnge and the junction of the Mandalay Canal with the Myitnge River and make their way into the hills south-east of Kyaukse.

Stopford had completed part of his task—the capture of Mandalay. But there was still an escape route in the vicinity of Kyaukse by which the remnants of *31st* and *33rd Division* of *15th Army* and the considerable Japanese force attacking Meiktila from the north could escape. Although he had to leave 20th Division to continue the fight in the Kyaukse area and keep contact with Meiktila, he was in a position to regroup the rest of his corps and change its front to face south-west ready to carry out his new task of advancing down the Irrawaddy valley. On the 20th March he issued orders for 2nd Division to hand over its responsibility in the Ava–Myitnge area to 19th Division, concentrate at Tadau and prepare to operate to the south-west towards Chauk, moving by routes which would be decided as the operations developed. Having mopped up Mandalay, 19th Division was to be ready to move to Meiktila and Thazi,[1] and 20th Division, after capturing Kyaukse and making contact with 17th Division at Wundwin, was to be ready to move south-west through Natmauk towards Magwe.[2] The 268th Brigade at Sagaing was to send one battalion immediately to Myotha, patrol widely from there and follow up with the rest of the brigade as soon as it was certain that there were no Japanese left around Sagaing. There was also to be a considerable redistribution of armour and artillery in order to get detachments back to their parent units and to concentrate the corps troops. The redistribution was not to take place, however, until all formations affected had concluded their current operations; this meant that, with the exception of 20th Division which continued fighting in the Kyaukse–Wundwin area till the end of March, and the immediate move of one battalion of 268th Brigade to Myotha, the regrouping began on the 23rd March.

Meanwhile 80th and 32nd Brigades of 20th Division had by the 18th March reached the Zawgyi River to the west of Kyaukse and to the south-east of Singaingmyo respectively, driving small but determined Japanese rearguards before them.[3] Since Kyaukse not only

---

[1] Stopford knew by this time that 36th Division of N.C.A.C. was to move to Mandalay and come under the orders of 14th Army as soon as it had reached Kyaukme and made contact with 50th Chinese Division. It was actually ordered to join 14th Army on the 30th March. See page 320.

[2] See Map 7, facing page 171.

[3] On the 18th Greeves was succeeded in command of 80th Brigade by Brigadier D. E. Taunton.

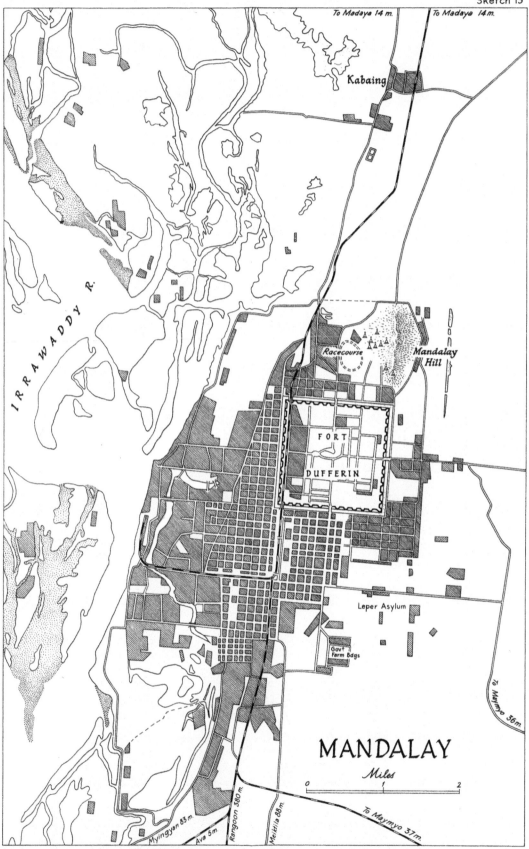

To Madaya 14 m. To Madaya 14 m.

Kabaing

IRRAWADDY R.

Racecourse

Mandalay
Hill

FORT

DUFFERIN

Leper Asylum

Govt
Farm Bdgs

To Maymyo 36 m.

MANDALAY

Miles

0   1   2

Myingyan 85 m.   Ava 5 m.   Rangoon 380 m.   Meiktila 88 m.   To Maymyo 37 m.

covered the main escape route for *15th Army* formations south of the
Myitnge River but was also reported in mid-March to be the headquarters of *31st Division*, it was expected that the enemy would defend
it resolutely. This proved to be the case, for 80th Brigade was soon
checked by well-organized defences in depth.

To comply with his orders to sweep south towards Wundwin,[1]
Gracey had formed a hard-hitting column of armour and lorried infantry under command of Lieut.-Colonel J. M. Barlow (Barcol), and
ordered it to advance in three bounds from Chaunggwa through
Pyinzi and Pindale to Wundwin, a distance of 70 miles.[2] There it was
to establish a firm base from which to harass and destroy enemy forces
attacking Meiktila from the north. Barcol began its advance on the
19th; moving swiftly, it surprised and routed the small enemy forces
which were defending the three towns, destroying communications,
supply dumps and convoys on the way. On the 22nd, columns were
sent out along all the roads and tracks from Wundwin, while the
engineers destroyed large dumps of stores and vehicles found in
the town which they could not use or move. One column captured
a train of sixteen trucks at Thedaw railway station loaded with
ordnance stores and a tank; another, moving down the road to
Meiktila, met no enemy and made contact with 17th Division. As
soon as he knew that Barcol had contacted the Meiktila garrison,
Gracey ordered it to move north on Kume which was reported to be a
rallying-point for *18th* and *33rd Divisions*. At 5 p.m. on the 23rd Barcol
surprised some three hundred Japanese in Kume and drove them
into the hills. For the next two days pursuit columns operated in
all directions, killing over a hundred and capturing twenty-seven
Japanese. These columns also captured large numbers of derelict and
damaged vehicles, assault boats, outboard engines, a gun and
twenty-three serviceable lorries. The raid by Barcol was most effective; the fact that it surprised post after post indicates the speed of its
movement and shows the extent to which the Japanese communications had broken down. One of the columns ran into trouble, however, on the Myittha road and in a brisk action, which continued well
into the night of the 24th, lost three tanks. While Barcol was completing its sweep towards Kume, the rest of 100th Brigade 'filled in'
behind it and secured all points of importance between Wundwin and
Myittha.

In the Singaingmyo area 32nd Brigade made contact with 62nd
Brigade of 19th Division on the 24th. As no Japanese were being
found in the area, Gracey ordered it to move to the south of Kyaukse,

---

[1] See page 294.
[2] Barcol consisted of 7th Light Cavalry (light tanks), 11th P.A.V.O. Cavalry (armoured
cars), each less two squadrons, one squadron 150th R.A.C. (medium tanks), 18th (S.P.)
Field Regiment less one battery, 4/10th Gurkhas (carried in lorries), 401st Field Squadron,
I.E. and a V.C.P.

passing behind 80th Brigade, and gave it the task of blocking all the roads and tracks running south-east from the town and of seizing, when ordered, the airfield four miles to its east. The brigade reached its new area on the 26th and made patrol contact with Barcol near Hamyinbo. Because of the many canals in the Kyaukse area which hampered movement, and the fact that enemy parties by-passed by the leading troops fought it out in well dug-in positions, confused fighting went on for three more days. On the 30th March, however, 9/12th F.F. Regiment, having worked its way round the north of Kyaukse the previous day, seized the pagoda-crowned hill east of the town, whereupon enemy opposition ceased. By this time 100th Brigade was in contact with 17th Division at Wundwin and was about to be relieved by 64th Brigade of 19th Division.[1]

While XXXIII Corps was breaking into Fort Dufferin and destroying what was left of the Japanese forces in the Mandalay area, the tempo of the battle for Meiktila, from Letse (west of the Irrawaddy) through Chauk and Taungtha to Myingyan, and around Meiktila itself, rose to its peak as a result of the desperate Japanese effort to annihilate IV Corps' forces in the Nyaungu bridgehead and at Meiktila.

At Nyaungu, to implement Messervy's orders of the 14th and 16th March,[2] and meet the situation indicated by the mass of information he now held on the Japanese intentions, Evans regrouped 7th Division. The enemy plan, known by IV Corps as the Yamamoto offensive, appeared to be a drive astride the Irrawaddy northward from Chauk towards Nyaungu and from Letse on the Myitche airfield.[3] Details of the plan indicated that two battalions (*188th* and *542nd* of *72nd I.M.B.*) were to advance north from the Pyinma Chaung to seize Nyaungu, and that *153rd Regiment* less a battalion (the *Katsu Force*), was to move up the Yaw Chaung to a point some fourteen miles north of Letse and then strike east to seize Myitche. The *187th Battalion* of *72nd I.M.B.* was to cover the left flank in the hills some twenty miles west of Letse, and *543rd Battalion* to hold the Chauk–Seikpyu area. It was known that there were two battalions of *112th Regiment* (the *Kanjo Force*) and an *I.N.A.* regiment in the Mount Popa area.

There was by now ample evidence that the strength of the enemy force west of the Irrawaddy was increasing.[4] This, and the effect of recent reverses inflicted on 28th (E.A.) Brigade, caused Evans

---

[1] The relief was in accordance with Stopford's orders of the 20th March under which his corps was to be regrouped. See page 302.

[2] See page 286.

[3] See Map 3, facing page 55.

[4] The *Koba Force* (*I/* and *II/154th Battalions*) had in fact arrived in the area from Arakan.

to reinforce the Letse area. To bring this about, he ordered 161st Brigade (5th Division), then crossing the river at Nyaungu, to Taungtha. There it was to relieve 1st Burma Regiment, which was to move to Nyaungu and be joined by 1/3rd Madras Regiment.[1] As soon as it was relieved by 7/2nd Punjab (less a company left on Wabo island), 2nd South Lancashire (114th Brigade) was to move from the Nyaungu bridgehead to the Letse area.[2] The rest of the 114th was to follow it as soon as possible.[3]

On the 17th March enemy pressure in both the Letse and Chauk sectors increased considerably. At Letse, a heavy attack was made on the 21st after a five hours' bombardment of the defences held by the East Africans. Two posts were overrun and some Japanese reached the supply area. The enemy was eventually driven back with the help of 4/14th Punjab, leaving behind 251 dead, all from *153rd Regiment*. About half of these lay in the barbed wire entanglement on to which they had hurled themselves regardless of whether or not it had been cut. On the 23rd, with the arrival of 2nd South Lancashire the previous day, the relief of the somewhat shaken African brigade began. Although their offensive towards Myitche had been brought to a halt, the Japanese held on until the end of the month to Point 534 some two miles to the south-east and overlooking the Africans' position at Letse.

East of the Irrawaddy a raid in force on the 17th by 4/8th Gurkhas, supported by tanks, on a position a mile to the north of Singu disclosed that the enemy strength in that area had increased, and provided identifications of *188th Battalion* and *I/61st (542nd) Battalion*. The raiders, having destroyed three guns, withdrew after dark, but after a second raid on the 20th they remained in occupation of the position. A Japanese attempt to retake it on the 23rd was halfhearted and made no progress.[4] The failure of the attacks on Letse and north of Singu was the end of Yamamoto's offensive. Meanwhile, enemy attempts to infiltrate into the bridgehead area had brought about some minor clashes, in one of which a Japanese officer with forty-nine men of the *I.N.A.* were surrounded; the officer and a third of the men were killed and the rest surrendered.

The arrival of 161st Brigade (5th Division) in the Taungtha area

---

[1] The 1/3rd Madras Regiment was temporarily allotted from 14th Army troops. The 1st Burma Regiment was to be replaced in 33rd Brigade by 1st Queen's Royal Regiment on its return to 7th Division from a period of rehabilitation. The 1st Burma Regiment was then to join 5th Division.

[2] The two companies of 2nd South Lancashire with Puffcol (see **page 269** fn. 4) were to be relieved by two companies of 7/2nd Punjab under command of Lieut.-Colonel T. Mainprise-King. Puffcol was then renamed Kingcol.

[3] At this time 7th Division was being maintained by road and river from the airhead at Myitche, with the exception of the formations operating in the Letse area which were on supply drop.

[4] The Japanese say that in the fighting north of Singu *542nd Battalion* was annihilated, only ten men surviving.

enabled 1st Burma Regiment to move into the bridgehead and
4/1st Gurkhas to be relieved so that it could join 4/15th Punjab for
the attack on Myingyan. Supported by a squadron of 116th R.A.C.,
139th Field Regiment and a machine-gun company, the two battalions
began the assault at 10 a.m. on the 17th. The 4/15th Punjab, supported by tanks, attacked from the south, and 4/1st Gurkhas (less two
of its companies still on their way from Taungtha) attempted to infiltrate into the town from the east.[1] At 1.30 p.m. the tanks, stopped
by an uncrossable ditch, withdrew to refuel and rearm while the
Punjabis secured and improved a way across it. The tanks were across
the ditch by 4.30 p.m., but the Gurkhas came up against a series of
defended posts covering the eastern approaches to the town, which
stopped further infiltration; the remaining two hours of daylight
were therefore spent in reconnaissance and consolidation. During the
18th and 19th the battle raged among a maze of sheer-sided dry
ravines. Success was largely due to the amazing courage of a young
Sikh, Lieutenant Karamjeet Singh Judge, who time after time
throughout the 19th directed tanks on to the carefully concealed
Japanese bunkers. On foot, alone and completely in the open, it was
miraculous that he survived until just before the tanks were forced by
darkness to withdraw, but by then the cotton mill area immediately
to the south of the town had been secured.[2] On the 21st the Gurkhas
were reinforced by some tanks, and the two battalions began to close
in on the town. Late in the afternoon of the 22nd, by which time a
company of 7/2nd Punjab from Wabo island had occupied the airfield,[3] the Japanese were driven from their positions and all resistance
ceased.[4] Thus on the 23rd March, with Myingyan secured and the
Japanese offensives at Letse and Chauk at a standstill, 33rd Brigade
was able to turn south to help 161st Brigade take the Taungtha hills,
and 123rd Brigade from Nyaungu could also move there in readiness
to push through to Meiktila.

In the middle of March the battle for Meiktila was at its most critical
stage, but reinforcements were on the way. The fly-in of 9th Brigade
(Salomons) began from Palel on the morning of the 15th.[5] It so
happened that the Japanese had started their offensive against the
Meiktila airfield during the preceding night and, although their first

---

[1] The town was held by *1/214th Battalion*, supported by *33rd Mountain Artillery Regiment*. The garrison was later reinforced by *215th Regiment* less two battalions.
[2] He was posthumously awarded the V.C. The citation records that he dominated the
entire battlefield by his numerous and successive acts of superb gallantry.
[3] See Map 9, facing page 320.
[4] The defenders had been given permission by *33rd Division* to withdraw through Pindale
to the Wundwin area. *En route* they ran into 4th Brigade of 2nd Division moving to the
Myingyan–Nyaungu area. See pages 297 and 362 fn. 3.
[5] See page 284 fn. 2.

effort achieved little success, the attacking force established itself near enough to make landing on the 15th a hazardous affair.[1] Nevertheless, during the day Headquarters 9th Brigade and 3/2nd Punjab landed with trifling loss, only one of the fifty-four aircraft which touched down being hit. It was clear, however, that until 99th Brigade, which was responsible for the defence of the area, could clear it, the fly-in of the rest of 9th Brigade would have to be suspended.

During the night of the 15th/16th there were many patrol clashes on the airfield, and at daybreak it was discovered that a Japanese force of unknown strength had succeeded in digging itself in on the eastern side of the runway, dominating the whole of it. During the 16th, 6/15th Punjab, supported by a squadron of Probyn's Horse and followed up by 1/3rd Gurkhas, cleared the area and established company posts at the north-eastern and south-eastern corners of the main runway. The same day 9th Brigade began to relieve the posts at Kyigon and the local reserve on the western side of the airfield. It was decided late on the afternoon of the 16th to risk resuming the fly-in, and by nightfall twenty-eight sorties had brought in the bulk of 4th Jammu and Kashmir Infantry at the cost of one aircraft destroyed by artillery fire and twenty-two casualties. On the 17th, in spite of continuous harassing fire and the appearance of Japanese fighting patrols on the runway twice during the day, another sixty sorties brought in the rest of 9th Brigade. By 6 p.m. that evening it had taken over the two new posts east of the runway and released 99th Brigade from all its existing static commitments, thus freeing it for mobile operations.

Cowan had intended to keep the airfield in operation by carrying out a sweep of the country round it every morning. The Japanese, however, had realized that in order to succeed they had to put 14th Army's airfields, and in particular Meiktila, out of action.[2] From the 17th they redoubled their efforts to gain control of the airfield and that night their patrols managed to set fire to a parked aircraft. It was now clear that the landing of aircraft was no longer possible and that from the 18th all supplies would have to be dropped.

Reinforced by 9th Brigade, Cowan was ready on the 17th to open a general offensive against the enemy forces closing in on Meiktila in a wide arc from the north-east to the north-west. He gave 9th Brigade the task of holding the firm base, and allotted the Wundwin road to 99th Brigade, the Pindale road to 48th Brigade and the Mahlaing road to 63rd Brigade. In the event, 48th Brigade became progressively

---

[1] See Sketch 16, facing page 360. The first attack was made by a column from *49th Division* from Pyawbwe headed by a commando-type unit 500 strong. From the 16th onwards all attacks on the airfield were made by *18th Division* from the north.

[2] See pages 295–96.

more involved in operations to hold off the increasing pressure on Meiktila from the south and south-east, and 9th Brigade in dealing with the incessant stream of Japanese patrols, snipers and even artillery units which made their way to some part of the airfield every night, and eventually in repelling a determined assault.

On the 19th it became clear that the Japanese were building up their strength at Nyaungbintha within a mile of the south-east corner of the airfield and at Kinde, south of 48th Brigade's harbour area. Columns from 9th and 48th Brigades were therefore sent out to try to disperse these concentrations. In an unsuccessful attack on Kinde on the 22nd a column from 48th Brigade lost three tanks, and the Japanese, following up the withdrawing column, attacked the brigade's harbour. A feature of this attack, which was made by *106th Regiment* supported by *49th Artillery Regiment*, was the bold handling of the Japanese artillery; a 75-mm. gun, for example, was brought into action within fifteen yards of a forward post held by 1/7th Gurkhas. When, after dark on the 23rd, the Japanese gave up the attack they left 198 dead, two guns and a large number of automatics on the battlefield.[1] The threat from the south was now so great that Cowan ordered 99th Brigade, which had just completed a successful four-day sweep in the Mindawgan Lake area as a follow-up to the successful action of the 11th,[2] to move with two battalions to make another attack on Kinde. This fared no better than that of the 22nd and two more tanks were lost. To have continued attacking in this area would have been to reinforce failure, so a battalion of 48th Brigade was detailed to watch and harass Kinde,[3] while 99th Brigade went back to the Mindawgan Lake area on the 25th to join 63rd Brigade in a final mopping-up. Operating under mutual arrangements between the brigade commanders, 99th Brigade advanced from the south-east and 63rd Brigade from the west and north-west. By the evening of the 28th, the Japanese, driven out of one position after another and in danger of being surrounded, began to withdraw north and then east across the Wundwin road.[4] The success of this operation cleared the Taungtha road as far as Mahlaing and thus made possible an early link-up with 5th Division.

At the airfield, 9th Brigade was under continuous pressure from the

---

[1] The Japanese accounts speak of the gallantry and skill of Colonel T. Uga, who commanded *49th Artillery Regiment* throughout the fighting south-east of Meiktila until he was killed at the end of March. Guns, often under his personal command, were used with the forward troops both in attack and defence. As a result, 255th Tank Brigade suffered its heaviest losses in tanks during the fighting in this area.

[2] See page 287. During this sweep seven guns (three of them 105-mm.) with tractors and two medium tanks were captured. The Japanese record that *56th Regiment* and an engineer battalion in that area were reduced to one-third of their original strength.

[3] The *106th Regiment* with some 400 men and nine guns held on to Kinde until the end of March.

[4] The 99th Brigade suffered ninety-one casualties against twenty known Japanese dead, and 63rd Brigade claimed to have killed 113 Japanese in its sector.

21st March for some five days.[1] The fighting was grim and at close quarters, so close that on the 22nd Lieut.-Colonel K. Bayley (officiating commander 9th Brigade) and his brigade major were both wounded by a shell fired at their command post at point-blank range.[2] Another attack on the night of the 22nd/23rd was driven off, the enemy leaving 103 dead on the battlefield, but snipers, left behind when the attackers withdrew, inflicted thirty-six casualties on 2nd West Yorkshires before being finally eliminated. The fighting in this area reached its climax on the 24th and 25th March. Late in the afternoon of the 24th a gun suddenly opened fire from the southern end of the runway, destroying two aircraft, and confused fighting followed. As darkness fell a tank drove unmolested straight down the runway, its nationality being discovered only when it was joined by two more tanks and some infantry and, supported by six guns, attacked a post held by 3/2nd Punjab on the western side of the airfield. A desperate fight followed, during which the tanks broke through the wire but were eventually driven off by fire from P.I.A.T.s. Later in the night other Japanese, found digging in on the airfield, were dispersed. On the morning of the 25th a gun opened fire from one of the aircraft bays, where yet another party had entrenched itself unnoticed. Drastic action was called for, and 48th Brigade, less the battalion watching Kinde, was ordered to clear the area, supported by two squadrons of medium tanks and 1st Indian Field Regiment. The attack was made from Kyigon in a south-easterly direction and took three days to achieve its object.[3]

On the 22nd, while the grim fighting was taking place around Meiktila, Messervy issued his orders for the final stage of the battle and for the redeployment of IV Corps for its advance on Rangoon. After the capture of Myingyan and the liquidation of all Japanese forces in the Meiktila–Thazi–Pyawbwe area, the corps, less 7th Division, was to concentrate in that area in preparation for the southward drive on Rangoon. Cowan (17th Division) was to complete the clearance of the Meiktila–Thazi area, send a column back towards Taungtha to meet 5th Division about the 27th March and begin his advance on Pyawbwe on the 29th.[4] Major-General R. Mansergh (5th Division)

---

[1] The first attack on the 21st was made by *II/106th Battalion*, which had 160 men killed in the action. Thereafter *18th Division* took over and the attacks were made by *55th* and *119th Regiments* supported by *18th Mountain Artillery Regiment*.

[2] Salomons, who had commanded the brigade with distinction for over a year, had been relieved of his command as a result of a disagreement with Cowan over the handling of his brigade.

[3] The 48th Brigade, though closely supported by tanks, suffered 102 casualties. It captured nine guns and found 212 Japanese dead. The Japanese say that *55th* and *119th Regiments* and their supporting artillery lost half their strength in men and guns during this action.

[4] On the 24th these dates were changed to the 29th March and the 1st April respectively.

was to take over from 7th Division the command of 17th Division's administrative base, resume command of 161st Brigade and, with it and 123rd Brigade already on its way forward, capture Taungtha and then break through to Meiktila. He was to relieve 17th Division at Meiktila by the 27th March and at Thazi by the 1st April.[1] Evans, having captured Myingyan, was to continue to inflict loss on the Japanese throughout 7th Division's area, complete the relief of 28th (E.A.) Brigade, and hand over 116th R.A.C. (less one squadron) and the squadron of 16th Cavalry then under his command to 5th Division. On the 1st April 7th Division was to pass to the command of XXXIII Corps in readiness for the southward advance along the Irrawaddy axis.

By the 25th, Mansergh was ready to attack Point 1788 at Taungtha from the west with 161st Brigade, while 33rd Brigade of 7th Division, temporarily under his command, attacked from the north.[2] As at Kyaukse, the Japanese fought to the death and 33rd Brigade, advancing down the Myingyan–Taungtha road, had to clear a series of strongpoints covering the town from the north. However, by the 28th Point 1788 was surrounded and most of its outlying posts had been mopped up. That night a convoy carrying supplies and ammunition to the Japanese garrison was intercepted and destroyed, and on the morning of the 29th, after an accurate airstrike with 500-lb. bombs on the summit, the hill was occupied without further fighting. As a parting gesture the Japanese made a fierce though unsuccessful attack on Point 676, which had just been taken over by the leading battalion of 123rd Brigade. Meanwhile, 17th Division had reoccupied Mahlaing and the way was now clear for 5th Division and the huge transport column with it to drive straight through to Meiktila.

With 5th Division on its way to Meiktila, Cowan could afford to evacuate the Mindawgan Lake area, and on the 30th he warned 99th Brigade to prepare for its next task—an advance on Pyawbwe by way of Thazi as part of the divisional plan to attack the town. Leaving a battalion to make sure that the mopping-up of the Mindawgan Lake area was complete, the brigade returned to its base in Meiktila. The same day an armoured column drove up the road to Wundwin to make physical contact with 100th Brigade of 20th Division, which was waiting to move south-westwards with the rest of the division as soon as it had been relieved by 64th Brigade of 19th Division.[3] On

---

[1] Mansergh, who had been Brigadier Royal Artillery in 5th Division, was appointed to command the division when Warren was killed in an air accident on his way back to Imphal from a conference at Headquarters IV Corps in February.

[2] See Map 9, facing page 320. The 33rd Brigade had handed Myingyan over to 1/3rd Madras Regiment sent there from Nyaungu. The 5th Brigade of 2nd Division also arrived at the town just as 33rd Brigade began to move to the south.

[3] See page 304.

the 31st, 5th Division (less 9th Brigade already there) arrived at Meiktila with 17th Division's and 255th Tank Brigade's administrative units and began to take over the area. On the 1st April the airfield was reopened for the landing of supplies.

The capture and defence of Meiktila from the crossing of the Irrawaddy to the end of March cost IV Corps 835 killed, 3,174 wounded and ninety missing, and the losses from sickness were roughly the same. Twenty-six tanks were destroyed in battle; forty-four were damaged by accident or enemy action, but were all repairable at or forward of the corps' workshops. These figures are high but the tanks were used boldly, inflicting severe losses on the enemy and saving hundreds of British and Indian lives. In the battle for Mandalay XXXIII Corps' losses amounted to 1,472 killed, 4,933 wounded and 120 missing, while sickness accounted for 3,571. When it is remembered that XXXIII Corps had one more division in action than IV Corps and was in action for nearly six weeks before IV Corps crossed the Irrawaddy, these figures are not dissimilar. The grand total of 14th Army's losses to the end of March was about 18,000, of which some 10,500 were battle casualties.

Throughout the battles for Mandalay and Meiktila, 221 Group R.A.F., supplemented when required by 224 Group,[1] provided 14th Army with close support in the form of airstrikes on selected targets, bombed the Japanese lines of communication to the south, and flew defensive patrols largely for the protection of transport aircraft on supply duties. Owing to the vast area over which the battle took place, March proved to be the peak month for the group, whose squadrons flew for more than 21,000 hours. To provide close support for 14th Army 4,360 sorties were flown, and attacks on the enemy's lines of communication accounted for 2,085 sorties; during these 1,560 tons of bombs were dropped. Another 2,300 sorties were flown to protect the transport aircraft, making a total of 8,745 sorties in the month. To maintain these operations, over 5,000 tons of bombs, ammunition and P.O.L. had to be flown into forward airfields by the C.C.T.F.[2]

Airstrikes in close support of 14th Army were of daily occurrence. Although they played a significant part in enabling 14th Army to overcome the fierce Japanese opposition, especially around Mandalay and Meiktila, only those of particular significance or interest have been mentioned, for all airstrikes of this nature followed a similar pattern.

The task of cutting the Japanese communications south of the line

[1] See page 254.
[2] See Appendix 24.

Meiktila–Heho was given to 908 Wing. The targets selected were bridges, locomotives and rolling stock on the main track between Thazi and Pegu, supply dumps, troop staging posts and pipelines in the oilfields. Attacks began in the first week of March, but it was found that the Japanese were quick to repair the railway bridges: for example, a bridge put out of action on the 5th was found to be in use on the 8th, a second attack that day caused further damage but the bridge was back in use on the 16th and a third attack had to be launched in order to put it completely out of action. So that 14th Army's advance on Rangoon should not be prejudiced, it was decided in the third week of March that no more attacks should be made on the railway, on bridges, on installations in the oilfields or on river craft on the Irrawaddy not in use. Thereafter the wing confined its activities to attacking enemy movements by road.

It is of interest to look at the battle for Meiktila between the 18th and 31st March from the Japanese point of view. On the 18th Honda ordered *18th Division* and its attached formations to secure their positions north of Meiktila and neutralize the main Meiktila airfield, *49th Division* to attack astride the Pyawbwe–Meiktila road, and *53rd Division* to withdraw immediately, moving west of Meiktila to the vicinity of Pyawbwe. This order reached *18th* and *49th Divisions* that night but did not arrive at *Headquarters 53rd Division* until late on the 19th. By the 25th Honda estimated that, during the severe fighting around Meiktila, *18th Division* had lost half its guns and had suffered heavy casualties, the losses of *49th Division* being even greater, and that there were only some twenty serviceable guns left in the two divisions. In the next few days it became evident to him that not only was *15th Army* being driven back in disorder into the mountains east of the railway but that *33rd Army's* offensive could no longer be sustained. Tanaka (*Burma Area Army* Chief of Staff) visited Honda's headquarters on the 28th and, after hearing the situation, agreed to the offensive being abandoned, but ordered *33rd Army* to maintain its existing positions to cover the withdrawal of *15th Army*. Honda replied that his army would continue the struggle to the last man, and asked for Tanaka's order to be confirmed in writing.

In orders issued next day Honda said that, in order to help *15th Army* to make good its retreat towards the mountainous country east of Wundwin, he intended to take up positions on a general line running south-west from Thazi to the south of Meiktila, behind which he could withdraw. The *18th Division* was to break contact on the night of the 29th March and move to positions covering Thazi, but was to keep the Meiktila airfield neutralized for as long as possible; *214th Regiment* (the *Sakuma Force*) was to withdraw at once, cross the railway south of Wundwin and rejoin its own division (*33rd*) in the mountains to the east of the town ; *49th Division* was to hold its existing positions and prevent any Allied forces moving south from Meiktila ; and *53rd Division* was to assemble at Yanaung, west of Pyawbwe.[1]

Three days later, on the 1st April, Honda ordered *18th Division* to withdraw to Pyawbwe, leaving a detachment to hold the defile at Hlaingdet, through which stragglers of *15th Army* were moving, and, as soon as *18th* and *53rd Divisions* had reached Pyawbwe and Yanaung respectively, *49th Division* was to withdraw to Yamethin.

The battles for Mandalay and Meiktila were over, and both *15th* and *33rd Armies* had suffered a major defeat. During the offensive for the recapture of Meiktila their losses were extremely heavy. According to their records, *18th Division* (excluding its attached formations) suffered 1,773 casualties (about one-third of its strength) and lost twenty-two out of forty-five guns, while *49th Division*, which began the battle with a strength of about 10,000, suffered 6,500 casualties and lost forty-five out of a total of forty-eight guns ; the casualties of the other units engaged are not available but would presumably be of a similar order. The casualties suffered by *15th Army* are not recorded but it is evident that they were equally heavy. *Burma Area Army* had virtually ceased to exist as a fighting force.

By the 31st March it was plain that the Japanese had abandoned all hope of recapturing Meiktila. The IV Corps was concentrating there and 17th Division was regrouping to attack Pyawbwe, where it was known that the enemy was preparing strong positions astride the road and railway to Rangoon. That these would be resolutely defended was to be expected, for, if they were lost, the Japanese could not hope to keep 14th Army from moving into southern Burma before the monsoon made movement by tanks and wheeled vehicles almost impossible, except on all-weather roads, and closed most of the airfields. As the comparative cool of early March gave way to the fierce humid pre-monsoon heat of April, an even greater sense of urgency and enthusiasm than before gripped the whole of 14th Army, for from its commander downwards everyone sensed that victory lay close ahead and that Rangoon could be reached in the comparatively short time that remained before the elements were added to their enemies.

---

[1] Although *53rd Division* had been ordered to withdraw from the Taungtha area on the 19th March, it had been unable to comply as it was unable to break contact. It did not in fact withdraw till the 28th.

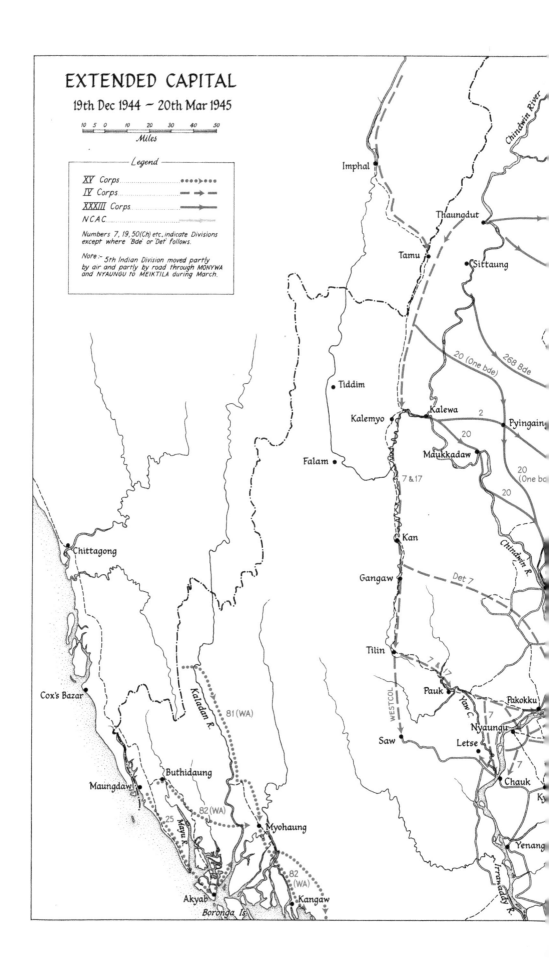

EXTENDED CAPITAL
19th Dec 1944 ~ 20th Mar 1945

10 5 0   10   20   30   40   50
Miles

─ Legend ─

XV Corps..................●●●●►●●●
IV Corps.....................▬ ▬►▬ ▬
XXXIII Corps................────►
N.C.A.C.

*Numbers 7, 19, 50(Ch) etc., indicate Divisions
except where 'Bde' or 'Det' follows.*

*Note :- 5th Indian Division moved partly
by air and partly by road through MONYWA
and NYAUNGU to MEIKTILA during March.*

Chindwin River

Imphal

Thaungdut

Tamu

Sittaung

20 (One bde)

268 Bde

Tiddim

Kalewa

2

Pyingain

Kalemyo

20

Falam

Maukkadaw

20
(One bde)

7 & 17

20

Chindwin R.

Kan

Chittagong

Gangaw

Det 7

Tilin

7 & 17

WESTCOL

Pauk

Pakokku

Cox's Bazar

Yaw C.

7

Nyaungu

Saw

Letse

Kaladan R.

81 (WA)

Chauk

Buthidaung

Maungdaw

82 (WA)

7

25

Mayu R.

Myohaung

Yenang

82
(WA)

Akyab

Kangaw

Boronga Is.

Irrawaddy R.

Myitkyina

Mogaung

Tengchung

Chindwin River

19

Banmauk

Indaw

50 (Ch)

36

Katha

Shwegu

Bhamo

Wanting

30 & 38 (Ch)

19

Pinlebu

Namhkam

50 (Ch)
& MARS

Kawlin

Irrawaddy River

36

MARS

Namhpakka

58 Bde

19

Shweli R.

50 (Ch)

Hsenwi

36

Myitson

Nammeik C.

Pyingaing

Twinnge

Mongmit

Namtu

30 & 38 (Ch)

2

Male

Lashio

20
(One bde)

Yeu

Thabeikkyin

Mogok

36

50 (Ch)

Hsipaw

38 (Ch)

Shwebo

Kyaukmyaung

Kyaukme

50 (Ch)

Budalin

20

Nyaungwun

Mu R.

2

Madaya

hindwin R.

20

19

19

Monywa

Myinmu

Maymyo

Allagappa

Sagaing

MANDALAY

Ngazun

2

Myitnge R.

Myotha

Kyaukse

20

akokku

Myingyan

7

Taungtha

Pyinbin

17

Wundwin

Loilem

7

hauk

Meiktila

Thazi

Taunggyi

Kyaukpadaung

Pyawbwe

Yenangyaung

DKP

CHAPTER XXVII

THE END OF N.C.A.C.

(March 1945)

See Maps 3 and 13 and Sketch 21

A FURTHER step towards settling the vexed question of the return of the American Chinese formations in N.C.A.C. to the China Theatre was taken in the middle of March. On the assumption that 14th Army would win the battle for Mandalay, the American Chiefs of Staff had by that time come to the conclusion that the removal of these forces would not jeopardize the conduct of further operations in Burma, and on the 16th March they sent the British Chiefs of Staff the draft of a telegram which they proposed to send to Sultan and Wedemeyer. In it they said that, although the overall responsibility for the security of Burma and the Burma Road lay with S.E.A.C., the provision of forces for the local security of that part of the road which lay in Burma was the function of the American and Chinese forces in N.C.A.C.[1] The employment of the American and Chinese forces under S.E.A.C.'s operational control should not be restricted geographically, provided that their employment did not prevent the fulfilment of their primary object of rendering support to the China Theatre and that they would be available for transfer when required by that theatre. They therefore proposed to direct Sultan to send Mars Force to China and to move the remaining Chinese divisions from N.C.A.C. at Wedemeyer's request on or after certain scheduled dates, viz., one division on the 1st June, one on the 15th June and one on the 1st July.[2] The transport aircraft to move and support these units were to be provided from those available to the China Theatre, N.C.A.C. and Air Transport Command. They did not contemplate that any of these three divisions or any transport aircraft already committed to the support of 14th Army operations would be withdrawn until after the capture of Rangoon, or until the 1st June, whichever date was earlier. The directive was subject to the condition that the forces remaining under N.C.A.C. would be sufficient to enable Sultan to provide for the local security of the Burma Road.

The Chiefs of Staff sent Mountbatten a copy of this draft telegram

---

[1] See Map 13 in end pocket.
[2] It will be noted that these dates were one month later than those proposed originally by Wedemeyer. See page 280.

and on the 17th March told him that, unless they heard to the contrary that day, they proposed to agree to the withdrawal of Mars Force from the 1st April, provided that the transport aircraft to move it were not found at the expense of the operations of the remainder of the N.C.A.C. forces or 14th Army. Since Mountbatten had overruled Leese's objection to the removal of 475th Regiment of Mars Force,[1] he felt he must consult him regarding the removal of the whole force, and instructed him to send his views direct to London. Next day Leese cabled that the removal of Mars Force would adversely affect 14th Army's battle, but on the 19th, after a conference at Headquarters 14th Army with Slim, Sultan and Stratemeyer, he changed his mind and told the Chiefs of Staff that, since all the N.C.A.C. forces were earmarked to go eventually to China, it was evident that he could not count on them to undertake further offensive operations. In these circumstances, and in order to relieve the administrative burden, he felt that the sooner they were moved to China the better: Mars Force at once, closely followed by one, or preferably two, Chinese divisions.[2] Leese stipulated, however, that the aircraft required for the move must not come from those allotted to S.E.A.C., since the removal of any of them would so prejudice his operations as to make their outcome extremely doubtful. He considered that the only contribution that N.C.A.C. could now make towards the outcome of the battle being waged by 14th Army was to direct 36th Division to Kyaukme and maintain it there, and he had directed Sultan accordingly. This move had as its object the release of 19th Division from Mandalay to take part in the battle raging around Meiktila, since without that division he felt there would not be enough troops to defeat the Japanese now reinforced by forces drawn into the 14th Army battle from the N.C.A.C. front.[3] The command of 36th Division would pass from N.C.A.C. to 14th Army on its arrival at Kyaukme, and the transport aircraft supplying the division would be transferred from 10th U.S.A.A.F. to the C.C.T.F. so that it could be maintained until the 1st May.

Mountbatten told the Chiefs of Staff that, while he agreed with Leese's views, he felt that he must reserve the right to retain one Chinese division to guard the Burma Road should this prove to be necessary. He again said that he could not spare aircraft to undertake the move, and explained that the agreement to release the N.C.A.C. forces so early had been made possible only by the complete change in the operational situation in the last few days; it was now essential

---

[1] See page 281.

[2] See Map 3, facing page 55. Mountbatten had told Leese that, in view of the tremendous importance to China of having Mars Force, he was to issue the necessary instructions for the move to begin on the 1st April unless, in his discussion with Sultan, he came definitely to the conclusion that such a move would have a really crucial effect on the battle.

[3] See Chapter XXV.

to give all available support to 14th Army in its battle and thereafter on its progress towards Rangoon. He pointed out that the text
of the draft American telegram implied that, although Wedemeyer
could not ask for the use of transport aircraft engaged in supplying
14th Army, he had the right to ask for those supporting N.C.A.C. In
his opinion all transport aircraft being used to maintain the fighting
formations in Burma had to be regarded as a single force, and he thus
reserved the right to switch any part of it from N.C.A.C. or XV
Corps to 14th Army or vice versa. He had in fact already had seriously to restrict XV Corps' operations by switching all the transport
aircraft supplying it to increasing the air supply to 14th Army;
despite this, and the fact that all transport aircraft were operating
above the recently increased sustained rates,[1] air supply to 14th Army
was falling short of requirements by some 130 tons a day, and there
was also a shortfall of 150 tons a day on the I.W.T. service from
Kalewa down the Chindwin.

On the 20th March the Chiefs of Staff agreed to the immediate
withdrawal of Mars Force, provided that the aircraft to move it were
found without jeopardizing the progress of N.C.A.C. and 14th Army
operations. The American Chiefs of Staff thereupon told Sultan of
the British agreement and proviso, and instructed him to move the
force in aircraft from either N.C.A.C., Air Transport Command, or
the China Theatre. They merely told the British Chiefs of Staff that,
in their opinion, there was no question of the provision of transport
aircraft to move the force prejudicing the progress of 14th Army or
N.C.A.C., adding that should any problem arise on this score it could
be discussed by the Combined Chiefs.

On the 21st Mountbatten informed Sultan that he was not to use
aircraft allotted to N.C.A.C. for the move of Mars Force, pending an
inquiry that he himself would hold at Monywa next day, at which
Park, Leese, Sultan, Stratemeyer and Slim would be present. Then
he would, if necessary, refer the matter back to the Chiefs of Staff in
accordance with the policy agreed at Argonaut. The conference was
duly held, and on the 27th March Mountbatten told the Chiefs of
Staff that the outcome of the major battle in the Mandalay–Meiktila–
Myingyan area would determine the tempo of the rest of the campaign. The strength of the opposition being met was greater than had
been expected, for the Japanese had withdrawn troops from the
Northern front and to some extent from Arakan. The Generalissimo
had instructed the Chinese troops still under N.C.A.C. not to advance
beyond the Lashio–Hsipaw area, and thus they could not be directed
to pursue the Japanese towards Loilem as planned. He had,

[1] See page 203. At this time the transport aircraft maintaining N.C.A.C., working well
above sustained rates, could deliver only 520 tons a day as against a requirement of 740
tons.

however, reached an agreement with Chiang Kai-shek under which Chinese troops would move south-west to Kyaukme to make contact with 36th Division, which had been directed there, and N.C.A.C. would undertake the protection of the Burma Road until Chinese divisions were sent from the China Theatre for the purpose.

The 14th Army was now operating 500 miles from its railhead at Dimapur and, despite the greatest possible development of the road and river lines of communication,[1] forward troops had to be maintained mainly by air supply which was delivering some 2,000 tons daily to the forward areas. The transport aircraft allotted to the Central front could not meet 14th Army's requirements in full, and thus, unless he could deploy all those available to S.E.A.C., he would be forced to withdraw up to two divisions at the end of the current battle. To provide for the increased strength of 14th Army necessitated by the transfer of Japanese forces from the Northern front, and to cover the deficit which would increase as the army moved further south, he would have to switch transport aircraft from N.C.A.C. to the Central front. This, he said, stressed 'the necessity to treat the campaign in Burma as a whole and the need to regard transport aircraft as interchangeable between different sectors of the front, as the progress of the campaign demands'. He could not increase the scale of the air effort, for all transport aircraft were already working some two-thirds above the sustained rates and, even if he were to switch all the aircraft from the Northern front, there would still be far fewer than were really needed. Forward stockpiling for the monsoon was therefore not being undertaken, civil supplies in the forward areas were tending to run out and commanders were being forced to adjust their plans to suit available air supply. Nevertheless, he was still confident that Rangoon could be occupied before the 1st June provided no transport aircraft were removed from his command. It would not, however, be possible to release transport aircraft for some two months after the port of Rangoon had become available and then only progressively as the tonnage it could handle increased. 'May I,' the telegram ended, 'have your firm and early assurance that all transport aircraft will be retained in support of my operations? We can then get on with the job to the best of our ability and with all possible speed.'

The Chiefs of Staff, who had not been sent a copy of the orders issued by the Americans to Sultan on the 20th March,[2] were astonished to hear that Sultan had been authorized to use aircraft from N.C.A.C. (10th U.S.A.A.F.) to move formations to China. They immediately requested the American Chiefs of Staff, in the light of assurances that they had already given, to provide the

---

[1] See Sketch 21, facing page 522.
[2] A copy reached them on the 28th.

assurance for which Mountbatten was now asking. So serious a view was taken in London of the situation that, on the 30th March, the Prime Minister asked Field-Marshal Sir Henry Maitland Wilson to convey his personal views orally and unofficially to General Marshall.[1] The Prime Minister pointed out that at Octagon he had expressed his dislike of undertaking a large-scale campaign in the jungles of Burma but, as the Americans had attached the greatest importance to it as a means of opening the Burma Road, he had agreed. Despite the fact that Mountbatten had not received the forces he wanted from Europe, the campaign had been conducted with the utmost vigour, the Burma Road had been opened,[2] and Mandalay captured.[3] The battle now being fought at the end of a very difficult line of communication was important not only for Burma but for the general wearing down of the Japanese military and air power. Once Rangoon had been occupied, powerful forces would be set free for further operations in combination with the general American offensive. He reminded Marshall that he had agreed to the retention in Italy of the three British/Indian divisions which Mountbatten had wanted for 'Dracula', and that this had made it possible for five British and Canadian divisions to be withdrawn from Italy to increase the strength of General D. Eisenhower's forces for the Second Front campaign. 'I feel therefore entitled,' Mr. Churchill continued, 'to appeal to General Marshall's sense of what is fair and right between us, in which I have the highest confidence, that he will do all in his power to let Mountbatten have the comparatively small additional support which his air force now requires to enable the decisive battle raging in Burma to be won.'[4]

Marshall replied on the 3rd April that it was the agreed American policy that the momentum of Mountbatten's offensive should continue, and that it was not intended to move American aircraft from Burma before the fall of Rangoon or the 1st June (the date given by Mountbatten for its capture). Mountbatten would be left with all he needed to secure Rangoon in the dry season, but it was necessary to reserve the right to transfer aircraft to China if, after all, the city were not occupied by the 1st June. Mountbatten had recently said that it might be necessary to retain all his transport aircraft for two months after the port of Rangoon was available; the reasons for this were not yet known and he was not therefore ready to agree to any extension beyond the limiting dates he had set.

Thus, after a long and exhausting wrangle, Mountbatten finally obtained the assurance that he could use all American resources then

[1] Wilson had succeeded Field-Marshal Sir John Dill as the Head of the Joint Staff Mission in Washington.
[2] See Chapter XVII.
[3] See Chapter XXV.
[4] Churchill, Volume VI (Cassell, 1954), pages 534–5.

at his disposal until at least the 1st June. It was not, however, until
the 3rd May (the day that Rangoon was reoccupied) that Wedemeyer
was told that the American and Chinese forces were to be moved from
N.C.A.C. to the China Theatre without the use of transport aircraft
from S.E.A.C. until the 1st June.

The advance on the Northern front had continued slowly against decreasing opposition, since headquarters and the bulk of *33rd Army* had
been drawn into the battle for Meiktila,[1] and the understrength but
still efficient *56th Division* was withdrawing to the south of the Burma
Road. Having established an airstrip at Mongmit, 36th Division
began its advance on Mogok on the 14th March.[2] The next day the
Japanese rearguard made its last stand in precipitous country and
inflicted casualties on 26th Brigade's advanced guard. A way round
the enemy position was found, and the Japanese withdrew. Mogok
was occupied on the 19th, Monglong on the 22nd, and on the 24th the
division set out for its final objective on the Burma Road, Kyaukme.
The same day Festing received a warning order that his division was
to be transferred to 14th Army and moved to the Mandalay area
as soon as he had made contact with 50th Chinese Division on his
left at Kyaukme. The advanced guard of 26th Brigade occupied
Namsaw on the 29th March and, pushing out patrols to the east,
contacted 1st Chinese Regiment at Kyaukme. Any hopes there may
have been of saving the viaduct over the Gokteik Gorge from destruction was dispelled when a report was received from the Kachin Levies
that it had been blown up on the 17th March. The division had now
completed its allotted task. On the 30th Festing was ordered to move
to the Mandalay area where he was to come under 14th Army's
command. The move began next day when an advanced party of
72nd Brigade was flown there, to be followed by the rest of the brigade
by road on the 2nd April.

Further to the east, 50th Chinese Division, moving south from
Namtu in a dilatory manner, entered Hsipaw on the 16th March. On
the 24th it made contact with 38th Chinese Division, which had
moved slowly down the Burma Road from Lashio, some seven miles
from Hsipaw, and on the 30th with 36th British Division.[3] The Burma
Road from Mandalay to the Chinese border, which had been in
Japanese hands since April 1942, was once again under Allied control.

---

[1] See pages 296 and 298.
[2] See Map 3, facing page 55.
[3] These moves by the Chinese took place as a result of Mountbatten's agreement with
the Generalissimo (see page 318).

CHAPTER XXVIII

PLANNING FOR THE CAPTURE
OF RANGOON
(March–April 1945)

See Maps 3, 7, 10, 11 and 13 and Sketches 20 and 21

IN commenting on Slim's planning directive of the 7th February,[1] A.L.F.S.E.A. gave him details on the 25th of the maintenance capacity likely to be available to 14th Army from March to May, and followed this up two days later with an operation instruction co-ordinating the efforts of 14th Army, N.C.A.C. and XV Corps for the capture of Rangoon.[2] It was evident that the plan envisaged in the directive of the 7th February would have to be modified for administrative reasons. Slim had anticipated this possibility and on the 5th March said he was preparing a fresh plan based on the maintenance capacity now at his disposal.

The first step was to prepare a new administrative appreciation covering the maintenance of 14th Army and 221 Group R.A.F. up to and including the capture of Rangoon and the opening of the port, to determine the size of the army and air force which could be maintained in the field and the scope of the operations within the limitations imposed by the available air and I.W.T. lift. It was based upon the assumptions that all airheads would be restricted to a 250-mile radius from air bases, delivery forward of airheads being by road, rail or I.W.T.; that the advanced base at Myingyan would be in operation by the 1st April; and that, to supplement air supply from the Akyab air base, which could deliver economically only as far south as Toungoo, a line of communication forward of Myingyan would have to be established by road to maintain forces operating down the Mandalay–Rangoon axis.[3] Maintenance had also to be arranged for the forces mopping up the Meiktila–Mandalay area, and those advancing down the Irrawaddy valley.

As regards air supply, Slim proposed to allot the whole of the

---

[1] See page 242–43.
[2] See page 249.
[3] See Sketch 20, facing page 412. It was assumed that the Akyab air base would begin operating on the 20th March and would be able to deliver 365 tons a day by the 1st April and 400 tons by the 1st May. In fact deliveries from Akyab during April were 365 tons a day (see Appendix 22).

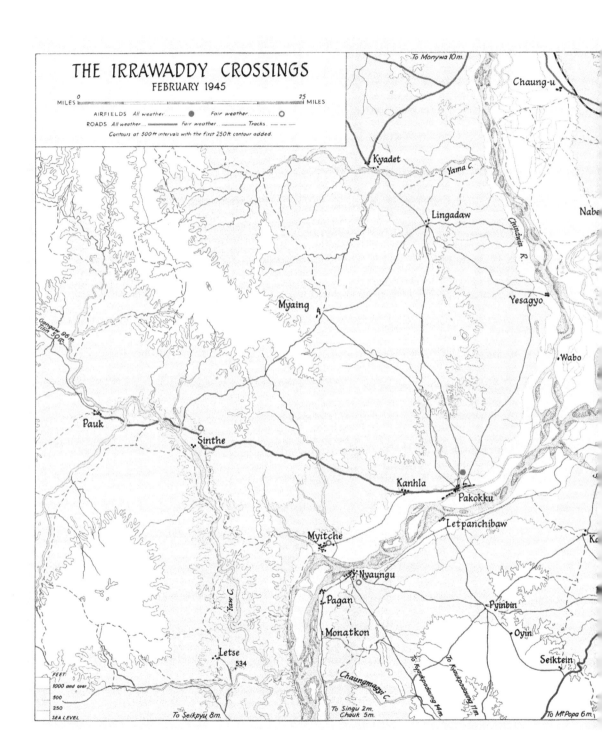

THE IRRAWADDY CROSSINGS
FEBRUARY 1945

AIRFIELDS *All weather* ●   *Fair weather* ○
ROADS *All weather* ━━━   *Fair weather* ━━━   *Tracks* ━ ━ ━
Contours at 500ft intervals with the first 250ft contour added.

To Monywa 10 m.

Chaung-u

Kyadet

Yama C.

Lingadaw

Nabe

Chindwin R.

Yesagyo

Myaing

Wabo

Gangaw 96 m.
Tilin 50 m.

Pauk

Sinthe

Kanhla

Pakokku

Letpanchibaw

Myitche

Ka

Yaw C.

Nyaungu

Pagan

Pyinbin

Monatkon

Oyin

Letse
534

Seiktein

FEET
1000 and over
500
250
SEA LEVEL

To Seikpyu 8 m.

Chaungmagyi C.

To Singu 2 m.
Chauk 5 m.

To Kyaukpadaung 14 m.
To Kyaukpadaung 11 m.

To Mt Popa 6 m.

Map 9

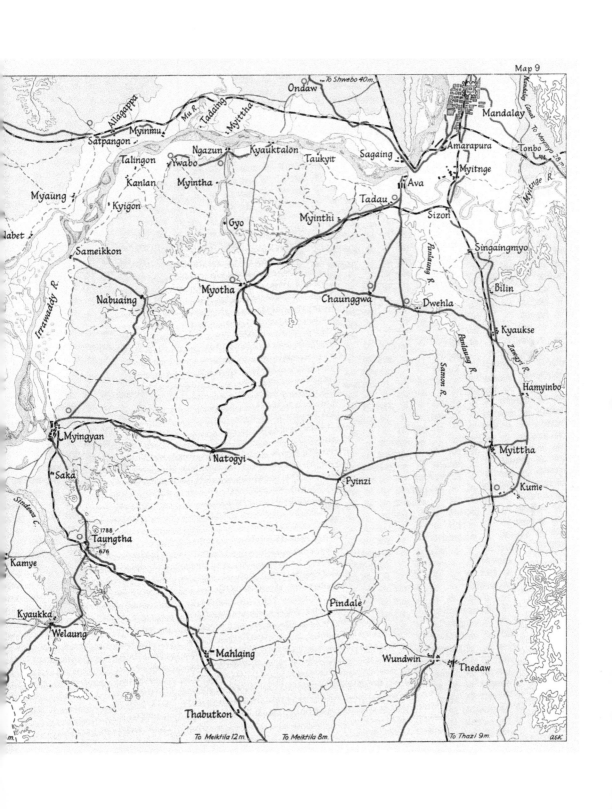

To Shwebo 40m.

Ondaw

Mandalay

Allagappa

Mu R.

Tadaing

Myittha

Mandalay Canal

To Maymyo 28 m.

Satpangon

Myinmu

Amarapura

Tonbo

Talingon

Ywabo

Ngazun

Kyauktalon

Taukyit

Sagaing

Myitnge

Kanlan

Myintha

Ava

Myitnge R.

Myaung

Kyigon

Tadau

Sizon

labet

Gyo

Myinthi

Singaingmyo

Sameikkon

Panlaung R.

Bilin

Irrawaddy R.

Nabuaing

Myotha

Chaunggwa

Dwehla

Kyaukse

Panlaung R.

Zawgyi R.

Samon R.

Hamyinbo

Myingyan

Natogyi

Myittha

Saka

Pyinzi

Kume

Sindewa C.

1788

Taungtha

676

Kamye

Pindale

Kyaukka

Welaung

Mahlaing

Wundwin

Thedaw

Thabutkon

To Meiktila 12m.

To Meiktila 8m.

To Thazi 9m.

a.s.k.

output from the Akyab air base to the force moving on the Mandalay–Rangoon road to the limit of its economic radius, any shortfall being made up from the Chittagong air base to Myingyan and thence by road. Maintenance for the force involved in the mopping-up operation would be from Imphal and Chittagong to airheads not beyond Myingyan, Myotha and Mandalay and thence by road. Maintenance for the Irrawaddy force would be from the Chittagong air base to airheads not beyond Magwe, and thence by road or I.W.T. to the destination. In addition to the existing airheads astride the Irrawaddy, north and west of Mandalay and at Meiktila, airheads capable of operating in all weathers would have to be established at Myingyan, Magwe and Toungoo.

To supplement the airlift and relieve the road lift, the greatest use would have to be made of the I.W.T. fleet built at Kalewa for service down the Chindwin and Irrawaddy Rivers. The service already operating from Kalewa to Alon would therefore have to be extended to Myingyan. Additional I.W.T. craft (mainly consisting of country boats and salvaged vessels), with a bulk lift of 500 tons a day and a lift of 370 tons for distribution in smaller craft, would have to be made available for the forces operating down the Irrawaddy axis. In the absence of any guarantee that Rangoon could be occupied before the monsoon, Slim decided that the fifteen days' Central Burma Stockpile would have to be established as far forward as Myingyan by the 15th May.[1] This involved a lift of 34,000 tons between the 1st March and the 15th May.

Calculations based on these assumptions showed that the combined air and I.W.T. lift would be insufficient for 14th Army's full requirements. To meet part of this shortfall, the L. of C. Transport Column, which was then operating from Dimapur to Kalewa, would have to extend its activities as far forward as the Sagaing area until the 1st April, despite the fact that any increase in its turnround would not be economic. After that date as much transport as possible would have to be released for use in the forward area. Since the army was advancing into an area where there was a railway system, every effort would have to be made to rehabilitate some of its lines to help in maintaining the army's advance. A careful balance would, however, have to be struck between the tonnage lost to the army by the lift required to bring forward locomotives, stores and railway units and the date by which a rail lift forward of Myingyan could support the maintenance of the army. It was considered that the only line which could be put into operation in time would be the one from Myingyan to Thazi, though repairs to sections of the Mandalay–Thazi line might produce a useful dividend in salvaged locomotives and trucks.

---

[1] See pages 248–49.

The assumption was made (based on possibilities discussed with A.L.F.S.E.A.) that, one month from the date of the occupation of Thazi, 150 tons a day could be delivered there by jeep train.

Since detailed calculations showed that the total possible lift would still not be sufficient to meet all the army's requirements, Slim decided that certain measures, however undesirable, would have to be taken.[1] These were: the fly-out of a division in the second half of April; a reduction in the maintenance tonnage available to the forces operating in the Mandalay–Meiktila area;[2] limitation of the maintenance tonnage allotted to 221 Group R.A.F. and to the army troops; and a reduction in the lift of engineer and transportation stores. Even so, there would almost certainly be an overall deficiency, since operational requirements during the last half of March and in April would make it necessary at times for a proportion of the airlift to be delivered beyond the economic range of 250 miles from air bases. Moreover, other unforeseen factors, such as bad flying weather, enemy action and interruptions or delays on the river and road lines of communication, might also reduce the tonnages delivered. To meet such a shortfall, either the monsoon stockpile would have to be used or the number of troops would have to be further reduced. Since Slim considered that the first would be administratively unsound, the fly-out of additional formations might have to be contemplated.

While this appreciation was being prepared, the operational situation did not develop as had been expected. As a result, some of the assumptions on which it was based no longer existed; Myingyan had not yet been captured and the advanced base could not therefore be functioning by the 1st April, and the road, rail and I.W.T. lines of communication giving access to the forward areas had not been cleared. It was, therefore, almost certain that IV Corps (designated for the advance on Rangoon) would have to begin its southward move before either the Myingyan base or the road communications could be established, and that mopping-up operations behind it would have to continue for a considerable period. Thus, when Slim sent the appreciation to A.L.F.S.E.A. on the 16th March, he said that, although the general policy set out in it still obtained, it was evident that supplies for IV Corps would have to be delivered direct to airheads established along the line of advance and at Rangoon, and that the rest of the army would have to bear the resulting overall loss in the airlift. To make IV Corps' advance possible, it was probable that another division as well as two brigades would have to be flown out by the middle of April. Any unforeseen reduction of the air

---

[1] See Appendix 24.

[2] The reduced tonnage would be 110–120 tons a day and would severely limit the radius of action of such forces.

or I.W.T. lift below the calculated figures would have to be met by a reduction in the Central Burma Stockpile or in the maintenance tonnage allotted to the forces not directly engaged in the main operation for the capture of Rangoon.

On the 23rd March Slim issued his final operation instruction for the advance on Rangoon.[1] His intention remained as before the destruction of the Japanese forces in central Burma, after which 14th Army was to capture Rangoon as soon as possible and at all costs before the onset of the monsoon. Yenangyaung, the airfields at Magwe and then Prome were to be seized, and the Myingyan–Mandalay–Maymyo–Meiktila–Chauk area and the road/rail communications from Meiktila to Rangoon secured.[2] The operations were to be carried out in three stages: the completion of the current battle, the regrouping and the southward advance.

In the first stage, IV Corps was to clear the Taungtha area as quickly as possible while containing the enemy astride the Irrawaddy on the general line Seikpyu–Chauk–Kyaukpadaung; it was to capture Pyawbwe by the 1st April, keep the Japanese rail/road communications cut at Thazi and finally concentrate in the Meiktila–Thazi area in readiness to advance on Rangoon. At the same time XXXIII Corps was to secure the Mandalay–Maymyo–Kyaukse area, destroy all Japanese forces as far south as Wundwin and then concentrate 20th Division there preparatory to an advance southwest to the Irrawaddy. It was to move 2nd Division to the Myingyan–Nyaungu area by brigade groups as they completed their tasks, and send first a brigade and eventually the whole of 19th Division to the Meiktila–Thazi area.

In the second and regrouping stage, which was to begin on the 1st April, 7th Division with its attached units was to pass from IV to XXXIII Corps, and 19th Division and 8th K.G.V's O. Light Cavalry were to come under direct command of 14th Army. The 7th Cavalry, less one squadron, and 18th (S.P.) Field Regiment were to pass from XXXIII to IV Corps as soon as possible. This regrouping, it should be noted, entailed practically no movement as most of the major formations concerned passed to their new commands *in situ*.[3] In the third stage, IV Corps was to take Rangoon by a direct thrust down the road/rail axis. To secure the corps' rear and left flank, 19th Division and 8th Cavalry under command of 14th Army would take over the Mandalay–Thazi area from XXXIII Corps and, as IV Corps' advance proceeded, secure the road and railway from Meiktila to Toungoo. The XXXIII Corps was to advance on Ran-

---

[1] See pages 297–98. This instruction was an amended version of the previous instruction issued on the 18th March.

[2] See Map 3, facing page 55, and Map 13 in end pocket.

[3] For details of the grouping see Appendix 21. It will be noted that the formations comprising IV Corps were fully mechanized and capable of undertaking a very rapid advance.

goon astride the Irrawaddy, capturing Seikpyu, Chauk, Yenang-yaung, Magwe and Prome on the way.

Owing to administrative limitations, those formations and units not needed in the third stage were to be withdrawn. Since their maintenance requirements were higher than those of Indian divisions, and the shortage of British manpower in S.E.A.C. largely as a result of repatriation under the 'Python' scheme prevented their being maintained at full fighting strength,[1] 2nd and 36th Divisions were selected to be flown out to India, the former between the 10th and 20th April and the latter under arrangements to be made later. All their transport was to be left behind. The 268th Brigade and some other units were also chosen to fly out, but the orders were cancelled almost at once.

The general maintenance policy was that supplies would be delivered into the army area from base airfields in India and Arakan and by I.W.T. from Kalewa, forward distribution from airheads and river ports being made by road and river. As much air supply as possible was to be made available to IV Corps which was, if necessary, to have priority; that this would entail delivery beyond economic range would have to be accepted. All other F.M.A.s had to be within economic range under all circumstances. It was intended to develop an army maintenance area at Myingyan, served by I.W.T. from Kalewa and by air. F.M.A.s were to be established by IV Corps at Meiktila, Pyinmana (Lewe), Toungoo and Nyaunglebin and by XXXIII Corps at Myitche, Yenangyaung and Magwe.[2] As the advance progressed, rear F.M.A.s would be taken over either by 14th Army or by 505 District when established.[3] To reduce the strain on air supply, an I.W.T. detachment was to work with XXXIII Corps on the Irrawaddy.[4] The provision of reinforcements and replacement of armour and transport would be restricted; units and formations were therefore to be brought up to strength in men and vehicles before the advance began, and replacements would be sent forward if and when possible.

The main medical centre was to be at Meiktila, with subsidiaries at Magwe and Toungoo. Evacuation from forward areas to casualty clearing stations was to be by light aircraft or ambulance, and from there transport aircraft and river craft would be used, supplemented if necessary by ambulance columns. Main Headquarters 14th Army/221 Group was to move to Meiktila as soon as possible and later to Toungoo and Rangoon. Army signals were to re-establish the civil telegraph system first between Meiktila, Toungoo and Rangoon, then

---

[1] See page 27.
[2] See Appendix 23 and Sketch 21, facing page 522.
[3] See page 204.
[4] This was an *ad hoc* detachment consisting of DUKWs, some power craft, Bailey rafting, barges and country boats. It was added to as and when craft became available.

between Myingyan and Meiktila and lastly between Mandalay and Meiktila.

An administrative instruction issued on the 28th March reiterated that the general policy would be to conserve airlift by using road transport from centralized corps F.M.A.s to the fullest possible extent, and that Myingyan would probably not be opened as the army maintenance area before the 15th April. It forecast that between the 1st April and the 31st May the airlift available to IV Corps would be 460 tons a day up to the 7th April and thereafter 470 tons, and to XXXIII Corps 550 tons a day up to the 7th April, falling thereafter by stages to 410 tons by the 23rd April; of these totals, 500 tons a day could be dropped, of which 250 would be allotted to Headquarters IV Corps, 150 to Headquarters XXXIII Corps and 100 kept in reserve. Nevertheless, every effort was to be made to keep the dropping of supplies to a minimum. The IV Corps was to operate the Meiktila airhead till relieved by 14th Army, and hand over the Myitche airhead to XXXIII Corps which was to transfer to it as much of the stock as possible from Ondaw, which could then be closed. The 36th Division was to take over the Mandalay North airhead and operate it until it was flown back to India.[1] The engineers were to concentrate on the speedy construction of the Myingyan base, the building and maintenance of roads, airfields and ferries, the production of timber and the building of boats and rafts. The I.W.T. service was to develop and rehabilitate the waterways on the Chindwin and Irrawaddy with a target capacity of 700 tons a day from Kalewa to Myingyan, and organize an I.W.T. flotilla to accompany XXXIII Corps' advance down the Irrawaddy. Railway development was to be confined to the provision of sidings at the Myingyan base, the repair of the railway from Myingyan through Meiktila to Thazi and thence southwards, and the repair of the Myingyan–Mandalay and the Mandalay–Thazi lines which might be necessary for the salvage and recovery of rolling stock and equipment. An army road transport column was to be formed with G.P.T. companies supplied by A.L.F.S.E.A. to undertake road deliveries forward of Myingyan.[2]

Meanwhile Leese had, on the 27th March, ordered 505 District (Major-General A. J. H. Snelling), which had been formed on the 9th, to be established with headquarters at Shwebo.[3] Snelling was to assume command of 551 L. of C. Sub-Area (Kalewa), 253 L. of C.

---

[1] When 36th Division was transferred from N.C.A.C. to 14th Army at the end of March, one combat cargo squadron (twenty-five aircraft) of 10th U.S.A.A.F. moved from Moran in Assam to Tulihal on the Imphal plain and continued to maintain the division until it was flown out of Burma.

[2] These would consist initially of four companies, rising to six by the 15th April, nine by the 1st May and twelve by the 15th May.

[3] See Map 3, facing page 55.

Sub-Area (Shwebo) and 552 L. of C. Sub-Area (Alon) from dates to be agreed with 14th Army, and any new sub-areas formed by 14th Army should an adjustment of its rear boundary make this necessary.[1] The boundary between 14th Army and 505 District was initially to be from Mount Victoria (six miles west of Kanpetlet) by way of Saw to the Irrawaddy opposite Chauk, thence along the river to Mandalay and the Burma Road to Kyaukme.

Leese had meanwhile discussed both current and future operations with Slim, Christison, Sultan and Stratemeyer at 14th Army Headquarters on the 19th March. Slim outlined his plans for the advance on Rangoon and pointed out that, since IV Corps' southward move had been delayed by the Japanese counter-offensive at Meiktila and as plans for maintaining it had been put out of gear by the failure to occupy Myingyan early in March, he might be unable to reach Rangoon overland by the time the monsoon broke. He therefore recommended that, as an insurance, an amphibious attack should be launched on Rangoon before the monsoon, i.e. early in May.

Leese met Mountbatten at the Monywa conference on the 22nd,[2] and told him that the build-up against 14th Army was greater than had been expected and asked him whether it would be feasible to conduct an operation against Rangoon during the latter part of April, for it was probable that at that time a brigade of 26th Division would be available. On his return to Ceylon next day Mountbatten instructed the Joint Planning Staff to examine the possibility of mounting such an operation, bearing in mind the effect of the unfavourable weather conditions which might be met at that time of the year.

On the 23rd March, the day that Slim issued his operation instruction for the advance on Rangoon, Mountbatten received a telegram from the Chiefs of Staff indicating that, in their view, operation 'Roger' (the capture of Phuket Island) should not be launched until it was clear beyond all doubt that the fall of Rangoon was imminent.[3] Leese, who had also received a copy of this telegram, told Mountbatten on the 26th that he agreed with the Chiefs of Staff over 'Roger' and, as he felt anxious that no plans were ready for an amphibious

---

[1] The 14th Army had established 551 Sub-Area on the 30th December 1944 to administer the Kabaw and Myittha valleys, 253 Sub-Area (released to the army by 202 Area on the 15th January 1945) on the 7th March to administer the Shwebo plain, Mandalay and Maymyo, and 552 Sub-Area on the 22nd March to administer the Chindwin River valley from Kalewa inclusive to Myingyan. The 505 District Headquarters opened at Shwebo on the 2nd April and took over 253 and 551 Sub-Areas that day and 552 Sub-Area on the 7th May. It also assumed responsibility for the internal security and protection of vital points in 553 Sub-Area (Myitkyina) on the 2nd April in an agreement between 14th Army and N.C.A.C.

[2] See page 317.

[3] See page 252.

assault on Rangoon to assist 14th Army, he recommended that an immediate study should be carried out with a view to using the 'Roger' force in a modified 'Dracula' operation to seize Rangoon between the 20th April and the 5th May. Mountbatten replied that a study on the lines suggested was already being made and that he was sending his Directors of Plans to Calcutta with all the available information; at the same time he warned Leese that, owing to naval difficulties, the odds against the assault being physically possible were considerable.

The Directors of Plans reported on the 29th March that the initiative for launching a modified 'Dracula' had come from 14th Army and that its tactical possibilities had not so far been studied in any detail by A.L.F.S.E.A., despite Leese's requests of the 22nd and 26th that the operation should be examined at Supreme Headquarters. It appeared that the operation was required as an administrative insurance: there was little doubt that 14th Army could reach Rangoon from the north but, so that it would not be forced to detach large forces to guard its line of communication, which was vulnerable to attack from the east, it was essential that it should be able to rely on there being adequate supplies and reinforcements available on its arrival at Rangoon. Without 'Dracula' there was a risk of a stalemate being reached, with 14th Army over-extended at the gates of the city. The timing of the operation would have to be closely linked with 14th Army's advance but, in view of the approach of the monsoon, D-day would have to be not later than the first week in May, even though that might entail a delay of some weeks before 14th Army and the 'Dracula' forces were able to link up. There were two possibilities: to use 23rd Division and 3 Commando Brigade from the 'Roger' force for the assault, with 81st (W.A.) Division available to follow up, or to form a composite force from the divisions already in Arakan, to be followed up by either 2nd or 36th Division, both of which were to be flown out from central Burma. Either alternative was practicable, but whichever was selected would cause a delay in operation 'Roger' of several weeks, since the necessary beach group would have to be found from 'Roger' force. A firm decision would have to be reached not later than the 2nd April.

On the 30th Leese told Mountbatten that, after full consideration, he recommended that an amphibious operation on Rangoon should be mounted from Arakan with a D-day not later than the 7th May, and earlier if possible. The operation should be carried out by 26th Division under the direction of XV Corps and an additional division (probably the 2nd) would be earmarked as a follow-up.

Mountbatten discussed the operation with his three Commanders-in-Chief at Kandy on the 2nd April. Power pointed out that the weather would be the main enemy, rather than the Japanese, and that

the operation would have to be mounted early in May. Leese stressed
the need for a follow-up division to be ready and made it clear that,
if a decision to launch the operation were taken, Slim, who could
have only three divisions for the final assault from the north, would be
able to accept far greater calculated risks during his advance. Mountbatten pointed out that, if 14th Army required the help of an amphibious operation, Slim would have to capture airfields north of and
within range of Rangoon before D-day, and since D-day could not be
postponed, his advance would have to be speeded up. He finally decided that in the first five days of May an amphibious assault would
be launched for the capture of Rangoon by one division, supported by
armour and one parachute battalion from 44th Indian Airborne
Division, and that preparations would be made to follow up with a
second division, should this prove to be absolutely necessary. With the
exception of the parachute battalion, and the beach group which had
to be found from 'Roger' force, the land and air forces would be
drawn from Arakan. Detailed planning was to be undertaken by the
Joint Force Commanders at Akyab without delay.

Next day Mountbatten told the Chiefs of Staff of his decision to
launch an amphibious operation against Rangoon and that, since he
would have to commit significant elements of 'Roger' force to support
the operation,[1] this would involve a delay of some six to nine weeks
both in operation 'Roger' and in any subsequent operations towards
Malaya and Singapore. Since the only suitable landing beaches were
inside the mouth of the Rangoon River, a small airborne force would
have to assist in the reduction of the defences at Elephant Point.[2]
He could find a parachute battalion from 44th Indian Airborne
Division, but the necessary transport aircraft could be made available
only at the direct expense of the already overstrained airlift to 14th
Army. He therefore asked for the loan of two fully-trained Dakota
transport squadrons, which should be available in the theatre by mid-
April.

The Chiefs of Staff replied on the 7th that, as they fully recognized
the immense importance of capturing Rangoon by the 1st June, they
would do everything possible to help but could not provide trained
transport squadrons by the 15th April. They would nevertheless try
to provide one squadron (which would not be trained for airborne
operations) by mid-May at the latest, and facilities by mid-April for
converting one of the existing heavy bomber squadrons in S.E.A.C.
to Dakotas. It seemed to them, they said, that the crux of the operation lay in its synchronization with the land advance, and they therefore assumed that no final decision would be taken to launch it until

---

[1] These included 41st Indian Beach Group and the necessary number of landing ships
and landing craft.

[2] See Map 11, facing page 414.

the land advance had progressed far enough to make it possible. They also expressed anxiety regarding the naval aspects of the operation, and wished to be assured that full consideration had been given to the difficulties of launching an amphibious operation at that time of the year. To this Mountbatten replied that the synchronization of 'Dracula' with the advance from the north mainly depended on the capture of the Toungoo group of airfields by 14th Army before D-day, which had to be very early in May.

On the 8th Leese told Mountbatten that, in order to ensure the success of 'Dracula', Stratemeyer had told him that two air commando squadrons would have to be withdrawn almost at once for training and rehearsals. Having weighed up the advantages of an airborne operation against the very serious disadvantages of depriving 14th Army of the services of these squadrons, he had reluctantly decided that the airborne operation as planned could not be carried out unless the two trained squadrons asked for arrived in India in adequate time.

On the 9th April, after discussing 'Dracula', and in particular Leese's suggestion of cancelling the airborne operation, with his naval and air Commanders-in-Chief, Mountbatten came to the conclusion that the operation could be carried out successfully only if Elephant Point was seized by an airborne attack before any attempt was made to enter the Rangoon River. He therefore decided to fly next day to see Leese at Calcutta. There on the 10th, during a private discussion with Leese, he insisted on the airborne operation being re-included in the plan for 'Dracula'. Later that day at a conference attended by Leese, the advanced headquarters senior staff officers, Stratemeyer and Coryton, he gave orders that 'Dracula' was to have overriding priority, however serious the effect on the dates of subsequent operations, and that the known weather hazards were to be accepted in order to accelerate the opening of the port of Rangoon. The troop carrier squadrons of both air commandos would be withdrawn from Burma for the airborne assault, and, should an airlift be required to 'leapfrog' troops forward, it would have to be found from transport squadrons then on air supply; the decision whether the loss of supplies thereby entailed should be borne by 14th Army or made up by flying transport aircraft still further above sustained rates would be made at the time. He accepted in principle the draft plan submitted by the Joint Force Commanders under which 26th Division was to be entrusted with the operation and made it clear that, as soon as possible after landing, the division was to assault Rangoon and occupy it before the monsoon broke or the American transport aircraft had to be sent to China. So that close air support could be provided, the completion of a 2,000-yards all-weather runway on Ramree Island for use by 224 Group R.A.F. was to be accelerated, and

14th Army was to make a supreme effort to capture an airfield at Toungoo or Prome for use by 221 Group R.A.F. Mountbatten also directed that 2nd Division should be prepared to follow up 26th Division, saying that his overriding reason was the need to get to Rangoon and have the port open before the monsoon, or, as he put it, Wedemeyer descended upon him, which he regarded as an even greater hazard.[1]

Since the object of the 1945 campaign had been confirmed as the occupation of Rangoon before the monsoon,[2] Mountbatten had, on the 28th February, ordered a plan to be prepared for the rehabilitation and opening up of the port and for the establishment of an advanced base there for the maintenance of 14th Army during the monsoon. The plan (operation 'Stanza') was to cater for the development of the port as soon as possible after its occupation to handle 7,500 tons a day (including 1,500 tons of bulk petrol), for the provision of storage for forty-five days' supplies and petrol for a force of two corps (six and two-thirds divisions) and an R.A.F. group, as well as for civilian requirements, and for the preparation of four all-weather airfields in the Rangoon area within four months of its occupation (to be increased to seven by the end of 1945). An appreciation of the administrative implications on this basis was prepared by A.L.F.S.E.A. and handed on the 11th March to Brigadier L. J. Woodhouse, who had been appointed to command a joint naval, army and air planning staff (later to become Headquarters No. 1 Area at Rangoon), with instructions to produce a first key plan and a first maintenance project by the 1st April with a view to their being put into operation should the Japanese withdraw or 14th Army capture Rangoon by the 1st May.

When it was decided on the 2nd April to carry out 'Dracula', it was evident that it would have to be dovetailed with 'Stanza' and, on the 5th, A.L.F.S.E.A. issued orders for this to be undertaken at once. Kyaukpyu was designated as the concentration area for 26th Division, Chittagong for corps troops and Calcutta for the follow-up (2nd) division. The responsibility for mounting the forces to sail from Kyaukpyu and Chittagong lay with A.L.F.S.E.A. (through L. of C. Command), and from Calcutta with G.H.Q. India. On the 16th April a provisional shipping programme up to D+13 was issued; the assault

---

[1] The 2nd Division, without its equipment and vehicles, was being flown out from Myingyan to Chittagong and was then being moved by rail to a concentration area north of Calcutta. The 6th Brigade was due to reach the area by the 12th April, divisional headquarters and 4th Brigade by the 16th, and 5th Brigade by the 30th. G.H.Q. India was making arrangements completely to re-equip each brigade on arrival at Calcutta so that the division could be ready for operations within a fortnight of the arrival of the last brigade.

[2] See page 247.

convoy was to sail from Kyaukpyu to arrive at the mouth of the Rangoon River on D-day (2nd May), and follow-up convoys were to sail from Calcutta and Kyaukpyu to arrive at the Rangoon River on D+5, D+8, D+11, D+12, D+13, D+17 and D+24. These first eight convoys were to transport 41,961 men, 2,686 vehicles, 19,850 tons of stores and 3,100 tons of P.O.L.

Mountbatten gave his general approval to the plan for 'Dracula' prepared by the Joint Force Commanders and A.L.F.S.E.A. on the 17th April. Four days later Leese issued a further administrative instruction. Since it was not clear whether 14th Army or XV Corps would occupy the city first, or whether the full number of follow-up convoys would be necessary, planning had to take account of a number of alternatives. On the assumption that XV Corps would occupy the city before 14th Army, it was to assume control of Rangoon until 26th Division had linked up with IV Corps; when this occurred, 14th Army would take charge. Since it was desirable that reconnaissance parties for 'Stanza' should enter Rangoon as soon as it was occupied, a small advanced party of Headquarters No. 1 Area was to be flown into Rangoon as soon as practicable; the rest of the area staff required for the initial reconnaissance would, travelling by road, arrive at Monywa by the 1st May and from there be moved forward to Rangoon under orders of 14th Army. The remainder of No. 1 Area staff and troops would be introduced by sea immediately after either 26th Division or, if a follow-up division were used, after the follow-up convoys. A further follow-up convoy was to reach the Rangoon River on D+31, after which 'Stanza' convoys would be scheduled to arrive at weekly intervals but, since it could not be certain that a follow-up division would be needed, arrangements were to be made so that the first 'Stanza' convoy could reach Rangoon on D+17 or D+24 instead of D+38.

While S.E.A.C. and A.L.F.S.E.A. were perfecting plans for the amphibious attack on Rangoon and the development of the port, Slim was taking action to enlarge the scope of the clandestine operations 'Character' and 'Nation' to assist his advance on the city.[1] On the 5th March he held a meeting at Headquarters 14th Army to discuss the employment and control of the Karen Levies which were in the process of being raised by Force 136 for 'Character'. That evening he wrote to Leese saying that, in his opinion, the main value of the Levies would be to prevent the Japanese from moving forces from north and central Burma into southern Burma by the Hopong–Loi-kaw–Bawlake–Toungoo route, a route which they might well try to use once 14th

---

[1] See pages 205–6.

Army had effectively blocked the main road and railway through Thazi,[1] and also to prevent reinforcements coming up from Moulmein into either the Sittang valley or the Rangoon area. He considered that the static Levies should be used to provide intelligence of any movement or activity within their respective areas and, in particular, movement along the Hopong–Toungoo road, the tracks leading into Siam and those from the Salween into the Sittang valley between Moulmein and Papun.[2] The mobile Levies could be used to keep a watch on the Martaban–Mokpalin line of communication, carrying out demolitions and harassing raids along it if ordered to do so, and on the line of the Sittang River between Mokpalin and Toungoo, reporting any movement across or up and down it. In addition, they could harass or impede enemy movements within the Karen Hills on the roads which were being watched by the static Levies and, if possible, report movements and activities along the Toungoo–Pegu–Mokpalin road and railway, if necessary carrying out demolitions and raids along it.

Slim recommended that the Levies should be under his command, since their operations would need to be closely co-ordinated with his own and any information they obtained would have to reach him without delay. He therefore proposed that Force 136 should establish a tactical headquarters not later than the 1st April alongside his own headquarters in direct touch by wireless with the Levies. Since the date on which it was desirable that the Levies should begin to operate would entirely depend on the progress of 14th Army, he felt that he should be the responsible authority for giving them the order to act. He thought it probable that he would have to activate the northern and central groups when his leading troops reached Yamethin, and the southern group when Pyinmana was occupied. These proposals were approved by A.L.F.S.E.A. on the 9th March.

Meanwhile, in the area covered by operation 'Nation', the team dropped by Force 136 near Toungoo had established an intelligence network as far north as Pyinmana.[3] On the 9th March Force 136 reported to Leese that both in Toungoo and Pyinmana local members of the A.F.O. were ready to turn actively against the Japanese, that men of the B.N.A. and *I.N.A.* had already begun to desert and that the A.F.O. had asked for an arms drop in the next ten days. By the middle of the month reports were received that the whole of the B.N.A. would place itself under A.F.O. leadership when the time came for action. At the same time it became known that Aung San had held a public farewell parade of the B.N.A. units in Rangoon before their departure to the front to fight the (unspecified) enemy.

---

[1] See Map 7, facing page 171.
[2] See Map 11, facing page 414.
[3] See page 206.

A Jedburgh team (two officers and a wireless operator) was dropped near Pyu on the 20th March with orders to contact the headquarters of the A.F.O. in the hills nearby.[1] Three days later the team reported that a general uprising of the A.F.O. and B.N.A. (armed with some 4,000 rifles) was inevitable in eight days time, independent, if necessary, of any British action. The report went on to say :

> 'Subsequent recovery of arms and present management of resistance depends on your co-operation. This is to be much more comprehensive than briefing. Failure to agree with proposal will mean loss of face of British and intelligence will suffer severely. Failure to agree within four days will have far-reaching consequences. Conversely, upon your agreement, co-operation will be very strong. Sorry to put it so strongly but that is the position.'

Leese immediately told Force 136 to discuss with 14th Army what assistance could be given to the rising. Slim, who welcomed it and hoped it would be on a maximum scale, recommended that it should be given every assistance. He could, however, offer no direct ground support for some three or four weeks, although he could arrange for airstrikes on suitable targets. He suggested that the rising should aim at the destruction of Japanese signal communications, dumps, military installations and the railways so as to disrupt movement along their lines of communication, but he asked that bridges should be neither attacked nor damaged.

Leese, reporting the position to Mountbatten, pointed out that, although the supply of arms to the A.F.O. as an organization was forbidden, Force 136 had been authorized to issue one hundred firearms for each commissioned officer, and that, if results were to be produced, involvement with the A.F.O. as an organization could not be avoided. He asked for an immediate decision since action could not be delayed. On the 27th Mountbatten agreed that the proposed rising should be given as much support as possible, and authorized Leese to arm guerrillas as was felt necessary. He did not consider, however, that the moment was ripe for action since the advance of 14th Army had been slower than had been hoped, and he suggested therefore that endeavours should be made to control the rising and ensure that it fitted in with 14th Army's advance. He had arranged that all Jedburgh teams sent into Burma should be given the following directive :

> '(a) Leaders of the movement are to be informed that their assistance is appreciated. If they raise the question of their past

---

[1] See Map 7, facing page 171.

offences against H.M. Government, they must be told that these have not been forgotten and that offenders may be required to stand their trials in due course. Any service to the Allied cause, however, will be taken into account.

(b) S.A.C. is seeking from H.M. Government approval for no arrests for political offences committed prior to the reoccupation of Burma to be made until re-establishment of the Civil Government and that such cases shall be tried under the law of Burma as it existed in 1941.

(c) No general amnesty will be given.

(d) The movement will be expected to disarm voluntarily when instructed but opportunities will be afforded for suitable volunteers to be enrolled in the Burma Armed Forces.

(e) Members of the movement will be enabled and expected to take part in the Civil reconstruction of the country.'

The same day Mountbatten told the Chiefs of Staff that a nationalist rising in Burma against the Japanese was imminent and expected before the end of the month: it was spontaneous and not fostered by the British in any way, but he hoped to delay it so that it would fit in more suitably with 14th Army operations. He touched on the political aspects of the rising and Slim's and Leese's views that the highest operation priority should be given to supporting it, and said that action by Force 136 would naturally involve extending a degree of recognition to the rising, which, from the aspect of civil affairs, might give offence to 'the more respectable elements of the population'. Moreover, Aung San, the commander of the B.N.A., was known to be guilty of treason in the past by virtue of his collaboration with the Japanese. The main political argument in favour of helping the rising was that knowledge of it could be kept from the outside world only by a rigorous censorship; if it became known that the British had refused to allow the Burmese to fight the common enemy, it would have repercussions in liberal circles at home and in the U.S.A. which it would be unwise to precipitate at that juncture. He therefore considered it essential to avoid any policy which might lead to his having to suppress the movement by force: this would involve an extra commitment of troops and possibly end in the army being bogged down in Burma; in addition the civil reorganization of the country would be gravely affected.

He had ordered officers from Force 136 to be sent in to south Burma at once and had issued them a directive to which they were to adhere strictly. Unless he received contrary instructions, he proposed to conduct a propaganda campaign stressing, among other things, that military resistance must be carried out only under orders from Allied forces, and that the British Government's aim was to assist

Burma to attain complete self-government within the Empire as soon as circumstances permitted.

On the 30th the Chiefs of Staff replied that the military aspects of the rising were being examined; the political implications had been reviewed as a matter of urgency, and the views of the War Cabinet were that the political consequences of S.E.A.C.'s support of the resistance movement and its leaders might be very far-reaching. Particular importance was attached, therefore, to ensuring that the movement was put into its right perspective in the eyes of the population of Burma as a whole. The section which now contemplated action was led by persons who had previously been actively pro-Japanese, and their action would be by way of retaliation against the Japanese who had let them down and not at all on Britain's behalf. It was important that any support to the leaders who had collaborated with the Japanese should not give the Burmese the impression that these leaders were regarded as in any sense the liberators of their country, or that other sections of the population were being asked to give their allegiance to these leaders. 'It is essential therefore,' they said, 'that we should make it abundantly clear to these leaders that we do not attach any great importance to their contribution and that they should be reminded more clearly than you propose that they have a lot of leeway to make up as ex-collaborators with Japanese, both in our eyes and in the eyes of their co-patriots who have suffered at the hands of the Japanese . . . We must at all costs avoid building up a Burma E.A.M. and E.L.A.S. with the unfortunate consequences that would result.'[1] They agreed that the resistance movement should be exploited by propaganda, but it should be conducted more on the lines that a large part of Burma had already been liberated, and the rest would be liberated very soon, by British and Indian (with American and Chinese) forces who had been helped in their victorious return by the many Burmese who had loyally stood by them in the hour of retreat. It was now the turn for all Burmese to take a hand in the final eviction of the Japanese, and, in accelerating the process, the help of any Burmese would be welcomed, even at that late hour. Such assistance, however, to be effective, must be rendered in conformity with the requirements of the Allied forces and under instructions from them.

As regards the attitude to be taken by officers of Force 136 towards Aung San and other leaders, para. (a) of the directive issued to them was approved, but the War Cabinet felt it might be made plainer to these leaders that they would have to 'work their passage home'. Para.(b) was *not* approved, since sufficient inducement was already afforded by para. (a). Para. (c) was approved; as for paras. (d) and

---

[1] E.A.M., a Communist-dominated resistance movement, was formed in Greece in 1941. E.L.A.S. was its military organization.

(e), it was agreed that the officers should make it plain to members of the resistance movement that they would have to give up their arms, and that they would be treated as any other law-abiding citizens and be expected to co-operate with the civil authorities in the rehabilitation of their country. The officers might add that, possibly as part of that process, room might be found for suitable volunteers among them to be enrolled in the Burmese armed forces—definite undertakings on this should, however, be avoided. If Aung San or any other leaders inquired about British intentions for the future government of Burma, or future policy, Force 136 should take the line that the British were not prepared to discuss political issues with them or any other isolated section of the community.

Next day the Chiefs of Staff told Mountbatten that, since there was a general shortage of transport aircraft, the support given to the rising must not lead to any additional demand for such aircraft. It must be made clear to the leaders of the movement that no additional air support could be given, other than what Mountbatten might decide to provide from his own resources.

The A.F.O. and B.N.A., the latter reported to be some 8,000 strong, began to rise against the Japanese about the 27th March, despite the efforts of Force 136 to delay action until 14th Army declared the time was ripe for it. By the end of the month reports were received that armed B.N.A. detachments were fighting at Pegu and in the Irrawaddy delta. Force 136 immediately flew in the rest of the Jedburgh teams which had been organized for operation 'Nation': two on the 30th March to Toungoo and Pyu respectively, two on the 1st April to the Tharrawaddy area and one on the 10th to the Pyinmana area. An additional team was dropped at Pyabon in the delta on the 3rd April to provide intelligence for operation 'Dracula' and another on the 24th in the same area. These teams set to work to raise and train A.F.O. guerrillas, but obtained little co-operation from the B.N.A. which acted only on orders received from Aung San. A.F.O. guerrillas attacked and cut the railway some twenty miles south of Toungoo and harassed Japanese road movements. The teams were able to pass back information on the location of supply and ammunition dumps, thus enabling useful airstrikes to be carried out, at times in co-operation with attacks by guerrillas.

Slim decided early in April that he ought to meet Aung San, so that the activities of the B.N.A. could be co-ordinated and the maximum value obtained from them.

> 'I had all along believed', he wrote later, 'that they [B.N.A.] could be a nuisance to the enemy but, unless their activities were closely tied in with ours, they promised to be almost as big a nuisance to us. It seemed to me that the only way satisfactorily to control them was to get hold of their Commander-in-Chief, Aung

San, and to make him accept my orders. This, from what I knew of him and the extreme Burmese nationalists, I thought might be difficult, but worth trying.'[1]

Force 136, although prepared to attempt Aung San's 'exfiltration', pointed out that to use and acknowledge him then and possibly try him later would have very serious political repercussions, since the 'exfiltration' would inevitably be regarded by Aung San and the B.N.A. as formal recognition of the British intention to forget the past. The proposal was referred through A.L.F.S.E.A. to Mountbatten who, on the 20th April, agreed to it, but said that the terms of the directive on the line to be taken with B.N.A. leaders must be made clear to Aung San by Slim.

At a meeting between Mountbatten and his Commanders-in-Chief at Calcutta on the 16th April, Sultan presented a detailed programme for the withdrawal of all American and Chinese forces from Burma. It proposed that the dates of the moves of the remaining Chinese divisions from N.C.A.C. should be some fifteen days earlier than those previously laid down by the Combined Chiefs of Staff,[2] that Headquarters 10th U.S.A.A.F. and 3rd and 4th Combat Cargo Groups (200 aircraft) should be moved in June, all the American tactical and strategic air groups during July and August and 1st Combat Cargo Group (seventy-five aircraft) in September 1945. Mountbatten accepted this programme with the proviso that he was not prepared to release any transport aircraft until the port of Rangoon had been opened; once it had been, he was willing to release 3rd and 4th Combat Cargo Groups during June on a phased timetable beginning as soon as supplies began to flow through the port.

Three days later Wedemeyer asked Sultan for the immediate release of a combat cargo squadron to help him to bring to a standstill a Japanese offensive directed towards Chihkiang, where there was one of the few remaining airfields from which aircraft of 14th U.S.A.A.F. could strike effectively against enemy forces in eastern China.[3] Sultan decided that he could make a squadron available from N.C.A.C. by directing 10th U.S.A.A.F. to fly at the maximum possible rates until the 15th May (the date when one squadron would be released from supplying 36th Division), by supplying as many formations as possible by road, by placing all of them on short supply for certain items and by reducing stocks held at airfields. In

[1] *Defeat into Victory*, page 515.
[2] See page 315.
[3] See Map 10, facing page 340. The Japanese launched an offensive north-westwards from the Changsha–Kweilin railway in the middle of April with a strength of about two divisions. The operation failed to achieve its object after being held up in the mountains some seventy-five miles south-east of Chihkiang, and was called off on the 9th May.

this way he considered he could avoid interfering with 14th Army's operations.

Leese felt that in the circumstances he had no option but to agree to Sultan's proposal. Mountbatten, too, agreed to the despatch of the squadron, provided that in return Wedemeyer was prepared to reduce the number of squadrons to be released in June by one and if the reduction in air supply were borne entirely by N.C.A.C. He reminded Sultan that it had already been agreed at the Monywa conference that every effort should be made to increase the air supply to 14th Army by pooling all transport aircraft for its benefit and reducing the use of air supply to both XV Corps and N.C.A.C.[1] Sultan replied that he was prepared to gamble on 10th U.S.A.A.F. maintaining a rate substantially above even the official sustained rate until the 15th May, which would obviate any reduction in the availability of transport aircraft for 14th Army's operations towards Rangoon. The squadron was duly despatched to China before the end of April.

---

[1] See pages 317–18.

Map 10

SHANTUNG

KANSU

Yellow R.
SHANSI
Loyang
Kaifeng
Haichow
Yellow R.
KIANGSU

Sian
HONAN
SHENSI

Nancheng
Laohokow
HUPEH
Hankow
Wuchang
Nanking
Shanghai
ANHWEI

SZECHWAN
Liangshan
Ichang
Enshih
CHEKIANG

Chengtu
Chungking
Wenchow

Yangtze R.
Changsha
Liuyang
KIANGSI

SIKANG
Chihkiang
HUNAN
Hengyang
Suichwan
FUKIEN

KWEICHOW
Leiyang
Lingling

Kweiyang
Pachai
Nanhsiung
Amoy

Tuhshan
Kweilin
Kukong
Pescadores

Kunming
Nantan
Swatow

KWANGSI
Ishan
Liuchow
FORMOSA

YUNNAN
Laipin
Wushuan
Tanchu
Hsi Chiang
Canton

Nanning
KWANGTUNG
Hong Kong

Suilu

CHINA SEA

Haiphong

INDO CHINA

CHINA
1944-45
Miles

HAINAN

0   100   200   300   400
AIRFIELD ⊙   ROADS ———   RAILWAYS ━ ━ ━
Provincial Boundaries ....

Formosa Strait

CHAPTER XXIX

THE ARAKAN FRONT
(February–April 1945)
The Coast and Bay of Bengal Cleared,
'Dracula' Mounted

See Maps 7, 11, 12 and 13 and Sketch 15

THE primary object of the Arakan operations, the provision of air bases to maintain the forces in central and south Burma, had been achieved with the capture of Akyab in January and Ramree in February 1945. It had, however, been decided early in February to continue XV Corps' offensive to prevent the Japanese withdrawing formations from Arakan to reinforce those opposing 14th Army in the Irrawaddy valley.[1] The offensive, which involved a series of amphibious operations on the Arakan coast, was made possible by the fact that control of the Indian Ocean had passed to the Royal Navy. Now consisting of the East Indies Fleet under command of Admiral Power,[2] it continued action from its base in Ceylon to consolidate its position and ensure that no Japanese ship could enter the Bay of Bengal without running the danger of destruction.[3]

Towards the end of February enemy merchant shipping once again made its appearance in the Andaman Sea. Consequently, with Mountbatten's approval, Power carried out a series of anti-shipping sweeps by destroyers in these waters; targets in the Andaman Islands were bombarded on the 24th and 25th February and again on the 3rd and 19th March, while an inshore sweep to the vicinity of Tavoy resulted in the sinking of a number of coastal sailing vessels on the 1st and 2nd March.[4] On the 26th March four destroyers sighted a Japanese convoy consisting of two merchant ships and two escorting submarine chasers in the Andaman Sea. The destroyers attacked and, after an unsatisfactory action during which ten torpedoes missed their target, two Liberators were called upon to sink the enemy. One of the merchant ships was then sunk by bombs, but one of the

---

[1] See Map 7, facing page 171, and page 218.
[2] See page 211.
[3] See Map 12, facing page 436.
[4] In the attack on the 19th March H.M.S. *Rapid* was hit and stopped by shore gun-fire and had to be towed back to Akyab.

Liberators crashed. Eventually the other merchant ship and one of the escorts were sunk by gun-fire and the other escort by a torpedo.[1] A number of destroyer sweeps were carried out in the same area in April, during which several small coasters and sailing craft were sunk, but no larger enemy vessels were seen. On the 11th April, however, Liberators of 222 Group R.A.F. sighted, attacked and sank an enemy merchant ship and its naval escort north-east of the Nicobar Islands, destroyers picking up survivors.

Meanwhile a carrier force, consisting of two escort carriers (*Empress* and *Ameer*), the cruiser *Kenya*, three destroyers and three frigates under command of Vice-Admiral H. T. C. Walker and accompanied by a tanker escorted by a frigate, carried out a number of photographic reconnaissances of the Hastings Harbour and Phuket Island area between the 26th February and the 4th March. On the 8th April Walker again sailed from Ceylon with the battleships *Queen Elizabeth* and *Richelieu*, the cruiser *London* and three destroyers, accompanied by two escort carriers (*Emperor* and *Khedive*), the cruiser *Cumberland* and two destroyers. Sabang and the area around it was bombarded on the 11th, two enemy aircraft being shot down; photographic re-connaissance of the Penang, Port Swettenham and Port Dickson areas was carried out on the 14th and 15th with the loss of one aircraft,[2] one enemy aircraft being shot down; and Padang was bombarded on the 16th and a number of coastal vessels sunk along the south-western coast of Sumatra before the force returned to Trincomalee on the 20th April. By this time the fighting in Arakan had virtually ceased and preparations for launching 'Dracula' were well advanced.

Soon after Christison had been told in the middle of February to con-tinue operations in Arakan, he had been warned by Leese that the need to use all available transport aircraft for the maintenance of 14th Army after it had crossed the Irrawaddy would mean that air supply for his corps would have to be drastically reduced from the end of the month.[3] Christison had just come to the conclusion that the northern group of *54th Division* in the An area was somewhat stronger than he had at first believed,[4] for a battalion of *121st Regiment* had been identi-fied at Ruywa. It therefore seemed possible that the whole regiment was holding the coast from Dalet southwards to exclusive Taungup instead of being, as previously thought, in Taungup. If that were so, then Taungup would probably be the responsibility of *55th Division* and the other two regiments of *54th Division* would be in the Dalet–An

---

[1] During the action the destroyers fired eighteen torpedoes, only one of which hit its target, and 3,160 rounds of 4·7-inch ammunition.
[2] For Port Dickson see Map 13 in end pocket.
[3] See page 224.
[4] See pages 222–23.

area. Unless he could destroy it he might fail to prevent the Japanese reinforcing the Irrawaddy front by way of the An Pass.[1] He therefore decided to concentrate as large a force as possible for the task while he still had air supply, establish sea lines of communication for the forces attacking An and Taungup and, at the same time, reduce the forces in the forward area to a size which could be easily maintained.

The Joint Force Commanders issued the necessary directives on the 18th February. An enveloping attack was to be made on An by 82nd (W.A.) Division (Stockwell) with 22nd (E.A.) Brigade under command. To bring this about, Stockwell, with the two brigades (1st and 4th) he had with him south-east of Kangaw,[2] was to press on by way of Kyweguseik and Dalet to attack An from the north; 2nd (W.A.) Brigade was to be passed through 25th Division's beachhead at Ruywa to attack it from the west; and 22nd (E.A) Brigade was to be passed through a beachhead to be established by 26th Division at Letpan to attack it from the south. In addition, 25th Division was to capture Tamandu and establish a maintenance centre there for the supply of the forces attacking An, clear the road southward to Kywegu and backload 51st Brigade and the commando brigade to Akyab by the 1st March. A very small detachment was to remain at Kangaw to keep the area clear and help 82nd (W.A.) Division, if necessary, to take Kyweguseik. One brigade group of 26th Division was to be used to secure Letpan and, after 22nd (E.A) Brigade had passed through towards An, was to be ready to advance to Taungup if ordered to do so by corps headquarters.

Miyazaki (*54th Division*) had also recast his plan in order to shorten his front. His northern group, consisting of *111th* and *154th Regiments*, was to establish a firm base at Letmauk with an outpost line along the Dalet Chaung, prepare defences covering An itself for possible use, and, in the first instance, keep a mobile reserve to counter-attack any force that succeeded in crossing the Dalet Chaung. His southern group (*121st Regiment*) was, as before, to cover the Taungup–Prome road and hold Taungup as its base. While the northern group was taking up its positions, *28th Army* ordered Miyazaki to send *Headquarters 54th Infantry Group* with *I/* and *II/154th Battalions* (the *Koba Force*) to Minbu in the Irrawaddy valley, the move to begin on the 26th February.[3] To meet the offensive by the four brigades under 82nd (W.A.) Division, Miyazaki's northern group now had only four infantry battalions and a reconnaissance battalion. He disposed the group in three task forces: *Headquarters 154th Regiment* with *II/154th Battalion* and *54th Reconnaissance Regiment* (less two companies) on the

---

[1] See Map 7, facing page 171.
[2] See page 223.
[3] At the conference of the 23rd February at Meiktila, *28th Army* had been ordered to co-operate in a counter-offensive by *15th Army* by attacking northwards about the 10th March astride the Irrawaddy from Chauk with as great strength as possible. See page 272.

Dalet Chaung; *Headquarters 111th Regiment* with *I/111th Battalion, 14th Anti-Tank Battalion* (less two companies) and *54th Artillery Regiment* (less two battalions) at Letmauk; and *II/111th Battalion* in the Tamandu area. He retained *III/111th Battalion* in reserve.

By the 27th February all the moves ordered in the directive of the 18th, except the attack on Letpan, were under way, but slowing down against determined opposition both in the Dalet area and between Ruywa and Tamandu. The 2nd (W.A.) Brigade, advancing east along a jungle track from Ruywa, had been halted at the foot of a precipitous ridge where the track ended abruptly several miles west of Sabagyi.[1] It was then instructed to turn north and make for the road between Letmauk and An. Headquarters 25th Division and 74th Brigade had been landed at Ruywa, which was already protected by 53rd Brigade.

This was the situation when Christison received an operation instruction from A.L.F.S.E.A. requiring him, with the resources at his disposal but without air supply, to contain the maximum enemy strength in Arakan by destroying the Japanese forces in the An area, and by operating towards Prome from a bridgehead established in the Taungup area.[2] So that he might have time to readjust his plans, air supply at the reduced rate of 120 tons a day would be continued up to the 7th March, after which it would stop altogether. Without air supply the wide encirclement necessary to bring about the complete destruction of the Japanese force at An was impossible, and even the possibility of pinning it down and inflicting loss on it would depend on the opening of the maintenance area at Tamandu by the time air supply ceased. On the 1st March, therefore, Christison gave 25th and 82nd Divisions fresh orders. Wood (25th) was to take Tamandu by the 4th March at latest and establish a brigade there to enable an F.M.A. to be opened; Stockwell (82nd), leaving 1st (W.A.) Brigade at Dalet to move on Letmauk from the north, was to take 4th (W.A.) Brigade and his divisional troops down the west bank of the Dalet Chaung to its mouth and thence along the coast road to Tamandu, from where he was to attack Letmauk from the west. Meanwhile 2nd (W.A.) Brigade, already on its way towards Letmauk from the south, was to establish a block on the road between Letmauk and An and patrol towards the latter. The idea of sending 22nd (E.A.) Brigade to Letpan to advance on An from the south was abandoned. When sending Leese the new plan, Christison warned him that until the promised reinforcements to his I.W.T. fleet arrived, of which there was as yet no sign, he would be unable to undertake any operations

---

[1] See Sketch 15, facing page 354.
[2] See page 249.

towards Taungup.[1] He would thus be unable to pin any part of *55th Division* to Arakan.

By the 3rd March 1st (W.A.) Brigade was concentrated at Dalet ready to attack Letmauk from the north. On the 4th, 74th Brigade of 25th Division entered Tamandu after a hard fought action a few miles south of it, during which 6th Oxford and Buckinghamshire Light Infantry, taking advantage of an exceptionally low tide, out-flanked and got behind the Japanese positions.[2] On the 6th, 2nd (W.A.) Brigade cut the Letmauk–An road but was quickly forced back into the Point 1269–Point 1106 area to the west of the road. On the 7th, Headquarters 82nd (W.A.) Division, 4th (W.A.) Brigade and the bulk of the divisional troops arrived at Tamandu from the north. Stockwell now planned to make a frontal attack along the Tamandu–Letmauk–An road as soon as the F.M.A. at Tamandu was function-ing. This took place on the 8th, by which time the Japanese had been cleared from the hills overlooking Tamandu from the east. It was evident, however, by now that the attack on An was going to take time, and the cessation of air supply made it essential that the number of troops in XV Corps forward areas should be reduced.

The deterioration of the tactical situation, which had looked so promising on the 7th March with Letmauk surrounded, was due to two factors: the skill with which Miyazaki had used his reserve to clear 2nd (W.A.) Brigade's block on the Letmauk–An road, and the cessation of air supply which had an immediate effect on the West African troops. They took it to mean that something had gone wrong and their morale suffered in consequence.[3]

On the 9th March, Joint Force Headquarters issued fresh orders to deal with the situation. The role of the corps was modified to that of driving the Japanese northern group east of An and containing it there until the monsoon, establishing a beachhead at Letpan, cutting the Taungup–Tamandu road and exploiting south to the Tanlwe Chaung to prevent, if possible, the withdrawal of troops of *54th* or *55th Division* from Taungup and the coastal area. It will be seen that there was no longer any mention of the destruction of the northern group or of an advance on Prome.

Lomax (26th Division) was to land a brigade group at Letpan before the 14th, establish a base there and then exploit south to the Tanlwe Chaung. His other two brigades were to remain on Ramree Island, ready to be sent back to India from the 20th March, and 22nd (E.A.) Brigade was to move on the 16th to Tamandu (instead of Let-pan as in the original plan) for operations in the An area under 82nd

---

[1] See page 245.

[2] During the fighting in the Tamandu area Rifleman Bhanbhagta Gurung, 2nd (K.E.O.) Gurkha Rifles, won the Victoria Cross.

[3] West African troops had previously shown that any setback quickly affected their morale and fighting value. See Volume III, page 154.

(W.A.) Division. Wood (25th Division) was ordered to withdraw his division from the Tamandu–Ruywa area to Akyab between the 13th and 31st March, handing over the Tamandu area to 82nd (W.A.) Division. Stockwell, having driven the Japanese northern group east of An, was to use 22nd (E.A.) Brigade (Johnstone) to contain it there until the monsoon began, and was to relieve the brigade of 26th Division in the Letpan–Tanlwe Chaung area. His task was then to destroy or contain the Japanese forces at Taungup and along the coast until the 15th May. Eventually 22nd (E.A.) Brigade was to be moved from An to Letpan to remain there during the monsoon, while 82nd (W.A.) Division withdrew to the Chittagong area. The directives to each division gave a forecast of the dates for the departure of units of 25th and 26th Divisions and parts of 82nd (W.A.) Division, and details of the shipping lift available.

The operations against An made little progress during the next week, for Miyazaki, having brought up his reserve battalion, launched a series of counter-attacks and the African troops fought half-heartedly. The 4th (W.A.) Brigade, supported by a troop of 19th Lancers (medium tanks) and 8th Field Regiment, advanced from Tamandu on the 12th March and the next day encountered the Japanese in the hills around Shaukchon. It took until the evening of the 14th to overcome this opposition and till the 17th to occupy Letmauk. Meanwhile 1st (W.A.) Brigade, finding itself unable to reach Letmauk from the north, had abandoned the attempt and had moved south to the Tamandu–Letmauk road; following up 4th (W.A.) Brigade, it reached Letmauk on the 20th. The same day 22nd (E.A.) Brigade disembarked at Tamandu. Stockwell now planned that both West African brigades should advance on An, making contact with 2nd (W.A.) Brigade still in the Point 1269 area west of the Letmauk–An road, where it had been on air supply since the 9th March.[1] Meanwhile 4th Indian Brigade (Forman) of 26th Division had landed at Letpan on the 13th unopposed and, having established its beachhead, began to exploit south and inland.[2] In the fighting that ensued a Japanese force with five light tanks was surrounded; three were destroyed and two and a 75-mm. gun captured, while the accompanying infantry was dispersed with loss. By the 19th March the forward troops were within five miles of the Tanlwe Chaung, where for the first time the Japanese offered determined resistance.

With 82nd (W.A.) Division in possession of Letmauk and closing on An, and 4th Indian Brigade nearing the Tanlwe Chaung, it must have seemed to Christison that the object of his orders of the 9th

---

[1] A special drop of 20 tons a day had been sanctioned for it while it was isolated.
[2] The 4th Indian Brigade had under command two troops 146th Regiment R.A.C. (medium tanks), 160th Field Regiment, one battery (less a troop) 6th Medium Regiment, 1st Indian Anti-Tank Regiment (less two batteries), 1/18th Royal Garhwal Rifles, 12th F.F. Regiment M.G. Battalion less two companies and 72nd Field Company, I.E.

March was about to be achieved, but at that stage he became aware that a large part of the Japanese northern group was apparently moving from An to the Irrawaddy. The operations towards An had clearly failed to achieve their object of containing the northern group. The rate of advance of the West African division had fallen far short of that envisaged in XV Corps' instruction of the 12th February and the Joint Force Commanders' directive of the 18th. Whether a more energetic advance could have prevented reinforcements being sent to the Irrawaddy is a matter for conjecture.

Christison now considered it more than ever important to prevent the transfer of troops from the Taungup area to the Irrawaddy, so the Joint Force Commanders, on the 21st March, issued new orders amplifying a warning order given on the 19th. Stockwell was instructed to contain the reduced northern group west of the An Pass for as long as possible. To increase the pressure on Taungup he was to send 22nd (E.A.) Brigade from Tamandu at once by road to Letpan, where it was to come under command of 26th Division. It was to be followed by a West African brigade not later than the 15th April. Strong diversionary raids were to be carried out along the coast near to and south of Taungup while these moves were taking place.[1] He was to be prepared to move his own headquarters to the Taungup area before the beginning of the monsoon and take over command from 26th Division. He was also to have one of his remaining two West African brigades in the An area ready to be moved back to Chittagong as soon as shipping became available after 25th Division had been moved out of Arakan. This would leave one West African brigade at An and that too was to be sent back to Chittagong before the monsoon by sea from Tamandu, which was then to be closed down.

Meanwhile 4th Indian Brigade continued to advance southwards. After driving Japanese rearguards out of several positions it reached the Tanlwe Chaung on the 22nd March, and next day secured a firm bridgehead on its southern bank. By the end of the month it had reached a point some four miles short of the Taungup Chaung, an F.M.A. had been established at Kindaunggyi and 22nd (E.A.) Brigade had concentrated at Letpan, having overcome slight enemy opposition on its way south from Tamandu. In the An area 1st (W.A.) Brigade, supported by 8th Field Regiment and a troop of 6th Medium Regiment, succeeded in making contact with 2nd (W.A.) Brigade to the south of Letmauk on the 24th March.[2] The 2nd Brigade, having evacuated its casualties, was then withdrawn to Tamandu for rest and

---

[1] In a diversionary raid near Taungup, Lieutenant C. Raymond, R.E., won the Victoria Cross. He subsequently died of his wounds.

[2] Brigadier A. T. Wilson-Brand succeeded Western in command of 2nd (W.A.) Brigade on the 23rd March.

rehabilitation. By the end of March, 25th Division had concentrated at Akyab in readiness for its return to India, and 71st Brigade of 26th Division, which had sailed from Kyaukpyu on the 25th, had arrived in Madras. The defence of Ramree Island had been taken over by 453 L. of C. Sub-Area with garrison troops, to be supplemented if necessary by units of 36th Brigade.

The operations in Arakan were now affected by the decision taken at the end of March to launch an airborne and amphibious assault on Rangoon early in May, with 26th Division providing the assault force.[1] On the 2nd April Christison issued a directive in which he said that the role of XV Corps remained unchanged except in respect of the proposed assault on Rangoon. The 26th Division was now to be concentrated on Ramree Island; 71st Brigade was to be recalled from Madras, and the tactical headquarters of 26th Division and 4th Brigade then in the Tanlwe–Taungup area were to be relieved as soon as possible by 82nd (W.A.) Division, whose task was to be re-cast. Stockwell was now to move his headquarters to the Tanlwe Chaung–Taungup area and take over command of all troops on the mainland, including 4th Brigade of 26th Division, by the 5th April, send 2nd (W.A.) Brigade (then at Tamandu) to the same area to arrive not later than the 15th April and the rest of the division, less 1st (W.A.) Brigade, as soon afterwards as possible; men and light equipment were to move by sea, and heavy stores and vehicles by road. The first brigade to arrive was to relieve 4th Indian Brigade. The 1st (W.A.) Brigade, under the direct orders of corps head-quarters, was to hold the F.M.A. at Tamandu and contain as large an enemy force as possible in the An area. On taking over command from 26th Division, Stockwell was to hold the Taungup area, provide protection for the F.M.A. at Kindaunggyi, secure Kyauktaga and exploit towards Yebawgyi on the Prome road. He was told that he could count on air supply up to 60 tons a day from Ramree and a further 60 tons by sea.

On the 5th April, 1st (W.A.) Brigade, advancing from Letmauk, occupied Point 990, the highest point on the road to An and some five miles from it, but could get no farther. During the next two days reports were received from 'V' Force that the Japanese were moving towards Dalet along a track running parallel with the Letmauk road. As the brigade's primary task was now the defence of Tamandu, Stockwell ordered it on the 8th to withdraw to Letmauk. It was con-centrated there by the 10th and for the next three days was counter-attacked by an enemy force which, on the 12th, formed a roadblock

---

[1] See pages 327–31.

behind it between Shaukchon and Kolan, thereby cutting its communications with Tamandu.[1] The roadblock was cleared with the aid of an airstrike, and the brigade was withdrawn on the 13th to Shaukchon. This counter-attack proved to be the last engagement in the An area, for that day the Japanese began to regroup for their withdrawal across the An Pass to Allanmyo which was to begin on the 19th. As a result, West African patrols reached An on the 23rd April, meeting with only a few Japanese.

In the Letpan area Stockwell took over command from Lomax, but for the time being 4th Indian Brigade remained under his command. The 22nd (E.A.) Brigade had arrived in the forward area from Letpan, and he planned to send it, supplied by air from Ramree, eastwards along the Tanlwe Chaung to establish a firm base at Palawa and from there strike south to the Taungup–Prome road and cut the line of retreat of all Japanese forces in south Arakan, believed, correctly, to consist of *121st Regiment* less its *II/121st Battalion* and some divisional troops and administrative units. They were then to be destroyed by 2nd (W.A.) Brigade advancing from Taungup along the road as soon as 22nd (E.A.) Brigade had established itself behind them. This was to be followed by the mopping-up of any Japanese left in Sandoway and Gwa.[2] The 4th (W.A.) Brigade was to hold a firm base in Taungup. While the African brigades were moving into position to carry out this plan, 4th Indian Brigade reached the Taungup Chaung and its patrols penetrated to the town and surrounding hills by the 14th. On the 17th it was relieved by 4th (W.A.) Brigade and began its move back to Ramree Island to prepare for 'Dracula'.

The 22nd (E.A.) Brigade reached Palawa on the 15th and as it moved south towards the Prome road began to meet opposition. On the 26th April it reached Mogyo near the Prome road, some ten miles east of Taungup, and the same day 2nd (W.A.) Brigade cleared Japanese from positions four miles north-east of the town. The following night 4th (W.A.) Brigade occupied the high ground south-east of Taungup and on the 29th occupied the town without opposition. Any hope of intercepting the enemy soon faded, for 22nd (E.A.) and 2nd (W.A.) Brigades made contact in the Mogyo area without meeting any Japanese. In fact the rearguards of *121st Regiment* had withdrawn from their positions in the hills east of Taungup on the 30th April.[3]

On the 1st May, 82nd (W.A.) Division came under direct command

---

[1] See Sketch 15, facing page 354. The counter-attack was carried out by *111th Regiment* (less *III/111th Battalion*), *154th Regiment* (less *I/* and *II/154th Battalions* already sent to the Irrawaddy front) and *54th Reconnaissance Regiment* (less two companies), organized into two columns and supported by two field artillery batteries. The *III/111th Battalion* remained holding Point 990. The roadblock was established by *II/111th Battalion*. All units were considerably under strength.

[2] See Map 11, facing page 414.

[3] See page 378.

of Headquarters A.L.F.S.E.A., and XV Corps' sole task became the control of the forces carrying out 'Dracula'. So ended the Battle of the Arakan Beaches. During the landings the Navy had fired 23,000 rounds of all calibres from 4- to 15-inch and carried 54,000 men, 800 animals, 1,000 vehicles and 14,000 tons of stores to the various beachheads. The losses in battle of XV Corps amounted to 5,089, of whom 1,138 were killed, while 224 Group R.A.F. lost 78 aircraft from all causes and believed it had destroyed 63 Japanese aircraft and damaged many others. The combined operations were remarkable because of the difficulties that were overcome in navigating uncharted chaungs without previous reconnaissance, while sloops, destroyers, minesweepers and motor launches carried out tasks they had never before been asked to attempt, and, owing to shortage in numbers, landing craft operated ceaselessly far from bases or depot ships. Last, but by no means least, the Joint Force Commanders had no precedent to guide them in their planning, for never before had combined operations been undertaken on such a seaboard or with such a heterogeneous collection of craft. It might be said that it was fortunate that there was never serious opposition to the many landings, but in fact it was flexibility in planning, speed in mounting attacks and bold navigation which achieved the surprise that made it impossible for the Japanese to foresee where the next blow might fall and make preparations to meet it.

The 1944-45 campaign in Arakan presented a most unusual paradox in that each side achieved its main object because its opponent had no interest in trying to prevent it from doing so. On the one hand, XV Corps was able to take Akyab without a shot being fired and Ramree Island with trifling loss; on the other, the Japanese with a comparatively small force fought to prevent XV Corps from breaking into the Irrawaddy valley, which it was not trying to do. In spite of all this, the campaign produced one of the bloodiest battles of the whole Burma campaign—Kangaw—and intensive manœuvring under extremely difficult conditions. It was in their secondary tasks that both sides failed: the Joint Force Commanders hoped to pin the whole of *54th* and *55th Divisions* to Arakan, while the Japanese *28th Army* hoped that, having prevented any advance across the Yomas by XV Corps, *54th Division* would join in the defence of Prome. In view of what is now known of Japanese intentions it seems probable that if XV Corps, having secured Akyab and Ramree Island, had been told to consolidate, return its two Indian divisions to India, and undertake no further major operations the Japanese plans would not have differed materially.

The Joint Force Commanders, however, did their utmost to destroy as much as possible of the *Matsu Detachment* of *54th Division*. Their attempt to do this in north Arakan by cutting its line of retreat brought on the fierce action at Kangaw, for Miyazaki had to get it away at all costs in order to retain a force large enough to enable him to carry out his mission. Had Christison succeeded in destroying the detachment, XV Corps would have been well on its way to achieving its secondary task of preventing reinforcements being sent from Arakan to the Irrawaddy. He failed to do so, but, had it been possible energetically to pursue the badly battered Japanese force withdrawing from Kangaw, the greater part of *54th Division* might well have been destroyed. Unfortunately from this moment onwards XV Corps suffered a series of frustrations, such as the unavoidable withdrawal of air supply, which made effective operations difficult. Even so, *54th Division* could have been hard hit had 82nd (W.A.) Division's advance not been so hesitant. When the urgent need to relieve Akyab and Ramree Island of the maintenance of XV Corps, so that the air bases at both could be ready in time to maintain 14th Army's drive on Rangoon, forced the withdrawal of 25th and 26th Divisions, the revival of pressure became impossible. Thus the campaign, which had begun with an unexpectedly quick success followed by hard fighting, dragged on to a frustrating and inconclusive end.

While the last stages of the Battle of the Arakan Beaches were being fought, the Joint Force Commanders and Headquarters XV Corps were engaged in mounting 'Dracula' at Kyaukpyu. On the 1st April Major-General H. M. Chambers had succeeded Lomax,[1] who had commanded 26th Division with distinction since he assumed command early in 1943 at the most critical stage of the disastrous first Arakan campaign.[2] Chambers was therefore appointed to Assault Force Headquarters as the army representative, together with Rear-Admiral Martin (who was also one of the Joint Force Commanders) and Group Captain H. Pleasance, R.A.F. The force for 'Dracula' was detailed in a planning directive issued by the Joint Force Commanders on the 9th April: 26th Division was to make the assault with 2nd Division following up; the armoured component was to be 19th Lancers (medium tanks) and the parachute operation was to be carried out by a Gurkha parachute battalion of 50th (P.) Brigade. The 41st Beach Group together with the necessary corps and administrative troops, but with a minimum of vehicles, made up the force.

The planning directive provided for a four-phase assault. D-day was to be the 3rd May—subsequently put forward to the 2nd, a date

---

[1] Chambers had been in command of 71st Brigade in succession to Cottrell-Hill for three weeks from the 1st March.

[2] See Volume II, pages 340–41. Lomax had been appointed to the command of a District in India.

which was not to be deferred except with the consent of the Naval Joint Commander (Martin). The first phase was to be a parachute drop on D – 1 to secure Elephant Point, followed on D-day by the landing of a brigade group on the west bank and a battalion group on the east bank of the Rangoon River estuary.[1] The second was to be the landing of the rest of 26th Division on the beaches thus secured, the establishment of a maintenance area at Kyauktan and exploitation northwards. The third phase, estimated to begin on D+9, was to be the landing of a brigade of the follow-up (2nd) division to hold the maintenance area while 26th Division captured Syriam. The fourth phase was to be the assault on Rangoon by 2nd Division which (less one brigade) was to embark at Calcutta in the middle of May.

Naval and air support—particularly the latter—was massive. It was thought that the garrison of Rangoon might number 10,000 and that a large part of *28th Army* might be in the area between Rangoon and Pegu. The operation had to be mounted hurriedly and since, with the monsoon approaching, any delay in establishing beachheads would be bound to have serious consequences, Mountbatten insisted that every available craft, sea and air, was to be available for instant action if needed. The naval element, apart from the East Indies Fleet, consisted of the 21st Assault Carrier Squadron (Commodore G. N. Oliver), H.M.S. *Phoebe* and two sloops and a large fleet of landing ships, landing craft and minesweepers. A huge air fleet of thirty-eight squadrons of fighters and bombers was detailed to undertake direct support but, as little of it was called on, need not be enumerated.

On the 17th April Mountbatten approved the outline plan submitted by the Joint Force Commanders (Christison, Martin and Bandon), and issued a final directive to his Commanders-in-Chief 'to carry out an amphibious and airborne operation with the object of the early capture of Rangoon should this not have been achieved by the advance of Fourteenth Army from the north'. The main points of Leese's instructions to the Joint Force Commanders based on this directive were the importance of the destruction of the enemy batteries on Elephant Point, and a rapid exploitation north by the assault division on both banks of the Rangoon River to protect the minesweepers which were expected to take four days to clear the river of mines, a large number of which had been laid by the R.A.F. For those four days maintenance was to be by air supplemented by sea, and thereafter by sea with air supply for use in emergency.

On the 22nd April, by which time 4th Indian Brigade had arrived in Ramree from Taungup, 26th Division's order for the assault was issued. It is sufficient here to record only the intention paragraph,

---

[1] See Map 11, facing page 414.

which read: '26th Indian Division, with naval and air support, will assault land in the Rangoon River and capture the general area Syriam–Kyauktan with a view to establishing a firm base there from which subsequent operations can be conducted against Rangoon.' In this intention lies the ultimate justification of the long, sometimes disastrous and always arduous campaign in Arakan which was at this moment drawing to its close.

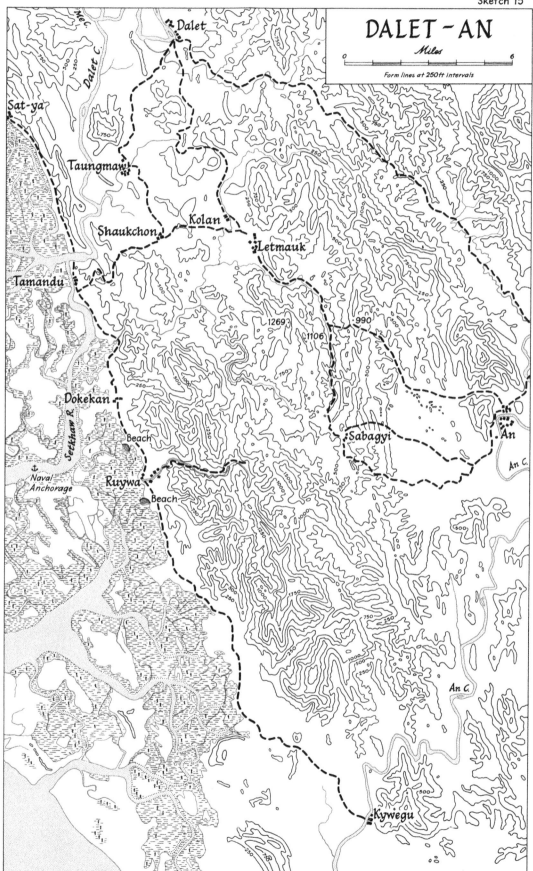

Sketch 15

DALET – AN

Miles

0   6

Form lines at 250ft intervals

Dalet

Sat-ya

Taungmaw

Kolan

Shaukchon

Letmauk

Tamandu

1269

1106

990

Dokekan

Sabagyi

An

Beach

An C.

Naval
Anchorage

Ruywa

Beach

Sethaw R.

An C.

Kywegu

CHAPTER XXX

THE CENTRAL FRONT

(1st–12th April 1945)

The Capture of Pyawbwe and the Advance towards Yenangyaung

See Maps 3 and 7 and Sketches 16 and 17

BY the 1st April 1945 the Japanese counter-offensive to recapture Meiktila and the Myitche–Nyaungu areas had completely failed: the remnants of *15th* and *33rd Armies* were in retreat, the former making its way in small parties from the Irrawaddy front to the hills east of Kyaukse and Kume, and the latter withdrawing from Meiktila to defend the Pyawbwe area. The *28th Army* in the Irrawaddy valley was holding the general line Mount Popa–Singu–Point 534 (south of Letse).[1]

The regrouping of 14th Army for the third stage of its operations for the final destruction of the Japanese armies in central Burma and for the capture of Rangoon,[2] now about to begin, was, like all Slim's moves, one of great simplicity. It involved an interchange of divisions *in situ*—7th Division from IV to XXXIII Corps and 19th Division from that corps to 14th Army command (and later to IV Corps). At the same time 2nd and 20th Divisions were, on completion of their existing tasks, to disengage and move south-west, passing behind IV Corps to their new area.

A summary of the dispositions of 14th Army is necessary for the proper understanding of the operations which were about to begin in the stifling heat and dust of a Burmese April, operations which were to complete the destruction of *Burma Area Army* and drive its remnants into the mountains east of the Sittang River and into Tenasserim. In the IV Corps sector 17th Division (Cowan) was advancing on a two-brigade front, with 48th Brigade making for Pyawbwe by the direct route and 99th Brigade by way of Thazi; both were in contact with the enemy by the evening of the 1st April. The 63rd Brigade was being relieved by 5th Division (Mansergh), which had resumed command of its 9th Brigade and was concentrating as a mobile reserve for IV Corps' thrust on Rangoon. The

---

[1] See Chapter XXVI and Map 3, facing page 55.
[2] See pages 324–25.

XXXIII Corps was in the process of changing its front from east to south-west to become the right wing of 14th Army in the Irrawaddy valley. The 7th Division (Evans), now under its command, was deployed astride the river with 114th Brigade on its west taking over from 28th (E.A.) Brigade in the Letse area, its right flank being protected by Westcol at Saw on the Kanpetlet track;[1] east of the river, 89th Brigade, in contact with the enemy in the Singu area, was awaiting orders to attack Chauk, and 33rd Brigade was being relieved by 2nd Division in the Taungtha–Myingyan area where fighting had ceased. Units of 33rd Brigade were moving to Nyaungu on relief to prepare for the attack on Yenangyaung in conjunction with an advance by 114th and 89th Brigades on Seikpyu and Chauk respectively. The 2nd Division (Nicholson) (less 5th Brigade advancing on Mount Popa) was beginning to concentrate in the Myingyan–Pyinzi–Mahlaing area preparatory to being flown out to India between the 10th and 20th April, and 268th Brigade was in Myingyan. The 20th Division (Gracey) was still mopping up in the Kyaukse–Myittha–Kume area, but was in process of being relieved by 19th Division, less a battalion which had to remain in Mandalay until the leading formations of 36th Division arrived there. Since the rundown of N.C.A.C. and the withdrawal of the Yunnan forces to China meant that *56th Division* in the Shan States would be free to harass the left flank of IV Corps' advance on Rangoon down the railway,[2] the void south of Mandalay, which would be created by the move of 2nd and 20th Divisions westwards, was to be filled by 19th Division moving south into the rear of IV Corps' area and by 36th Division from Kyaukme moving into Mandalay on coming under command of 14th Army.[3]

At Myingyan 45th Beach Group was operating the newly-opened river port, and work on the construction of the 14th Army base was in progress. The airhead at Myitche was in process of being taken over by XXXIII Corps, Headquarters IV Corps was on its way to Meiktila where the airfield was being organized as the corps airhead, and 505 District was taking over administrative responsibility north of the Irrawaddy. There was, however, still anxiety over the air supply situation, for it was not until the 3rd April that the Americans gave Mountbatten the assurance, for which he had fought so hard, that their aircraft would not be withdrawn from S.E.A.C. until the fall of Rangoon or the 1st June, whichever was earlier.[4]

·   ·   ·   ·   ·

[1] For Westcol see pages 256 and 284.
[2] See Chapter XXVII.
[3] See Chapter XXVIII.
[4] See page 319.

On orders from *Southern Army, Burma Area Army* was at this time planning to defend southern Burma. Kimura's intention was to withdraw to and hold the general line Loi-kaw–Toungoo–Prome with *15th* and *33rd Armies* in the Sittang valley and *28th Army* in the Irrawaddy valley.[1] The *33rd Army* was to cover the withdrawal of *15th Army* from the Mandalay–Irrawaddy battlefield to positions north of Pyinmana by holding the general line Thazi–Pyawbwe–Yanaung. As soon as *15th Army* was in position, *33rd Army* was to withdraw through it and regroup north of Toungoo, which was then to be held by both armies, with *56th Division* covering the right flank from Loi-kaw. The *28th Army* was to hold the Mount Popa–Chauk–Seikpyu–Yenangyaung area with *72nd I.M.B.* and its attached units for as long as possible to give time for the main body of *54th Division* to withdraw from Arakan and concentrate in the vicinity of Magwe for the defence of the Allanmyo–Prome area.[2] As will be seen, the speed of the Allied advance rendered these plans ineffective; the Pyawbwe–Yanaung line was taken and Pyinmana overrun long before *15th Army* could get into position, with the consequence that *33rd Army* had to retreat unaided as best it could to Toungoo, and Yenangyaung was lost before *54th Division* could get into position in the Irrawaddy valley.

In the Japanese account covering *33rd Army's* operations in April it is contended that *Burma Area Army*, with its headquarters 250 miles to the rear and with bad communications, was out of touch with the situation in the forward areas, and that Kimura's order to Honda to hold such an extended covering position as the general line Thazi–Pyawbwe–Yanaung in open country against an enemy vastly superior in armour gave him an impossible task. This resulted in such heavy losses that no organized force was left with which to hold the main Toungoo position. In fact, the strength of the three divisions of *33rd Army* had dropped to less than that of one division, and many men still in the ranks were walking wounded. It had few guns, its ammunition was almost exhausted and its strength in anti-tank weapons was about half of what was normal for one division.

One can assume that, left to himself, Honda would have broken contact and withdrawn to a position difficult to outflank, such as the Shwemyo gorge which he later tried to hold with the remnants of his force defeated at Pyawbwe.

Messervy had given 17th Division (Cowan) the task of capturing Pyawbwe, which covered the entrance to the Sittang valley. The object, as in all operations of 14th Army, continued to be the destruction of Japanese forces, and Cowan therefore planned to envelop the

---

[1] See Map 7, facing page 171.
[2] For the withdrawal of *54th Division* from Arakan see Chapters XXIX and XXXI.

defences covering the town completely before attacking it. The 48th Brigade (Hedley) was to attack frontally down the main road; 63rd Brigade (Burton) was to attack from the west by way of Yanaung; a powerful armoured column (Claudcol) under Pert (255th Tank Brigade) was to by-pass Pyawbwe to the west, cut the Rangoon road and attack from the south; while 99th Brigade (Brigadier M. V. Wright) was to come in from the north-east, by way of Thazi.[1] The final assault was to be co-ordinated by Cowan from Yindaw, which was to become the divisional firm base.

The 99th Brigade, which had the farthest to go, had begun its advance on the 30th March, when 1/3rd Gurkhas and a squadron of 9th Royal Horse, which had established a patrol base some four miles east of Meiktila, reported before nightfall that there was no enemy within striking distance of the Thazi road as far as MS 10. By the early morning of the 2nd April the brigade was disposed in depth along the Meiktila–Thazi road, with its leading battalion (1st Sikh Light Infantry) in contact with enemy in prepared positions covering Thazi. The same morning 48th Brigade, which had moved out from Meiktila on the 1st, ran into determined opposition at Kandaung.[2] After an air bombardment beginning at 10 a.m. on the 3rd, followed by artillery concentrations from 10.30, Hedley's leading battalion (4/12th F.F. Regiment) by-passed the position and attacked it from the south-west in conjunction with a frontal attack by 1/7th Gurkhas. Throughout the day the Japanese who, under Colonel Uga, had already resisted three deliberate attacks in the area during the latter part of March,[3] held on, but, threatened with encirclement and annihilation, the remnants evacuated their positions during the night. The next day 1st West Yorkshires with 9th Royal Horse, less one squadron, were ordered to by-pass Kandaung to the west and make for Yindaw from where the divisional attack on Pyawbwe was to be mounted, while 1/7th Gurkhas, having mopped up, advanced on it from the north. The Gurkhas met strong opposition at the Chaunggauk Chaung crossing some two miles south of Kandaung, and it was not until 2 p.m. on the 5th that resistance ceased and the Japanese withdrew down the road to Yindaw.[4] That afternoon 99th Brigade, which had been relieved at Thazi on Messervy's orders by a brigade of 5th Division and was moving south, struck the retiring Japanese in flank, inflicting very heavy losses.[5] By evening 48th Brigade was

---

[1] Wright had replaced Tarver on the 25th March.
[2] See Sketch 16, facing page 360.
[3] See page 308 fn. 1.
[4] See Map 7, facing page 171.
[5] The Japanese losses were 253 counted dead, two field guns and a number of horses stampeded. Identifications were of I/ and III/106th Battalions and 49th Reconnaissance Regiment. Known losses here and at Kandaung were 583 dead and nine guns. The Japanese account states that in the fighting near Yindaw half 49th Division's headquarters staff were killed or wounded and that, as communications with 33rd Army were totally disrupted, the division had no choice but to make its way as best it could towards Toungoo.

closing on Yindaw from north and west and the 99th from north-east, and 63rd Brigade was on its way to Yanaung. The 99th Brigade's losses had been negligible and those of 48th Brigade amounted to a little over 100, of whom only a small proportion were killed.

During the 6th Yindaw was occupied and Cowan made his final arrangements for surrounding Pyawbwe. Claudcol,[1] with 7/10th Baluch Regiment of 63rd Brigade temporarily under command, moved off early on the 7th for Yanaung, followed by 63rd Brigade less a battalion. The first objective was Point 900 overlooking Yanaung from the east;[2] there a Japanese force, taken by surprise early on the 8th, was dispersed, leaving behind 201 dead and four guns and providing identifications of both *49th* and *53rd Divisions.* Leaving 7/10th Baluch, which had taken the hill, to hold it and a nearby roadblock till the arrival of the rest of 63rd Brigade, Claudcol pushed on to cut the road south of Pyawbwe. Having given Claudcol and 63rd Brigade a day's start, Cowan got 48th and 99th Brigades on the move on the morning of the 8th, the former on the axis of the main road and the latter to the east of it with orders to secure the hills between the road and the railway. Each brigade had a squadron of 9th Royal Horse under command. The advanced guard of 48th Brigade,[3] in a two-hour action at the Myingya Chaung crossing dispersed a Japanese force, of which 135 were killed, and that same evening 99th Brigade on the left secured the dominating Point 796.

The advance continued on the 9th, 48th Brigade, against minor opposition, reaching Nyaungnwe, some four miles north of Pyawbwe. On the right, 63rd Brigade, moving across country from Yanaung, reached Kyauktaing, four miles west of Pyawbwe, where 1/10th Gurkhas cleared the village, and armoured cars and tanks intercepted and routed a Japanese column on the move. Known Japanese losses amounted to eighty-nine dead, six prisoners and nine guns. Claudcol surprised and attacked an enemy force at Ywadan, seven miles to the south of Pyawbwe, killing some 220 men and capturing four guns, including two 150-mm. heavy field artillery weapons. This attack actually surrounded *33rd Army Headquarters* and destroyed its remaining transport. The Japanese records state that the tanks did not recognize the headquarters for what it was, and at about 3 p.m. lifted the siege and moved north to attack *18th Division.* Wireless communications were disrupted and, from that time onwards, it became impossible to disseminate army orders except by

---

[1] Claudcol consisted of 5th (Probyn's) Horse less one squadron, one squadron 16th Light Cavalry (armoured cars), 6/7th Rajput Regiment, D Company 4/4th Bombay Grenadiers, 59/18th (S.P.) Field Battery and one troop 36th Field Squadron, I.E.

[2] See Sketch 17, facing page 368.

[3] The 4/12th F.F. Regiment, one squadron 9th Royal Horse (medium tanks) and one troop 16th Cavalry (armoured cars).

means of liaison officers on foot. The army commander (Honda) and his staff got away on foot to Yamethin, where they joined up with the remnants of *18th Division* in its retreat to Shwemyo. By evening Claudcol had established a roadblock of armoured cars and infantry on the main road near Sedwin, about six miles south of Pyawbwe. On the left (east) flank, 99th Brigade, with the help of two airstrikes and the divisional artillery, cleared the whole of the Point 796 group of hills, while its armour overran the airstrip north of Pyawbwe. Confused fighting went on all day, and by the end of it 302 Japanese, mostly caught in the open by armour, lay dead on the battlefield, but among the dead were twenty-six killed during a counter-attack on Headquarters 99th Brigade, which indicates the closeness of the fighting. By the evening of the 9th Pyawbwe was surrounded, except for a gap to the east where a track ran towards the hills, which 99th Brigade had been unable to close since it was fully involved in the dog-fight north-east of the town. On Cowan's orders 48th Brigade sent a company of 4/12th F.F. Regiment and a troop of tanks to close the gap; this they successfully did, after passing behind and around 99th Brigade's battle area to get there.

On the 10th, nine days behind the original schedule, 17th Division closed in on Pyawbwe from all directions.[1] Since the last gap in the circle round Pyawbwe had been closed, the garrison had to fight its way out, die or surrender. It chose a combination of the first two, and when Pyawbwe was entered 1,110 dead and thirteen guns were found in the town.[2] Pyawbwe was the only large action in the Battle of the Rangoon Road and it finally shattered *33rd Army*.

The very heavy losses suffered by the Japanese arose partly from the fact that the garrison was caught in the act of pulling out, for, on the 9th April, Honda had given orders for the evacuation of Pyawbwe to begin that night. The *18th Division*, moving east of the main road, was to occupy positions on the plateau north-east of Shwemyo on the eastern side of the Sinthe Chaung, *53rd Division*, moving west of the road, was to hold the line of the chaung in the area where it was crossed by the railway bridge, and *49th Division* was to take up a position in rear of *18th Division*.[3]

The exact strength of the Japanese forces involved at Pyawbwe is

---

[1] In Messervy's instruction the move on Pyawbwe was to begin on the 29th March. To implement it, Cowan had on the 23rd March issued a forecast of operations which included a converging attack on the town on the 1st April. Circumstances forced the starting time of the move on Pyawbwe to be put back by three days. This and the stubborn fight put up by Japanese rearguards covering Pyawbwe caused further delay.

[2] Among the dead were men of *4th Regiment* of *2nd Division*. Information from P.O.W.s and captured documents indicated that elements of the regiment, which was on its way to Indo-China, were stopped at Pegu at the end of March and sent back to Pyawbwe. Japanese accounts state that Regimental Headquarters and one composite battalion of *4th Regiment* remained in Burma.

[3] See Map 7, facing page 171. By this time *49th Division* was out of touch with *33rd Army* and did not receive this order.

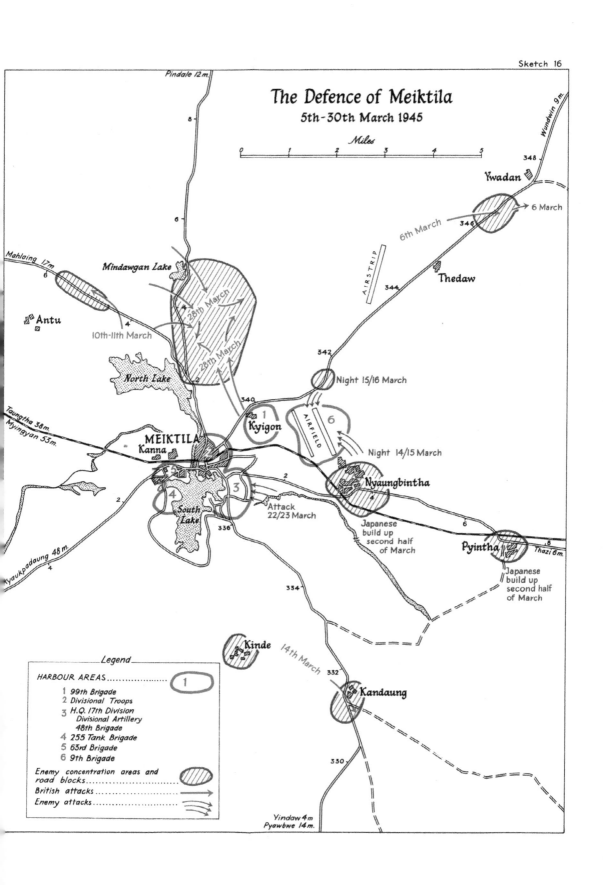

Sketch 16

The Defence of Meiktila
5th–30th March 1945

Miles
0   1   2   3   4   5

Pindale 12 m.

Wundwin 9 m.

348

Ywadan

346   6 March

6th March

Thedaw

AIRSTRIP

344

Mahlaing 17 m.

Mindawgan Lake

Antu

28th March

10th–11th March

28th March

North Lake

342

Night 15/16 March

Taungtha 38 m.
Myingyan 55 m.

340

1 Kyigon

AIRFIELD   6

MEIKTILA
Kanna

Night 14/15 March

5   2

4   3   Nyaungbintha

South Lake   Attack 22/23 March

Japanese build up second half of March

2.   336

6

Pyintha   8

Thazi 6 m.

Kyaukpadaung 48 m.

Japanese build up second half of March

334

Kinde

14th March   332

Kandaung

Legend

HARBOUR AREAS   1

1 99th Brigade
2 Divisional Troops
3 H.Q. 17th Division
    Divisional Artillery
    48th Brigade
4 255 Tank Brigade
5 63rd Brigade
6 9th Brigade

Enemy concentration areas and
road blocks ....

British attacks ....

Enemy attacks ....

330

Yindaw 4 m.
Pyawbwe 14 m.

difficult to assess, the only firm figure being that the core of the defence, *18th Division*, was 5,000 strong with twenty-two guns. Of this there was a detachment at Hlaingdet which, in view of the determined resistance met there, might have been as much as 1,000 strong. The *53rd Division* was very much under strength, and had no artillery except battalion guns; it seems probable that it was not more than 3,000 strong. What was left of the detachment of *49th Division* which fought at Kandaung and Yindaw did not take part in the close defence of Pyawbwe. It therefore seems reasonable to assume that the defenders of the town on the 3rd April, when positions were taken up, numbered about 7,000 with twenty-two guns. In addition there were four medium and five light tanks, all of which were destroyed.[1] The reaction of Japanese troops to orders to fight to the end is exemplified by an incident on the 10th when a column about 150 strong was seen marching in formation towards the town from the north. Small arms and mortar fire was brought down on it, and though it left more than a third of its strength dead in its track the column did not break formation. It belonged to *II/16th Battalion* (possibly all that was left of it), which had been roughly handled near Taungtha in February.[2]

From the 11th April the battle developed into a running fight, as 5th Division, less its air-transportable 9th Brigade, moved forward to take up the pursuit, leaving 17th Division to mop up in and around Pyawbwe.

The absent 9th Brigade (Brigadier H. G. L. Brain)[3] was under command of 19th Division and had been engaged, in co-operation with 64th Brigade (Flewett), in clearing the Thazi–Hlaingdet area. To this the Japanese clung tenaciously as it covered the road to Kalaw, the last escape route for stragglers from the Mandalay and Meiktila battles and along which *56th Division* might operate from the Shan Hills to harass the left flank and communications of 14th Army as it moved south on Rangoon.[4] On the 5th April the command of 19th Division (Rees) was transferred from 14th Army to IV Corps, and Rees took over operational control of the area from the Meiktila–Thazi road northwards as far as Kume. At the same time 36th Division (Festing) became responsible for the Mandalay–Maymyo–Kyaukse area.

·   ·   ·   ·   ·

---

[1] Known Japanese losses from the 3rd to the 10th April were 2,900 killed, twenty-nine prisoners, forty-four guns, six medium tanks and seventy M.T. vehicles. The forty-four guns and six medium tanks claimed by IV Corps include losses at Kandaung and elsewhere north of Pyawbwe, and the claim does not therefore conflict with the Japanese figures.

[2] See page 268.

[3] Brain was the replacement for Salomons as from 26th March (see page 309 fn. 2).

[4] See Map 3, facing page 55.

While IV Corps was capturing and clearing the Pyawbwe area during the first twelve days of April, XXXIII Corps was preparing for its drive down the Irrawaddy. On the 29th March Stopford had allotted his divisions and 268th Brigade their tasks. Evans (7th Division) was to capture Seikpyu and Chauk.[1] He was to be prepared to operate with one brigade water-borne; the corps engineers were therefore to assemble the necessary rafts and power craft at Chauk as soon as it was captured.[2] Nicholson (2nd Division) was to send one brigade (5th) to advance by way of Welaung on Kyaukpadaung, from where it was to assist 7th Division to capture Chauk; 6th Brigade was to concentrate at Myingyan, and the 4th was to mop up the Pyinzi–Mahlaing area.[3] All three brigades were to be flown out to India beginning on the 10th April. Gracey (20th Division) was to concentrate in the Myittha–Wundwin area as soon as he had cleared Kyaukse and handed it over to 19th Division, and prepare to advance at speed on Magwe by way of Meiktila, Zayetkon and Natmauk. The 268th Brigade was to take over the protection of the right flank of the corps west of the Irrawaddy from Westcol (this role being later changed). Owing to the very wide dispersal of his formations, Stopford allotted most of the corps armour and artillery to divisions.[4] The ferry at Ava was to be taken over by 505 District and those at Kyauktalon and Nyaungu by C.A.G.R.E. 14th Army; the army was also to take over responsibility for the security of the airfields at Tadau, Myingyan, Taungtha, Nyaungu, Myitche and Sinthe.

On the day the corps order was issued, the two battalions of 114th Brigade (7th Division) operating in the Letse area under command of 28th (E.A.) Brigade were in close contact with enemy on Point 534 south-east of Letse and in the group of hills four miles to the south of it on the road to Seikpyu.[5] On the 1st April, after a heavy and accurate air attack by two squadrons of Hurricanes and two of Thunderbolts, the Japanese resistance on Point 534 finally collapsed and they made no attempt to retake the hill. There were, however, still Japanese detachments to the north of Letse but, as they were now isolated, it was hoped (as it turned out with undue optimism) that they would have little effect on operations.

The next day (2nd April) Evans issued an instruction for the regrouping of 7th Division. The Taungtha area was now to become the

---

[1] See Maps 3 and 7, facing pages 55 and 171.

[2] From the date of this order 7th Division operated under command of XXXIII Corps, but continued to be administered for the next few days by IV Corps.

[3] While mopping up this area, 4th Brigade intercepted and dispersed a Japanese column which was probably the remnants of the Myingyan garrison. See page 306 fn. 4.

[4] 2nd Division: Carabiniers, less two squadrons, and a detachment of flame-throwers; 7th Division: one squadron Carabiniers, 2nd Indian Field Regiment and 8th Mahratta Anti-Tank Regiment; 20th Division: 150th R.A.C., less one squadron, 53rd Deception Company, one battery 1st Medium Regiment and a troop of 44th L.A.A. Battery; 268th Brigade: one battery 99th Field Regiment (from 2nd Division).

[5] See page 305.

responsibility of 268th Brigade operating under command of 2nd Division.[1] Headquarters and units of 33rd Brigade still at Taungtha were to move to Nyaungu and prepare to attack Yenangyaung. Headquarters 114th Brigade was to move with its remaining battalion from Nyaungu to Letse and complete the relief of 28th (E.A.) Brigade, which was then to be flown out to India. While these changes were being made, fighting patrols of 114th Brigade (Dinwiddie), whose orders were to attack Seikpyu on or before the 11th April, probed the Japanese positions covering the village. The Japanese retaliated strongly and as a result losses were, for this type of fighting, severe. In the Chauk sector, 89th Brigade found the Singu defences fully manned and it was clear that the Japanese intended to hold Seikpyu and Chauk for as long as possible.[2]

The advance of 5th Brigade (Alston-Roberts-West), with 2nd Reconnaissance Regiment, one squadron Carabiniers (medium tanks) and 10th Field Regiment R.A. under command, had meanwhile begun on the 1st April from Welaung, where its forward troops were in touch with Kingcol of 7th Division.[3] The first objective was Legyi on the Taungtha–Kyaukpadaung road, some six miles north of Mount Popa. The advance met minor opposition from *I.N.A.* patrols, many of which surrendered without a fight. Information was copious but conflicting, but it became clear that Legyi was held and indications were that the force there might be an *I.N.A.* battalion with about 100 Japanese and some guns. An airstrike on Legyi was called for and made on the 2nd, setting the village on fire, but carriers of 2nd Reconnaissance Regiment, attempting to pass through the village, were met by machine-gun and anti-tank gun-fire and stopped. On the 3rd the reconnaissance regiment was sent to find out whether Kyaukpadaung could be reached by way of the Pyinbin–Kyaukpadaung road, leaving a battalion, if necessary, to mask Legyi; it reported, however, that the road was impassable for mechanized units. The same day 5th Brigade surrounded Legyi and attacked it without success, and for the next four days made no progress.[4]

Meanwhile Evans had, on the 4th April, issued an operation instruction for the capture of Seikpyu and Chauk, the latter by an enveloping attack, but, since 5th Brigade, whose task was to capture

---

[1] Stopford had given a verbal order for 268th Brigade to be retained in the Taungtha area instead of moving west of the Irrawaddy as originally intended.

[2] The IV Corps' Intelligence staff estimated Japanese strength in the area Seikpyu–Chauk–Kyaukpadaung—Mount Popa–Yenangyaung as: *153rd Regiment* (the *Katsu Force*) about 1,000 strong, *72nd I.M.B.* (four battalions), two battalions *154th Regiment* (the *Koba Force*), two battalions *112th Regiment* (the *Kanjo Force*), and elements of *2nd I.N.A. Division*.

[3] For Kingcol see page 305 fn. 2.

[4] The *Koba Force* (*I|* and *II|154th Battalions*) had arrived in the Kyaukpadaung area from Letse on the 25th March, with orders to advance on Seiktein, two miles north-east of Legyi. The *I|154th Battalion* had recently arrived at Legyi when 5th Brigade attacked it on the 2nd. An *I.N.A.* battalion was also there, but most of it, according to Japanese accounts, surrendered when attacked.

Kyaukpadaung, was held up at Legyi, he was forced to change his intention. A glance at the map shows that Kyaukpadaung, the oilfield railhead and focal point of all motorable roads in the area, had to be secured before an attempt to envelop Chauk or attack Yenangyaung could be made. Evans was also anxious about the security of his left flank, for he had received information that *154th Regiment* was in the Mount Popa area, which indicated that the enemy strength there might be as much as five battalions and an *I.N.A.* division. The quick capture of Kyaukpadaung was vital if he were to succeed in enveloping Chauk. On the 8th, therefore, he issued a fresh instruction in which he stated that his intention was now to clear the Japanese from the Mount Popa–Kyaukpadaung–Gwegyo area in preparation for the capture of Chauk. He ordered 33rd Brigade (A/Brigadier Pugh) to attack Kyaukpadaung from the north and 268th Brigade (then at Pyinbin), which Stopford had on the 6th once again placed at his disposal, to cut the road between Kyaukpadaung and Mount Popa to prevent any interference from the Mount Popa area with 33rd Brigade's attack.[1]

Between the 8th April and the 11th, when 33rd Brigade attacked Kyaukpadaung, the Japanese had again regrouped their forces. Their original plan had been that, during the last week of March, the *Koba Force* (*154th*) was to attack north-east from Legyi while the *Kanjo Force* (*112th*) from Mount Popa attacked Pyinbin to strike the flank of the IV Corps column (5th Division) making for Meiktila by way of Taungtha. The *Koba Force*, as has been seen, was stopped at Legyi. The *Kanjo Force* attacks towards Pyinbin resulted in several skirmishes with Kingcol of 7th Division, during which many *I.N.A.* troops deserted; the Kingcol base south-west of Pyinbin was shelled and both sides had a few casualties. When he learned that *33rd Army* had abandoned the attempt to regain Meiktila, Sakurai (*28th Army*) ordered the forces based on Yenangyaung under Yamamoto to go over to defence. The *Kanjo Force* was to hold Mount Popa; *72nd I.M.B.* was to withdraw its battalion from the extreme western flank and concentrate the whole brigade for the defence of the Gwegyo–Yenangyaung area; the *Koba Force* was to return to the west of the Irrawaddy and hold the Salin area; and, on its arrival there, the *Katsu Force* (*153rd*), at this time covering Seikpyu after being driven out of the Letse area, was to cross the river to Chauk and hold it for as long as possible. This regrouping made the *Koba Force* (*54th Division*) responsible for operations west of the Irrawaddy, and *72nd I.M.B.*, with the *Kanjo* and *Katsu Forces* under command, (now named the *Kantetsu Group*), responsible for the Chauk–Mount Popa–Yenangyaung area. On the 9th April the concentration of the *Kantetsu Group*

---

[1] Lieut.-Colonel Pugh took over command of 33rd Brigade from Collingwood with the rank of A/Brigadier on the 28th March.

was complete and Major-General K. Ohara succeeded Yamamoto in command.[1]

On this same day (the 9th), as a result of Evans's revised orders, 33rd Brigade and 268th Brigade began to advance south. Although the Pyinbin–Kyaukpadaung road had been reported as impassable, 268th Brigade managed to move down it with its transport and, after a sharp fight in which its leading battalion suffered twenty casualties, had by the early morning of the 12th cut the Taungtha–Kyaukpadaung road south-west of Mount Popa; by the same morning 33rd Brigade had cut the roads running west and south from Kyaukpadaung. The Japanese held on all day in Kyaukpadaung; and what was left of the garrison slipped away during the night, leaving 125 dead, six Japanese and thirty-two *I.N.A.* prisoners, a serviceable 15-cm. howitzer and its ammunition, and a large amount of oilfield machinery and railway rolling stock. By this time 114th Brigade should have been attacking Seikpyu in accordance with divisional orders of the 2nd April, and have been in a position to co-operate with 33rd Brigade in an enveloping attack on Chauk, but until the 9th only two battalions of the brigade were west of the river.[2] Of these, 4/14th Punjab was engaged in mopping up the Japanese parties in the Letse area and carrying out the relief of 28th (E.A.) Brigade, leaving the understrength 2nd South Lancashires to advance on Seikpyu; in attempting to do so the battalion incurred further casualties in fighting with the *Katsu Force* (*153rd*). It was not until the 10th that Dinwiddie was able to organize an all-out drive to mop up the Japanese, some of whom were still in the area north of Letse. As a result, 114th Brigade had not started its advance on the 12th when Kyaukpadaung fell. Nevertheless 7th Division, with 268th Brigade under command, was now in a position to encircle Seikpyu, Chauk and Mount Popa, the first objectives in its drive south down the Irrawaddy valley.

On the left wing of XXXIII Corps, 20th Division's advance was also under way. On the 7th April Slim ordered reliefs between 19th, 20th and 36th Divisions to bring about the immediate release of 20th Division from the area north of Meiktila and the concentration of 19th Division for operations in support of IV Corps. As a result of this the advanced guard of 20th Division, consisting of a battalion of 32nd Brigade (Brigadier E. C. J. Woodford) with a squadron of light tanks and two of armoured cars, advanced on Zayetkon on the 10th.[3] From there it turned south and by the 12th had reached Natmauk, an

---

[1] Yamamoto was promoted Lieut.-General and posted to *Imperial General Headquarters, Tokyo.* This change in command was partly responsible for the return of *154th Regiment* to the west bank, for Koba was senior to the new commander of *72nd I.M.B.*

[2] There was no armour west of the river at this time.

[3] See Map 7, facing page 171. Woodford succeeded Mackenzie on the 25th March on the latter's transfer to an appointment in India on completion of his tenure of command.

advance of sixty miles in three days, and the rest of the brigade had reached Zayetkon. At this stage 1st Northamptonshire Regiment was replaced in 32nd Brigade by 1st Gurkha Rifles, and used under direct command of 20th Division for operations along the Zayetkon–Kyaukpadaung road to link up with 268th Brigade west of Mount Popa in an effort to isolate its garrison.[1] This arrangement left 32nd Brigade free to carry out its primary task as advanced guard to the division's thrust on Magwe. The other two brigades of the division were at Meiktila and Wundwin; they were about to be relieved by 19th Division which had one brigade on the Kalaw road east of Thazi and the other two on the railway, one south-east and one north of Wundwin.[2] All three brigades were involved in small-scale fighting with enemy escaping south-east, capturing guns, vehicles and a few tanks. The 36th Division was deployed behind 19th Division with one brigade at Kume, a second divided between Kyaukse and Mandalay and the third still back at Maymyo.

By the 12th April 14th Army had deployed five divisions for its drive on Rangoon on the general line Letse–Kyaukpadaung–Zayetkon–Pyawbwe: the 7th astride the Irrawaddy closing on the Chauk–Yenangyaung oilfields, the 20th pushing south for Magwe, the 5th beginning to pass through the 17th making for Pyinmana, and the 19th ready to follow up IV Corps and cover its left flank. The pursuit had begun.

To provide continuous close support for the very rapid advance which was expected to take place, the R.A.F. began to redeploy on the 12th April. A mobile advanced group control centre was formed with orders to take position alongside the most forward short-range wing. There were two of these (906 and 909) in support of IV Corps and one (907) in support of XXXIII Corps. In the Irrawaddy valley, 907 Wing was to move from Sinthe to Magwe and thence to Prome as these places were captured. On the Rangoon road, 909 and 906 Wings were to 'leapfrog' in turn to Meiktila, Pyinmana, Toungoo, Nyaunglebin and Mingaladon (Rangoon).[3] As might be expected, the control centre moved with the direct advance along the Rangoon road and controlled 907 Wing in the Irrawaddy valley by wireless and liaison officers. The main 14th Army/221 Group Headquarters, which was to be set up in Meiktila as soon as possible, was to exercise direct control over the long-range 908 and 910 Wings (Mosquitos and Thunderbolts) and indirect control over the short-range wings through the advanced group control centre.

A.L.F.S.E.A.'s deception plans for this phase of 14th Army's

---

[1] This relief was part of the exchange of British and Indian battalions between 20th and 36th Divisions to make the latter an all-British division. See Appendix 18.

[2] See Map 3, facing page 55.

[3] 909 Wing flew into Meiktila airfield on the 12th April.

operations depended mainly on the R.A.F. which, with the help of the Royal Navy, was to simulate an assault on Bassein; and, with the help of Force 136 and its guerrilla bands, the American O.S.S. and 'D' Division (strategical and tactical deception units), all of which had representatives at 14th Army Headquarters, it was also to create the impression that paratroops were being dropped along the Thazi–Taunggyi–Loilem road to isolate and destroy all Japanese forces to the north of it. Although for a time it seemed that this operation, known as 'Conclave', was achieving some success and it was even reported that Japanese were retreating towards the Salween, it was in fact ineffective. The Japanese either ignored it or were unaware of it.

As 14th Army began its drive south down the Irrawaddy valley and the Rangoon road, it passed from the dry belt into an area of maximum rainfall, and the monsoon was approaching. The operations in the chapters which follow took place under gradually worsening weather conditions, which have been described by one who took part:

> 'The heavy storms of the pre-monsoon period rapidly made all unmetalled roads impassable to wheels and tracks, while sudden spates turned shallow streams into waist-deep roaring torrents. Between storms the sun came out and man and beast and vegetation sweated and steamed in the lifeless, humid and superheated air. Many collapsed with heat exhaustion and battalions that a couple of months before had covered twenty-five miles or more a day and been quite prepared to go into action at the end of it, were now in no condition to mount an attack after a ten- or twelve-mile march.'

Almost every man suffered from the tortures of prickly heat or jungle sores or both. The monsoon, when it eventually arrived, made the going even worse, but the more continuous rain and cooler breezes were a relief to man and beast. For pilots and aircrews the fast-moving storms and piled-up cumulus clouds were a constant source of peril, for in a matter of moments any aircraft unlucky enough to be caught in them could be broken up. Nevertheless, countless sorties were flown in spite of warnings of danger issued by the meteorological service.

Both in the air and on land, neither peril nor hardship was allowed to slow down the tempo of the final effort to destroy the enemy, to efface the memory of the disastrous defeats of the first eighteen months of the war and to reach Rangoon before the monsoon.

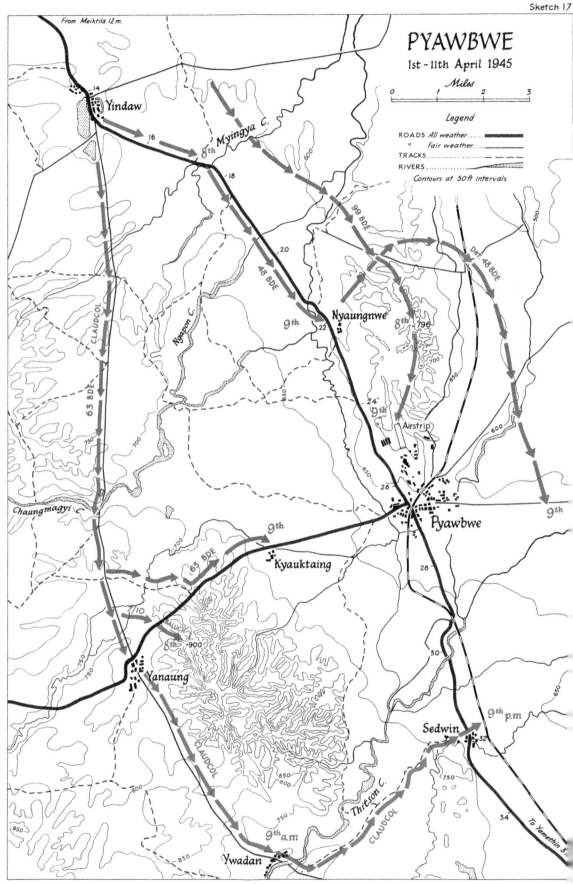

Sketch 17

PYAWBWE
1st – 11th April 1945

Miles
0   1   2   3

Legend
ROADS All weather.........
" Fair weather.....
TRACKS.............
RIVERS.............
Contours at 50ft Intervals

From Meiktila 12 m.

Yindaw
Myingya C.
8th
99 BDE
Det. 48 BDE
48 BDE
9th
Nyaungnwe
8th
796
9th
24"
9th
Airstrip
9th
Pyawbwe
Ngapon C.
CLAUDCOL
63 BDE
Chaungmagyi C.
9th
63 BDE
Kyauktaing
10
BALUCH
8th
900
Yanaung
CLAUDCOL
9th p.m
Sedwin
9th a.m
Thitson C.
CLAUDCOL
Ywadan
To Yamethin 3

CHAPTER XXXI

THE CENTRAL FRONT
(April–May 1945)
The Battle of the Irrawaddy

See Maps 7 and 11 and Sketch 19

ON the 12th April 14th Army had five divisions deployed for a double thrust on Rangoon by way of the Irrawaddy valley and the Mandalay–Rangoon road and railway, of which two (7th and 20th) were on XXXIII Corps front in the Irrawaddy valley. The 7th Division's objectives were Seikpyu and Salin on the west bank of the river and Chauk and Yenangyaung on the east. The advanced guard of 20th Division had reached Natmauk, some thirty-five miles from its objective, Magwe. The Chauk and Magwe operations would, between them, isolate Mount Popa, whose garrison was to be destroyed by 268th Brigade attacking from the west, 1st Northamptons (detached from 20th Division) under command attacking from the south, and 5th Brigade of 2nd Division attacking from the north-east.[1]

Although the Japanese had no knowledge of the forward redeployment of 221 Group R.A.F., they were well aware that 14th Army had begun a drive south and where its forward units were. The defeat at Pyawbwe meant that the right sector of *Burma Area Army's* resistance line was crumbling; this presented a grave threat to Sakurai (*28th Army*), many of whose troops were still in Arakan and would be trapped should 14th Army succeed in driving south down the Rangoon road and Irrawaddy valley. When he heard of the defeat at Pyawbwe, Sakurai took steps on the 12th to enable him to extricate his forces still in Arakan: he instructed the *Kantetsu Group* (Ohara), now consisting of *72nd I.M.B.* and the *Kanjo Force (I/ and II/112th Battalions)*,[2] to continue to hold the Mount Popa and Yenangyaung areas,[3] and warned Miyazaki (*54th Division*) to be prepared to hold the Salin–Sidoktaya area west of the Irrawaddy and to withdraw three battalions from Arakan to Allanmyo. On the same day he moved his headquarters from Allanmyo to a village on the Prome railway forty miles north-west of Rangoon, so that he would be in

---

[1] See page 366 and Map 7, facing page 171.
[2] For the *Katsu Force* see page 377.   [3] See pages 364–65.

closer touch with *Headquarters Burma Area Army*.[1] On the 13th he visited Kimura to obtain permission, should the Allies advance south of Toungoo, for the withdrawal of *28th Army* to the Pegu Yomas, from where he proposed to carry out guerrilla operations. At the same time he urged that *Headquarters Burma Area Army* should be moved to the Shan plateau, but to this Kimura would not agree, giving as his reason his intention to hold Rangoon to the last. Sakurai had no delusions about the shape of things to come, and his foresight undoubtedly saved *28th Army* from complete destruction in the Irrawaddy valley.

The XXXIII Corps began to close on the Chauk–Yenangyaung oilfields on the 13th April when 33rd Brigade of 7th Division, having completed the occupation of Kyaukpadaung, turned west to attack Chauk from the south and east in conjunction with 89th Brigade from the north. It was realized that 114th Brigade, west of the river, would not be able to co-operate in the operation by taking Seikpyu, as it was still engaged in clearing the area around Letse and the one battalion advancing on Seikpyu had made little progress.[2] On the 14th, quickly overcoming the spirited resistance of its small garrison, 33rd Brigade (Pugh) occupied Gwegyo, the junction of the roads from Chauk and Kyaukpadaung to Yenangyaung. Having handed over Kyaukpadaung to 268th Brigade,[3] and Gwegyo to 7/2nd Punjab (7th Division reconnaissance battalion), 33rd Brigade got ready to close on Chauk from east and south.

Chauk, with its oilfield and network of roads, was situated in a triangular group of hills in the angle between the Irrawaddy and the Pyinma Chaung, some five miles deep from its apex to its four-mile-wide base. Spurs from the main ridge, which formed the east side of the triangle, ran west to the Irrawaddy and ended in cliffs. Between the spurs there were usually sheer-sided ravines and this, combined with the fact that there was no vegetation to give cover to attackers, made the area ideal for defence by small numbers. A commanding hill on the main ridge near the south-east corner of the triangle dominated most of the area and was expected to be held strongly. Patrols, however, found it unoccupied and, during the night of the 16th/17th, 4/15th Punjab and 4/1st Gurkhas were rushed up in lorries and occupied the whole feature. Although during the day there were rumours that the Japanese were evacuating Chauk, 89th Brigade found Singu and the north end of the Chauk ridge still held. On the

---

[1] See Map 11, facing page 414.
[2] See page 365.
[3] Kyaukpadaung was taken over by 1st Chamar Regiment just released by corps from airfield protection duty at Myitche.

18th it became clear that the enemy, instead of withdrawing as expected into the arms of 33rd Brigade, had crossed the river to Seikpyu, but 114th Brigade, though aware of the movement, was too far away to intercept effectively. The escaping columns were attacked by aircraft and artillery fire, but they got away with little loss. Evans now ordered 114th Brigade to push south as fast as possible to Salin, 33rd Brigade to advance on Yenangyaung with its left covered by 7/2nd Punjab from Gwegyo, and 89th Brigade to concentrate at Chauk in divisional reserve.[1]

At this stage the Japanese resistance on Mount Popa collapsed. The 268th Brigade had attacked on the 13th with its two available battalions, 1/3rd Madras and the Nepalese Mahindra Dal Regiment. The strong Japanese artillery was active, and on the night of the 14th/15th a bush fire started by it forced 1/3rd Madras to vacate its positions. The battalion, instead of withdrawing, moved forward and so escaped the artillery concentration put down behind the fire, but much of its transport was burned. Both battalions made steady progress, although frequently subjected to heavy and accurate artillery fire. On the 19th, the left battalion made contact with 5th Brigade north of Mount Popa and the right battalion gained a footing on the ridge running south from it, where 1st Northamptons, advancing from Zayetkon, made contact with it. As darkness fell on the 19th, fires broke out all over the mountain as the Japanese destroyed their stores. The 268th Brigade, closing in, intercepted many parties of retreating Japanese during the 20th, and captured five 105-mm. guns and seventeen 3-ton lorries.

On the 12th Gracey (20th Division) had told Woodford (32nd Brigade), whose advanced guard had reached Natmauk that same day,[2] to take Taungdwingyi, the meeting point of the rail and road connections between the Irrawaddy and Sittang valleys. At the same time he brought 80th Brigade (Taunton) up from Zayetkon, and ordered it to fork south-west at Natmauk for Magwe, and placed 150th R.A.C., a squadron of 11th Cavalry and two companies of 3/4th Bombay Grenadiers under its command. Taungdwingyi, which the enemy made no attempt to hold, was occupied on the 15th, its garrison escaping west to Magwe. The leading troops of 80th Brigade reached the northern outskirts of Magwe on the 19th, surprising a mixed force of Japanese and *I.N.A.* A few were killed, most of the *I.N.A.* surrendered and the rest of the force withdrew to the southern part of the town. By nightfall all the roads leading into Magwe were blocked, but 80th Brigade's blocks on the north were soon attacked from the direction of Yenangyaung. The attackers

---

[1] See Sketch 19, facing page 400.
[2] The 32nd Brigade's advanced guard consisted of 9/14th Punjab, two squadrons 11th Cavalry (armoured cars) and a squadron of 7th Light Cavalry (light tanks).

disappeared at dawn, leaving twelve abandoned lorries, eighty-five dead,[1] and five prisoners-of-war from whom it was learned that there were about 1,000 Japanese in Yenangyaung unaware that Magwe had been taken. On the 20th, 150th R.A.C. with two companies of 3/4th Bombay Grenadiers mopped up south Magwe and captured a whole battalion of *I.N.A.* 650 strong with eleven guns, mostly anti-aircraft, and large quantities of stores. It had been thought that, after taking Magwe, 20th Division might have to turn north to help take Yenangyaung, but, as will be seen, this was unnecessary and 20th Division was able to continue its advance on Allanmyo.

It was on this day, the 20th April, as XXXIII Corps broke into Magwe and IV Corps cleared Pyinmana and Lewe,[2] thus securing for 14th Army both ends of the only all-weather lateral route across the Pegu Yomas, that Slim issued an instruction to Stopford and Messervy giving details of the coming amphibious attack on Rangoon. Its contents were not to be divulged to anyone below principal staff officers at corps and divisional headquarters. The instruction ended by telling corps commanders to make a supreme effort to capture Prome and Toungoo respectively as quickly as possible.

The terrain at Yenangyaung was similar to that at Chauk. It consisted of a rectangle six by four miles, surrounded on three sides by bare, eroded hills rising to about 600 feet and on the fourth by the Irrawaddy. Within it lay a maze of deep ravines separating the three main east-west spurs. A network of excellent roads covered the area and air photographs showed that the spurs overlooking all road junctions were heavily entrenched, as were the possible river beaches. A mass of oil derricks, damaged buildings, power houses, oil storage tanks and a large built-up area completed the picture. Its capture looked like being a formidable task. Evans's plan of attack was for 33rd Brigade (Pugh) to deploy on the north and east face of the area, while 89th Brigade (Crowther), moving wide to the east, came in from the south and south-east. Supported by every available gun and aircraft, both brigades were to attack simultaneously. The 1st Queen's, leading 33rd Brigade, reached the Pin Chaung, which marked the north edge of the oilfield, on the morning of the 20th and managed to get a strong patrol across it in spite of considerable artillery fire. Almost immediately dense clouds of smoke began to rise from all over the oilfield, indicating wholesale demolitions. Pugh at once sent back all available transport to bring up his reserve (4/15th Punjab) from Gwegyo while the Queen's crossed the chaung in strength to secure the ford. Meanwhile 4/1st Gurkhas had crossed the

---

[1] The 80th Brigade's losses were very small: three killed and ten wounded.
[2] See page 385.

Pin Chaung near its mouth and begun to work its way down the river bank towards the town.

Seeing an opportunity, Evans, instead of waiting for 89th Brigade to get into position, ordered 33rd Brigade to attack at once and switched all artillery to its support. An indication of the speed at which the order was carried out is that Stopford, on his way forward in his jeep to watch the battle, was overtaken by a medium battery moving into position. As a result, by 4.30 p.m. the Queen's had secured the shoulders of the defile through which the main road from the north entered the oilfield area. As they did so, Japanese with torches emerged from caves in the cutting, set fire to stacked petrol drums and then began to roll containers down the hillside to keep the conflagration going and the tanks out. On the 21st, while the Gurkhas making for the beaches were held up on the northern outskirts of the town, the Queen's and 4/15th Punjab attacked the eastern defences with tank and artillery support, and by 5 p.m. the town was surrounded on the landward side. To prevent the garrison from escaping across the river, as had happened at Chauk, it was arranged for patrols of Small Operations Group to operate on the river during the hours of darkness and for night-fighter aircraft to join in when the moon rose. Hopes of destroying the garrison ran high, but at this stage the weather intervened. Cloud and heavy rain reduced visibility to nothing and, though S.O.G. patrols sank one or two boats that night and artillery a few more on the morning of the 22nd, the bulk of the garrison escaped. The known enemy losses amounted to seventy dead, ten guns, twelve heavy machine-guns, a light tank and 200 motor vehicles, most of which had been made useless. Japanese dissatisfaction with the way in which *72nd I.M.B.* conducted itself in this action is to some extent justified by the fact that 33rd Brigade's losses in the attack on the town itself amounted to only seven killed and four wounded.

With a view to cutting off and destroying the Japanese opposing 114th Brigade in the Salin area and preventing their junction with the force which had withdrawn across the river from Yenangyaung, Evans ordered 89th Brigade to cross as soon as the 'river fleet' could be brought forward.[1] The infantry got across on the night of the 24th/25th April. On the morning of the 25th the tank and vehicle rafts arrived, and a squadron of Carabiniers, 136th Field Regiment, R.A., and some engineer stores were ferried to the west bank. The leading tank raft stuck on a sandbank and remained there for two days, some bulldozers and a tank 'dozed' themselves into quicksands on landing, and wheeled vehicles were marooned for some hours on the river bank by lack of motorable tracks until the engineers, as usual, were able to

---

[1] See page 362.

overcome the natural hazards. Nevertheless the brigade with most of its supporting arms was across before dark and, leaving its bogged vehicles, moved on to the road running south from Salin without further mishap.

The same day Westcol (Chin Hills Battalion and Lushai Scouts), moving along the foothills some fifteen to twenty miles to the west, was making for Sidoktaya, and 4/5th Gurkhas of 114th Brigade drove in the enemy force covering Salin. By the evening of the 25th, when 114th Brigade made contact with 89th Brigade south of Salin, there were no signs of Japanese except for some fifty dead left in the defences north of the town. Patrols from 33rd Brigade east of the river were meanwhile making for Magwe as quickly as possible to contact 20th Division.

All XXXIII Corps' first objectives having been gained, Stopford issued a brief order on the 26th April for the next phase of operations. The 20th Division was to move at once on Allanmyo and then on to Prome and Tharrawaddy, leaving all mopping-up to 268th Brigade which was placed under its command for this purpose. The 33rd Brigade of 7th Division from Yenangyaung was to take over the defence of Magwe, Allanmyo and Prome in turn as soon as each was captured. The rest of 7th Division, completely supplied by air, was to clear the west bank of the Irrawaddy in two bounds: the first to the line of the Ngape–Minbu road, thus blocking the An Pass route from Arakan, and the second to the line of the Mindon–Thayetmyo road where the Japanese withdrawing from Arakan might try to cross the Irrawaddy. The 254th Tank Brigade, less detachments with forward formations, was in reserve.

The Japanese plan to carry out a staged withdrawal on the Irrawaddy axis through Yenangyaung and Allanmyo to Prome, with *72nd I.M.B.* and part of *54th Division* from Arakan, had already been disrupted by the quick defeat at Yenangyaung and the subsequent withdrawal of its garrison across the river. This left Allanmyo and Prome virtually undefended against the rapid armour-supported thrust of 20th Division.

In the rear area of XXXIII Corps, 268th Brigade had by this time completed the mopping-up of the Mount Popa area, the scattered garrison of which was making its way southward across country in small parties, and was under orders to join 20th Division at Taungdwingyi.[1] The whole of 2nd Division, except for the rear parties of 5th Brigade which had not been withdrawn from the Mount Popa area until the 22nd, had left for India.

On the 28th April, having cleared the Salin area, 114th Brigade, with its right covered by the Chin Hills Battalion on the Mwe

---

[1] The 268th Brigade was now back to its late 1944 composition: 4/3rd Madras Regiment, 1st Chamar Regiment and Mahindra Dal Regiment.

Chaung twenty-four miles west of Seikpyu and by the Lushai Scouts
on the Mon Chaung almost due west of Salin, moved south on a broad
front. The same day the leading troops (2nd K.O.S.B.) of 89th
Brigade, which had been moving south along the west bank of the
Irrawaddy, were within eight miles of Minbu, and 33rd Brigade was
at Yenangyaung ready to move to Magwe. The 100th Brigade (20th
Division), moving by the main road through Nyaungbintha, reached
Allanmyo that day, while 32nd Brigade, having handed over
Taungdwingyi to 268th Brigade, was close behind it, and 80th
Brigade, advancing south along the river bank from Magwe, was
about half-way (twenty-eight miles) to Allanmyo and had taken the
surrender of 500 men of the *I.N.A.* The 100th Brigade met only
sporadic opposition, but west of the river the opposition to 89th
Brigade increased steadily as it approached the Man Chaung, which
enters the Irrawaddy a few miles north of Minbu.

The same day (28th) Slim told Stopford that, having seized Prome,
he was to destroy any enemy forces attempting to escape eastwards
across the Irrawaddy and push on to Rangoon with the largest force
which he could maintain. The limiting factors were that, out of his
air supply allotment of 450 tons a day, only the forty-five tons which
came from Akyab could be delivered to Prome without loss. The remaining 405 tons, which had to come from Chittagong, could not be
delivered south of Magwe without the loss of a tenth for each thirty
miles further south. This meant that no more than a brigade could
make for Rangoon, and even that would mean making economies
elsewhere. It was therefore evident that XXXIII Corps' advance on
Rangoon could be only a diversion to assist IV Corps and 'Dracula'.

The general concept of XXXIII Corps' operations had from the
outset been that 20th Division with an armoured spearhead would
drive south down the Allanmyo–Prome road, keeping pace with IV
Corps' advance, to cover its right, and at the same time intercept
forces trying to escape from Arakan so that 7th Division could destroy
them west of the Irrawaddy. After the capture of Pyinmana and the
dispersal of *33rd Army* on the 20th, IV Corps' advance had outpaced
that of XXXIII Corps, so on the 30th Stopford held a conference at
Allanmyo with Evans (7th Division), Gracey (20th Division) and
Dyer (268th Brigade) to consider means of speeding up the advance
and continuing it to Rangoon. The outcome was that on the 1st May
Gracey ordered 100th Brigade (Rodham), with the Carabiniers
less one squadron and a squadron of 11th Cavalry (armoured cars)
under command, to seize Prome. As soon as Prome was secured,
32nd Brigade (Woodford) with an armoured advanced guard was
to pass through and make for Rangoon, while 80th Brigade
(Taunton) established a cordon along the Allanmyo–Prome road.
The 268th Brigade was to cross the river to Thayetmyo to intercept

Japanese forces withdrawing before 7th Division and assist in their destruction.

On 7th Division's front west of the Irrawaddy, the forward troops of 89th Brigade, consisting of 2nd K.O.S.B. with a squadron of Carabiniers operating westwards along the Minbu–Ngape road, were involved in two actions between the 29th April and the 1st May with Japanese using hidden single guns at point-blank range to stop tanks, which in this hilly and forested country were confined to the road. This determined opposition lent colour to a reliable report of 4,000 Japanese from Arakan collecting at Padan, whose eventual destination would undoubtedly be Thayetmyo. Evans now decided to intercept this force with 89th Brigade, and then destroy it by a southward sweep by 114th Brigade from the Salin area. He divided the country west of the Irrawaddy into two brigade sectors, the dividing line being the fair-weather road running westwards from Minhla to Yenanma. On the 1st May he ordered 89th Brigade (Crowther) to hand over the Minbu–Ngape road to 114th Brigade (Dinwiddie) and move south along the river bank to Minhla and thence south-west to Yenanma and Shandatkyi. He also told Crowther that he was not to leave that area until he was sure that the whole Japanese force caught between the two brigades had been destroyed or dispersed. The 33rd Brigade (Pugh), based on Magwe on the east bank, was to be in divisional reserve and prevent any Japanese escaping across the river into the Pegu Yomas behind 20th Division.

Between the 1st and 3rd May, 114th Brigade combed the northern sector southwards as far as the Minbu–Ngape road and met very little opposition. On reaching the road, 4/5th Royal Gurkhas was ordered to take over the Carabinier squadron and the responsibility for the road from 2nd K.O.S.B., which was then to move south with 89th Brigade. For some days the weather had been deteriorating, and torrential rain on the 3rd temporarily brought everyone to a standstill.[1] By the 5th, however, conditions had improved and the advance of both brigades was resumed. Fighting flared up when the Gurkhas found the ridge astride the road north-east of Padan held. Their advanced guard was ambushed, a tank was destroyed, the artillery forward observation officer was killed and two officers of the Gurkhas wounded. A battalion attack was quickly mounted and the enemy driven off the ridge, leaving behind forty-seven dead. Also on the 5th, twenty-five miles to the south-east, the vanguard company of 1/11th Sikhs, leading 89th Brigade, came face to face in Yenanma with a similar force of Japanese. The Sikhs, charging with Bren guns blazing, scattered the Japanese, killing twenty-one and taking one prisoner. From these two actions it looked as though 89th Brigade had

---

[1] This was the day 26th Division occupied Rangoon.

arrived in time to cut the line of retreat of the Japanese force reported at Padan. There ensued a pause while 89th Brigade hurried forward its rear battalions to close both the Yenanma and Shandatkyi routes and the Japanese concentrated for a break-through. Meanwhile 268th Brigade, under orders to seize Thayetmyo, got a battalion across the Irrawaddy against slight opposition to the west bank a few miles north of Allanmyo, which the rest of the brigade took over from 20th Division.

By the 16th April Sakurai had realized that his orders of the 12th would have to be modified in order to speed up the withdrawal of *54th Division* from Arakan.[1] An essential part of any plan for the withdrawal from Arakan was that Yenangyaung and Mount Popa should be held until the main body of *54th Division* had concentrated in the Irrawaddy valley. The arrival of a strong and aggressive force of armour and infantry in the Natmauk area within striking distance of Magwe, of which he was now aware, meant that communications to his forces at Yenangyaung and Mount Popa were in great danger. To deal with this situation and to comply with *Burma Area Army's* instructions regarding the defence of Prome and the road from there to Rangoon, Sakurai issued fresh orders on the 16th. Miyazaki was to withdraw with the main body of *54th Division* from the An area to Allanmyo, take up a position on the east bank of the Irrawaddy covering Allanmyo and block the roads from Arakan at Mindon and the Taungup pass. The *Kantetsu Group* (*72nd I.M.B.* at Yenangyaung and the *Kanjo Force* at Mount Popa) was to stand fast until Miyazaki reached Allanmyo, and then itself withdraw to Prome on orders of Ohara, the group commander. Two battalions of *121st Regiment* and an artillery battalion from Taungup were to move to Okpo as reserve under direct command of *28th Army*, the move to begin on the 21st April and be completed by the 29th. The *Katsu Force* (*II/* and *III/-153rd Battalions* of *49th Division*) and the *Shin-i Force* of *55th Division* were to come under Miyazaki's command; the latter, which was on the road north-east of Allanmyo, was to cover the town pending Miyazaki's arrival there.[2] The three infantry battalions which had been ordered to Allanmyo on the 12th were to revert to command of *54th Division*.

On the 17th April Miyazaki issued his orders. His northern group, leaving one battalion (*II/111th*) as rearguard covering An, was to

---

[1] See pages 369–70.

[2] The *Shin-i Force* consisted of *I/143rd Battalion, 55th Reconnaissance Regiment* (less one company), one mountain artillery battalion (less one battery), a platoon each of heavy field artillery and engineers, and a transport detachment. It was formed in January to assume responsibility for the Allanmyo–Prome area where it was thought the Allies might make airborne landings.

withdraw to Thayetmyo in two columns by way of Ngape, Padan and Yenanma. The leading column (*Headquarters 154th Regiment, I/111th and III/154th Battalions* and some artillery) was to move on the 19th April, and the main body of the force (*Headquarters 111th Regiment, III/111th Battalion* and *54th Reconnaissance Regiment*) was to follow with divisional headquarters and the bulk of the divisional field artillery and engineer regiments. The *Koba Force* was to hold the Salin–Sidoktaya area until the main body of the division, withdrawing from An, had passed through Padan, and was then to become the rearguard and cover its retreat to Thayetmyo. His southern group was to send one battalion (*II/121st*) to Pyalo on the 21st April and the rest of *121st Regiment* on the 29th to Okpo.

The success of *28th Army's* plan of withdrawal was jeopardized at an early stage by the loss of Chauk, Yenangyaung and Mount Popa. The *Kantetsu Group* (*72nd I.M.B.* and the *Kanjo Force*), which was to have delayed any advance by XXXIII Corps on Allanmyo long enough to enable Miyazaki to get there unopposed, had disintegrated. All four battalions of *72nd I.M.B.* had crossed to the west bank in some disorder, and the *Kanjo Force*, after evacuating Mount Popa, was scattered and completely out of touch. Miyazaki, commanding the forces west of the Irrawaddy, was now faced with the probability of having to fight his way across the Irrawaddy valley to the Pegu Yomas and the possibility of having to make an opposed crossing of the river itself.

Miyazaki and his headquarters reached Padan on the 24th April, and it would seem that on arrival he heard of the loss of Yenangyaung, which exposed his northern flank, because he sent *III/111th Battalion* to block the Minbu–Padan road and *54th Reconnaissance Battalion* to Kyunbya to block the Minbu–Yenanma road. The former was to rejoin Miyazaki when relieved by the *Koba Force* and the latter was to come under its command. Koba was to hold both positions till the main body was clear of Yenanma. The *II/111th Battalion* left at An as rearguard was to begin to withdraw on the 1st May. The *Katsu Force* (*153rd Regiment* less one battalion) was to withdraw independently to Thayetmyo through Seikpyu.

The leading column of Miyazaki's force reached Thayetmyo on the evening of the 28th April, only to learn that its final objective, Allanmyo, had been lost that day. However, by this time Sakurai (*28th Army*) knew that *Headquarters Burma Area Army* had left Rangoon for Moulmein on the 23rd and all wireless communication with it had ceased. Coming to the conclusion that to fight for the Allanmyo–Prome area was futile, he decided to move *28th Army* into the Pegu Yomas at once. The object of Miyazaki's leading column now became that of securing a bridgehead across the Irrawaddy at any suitable place as quickly as possible. The *III/154th Battalion* was therefore sent southwards to find an alternative site to Allanmyo and, having crossed the Irrawaddy near Pyalo, fought an action with units of 100th Brigade advancing on Prome. The *I/111th Battalion*, however, remained west of the Irrawaddy to await the arrival of Miyazaki and the main body, which had left Padan on the 26th. On the 1st May, Miyazaki was joined by the *Katsu Force* (now a composite battalion formed from the remnants of the two battalions of *153rd Regiment*) on the road ten miles west of Thayetmyo. The force cut off by the arrival of 89th Brigade at Yenanma was the rearguard of Miyazaki's force, consisting of the *Koba Force* (*154th Regiment* less one battalion), *II/111th Battalion*, *III/111th Battalion*, *54th Reconnaissance Battalion* and some engineers and transport with 700 sick and wounded. With Miyazaki, north-west of Thayetmyo, were *I/111th Battalion*, the composite battalion of *153rd Regiment* and the bulk of the divisional artillery and engineers. East of the river he had *III/154th Battalion* and *I/143rd Battalion* which, after being joined by *II/121st Battalion* from Taungup, had ineffectively tried to prevent 20th Division from taking Allanmyo. These three battalions then took up positions in the hills on the east bank covering the selected crossing place at Kama pending the arrival of *54th Division* and formations under its command.[1] It was the 6th May before the column from Thayetmyo assembled at Kama, and by then Koba with the rearguard was fighting his way out of the trap set by Evans in the Shandatkyi area. Miyazaki, having secured a bridgehead, decided to await Koba's arrival before making his break-through to the Pegu Yomas.

In 20th Division's sector, 100th Brigade (Rodham) had a short but grim fight near Pyalo on the 1st May in which 14/13th F.F. Rifles, 1/1st Gurkhas and a squadron of Carabiniers took part. The Japanese, though outnumbered, fought desperately, and on several occasions men with explosives strapped to them threw themselves in the path of tanks, with little effect. On the 3rd May the brigade entered Prome from the north and east; there was no fighting and some 400 I.N.A. surrendered. That evening, as news of the capture of Rangoon was received,[2] 1/1st Gurkhas and the Carabiniers reached Shwedaung, and patrols of 4/10th Gurkhas crossed the river and began to work their way along the Taungup road, where they were soon in contact with small parties of Japanese. On the 5th, 32nd Brigade passed through 100th Brigade outposts at Shwedaung on the Rangoon road with orders to extend the cordon, which already stretched from Allanmyo (268th Brigade) through Dayindabo (80th

---

[1] Two battalions of *72nd I.M.B.* (*542nd* and *543rd*) had already withdrawn through Thayetmyo and linked up with *121st Regiment* (less *II/121st Battalion*) from Taungup.

[2] A unit war diary recording the fact says that 'the announcement was received with interest'—a good example of the small impact which events on other fronts have on troops in action.

Brigade) and Prome (100th Brigade) to Shwedaung. The same day 80th Brigade sank ten out of twelve boatloads of Japanese seen crossing the river at Kama,[1] but only one boatload which had stranded in shallows was recovered, with fifteen bodies in it.

On the 6th May Stopford held a second conference at Allanmyo at which he outlined the pattern of operations on the Irrawaddy front for the next three weeks. The Japanese trying to cross the Irrawaddy from west to east had up to date consisted mainly of administrative troops and sick, but fighting troops were now beginning to arrive in increasing numbers. It was expected that the enemy would use two main escape routes: a northern one by way of Kama to Paukkaung, twenty-two miles east-north-east of Prome, and a southern by way of Shwedaung to Pauktaw, twenty-eight miles south-east of Prome. By alertness and aggressive action at all levels the greatest possible loss was to be inflicted on them and every care taken to prevent them from capturing stores, particularly food. There were therefore to be no night convoys on any of the roads in the escape area, and every precaution was to be taken to ensure that roads about to be used by convoys during daylight were clear of the enemy.

By the 6th May the last Japanese had left Arakan; 82nd (W.A.) Division, now under direct control of A.L.F.S.E.A., was about to go into monsoon quarters at Taungup, while 22nd (E.A.) Brigade was preparing to cross the Arakan Yomas by way of the Taungup–Prome road to join XXXIII Corps. The Japanese had delayed their evacuation of Arakan too long, and in consequence the main body of *54th Division*, split into two parts, was trapped west of the Irrawaddy. The same day XXXIII Corps' orders for the establishment of a cordon on the east bank of the river began to take effect, and 7th Division was hurrying the rest of 89th Brigade to Shandatkyi to ensure that *54th Division's* rearguard under Koba could not rejoin its main body without heavy loss. *Headquarters 28th Army* was in the Pegu Yomas with elements of *54th* and *55th Divisions* and various administrative units. Sakurai could do nothing to help the main body of *54th Division* cross the Irrawaddy, for the few mobile troops he had were being sought out and attacked by 20th Division. To the east, IV Corps was also beginning to lay a cordon in the Sittang valley to ensure that *28th Army*, even if it succeeded in concentrating a considerable force in the Pegu Yomas, would not be able to link up with *33rd* and *15th Armies*.

Isolated, with its two wings separated by the wide Irrawaddy, which was under constant observation by air, by river patrols and by strong mobile forces, and its only refuge the barren, trackless thorn scrub-covered Pegu Yomas, *28th Army* was doomed, unless *33rd Army* could at least temporarily break the IV Corps cordon and open an escape route.

---

[1] It was at Kama that the main body of *54th Division* and the remnants of *72nd I.M.B.* later crossed the Irrawaddy.

CHAPTER XXXII

THE CENTRAL FRONT
(April–May 1945)
The Battle of the Rangoon Road and the
Reoccupation of Rangoon

See Maps 7, 11 and 13 and Sketches 18 and 19

ON the 10th April, as 17th Division and the powerful armoured column from 255th Tank Brigade closed on Pyawbwe, Honda's shattered *33rd Army* began its retreat, hoping to re-form and offer battle at Shwemyo and the Sinthe Chaung.[1] The tenacity of the Japanese forces and the heavy losses incurred by them in attempting to hold Pyawbwe were in vain, for the trap had closed on them and they were unable to extricate themselves in good order. From this moment the speed of IV Corps' advance steadily increased, and Honda's troops were hustled out of all the positions he hoped to hold before they had time to occupy them properly, and every attempt to make a stand resulted in increased confusion. The position of the Japanese forces in the Pyawbwe area was somewhat similar to that of the British force in Rangoon in March 1942, which escaped unscathed only because the Japanese in their hurry to reach the city left its line of retreat open for twenty-four hours.[2] Messervy made no such mistake. As early as the 7th April he had 5th Division (Mansergh) ready, as soon as Pyawbwe was clear, to take up the pursuit with orders to seize Toungoo and its all-weather airfield by the 25th at all costs, and then drive on to the Pyu area to cover the establishment by 19th Division of a firm base and airhead at Toungoo from which the final thrust on Rangoon could be maintained.

On the 7th, 123rd Brigade (Denholm-Young) of 5th Division, with 3/9th Jats and an armoured advanced guard under command,[3] moved south from Meiktila, with a battalion group (2/1st Punjab with armour and artillery) covering its left flank. Although 17th

---

[1] See page 360, and Map 7, facing page 171.
[2] See Volume II, pages 97–99.
[3] The armoured advanced guard consisted of 116th R.A.C. (medium tanks) less one squadron, 7th Light Cavalry (light tanks) less two squadrons, one squadron 16th Light Cavalry (armoured cars), 18th (S.P.) Field Regiment less two batteries, one battery 5th Mahratta Anti-Tank Regiment, two companies 1/17th Dogras carried on tanks, one company 4th Bombay Grenadiers, a V.C.P. and artillery and engineer reconnaissance parties.

Division had passed over the ground, the flank guard at once ran into fierce opposition, which it had only just overcome when 123rd Brigade was told to take up the pursuit. Even then, the last of the enemy on the flank had not been seen, for on the 10th, when the brigade began to move forward to pass through 17th Division, the leading troops of the flank guard fell into an ambush three miles east of Pyawbwe in an area they believed to be in possession of 17th Division. In spite of this early set-back, the day's fighting ended in the capture of five guns (including two 155-mm. howitzers), a dozen lorries and an ammunition dump. On the 11th, as the brigade approached Yamethin, the flank guard was withdrawn into the main body, a move which proved to be premature, for that evening, when the leading group of the main body tried to follow the advanced guard through Yamethin, it found the road blocked and came under heavy fire from enemy who appeared in the eastern part of the town. The brigade was forced to harbour for the night north of Yamethin, five miles from its advanced guard which was already to the south of the town. Early on the 12th the brigade harbour was machine-gunned by low-flying Japanese aircraft; this attack caused few casualties, but the solitary bomb which was dropped hit a petrol lorry and the ensuing fire destroyed twenty-eight vehicles, including several petrol and ammunition lorries.

All efforts to infiltrate into Yamethin during the morning of the 12th having failed, a deliberate attack with heavy air and artillery support was made in the afternoon by 7th York and Lancaster and 3/9th Jats, but by 4.30 p.m. this too was held up. During the night the Jats north-west of the town were vigorously attacked twice; in the morning, however, they hit back and cleared the town west of the road, thus enabling 2/1st Punjab and a squadron of 116th R.A.C. to break through and make contact with the advanced guard. Since 7th York and Lancaster was unsuccessful in its efforts to clear the eastern section of Yamethin, it remained impossible for unarmoured vehicles to drive through the town until 2/1st Punjab, attacking from the west and south-west with tank support, cleared it by midday on the 14th.[1] The capture of Yamethin cost 123rd Brigade 126 casualties; 116th R.A.C. lost two tanks, and about eighty dead Japanese were found. Information obtained during the fighting indicated that there were only about a hundred Japanese in Yamethin when the advanced guard passed through, but that a column of about 400 to 500 had arrived from the east soon after firing began.[2] To IV Corps, already nine days behind schedule,[3] the delay at Yamethin was serious, so, while mopping-up was still going on, 161st Brigade (Brigadier E. H.

[1] See Sketch 19, facing page 400.
[2] This column presumably came from *18th Division* which, in accordance with Honda's orders, was withdrawing to Shwemyo, by-passing Yamethin to the east.
[3] See page 360.

65. Mount Popa from the north-west. Summit not visible, crater in saddle

66. Looking west from the summit of Mount Popa. Lip of crater right foreground, Pyinma Chaung in the distance

67. Chauk oilfield

68. Yenangyaung. Burnt storage tanks and camouflage of one on fire

69. Paddy fields near Prome

70. Motors and a Stuart tank bogged near Prome

71. Remains of Yamethin railway station

72. Jeep train on the Myingyan–Meiktila railway

73. Transport crossing an extemporised bridge over the Pyu River

74. Japanese prisoners taken at Penwegon

75. Major-General E. C. R. Mansergh,
5th Indian Division

76. Major-General H. M. Chambers,
26th Indian Division

77. Gurkha paratroops dropping to
attack Elephant Point

78. Japanese machine-gun post at
Elephant Point

79. Landing Craft on the Rangoon River

80. Vice-Admiral H. C. T. Walker,
2nd in Command, East Indies Fleet

Grimshaw) was given control of the armoured advanced guard and by 1 p.m. on the 14th was on its way south.[1] Before describing its advance it is of interest to see what 19th and 36th Divisions, behind IV Corps, had been doing, and how the Japanese withdrawal, as ordered on the 9th April,[2] was progressing.

During the fighting at Pyawbwe and Yamethin, 19th Division, less 64th Brigade, was east and north of Wundwin rounding up parties of Japanese trying to make their way into the mountains to the east, while 64th Brigade, in co-operation with 9th Brigade of 5th Division at Thazi, was closely engaged with Japanese in the Hlaingdet area.[3] The clearance of this area by 64th Brigade on the 13th April and the departure of the last brigade of 20th Division from Meiktila towards the Irrawaddy valley enabled 19th Division (Rees) to concentrate forward for its next task; this, in turn, freed 9th Brigade to rejoin 5th Division, now leading the corps advance with Toungoo as its main objective. As 19th Division moved forward, 36th Division was, on Slim's orders, to take over the areas it vacated, concentrate in the Thazi area and send one brigade to operate eastwards along the Kalaw road. The division was to be maintained by road from Meiktila. As no extra airlift was available, supply-dropping had to be limited to the forward troops of the brigade on the Kalaw road. On the 16th April Rees ordered 62nd Brigade (Brigadier G. H. B. Beyts[4]) to Yamethin, the 98th (Jerrard) to Pyawbwe, and the 64th (Flewett) to Meiktila as soon as possible after its relief on the Kalaw road by 36th Division. The general concept of operations was that as 5th Division moved forward from Yamethin the 19th would move into position in depth behind it, the 36th would take over the final clearing up of the country north and east of Meiktila, and the 17th would be reorganized in readiness to resume the lead in IV Corps' advance on Rangoon as soon as the 5th had reached its final objective, Pyu.

Honda's order of the 9th April for the withdrawal of *33rd Army* from Pyawbwe to the Shwemyo–Sinthe Chaung positions was compromised from the very beginning, since its timing coincided with the surrounding of the bulk of his forces in the Pyawbwe–Yanaung area. By the time that the battered *18th* and *53rd Divisions* and *Headquarters 33rd Army* escaped from the trap which was closing on them at Pyawbwe, 123rd Brigade was attacking Yamethin and threatening a second encirclement. Although the Japanese rearguard at Yamethin

---

[1] Grimshaw had succeeded Poole on the 3rd March.
[2] See page 360.
[3] See page 361.
[4] Beyts commanded in the absence of Morris from the 3rd April until the 15th June.

managed to hold up the advance throughout the 12th and 13th, 5th Division's advanced guard was probing the Sinthe Chaung positions before *18th* and *53rd Divisions* had fully occupied them. This and the fact that the almost dry Sinthe Chaung was found to be of little value as an obstacle made Honda decide on the 16th to withdraw to Pyinmana, which he had been given to believe was held by the main body of *55th Division*.[1] Both divisions were to carry out fighting withdrawals: the *18th* to positions east and the *53rd* to positions west of Pyinmana, co-ordinating their dispositions with those of *55th Division*. The order did not reach *49th Division*, which was to take post behind *18th Division*.[2]

It will be recalled that 161st Brigade passed through Yamethin on the 14th April within an hour of its capture. By 4 p.m. its armoured advanced guard was in contact with the Japanese on the Sinthe Chaung twenty-two miles to the south. It was too late to mount an attack that evening, and the brigade formed harbour for the night astride the road and railway near Tatkon, some two miles north of the chaung crossing.[3] The next morning the advanced guard was held up at Shwemyo village, and when the main body of 161st Brigade reached the chaung it became involved with enemy holding the escarpment east of the road, which became known as the Shwemyo bluff. Mansergh, who had estimated that to reach Toungoo on time he had to occupy Pyinmana by the 15th, now decided to bring up 123rd Brigade to attack the Shwemyo bluff while the 161st pushed on to Pyinmana, and ordered the divisional engineers to make a track to enable it to by-pass Shwemyo to the west. On the 16th the armoured advanced guard broke into Shwemyo village, but Japanese from the bluff, evading the armour, attacked the engineers making the by-pass, so little progress was made that day. On the 17th, 123rd Brigade cleared the bluff, but the 161st, which had by-passed the village, got only a short way beyond it before being again held up. Mansergh now gave 161st Brigade a squadron of 5th (Probyn's) Horse (medium tanks), but in spite of this only six miles were gained on the 18th. On this day, desperately concerned lest 14th Army should fail to reach Toungoo in time to open its airfields for the sup-

---

[1] The main body of *55th Division* (*144th Regiment, III/112th Battalion*, one battalion *55th Mountain Artillery Regiment*, and *55th Engineer, Transport* and *Signal Regiments* less detachments) began to move from south-west Burma to the Rangoon road in mid-March. Its first unit reached Toungoo on the 31st March and became involved in quelling a revolt of the Burma National Army (see page 388). On the 10th April *144th Regiment* was ordered to the Sinthe Chaung, but most of it got no farther than Pyinmana.

[2] Honda had lost touch with *49th Division* (less *153rd Regiment* on the Irrawaddy front) when what was left of it withdrew from Yindaw, and regained it only during the action at Toungoo over a fortnight later.

[3] An airhead was opened at Tatkon on the 20th April; see Appendix 23.

port of 'Dracula', Mountbatten paid a visit to the Central front. He saw both Slim at Monywa and Messervy at Meiktila and urged them to speed the advance at any cost. The reasons for Mountbatten's anxiety are understandable but, as it turned out, his visit was unnecessary. Everyone was already doing his best to reach Toungoo on time and, in fact, the outcome of the battle had been decided by the fighting of the previous five days and by orders issued by 5th Division early on the 18th for the encirclement of Pyinmana. By the morning of the 19th it became evident that *33rd Army* had reached breaking-point.

During the night of the 18/19th the Japanese attacked 161st Brigade (Grimshaw) on the road and the 123rd in the hills to the east, but it soon became clear that these were but diversions to cover the beginning of a general retreat by both *18th* and *53rd Divisions*. By 6 a.m. on the 19th the armoured advanced guard of 161st Brigade had captured the bridge north of Pyinmana intact, although it was fully prepared for demolition, and by 7.30 a.m. had secured the airfield. While Grimshaw mounted a two-battalion (1/1st Punjab and 4/7th Rajput) attack, supported by the squadron of Probyn's Horse at his disposal, on Pyinmana town, the advanced guard by-passed it and, in a village six miles south of the town, fell on a Japanese position, believed to be an army headquarters. This was, in fact, *33rd Army Headquarters*, and for the second time in ten days Honda and his staff after a grim fight had to escape on foot across country.[1]

By the evening of the 19th, 161st Brigade had secured the northern half of Pyinmana and established a roadblock south of the town. The advance was now only four days behind schedule and moving fast. Next morning 4th Royal West Kents and a detachment of Probyn's Horse moved south-west and occupied Lewe on the railway to Taungdwingyi and the Irrawaddy valley. As soon as Lewe was occupied, airfield engineers, who always moved near the head of the main body despite the fact that in that position they were a tactical embarrassment, moved on to the airstrip and set to work with bull-dozers, crash-landed in American gliders. As a result, the airhead at Lewe was opened on the 23rd April.[2] At Pyinmana and Lewe, 161st Brigade's casualties were trifling; the known Japanese losses amounted to only fifty-three dead, but that their forces had been scattered was clear from the brigade's war diary of the 20th April which recorded that local inhabitants were reporting so many small parties of Japanese in so many places that it was quite impossible to deal with them all.[3]

While 161st Brigade cleared Pyinmana and Lewe, 123rd Brigade

---

[1] See pages 359–60.
[2] See Appendix 23.
[3] On this day (20th) Slim issued the order giving his corps commanders details of 'Dracula' and requiring them to capture Prome and Toungoo as quickly as possible. See page 372.

took the lead and by the evening of the 21st its main body was thirty miles south of Pyinmana, while its armoured advanced guard reached Yedashe, within sixteen miles of Toungoo. On the 22nd, three days ahead of schedule, Toungoo airfield was taken without opposition, and 7th York and Lancaster, mopping up behind the armoured advanced guard, found the town deserted except for a few stragglers.[1] A two-company column with a troop of light tanks pushed on to Oktwin, eight miles to the south. As the column, led by its light tanks, reached the town, it was waved on by a Japanese traffic control post. The post was overrun, as was a small party of Japanese with a captured British Bren carrier escorting a convoy of bullock carts a few miles farther on. The day's operations were completed without loss until the column in Oktwin was unfortunately mistaken for Japanese and attacked by R.A.F. fighters. It is evident that even the forward group control centre had been unable to keep pace with the advance. Known enemy losses were thirty-five Japanese killed and 135 *I.N.A* prisoners-of-war.

It has already been shown that *33rd Army Headquarters* had virtually lost control and it is clear that this state of affairs was widespread throughout *Burma Area Army*, for a *55th Division* order of the 16th April, captured at Toungoo on the 22nd, instructed *144th Regiment* to take up positions north of Pyawbwe, which by the 16th had been in possession of IV Corps for five days[2]. The extent of the disorganization within Japanese formations can be gauged by the fact that, nearly a hundred miles behind the forward troops, 9th Brigade of 5th Division, moving forward by road from Pyawbwe to take over Pyinmana and Lewe from 161st Brigade, time and again ran across parties of escaping Japanese, who avoided action when possible but fought back when intercepted. The pursuers were in fact outstripping the pursued.

On the 23rd April, 161st Brigade, having handed over the Pyinmana area to 9th Brigade, moved forward to Toungoo in readiness to go through 123rd Brigade and capture 5th Division's final objective, Pyu. As it drove south it rounded up parties of dispirited *I.N.A.*, whose only anxiety appeared to be to find out where to 'report in'. Quantities of abandoned rations and equipment lay everywhere; the few Japanese stragglers who were met died fighting or committed suicide rather than surrender. On the 23rd, 161st Brigade harboured for the night just north of Toungoo where, before it began to move on the morning of the 24th, it was attacked by eight Japanese fighters

---

[1] An airhead was opened at the main Toungoo all-weather airfield on the 24th April; see Appendix 23.

[2] The order gave the strength of the regiment as follows: *1st Battalion*, 570; *2nd*, 560; *3rd*, 420; total regiment including attached troops, 2,131. Other documents showed that *3rd Company, 55th Division Reconnaissance Regiment* was present with five tanks and seven armoured cars.

with anti-personnel bombs and machine-gun fire and suffered thirty-
four casualties. This did not, however, delay the beginning of the
advance as the 4th Royal West Kent group, which was to lead the
main body, had already moved forward to Oktwin from where the
brigade was to take over the lead, headed by a reorganized armoured
advanced guard.[1] There was little opposition, but delays were caused
by parties of *I.N.A.* and B.N.A. surrendering, and by frequent rain
storms which made it difficult to cross chaungs where culverts and
bridges had been destroyed. The only opposition met was at the Pyu
Chaung, where one tank of the advanced guard was destroyed by a
concealed 75-mm. gun firing hollow charge shell, the most effective
anti-tank projectile the Japanese possessed. By daybreak on the 25th
the advanced guard and leading group of 161st Brigade had crossed
the Pyu Chaung, and shortly afterwards *1st I.N.A. Division* surrendered.[2] By that evening the advanced guard had reached Penwegon.
That night 161st Brigade harboured five miles south of Pyu and
123rd Brigade, following up, consolidated the town.[3] Toungoo was
now secure and the task of 5th Division completed. The 17th Division
therefore moved up to continue the advance to Pegu, and 19th
Division hurried forward to Toungoo to consolidate and meet the
threat offered by an enemy force, reliably reported to be steadily
increasing in strength, to the east on the Mawchi road.

The force with which 19th Division (less 64th Brigade) came into
contact as soon as it attempted to gain elbow room east of Toungoo
was not, as thought, an enemy concentration for a counter-offensive,
but the remnants of *18th, 49th* and *53rd Divisions of 33rd Army*, scattered
and out of Honda's control as the direct result of the speed and power
of IV Corps' southward drive. On the 27th April, Kimura (*Burma
Area Army*) gave orders that *15th Army*, which having moved south
through the Shan and Karen Hills had reached the Bawlake–
Kemapyu area,[4] was to remain there, its *15th Division* holding the

---

[1] Vanguard: A Squadron 5th Horse carrying one company 1/17th Dogras, one battery
18th (S.P.) Field Regiment and a detachment 36th Field Squadron; Mainguard (Lieut.-
Colonel M. R. Smeeton): V.C.P., 5th Horse scout and regimental headquarters troops
carrying the defence platoon of 1/17th Dogras, C Squadron 5th Horse carrying one company
1/17th Dogras, 36th Field Squadron (less detachment) carrying two scissors bridges, 18th
Field Regiment (less two batteries), B Squadron 5th Horse carrying one company 1/17th
Dogras, an advanced dressing station and B echelon of all unit transport; Rearguard:
1/17th Dogras (less three companies).
[2] The 255th Tank Brigade War Diary states that the surrendered *I.N.A.* division consisted of three guerrilla regiments, with detachments of a fourth, and a medical staging
section. The approximate strengths were: 3,000 fit men, 440 hospital patients and over
1,500 convalescents. The division was disarmed by 5th Division.
[3] See Map 11, facing page 414.
[4] Slim had ordered the two northern groups of Levies under operation 'Character' (see
pages 249-50) to begin operations about the 13th April. These groups carried out demolitions on the Loi-kaw–Bawlake–Kemapyu road and on the Mawchi–Toungoo road, and in
general did their best to harass the withdrawal of *15th Army*.

Toungoo–Mawchi road until *33rd Army*, attempting to re-form in the same area east of Toungoo, had withdrawn to the Sittang estuary where it was to keep open an escape route by way of the Sittang bridge. The subsequent task of *33rd Army* was to cover the flank of *15th Army* and *56th Division* as they withdrew from Kemapyu to Moulmein. On the 28th, Honda once more gained touch with his divisions collecting east of Toungoo and issued orders for the move of *33rd Army* to the Sittang estuary by way of the east bank of the river. Owing to the number of unbridged tributaries that would have to be crossed, all wheeled artillery and vehicles were to move southwards along the main road by way of Mawchi. The withdrawal began as soon as it was dark on the 29th, hampered by pouring rain which had begun that afternoon, rising streams and harassing artillery fire from 19th Divisional artillery sited on the west bank of the Sittang. There was, however, no appreciable slackening of resistance to 98th Brigade (Jerrard) of 19th Division on the Mawchi road sector, since *15th Division* had been placed there with the task of opposing any advance eastwards along the road.

The defence of Toungoo had been entrusted to the main body of *55th Division* from south Burma.[1] After *144th Regiment* arrived at Toungoo at the end of March it was ordered to Pyinmana, but, because it had to deal with B.N.A. units which had changed sides, it did not get there until the 19th April, just as 5th Division armour and 161st Brigade broke through the defences. It was thrown into confusion and was not able to get back to Toungoo which, in consequence, was virtually undefended. Thus Honda's efforts to organize a line of defence between Pyinmana and Toungoo resulted in the overrunning of what was left of his headquarters and the loss of all its wireless equipment.

On the 26th April IV Corps Headquarters moved into Toungoo, where there were two all-weather airfields—Main and Tennant. The airfields were fit for use, although the runways were in poor condition, and orders were issued for 906 and 909 (Spitfire and Hurricane) Wings as well as 166th Liaison Squadron U.S.A.A.F. and IV Corps Communication Flight to fly in that day, to be followed on the 30th by 910 (Thunderbolt) Wing, required for the support of 'Dracula'. The defence of the airfields was to be undertaken by 19th Division in close co-operation with the R.A.F. station commanders and wings of the R.A.F. Regiment. In rear of IV Corps the fly-out of 36th Division was about to begin, and Slim had urged Festing to speed up 29th Brigade's operations to capture Kalaw; 19th Division, less 64th Brig-

---

[1] For its composition see page 384 fn. 1.

ade which remained at Meiktila and was later to relieve 29th Brigade on the Kalaw road, had taken over the task of protecting Toungoo and its airfields and securing the Mawchi road to cover the left flank of IV Corps. In the forward area, 17th Division was about to pass through 5th Division (which was consolidating the Pyu area) to attack Pegu.

The advance of 17th Division on Pegu began when 63rd Brigade passed through the forward troops of 5th Division at Penwegon on the 28th April.[1] At 9 a.m. twenty-two miles to the south, at MS 100 from Rangoon, the armoured advanced guard (Pert) met an enemy detachment on the move and, in a running fight lasting until 4 p.m., captured two trains, three engines, a hundred horses and three prisoners; it estimated that it had killed close on a hundred Japanese. The next day Japanese were found in position astride the road at Pyinbongyi with their right protected by the Moyingyi Reservoir. A deliberate attack by 6/7th Rajputs and 9th Royal Horse cleared the position by evening, and the advanced guard halted for the night on the ground gained. As expected, this position was merely a covering one, and early on the 30th April Japanese were found in a strong position at the south-west corner of the reservoir, covered by minefields.[2] Attempts by tanks to outflank the position failed owing to natural obstacles, and Pert ordered a two-squadron frontal attack by 9th Royal Horse for 9.30 a.m. Each squadron was supported by the company of 6/7th Rajputs which had been riding its tanks throughout the advance. The leading troops of the right squadron found themselves hemmed in by the road and railway embankments and they and their accompanying infantry incurred considerable losses, but, on the left, one troop broke right through the position and established a block on the road south of it. The Japanese, however, fought on, and at 3 p.m. Pert sent in 1/3rd Gurkhas, less one company, with the third squadron of 9th Royal Horse. By 5 p.m. the position was taken: at 6.30 p.m. contact was made with the roadblock to the south and resistance ceased.[3] Meanwhile, about seven miles to the east a small column of infantry and armoured cars cut the Payagyi–Waw road, the last escape route from Pegu and Rangoon, and played havoc for twenty-four hours with a stream of cars and lorries making for the Sittang. On the 29th, after a heavy airstrike and bombardment, 63rd Brigade occupied Payagyi without meeting any opposition, and from

---

[1] The 17th Division was organized in three brigade groups, and a very powerful armoured advanced guard consisting of Headquarters 255th Tank Brigade, 9th Royal Horse (medium tanks), 7th Light Cavalry (light tanks) less one squadron, 16th Cavalry (armoured cars) less one squadron, 18th (S.P.) Field Regiment, 6/7th Rajputs riding on tanks, 1/3rd Gurkhas in lorries, 36th Field Squadron, I.E., and one company 4/4th Bombay Grenadiers.

[2] The 'mines' included Japanese soldiers with hand-detonated charges sitting in holes waiting for tanks to pass over them. See photograph No. 52, following page 286.

[3] Japanese losses were over 200 killed and several dumps of ammunition and stores together with an assortment of vehicles captured. The 17th Division losses were sixty-five killed and wounded and three medium tanks destroyed.

there sent forward columns to reconnoitre the defences of Pegu and secure points of tactical importance.[1]

It had in the meantime become known at IV Corps Headquarters that a large force of Japanese was moving south down the east bank of the Sittang (this of course being the move of *33rd Army* to the Sittang estuary). Messervy thereupon ordered the air-transported 9th Brigade (Brain) of 5th Division to be flown from Lewe to forward airfields to operate against it in the Shwegyin–Waw area. The brigade was to secure the ferries at Shwegyin and the road to them from Nyaung-lebin, patrol the road eastwards from the ferries, reconnoitre the road south to Mokpalin, and finally control the rail and roads eastwards from Waw to the Sittang. The leading battalion (1st Burma Regiment) flew to Pyuntaza airstrip on the 29th,[2] where it was joined by a battery of 24th Mountain Regiment and a troop of armoured cars of 16th Light Cavalry, and at once moved to the Shwegyin area. There it was soon in contact with Japanese moving south along the east bank, and collected ten prisoners-of-war in the first twenty-four hours. The rest of the brigade, on relief at Lewe by troops of 19th Division, was flown to Payagyi on the 1st May and set up its headquarters near Waw. From there fighting patrols fanned out eastwards, one of which (a company of 2nd West Yorkshires and a troop of 7th Light Cavalry) dispersed a Japanese patrol about sixty strong, killing twenty-eight men all from *128th Regiment* of *53rd Division*.[3]

The arrival of 9th Brigade in the Waw area secured the left flank of 17th Division during its attack on Pegu, which had begun on the 29th with an attempt by two companies of 7/10th Baluch to occupy a small group of hills north-east of the town near Shweban, while a company of 1/10th Gurkhas secured the railway bridge north of the town.[4] Both attempts were supported by 5th (Probyn's) Horse but were unsuccessful, as was an attempt by 9th Royal Horse to ford the Pegu River west of Payagyi on the Sitpinzeik track.

While these moves were in progress, a British officer who had been captured at Singapore appeared at 48th Brigade Headquarters at Kadok and reported that there were 437 British prisoners-of-war in a village on the railway seven miles north-east of Pegu.[5] They had been on their way to Moulmein from Rangoon and had been turned loose by the Japanese when the Waw road was cut on the 27th. It now seemed certain that the Japanese had left Rangoon, and hopes ran high that 14th Army might yet get there before the sea-

---

[1] An airhead was opened at Payagyi on the 30th April; see Appendix 23.
[2] An airhead was opened on this airstrip on the 30th April; see Appendix 23.
[3] The *33rd Army* had sent foraging teams ahead to the Sittang estuary area on the 27th April.
[4] See Sketch 18, facing page 398.
[5] They had scattered to avoid R.A.F. attacks but were all found during the next two days.

borne assault, provided the resistance at Pegu could be quickly overcome. Of this there could be no certainty, because it was evident from
the unsuccessful efforts to occupy vantage points on the 29th that the
town was strongly held. Identification of a battalion of *24th I.M.B.*
(from Tenasserim) in the area led to the belief that the whole brigade
might be holding the town.

An independent mixed brigade was in fact holding Pegu but it was
not the *24th*, although one of its battalions was in the Waw–Mokpalin
area. The Japanese had formed a *Rangoon Defence Force* under command of Major-General H. Matsui, consisting of *105th I.M.B.*, an
anti-aircraft battalion, a provisional brigade,[1] an airfield battalion,
three infantry units consisting of training personnel, trainees and reservists and two naval guard units of about company strength. Its
total strength was about 7,000.

It was part of this force, consisting of the bulk of the provisional
brigade and one of the training personnel units, in all numbering
some 1,700 men, which had held the covering positions at Pyinbongyi
and Payagyi. When these positions were overwhelmed, the remnants
were driven eastwards and joined up with the battalion of *24th I.M.B.*
at Waw. The Japanese estimate that its losses included at least 350
killed. Pegu itself was defended by the rest of the *Rangoon Defence
Force*. The final evacuation of Rangoon had taken place on the 29th
after the last of the hospital staff and patients, about 500 in all, had
left by sea. It seems probable that on the 29th, when 17th Division
made the first probing attack on Pegu, its garrison was approximately
5,000 men with a few tanks, presumably the remnants of *14th Tank
Regiment*. Nearly all guns, both field and anti-aircraft, were found,
after the battle, to have been sited for anti-tank defence.

In an operation instruction issued on the 28th April, Messervy
estimated that, although the Japanese were evacuating Rangoon, it
was possible that considerable numbers from Arakan and the Irrawaddy valley, withdrawing before XXXIII Corps, might move into
the city.[2] His plan for the capture of the port of Rangoon was to make
a concentric attack by 17th and 5th Divisions, the former from the
north after it had taken Pegu and secured its airstrips, and the latter
(less 9th Brigade) from north-east and east, striking south from Zayatkwin after crossing the Pegu River behind 17th Division. The
course of events rendered the attack by 5th Division unnecessary and
it was cancelled; in any case the weather would have made it impossible.

Cowan's orders for 17th Division's attack on Pegu were issued early

---

[1] Formed from Japanese civil population, sea, rail and other administrative units,
convalescents and soldiers under sentence in military prisons.

[2] Kimura had in fact ordered *28th Army* to defend Rangoon to the last, but the order
could not be complied with.

on the 30th April. The 48th Brigade was to send a battalion to cross the Pegu River at Okpo and move down the west bank to capture the railway station; 63rd Brigade, supported by a squadron of 9th Royal Horse, was to seize the low hills at Shweban and then push down the main road to seize the road bridge in the town; and 255th Tank Brigade (less 116th R.A.C. and one squadron of 9th Royal Horse)[1] with 1/3rd Gurkhas under command was to seize the village of Kamanat, and from there deliver an infantry attack on Pegu from the east, supported by armour, while the rest of the armour encircled the town to the south-east and then struck north to meet 63rd Brigade at the bridge in the town. The 99th Brigade in reserve at Payagyi was to close all escape routes from Pegu to the east.

Hedley (48th Brigade) detailed 4/12th F.F. Regiment to capture Pegu railway station, by way of Okpo. It found both bridges blown but succeeded in getting a company across at the northern railway bridge by 3 p.m., but was unable to exploit south that day. The 63rd Brigade (Burton), advancing astride the road, made little progress and, although only one tank was destroyed, its supporting armour suffered considerable damage from well-concealed guns. The 255th Tank Brigade (Pert) reached Kamanat without difficulty by 11.30 a.m., but it took 1/3rd Gurkhas and 5th (Probyn's) Horse until 5 p.m. to secure the 200-foot-high pagoda-topped hill between the village and Pegu. The rest of 255th Tank Brigade worked its way to the south-east of Pegu but was then confronted by a tank-proof ditch.[2] No way across it had been found by nightfall and the tanks had to withdraw to harbour for the night. The day's gains thus amounted to a company bridgehead north of Okpo and the hill west of Kamanat.

After dark on the 30th, patrols of 63rd Brigade made their way into Pegu and reported that the Japanese were withdrawing. Preparations for a deliberate attack on the 1st May were therefore suspended, and fighting patrols were sent to follow up the retreat and, if possible, secure the main bridge in Pegu. At daybreak tanks joined in, and by 8 a.m. on the 1st May the whole of Pegu east of the river was clear; it was evening, however, before the engineers finished clearing the many mines and booby traps.[3] The whole of 4/12th F.F. Regiment had meanwhile crossed the river near Okpo and, striking south, had seized the railway station. By the evening of the 1st May the whole division was concentrated in and north of Pegu ready to advance on

---

[1] The 116th was with 19th Division.

[2] This column consisted of 9th Royal Horse less one squadron, a composite squadron of light tanks and armoured cars (7th and 16th Light Cavalry) and a detachment of 4/4th Bombay Grenadiers.

[3] One hundred and thirty-three Japanese dead, twenty-four guns (eight of them British), eight Vickers guns and a large ordnance dump were found. Nearly all the guns were serviceable.

Rangoon, only fifty miles distant, as soon as the river was bridged.[1] The only suitable site for rapid construction of a Bailey bridge was at the main line railway bridge three and a half miles north of the town. Work on a bridge there and on its approaches began at 7 a.m. on the 2nd. At 2 p.m. the armoured advanced guard, followed by 1/7th Gurkhas of 48th Brigade, was able to cross, and the race for Rangoon was resumed. It was, however, to prove a false start for, as night fell on the 2nd May, the frequent heavy showers which had been falling gave place to continuous torrential rain. The river began to rise and the approaches to the recently opened bridge were flooded and rendered useless.

The heavy rain which began on the 2nd and continued for some days flooded the two airfields at Toungoo, putting Tennant, from which 906, 909 and 910 Wings R.A.F. were operating, out of action. To prevent the wings being bogged down for an indefinite period, arrangements were made to fly them out as soon as conditions permitted. By the 7th, 906 and 909 Wings had flown back to Meiktila, leaving one squadron behind for local protection, and 910 Wing had flown to Myingyan. Toungoo Main was kept open with difficulty for use by transport aircraft and the squadron of fighters. Air support for 14th Army was taken over from the 8th by the two long-range wings (908 and 910) from Myingyan.

While the frustrated 14th Army struggled to get across the Pegu River, the amphibious operation for the capture of Rangoon was launched. It began on the 27th April when two naval forces set out from Trincomalee to give long-range protection to the convoys during their voyage to the mouth of the Rangoon River and to intercept Japanese forces attempting to leave Rangoon by sea. The first under Vice-Admiral Walker sailed from Trincomalee with two battleships, the *Queen Elizabeth* and *Richelieu*, four cruisers, the *Cumberland*, *Suffolk*, *Ceylon* and *Tromp*, two escort carriers, the *Empress* and *Shah*, and five destroyers, the fleet being accompanied by two oilers escorted by a sixth destroyer. This force bombarded airfields and other targets on the Nicobar Islands on the morning of the 30th and then set course for Port Blair in the Andamans where, in the evening, airfields, batteries and shipping were attacked by airstrikes and by gunfire. The force remained in the area until the 7th May, during which time it attacked Mergui, Victoria Point, and Port Blair and the Nicobars

---

[1] It is of interest that Pegu was retaken by 17th Division (still commanded by Cowan) which had been driven out of it three years previously (see Volume II, pages 89–92), and that the leading part in its recapture was played by the five battalions (7/10th Baluch, 4/12th F.F.R. and 1/3rd, 1/7th and 1/10th Gurkhas) which had remained with the division throughout the Burma campaign.

for the second time.[1] Throughout the operation no Japanese warship was sighted, and the force returned to Trincomalee on the 9th. The second force of three destroyers under command of Commodore A. L. Poland patrolled the Gulf of Martaban from the 29th April to 2nd May. During its first night in the gulf it encountered a convoy of about ten small craft and sank most of them. A search at daybreak revealed only two grounded wrecks, from which five Japanese survivors were rescued. From them it was learned that the vessels were part of a convoy carrying about a thousand men from Rangoon to Moulmein.

The assault on Rangoon began with the airborne attack on Elephant Point by a composite battalion of 50th (P.) Brigade carried by 317 and 319 Troop Carrier Squadrons of No. 1 Air Commando.[2] Two pathfinder aircraft took off from Akyab at 2.30 a.m. on the 1st May and dropped an advanced party consisting of a Visual Control Post and a detachment from Force 136 in the selected dropping zone, some five miles west of Elephant Point. The parachute battalion (less one company) followed half an hour later in thirty-eight Dakotas and was dropped at 5.45 a.m. without opposition in the marked zone.[3] Although it was raining the wind was not strong, and the drop was accomplished with only five minor casualties. The battalion halted two and a half miles west of Elephant Point while Liberators bombed it. Here a stick of bombs fell short, causing thirty-two casualties among the Gurkhas. By this time visibility was becoming so bad that at 11 a.m. the V.C.P. ordered no further bombing except on its instructions. The attackers struggled on in pouring rain through floods and across the numerous creeks, and it was not until 4 p.m. that the leading company of Gurkhas made contact with the Japanese holding a position just north of Elephant Point and attacked with flame-throwers. The fight was short and fierce. Of the thirty-seven Japanese holding the post only one remained alive to be taken prisoner, while the Gurkhas lost another forty-one, bringing their total casualties to twenty-one killed and fifty-seven wounded. There was no further opposition, and the force bivouacked for the night on any patches of ground it could find above water. The way was now clear for the landing craft carrying the assault troops to enter the river as soon as the mines off its entrance had been swept.

During the night a report was received that aircraft flying over

---

[1] See Map 13 in end pocket.
[2] See Map 11, facing page 414. Many men of the parachute brigade were on leave in Nepal when the decision was taken to launch 'Dracula' and a composite battalion was formed from its two Gurkha battalions. The aircraft were American and, since the British system of jumping differed from that normally used by the Americans, Royal Canadian Air Force jumpmasters were carried in each aircraft. This was the first and only time that any parachute unit was used in its proper role in Burma.
[3] The remaining Gurkha company was dropped in the marked zone at 2.45 p.m. and later in the afternoon there was a supply drop.

Rangoon during the afternoon of the 1st May had seen the words 'Japs gone' and 'Extract Digit' painted on the roof of a building which was identified as the Rangoon gaol where British prisoners-of-war were known to be in custody.[1] This confirmed the reports which had been reaching A.L.F.S.E.A. since the 24th April that there were signs that the Japanese were evacuating the city, none of which had been sufficiently definite to call for any adjustment in the timings for 'Dracula'. Therefore, as planned, six convoys left Kyaukpyu and Akyab between the 27th and 30th April for the Rangoon River, covered by aircraft from escort carriers and 224 Group R.A.F.[2] The minesweepers preceding the assault force convoys arrived off the river mouth on the 1st May, swept the outer approaches and laid marker buoys for the assault convoys. The convoys arrived at their lowering positions at 2.15 a.m. on the 2nd. In the dark, in pouring rain and with a heavy swell running the troops were transferred to their landing craft, which then began the long journey of some thirty miles to the beaches. Air bombardment of the assault areas on both banks of the river was carried out from 5 a.m. to 6.30 a.m. and at about 7 a.m., covered by fire from five L.C.G.s and two flotillas of motor launches, two battalions of 36th Brigade (Brigadier I. C. A. Lauder)[3] landed on the west bank due east of Wabalaukthauk, and about an hour later one battalion of 71st Brigade (Brigadier H. P. L. Hutchinson) landed on the east bank south-west of Kyauktan.[4] Both landings were unopposed. The battalion on the east bank learned that the Japanese had left five days earlier and that a B.N.A. unit in Syriam was likely to be friendly. A reconnaissance party in motor launches and landing craft, which had moved upstream, reached the mouth of the Pegu River without opposition. Since it was evident that the Japanese had evacuated the area, the build-up of 71st Brigade was accelerated and a mobile column was formed to push on to Syriam at first light on the 3rd. The day was marred by one tragedy when a landing craft carrying key engineer and medical personnel struck a mine and was destroyed. There were few survivors. Every officer on board, including the Assistant Director of Medical Services of 26th Division, was killed and the complete equipment of a mobile surgical unit was lost.

Wing Commander A. E. Saunders (Commanding 110 Squadron R.A.F.) had meanwhile flown low over Rangoon on reconnaissance

---

[1] 'Extract Digit' was R.A.F. slang for 'wake up', and was painted on the roof to indicate to R.A.F. pilots that the words 'Japs gone' were not an enemy ruse.

[2] The carrier force (Commodore Oliver) consisted of the cruiser *Royalist* and the escort carriers *Hunter*, *Stalker*, *Khedive* and *Emperor*, carrying eighty-four fighters and fighter-bombers, accompanied by an escort of four destroyers.

[3] Lauder was acting for Brigadier K. S. Thimayya who was in hospital on Ramree Island.

[4] Hutchinson succeeded Chambers when the latter became commander of 26th Division; see page 351.

on the afternoon of the 2nd. Seeing no signs of the enemy, and encouraged by the R.A.F. slang on the roof of the gaol, he landed on the Mingaladon airfield. The runways, however, had been extensively cratered by Allied bombing and his Mosquito sustained enough damage to prevent it from taking off again. Saunders and his navigator made their way to the Rangoon gaol, where there were some 1,400 Allied prisoners-of-war. On arrival they were told that the Japanese guards had been withdrawn after dark on the 29th April, leaving the following message pinned to the main gate:

> Rangoon
> 29th April, 1945
>
> To the whole captured persons of Rangoon Jail. According to the Nippon Military Order, we hereby give you liberty to leave this place at your will.
>
> Regarding other materials kept in the compound, we give you permission to consume them as far as necessity is concerned. We hope that we shall have an opportunity to meet you again at battlefield of somewhere. We shall continue our war effort in order to get the emancipation of all Asiatic races.
>
> (*Sgd*) HARUO ITO
> Chief Officer, Rangoon Branch Jail.[1]

Saunders immediately made his way to the docks, commandeered a sampan and sailed down the river; early on the 3rd he was picked up by a patrolling motor launch and taken to Joint Force Headquarters to report on the situation in Rangoon.

Saunders's news arrived too late to affect the issue, for it was already evident by the evening of the 2nd that there would be little if any resistance to an immediate advance on Rangoon and it had been decided to make straight for the city without waiting for 4th Brigade of 26th Division. During the night of the 2nd/3rd May orders were issued for 36th Brigade and elements of 71st Brigade to re-embark and push on to the city as quickly as possible. Chambers, the divisional commander, himself went up the river early on the 3rd to supervise the advance. Lauder (36th Brigade), whose troops were deployed some way from the beaches, said he could re-embark them and be in the city by 4 p.m. Hutchinson (71st Brigade), whose mobile column occupied Syriam that morning, had 1/18th Royal Garhwal at Kyauktan. This battalion began to embark at 10.30 a.m. and should have been the first unit to reach Rangoon, but there was insufficient water to float the loaded craft which settled on the mud and could not be moved until high water some six hours later. The 36th Brigade re-embarked as planned and, preceded by mine-sweepers, moved up the river. The 5/9th Jats landed at Dala on the afternoon of the 3rd and

---

[1] The Japanese garrison began to withdraw from the city on the 23rd and the last elements left during the night of the 29th/30th April.

began to work its way up the west bank of the river, while 8/13th F.F. Rifles and 1/8th Gurkha Rifles landed at the docks at about 4 p.m. as forecast and made their way into the city.

Rangoon, which had been in enemy hands for almost exactly three years and two months, was thus, two days before the surrender of Germany, occupied without fighting, just as the Japanese had occupied it without a shot being fired in 1942. The population of the city turned out in force to give the troops an enthusiastic welcome. Rangoon itself was in a sorry state owing to the breakdown, through neglect, of the hospital and sanitation services and the water supply, and because of the deliberate destruction of the electricity supply system by the retreating Japanese. In the circumstances the enthusiasm shown was genuine, perhaps partly caused by relief that the city had been spared bombing and fighting in the streets, with all the destruction that would have entailed.[1]

The Garhwalis landed at dawn on the 4th; the rest of 71st Brigade moved into the city during the day and then advanced into its northern suburbs. On the 5th Mingaladon airfield was occupied, Headquarters 26th Division was established at Government House, all Allied prisoners-of-war found in Rangoon were flown to India and 71st Brigade began to move towards Pegu to meet 14th Army. On the 6th the forces in Rangoon came under command of 14th Army, bringing to an end the operational career of XV Corps.

Fifty miles to the north, at Pegu, engineers had been working day and night since the evening of the 2nd May to bridge the river, and at 9.30 a.m. on the 4th traffic began to cross. The armoured advanced guard, which had crossed on the 2nd by the now useless northern bridge[2], had been held up by another destroyed bridge ten miles south of Pegu, where the road entered a belt of thick jungle and was heavily mined. The 1/7th Gurkhas of 48th Brigade, following up the advanced guard, now took the lead on foot. The bridge was repaired while the battalion worked its way through the jungle astride the road against sporadic but at times fierce opposition, and the engineers cleared no fewer than 500 mines off the road. By the evening of the 3rd the advanced guard had reached the deep tidal chaung a mile east of Zayatkwin to find that bridge also blown. As soon as the bridge in Pegu opened on the 4th, bridging material was rushed forward and by evening the engineers, protected by 7th Gurkhas whose pioneers had made a footbridge, had built a bridge capable of taking light tanks and armoured cars, and the advance was resumed. During the

---

[1] For further details on the state of Rangoon see Donnison, *British Military Administration in the Far East, 1943–46* (H.M.S.O., 1956), Chapter VII.

[2] The appoaches were flooded; see page 393.

5th, 1/7th Gurkhas with a composite squadron of 7th and 16th Cavalry cleared Hlegu against slight opposition, and early on the 6th May a company of Gurkhas crossed the blown-up bridge west of the town by clambering along the broken spans under cover of a smoke screen put down by mortars. The last action of operation 'Capital', which had begun nine months earlier at the southern exits of the Imphal plain, had been fought, for at 4.30 p.m. a column of the Lincolns from 26th Division linked up with the Gurkha company in its bridgehead west of Hlegu.

The Battle of the Rangoon Road was over. Messervy had already warned 17th Division on the 5th that it was not to go to Rangoon but was to turn about and move north to the line Pyinbongyi–Pyu and destroy any Japanese from the Pegu Yomas attempting to escape east to the Sittang, and that the Pegu area was to become the responsibility of 5th Division. At the same time 255th Tank Brigade concentrated at Pegu in readiness to move to monsoon quarters. North of the new 17th Division area, 19th Division already held Toungoo and was operating along the Thazi–Kalaw and Toungoo–Mawchi roads, while 36th Division was on its way back to India by air. The pursuit from Pyawbwe to Hlegu, a distance of 300 miles covered in twenty-six days, cost IV Corps 446 dead, 1,706 wounded and 14 missing, little by comparison with the heavy Japanese losses of 6,742 counted dead, 273 prisoners, 15 tanks, 127 guns and 434 lorries captured or destroyed.

It is perhaps a fitting end to the story to record that on the 1st May Slim and Messervy, having had reports that Rangoon was clear of enemy and that messages to that effect were displayed on roof-tops, decided to go and see for themselves. They set off in Slim's Dakota from Payagyi airfield with a Royal Air Force pilot, observer and wireless operator and accompanied by Colonels Fullerton and Lyons of the United States Army, who were attached to 14th Army Headquarters staff. Extracts from a letter written by Messervy describe what happened:

'We flew straight down the Pegu–Rangoon road at 2,000 feet. When we were about half-way, thirty miles or so from Pegu, there was suddenly a bit of a noise, like somebody dropping a tray on the kitchen floor and we soon saw that contrary to their custom the Japs had fired on us. I had flown many times low over Jap positions by courtesy of the U.S.A. L.5 squadrons and never been fired at as far as I knew except once over Pegu during 17 Div.'s attack on it . . . Bill Slim was in front a few feet from the wireless which was hit, and two or possibly three more projectiles came through the under side of the fuselage. None did any damage except one which got poor Fullerton in the leg . . . Of course the pilot turned for home. On the airfield was an M.D.S. with a forward surgical team including Bruce, 14th Army chief surgical

Tandawgyi 4 m.

To Nyaunglebin 37m.

Payagyi

To Kyaikhla 3m. Waw 8m.

60

Sitpinzeik

58

To Kyaikhla 4 m. Waw 7 m.
Sittang Bdge. 24 m.

Pegu R.

R.S

58

R.S

56

R.S

Shanywagyi

54

Kawwin 4 m.

17 DIV. Engr.
TRESTLE BDGE

Okpo

Shweban

Club

Pegu

Kamanat

DISUSED

Pepaungdaw

AIRFIELD

Kyaikpun

Thanatpin

46

R.S

Payathonzu

44

PEGU-SITTANG CANAL

42

PEGU May 1945

Tawa

Miles

0   1   2   3   4

Legend

ROADS All weather...............

Fair weather.............

TRACKS............................

RAILWAYS Double Track.....

" Single ....

RIVERS. LAKES...........

Hilly areas covered
by jungle..........

40

R.S

38

300m
50 m

Intagaw

To Kawa 9m.

To Rangoon 35 m.

specialist. In spite of this Fullerton lost his leg . . . I often wonder what we would have done had we got to Rangoon. I feel that if we had found the airfield clear and possible for landing we would probably have done so and Bill Slim could have personally re-occupied Rangoon. What fun that would have been!'

It would indeed have been a splendid climax to the reconquest of Burma.

The period of unsettled weather which began on the 29th April and the heavy storms early in May which put forward airstrips out of action, together with the difficulty of distributing supplies since vehicles were unable to move off the main roads, forced IV Corps on to half rations.[1] On the 3rd May Messervy said that he could no longer rely on air supply and asked that corps troops, 5th Division and 255th Tank Brigade (the formations nearest to Rangoon) should be supplied through the port. The difficulty of supplying IV Corps, the nearness of the monsoon and the impending reduction of the number of transport aircraft available, with the withdrawal of the American combat cargo groups to China,[2] made it a matter of urgency that Rangoon port should be opened as quickly as possible and the city developed as a base for the maintenance of the formations of 14th Army in southern Burma. As soon as the city had been occupied, therefore, a survey of the dock area was begun. Although bombing had completely blocked all the exits from it, three berths for ocean-going ships were usable and a few cranes were in working order. Work on clearing the exits from the docks was immediately begun by local labour, of which there was an abundance, and minesweeping was continued without a break. By the 7th most of the mines known to be in the river had been cleared, and on the following day three stores ships berthed and began unloading. By the 10th the river was fully opened for ocean-going ships and some more berths were available for their use.[3] The same day the Port Commandant, accompanied by the port and base development reconnaissance party which had moved by road with 14th Army, reached Rangoon.[4]

On the 4th Leese had given orders for the despatch of 2nd Division (less 6th Brigade) to be delayed, the number of corps troops to be sent to Rangoon to be cut to a minimum, and the pre-arranged follow-up convoys to be adjusted; the convoy due to arrive at Rangoon from Kyaukpyu on the 14th May (D+12) was now to carry all the

---

[1] For about three weeks IV Corps had to exist on 175 tons a day dropped instead of 450 tons landed at forward airheads.

[2] See pages 318–19.

[3] During the operations one L.C.T. was sunk and one L.S.T. damaged by hitting mines off Elephant Point and within the river respectively.

[4] See page 332.

administrative units standing by to embark in the first three Stanza convoys, and the convoy due to arrive on the 19th (D+17) was to become the first Stanza convoy instead of the one due to arrive on the 9th June (D+38), thus saving three weeks.[1]

The launching of 'Dracula', asked for by Slim as an administrative insurance in the middle of March, resulted in the reoccupation of Rangoon on the 3rd May, about a week earlier than it could have been entered by 14th Army and enabled the port to be opened much earlier than it would have been had the reoccupation been left to 14th Army and the opening of the port to operation 'Stanza' as originally planned. From an administrative point of view, the saving of three weeks of pre-monsoon weather justified the decision to undertake the operation.

---

[1] See page 322. From the 8th to the 17th May, stores were landed at the average rate of 1,200 tons a day; by the end of the month this figure had increased to 2,075 tons.

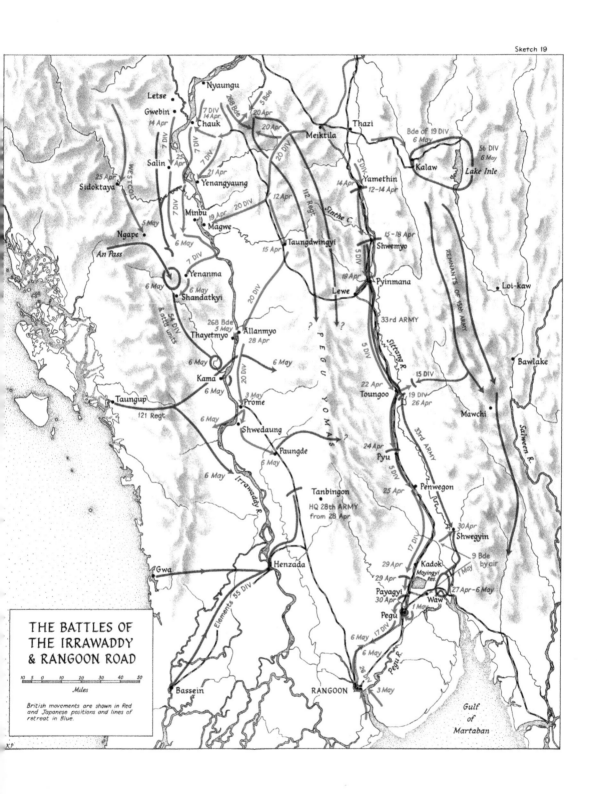

THE BATTLES OF
THE IRRAWADDY
& RANGOON ROAD

10 5 0   10   20   30   40   50
Miles

British movements are shown in Red
and Japanese positions and lines of
retreat in Blue.

CHAPTER XXXIII

AIR WARFARE IN SOUTH-EAST
ASIA
(August 1944–May 1945)

See Maps 7, 10, 11 and 13 and Sketch 20

B Y June 1944, as described in Volume III, the Allies had gained absolute air superiority over the greater part of Burma.[1] During the period covered by this volume the aim was to retain and extend the range of that superiority throughout South-East Asia. The air forces were also to disrupt the Japanese lines of communications into, as well as within, Burma, provide close support as required for the Allied armies during their sustained offensive, and undertake the vital and complicated task of supplying them as they advanced deeper and deeper into Burma.

When 14th Army began its advance across the Chindwin early in December 1944, Eastern Air Command, with bases in eastern Bengal and Assam, had forty-eight squadrons of fighters and bombers with a first-line strength of 650 fighters (464 R.A.F. and 186 U.S.A.A.F.) and 177 bombers (74 R.A.F. and 103 U.S.A.A.F.),[2] six photographic reconnaissance squadrons and four troop carrier squadrons; in addition there were two fighter squadrons for the air defence of Calcutta.[3] It also had sixteen transport squadrons (four R.A.F. and twelve U.S.A.A.F.), increasing to nineteen during March and April and twenty in May (ten R.A.F. and ten U.S.A.A.F.), with a first-line strength of some 500 aircraft.[4]

The Japanese *3rd Air Army*, with headquarters at Singapore, comprised three air divisions: the *5th* in Burma, the *7th* in Java and the *9th* in Sumatra. After the return in January 1945 of two air regiments

---

[1] See Volume III, page 388.

[2] The forty-eight squadrons were made up as follows: seventeen fighter, twelve fighter-bomber, three fighter-reconnaissance, ten heavy bomber, five medium bomber and one light bomber.

[3] See Appendix 4. Although the wings in each group (221 and 224 R.A.F.) remained constant between January and May 1945, the actual number of squadrons they controlled fluctuated according to the availability of forward airfields and the changing tactical situation, and when, as new squadrons became operational, other squadrons were withdrawn from the forward area for re-equipment. The strength of Eastern Air Command thus varied from month to month.

[4] See Appendix 15.

and two heavy bomber squadrons to Japan,[1] the first-line strength of the three air divisions, excluding an air training organization at Singapore and its advanced echelon in Burma, was reduced to 195 aircraft, of which *5th Air Division's* share in Burma was sixty-six aircraft, mainly fighters.[2] Since *3rd Air Army* received no reinforcements or replacements from January 1945 onwards and had to make do with the aircraft it had and with some of its training aircraft used in an operational role, its strength, despite strenuous efforts to repair damaged aircraft while there were still spare parts available, gradually diminished, and by April had fallen to 158 aircraft. The *5th Air Division*, part of which was moved from Burma to Indo-China between February and April,[3] was reduced to some fifty serviceable aircraft by April. The performance of all types of Japanese aircraft at this stage in the war in no way compared with the more modern aircraft with which the Allied air forces were equipped.[4]

With such a preponderance of strength, the Allies had no difficulty in maintaining air supremacy in Burma. Although it is now known that *3rd Air Army* had been left to waste away from January 1945 onwards, to those in charge of air operations in South-East Asia there was always the possibility that it might be reinforced by aircraft withdrawn from the Philippines, or from Japan by way of China and Indo-China. There was also the danger that the Japanese might attack the stream of unarmed transport aircraft on which 14th Army and N.C.A.C. had to rely for supplies as they penetrated into Burma. Though fighter cover and standing patrols were to be provided in the forward areas as and when possible, there would be times when, as the Allied armies progressed deeper into Burma, transport aircraft might have to operate in front of any warning system and without protection.

The *5th Air Division*, however, conformed rigidly to its main role of providing close support for *15th* and *33rd Armies*. It therefore undertook surprise raids at infrequent intervals against the many, though fleeting, targets that existed, and thus frittered away what little strength it had in ineffectual attacks which, although sometimes causing casualties, had no effect on the progress of the Allied offensive. Had its role been changed to that of attacking transport aircraft, particularly those operating near the battle line, *5th Air Division* could, despite its diminishing numbers, have been considerably more effective. On the one occasion that such an attack was made on Onbauk, it forced the Allies for a short time to resort to night flying to lessen the risk.[5]

---

[1] See page 233.
[2] See Appendix 17, note 3.
[3] See page 188 and fn. 2.
[4] See Volume III, Appendix 28.
[5] See page 179.

Owing to the difficulty of intercepting Japanese fighters making surprise raids, it was decided to undertake intruder raids by long-range fighters against the airfields thought to be used by *5th Air Division*. These raids were at first concentrated against the Rangoon group of airfields. When, in the spring of 1945, *5th Air Division* began to withdraw into Siam and Indo-China, these operations became almost a specialist task undertaken by the Mustang squadrons of 1st U.S. Air Commando Group. On several occasions these squadrons made round flights of 1,500 miles to attack enemy-occupied airfields, and on the whole obtained good results, destroying or damaging a considerable number of aircraft on the ground.

By March 1945 the Japanese air effort in Burma had become negligible. Not only could transport aircraft fly to their destination, land, unload and return without close protection, but long columns of troops and motor transport could move forward by day unmolested with almost complete disregard for anti-aircraft precautions, while behind the enemy lines no movement by day was possible. There could be no clearer proof of the overwhelming advantages of air superiority.

The offensive undertaken by the Strategic Air Force during the 1943–44 campaign was continued on a much reduced scale during the 1944 monsoon, since the weather, especially over Malaya and Siam, made long distance raids impossible,[1] and 7th Bombardment Group U.S.A.A.F. had been diverted in June 1944 to ferry aviation petrol to 14th U.S.A.A.F. in China.[2] Nevertheless, taking advantage of the infrequent spells of fair weather, the force was able to make night attacks on the railway system between Mandalay and Bangkok and to continue with its task of laying mines off Moulmein, Tavoy, Mergui and Port Blair.[3]

The Strategic Air Force was brought up to its full strength on the 1st October 1944 when 7th Bombardment Group rejoined it. Since the likelihood of heavy bombers being intercepted by enemy fighters, even on long distance flights, had by then become slight, it was decided that, when the monsoon ended, all strategic air operations, other than mine laying, should be undertaken by day instead of by night. The advantage of this would be that relatively small targets could be more easily identified. The objectives laid down were, in order of priority, enemy naval and merchant vessels (as opportunity offered), communications by sea and land to Burma, airfields and installations within Burma, and finally ports, military depots and supply dumps. The mine-laying operations were, as before, to be carried out on moonlight nights.

[1] For the strategic air offensive in the 1943–44 campaign see Volume III, Chapter XXVII.
[2] See Volume III, pages 389–90.
[3] See Map 13 in end pocket.

The first attack during the 1944–45 dry weather was a raid by two formations each of sixteen bombers on the 6th October on the Bangkok–Chiengmai railway, believed to be used by the Japanese as a means of getting supplies into Burma, in which bridges were wrecked, sections of the track blown up and locomotives and rolling stock machine-gunned. But the main target selected for both medium and heavy bombers was the Pegu–Moulmein–Ban Pong–Bangkok railway. Since for most of its length the track followed a winding course through jungle-covered hills, it was unsuitable for low-level air attacks; the bombers therefore were ordered to concentrate on the destruction of bridges. From January to May 1945 they kept an average of nine bridges unfit for use between Bangkok and Pegu, despite the skill of the Japanese engineers in constructing diversions with temporary wooden bridges. Attacks were also made on the railway across the Kra Isthmus to Victoria Point and on the main line between Bangkok and Singapore. These attacks were carried out by formations of twelve to sixteen aircraft and were repeated systematically to ensure that breaches on the railways, once made, were kept open. On occasions the Strategic Air Force was diverted to give close support to the army : for instance some eighty-five heavy bombers were used to attack specific targets during the assault on Ramree Island in January; and from the 22nd January to the middle of March 12th Bombardment Group operated under 221 Group R.A.F. in close support of 14th Army, and up to half of the heavy bombers were put at the group's disposal to assist in isolating Mandalay and preventing reinforcements from reaching Meiktila.

Towards the end of January 1945, 20th Bomber Command gave up its forward airfields in China and concentrated at its base airfields at Kharagpur near Calcutta preparatory to being transferred to the Marianas, from where the long-range B.29s could be used more effectively against targets in Japan. Since the new bases in the Marianas would not be ready to receive the aircraft until April it was arranged that they could be used for limited operations within S.E.A.C.[1] As industrial targets suitable for B.29s were few, it was decided to direct them against major ports, naval bases and large railway installations. In an effort to prevent enemy naval vessels making use of the repair facilities at the Singapore naval base, seventy-six B.29s laid six minefields in the approaches to Singapore Island on the 25th January. A month later twelve B.29s laid minefields in the Johore Strait and fifteen Liberators of 231 Group R.A.F. laid some sixty mines in the approaches to Penang harbour. On the night of the 1st February eighty-eight B.29s bombed the Singapore naval base, damaging workshops and other installations and sinking a floating

[1] See pages 89 and 133.

dock together with a ship under repair in it, for the loss of two aircraft. On the 6th February Mountbatten directed that no more attacks were to be made on naval installations at Singapore or Penang, as these might later be of use to the Allies. The B.29s were therefore used to attack Saigon, Bangkok and certain targets such as oil storage tanks in and around Singapore Island.

Early in March, at the request of Chennault (14th U.S.A.A.F.), a few B.29s were diverted to lay mines in the Yangtze River, which was being used as a main supply route by the Japanese armies in China.[1] These mine-laying sorties were repeated later in the month without loss. The last raid by B.29s against objectives in South-East Asia was made on the night of the 29th March when some fifty aircraft attacked oil storage depots on islands off Singapore, causing several fires and the destruction of a number of oil tanks. On the 1st April, 20th Bomber Command was transferred to the Pacific, staging through Bhamo, Luliang in south China and Luzon to Guam. On arrival in the Marianas its squadrons came under the command of 21st Bomber Command, whereupon Headquarters 20th Bomber Command was withdrawn to the United States.

At the same time as these attacks on the Japanese lines of communication to Burma were taking place, systematic daylight attacks were being made by heavy and medium bombers with high explosive and incendiary bombs on the reserve stocks which the Japanese were known to have built up in the vicinity of Rangoon. Although these were dispersed in camouflaged and well protected dumps around the northern perimeter of the city, aerial photographs showed that a considerable proportion of the dumps had been hit and their contents destroyed. In the course of these raids *Headquarters Burma Area Army* in Rangoon was attacked on the 29th March; a report of this attack and the fact that it had caused many casualties reached the Allied prisoners-of-war in the Rangoon gaol, who were overjoyed at the news.

From December 1944 onwards the tactical air forces in S.E.A.C. consisted of 224 Group (Bandon), 221 Group (Vincent) and 10th U.S.A.A.F. (Davidson) in support of XV Corps, 14th Army and N.C.A.C. respectively. Fighter sweeps to protect transport aircraft were a daily routine. Close support operations on selected targets or in reply to calls for air support by V.C.P.s were undertaken almost daily by 221 and 224 Groups throughout the campaign. A detailed description of them all would be purely repetitive, but this omission in no way discounts the enormous help they gave to the army. Descriptions of operations of special significance in support of army

---

[1] See Map 10, facing page 340.

formations have, however, been included in the appropriate chapters of this volume. Tactical squadrons also undertook photographic reconnaissance when required. During the crossings of the Irrawaddy in February 1945, for instance, the ever-changing channels in the river-bed were photographed daily so that up-to-date information was always available on the position of sandbanks and other snags which might affect the operations. The almost continuous presence of Allied aircraft over the battle area meant that troops could move freely by day, and was one of the many factors which helped to maintain the army's high morale.

Tactical squadrons also had the role of attacking traffic on railways, roads and rivers on the Japanese lines of communication, using bombs, rockets, cannons or machine-guns as appropriate. By January 1945 the Japanese had virtually stopped running railway trains during daylight, and kept their locomotives and rolling stock dispersed and camouflaged until sunset. Low-flying attacks were therefore made by night in order to catch trains on the move; such attacks not infrequently had spectacular results—engine boilers exploding, rolling stock blazing and trucks carrying ammunition detonating. Nevertheless the permanent ways were kept under close observation by day, and many stationary locomotives were located and put out of action.

As any movement by day on the roads was attacked, the Japanese usually ran motor vehicle and bullock cart convoys at night. Roads were therefore kept under observation during the hours of darkness and on occasions motor transport was spotted. A convoy of some fifty lorries travelling westwards from Meiktila on the 5th February was successfully attacked, and Beaufighters located and attacked motor convoys on the night of the 15th/16th moving eastwards on the Chauk–Meiktila road.[1] A little later, on the night of the 27th/28th a convoy of over a hundred vehicles with some armoured cars and tanks was found moving northwards from Taungdwingyi; this was attacked by Mitchell bombers, and it was estimated that about forty vehicles were destroyed and others set on fire. As the advance into southern Burma progressed, such targets became more frequent. In March a Hurricane squadron located and attacked about forty heavily loaded and camouflaged motor vehicles halted nose to tail just south of Pyinmana, and left some seventeen in flames and many more severely damaged. Towards the end of April, Hurricanes spotted an even larger number near the wrecked bridge over the river at Sittang and, in the attack that followed, it was estimated that forty-three lorries were burnt out and many more damaged. In Arakan, the track over the An Pass to Minbu and the road from Taungup to the rail-

---

[1] See Map 7, facing page 171.

head at Prome were kept under continuous air observation and attack. During March and April the road became the principal objective of 224 Group, and attacks by fighter-bombers were made almost daily with the object of cratering its surface or causing landslides to prevent the Japanese from using it for their withdrawal from the coastal strip.

Attacks on river craft on the Irrawaddy, along the Arakan coast and on the waterways in south-west Burma were made by ground attack fighters almost as a routine. Enemy movement on the waterways, as on the railways and roads, was mainly by night. Nevertheless large numbers of craft, including many power-driven, were attacked and either sunk or left severely damaged. In the latter part of April the tactical squadrons extended their operations to cover the Bassein area to prevent the Japanese from moving reinforcements eastwards to the Irrawaddy front.[1] Motor launches operating in and around Bassein were successfully attacked on a number of occasions, the most successful being on the 25th April when twenty-seven Beaufighters and Mosquitos bombed and machine-gunned their camouflaged base south-west of Rangoon.

On the Northern front the tactical squadrons of 10th U.S.A.A.F. followed a similar procedure to that of the R.A.F. groups but, when at the end of March contact was lost with the enemy, they concentrated on the disruption of communications along the Japanese lines of retreat through the Shan States towards Siam.

From the middle of 1942 air operations in South-East Asia in support of the clandestine organizations had been carried out only in a small way, but early in 1945, with the mounting of operations 'Character' and 'Nation', there was a great increase in this form of air activity.[2] A base for such operations had by this time been established at Jessore (fifty miles north-east of Calcutta), and 357 (Special Duties) Squadron R.A.F., consisting of Liberators for long-range and Hudsons (later replaced by Dakotas) for short-range sorties, had been especially allotted for the purpose. The task of the squadron was to drop agents or Force 136 detachments into enemy-occupied territory during the moonlight phases in each month, and subsequently to maintain them with arms and supplies. From January 1945 onwards the Dakotas flew on an average 180 sorties a month into Burma, while the Liberators made some six to eight sorties a month to destinations in Siam and Malaya, which often involved very long flights of up to twenty-two hours' duration, and to French Indo-China, which necessitated a stop at Kunming for refuelling. The

---

[1] See Map 11, facing page 414.
[2] See Chapters XVIII, XXII and XXVIII.

requirements of Force 136 in Burma had by March become a major commitment, and during the next two months sorties were flown on every suitable night.

The presence of the Force 136 detachments in Burma proved to be of considerable value to the tactical air forces. Thanks to the information passed back, both 221 and 224 Groups were able to attack many targets which might otherwise have never been found, such as enemy headquarters, concealed supply dumps and stationary camouflaged troop trains. On one occasion towards the end of April, as a result of such information, a pagoda being used by the Japanese as a petrol and ammunition store was attacked by fighter-bombers and blown up. Aircraft engaged on clandestine operations were also used while on their way to their operational areas to drop leaflets printed in Burmese and Japanese at selected points in central and southern Burma.

Owing to the somewhat meagre intelligence available from other sources in much of the area covered by S.E.A.C., photographic reconnaissance was of particular importance not only to Supreme Headquarters but in the conduct of strategic air operations, for it provided valuable intelligence on the location of enemy aircraft and on likely bombing objectives. The Photographic Reconnaissance Force based on Alipore (near Calcutta) consisted of two R.A.F. and four U.S.A.A.F. squadrons,[1] with Spitfires, Lightnings, Mosquitos, Mitchells, Warhawks and Liberators, modified for high altitude reconnaissance or other photographic tasks. The primary role of the force was the methodical coverage of enemy airfields and communications, as well as possible bombing objectives and areas for mine-laying, but it was also used extensively to take photographs required by the Intelligence services and to undertake aerial survey for the production of maps.[2] Mosquito aircraft with their long range were used for such tasks as the photographic reconnaissance of the railway between Bangkok and Singapore, which involved a flight of some 2,500 miles in just over eight hours—a record for this type of aircraft in any theatre of war. The main difficulty faced by the photographic reconnaissance aircraft was the presence of cloud cover over operational areas, and because of this little photography could be undertaken during the monsoon. As conditions improved at the end of the monsoon a great increase in sorties became possible and, in January 1945, some 350,000 separate prints were produced. By February the force had completed three-quarters of the survey

---

[1] See Appendix 4.
[2] These tasks were in no way connected with the photography required by army formations, for which the tactical squadrons giving close support were entirely responsible.

required for the production of a series of 1/25,000 maps from Dimapur to Rangoon and on towards Moulmein.

The Allied armies could not have carried 'Extended Capital' to a successful conclusion in 1945 had it not been possible to supply the greater part of their needs by air. The N.C.A.C. had the advantage of the Ledo Road, which was extended as it advanced to Bhamo (and thence to China), and XV Corps had that of a sea line of communication, yet both were dependent on air supply to a considerable extent. Comparative figures for deliveries by air to N.C.A.C. are not available, but between the 2nd January and the 21st May 1945 XV Corps received some 7,500 tons of supplies, an average of about 54 tons a day; these supplies were almost all dropped to those formations operating well inland and out of reach of the sea communications.[1]

Once it had crossed the Chindwin, 14th Army was dependent during its rapid advance into central and southern Burma on air supply, supplemented by what little could be carried forward by road from Kalewa and by the tonnage carried by the extemporized I.W.T. service down the Chindwin and Irrawaddy Rivers. From the 2nd January to the 21st May the army received some 210,000 tons of supplies by air and 5,500 tons by road.[2] Between the 1st February, when the I.W.T. service built up at Kalewa began to operate, and the 23rd May it delivered to Alon and Myingyan some 38,600 tons.[3] From these figures the vital importance of air supply will be obvious.

To carry out this vast undertaking Eastern Air Command had two separate formations: 3rd (American) Combat Cargo Group consisting of four Dakota squadrons (reduced to three in May 1945) under command of 10th U.S.A.A.F. which, in addition to the task of supplying N.C.A.C., had certain commitments to the China theatre, and the Combat Cargo Task Force, which in December consisted of twelve squadrons (four R.A.F. and eight U.S.A.A.F.) rising by May 1945 to seventeen (ten R.A.F./R.C.A.F. and seven U.S.A.A.F.),[4] and had the task of supplying 14th Army and XV Corps. There were in addition four U.S. troop carrier squadrons but, as these were not suitably equipped for air supply, they could be used in that role only in emergency.[5]

---

[1] See Appendix 22.
[2] See Appendix 22.
[3] See Appendix 16. From December to May inclusive the L. of C. Transport Column ferried some 72,000 tons from Dimapur by way of Imphal to Yazagyo and Indainggyi and some 81,000 tons to Kalewa, but carried forward only about 5,500 tons by road to Monywa, Yeu and Shwebo and eventually to Myingyan.
[4] See Appendix 15. One R.A.F. squadron operated throughout the period from Comilla ferrying forward reinforcements and evacuating casualties.
[5] See Appendix 4.

The removal of three combat cargo squadrons to China in December 1944 threatened at one time to bring 'Capital' to a halt astride the Irrawaddy.[1] The return of two of these three squadrons at the end of January and the arrival about the same time of two R.C.A.F. squadrons gave S.E.A.C. what was estimated to be sufficient carrying capacity to meet all requirements, provided that squadrons were so deployed that they were not called on to operate beyond their economic range of 250 miles. For this it was essential to establish air bases supplied by sea at Akyab and Ramree, since without them the land forces operating south of the general line Pakokku–Myingyan–Mandalay would be beyond the economic range of transport aircraft working from the existing bases on the Imphal plain and eastern Bengal.[2]

With Akyab occupied early in January and Kyaukpyu on Ramree Island in February, everything depended on whether the necessary airfields and installations at these two places could be built and stocked in time to be ready to supply 14th Army during its advance on Rangoon. Thanks to the great work performed by the engineers and the administrative services, Akyab began to operate on the 20th March just in time to supply IV Corps during its advance from Meiktila to Rangoon, and Ramree came into use on the 15th April just at the moment when IV Corps began to pass out of the economic range of Akyab.[3]

The actual deliveries by air from January to May 1945 were :[4]

Period	Tons delivered			Tons a day	Number of squadrons operating	Average lift a day per squadron
	14th Army	XV Corps	Total			
2/1–29/1	26,429	2,442	28,871	1,031	10	103
30/1–26/2	41,951	2,149	44,100	1,575	12	131
27/2–26/3	47,130	1,669	48,799	1,740	14	124
27/3–23/4	50,014	400	50,414	1,800	14	128
24/4–21/5	44,706	841	45,547	1,625	16	102

The tonnage delivered by air to 14th Army in January fell short of its full requirements. This was due to the temporary shortage of transport aircraft, to days lost through bad weather and the redeployment of squadrons, to the inability of pilots at times to locate the dropping zones of swiftly moving forward formations and to the 'teething troubles' of the newly-formed ground organization.[5] There were also at times unavoidable delays in bringing forward airfields

---

[1] See page 201.
[2] See page 200.
[3] See Appendix 22 and Sketch 20, facing page 412.
[4] For details see Appendix 22.
[5] See pages 183 and 203–5.

into use, especially where extensive engineering work was necessary. Furthermore, airheads could not always operate at full efficiency when first opened to traffic. This resulted in aircraft having to circle and wait their turn to land, and therefore increased the turnround period. In consequence the sustained rate of 100 hours a month for each aircraft was raised to 125 hours on the 1st February, which meant that the intensive rate (which could normally be maintained for only a month) became 185 hours.[1] This, with the arrival of two additional squadrons and no days being lost owing to bad weather, increased the deliveries during February by fifty per cent, and supplies reaching 14th Army were adequate to enable it to undertake the difficult operation of crossing the Irrawaddy, though insufficient to enable the Central Burma Stockpile to be built up to the tonnage originally planned.

Slim's plans from the 1st March onwards were based on A.L.F.S.E.A.'s forecast of deliveries, averaging 1,860 tons a day in March, 1,921 in April and 2,075 in May up to the 15th when the monsoon was expected to set in.[2] These figures were calculated on the basis that aircraft would be flying at their economic range of 250 miles,[3] and on the airhead at Myingyan (250 miles from all the principal air bases) being ready to operate by the 1st April. The actual deliveries were in fact considerably less than these estimated figures, since the ideal conditions on which they were calculated did not obtain. Myingyan was not captured till the 23rd March, and did not begin to operate until a month later. Aircraft had therefore to deliver direct to airheads in the forward areas south of Meiktila. This entailed their flying well beyond their economic range, with a consequent reduction in their daily carrying capacity. Although every effort had been made to place stores so as to ensure the most economical use of transport aircraft by having all air bases on an all-commodity basis, the shortage of certain stores and of trained storemen capable of recognizing a particular ordnance item required out of some three-quarters of a million articles made this impossible to achieve. Thus, for example, Akyab held stores only for Indian troops, British troops had to be maintained from Chittagong, and spare parts for armoured units, even when operating well to the south of Meiktila, had to be delivered from the Imphal air bases. This factor, too, resulted in aircraft having to fly beyond their economic range.

In the administrative appreciation written early in March,[4] Slim had kept the demands on air supply within the limits which had been set by A.L.F.S.E.A. on the 25th February, making up the deficit as

[1] See page 204 and footnote.
[2] See Appendix 24.
[3] See page 247.
[4] See Chapter XXVIII.

far as possible by deliveries by road and I.W.T. Having made allow-
ances for the additional distances that aircraft would have to fly
above 250 miles and for the losses incurred by dropping supplies, the
requirements for daily air supply tonnages were 1,792 in March,
1,791 in April, and 1,755 from the 1st to the 15th May. The daily
tonnages actually delivered by air were 1,682 in March, 1,789 in
April and 1,605 from the 1st to the 15th May.[1] It will be seen that the
air force delivered nearly all that was expected of it in March and all
in April, but in May, owing to heavy pre-monsoon storms, deliveries
inevitably fell to something near to A.L.F.S.E.A.'s estimated figures
(1,563) for the monsoon period. That deliveries reached the figures
they did is in itself a tribute to the aircrews and ground maintenance
staffs of all the transport squadrons whose aircraft were flown at intensive rates or more for months on end,[2] to the will that existed on the
part of all army units concerned in air supply to overcome every
difficulty as it arose and to the very close co-operation between the
army and air force units involved.

It will be seen from Appendix 24 that supplies delivered by air,
road and I.W.T. never fully met 14th Army's requirements. Slim
knew that this would be so, and during the advance on Rangoon allowed for it by ensuring that formations involved in the actual fighting
received all that was necessary and that the deficit was borne by formations in rear areas. The only period when fighting troops were short
of supplies was when the pre-monsoon storms reduced air deliveries
at the end of April and early in May before the port of Rangoon
was opened. It can be confidently said that, although 14th Army was
at times short of supplies and specific items of equipment and had
therefore to improvise to a considerable extent, its advance was never
checked by a breakdown in air supplies whatever the conditions.

The evacuation of casualties by air was not strictly a function of the
transport squadrons, but throughout the operations in central and
southern Burma it was accepted in principle that casualties should be
flown back to India from the forward areas by these aircraft on their
return flights after landing supplies. Had all returning transport aircraft evacuated casualties, however, the seriously wounded and sick
would have had to be sent to different base airfields where the
necessary medical facilities might not have existed. The system therefore adopted was that light aircraft (capable of landing and taking off
from narrow airstrips some 450–600 yards in length) were used to fly

---

[1] See Appendix 24.
[2] The aircrews engaged on air supply had to fly for long hours—up to 150 hours a
month from February to April. Sometimes they flew ten hours a day making three sorties,
beginning before dawn and ending at dusk.

Myitkyina

Sylhet

Silchar

IMPHAL

R. Chindwin

Indaw

R. Irrawaddy

AGARTALA   250 MILES

250 MILES

COMILLA

FENI

Kalewa

250 MILES

CHITTAGONG

Yeu

Shwebo

Alon   Monywa

Mandalay

Myotha

Kyaukse

Pakokku   Myingyan

Chauk

Thazi   Heho

Meiktila

Loilem

Magwe

AKYAB

Pyinmana

R. Salween

BAY

OF

BENGAL

250 MILES

RAMREE

Taungup   Prome   Toungoo

R. Irrawaddy

R. Sittang

250 MILES

Henzada

Pegu

Rangoon

The Economic Radius of Transport
Aircraft from Air Bases,
January–May 1945

Moulmein

10 0   20   40   60   80   100   120
Miles

Gulf
of
Martaban

D.K.P.

seriously wounded or sick back to the nearest airhead from where, after receiving temporary medical attention, they were transferred to Dakotas and flown back to the main hospitals located at Comilla, a special squadron being allotted for this purpose and for the fly-in of reinforcements.[1] The only alternative to air evacuation meant a difficult journey lasting for several days, with many changes by road, river and rail, and the spread of the available medical facilities over great distances.

The use of air transport made it possible to evacuate casualties who could not possibly have been moved safely by any other means. Not only did this save many lives and eliminate long painful journeys over bad roads, but the knowledge that the seriously sick and wounded could be in well-equipped base hospitals within a few hours was a potent factor in maintaining the high morale of the army. From the 2nd January to the 19th May some 40,000 casualties were flown out and about 31,000 reinforcements flown in by the aircraft used for this purpose.

The squadrons engaged in seaward reconnaissance were responsible, in co-operation with the navy, for the security of the long lines of sea communications on which the Allies in South-East Asia depended for reinforcements and supplies of all kinds. Land-based Liberators and Wellingtons together with Catalina and Sunderland flying-boats continually reconnoitred a vast area of the Indian Ocean and the Bay of Bengal. So long as the submarine threat remained, the squadrons flew patrols in all weathers, sometimes to the limit of endurance of their aircraft and often with no enemy sighting to reward them. There is no doubt, however, that these constant patrols helped to preserve the almost complete immunity to attack enjoyed by Allied shipping in these waters at this period.[2]

After the submarine threat had come to an end in January 1945, 222 Group in Ceylon and 225 Group in southern India laid some 800 mines between February and May in the approaches to ports and river estuaries known to be used by the Japanese. In the same period low-level anti-shipping strikes along the Malayan and Burmese coasts and sweeps by the East Indies Fleet made it virtually impossible for the Japanese to move supplies by sea during daylight and forced them, as a last resort, to sail only by night.[3]

---

[1] See Appendix 15.
[2] See pages 213–14.
[3] See Chapter XXIX.

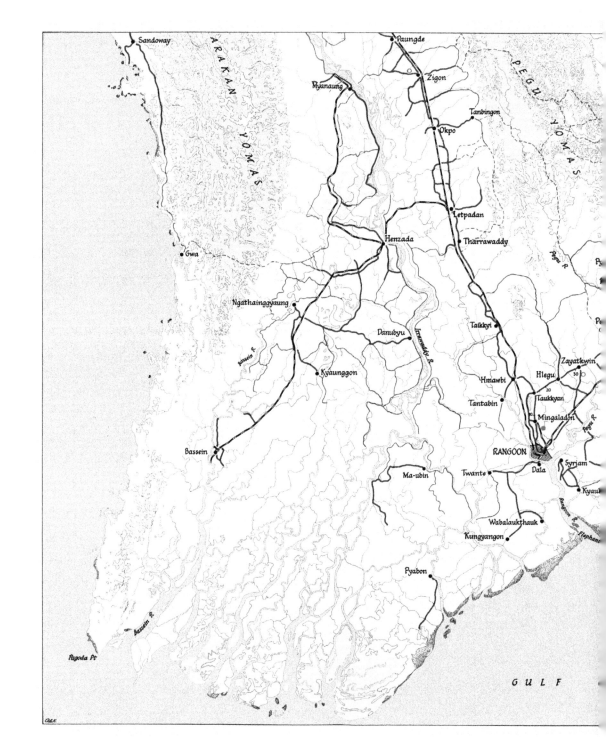

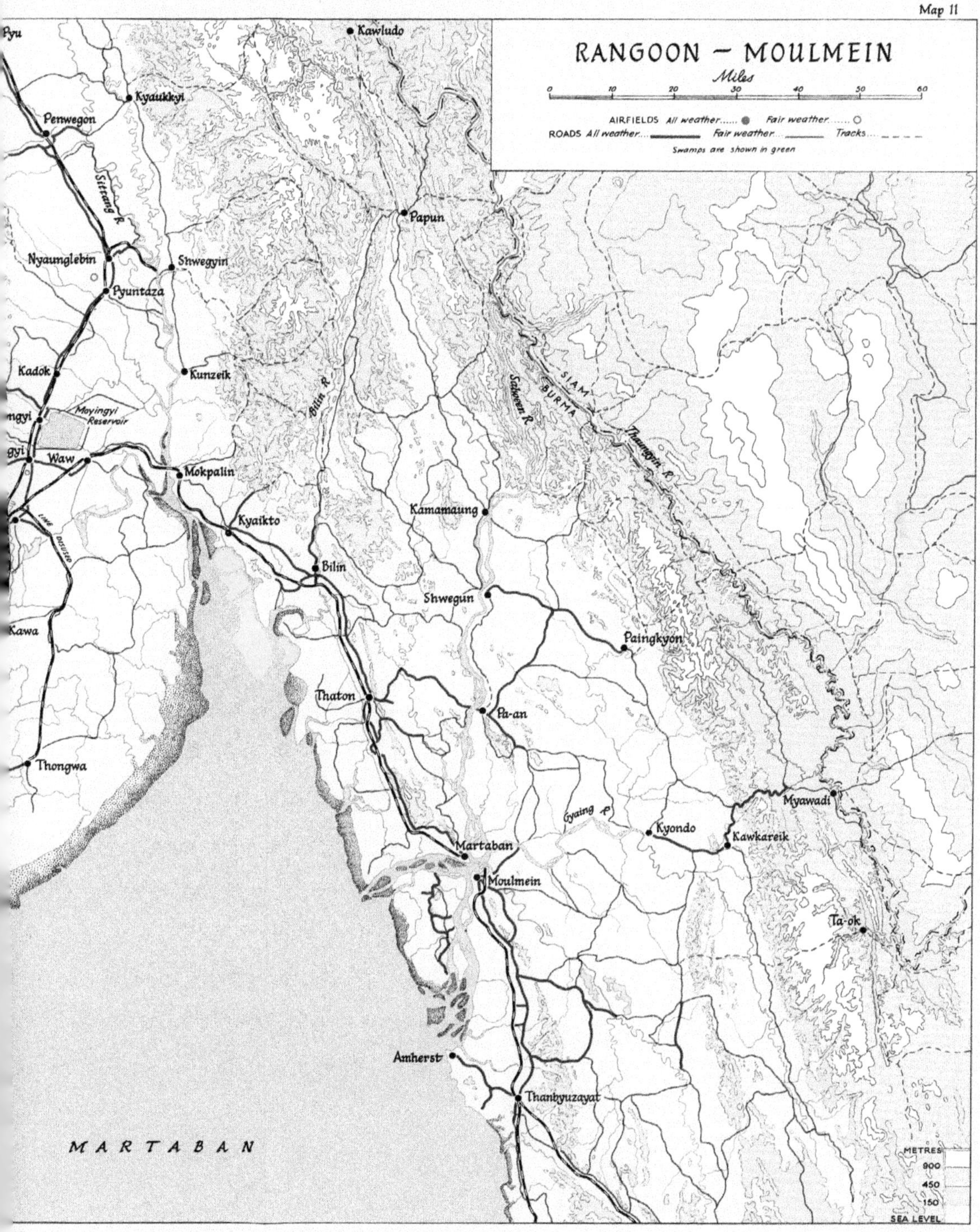

Map 11

RANGOON — MOULMEIN
Miles

AIRFIELDS *All weather* ...... ● *Fair weather* ...... ○
ROADS *All weather* .... _____ *Fair weather* _____ *Tracks* ____ ____
Swamps are shown in green

M A R T A B A N

CHAPTER XXXIV
RETROSPECT

See Maps 1, 3, 7, 8, and 13 and Sketch 20

AT the end of June 1944 the Japanese *15th Army* attacking the Imphal plain was facing decisive defeat and possible disaster —a possibility which was to become a certainty within a few weeks.[1] The defeat of *15th Army* produced the conditions necessary for the fulfilment of the second part of the Combined Chiefs of Staff directive of the 3rd June 1944—to exploit the development of over-land communications to China.[2]

By the 14th July the planning staffs at 11th Army Group, 14th Army, N.C.A.C. and Supreme Headquarters had prepared a number of alternative plans for an offensive into northern Burma, and, since Mountbatten had been invited to submit plans for the capture of Rangoon, Supreme Headquarters had in addition prepared one for an amphibious assault directed against that city. After discussing these with his Commanders-in-Chief, Mountbatten decided to submit to the Chiefs of Staff two alternative plans—'Capital' (the direct advance into north Burma) and 'Dracula' (the amphibious assault on Rangoon).[3]

Mountbatten knew that an assault on Rangoon, which was no new idea, was likely to be considered carefully by the Chiefs of Staff, and particularly by the Prime Minister who had throughout shown his preference for bold amphibious operations to strike the Japanese in rear. As he had surmised, he found, when he visited London early in August 1944, that the Chiefs of Staff and the Prime Minister had come down heavily on the side of 'Dracula' rather than 'Capital'. They realized that, if the Allies remained quiescent in north Burma, they would lose the initiative so recently gained, but they feared that operations on the lines of 'Capital' would inevitably expand and involve a slow and costly reconquest of the country from the north. They therefore preferred to keep operations in the north to a mini-mum and stake all on launching 'Dracula' in March 1945, the earliest date by which the resources required from Europe could be ready for action in S.E.A.C.[4]

As might have been expected, the Chiefs of Staff's decision to accept

---

[1] See Volume III, Chapter XXV, and Map 13 in end pocket.
[2] See page 1.
[3] See pages 3–5.
[4] See pages 7–8.

'Dracula' as the main operation for 1944–45 in preference to 'Capital' renewed the controversy, of which the readers of the earlier volumes of this history will be well aware, between the British and American Chiefs of Staff over strategic policy in Burma. The former to some extent, and the Prime Minister whole-heartedly, favoured an amphibious strategy, while the latter had always insisted that the direct approach across north Burma to open the road to China must have priority. So it was again: the Americans considered that 'Dracula' should be carried out only if it did not interfere with 'Capital', which should be the main operation.[1] Eventually both operations were approved at the Octagon Conference in September 1944,[2] which made it necessary for the British Chiefs of Staff to find from Europe the additional resources required to enable 'Dracula' to be mounted. The delay in the defeat of Germany made this impossible, and thus 'Dracula' had to be postponed until the necessary resources could be found, and 'Capital' became the accepted plan for the 1944–45 campaign.[3]

The exchange of views in London and later between Washington and London naturally resulted in delay in reaching a decision. This might have had serious repercussions but for the fact that Giffard, in pursuance of Mountbatten's directive of the 9th June,[4] had authorized Slim to press the retreating Japanese and seize crossings over the Chindwin as soon as possible: operations which Slim was only too ready to carry out with all the resources at his disposal. The extent to which the submission of an alternative plan jeopardized these operations is exemplified by the telegram which, after hearing the views of the Prime Minister and the Chiefs of Staff, Mountbatten sent from London to his deputy, Stilwell, and to his three Commanders-in-Chief. In an effort to prevent forces being drawn into 'Capital' which would be needed for 'Dracula', he suggested that the pursuit of the defeated Japanese might be discontinued and asked for their opinion on whether a withdrawal on the Central front to the Imphal plain could be made without prejudicing the situation on the Northern front, where Stilwell, with N.C.A.C., was under orders to open the land route and pipeline to China.[5] This suggestion meant abandoning the substance of the very real initiative on the Central front for the shadow of a greater and more decisive, but by no means certain, initiative by taking Rangoon and so cutting off in one stroke all the Japanese forces in Burma. An attractive concept, but at that stage

---

[1] See page 11.
[2] See pages 12–13. The two operations together were similar to operation 'Anakim', conceived by Wavell in 1942 and abandoned for the lack of resources. See Volume II, Chapter XXI.
[3] See page 108.
[4] See page 2.
[5] See pages 9–10.

81. Myitnge bridges destroyed by the R.A.F.

82. Bridge at Natmauk (probably destroyed by Japanese)

83. Japanese supply train set on fire by the R.A.F. near Pegu

84. Bridge on Bangkok railway after attack by R.A.F. Liberators

89. Hurricane Fighter-Bomber

90. Spitfire Fighter

91. Mosquito Light Bomber

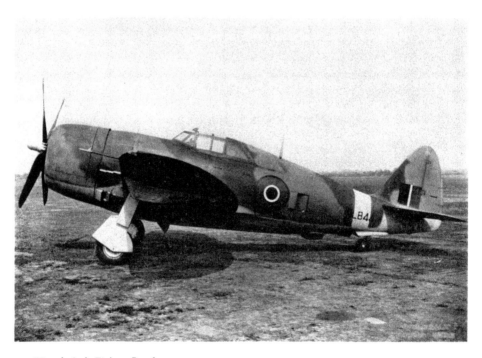

92. Thunderbolt Fighter-Bomber

quite definitely a shadow. Stilwell and the Commanders-in-Chief in reply pointed out that it was essential to retain the initiative and unsound to limit the extent and scope of the pursuit, which could be carried out without using more troops than would be required for a defensive strategy.[1] Mountbatten, who had no desire to stop 14th Army's advance, did not press the point and the pursuit continued, with the result that, when the Chiefs of Staff eventually sanctioned the first two phases of 'Capital', they were well on the way to completion, and thus the lengthy discussions over 'Dracula' did not delay the invasion of Burma.[2]

In July 1944, Mountbatten had proposed the replacement of 11th Army Group and its commander by an Allied land force headquarters and a new Commander-in-Chief acceptable to the Americans so that he would have one man controlling all the three fronts in Burma. The Chiefs of Staff could not, however, come to any agreement with their American colleagues and the matter was temporarily dropped. In September Mountbatten reopened it and pressed for an early relief for Giffard so that the new Allied Commander-in-Chief could take part in framing the plans for the 1944–45 campaign. It was not till October 1944, when Chiang Kai-shek demanded the recall of Stilwell, in whom he had lost confidence, that the long-needed changes in the unsatisfactory system of command in S.E.A.C. were set in motion. The Americans then accepted the obvious solution—the division of the C.B.I. Theatre into the India–Burma and China Theatres. Stilwell's various appointments were divided among three men, Sultan taking command of the India–Burma Theatre and N.C.A.C., Wheeler becoming Deputy Supreme Commander with no duties outside Supreme Headquarters and Wedemeyer (Mountbatten's Deputy Chief of Staff) becoming commander of the American forces in China and Chief of Staff to Chiang Kai-shek.[3] This reorganization made it possible to do away with the unsatisfactory compromise, adopted owing to Stilwell's intransigence, by which the Supreme Commander was directly responsible for operations on the Northern front. It was not, however, till mid-November that A.L.F.S.E.A. came into being and Leese replaced Giffard. By this time operations for the reconquest of Burma were well advanced and 14th Army's drive was gaining momentum. There could scarcely have been a worse time for 'swopping horses.' Leese made matters more difficult for himself by replacing many of the senior and experienced 11th Army Group staff officers by officers

---

[1] See page 10.
[2] See pages 10–11 and 42.
[3] See Chapter X.

from the United Kingdom and the Middle East with no knowledge of
the theatre. The consequences might have been at least unfortunate,
but for the fact that Slim had taken complete control of the main
offensive and allowed nothing to deflect him from his purpose of destroying the Japanese armies in north and central Burma.

The formation of an integrated land force headquarters and the
appointment of one of Mountbatten's principal staff officers to the
China Theatre should have solved all the difficulties which had beset
the Supreme Commander's relations with Chiang Kai-shek and with
the American headquarters in his theatre. In some ways, however,
the situation became worse. Wedemeyer, on arrival in Chungking,
allowed himself to be influenced by Chiang Kai-shek's fears, real or
imaginary, and at once began to press for the transfer of the Chinese-
American formations in N.C.A.C. to China together with a large number of the American transport aircraft squadrons allotted to S.E.A.C.[1]
His minimum demand was for two divisions and five transport squadrons, all of which Mountbatten considered at that time were necessary for the prosecution of the offensive to which he was already
committed. Despite his protests, the Chiefs of Staff decided that there
was no option but to agree to the transfer of two Chinese divisions
from N.C.A.C. to China by the 1st January 1945. Finding in mid-
December 1944 that there would be a surplus of air transport for
'Capital' until the end of February, though thereafter there would
be a deficit, Mountbatten felt obliged to meet Wedemeyer's demands,
and agreed reluctantly to China Command being sent one transport
squadron permanently and being lent three others temporarily till the
1st March 1945.

Almost simultaneously with the despatch of these squadrons to
China, Slim adopted the 'Extended Capital' plan, which involved
fighting the main battle south of the Irrawaddy and would therefore
eventually place extra demands on air supply. It thus became a
matter of urgency for the loaned squadrons to be returned to S.E.A.C.
or replaced from elsewhere, and Mountbatten had to send his Chief
of Staff to London to press the Chiefs of Staff to take immediate
action. The problem was solved by the end of January, for Wedemeyer agreed to return two squadrons by the 1st February and the
Chiefs of Staff to provide two additional R.A.F. squadrons to reach
India in mid-February and by the end of March respectively.[2] With
fifteen transport squadrons (eight R.A.F. and seven U.S.A.A.F.) all
seemed set fair, but Mountbatten's troubles were still not at an end,
for the Americans insisted that all their resources deployed in the
India–Burma Theatre had been provided to give direct or indirect
support for China. They thus reserved the right at any time to use

[1] See Chapter XI.
[2] See page 207.

these resources to fulfil their primary object, although they did not contemplate any change in their agreement to the resources being used in S.E.A.C.[1] They agreed, however, that any proposal to transfer resources from S.E.A.C. already engaged in approved operations, which in the opinion of the Chiefs of Staff would jeopardize such operations, would be a matter for discussion by the Combined Chiefs of Staff.[2]

The reservation resulted in Wedemeyer making renewed attempts in March 1945 to obtain the agreement of the American Chiefs of Staff to the transfer of further formations from N.C.A.C. to China and the use of transport aircraft allotted to N.C.A.C. for moving them.[3] By this time, however, the success of 14th Army's offensive had altered the strategic picture in Burma. The American/Chinese formations in N.C.A.C., whose progress had been slow, had now become more of a liability than an asset, since their maintenance involved the use of transport aircraft which could be employed more profitably in maintaining 14th Army's drive on Rangoon about to begin. Mountbatten therefore agreed to their transfer to China except for one division required to protect the newly-opened Burma Road. He made the proviso, however, that the move would have to be effected by aircraft other than those allotted to S.E.A.C.[4] Nevertheless the Americans, despite their agreement on the transfer of resources and without informing the Chiefs of Staff, instructed Sultan, in his capacity as Commanding General, Burma–India Theatre, to move the formations in aircraft from China, from Air Transport Command or from those maintaining N.C.A.C.[5] Sultan, who retained a realistic sense of his responsibility towards Mountbatten, warned the Supreme Commander of this order. Mountbatten promptly refused to allow any aircraft already allotted to S.E.A.C. to be used for the purpose and took the matter up with the Chiefs of Staff, who, with the assistance of the Prime Minister, eventually got an agreement from the Americans that no aircraft allotted to S.E.A.C. would be removed until Rangoon had been occupied or until the 1st June 1945, whichever was earlier.[6]

The orders to Sultan not only disregarded the agreed method of issuing directives regarding operations in S.E.A.C., but repeated a practice which had in the past caused friction.[7] This illustrates the difficulties Mountbatten had to contend with over the allocation of American resources in this campaign and the danger of a Supreme

---

[1] See page 208.
[2] See pages 208–9.
[3] See page 315.
[4] See pages 316–17.
[5] See page 317.
[6] See pages 318–19.
[7] See Volume III, Chapter XVII.

Commander not being able to exercise control over all resources in his theatre.

Mountbatten fortunately had the personality to withstand pressure from the highest levels. He was loyally supported by Sultan and Stratemeyer (the two senior American commanders in the theatre), and he had the tact and diplomacy to make concessions, provided they did not jeopardize plans which he believed essential for success, in order to ensure that he obtained what he considered absolutely necessary. Thus the worst consequences of the importunities of Wede-meyer and the efforts to by-pass S.E.A.C. Headquarters were avoid-ed. Seldom has a campaign which had to face so many serious diffi-culties at high command level achieved such outstanding success as that of the 1944–45 campaign in Burma. That it did so is attribut-able to the leadership shown by Mountbatten, who not only solved the many complex inter-Allied problems, thereby ensuring that his Commanders-in-Chief had the tools with which to carry out their allotted tasks, but also kept in close touch with the course of operations, intervening only when absolutely necessary.

By the time that A.L.F.S.E.A. was formed in November 1944, the plan for the reconquest of Burma ('Capital') had been finalized and was in progress. On the Arakan front, XV Corps had the task of clearing north Arakan and capturing Akyab, after which two divi-sions and engineer and administrative units were to be withdrawn for operations elsewhere; on the Central front, 14th Army was to cross the Chindwin, clear the Yeu–Shwebo plain and link up with N.C.A.C., which was to secure the general line Mogok–Lashio. Both were then to be prepared to exploit southwards with the general object of destroying the Japanese forces and securing the air and road link with China.[1]

By the end of November 1944, 14th Army, after its costly and arduous monsoon campaign, had closed up to the Chindwin on a front of 100 miles from Kalewa to Thaungdut and had secured bridge-heads at Yuwa, Sittaung and Thaungdut.[2] Slim hoped to bring the Japanese *15th Army* to battle on the Shwebo plain where his armour would be a decisive factor.[3] Believing that the Japanese, in spite of their heavy defeat at Imphal, would fight to hold the precipitous Zibyu Taungdan with its few passes, he planned to pin them in the plain by advancing on it from the north and west.[4] Consequently

---

[1] See Chapter IX.
[2] See Map 1, facing page 15.
[3] See pages 149–50.
[4] Slim had learned in October that Kawabe and Mutaguchi had been replaced by Kimura and Katamura. He considered that Kimura would run true to form, seeing 'the Chindwin behind us, not the Irrawaddy behind him.' See *Defeat into Victory*, pages 379–80.

he ordered XXXIII Corps to advance from the Kalewa area directly on to Yeu and Shwebo, while IV Corps on its left moved rapidly eastwards from the Thaungdut area in a wide enveloping movement to contact the right wing of N.C.A.C. in the Indaw area with its outer flank, and then swung south towards the Yeu–Shwebo area, thus catching the Japanese between the two corps.[1] As is now known, Kimura, instructed late in September to regroup his forces to cover vital strategic areas in southern Burma, had decided to defend a general line from the Monglong Range through Mandalay and Yenangyaung to the Arakan coast. As a result of this decision, Katamura (*15th Army*) decided to begin his withdrawal on the 1st December 1944 so that he would be ready to fight on the line of the Irrawaddy by the middle of January.[2]

Lack of opposition east of the Chindwin early in December made Slim suspect that *15th Army* was withdrawing across the Irrawaddy.[3] If this proved to be correct he would be unable to pin and destroy it, as he had hoped, between the Chindwin and the Irrawaddy, and would have to find another battleground. He came to the conclusion that the only alternative was to cut the Japanese communications in the Meiktila–Thazi area and then destroy the enemy forces in north Burma between Meiktila and Mandalay where, as on the Shwebo plain, his armour could exert its full power. When suspicion became a certainty on the 16th December, he had a revised plan ready; he sent Leese the gist of it on the 17th and on the 18th issued verbal orders to his two corps commanders, who began to put them into effect next day.[4] The new plan involved a simple exchange of formations *in situ* between IV and XXXIII Corps, while IV Corps, having relinquished its forward division (19th) east of the Chindwin, was able to deploy on the right of XXXIII Corps without any switching of formations and advance under a cloak of secrecy up the Myittha valley with Meiktila as its objective, the capture of which would cut off all Japanese forces in north Burma from their base at Rangoon and precipitate a major battle in country suitable for the use of armour. At the same time Slim warned his corps commanders that the capture of Meiktila, known as 'Extended Capital', might be followed by a drive southwards to secure a port, preferably Rangoon; this plan was known within 14th Army Headquarters as 'Sob' (Sea or Bust) for without a port the army could not be maintained in south Burma during the monsoon.[5]

'Extended Capital' was bold and imaginative and, if the thrust to Meiktila succeeded, would give Slim the opportunity of destroying at

[1] See page 157.
[2] See pages 58–60.
[3] See pages 163–64 and Map 3, facing page 55.
[4] See pages 164 and 168.
[5] See Chapter XV.

one stroke the Japanese armies in northern and central Burma.
Much, however, depended on the success of the deception plan which
was an integral part of it, for IV Corps had to be got across the
Irrawaddy without arousing Japanese suspicions that it was the main
thrust aimed at their most vital area. Slim believed that the Japanese
knew that 19th Division formed part of IV Corps and that its continued presence on the left of XXXIII Corps would create the impression that the whole army was advancing east. He therefore took
steps to increase this impression and to conceal the movement of the
reconstructed IV Corps up the Myittha valley by heading its advance
with an East African brigade, ostensibly belonging to 11th (E.A.)
Division which had been operating for weeks at the junction of the
Kabaw and Myittha valleys.

By the end of January XXXIII Corps had practically closed up to
the Irrawaddy on a front of 120 miles from its confluence with the
Chindwin to Thabeikkyin, and had established two bridgeheads
across it some fifty and seventy miles north of Mandalay,[1] while the
leading division of IV Corps had reached Pauk.[2] That the Japanese
had at that time no suspicion of IV Corps' move up the Myittha
valley and the danger it represented is shown by their dispositions.
The *15th Army* had *15th Division* north of Mandalay, *31st Division*
holding the Irrawaddy from Mandalay westwards to Myinmu, *33rd
Division* holding from the hilly ground south of Myinmu to Pakokku
and *53rd Division*, withdrawn after its abortive attacks on 19th
Division's bridgeheads, in reserve near Kyaukse, dispositions clearly
designed to meet an enveloping attack on Mandalay from north and
west. The bulk of *28th Army's* strength in the Irrawaddy valley was
the two regiments in the Yenangyaung area and there was only an
I.N.A. regiment in the Nyaungu–Pagan area in touch with the left of
33rd Division.[3] The advance of 14th Army from the Chindwin had
been far more rapid than the Japanese had expected, and in consequence they had had insufficient time for reorganization and for the
preparation of their new defensive positions on the Irrawaddy. The
failure of their attempts in the second half of January to destroy the
bridgeheads gained by 19th Division north of Mandalay made their
situation worse, for it resulted in severe losses, which they could ill
afford, without any corresponding gain.[4] The Japanese situation was
far from satisfactory, but 14th Army, except north of Mandalay, had
still to cross the Irrawaddy.

The 14th Army's crossing of the river presented Slim with a difficult
problem. The equipment he had was barely adequate to enable one

---

[1] See pages 183–86.
[2] See page 182.
[3] See pages 187–88.
[4] See pages 185 and 187.

division in each corps to get a big enough 'first wave' across the river to establish a bridgehead capable of holding out against serious attack until the 'second wave' could join it. What equipment there was had suffered considerable damage during its difficult 350-mile journey over mountainous roads from the railhead at Dimapur, and had to be repaired by field workshops. It was of primary importance that the IV Corps bridgehead at Nyaungu should be established and the Meiktila striking force concentrated in it so quickly that the Japanese would have no chance of discovering what was afoot, so that the thrust on Meiktila would come as a complete surprise. Slim therefore had to wait until the division which was to make the Nyaungu crossing was ready to strike.

His timing of the various crossings is the main point of interest. By the 10th February, 7th Division of IV Corps was in a position to make its final reconnaissance for the crossing at Nyaungu. That day Slim ordered 19th Division, nearly 200 miles farther up the river, to begin to break out of its Kyaukmyaung bridgehead. He gave the Japanese two days in which to try to discover where the next blow would fall, during which 2nd Division was to draw attention to the river bank opposite Mandalay by active reconnaissance. At nightfall on the 12th he loosed 20th Division to cross at two points near Myinmu, an area which would appear to the Japanese as the obvious one for the right arm of an enveloping attack on Mandalay. As he expected, the Japanese immediately began to move their reserves to counter-attack 20th Division. When, in the early hours of the 14th, the crossing by 7th Division at Nyaungu took place, the Japanese did not take it seriously; they were in fact far more concerned with the East African brigade's move towards Seikpyu and the threat it implied to Yenang-yaung than with the situation at Nyaungu. They therefore directed their immediate counter-attack on 20th Division's bridgehead at Myinmu and on the East Africans west of the Irrawaddy, so 7th Division was able, without meeting serious opposition, to establish its bridgehead and 17th Division with its armour to concentrate in it without being molested.[1]

Even if the message saying that a force with 200 vehicles was advancing on Meiktila had been correctly received,[2] the Japanese, with all their immediately available reserves committed, were temporarily helpless, and could not have held up or delayed 17th Division's thrust. By the 4th March the division was in full possession of the town and surrounding country. Slim had succeeded in so misleading his opponents that he had been able to place a division and an armoured brigade astride their main line of communication in Burma with the minimum loss of time, men and material.

[1] See Chapter XXIII.
[2] See page 272.

The most difficult problem raised by operation 'Capital' was that of maintaining 14th Army once it had crossed the Chindwin. The Imphal road had to be repaired and extended as a fair-weather road down the Kabaw Valley to Kalewa and from Shwegyin across the river to the Yeu–Shwebo plain so that the army could be concentrated forward. It was evident that this one road could not also carry the daily maintenance requirement of the army and that this would have to be carried by air to forward delivery points established by the forward troops, and by I.W.T. down the Chindwin from Kalewa to the Alon–Monywa area. Such engineer resources as remained after dealing with the repair, construction and maintenance of roads in the forward area, the establishment of the I.W.T. service and the provision of airfields and of forward bases would have to be used to build an all-weather road from Tamu to Kalewa so that the I.W.T. service could be operated throughout the monsoon.

The air supply of 14th Army did not appear in the latter part of 1944 to offer any insuperable difficulties since the objective, then the Pakokku–Mandalay line, was within the economic range of Dakota aircraft operating from air bases on the Imphal plain supplied by the northern line of communications from India, and the number of British and American transport aircraft was at the time sufficient to meet the expected load.[1] The whole situation suddenly altered in December 1944 when, soon after Mountbatten had justifiably agreed to loan three transport squadrons to the China Theatre to meet Wedemeyer's urgent requests for help, Slim found it necessary to change the original plan and introduce 'Extended Capital'.

The new plan not only meant that the major battle in Burma would be fought south of the Irrawaddy in an area which was outside the economic range of Dakota aircraft working from Imphal, but also that an attempt was likely to be made to capture Rangoon from the north before the monsoon. This made it essential that new air bases were established within economic range of the whole of south Burma, that the aircraft lent to Wedemeyer were returned and that the total number of aircraft was increased. Supreme Headquarters and A.L.F.S.E.A. were thus posed with a new problem to which an immediate solution had to be found if 14th Army were to be maintained. Mountbatten was able to ensure the supply of aircraft, but the provision of air bases within economic range of south Burma was more difficult. Suitable airfields existed around Chittagong and immediate steps were taken to move there the existing air base from Agartala; this eased the situation in the Myingyan area and down the Irrawaddy as far as Magwe and enabled all the transport

---

[1] See page 129 and Sketch 20, facing page 142.

squadrons to be deployed, but did not bring south Burma within range. The only other places safe from enemy interference where ports could be developed, airfields built and air bases easily established were Akyab and Ramree Islands; the former brought Toungoo and Prome within range and the latter the rest of south Burma including Rangoon.[1]

The offensive for the capture of Akyab was well under way and it was thought that it would be occupied before the end of January 1945. The Japanese made matters much easier and saved A.L.F.S.E.A. much time by evacuating the island, and it was occupied without opposition some three weeks earlier than expected, weeks which were to prove invaluable. Immediate steps were then taken to capture Ramree Island, and Kyaukpyu, the proposed site for the air base, was occupied by the end of January.[2]

The maintenance of 14th Army had now to be progressively transferred from the air base at Imphal to the bases at Chittagong, Akyab and Kyaukpyu. This meant that maintenance for an army of six divisions, two independent brigades, two tank brigades and corps and army troops, totalling some 260,000 men, had to be transferred from the northern to the southern line of communications. Since all the reserves for 14th Army had been stockpiled on the northern line and the southern line had been developed and stocked to maintain only XV Corps of four divisions, A.L.F.S.E.A. administrative staffs and India Base were faced with a vast 'crash' programme entailing considerably increased demands on engineer resources and shipping tonnage. This included developing two ports, constructing an adequate number of airfields and providing storage space for the necessary reserve of supplies of all kinds at Akyab and Kyaukpyu, and stocking these air bases within a very limited period of time.[3]

The development of the new air bases at Akyab and Kyaukpyu was made more difficult by the fact that both ports were being used for the maintenance of XV Corps engaged on operation 'Romulus'— the clearance of north Arakan. Since 'Romulus' would not necessarily contain the Japanese on the Arakan coast or assist 14th Army's offensive, the Supreme Commander decided towards the end of January to extend XV Corps' role, and early in February instructed Leese to establish a bridgehead at Taungup and open up the Taungup–Prome road as a fair-weather supply route.[4]

It became evident by the middle of February, however, that the air supply allotted to XV Corps would have to be transferred to 14th Army as soon as the army had crossed the Irrawaddy, and that the

---

[1] See Sketch 20, facing page 412, and Chapter XVIII.
[2] See Chapter XIX.
[3] See Chapter XVIII.
[4] See page 241.

dates fixed for the opening of the forward air bases at Akyab and Kyaukpyu would be far too late. Since an acceleration in the dates of readiness of these bases could be achieved only by relieving the ports and their installations of the burden of maintaining XV Corps, its maintenance had to be switched to Chittagong. This port was already congested and could not bear the whole of the additional burden. As it was essential that 14th Army's advance on Rangoon should not be checked, Leese had no alternative but to reduce the corps to one division, which virtually put an end to its operations on the Arakan coast.[1] Nevertheless the operations of XV Corps and the ever-present threat of a landing at Rangoon succeeded in containing eleven Japanese battalions in Arakan and south Burma until April, by which time *Burma Area Army* had lost control and the disintegration of the Japanese army in Burma had begun.[2]

By establishing advanced air bases at Chittagong and along the Arakan coast (though those at Akyab and Kyaukpyu were able to operate only just in time) and by operating all the available aircraft for long periods over even the intensive rate, air transport was enabled to carry seventy-seven per cent of the supplies delivered to 14th Army and the balance was carried by the I.W.T. fleet operating on the Chindwin and Irrawaddy. It will be noted, however, that, despite the enormous exertions of all those engaged in the maintenance of 14th Army, deliveries fell short of its full requirements by some 380 tons a day in March (fifteen and a half per cent) and 450 tons a day in April (sixteen and a half per cent).[3] This shortage did not deter 14th Army, which by improvisation made do with what it got.

The creation of an I.W.T. fleet (capable of carrying 600–700 tons a day) in the upper reaches of the Chindwin, with material brought hundreds of miles along indifferent roads and augmented by local material, was a fine piece of imaginative planning implemented by the determination and skilful improvisation of those who carried it out. The development of the ports and air bases at Akyab and Kyaukpyu in three months was also a fine feat. A tribute must be paid to all those engaged on these projects, the army and air units engaged in operating the air supply and the units building up and operating the I.W.T. organization, for, had they failed, 14th Army could not have carried its pursuit to a victorious conclusion. But it must be remembered that air supply, on which so much depended,

---

[1] See pages 245–46.

[2] It is of interest to note that, of the nine battalions that were despatched from *54th* and *55th Divisions* to the Irrawaddy front, only four (two battalions of *154th Regiment* in the Letse area and two of *112th Regiment* at Mount Popa) made any appreciable impact on operations on the Central front.

[3] See Appendix 24.

would not have been possible if the Allied air forces had not first obtained and then retained complete air superiority.

The loss of Meiktila created for the Japanese a desperate situation and they reacted characteristically by concentrating all the troops they could spare in an all-out counter-offensive to retake it. This led to a battle which raged throughout March 1945 and ended with the complete defeat of the Japanese armies and their hurried retreat.[1] This battle, however, not only delayed the start of 14th Army's drive towards Rangoon but also the development of its line of communication, since the Japanese holding the ring for their forces attacking Meiktila hung on to Myingyan for as long as possible. The work on developing Myingyan as a river port and main base for 14th Army's southward advance could not thus begin until the end of March, instead of the beginning as had been hoped.[2]

Slim realized that these delays might well prevent 14th Army from reaching Rangoon before the onset of the monsoon. Without a seaport the army could not be maintained in south Burma, and would be faced with a withdrawal which would be a military and political disaster. He therefore asked Leese to arrange for an amphibious attack to be launched on Rangoon before the monsoon as an administrative insurance.[3] Although, as events turned out, it is certain that 14th Army would have occupied Rangoon by the end of the first week in May without the aid of an amphibious operation, Slim was justified in asking for the operation since even the remotest risk of failure was unacceptable.

The possibility of mounting an amphibious operation against Rangoon had been raised by Leese in February and, owing to its earliest timing being at the end of April, had eventually been discarded as being too late to asssist 14th Army.[4] Slim's request did not therefore raise a new issue and, in view of the short time remaining before the monsoon, it should have been evident that immediate action was necessary. Although Slim made his request on the 19th March, Leese took no action till the 22nd and then merely asked Mountbatten, whom he met at Monywa, whether such an operation would be feasible at the end of April, when a brigade from Arakan would be available.[5] It was not till the 26th that he made a definite request for the operation, by which time seven valuable days had been lost. Mountbatten, who had always advocated the operation and was well aware of the importance of the time factor, thereupon sent

[1] See Chapters XXV and XXVI.
[2] See page 323.
[3] See page 327.
[4] See pages 241–42 and 243–4.
[5] See page 327.

his Directors of Plans to A.L.F.S.E.A. Headquarters at Calcutta from where they reported on the 29th that no plans had been prepared. It was not till the 30th, after eleven days delay, that Leese recommended that the operation should be launched from Arakan by a division of XV Corps.

A plan was then quickly evolved for a seaborne assault, preceded by an operation by parachute troops to capture Elephant Point where there were guns covering the entrance to the Rangoon River. The aircraft for this operation had to be supplied from within A.L.F.S.E.A.'s resources, and Leese, who was averse to their use for this purpose, proposed to do without the airborne operation. Since, with Elephant Point in enemy hands, an amphibious operation might have incurred heavy losses and been checked, Mountbatten made a special trip to Calcutta and overruled Leese.[1] In view of the disastrous consequences that might have resulted if 14th Army had been held up by the monsoon before it could reach Rangoon, Leese's delay in ordering preparations to be made for 'Dracula' appears surprising, as also does his willingness to accept the risk to the seaborne assault force if Elephant Point remained in enemy hands.

The speedy and overwhelming success of 14th Army's advance from the Chindwin to Rangoon was largely due to the flexibility in planning, tactics and organization shown by Slim and his commanders. Flexibility in planning is exemplified by Slim's major change of plan in December when he discovered that the Japanese had no intention of fighting between the Chindwin and the Irrawaddy. Flexibility in tactics is well illustrated by the way 14th Army took in its stride the switch from close jungle fighting with tanks acting as mobile pillboxes, when half a mile a day was good progress, to wide-ranging moves by infantry in lorries led by powerful armoured spearheads, which often covered twenty to thirty miles a day. Only highly trained troops led by commanders possessing boldness and skill could have taken such changes in their stride without faltering. The same flexbility, though in a different way, was shown in Arakan when complex amphibious operations on a coast studded with islands and only approachable through narrow mangrove-fringed creeks were carried out by ordinary standard divisions without previous training, and by naval units often with craft not designed for the tasks required of them. The foresight and initiative shown by the motorization and reorganization at short notice of the two divisions earmarked for the thrust to capture Meiktila and the pursuit of the enemy to Rangoon, so that they could move fast with armour across waterless country, is a fine example of flexibility in organization.

[1] See page 330.

A dominating factor was the invaluable and constant close support provided by the R.A.F., whose aircraft destroyed enemy communications and were continually available at short notice to bring devastating destructive fire on enemy-held strongpoints. Yet another dominating factor was the medium tank. The Japanese had no means of dealing with heavily armoured, fast-moving tanks except by misusing their field, mountain and anti-aircraft guns by siting them to fire at point-blank range in the hope of getting in one effective shot before being overwhelmed. Used boldly in wide enveloping movements, 14th Army's armour often caught the Japanese in the open and inflicted heavy casualties. Although the armoured units' losses were by no means inconsiderable—for the risk of running into concealed guns at point-blank range was accepted—they saved the lives of many hundreds of infantry. Tanks were frequently used to ferry infantry across country, the troops dismounting only when close-range small-arms fire forced them to take up the fight on foot, either supporting or being supported by the tanks. Thus the army was able to pursue at a speed which eventually caused the complete breakdown of the Japanese command and supply organization, with the result that their formations became scattered and lost all cohesion.

Finally, the fact that the Allied forces could be supplied very largely, and on occasions entirely, by air freed them to a considerable extent from being tied to roads, and enabled them to undertake operations which would otherwise have been impossible to maintain for more than a few days. If it is true, as Napoleon said, that armies march on their stomachs, it is equally true that 14th Army was carried to victory on the wings of the Allied air forces.

It will be evident to the reader of this volume that, from the time that 14th Army began its advance from the Imphal plain until it reached the gates of Rangoon, the foresight which saw both the opportunities and dangers, and the initiative in seizing the former and forestalling the latter, stemmed from one man—Slim. Backed by able subordinates, he saw to it that the defeated *15th Army* was relentlessly followed up and given no time to reorganize. Its every move was watched with a view to pinning it on a battleground where Slim could use his armour with full effect to bring about its final destruction. The bold thrust to Meiktila, later aptly described by Kimura as the master-stroke, placed an infantry division and an armoured brigade astride the Japanese main line of communications. Seldom has a move of this magnitude, which incidentally involved an opposed crossing of one of the great rivers of Asia, been carried out in such complete secrecy. The presence of IV Corps in the Meiktila area disrupted the Japanese plans and held all their forces in north Burma in a vice-like grip until they were broken and dispersed. Within hours of the collapse of the fierce enemy counter-stroke, carried out with all the grim determination and courage of the Japanese soldier, there began one of the outstanding pursuits in the annals of British arms.

It is of interest to note that in the 1944 campaign, described in Volume III of this series, there were many special formations. No fewer than nine brigades were organized and trained for special tasks: two four-battalion brigades of 36th Division trained for amphibious operations, one commando brigade and six brigades of Special Force (Chindits). In the 1944 campaign 36th Division, temporarily employed in Arakan as a normal infantry division, was used sparingly so that it should avoid losses and remain available for amphibious operations. The brigades of Special Force were in action for periods varying from three to four months only. They incurred serious battle casualties, and the wastage from sickness and malnutrition was such that, on withdrawal, they were unfit for active service for a very long period.

In the 1944–45 campaign forces designed and trained for special tasks almost entirely disappeared. The 36th Division was reorganized as a standard division to meet the urgent need for such a formation in N.C.A.C. The commando brigade fought with distinction in Arakan, but only for a few weeks. Special Force was not used at all. By the end of 1944 its heavy losses had not been replaced and, as no task had been found for it, it was broken up in January 1945, two of its brigades being transferred to the Indian airborne division (which came into being too late to be of any use during the war) and the remainder of its manpower to other units.

The campaign of 1944–45 amply bears out the contention, made by Auchinleck and Giffard at the time the Chindits were increased, that a well-trained standard division could carry out any operational task with little special training, and underlines the waste of manpower in forming forces fitted for particular tasks which, as opportunities for their use in the role for which they were designed are likely to be limited, may spend the greater part of the period of hostilities in inactivity.

It may appear to the reader as the story of the advance into central and south Burma unfolds that the country was almost depopulated since, unlike previous volumes, there is seldom any mention in this volume of inhabitants except in relation to the activities of Force 136. Throughout 1943 and most of 1944, 14th Army, which then included XV Corps, was operating in the Naga and Chin Hills and in north Arakan. The Nagas and Chins, who hated the Japanese, were friendly, and the Arakanese Muslims were also friendly for they hated the Arakan Buddhists, who from the outset had tended to throw in their lot with the Japanese. Refugees who had left their homes in the areas occupied by the Japanese had been housed and cared for by the Indian refugee organization and by the army. Of those who stayed in their homes, many were willing to help Allied troops by giving information to 'V' Force, when they could do so without incurring the suspicions of the Japanese.

When the general advance began in late 1944 the Allied forces were moving into territory which had been in Japanese occupation for two and a half years, and it was at least possible that some of the inhabitants had in that time become pro-Japanese. Burma, unlike India, is sparsely populated and it was easy for its inhabitants, even in large towns, to disappear from areas where battle was imminent. Thus the forward troops usually found villages and towns almost deserted,[1] and the few inhabitants they met were at first afraid to be co-operative. The Japanese, as they withdrew, had taken with them most of the senior local officials but, as the advance progressed, the inhabitants of the reoccupied territory began to flow back, and it soon became quite common for minor civil officials and police to report back for duty. As the war diary of one unit which had been in the retreat from Burma commented, the friendliness of the Burmans was in marked contrast to their attitude in 1942.

At the time S.E.A.C. was established in 1943, large-scale amphibious operations were contemplated. Mountbatten therefore established his headquarters at Kandy in Ceylon, where he would be in close touch with his naval Commander-in-Chief and at the centre of the periphery of possible amphibious operations.[2] Kandy was, however, some seventy miles from the nearest suitable airfield, 1,500 air miles from Delhi, from where Auchinleck controlled India Base on which S.E.A.C. was entirely dependent, and 1,300 air miles from Calcutta, which was the nerve centre of the lines of communication to the north-east frontier and the headquarters of Eastern Air Command.[3] A supreme Commander should have his three Commanders-in-Chief alongside him, and Mountbatten naturally wished to have them in Ceylon. This led to a difference of opinion between himself and his land and air Commanders-in-Chief, Giffard and Peirse. Although responsible for the garrisons of various islands in the Indian Ocean,

---

[1] The pre-war population of Mandalay was some 160,000 but when the city was reoccupied there were, it was estimated, not more than 7,000 inhabitants.

[2] See Volume III, pages 51–52.

[3] The journey by rail and road from Kandy to the airfield took some two and a half hours; from there, in a Dakota, the flying time to Delhi was between eight and nine hours and to Calcutta between seven and eight hours.

Giffard had at the time the overriding task of controlling land operations on the India–Burma border. This necessitated his having a headquarters located close to the nerve centre of his communications and supporting air formations, and in a position from which he could easily visit the Arakan and Central fronts in all weathers. It is not therefore surprising that he established his main headquarters at Calcutta and remained adamant in his refusal to meet Mountbatten's wishes to move them to Ceylon. There is little doubt, when reviewing the course of the decisive battles of 1944, that Giffard's decision to remain at Calcutta was justified. On the formation of A.L.F.S.E.A. in November 1944 and the replacement of Giffard by Leese, Mountbatten insisted on Leese establishing his main headquarters at Kandy, using Calcutta as an advanced headquarters.[1] Whatever names were given to the various echelons of A.L.F.S.E.A.'s headquarters, Leese, heavily involved in 'Capital', found that Calcutta became of necessity his main headquarters in deed if not in name. Peirse also was not prepared to move to Kandy, which was a long way from both Eastern Air Command (his main operational headquarters in Calcutta) and his maintenance echelons based on Delhi. The fact that Supreme Headquarters was located at Kandy thus was convenient for neither Mountbatten nor his land or air Commander-in-Chief.

Since land operations in Burma were in 1944 and the early part of 1945 the main preoccupation of S.E.A.C., it would have been more convenient for all concerned had the Supreme Commander established an advanced element of his headquarters in or near Calcutta during 1944,[2] where he could have had his land and air Commanders-in-Chief alongside him throughout the campaign for the reconquest of Burma; his possible separation from his naval Commander-in-Chief, had the latter refused to leave Ceylon, would have been of no great significance in view of the fact that amphibious operations on a large scale had been abandoned owing to lack of resources.

By August 1944 *Imperial General Headquarters* were faced with a very serious situation. Repeated efforts by Japanese soldiers and statesmen to bring about mediation between the U.S.S.R. and Germany had failed, and it was evident that Russia had no intention of making a separate peace with Germany. It seemed, too, that Germany was

---

[1] See Chapter X.

[2] Between the 14th December 1944 and the end of March 1945 Mountbatten made five trips to the forward areas and was away from Kandy for thirty-eight days. During these trips he saw Leese seven times and Slim six times, and took most of his important operational decisions in Calcutta or even farther forward. During his visit to Calcutta Mountbatten made use of offices in Fort William. In the same period Leese paid only one visit of two days to Kandy.

doomed to defeat by the end of 1944 or early 1945, and that the Allies would invade Burma in overwhelming strength as soon as the 1944 monsoon ended.

The swift advance by the Americans across the Pacific was threatening the Philippines, Formosa and the sea lines of communication to the Southern Region, already in a parlous state owing to the heavy losses in merchant shipping which could no longer be made good.[1] Unless a decisive defeat could be inflicted on the American forces when they attacked the Philippines, it would be only a matter of time before the Southern Region was isolated and there would be a serious threat to the Japanese mainland. It was therefore vitally important for the very existence of Japan that the maximum naval, military and air strength should be concentrated in the Pacific and an all-out effort made to throw back the American offensive.

All theatres in the Southern Region thus had become subservient to the needs of the war in the Pacific, and it was clear that all the occupied territories in the Southern Region could not be held. Burma was the farthest from Japan, of no economic value since command of the sea had been lost, and was difficult to defend. In their operation instructions to *Southern Army* issued in September 1944, *Imperial General Headquarters* made it clear that the vital fronts were those facing the Pacific and that Burma was of secondary importance.[2] Nevertheless, although a complete withdrawal from Burma was considered, it was rejected on the grounds that the security of the whole chain of defences from Burma to Sumatra which covered *Southern Army's* flank would thereby be endangered. Thus, although reinforcements could no longer be sent to Burma to replace the heavy losses suffered in the battle for Imphal, and *Burma Area Army* was not strong enough to hold sufficient territory in Burma to keep communications between India and China severed, it was ordered to secure strategic areas covering southern Burma.

In the autumn of 1944 Kimura was set an almost impossible task and one which was made even more difficult when, at the height of his struggle to keep the Allies out of south Burma, he was ordered to transfer one of his divisions and his remaining air strength to Indo-China.[3] His formations were much below strength and he could not expect to receive reinforcements, he had nothing with which to meet his opponent's strong armoured forces and his few remaining reconnaissance aircraft could not, in face of Allied air superiority, obtain for him adequate intelligence of his enemy's movements. His land forces had little hope of defeating the Allied offensive.

It would appear that his only hope, and a very slender one at that,

---

[1] See Map 8, facing page 252.
[2] See Chapter V.
[3] See page 188.

of delaying the Allies' progress and keeping them out of south Burma till the 1945 monsoon made movement difficult and air supply precarious lay in interfering with their extended lines of communication. There were only two ways in which he could have tried to do this: by using his remaining air strength in surprise attacks on the unarmed transport aircraft at newly-established airheads, and by preventing, regardless of the cost, the establishment of air bases within range of south Burma, thus increasing the distance supplies had to be carried. No attempt was made to take either of these steps.

The Japanese army air force had as its normal task the provision of close support for the army, and by conforming rigidly to this role was of no help to *Burma Area Army* in the serious situation in which it found itself. Except for an attack on the Onbauk airfield which stopped daylight landings of transport aircraft for five days, the air force was wasted on sporadic and ineffectual attacks on military targets in the forward areas.[1]

Akyab, the key point on the Arakan coast within reach of most of south Burma, was abandoned early in January 1945 without a shot being fired. Its evacuation came about as the result of sound military decisions based on the policy laid down by Kimura, whose predecessor had reduced the strength of *28th Army* by a division in order to mount what proved to be a costly offensive against the Chinese Yunnan armies.[2] This was not replaced, and Sakurai was left with insufficient troops to defend the Arakan coast, the Irrawaddy valley and south Burma adequately. He therefore gave Miyazaki (*54th Division*) orders to secure the flank of *15th Army* by defensive action to cover the An Pass and the Taungup–Prome road.[3] Miyazaki was responsible for an area of Arakan from the Kaladan valley and Akyab in the north to Taungup in the south. Given the overall strategic position as presented to him, Akyab island appeared to have little tactical value and, as he could not afford to have part of his division cut off or destroyed, he withdrew to the mainland and disposed his forces to cover the passes across the Arakan Yomas.

It would appear that *Imperial General Headquarters* might have been better advised to abandon altogether the attempt to keep the communications between India and China severed. Kimura was told that this task was of secondary importance,[4] and thus he could justifiably have strengthened *28th Army* on his left at the expense of his right flank so that the Allies would have had to fight for Akyab as in the years 1942–44. In the wider field the Japanese effort to hold south Burma against overwhelming odds was courageous, but *Imperial*

---

[1] See page 179 and page 402.
[2] See Chapter V.
[3] See Map 7, facing page 171.
[4] See page 58.

General Headquarters might have been better advised to order a withdrawal from Burma in the autumn of 1944.

In August 1944 Japan was facing defeat; the Tojo Government fell and was replaced by a Government under the joint leadership of General Koiso and Admiral Yonai.[1] *Imperial General Headquarters* realized that, if the position were to be saved, the Philippines had at all costs to be held, and began to make feverish preparations to defend that area.[2] The speed with which the American offensive developed was too great and, when the invasion of Leyte took place, these preparations were far from complete. The *14th Area Army*, entrusted with the defence of the Philippines, was not fully concentrated and the vital fighter aircraft were not in position. The *Combined Fleet*, which was to be the spearhead of the effort to destroy the American invasion fleets, was still recovering from its losses in the Battle of the Philippine Sea. Owing to the shortage of oil fuel it was split between Singapore and Japan, was limited both in its radius of action and in its tactical freedom, and was without fully operational aircraft carriers. Committed to action without proper air cover, it suffered a crushing defeat.[3] The slender possibility of throwing back the American offensive had now disappeared altogether. The fact that *Imperial General Headquarters* and *Southern Army* overruled their commander on the spot (Yamashita) and made a vain attempt, expensive in ships, aircraft and men, to reinforce Leyte after the American forces were safely ashore, resulted in both Leyte and Luzon being lost in a comparatively short period of time. The line of communication from Japan to the Southern Region was now completely severed.

By January 1945 it was evident that the Ryukyus were gravely threatened, and that Japan herself faced invasion before the end of the year. *Imperial General Headquarters* had therefore once again to recast their plans, and this time to take measures to defend the homeland against air and amphibious attacks as well as provide for the defence of Formosa, east China and the Ryukyu Islands, all of which offered the Americans advanced bases for an invasion of Japan and any of which might therefore be attacked.[4] The new plans, drawn up during January, could not be implemented quickly, especially those affecting the concentration of the available air forces in Japan and the formation of *Kamikaze* squadrons, which were to be the main instrument of destruction in the final attempt to prevent the American fleets from approaching close to Japan. For this reason, when Nimitz

---

[1] See page 53.
[2] See pages 53–4 and Map 8, facing page 252.
[3] See Chapter VII.
[4] See Chapter XX.

launched his amphibious attack on Iwojima in February, no real attempt was made to attack the American armada which lay off the island for many weeks.[1]

With the loss of Iwojima, the imminence of an attack on Okinawa and the likelihood of intensified incendiary bomb attacks on her major cities, against which there was no defence, Japan's position was now desperate. The Koiso Government, having failed to arrest the onward surge of the American offensive, resigned on the 4th April, and Japan had to set about finding a new Government capable of facing the ever-growing crisis.

---

[1] See Chapter XXI.

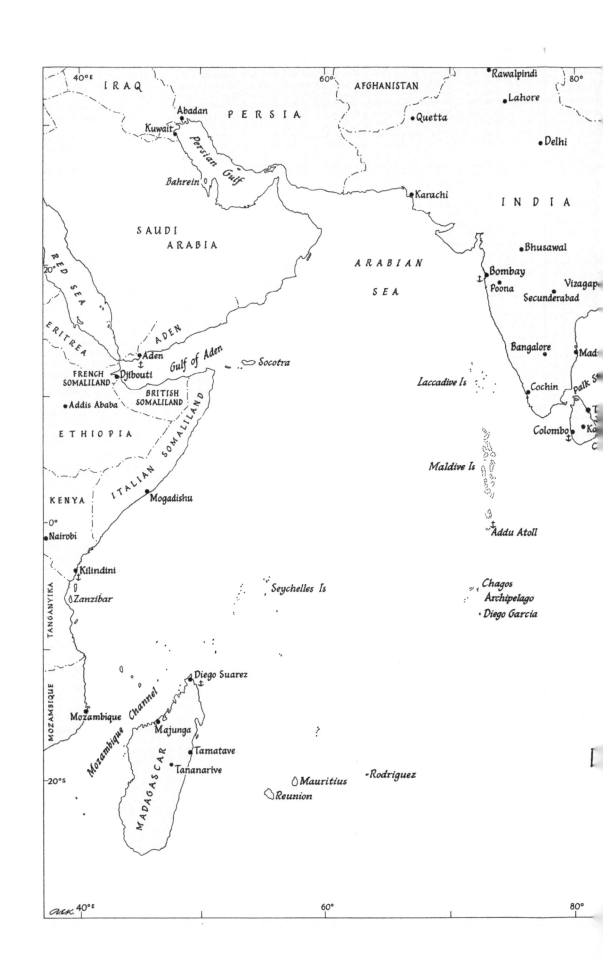

Map 12

• Rawalpindi

80°

T I B E T

C H I N A

100°

• Lahore

• Chunking

• Delhi

Ledo •

BURMA ROAD

• Kunming

• Benares

Imphal •

• Ranchi

Lashio •

• Canton

I N D I A

Calcutta •

Chittagong •

• Mandalay

Langson •

Hanoi •

HongKong

20°N

• Bhusawal

Akyab •

B U R M A

I N D O - C H I N A

HAINAN

• Bombay

Poona •

• Vizagapatam

B A Y

of

Ramree I.

• Secunderabad

• Cocanada

B E N G A L

Rangoon •

S I A M

CHINA
SEA

• Bangalore

• Madras

Tavoy •

Bangkok •

Camranh
Bay

Andaman Is •

Mergui •

• Cochin

Palk Str

• Port Blair

Saigon •

• Trincomalee

Victoria Pt •

Kra Isthmus

Colombo •

• Kandy

0

CEYLON

Nicobar Is

Phuket I.

Sabang •

Penang •

Lhoknga •

• Taiping

Belawan Deli •

MALAYA

• Port Swettenham

• Addu Atoll

Singapore

Padang •

S U M A T R A

B O R N E O

0°

Balikpapan •

Chagos
Archipelago

Diego Garcia

Palembang •

J A V A

Batavia •

SEA

Sourabaya •

Sunda Str

J A V A

Lombok Str

Cocos Is

I N D I A N   O C E A N

1944 - 45

20°S

Fleet Base........

AUSTRALIA

80°

100°

SARAWAK

Malacca Str

APPENDIX 1

The Chain of Command, South-East Asia, 20th June 1944

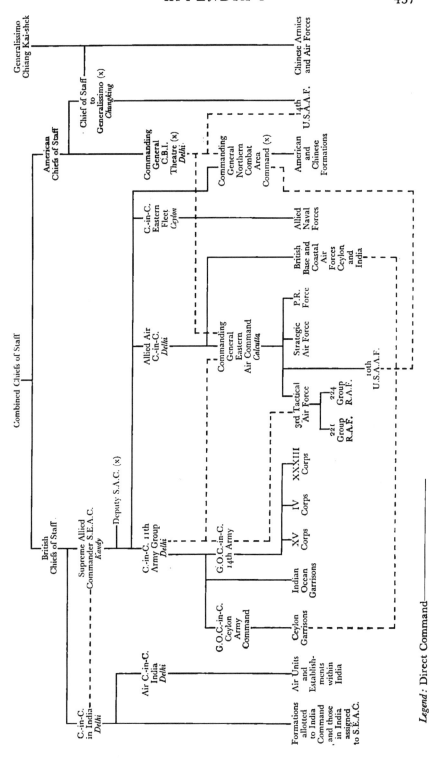

Legend: Direct Command ———
Liaison - - - - -

Notes: (a) Appointments marked (x) were all held by Lieut.-General J. W. Stilwell (U.S. Army).
(b) Air Transport Command (air ferry to China) and 20th Bomber Command (B.29 bombers to operate from China) were both controlled directly from Washington through H.Q. C.B.I. Theatre.

APPENDIX 2

Allied Oil Pipelines Completed, Under Construction and Projected, August 1944

	Size	Length in miles	Theoretical capacity tons/month	Remarks
A. Brahmaputra River System				
1. Dhubri Station–Dhubri Ghat	4-inch	2	10,000	Completed
2. Tezpur–Misamiri	4-inch	34	10,000	Completed
3. Neamati–Jorhat	4-inch	16	10,000	Completed
4. Dibrugarh–Tinsukia–Sookerating	4-inch	55	10,000	Completed
5. Tinsukia–Dinjan	4-inch	20	5,000	Completed
6. Tinsukia–Dibrugarh	4-inch	45	5,000	Completed } Used for kerosene from the Digboi
7. Dhubri Ghat–Dhubri Station	4-inch	2	5,000	Completed } oilfield required in India
B. Chittagong–Kalewa System				
8. Chittagong–Chandranathpur	4-inch	290	15,000	In hand. Completed 9/2/45
9. Chandranathpur–Dimapur	4-inch	160	13,000	Completed
10. Dimapur–Imphal (Kamrol) [1,2]	4-inch	134	10,000	Under construction. Completed 1/3/45.
11. Imphal–Tamu (Moreh)–Kalewa [2]	4-inch	184	10,000	Projected. Completed to Tamu (66 miles beyond Imphal) by the end of May 1945. Extension to Kalewa abandoned
C. Calcutta } Tinsukia–Myitkyina System **Chittagong }**				
12. Calcutta–Parbatipur–Tinsukia	6-inch	751	33,000	Completed
13. Chittagong–Dimapur–Tinsukia	6-inch	570	33,000	Projected. Work began in October 1944 and was completed 31/3/45
14. Tinsukia–Myitkyina	4-inch	292	16,000	Under construction. Completed 2/10/44
15. Tinsukia–Myitkyina	4-inch	292	16,000	Under construction. Completed 19/11/44
16. Tinsukia–Myitkyina	6-inch	292	33,000	Projected. Completed June 1945
D. Myitkyina–Bhamo–Kunming System				
17. Myitkyina–Bhamo	4-inch	101	16,000	Projected. Completed end of May 1945
18. Myitkyina–Bhamo–Kunming [3]	4-inch	677	16,000	Projected. Completed June 1945
19. Myitkyina–Bhamo–Kunming	6-inch	677	33,000	Projected. The construction of this pipeline was abandoned early in 1945

[1] A gravity pipeline was run from MS 102 on the Imphal Road (near Kangpopki) to feed the airfields at Imphal, Tulihal and Kangla.

[2] Barrel-filling plants were installed at the tank farms at Imphal (Kamrol) and Tamu (Moreh).

Kunming (750 miles) only in May, but its remaining 217 miles were not opened till June 1945. It was then extended

APPENDIX 3

The Principles of Joint Land/Air Action Defined by the Supreme Commander, South–East Asia, 17th June 1944

Relationship between Land and Air Forces

1. Land power and air power are coequal and interdependent forces. Neither is an auxiliary of the other.

Flexibility of Air Forces

2. The greatest asset of air power is its flexibility which enables it to be switched quickly from one objective to another in the theatre of operations. Properly commanded and controlled this enables the whole weight of available air power to be used in selected areas in turn. This concentrated use of the Air Striking Force is a battle-winning factor of the first importance.

Centralized Control

3. In order to exploit the flexibility of the air forces to the full, it is essential that their control be centralized and command exercised through Air channels.

Command

4. The soldier commands the land forces, the airman the air forces. Both Commanders work together and operate their respective forces in accordance with a Combined Army/Air plan, the whole operation being directed by the Army Commander.

5. In order to implement the principles of command enunciated in the previous paragraph, Army and Air Commanders at appropriate levels should work from a joint headquarters.

6. In this technical age it needs a life of study for a soldier or an airman to learn his own profession. Hence it is wrong for either to command the other's forces. Nothing could be more fatal to successful results than to dissipate the air resources into small packets placed under the command of Army Formation Commanders with each packet working on its own plan. The soldier must not expect or wish to exercise direct command over Air Striking Forces.

Capture and Security of Landing Grounds

7. The land forces cannot fight successfully without the closest co-operation of the air. This close co-operation cannot be given in full measure and without interruption unless the land forces are active in securing airfields and

landing grounds and unless they ensure that these and essential air installations are at all times adequately protected against ground or air attack. This factor must be kept to the fore in all planning.

Land Co-operation with Air Forces

8. Air forces cannot fight successfully without the closest co-operation of the land forces. This factor must be kept to the fore in all planning.

APPENDIX 4

Outline Order of Battle of Air Command, South–East Asia, 12th December 1944

HEADQUARTERS, AIR COMMAND S.E.A.: Kandy, Ceylon
(*Air Marshal Sir Guy Garrod*[1])

I. EASTERN AIR COMMAND: Calcutta
(*Lieut.-General G. E. Stratemeyer, U.S.A.A.F.*)
(Deputy Commander, *Air Marshal A. E. Coryton*)

(a) 221 GROUP R.A.F.: Imphal (*Air Vice-Marshal S. F. Vincent*)

906 Wing: Imphal

1 (F.R.) Squadron (R.I.A.F.)	Hurricane
42 (F.B.) Squadron	Hurricane
60 (F.B.) Squadron	Hurricane

907 Wing: Tamu

152 (F.) Squadron	Spitfire
11 (F.B.) Squadron	Hurricane

908 Wing: Kumbhirgram

45 (L.B.) Squadron	Mosquito

909 Wing: Palel

17 (F.) Squadron	Spitfire
155 (F.) Squadron	Spitfire
607 (F.) Squadron	Spitfire
34 (F.B.) Squadron	Hurricane
113 (F.B.) Squadron	Hurricane

910 Wing: Wangjing

79 (F.B.) Squadron	Thunderbolt
146 (F.B.) Squadron	Thunderbolt
261 (F.B.) Squadron	Thunderbolt

(b) 224 GROUP R.A.F.: Cox's Bazar (*Air Vice-Marshal The Earl of Bandon*)

901 Wing: Chiringa

27 (L.R.F.) Squadron	Beaufighter
177 (L.R.F.) Squadron	Beaufighter
211 (L.R.F.) Squadron	Beaufighter

---

[1] Acting Allied Air C.-in-C. until the 23rd February 1945, when Air Chief Marshal Sir Keith Park assumed the appointment of Allied Air C.-in-C.

902 Wing : Chittagong
    9 (F.) Squadron (R.I.A.F.)   Hurricane
    30 (F.B.) Squadron   Thunderbolt
    135 (F.B.) Squadron   Thunderbolt
    459 (L.R.F.) Squadron (U.S.A.A.F.)   Lightning (P.38)

903 Wing : temporarily at Comila
    67 (F.) Squadron   Spitfire

904 Wing : Cox's Bazar
    2 (F.R.) Squadron (R.I.A.F.)   Hurricane
    4 (F.R.) Squadron (R.I.A.F.)   Hurricane
    273 (F.) Squadron   Spitfire

905 Wing : near Chiringa
    134 (F.B.) Squadron   Thunderbolt
    258 (F.B.) Squadron   Thunderbolt

(c) 10TH U.S.A.A.F. : Myitkyina (*Major-General H. C. Davidson, U.S.A.A.F.*)

80th Fighter Group : Myitkyina area
    88 (F.) Squadron   Thunderbolt (P.47)
    89 (F.) Squadron   Thunderbolt (P.47)
    90 (F.) Squadron   Thunderbolt (P.47)

33rd Fighter Group : Myitkyina area
    58 (F.) Squadron   Lightning (P.38)
    59 (F.) Squadron   Lightning (P.38)
    60 (F.) Squadron   Lightning (P.38)
    490 (M.B.) Squadron   Mitchell (B.25)

3rd U.S. Combat Cargo Group : Dinjan
    9 (C.C.) Squadron   Dakota (C.47)
    10 (C.C.) Squadron   Dakota (C.47)
    11 (C.C.) Squadron   Dakota (C.47)
    12 (C.C.) Squadron   Dakota (C.47)

443rd U.S. Troop Carrier Group : Ledo
    1 (T.C.) Squadron   Dakota (C.47)
    2 (T.C.) Squadron   Dakota (C.47)
    315 (T.C.) Squadron   Dakota (C.47)

(d) COMBAT CARGO TASK FORCE : Comilla (*Brig.-General F. W. Evans,*
                                                 U.S.A.A.F.)

1st U.S. Combat Cargo Group : Tulihal
    1 (C.C.) Squadron   Dakota (C.47)
    2 (C.C.) Squadron   Dakota (C.47)
    3 (C.C.) Squadron   Dakota (C.47)
    4 (C.C.) Squadron   Dakota (C.47)

177 (Transport) Wing R.A.F. : Comilla
    31 (Tpt.) Squadron   Dakota
    62 (Tpt.) Squadron   Dakota
    117 (Tpt.) Squadron   Dakota
    194 (Tpt.) Squadron   Dakota

4th U.S. Combat Cargo Group: Sylhet/Agartala

13 (C.C.) Squadron	Dakota (C.47)
14 (C.C.) Squadron	Dakota (C.47)
15 (C.C.) Squadron	Dakota (C.47)
16 (C.C.) Squadron	Dakota (C.47)

1st U.S. Air Commando Group: Comilla/Ledo

319 (T.C.) Squadron	Dakota (C.47)

(e) STRATEGIC AIR FORCE: Calcutta (*Air Commodore F. J. Mellersh, R.A.F.*)

231 Group R.A.F.: Calcutta
175 Wing

99 (H.B.) Squadron	Liberator

184 Wing

355 (H.B.) Squadron	Liberator
356 (H.B.) Squadron	Liberator

185 Wing

159 (H.B.) Squadron	Liberator
215 (H.B.) Squadron	Liberator
357 (H.B.) Squadron	Liberator

7th Bombardment Group, U.S.A.A.F.: Calcutta

9 (H.B.) Squadron	Liberator (B.24)
436 (H.B.) Squadron	Liberator (B.24)
492 (H.B.) Squadron	Liberator (B.24)
493 (H.B.) Squadron	Liberator (B.24)

12th Bombardment Group, U.S.A.A.F.: Feni

81 (M.B.) Squadron	Mitchell (B.25)
82 (M.B.) Squadron	Mitchell (B.25)
83 (M.B.) Squadron	Mitchell (B.25)
434 (M.B) Squadron	Mitchell (B.25)

(f) PHOTOGRAPHIC RECONNAISSANCE FORCE: Alipore, Calcutta
(*Group Captain S. G. Wise, R.A.F.*)

R.A.F.

681 (P.R.) Squadron	Spitfire XI
684 (P.R.) Squadron	Mosquito/Mitchell

U.S.A.A.F.

9 (P.R.) Squadron	Lightning (F.5)
20 (Tac.R.) Squadron	Warhawk (P.40)
	Mitchell (B.25)
24 (C.M.) Squadron	Liberator (F.7)
40 (P.R.) Squadron	Lightning (F.5)

(g) 293 WING R.A.F.: Air Defence of Calcutta

69 (N.F.) Squadron	Beaufighter
615 (F.) Squadron	Spitfire

2. DIRECTLY UNDER COMMAND OF AIR HEADQUARTERS S.E.A.C.

222 Group R.A.F.: Colombo (*Air Marshal A. Durston*)

17 (F.) Squadron	Spitfire
81 (F.) Squadron	Spitfire
136 (F.) Squadron	Spitfire
22 (N.F.) Squadron	Beaufighter
176 (N.F.) Squadron	Beaufighter
217 (L.R.F.) Squadron	Beaufighter
205 (Fg.Bt.) Squadron	Catalina
209 (Fg.Bt.) Squadron	Catalina
259 (Fg.Bt) Squadron	Catalina
262 (Fg.Bt) Squadron (S.A.A.F.)	Catalina
265 (Fg.Bt.) Squadron	Catalina
321 (Fg.Bt.) Squadron (Netherlands)	Catalina
413 (Fg.Bt.) Squadron (R.C.A.F.)	Catalina
230 (Fg.Bt.) Squadron	Sunderland
8 (G.R.) Squadron	Wellington
224 (G.R.) Squadron	Wellington
621 (G.R.) Squadron	Wellington
160 (G.R.) Squadron	Liberator
354 (G.R.) Squadron	Liberator

225 Group R.A.F.: Bangalore (*Air Vice-Marshal N. L. Desoer*)

20 (F.B.) Squadron	Hurricane
191 (Fg.Bt.) Squadron	Catalina
212 (Fg.Bt.) Squadron	Catalina
240 (Fg.Bt.) Squadron	Catalina
200 (G.R.) Squadron	Liberator
357 (S.D.) Squadron	Liberator/Hudson

3. NON-OPERATIONAL SQUADRONS

U.S.A.A.F.

(F.B.) Squadron	Mustang (P.51)
(F.B.) Squadron	Mustang (P.51)
164 (L.) Squadron	Sentinel (L.5)
165 (L.) Squadron	Sentinel (L.5)
166 (L.) Squadron	Sentinel (L.5)

R.A.F. [1]

5 (F.) Squadron	Thunderbolt
123 (F.) Squadron	Thunderbolt
47 (L.B.) Squadron	Mosquito
82 (L.B.) Squadron	Mosquito
84 (L.B.) Squadron	Vengeance
110 (L.B.) Squadron	Mosquito
203 (G.R.) Squadron	Wellington
358 (H.B.) Squadron	Liberator

R.C.A.F. [1]

435 (Tpt.) Squadron	Dakota
436 (Tpt.) Squadron	Dakota

[1] These squadrons in varying states of re-equipment and training were located in 225 Group area.

R.I.A.F. [1]
        7 (F.B.) Squadron   Hurricane
        8 (F.) Squadron   Spitfire
        10 (F.) Squadron   Hurricane

Notes:

1. The establishment of U.S. troop carrier squadrons was 16 aircraft each; the establishment of U.S. combat cargo and R.A.F. transport squadrons was 25 aircraft each.

2. 1st U.S. Air Commando Group absorbed the original No. 1 Air Commando withdrawn from operations in June 1944. The new air commando group as reconstituted comprised two Mustang (P.51) fighter-bomber squadrons, one Dakota troop carrier squadron (16 aircraft), thirty-two gliders (C.G.4a) and three light Sentinel (L.5) squadrons (each with 32 aircraft). The group was an entirely independent American formation, but its one transport squadron (319) operated as part of the Combat Cargo Task Force.

3. A U.S. group was the equivalent of an R.A.F. wing.

4. Abbreviations: F.—Fighter; F.B.—Fighter-Bomber; F.R.—Fighter-Reconnaissance; Fg.Bt.—Flying Boat; G.R.—General Reconnaissance; L.B.—Light Bomber; M.B.—Medium Bomber; H.B.—Heavy Bomber; N.F.—Night Fighter; L.R.F.—Long-Range Fighter; P.R.—Photographic Reconnaissance; T.C.—Troop Carrier; C.C.—Combat Cargo; Tpt.—Transport; Tac.R.—Tactical Reconnaissance; L.—Liaison; S.D.—Special Duties; C.M.—Combat Mapping.

---

[1] These squadrons in varying states of re-equipment and training were located in 225 Group area.

APPENDIX 5

The Organization of Eastern Air Command, August 1944

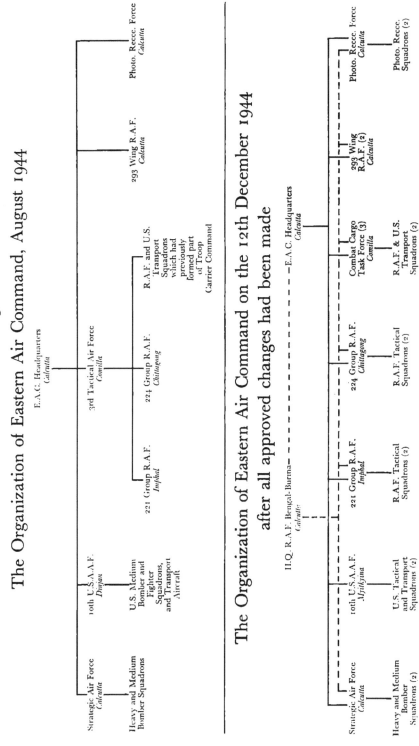

The Organization of Eastern Air Command on the 12th December 1944 after all approved changes had been made

Notes: (1) ———— denote command and tactical control; – – – – denotes R.A.F. administrative control.

(2) For details of squadrons see Appendix 4.

(3) Combined Army-Air Transport Organization (C.A.A.T.O.) had its H.Q. alongside C.C.T.F.

APPENDIX 6

Distances in Miles by Air from Air Bases in Assam, Eastern Bengal and Arakan to Principal Points in Central and Southern Burma

	Shwebo	Kyaukse	Maymyo	Myingyan	Meiktila	Heho	Loilem	Chauk	Magwe	Prome	Pyinmana	Toungoo	Mokpalin	Henzada	Rangoon
Imphal · ·	180	270	250	250	300	330	360	280	330	420	380	430	540	500	—
Chittagong · ·	240	270	290	240	270	340	370	210	250	330	330	380	470	390	—
Akyab · ·	240	230	270	190	200	250	310	140	130	180	220	240	320	240	—
Ramree · ·	260	220	270	180	180	230	275	130	100	90	160	170	220	140	230

Note: The maximum economic range for transport aircraft used for air supply was 250 miles; see Sketch 20.

APPENDIX 7

The Distribution of the Japanese Army and Army Air Forces in August 1944, showing Changes up to 31st January 1945

Location	Command	Army Headquarters	Divisions	No. of divisions	Remarks
A. Japan	General Defence Command	Eastern Command Central Command Western Command 1st Air and Training Air Armies	1st and 3rd Guards, 44th, 47th, 72nd, 73rd, 81st, 84th, 86th and 93rd 4th Armoured 10th, 11th and 12th Air	10 1 Armd. 3 Air	The Training Air Army was redesignated 6th Air Army in December 1944
B. North-East Front	5th Area Army	27th	7th, 42nd, 77th and 91st 1st Air	4 1 Air	This front included the Kurile Islands, Sakhalin and Hokkaido
C. Korea	Korea Army (under General Defence Command)	—	19th	1	The 19th Division was posted to 14th Area Army late in 1944
D. Manchuria	Kwantung Army	2nd, 3rd, 4th, 5th, 6th and 20th 2nd Air	11th, 12th, 23rd, 25th, 57th, 71st, 107th, 108th, 111th and 112th 1st Armoured	10 1 Armd.	No air divisions. The 2nd Air Army consisted of two mixed air brigades. The 12th Division was sent to Formosa and the 23rd to the Philippines late in 1944. They were replaced by two newly-formed divisions, the 119th and 120th

Location	Command	Army Headquarters	Divisions	No. of divisions	Remarks
E. China	China Expeditionary Army	1st, 11th, 12th, 13th, 23rd and Mongolia Garrison 5th Air	3rd, 13th, 22nd, 27th, 34th, 37th, 39th, 40th, 58th, 59th, 60th, 61st, 63rd, 64th, 65th, 68th, 69th, 70th, 104th, 110th, 114th, 115th, 116th, 117th and 118th 3rd Armoured 3rd Air	25 1 Armd. 1 Air	H.Q. North China Area Army controlled 1st, 12th and Mongolia Garrison Armies. On the 15th September, 6th Area Army was formed to control 11th and 23rd Armies and a newly-formed 34th Army
F. Central Pacific	31st Army	31st	14th, 29th, 43rd, 52nd and 109th (Bonin Force)	5	—
G. Ryukyu Islands	32nd Army	32nd	9th, 24th, 28th and 62nd	4	—
H. Formosa	Formosa Army	—	10th, 50th and 66th 8th Air	3 1 Air	The 10th Division was posted to 14th Area Army in November and replaced by 12th Division from Manchuria
J. South-East Pacific	8th Area Army	17th	6th, 17th and 38th	3	—
K. Operations controlled by Southern Army	Southern Army (Field-Marshal Count H. Terauchi)	—	—		—
(1) New Guinea and New Britain	Southern Army	18th 3rd Air	20th, 41st and 51st	3	The 3rd Air Army had under command 5th, 7th and 9th Air Divisions

Location	Command	Army Headquarter	Divisions	No. of divisions	Remarks
(2) Philippines	14th Area Army	35th 4th Air	1st, 8th, 16th, 26th, 30th, 100th, 102nd, 103rd and 105th 2nd Armoured 2nd and 4th Air	9 1 Armd. 2 Air	The 1st Division and 2nd Armoured Division in Shanghai and Manchuria were posted to 14th Area Army on the 22nd September and the 4th August 1944 respectively. Later in the year the area army was reinforced by 10th Division from Formosa and 23rd Division from Manchuria
(3) North Australian Front	2nd Area Army	2nd and 19th	5th, 32nd, 35th, 36th, 46th and 48th 7th Air	6 1 Air	—
(4) Indian Ocean Java . Sumatra . Malaya . Borneo .	7th Area Army	16th 25th 29th Borneo Garrison Army	Garrison units 4th and 2nd Guards and 9th Air 94th Division and garrison units Garrison units	3 1 Air	Orders were issued on the 29th August 1944 for 9th Air Division to be formed. The Borneo Garrison Army was redesignated 37th Army on the 12th October 1944
(5) Burma .	Burma Area Army	15th 33rd 28th Area Army Reserve	15th, 31st and 33rd 2nd, 18th, 53rd and 56th 54th and 55th 49th 5th Air	10 1 Air	The 53rd Division was transferred to 15th Army and 2nd Division to Area Army reserve during the later months of 1944

Location	Command	Army Headquarters	Divisions	No. of divisions	Remarks
(6) Siam .	Siam Garrison Army	—	—	—	The Siam Garrison Army was redesignated 39th Army in December 1944 and reinforced by 4th Division from Sumatra
(7) Indo-China .	Indo-China Garrison Army	—	21st	1	The Indo-China Garrison Army was redesignated 38th Army in December 1944 and arrangements were made to reinforce it with 22nd and 37th Divisions from China, moving by road

Notes:

1. This appendix should be compared with Appendix 12 of Volume III.

2. The Japanese military forces which in 1941 consisted of 51 infantry divisions and 5 air divisions had by August 1944 been expanded to 97 divisions, 4 armoured divisions and 11 air divisions (6th Air Division had been abolished). By the end of the year the infantry divisions numbered 99.

3. This appendix does not show Japanese formations below a division.

APPENDIX 8

Skeleton Order of Battle of Burma Area Army, 15th November 1944

15th Army: (*Lieut.-General S. Katamura*)

15th Division

51st Infantry Regiment
60th Infantry Regiment
67th Infantry Regiment
21st Field Artillery Regiment (less I/21st Field Artillery Battalion)

31st Division

58th Infantry Regiment
124th Infantry Regiment
138th Infantry Regiment
31st Mountain Artillery Regiment
I/21st Field Artillery Battalion
Elements of 3rd Heavy Field Artillery Regiment
Three anti-tank batteries
31st Engineer Regiment
20th Independent Engineer Regiment

33rd Division

213th Infantry Regiment
214th Infantry Regiment
215th Infantry Regiment
33rd Mountain Artillery Regiment
Elements of 18th Heavy Field Artillery Regiment
III/2nd Field Artillery Battalion
33rd Engineer Regiment
4th Independent Engineer Regiment

53rd Division

119th Infantry Regiment
128th Infantry Regiment
151st Infantry Regiment
53rd Field Artillery Regiment (less III/53rd Field Artillery Battalion)[1]

28th Army: (*Lieut.-General S. Sakurai*)

54th Division

54th Infantry Group Headquarters
111th Infantry Regiment

---

[1] This battalion was not in Burma.

121st Infantry Regiment
154th Infantry Regiment
54th Field Artillery Regiment
54th Engineer Regiment

55th Division

55th Infantry Group Headquarters
112th Infantry Regiment
143rd Infantry Regiment
144th Infantry Regiment
55th Mountain Artillery Regiment
55th Engineer Regiment

72nd Independent Mixed Brigade

72nd Infantry Mixed Brigade Headquarters (organized from 33rd Divisional Infantry Group Headquarters)
187th Infantry Battalion
188th Infantry Battalion
542nd Infantry Battalion ⎤ reorganized from 61st Infantry
543rd Infantry Battalion ⎬ Regiment (less one battalion) of 4th
　　　　　　　　　　　 ⎦ Division
72nd Brigade artillery unit
72nd Brigade engineer unit

33rd Army: (*Lieut.-General M. Honda*)

18th Division

55th Infantry Regiment
56th Infantry Regiment
114th Infantry Regiment
18th Mountain Artillery Regiment
12th Engineer Regiment

56th Division

113th Infantry Regiment
146th Infantry Regiment
148th Infantry Regiment
56th Field Artillery Regiment
56th Engineer Regiment

Burma Area Army Reserve:

2nd Division

4th Infantry Regiment
16th Infantry Regiment
29th Infantry Regiment
2nd Field Artillery Regiment (less III/2nd Field Artillery Battalion)
2nd Engineer Regiment

49th Division

    106th Infantry Regiment
    153rd Infantry Regiment
    168th Infantry Regiment
    49th Mountain Artillery Regiment
    49th Engineer Regiment

24th Independent Mixed Brigade

    138th Infantry Battalion
    139th Infantry Battalion
    140th Infantry Battalion
    141st Infantry Battalion
    24th Brigade artillery unit
    24th Brigade engineer unit

Note : 1. Sub-units of 14th Tank Regiment were allotted to the armies as required.

    2. Some of the divisions had reconnaissance battalions.

APPENDIX 9

Japanese Merchant Navy Gains and Losses of Vessels over 500 Tons, December 1941–August 1945

Month	Number of ships lost	Gross tonnage lost including tankers	Captured or salvaged	Built	Net lossess	Tonnage available at end of year	Remarks
Total December 1941 to end of 1942	241[1]	1,123,156	672,411	272,963	177,782	5,818,825	On the 7th December 1941 the total tonnage available was 5,996,607
Total 1943	434[2]	1,820,919[2]	109,028	769,085	942,806	4,876,019	
1944							
January	95	355,368					
February	112	518,697					
March	67	263,805					
April	38	128,328					
May	64	258,591					
June	71	278,484					
July	66	251,921					
August	66	295,022					
September	120	419,112					
October	130	512,378					
November	97	421,026					
December	43	188,287					
Total 1944	969[3]	3,891,019[3]	35,644	1,699,203	2,156,172	2,719,847	

Month	Number of ships lost	Gross tonnage lost including tankers	Captured or salvaged	Built	Net losses	Tonnage available at end of year	Remarks
1945							
January	101	434,648					
February	33	101,541					
March	81	194,649					
April	52	125,673					
May	118	270,703					
June	123	245,930					
July	145	309,902					
August	48	99,094					
Total 1945	701[4]	1,782,140[4]	5,880	559,563	1,216,697	1,503,150	
Grand Totals	2,345	8,617,234	822,963	3,300,814	4,493,457		

[1] Tanker losses to end of 1942 were 2 tankers of 9,538 tons
[2] Tanker losses during 1943 were 23 tankers of 169,491 tons
[3] Tanker losses during 1944 were 131 tankers of 754,889 tons
[4] Tanker losses during 1945 were 103 tankers of 351,028 tons

Total tanker losses were 259 ships of 1,284,946 tons or approximately fifteen per cent of total tonnage lost.

APPENDIX 10

Japanese Naval Order of Battle, 25th October 1944

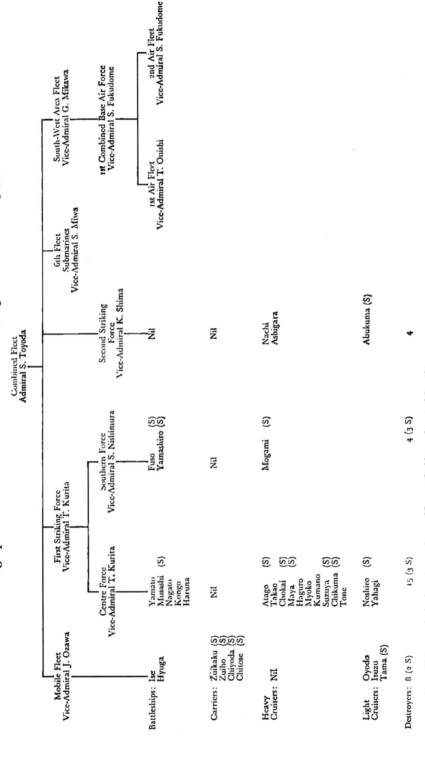

Combined Fleet
Admiral S. Toyoda

Mobile Fleet
Vice-Admiral J. Ozawa

First Striking Force
Vice-Admiral T. Kurita

Centre Force
Vice-Admiral T. Kurita

Southern Force
Vice-Admiral S. Nishimura

Second Striking Force
Vice-Admiral K. Shima

6th Fleet
Submarines
Vice-Admiral S. Miwa

South-West Area Fleet
Vice-Admiral G. Mikawa

1st Combined Base Air Force
Vice-Admiral S. Fukudome

1st Air Fleet
Vice-Admiral T. Onishi

2nd Air Fleet
Vice-Admiral S. Fukudome

	Mobile Fleet	Centre Force	Southern Force	Second Striking Force
Battleships:	Ise Hyuga	Yamato Musashi (S) Nagato Kongo Haruna	Fuso (S) Yamashiro (S)	Nil
Carriers:	Zuikaku (S) Zuiho (S) Chiyoda (S) Chitose (S)	Nil	Nil	Nil
Heavy Cruisers:	Nil	Atago (S) Takao Chokai (S) Maya (S) Haguro Myoko Kumano Suzuya (S) Chikuma (S) Tone	Mogami (S)	Nachi Ashigara
Light Cruisers:	Oyodo Isuzu Tama (S)	Noshiro (S) Yahagi		Abukuma (S)
Destroyers:	8 (2 S)	15 (3 S)	4 (3 S)	4

Note: Ships sunk during the actions of Leyte Gulf are denoted by (S)

APPENDIX 11

Proposed Maintenance and Forward Stocking Programme for 'Capital', including R.A.F. Requirements, August 1944

Daily tonnage in long tons

Phase	Dates of Phase	BY ROAD				G.P.T. Coys. in terms of 3-ton Coys.		BY AIR	
		Dimapur to Imphal/Palel	Palel to Indainggyi	Indainggyi to Shwebo	Shwebo to Mandalay	Required	Available	From East Bengal	From Imphal
Prelim.	16 Oct.–15 Dec. '44	2,211	260	—	—	28·1	29·5	146	230
I (a)	16 Dec. '44–15 Jan. '45	2,144	521	—	—	30·8	30·5	374	170
I (b)	16 Jan.–31 Jan. '45	1,694	1,171	—	—	34·4	34·5	166	270
II (a)	1 Feb.–28 Feb. '45	1,700	1,114	445	—	38·3	38·5	381	355
II (b)	1 Mar.–15 Mar. '45	2,228[1]	1,296	1,030	—	48·3	48·5	386	355
III	15 Mar.–15 May '45	2,279[1]	1,524	1,245	50	57·4	57·0	491	370
IV	16 May–15 Jul. '45	2,250[1]	1,269	890	515	50·3	59·5	221	360

[1] Including 350 tons a day petrol reaching the Imphal plain by pipelines.

Note:

1. The basis of calculation for the lift by road was as follows: average payload per vehicle, 2¾ tons; turnround by L. of C. Road Transport Dimapur–Palel, one ton per vehicle per day; turnround Palel–Indainggyi, four days, Indainggyi–Shwebo, three days, Shwebo–Mandalay, two days.

2. It was assumed that the depot at Palel would have been stocked with thirty days' supplies for four divisions by the 15th October.

Revised Chain of Command, South-East Asia, Resulting from Changes Introduced Between 12th November and 4th December 1944

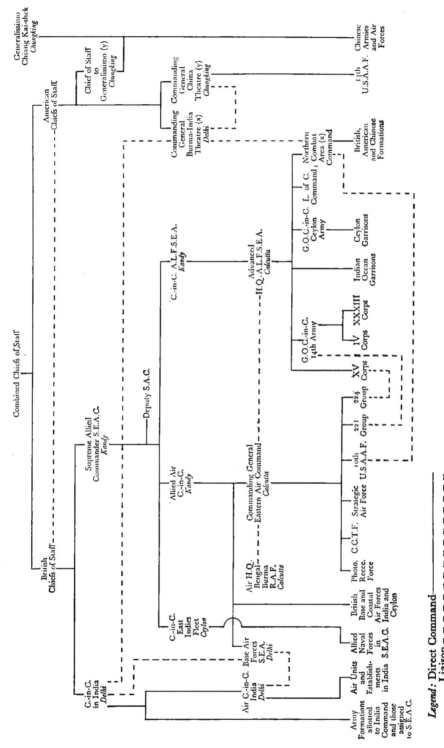

Legend: Direct Command ————
Liaison – – – – – – – –

Notes: (a) Appointments marked (x) were held by Lieut.-General D. I. Sultan (U.S. Army).
(b) Appointments marked (y) were held by Lieut.-General A. C. Wedemeyer (U.S. Army).
(c) Air Transport Command (air ferry to China) and 20th Bomber Command (B.29 bombers to operate from China) were controlled directly from Washington through Commanding General, Eastern Air Command.

APPENDIX 13

The Assessment by 14th Army of Aircraft Required and the Airlift Available from 16th December 1944 to 15th May 1945, as Calculated on 11th December 1944

Period	14th Army Requirements (long tons a day)[1]	Available Airlift[2]			Surplus or Shortage	Remarks
		Imphal	E. Bengal	Total		
16–31 Dec.	705	238	420	658	− 47	
1–15 Jan.	688	300	388	688	± 0	
16–31 Jan.	813	340	473	813	± 0	
1–15 Feb.	763	460	303	763	± 0	
16 Feb.–2 Mar.	906	460	446	906	± 0	No aircraft availabe for
3–17 Mar.	1,190	540	528	1,068	−122	fly-in of formations
18–31 Mar.	1,270	540	517	1,057	−213	
1 Apl.–15 May	1,205	540	519	1,059	−146	
Thereafter	1,200	400	300	700	−500	Approximate figures only

Note: The basic daily maintenance requirements within 14th Army were calculated at this time to be:

Infantry division	100 tons
Tank brigade	70 tons
Corps and L. of C. troops	150–200 tons ⎱ depending on number of divisions and
R.A.F.	80–120 tons ⎰ squadrons operating in the forward areas.
Royal Engineers (Works)	90–120 tons

[1] These figures are requirements for maintenance. In addition, 14th Army needed 5,000 sorties from the 16th February to the 17th March for the fly-in of air-transported forces and, throughout the whole period, twenty-one sorties a day for the fly-in of reinforcements and fresh supplies (and the evacuation of casualties).

[2] These figures represent the lift available after the deduction of the lift of the squadrons to be transferred to China and the requirements of the N.C.A.C. front and of XV Corps in Arakan.

APPENDIX 14

The Cost of the Monsoon Campaign

The average weekly strength of XXXIII Corps from the 22nd June to 16th November 1944 was 88,578. Including those who were engaged on administrative duties in forward areas, less than half of this number were engaged in active operations against the enemy, two divisions, the armour and most of the artillery being for the greater part of the period in healthy rest camps in the Imphal–Maram–Kohima area. The numerically stronger of the two forward divisions—11th (E.A.) Division—had a reputed high resistance to malaria, and all troops were on prophylactic mepacrine.[1]

The corps casualties for the period totalled 50,387 made up as under:

	Sickness	Battle Casualties
Malaria and other fevers	20,430	
Dysentery and allied diseases	6,849	
Typhus	2,245	
Wounded		1,484
Injuries due to active service		1,384
Missing		49
Killed in action		372
Miscellaneous complaints	17,574	
	47,098[2]	3,289

---

[1] General Stopford, the corps commander, said later that the reputed high resistance was not confirmed by events.

[2] Of these, more than half were evacuated from the corps area and took no further part in the monsoon campaign.

APPENDIX 15

The Redeployment of Transport Squadrons of C.C.T.F. in Support of 14th Army and XV Corps, December 1944–May 1945

	December 1944		January 1945		February 1945		March 1945		April 1945		May 1945		Remarks
	Sqns.	Total	Sqns.	Total	Sqns.	Total	Sqns.	Total	Sqns.	Total	Sqns.	Total	
Imphal Plain	1, 2, 3, 4 U.S.A.A.F.	4	435, 436 R.C.A.F. 3 U.S.A.A.F.	3	435, 436 R.C.A.F. 2, 3, 4 U.S.A.A.F.	5(b)	435, 436 R.C.A.F.	2	435 R.C.A.F.	1	435 R.C.A.F. 215 R.A.F.(f)	2	—
Agartala	13, 14, 15, 16 U.S.A.A.F.	4	13, 14, 15, 16 U.S.A.A.F.	4	—	—	—	—	—	—	—	—	—
Comilla	31, 62, 117, 194 R.A.F.	4	31, 62, 194 R.A.F.	3	194 R.A.F.	1	238 R.A.F.(c)	1	238 R.A.F.	1	238 R.A.F. 96 R.A.F.(f)	2	Comilla was used for despatch of reinforcements and evacuation of casualties but remained available as a supply base in emergency
Chittagong Area (including Hathazari and Dohazari)	—	—	117 R.A.F.	1	13, 14, 15, 16 U.S.A.A.F. 31, 62, 117 R.A.F.	7	2, 3, 4, 13, 14, 15, 16 U.S.A.A.F. 31, 62, 117, 194, 267 R.A.F.(c)	12	2, 3, 4, 13, 14, 15, 16 U.S.A.A.F. 31, 117 R.A.F.	9	2, 3, 4, 13, 14, 15, 16 U.S.A.A.F.	7	117 R.A.F. maintained XV Corps till end of March

	December 1944		January 1945		February 1945		March 1945		April 1945		May 1945		Remarks
	Sqns.	Total	Sqns.	Total	Sqns.	Total	Sqns.	Total	Sqns.	Total	Sqns.	Total	
Akyab	—	—	—	—	—	—	—	—(d)	62, 194, 267 R.A.F. 436 R.C.A.F.	4	62, 194, 267 R.A.F.	3	—
Ramree	—	—	—	—	—	—	—	—	—	—(e)	31, 117 R.A.F. 436 R.C.A.F. (g)	3	—
Total available	12(a)		11		13		15		15		17		

(a) 1, 2 and 4 Sqns. U.S.A.A.F. moved to China during December 1944. See Appendix 4.
(b) 2 and 4 Sqns. U.S.A.A.F. returned from China on the 1st February 1945.
(c) 238 and 267 Sqns. R.A.F. arrived in S.E.A.C. from overseas.
(d) 62, 194, 267 Sqns. R.A.F. and 436 Sqn. R.C.A.F. moved forward to Akyab where 194 and 436 Sqns. began operating on the 20th March, and 62 and 267 Sqns. on the 1st April.
(e) Detachments 31, 62 Sqns. R.A.F. and 436 Sqn. R.C.A.F. began operating from Ramree on the 16th April.
(f) 96 and 215 Sqns. R.A.F. were formed and equipped in India for S.E.A.C.
(g) 31, 117 Sqns. R.A.F. and 436 Sqn. R.C.A.F. moved to Ramree early in May when det. 62 Sqn. R.A.F. returned to Akyab.

Note:

1. Location of R.A.M.O.s. (Rear Airfield Maintenance Organization).
Imphal Plain: No. 1 until the 7th March 1945, then moved to Akyab; No 2. until the 24th March, then moved to Ramree; No. 6.
Agartala: No. 4 until the 28th January, then moved to Chittagong area.
Comilla: No. 3.
Chittagong Area: No. 4 from the 16th February; No. 5; No. 7 from the 22nd January.
Akyab: No. 1 from the 20th March.
Ramree: No. 2 from the 7th April.

2. In addition to the squadrons supporting 14th Army and XV Corps there was 3rd U.S. Combat Cargo Group (9, 10, 11 and 12 Squadrons) which, based on Dinjan and under command of 10th U.S.A.A.F., supplied N.C.A.C.; all but one of its squadrons was transferred to China at the end of April 1945 (see Chapter XXVII). The total number of transport squadrons in S.E.A.C. was therefore: in December 16, in January 15, in February 17, in March 19, in April 19 and in May 18.

APPENDIX 16

The Build-up of the Inland Water Transport Service on the Chindwin in 1945

During a visit to India, Major-General D. J. McMullen (the Director of Transportation at the War Office) appreciated that a British offensive to drive the Japanese out of Burma would likely have to follow the same route as that taken by the Allies during the withdrawal from Burma into Assam in the early months of 1942; river craft in considerable numbers would therefore be required on the Chindwin and the Irrawaddy. Such craft would have to be of shallow draught and capable of being transported in sections by the broad and narrow gauge railways to Dimapur and thence along a 300-mile mountain road to the Chindwin and reassembled there. On his return to London he ordered a prototype tug and barge to be built of light steel plates on the Meccano principle, which could be riveted together on the banks of the Chindwin. Successful trials were carried out in the United Kingdom and by mid-1944 large-scale production of Unicraft tugs and barges had begun, the contracts being placed with small workshops and garages all over the countryside. The various parts were then assembled at a central depot and shipped to India.

Wooden shallow-draught craft had already been designed in Canada and America for use on rivers and sheltered waterways. Amongst these were the ramped cargo lighter (R.C.L.) with a pay load of 25 tons, and the Higgins barge with a pay load of 60/70 tons deadweight. These craft had the advantage over Unicraft in that, being fully decked, they could carry vehicles and bulky loads and were easier and quicker to erect than steel craft. The Higgins barge could also be used as a terminal pontoon for loading and offloading.[1] India Command itself was not lacking in foresight: in 1942 Eastern Army had designed craft (which became known as Eastern Army boats) made from local timber, 40 feet in length and 6 feet in beam. These could be used as pontoons for improvised bridging, or, if formed into rafts of three boats each, had a cargo capacity of 30 tons and could be driven by outboard motors.

The original plan for the second phase of 'Capital', as drawn up in August and September 1944, envisaged an advance eastwards from Kalewa to the Yeu–Shwebo area which did not follow the course of the Chindwin. The 14th Army demands on an I.W.T. service were therefore limited to:

(a) A ferry from Kalewa to Shwegyin (seven miles) with a capacity of 500 tons a day.

(b) A ferry from Sagaing to Ava (three miles) with a capacity of 500 tons a day.

(c) An I.W.T. service from Monywa to Pakokku (seventy miles) with a capacity of 100 tons a day.

---

[1] For details of all the various craft used see Table 1.

(d) A ferry service across the Irrawaddy near Pakokku (six miles) with a capacity of 200 tons a day.[1]

To meet these requirements, which totalled 13,800 ton-miles a day, it was estimated that 32 R.C.L.s, 25 Higgins barges, 50 Burley boats, 8 Rodda craft, 50 G.P. launches and 100 outboard motors would be required. To operate the service two I.W.T. operating companies, an Indian river salvage company (to salvage sunken and damaged craft along the river) and detachments from an I.W.T. store and I.W.T. workshop companies would be required.

To prove that it was feasible to move boats by road to the Chindwin, one R.C.L., one Rodda craft and two Burley boats were sent by rail from Calcutta to Dimapur and onwards by road to the banks of the Yu River. They reached their destination on the 23rd October 1944, were erected and, with the help of elephants, were successfully launched, and floated down to Yuwa on the Chindwin. They reached Sittaung on the 28th November and were used to assist 19th Division to cross the river.[2] Since this experiment was successful, A.L.F.S.E.A. decided that the craft and units required to operate the I.W.T. service as then planned should be phased forward to Dimapur in weekly batches between the 19th December 1944 and the 19th February 1945 so that an even movement along the Imphal Road could be maintained.

On the 10th December, when a review was being made of the supply capabilities of the available air transport squadrons and the effect on the current operations if any were diverted,[3] 14th Army, which had by that time realized the need to develop a river line of communication south from Kalewa, asked A.L.F.S.E.A. to provide craft to enable the original planned capacity of the I.W.T. service to be increased to 200 tons a day over 100 miles, plus 300 tons a day over 275 miles (a total of 112,500 ton-miles a day). To meet this greatly increased demand, A.L.F.S.E.A. agreed to send forward an additional eighteen R.C.L.s, forty-five Higgins barges and fifteen Unicraft single-screw tugs,[4] two additional I.W.T. operating companies, an Indian railway workshop company and an additional erection company, which was to include a team of riveters for the assembly of Unicraft tugs and barges, and a special detachment trained in the erection of Higgins barges.

It was then agreed that the transportation services (working under A.L.F.S.E.A. control) would be responsible for the move forward of all craft to the Chindwin, for the erection of Unicraft tugs and Higgins barges and for the delivery at the erection site of the two end sections, ramps and machinery of the R.C.L.s. The centre sections of the R.C.L.s were to be built of local wood by 14th Army engineers, who were also to build about 100 Eastern Army boats to make rafts for which the transportation services

---

[1] A ferry was eventually established in the Pakokku area at Nyaungu.
[2] See Chapter XIV.
[3] See page 129.
[4] Powered craft were at first allowed at the rate of one to 1,730 ton-miles. This in practice did not allow sufficient margin for repairs, and was later adjusted to one to 1,160 ton-miles as more Unicraft tugs became available.

would provide outboard motors.[1] All craft and machinery to be provided by the transportation services would be delivered at Kalewa by the 15th April.

As soon as Kalewa was captured, a site for the erection and building of the craft was selected on a sandy stretch of the river bank immediately to the north of Kalewa, upstream from the Bailey bridge. This bridge was now required by the engineers in the forward area and was replaced by a pontoon (Falls) bridge with a high level centre span to allow the passage of river craft.

When the original 'Capital' operation was replaced by 'Extended Capital' and it was decided that the Shwegyin–Yeu road would be maintained to a fair-weather standard only, thus making it of little value in the monsoon, the I.W.T. link from Kalewa to Alon (near Monywa) and later to Myingyan to join with the all-weather Burma Road system and the Burma railways became of vital importance. The 14th Army now required a lift of some 115,000 ton-miles a day (110 tons a day from Kalewa to Alon by the 1st March and 500 tons a day to Myingyan by the 1st May).[2] The target for deliveries to Myingyan was later increased to 575 tons a day by the 15th May and 700 by the end of that month. This necessitated a greater number of craft of all kinds, as well as larger facilities for the erection and the operation of the river fleet; the foundations of the plan were, however, sound and the necessary expansion proved to be feasible.

Work on the erection site at Kalewa began on the 24th December 1944. The same day an airlift of Unicraft single-screw tugs and Unicraft barges from Chittagong to Indainggyi began.[3] By the end of the month ten tugs and five barges, less bow sections and engines (a total weight of 100 tons), had been delivered by C.46 aircraft. The engines, which were not required early, and the bow sections, which were too bulky to be loaded into the aircraft, reached Kalewa by road on the 9th January. Boat-building and salvage of sunken craft began on the 2nd January 1945.[4] The buoying of the channel began the same day, and progressed as the tactical situation permitted. Members of the original Burma Government River Conservancy Board had been recruited, and, with their help, locally raised demolition and manhandling parties were established as and when possible at all points along the river where there was likely to be difficulty in keeping the channel open or when the grounding of craft was a possibility.

By the 28th January, 45th Beach Group had concentrated at Alon to open a 14th Army maintenance area to receive stores by river and by air. On the 4th February the I.W.T. service began to deliver stores there.[5]

---

[1] The number of Eastern Army boats eventually built was 541. Timber for the R.C.L. centre portions and for the Eastern Army boats was cut locally and, with the help of the 14th Army Elephant Company, dragged to the river and floated down to the erection site.
[2] See page 166.
[3] The Unicraft tugs and barges had begun to arrive in India during December. Indainggyi was the nearest suitable airfield to Kalewa.
[4] The planned rate of production was for five Unicraft tugs, seven Unicraft barges and seven Higgins barges a week. In the middle of April efforts were made to step up the rates of the first two to ten and fifteen respectively.
[5] The turnround from Kalewa to Alon was ten days and, when the service began, the capacity of the available craft was 300 tons, giving an initial delivery of 30 tons a day.

During February deliveries averaged 76 tons a day, but rose to an average of some 140 tons during the first half of March as more craft became available.[1] To increase the capacity during this period, locally constructed bamboo and tarpaulin rafts were used to carry supplies, and P.O.L. was sent down river in drums made up into rafts with a strong framework of bamboo and propelled by a small outboard motor.

On the 22nd March, 552 L. of C. Sub-Area took over the control and working of the maintenance centre at Alon, and 45th Beach Group stood by to move to Myingyan as soon as it was captured.[2] Myingyan was cleared on the 23rd and the following day the beach group moved forward. The I.W.T. service to the new 14th Army maintenance area at Myingyan began on the 26th March.

The deliveries by I.W.T. forward of Kalewa from February to May inclusive were:

Period	Kalewa to Alon	Kalewa to Myingyan	Alon to Myingyan	Total in period	Average daily tonnage
1st–28th February	2,140	—	—	2,140	76¼
1st–28th March	5,453	—	—	5,453	190½
29th March–25th April	387	8,790	3,663	12,840	458¼
26th April–16th May	306	11,933	1,589	13,828	660
17th May–30th May	327	8,314	631	9,272	662
Totals	8,613	29,037	5,883	43,533	365

Note:

1. All figures are in long tons.

2. From February to May inclusive the I.W.T. service on the Chindwin also carried some 6,500 men and 125 vehicles from Kalewa.

The conception and planning of the whole project was brilliant. The establishment of an *ad hoc* shipbuilding establishment on the upper reaches of a river, and the moving forward of all the components required (other than timber cut locally) along a complicated and difficult line of communication many hundreds of miles in length were feats of extemporization seldom surpassed in the history of war.

The Chindwin Flotilla

When it became evident early in January 1945 that suitable craft could be built, Slim conceived the idea of constructing four gunboats so that he would have a naval force with which to interfere with the Japanese withdrawal across the Irrawaddy. Although he knew that the construction of these craft would reduce the output of Eastern Army rafts by some twenty-five a month, he told A.L.F.S.E.A. of his proposal and asked that the

---

[1] By the middle of March the river fleet in operation consisted of 8 R.C.L.s, 48 Burley boats, 25 G.P. launches, 13 Higgins barges, 12 Rodda craft, 18 single-screw Unicraft tugs, 25 Unicraft barges, 43 Eastern Army three-boat rafts, 10 salvaged steel craft and 103 salvaged wooden craft.

[2] Deliveries to Alon in the second half of March averaged 240 tons a day.

necessary guns, fittings and engines, should be supplied and sent forward to Kalewa between the 7th and 31st March.

Work was begun in mid-January on the construction of four craft to the following specifications: length 50 ft., beam 13 ft., depth $7\frac{1}{2}$ ft., draught $2\frac{1}{4}$ ft., scow-shaped in elevation and rectangular in plan; each craft was to be driven by a Ford V.8 engine and carry fuel for twenty hours' endurance at a speed of ten knots; the armament was to consist of two single Oerlikon guns forward and one aft, with twin Vickers machine-guns on the bridge. The crews were to consist of one naval officer and eight ratings. A shore base, consisting of a few naval ratings with the necessary military adminis-trative units attached, was to be established on the banks of the Chindwin.

The advance of 14th Army was, however, so rapid that the gunboats were not ready in time to be used in the role Slim had envisaged for them. He therefore changed it to that of providing anti-aircraft protection for I.W.T. craft on the river and of supporting operations as necessary on the Irrawaddy. Two gunboats were commissioned at the end of March and the other two in the middle of April 1945.

Table of I.W.T. Craft on next page.

Table 1 to Appendix 16

DESCRIPTION OF I.W.T. CRAFT IN USE ON THE CHINDWIN IN 1945

	Unicraft Tug	Unicraft Barge	Ramped Cargo Lighter (R.C.L.)[1]	Higgins Barge[1]	Rodda Craft	Burley Boat
Description	Two types: single-screw with one 40-h.p. engine, and twin-screw with two similar engines. Steel riveted craft[2]	Steel riveted dumb craft, 60 ft. long	Flat-bottomed wooden craft with ramped bow and stern. 54 ft. 6 in. long and powered by two 90-h.p. engines	Flat-topped wooden barge, 60 ft. long	Wooden construction, powered by Ford V.8 engine	Wooden construction, powered by outboard motor
Loaded Draught	2 ft. 6 in.	2 ft. 6 in.	2 ft. 6 in.	4 ft.	2 ft. 3 in.	1 ft. 6 in.
Theoretical cargo capacity	Nil	35 tons	24 tons (in practice it was found that 15 tons was the maximum safe load)	60-70 tons at full draught	Nil	3 tons
Total weight	10 tons	7 tons	25 tons	18 tons (approx.)	2 tons	21 cwt.
Method of overland transport	Knocked down	Knocked down	Knocked down	Knocked down	Knocked down	Knocked down
Size and weight of largest component	14 ft. × 14 ft. 6 in. × 1 ft. 6 in. 17 cwt.	15 ft. × 6 ft. 6 in. × 1 ft. 6 in. 6 cwt.	14 ft. 6 in. × 9 ft. 2 in. × 7 ft. 4 tons 8 cwt.[3]	20 ft. × 6 ft. × 1 ft. Not known	12 ft. 6 in. × 6 ft. 6 in. × 3 ft. 6 in. 1¼ tons approx.	8 ft. × 6 ft. 6 in. × 6 ft. 1¼ cwt.

[1] These craft could be decked and could therefore carry vehicles and bulky loads as well as cargo.

[2] The twin-screw tugs were not in operation till the end of April 1945.

[3] The bow and stern identical sections, the swims and ramps together with winches, steering-gear and engines were despatched by road, and the centre portions (an awkward load for road transport) were built at Kalewa by 14th Army engineers.

APPENDIX 17

Composition of the Japanese 3rd Air Army, November 1944–April 1945

Formation	Area	Type	Maximum Strength	Remarks
3rd Air Army	Southern Army	—	—	
5th Air Division	Burma Area Army			Moved to French Indo-China in February 1945
50th Air Regiment		Fighter	20	
64th Air Regiment		Fighter	20	
13th Air Regiment		Fighter	10	Transferred from Philippines in January 1945
8th Air Regiment		Lt. Bomber	13	
81st Air Regiment		Recce.	15	
204th Air Regiment		Fighter	2	Transferred from Philippines in December 1944
58th Air Regiment	French Indo-China	Heavy Bomber	15	Moved from Sumatra in February 1945
9th Air Division	7th Area Army (Sumatra)	—	—	
87th Air Regiment		Fighter	20	
71st Independent Air Squadron		Fighter	10	
74th Independent Air Squadron		Recce.	6	
26th Air Regiment		Fighter	5	Transferred from Philippines in December 1944
33rd Air Regiment		Fighter	4	Transferred from Philippines in December 1944
24th Independent Air Squadron		Fighter	—	Transferred from Philippines in December 1944
21st Air Regiment		Fighter	20	Transferred from Celebes in January 1945
7th Air Division	7th Area Army (Java)	—	—	
12th Air Regiment		Heavy Bomber	5	
73rd Independent Air Squadron		Lt. Bomber	6	
70th Independent Air Squadron		Recce.	3	
10th Independent Air Brigade	7th Area Army (N. Borneo)	—	—	

Formation	Area	Type	Maximum Strength	Remarks
83rd Air Regiment		Fighter & Lt. Bomber	12	Transferred from Philippines in mid-January 1945
58th Air Regiment	Sumatra	Heavy Bomber	15	Moved to French Indo-China in February 1945
61st Air Regiment	Malaya	Heavy Bomber	20	Transferred from Japan in December 1944
109th Air Transport Regiment	Malaya	Transport	10	Placed under direct command Southern Army in January 1945
1st Field Replacement Unit	Malaya	Mixed	30	12 fighter, 6 heavy and 6 light bomber, and 6 recce. squadrons

Notes:

1. There were in addition two training units:
55th Air Training Division at Singapore with about 150 aircraft.
8th Advanced Training Regiment in Burma with about 15 fighter aircraft.

2. After the battle for Leyte began in October 1944 3rd Air Army was unable to obtain either replacement aircraft or aircrews. Every effort was made to repair damaged aircraft but the strength declined by some ten per cent a month.

3. Despite air units transferred from the Philippines between December and February, the total estimated operational strength of 3rd Air Army, which was 159 aircraft in November 1944, eventually declined. The approximate monthly strength was: December 165, January 195, February 195, March 175, April 158. The monthly strength of 5th Air Division in Burma was approximately: November 68, December 63, January 66, February 60, March 54 and April 50.

4. In 1944–45 the Japanese were using the same types of aircraft as in 1942–43. The performance of these aircraft could not compare with that of the more modern British and American aircraft used by the Allies at this period. For performances see Volume III, Appendix 28.

APPENDIX 18

Outline Orders of Battle, Land Forces, S.E.A.C., September 1944–May 1945

Commanders, Principal Staff Officers and Heads of Services of
Headquarters S.E.A.C., Royal Navy, 11th Army Group,
A.L.F.S.E.A. and Air Command, S.E.A.   page 473

14th Army H.Q. and Army Troops   475

IV Corps H.Q. and Corps Troops   477

XXXIII Corps H.Q. and Corps Troops   478

Divisions of 14th Army:

  2nd Division   479

  5th Indian Division   480

  7th Indian Division   481

  11th East African Division   482

  17th Indian Division   483

  19th Indian Division   484

  20th Indian Division   485

  36th Division (see N.C.A.C.)

Independent Brigades of 14th Army:

  268th Indian Infantry Brigade ⎫

  Lushai Brigade   ⎬   486

  28th East African Brigade ⎭

XV Corps H.Q. and Corps Troops   487

Divisions of XV Corps:

  25th Indian Division   489

  26th Indian Division   490

  81st West African Division   491

  82nd West African Division   492

Northern Combat Area Command:

  Mars Task Force   ⎫

  New Chinese First Army   ⎬   493

  New Chinese Sixth Army   ⎭

  36th Division   494

Line of Communication Areas   495

COMMANDERS, PRINCIPAL STAFF OFFICERS
and
HEADS OF SERVICES
of
HEADQUARTERS S.E.A.C., ROYAL NAVY, 11th ARMY GROUP, A.L.F.S.E.A. and AIR COMMAND, S.E.A.

SOUTH-EAST ASIA COMMAND

Supreme Allied Commander
Admiral the Lord Louis Mountbatten
Deputy Supreme Commander
General J. W. Stilwell, U.S. Army (till 21.10.44)
Lieut.-General R. A. Wheeler, U.S. Army (from 12.11.44)
Prime Minister's and Supreme Allied Commander's Representative
(i) in Chungking
Lieut.-General Sir Adrian Carton de Wiart, V.C.
(ii) at South-West Pacific Command Headquarters
Lieut.-General C. H. Gairdner (from 16.3.45)
Supreme Allied Commander's Representative in Delhi and Commander, Rear H.Q. S.A.C.S.E.A.
Major-General C. R. C. Lane
Chief of Staff
Lieut.-General Sir Henry Pownall
Lieut.-General F. A. M. Browning (from 26.12.44)
Deputy Chief of Staff (Information and Civil Affairs)
Air Marshal Sir Philip Joubert de la Ferté
Principal Administrative Officer
Lieut.-General R. A. Wheeler, U.S. Army (also Deputy S.A.C. from 12.11.44)
Deputy Principal Administrative Officer
Major-General R. F. S. Denning

ROYAL NAVY

Commander-in-Chief, Eastern Fleet
Admiral Sir Bruce Fraser (till 21.11.44)
Commander-in-Chief, East Indies Fleet
Admiral Sir Arthur Power (from 22.11.44)
Commander, 3rd Battle Squadron
Vice-Admiral H. T. C. Walker
Flag Officer Force 'W'
Rear-Admiral B. C. S. Martin

11th ARMY GROUP (became A.L.F.S.E.A. 12.11.44)

Commander-in-Chief
General Sir George Giffard
Major-General General Staff
Major-General I. S. O. Playfair

Major-General Administration
Major-General E. N. Goddard
Director Medical Services
Major-General T. O. Thompson

ALLIED LAND FORCES, SOUTH-EAST ASIA

Commander-in-Chief
Lieut.-General Sir Oliver Leese
Chief of General Staff
Major-General G. P. Walsh
Major-General General Staff
Major-General I. S. O. Playfair
Brigadier Royal Artillery
Brigadier L. C. Manners-Smith
Engineer-in-Chief
Major-General K. Ray
Chief Signal Officer
Major-General D. H. Steward
Major-General Administration
Major-General E. M. Bastyan
Director Medical Services
Major-General T. O. Thompson
Major-General W. E. Tyndall (from 7.4.45)

AIR COMMAND, SOUTH-EAST ASIA

Allied Air Commander-in-Chief
Air Chief Marshal Sir Richard Peirse
Air Marshal Sir Guy Garrod (acting, from 27.11.44)
Air Chief Marshal Sir Keith Park (from 24.2.45)
Commander, Eastern Air Command
Major-General G. E. Stratemeyer, U.S.A.A.F.
Headquarters R.A.F. Burma
Air Marshal W. A. Coryton

14TH ARMY HEADQUARTERS AND ARMY TROOPS
Lieut.-General Sir William Slim

Brigadier General Staff	*Brigadier S. F. Irwin*
	Brigadier J. S. Lethbridge
	(from September 1944)
Deputy Adjutant & Quartermaster	*Major-General A. H. J. Snelling*
General	*Brigadier F. J. Walsh* (from 9.3.45)
Chief Signal Officer	*Brigadier W. O. Bowen*
Deputy Director Medical Services	*Brigadier G. F. Macalevey*

Armour
> 8th K.G.V's O. Light Cavalry
> 11th Cavalry (P.A.V.O.) (armoured cars)
> 6th Armoured Fighting Vehicles Maintenance
>   Troop
> 2nd Indian Tank Delivery Squadron

Artillery   *Brigadier G. de V. Welchman*
> 18th (Self-Propelled) Field Regiment, R.A.
> 134th Medium Regiment, R.A.
> 52nd Heavy Anti-Aircraft Regiment, R.A.
> 69th Light Anti-Aircraft Regiment, R.A.   } detachments to
> 2nd Indian Field Regiment   corps as necessary
> 2nd Indian Light Anti-Aircraft Regiment
> 5th Mahratta Anti-Tank Regiment
> 656 Air O.P. Squadron, R.A.F.

Engineers   *Brigadier W. F. Hasted*
> Four artisan works companies, I.E.
> Two bridging companies, I.E.
> Three bridging platoons, I.E.
> Three engineer battalions, I.E.
> Four field companies, I.E.
> H.Q. 459th Forward Airfield Engineers, I.E.   } detachments to
>   One engineer battalion, I.E.   corps as necessary
>   Two field companies, I.E.
>   One mechanical equipment platoon, I.E.
> Two mechanical equipment companies, I.E.
> Three works sections, I.E.
> One quarrying company, I.E.

Infantry
> 1/3rd Madras Regiment
> 1st Assam Rifles
> 3rd Assam Rifles
> 4th Assam Rifles
> Chin Hills Battalion
> 25th Gurkhas Rifles
> Western Chin Levies
> Lushai Scouts

R.A.S.C./R.I.A.S.C.

590th Company, R.A.S.C. (tank transporters)
Elephant Company, R.I.A.S.C.
387th Divisional Troops Company, R.A.S.C. (DUKWs)
127th G.P.T. Company, R.I.A.S.C.
Four animal transport companies, R.I.A.S.C.
5th Indian Field Ambulance

IV CORPS HEADQUARTERS AND CORPS TROOPS

Lieut.-General Sir Geoffry Scoones
Lieut.-General F. W. Messervy
(from 8.12.44)

Brigadier General Staff	*Brigadier K. Bayley*
	Brigadier E. H. W. Cobb
	(from November 1944)
Deputy Adjutant & Quartermaster General	*Brigadier L. R. Mizen*
Deputy Director Medical Services	*Brigadier D. F. Panton*

Armour

    255th Indian Tank Brigade   *Brigadier C. E. Pert*
      116th Regiment, R.A.C. (Gordon Highlanders)
      5th (Probyn's) Horse
      9th (Royal Deccan) Horse
      16th Light Cavalry (armoured cars)
      4/4th Bombay Grenadiers
      36th Field Squadron, I.E.
      3rd Independent Bridging Troop, R.A.C.

Artillery   *Brigadier C. Goulder*

      8th Medium Regiment, R.A.
      1st Indian Light Anti-Aircraft Regiment
      67th Indian Heavy Anti-Aircraft Regiment
      1st Survey Regiment, R.A.

Engineers   *Brigadier W. W. Boggs*

      H.Q. 471 Army Group Engineers
      H.Q. Corps Troops Engineers
      12th Engineer Battalion, I.E. (from 14th Army)
      75th Field Company, I.E.
      424th Field Company, I.E.
      94th (Faridkot) Field Company, I.S.F.
      305th Field Park Company, I.E.
      One mechanical equipment platoon, I.E.

Signals   *Brigadier E. V. McCormack*

      IV Corps Signals

Infantry

      78th Indian Infantry Company

Miscellaneous Forward Troops

      51st Indian Company, 'D' Division (Deception)
      No. 1 Control Centre Forward Maintenance Area
      No. 2 Control Centre Forward Maintenance Area
      B Group 'V' Force Operations H.Q.

XXXIII CORPS HEADQUARTERS AND CORPS TROOPS

Lieut.-General Sir Montague Stopford

Brigadier General Staff	*Brigadier G. N. Wood*
	Brigadier F. C. Scott
	(from 13.10.44)

Deputy Adjutant & Quartermaster
    General   *Brigadier D. F. Wilson-Haffenden*

Deputy Director Medical Services   *Brigadier G. J. V. Crosby*

Armour

    254th Indian Tank Brigade   *Brigadier R. L. Scoones*
        Carabiniers (3rd Dragoon Guards)
        150th Regiment, R.A.C.
        7th Light Cavalry[1]
        3/4th Bombay Grenadiers
        401st Field Squadron, I.E.
        2nd Independent Bridging Troop
        One troop 400th Scorpion Squadron (flame-throwers)

Artillery   *Brigadier D. J. Stevens*

    1st Medium Regiment, R.A.
    44th Light Anti-Aircraft Regiment, R.A.
    101st Heavy Anti-Aircraft Regiment, R.A.
    1st Indian Survey Regiment
    8th Mahratta Anti-tank Regiment

Engineers   *Brigadier J. F. D. Steedman*

    H.Q. 474 Army Group Engineers
    H.Q. Corps Troops Engineers
        10th Engineer Battalion, I.E. (from 14th Army)
        67th Field Company, I.E.
        76th Field Company, I.E.
        361st Field Company, I.E.
        322nd Field Park Company, I.E.
        One mechanical equipment platoon, I.E.

Signals   *Brigadier C. N. Stafford*

    XXXIII Corps Signals

Infantry

    2nd Suffolk Regiment
    (from March 1945)

---

[1] Transferred (less one squadron) to 255th Tank Brigade in April 1945. (See also Appendix 21.)

DIVISIONS OF 14TH ARMY

2ND DIVISION

Major-General C. G. G. Nicholson

Divisional Reconnaissance
　2nd Reconnaissance Regiment, R.A.C.

Artillery　　　　　　　　　　　*Brigadier H. S. J. Bourke*
　10th Field Regiment, R.A.
　16th Field Regiment, R.A.
　99th Field Regiment, R.A.
　100th Anti-Tank Regiment (Gordon Highlanders)

Engineers
　5th Field Company, R.E.
　208th Field Company, R.E.
　506th Field Company, R.E.
　21st Field Park Company, R.E.

Signals
　2nd Divisional Signals

Divisional Machine-Gun Battalion
　2nd Manchester Machine-Gun Battalion

Infantry
　4th Infantry Brigade　　　　　*Brigadier R. S. McNaught*
　　1st Royal Scots
　　2nd Royal Norfolk Regiment
　　1/8th Lancashire Fusiliers

　5th Infantry Brigade　　　*Brigadier M. M. Alston-Roberts-West*
　　7th Worcestershire Regiment
　　2nd Dorsetshire Regiment
　　1st Queen's Own Cameron Highlanders

　6th Infantry Brigade　　　　*Brigadier W. G. Smith*
　　1st Royal Welch Fusiliers
　　1st Royal Berkshire Regiment
　　2nd Durham Light Infantry

5TH INDIAN DIVISION

Major-General G. C. Evans

Major-General D. F. W. Warren (from 23.9.44.)
(killed in flying accident, 9.2.45)

Major-General E. C. R. Mansergh (from 22.2.45)

Artillery — *Brigadier G. B. J. Kellie*

    4th Field Regiment, R.A.
    28th Field Regiment, R.A.
    56th Anti-Tank Regiment, R.A.
    24th Indian Mountain Regiment

Engineers

    2nd Field Company, I.E.
    20th Field Company, I.E.
    74th Field Company, I.E.
    44th Field Park Company, I.E.

Signals

    5th Indian Divisional Signals

Divisional Infantry

    3/9th Jat Regiment (reconnaissance battalion)
    7/14th Punjab Regiment (H.Q. battalion),
        replaced March 1945 by 4th Jammu and Kashmir Infantry,
        I.S.F.
    17th Dogra Machine-Gun Battalion

Infantry

    9th Indian Infantry Brigade — *Brigadier J. A. Salomons*
        2nd West Yorkshire Regiment — *Brigadier H. G. L. Brain*
        3/2nd Punjab Regiment — (from 26.3.45)
        4th Jammu and Kashmir Infantry, I.S.F.,
            replaced March 1945 by 1st Burma Regiment

    123rd Indian Infantry Brigade — *Brigadier E. J. Denholm-Young*
        2nd Suffolk Regiment, replaced March 1945
            by 7th York and Lancaster Regiment
        2/1st Punjab Regiment
        1/17th Dogra Regiment

    161st Indian Infantry Brigade — *Brigadier E. G. C. Poole*
        4th Royal West Kent Regiment — *Brigadier E. H. W. Grimshaw*
        1/1st Punjab Regiment — (from 3.3.45)
        4/7th Rajput Regiment

7TH INDIAN DIVISION

Major-General F. W. Messervy
Major-General G. C. Evans
(from 29.12.44)

Artillery   *Brigadier A. F. Hely*

 136th Field Regiment, R.A.
 139th Field Regiment, R.A.
 24th Anti-Tank Regiment, R.A.
 25th Indian Mountain Regiment

Engineers

 62nd Field Company, I.E.
 77th Field Company, I.E.
 421st Field Company, I.E.
 331st Field Park Company, I.E.

Signals

 7th Indian Divisional Signals

Divisional Infantry

 7/2nd Punjab Regiment (reconnaissance battalion)
 13th Frontier Force Rifles Machine-Gun Battalion
 2nd Baroda Infantry, I.S.F. (H.Q. battalion)

Infantry

 33rd Indian Infantry Brigade *Brigadier R. G. Collingwood*
  4/15th Punjab Regiment *A/Brigadier L. H. O. Pugh*
  4/1st Gurkha Rifles   (offg.) (from 28.3.45)
  1st Burma Regiment (until return of 1st Queen's
   Royal Regiment (West Surrey) in April 1945)

 89th Indian Infantry Brigade *Brigadier W. A. Crowther*
  2nd King's Own Scottish Borderers
  1/11th Sikh Regiment
  4/8th Gurkha Rifles

 114th Indian Infantry Brigade *Brigadier H. W. Dinwiddie*
  2nd South Lancashire Regiment
  4/14th Punjab Regiment
  4/5th Royal Gurkha Rifles

Major-General C. C. Fowkes

Artillery   *Brigadier J. V. D. Radford*

    302nd (E.A.) Field Regiment
    303rd (E.A.) Field Regiment
    304th (E.A.) Anti-Aircraft/Anti-Tank Regiment

Engineers

    54th (E.A.) Field Company
    58th (E.A.) Field Company
    64th (E.A.) Field Company
    62nd (E.A.) Field Park Company

Signals

    11th (E.A.) Divisional Signals

Divisional Infantry

    5th King's African Rifles (reconnaissance battalion)
    13th King's African Rifles (H.Q. battalion)

Infantry

    21st (E.A.) Infantry Brigade   *Brigadier J. F. Macnab*
       2nd King's African Rifles
       4th King's African Rifles
       1st Northern Rhodesia Regiment

    25th (E.A.) Infantry Brigade   *Brigadier N. C. Hendricks*
       11th King's African Rifles
       26th King's African Rifles
       34th King's African Rifles

    26th (E.A. Infantry Brigade)   *Brigadier V. K. H. Channer*
       22nd King's African Rifles   *Brigadier A. P. Walsh*
       36th King's African Rifles   (from 18.11.44)
       44th King's African Rifles

17TH INDIAN DIVISION

Major-General D. T. Cowan

Artillery
    129th Field Regiment, R.A.
    1st Indian Field Regiment
    21st Indian Mountain Regiment
    82nd Anti-Tank Regiment, R.A.

Brigadier the Baron de Robeck
Brigadier H. K. Dimoline
(from 25.10.44)

Engineers
    414th Field Park Company, I.E.
    60th Field Company, I.E.
    70th Field Company, I.E.
    Tehri Garhwal Company, I.S.F.

Signals
    17th Indian Divisional Signals

Divisional Infantry
    6/7th Rajput Regiment (H.Q. battalion), replaced
        April 1945 by 6/15th Punjab Regiment
    6/9th Jat Regiment (reconnaissance battalion),
        replaced April 1945 by 6/7th Punjab Regiment
    9/13th Frontier Force Rifles (Machine-Guns)

Infantry
    48th Indian Infantry Brigade   *Brigadier R. C. O. Hedley*
      1st West Yorkshire Regiment
      4/12th Frontier Force Regiment
      1/7th Gurkha Rifles

    63rd Indian Infantry Brigade   *Brigadier G. W. S. Burton*
      9th Border Regiment
      7/10th Baluch Regiment
      1/10th Gurkha Rifles

    99th Indian Infantry Brigade   *Brigadier G. L. Tarver*
      6/15th Punjab Regiment, replaced   *Brigadier M. V. Wright*
        April 1945 by 1st East Yorkshire   (from 25.3.45)
        Regiment
      1st Sikh Light Infantry
      1/3rd Gurkha Rifles

APPENDIX 18

19TH INDIAN DIVISION

Major-General T. W. Rees

Artillery   *Brigadier J. A. Macdonald*

    115th Field Regiment, R.A.
    33rd Anti-Tank Regiment, R.A.
    4th Indian Field Regiment
    20th Indian Mountain Regiment

Engineers

    29th Field Company, I.E.
    64th Field Company, I.E.
    65th Field Company, I.E.
    327th Field Park Company, I.E.

Signals

    19th Indian Divisional Signals

Divisional Infantry

    1/15th Punjab Regiment (H.Q. battalion)
    11th Sikh Machine-Gun Battalion
    1st Assam Regiment (reconnaissance battalion)

Infantry

    62nd Indian Infantry Brigade   *Brigadier J. R. Morris*
      2nd Welch Regiment   *Brigadier G. H. B. Beyts*
      3/6th Rajputana Rifles   (from 3.4.45)
      4/6th Gurkha Rifles

    64th Indian Infantry Brigade   *Brigadier G. A. Bain*
      2nd Worcestershire Regiment   *Brigadier J. G. Flewett*
      5/10th Baluch Regiment   (from 8.2.45)
      1/6th Gurkha Rifles

    98th Indian Infantry Brigade   *Brigadier C. I. Jerrard*
      2nd Royal Berkshire Regiment
      8/12th Frontier Force Regiment
      4/4th Gurkha Rifles

20TH INDIAN DIVISION

Major-General D. D. Gracey

Artillery   *Brigadier J. A. E. Hirst*

    9th Field Regiment, R.A.
    114th Field Regiment, R.A.
    111th Anti-Tank Regiment, R.A.
    23rd Indian Mountain Regiment

Engineers

    92nd Field Company, I.E.
    422nd Field Company, I.E.
    481st Field Company, I.E.
    332nd Field Park Company, I.E.

Divisional Infantry

    4/2nd Gurkha Rifles (reconnaissance battalion)
      from March 1945
    4/17th Dogra Regiment (H.Q. battalion)
    9th Jat Machine-Gun Battalion

Infantry

    32nd Indian Infantry Brigade   *Brigadier D. A. L. Mackenzie*
      1st Northamptonshire Regiment[1] *Brigadier E. C. J. Woodford*
      9/14th Punjab Regiment   (from 25.3.45)
      3/8th Gurkha Rifles

    80th Indian Infantry Brigade   *Brigadier S. Greeves*
      1st Devonshire Regiment[1] *Brigadier D. E. Taunton*
      9/12th Frontier Force Regiment (from 18.3.45)
      3/1st Gurkha Rifles

    100th Indian Infantry Brigade   *Brigadier C. H. B. Rodham*
      2nd Border Regiment[1]
      14/13th Frontier Force Rifles
      4/10th Gurkha Rifles

36TH DIVISION

Major-General F. W. Festing

Under 14th Army from the 1st April 1945
(For details see order of battle of N.C.A.C.)

---

[1] Between the 12th and 18th April 1945 the three British battalions of 20th Division exchanged with Indian Army battalions from 36th Division: 1st Northamptonshire Regiment with 1/1st Gurkha Rifles, 1st Devonshire Regiment with 1/19th Hyderabad Regiment, and 2nd Border Regiment with 2/8th Punjab Regiment.

INDEPENDENT INFANTRY BRIGADES OF 14TH ARMY

268TH INDIAN INFANTRY BRIGADE

Brigadier G. M. Dyer

4/3rd Madras Regiment
1st Chamar Regiment
Mahindra Dal Regiment (Nepalese)

LUSHAI BRIGADE

Brigadier P. C. Marindin

Signals

Brigade Signals Section

Infantry

1st Royal Battalion, 9th Jat Regiment
1st Bihar Regiment
Chin Hills Battalion, replaced
December 1944 by 7/14th Punjab
Regiment
1st Assam Rifles (less two companies)

28TH EAST AFRICAN INFANTRY BRIGADE

Brigadier W. A. Dimoline
Brigadier T. H. S. Galletly
(from 21.2.45)
7th King's African Rifles
46th King's African Rifles
71st King's African Rifles
63rd (E.A.) Field Company
28th (E.A.) Infantry Brigade
Defence Platoon

XV CORPS HEADQUARTERS AND CORPS TROOPS

Lieut.-General Sir Philip Christison

Brigadier General Staff	*Brigadier D. C. Hawthorn*
	Brigadier N. D. Wingrove
	(from 24.3.45)
Deputy Adjutant & Quartermaster General	*Brigadier N. D. Wingrove*
	Brigadier A. C. L. Maclean
	(from 24.3.45)
Deputy Director Medical Services	*Brigadier A. N. T. Meneces*

Armour

50th Indian Tank Brigade   *Brigadier G. H. N. Todd*
146th Regiment, R.A.C.
19th Lancers
45th Cavalry
2/4th Bombay Grenadiers
37th Field Squadron, I.E.
1st Independent Bridging Troop, R.A.C.
3rd Independent Tank Delivery Squadron, I.A.C.

Artillery   *Brigadier L. A. Harris*

6th Medium Regiment, R.A.
8th (Belfast) Heavy Anti-Aircraft
   Regiment, R.A.
36th Light Anti-Aircraft Regiment, R.A.
2nd Survey Regiment, R.A.
C Flight 656th Air O.P.
   Squadron, R.A.

Engineers   *Brigadier L. I. Jacques*

H.Q. Corps Troops Engineers   *Brigadier D. C. T. Swan*
H.Q. 472nd Army Group Engineers   (from 9.4.45)
16th Engineer Battalion, I.E.
17th Engineer Battalion, I.E.
20th Engineer Battalion, I.E.
73rd Field Company, I.E.
483rd Field Company, I.E.
Malerkotla Field Company, I.S.F.
403rd Field Park Company, I.E.
855th Bridging Company, I.E.

Signals   *Brigadier D. W. R. Burridge*

XV Indian Corps Signals

Infantry

79th Indian Infantry Company

22nd East African Brigade   *Brigadier R. F. Johnstone*
 1st King's African Rifles
 3rd Northern Rhodesia Regiment
 1st Royal African Regiment
 59th (E.A.) Field Company
 22nd (E.A.) Brigade Signal Section

Commandos

3 Commando Brigade   *Brigadier C. R. Hardy*
 1 Commando
 5 Commando
 42 Royal Marine Commando
 44 Royal Marine Commando

DIVISIONS OF XV CORPS

25TH INDIAN DIVISION

Major-General G. N. Wood

Artillery   *Brigadier A. J. Daniell*
    8th Field Regiment, R.A.   *Brigadier N. P. H. Tapp*
    27th Field Regiment, R.A.   (from 7.4.45)
    33rd Indian Mountain Regiment
    7th Indian Anti-Tank Regiment

Engineers
    63rd Field Company, I.E.
    93rd Field Company, I.E.
    425th Field Company, I.E.
    325th Field Park Company, I.E.
    16th Bridging Section, I.E.

Signals
    25th Indian Divisional Signals

Divisional Infantry
    9th York and Lancaster Regiment (H.Q. battalion)
    12th Frontier Force Regiment Machine-Gun Battalion

Infantry
    51st Indian Infantry Brigade   *Brigadier T. H. Angus*
        16/10th Baluch Regiment   *Brigadier R. A. Hutton*
        8/19th Hyderabad Regiment   (from 6.11.44)
        2/2nd Punjab Regiment

    53rd Indian Infantry Brigade   *Brigadier A. G. O'C. Scott*
        17/5th Mahratta Regiment   *Brigadier B. C. H. Gerty*
        7/16th Punjab Regiment   (from 29.12.44)
        4/18th Royal Garhwal Rifles

    74th Indian Infantry Brigade   *Brigadier J. E. Hirst*
        6th Oxfordshire and Buckinghamshire
          Light Infantry
        14/10th Baluch Regiment
        3/2nd K. E. O. Gurkha Rifles

APPENDIX 18

26TH INDIAN DIVISION

Major-General C. E. N. Lomax
Major-General H. M. Chambers
(from 1.4.45)

Artillery
    160th Field Regiment, R.A.
    7th Indian Field Regiment
    30th Indian Mountain Regiment
    1st Indian Anti-Tank Regiment

Brigadier C. J. G. Dalton
Brigadier the Baron de Robeck
  (from 10.10.44)
Brigadier T. E. D. Kelly
  (from 7.4.45)

Engineers
    28th Field Company, I.E.
    72nd Field Company, I.E.
    98th Field Company, I.E.
    328th Field Park Company, I.E.
    7th Bridging Platoon, I.E.

Signals
    26th Indian Divisional Signals

Divisional H.Q. Infantry
    5/9th Jat Regiment

Infantry
    4th Indian Infantry Brigade
      2nd Green Howards
      2/13th Frontier Force Rifles
      2/7th Rajput Regiment

Brigadier A. W. Lowther
Brigadier J. F. R. Forman
  (from 19.1.45)

    36th Indian Infantry Brigade
      8/13th Frontier Force Rifles
      1/8th Gurkha Rifles
      2nd Ajmer Regiment, I.S.F.

Brigadier L. G. Thomas
Brigadier K. S. Thimayya
  (from 1.4.45)

    71st Indian Infantry Brigade
      1st Lincolnshire Regiment
      5/1st Punjab Regiment
      1/18th Royal Garhwal Rifles

Brigadier R. C. Cottrell-Hill
Brigadier H. M. Chambers
  (from 1.3.45)
Brigadier H. P. L. Hutchinson
  (from 22.3.45)

81ST WEST AFRICAN DIVISION

Major-General F. J. Loftus-Tottenham

Artillery

    21st (W.A.) Anti-Tank Regiment
    41st (W.A.) Mortar Regiment
    101st (W.A.) Light Regiment

Engineers

    3rd (W.A.) Field Company
    5th (W.A.) Field Company
    6th (W.A.) Field Company
    8th (W.A.) Field Park Company

Signals

    81st (W.A.) Divisional Signals

Divisional Reconnaissance Battalion

    81st (W.A.) Reconnaissance Battalion

Infantry

    5th (W.A.) Infantry Brigade   *Brigadier P. J. Jeffreys*
       5th Gold Coast Regiment
       7th Gold Coast Regiment
       8th Gold Coast Regiment

    6th (W.A.) Infantry Brigade   *Brigadier A. A. Crook*
       1st Gambia Regiment
       4th Nigeria Regiment
       1st Sierra Leone Regiment

Note: The remaining brigade of the division (3rd) was part of Special
Force (3rd Indian Division). See Volume III, Appendix 16.

APPENDIX 18

82ND WEST AFRICAN DIVISION

Major-General G. McI. I. S. Bruce
Major-General H. C. Stockwell
(from 9.2.45)

Artillery

    22nd (W.A.) Anti-Tank Regiment
    42nd (W.A.) Mortar Regiment
    102nd (W.A.) Light Regiment

Engineers

    1st (W.A.) Field Company
    2nd (W.A.) Field Company
    4th (W.A.) Field Company
    9th (W.A.) Field Park Company

Signals

    82nd (W.A.) Divisional Signals

Divisional Reconnaissance Battalion

    82nd (W.A.) Reconnaissance Battalion

Infantry

    1st (W.A.) Brigade   *Brigadier C. R. A. Swynnerton*
      1st Nigeria Regiment
      2nd Nigeria Regiment
      3rd Nigeria Regiment

    2nd (W.A.) Brigade   *Brigadier E. W. D. Western*
      1st Gold Coast Regiment   *Brigadier A. T. Wilson-Brand*
      2nd Gold Coast Regiment   (from 23.3.45)
      3rd Gold Coast Regiment

    4th (W.A.) Infantry Brigade   *Brigadier A. H. G. Ricketts*
      5th Nigeria Regiment
      9th Nigeria Regiment
      10th Nigeria Regiment

NORTHERN COMBAT AREA COMMAND
Lieut.-General D. I. Sultan

Mars Task Force   *Brig.-General J. P. Willey*
    612th (American) Field Artillery Battalion (Pack)
    475th (American) Infantry Regiment
    124th (American) Cavalry Regiment
    1st Chinese Regiment

New Chinese First Army   *General Sun Li-Jen*
    30th Division
        88th Infantry Regiment
        89th Infantry Regiment
        90th Infantry Regiment

    38th Division
        112th Infantry Regiment
        113th Infantry Regiment
        114th Infantry Regiment

New Chinese Sixth Army   *General Liao Yueh-shang*
    14th Division
        40th Infantry Regiment
        41st Infantry Regiment
        42nd Infantry Regiment

    22nd Division
        64th Infantry Regiment
        65th Infantry Regiment
        66th Infantry Regiment

    50th Division
        148th Infantry Regiment
        149th Infantry Regiment
        150th Infantry Regiment

36TH (BRITISH) DIVISION

Major-General F. W. Festing

Artillery   *Brigadier G. H. Inglis*

122nd Anti-Tank Regiment, R.A.
130th Field Regiment, R.A.
178th Field Regiment, R.A.
3rd Meteorological Detachment, R.A.
32nd Indian Mountain Regiment

Engineers

10th Bridging Platoon, I.E.
12th Bridging Platoon, I.E.
15th Engineer Battalion, I.E.
30th Field Company, I.E.
58th Field Company, I.E.
236th Field Company, R.E.
324th Field Park Company, I.E.

Signals

36th Divisional Signals

Divisional Infantry

'D' Company 2nd Manchester Machine-Gun Battalion
88th Indian Infantry Company (H.Q. company)

Infantry

26th Indian Infantry Brigade   *Brigadier M. B. Jennings*
  2nd Buffs
  1/19th Hyderabad Regiment[1]
  2/8th Punjab Regiment,[1] replaced
    March 1945 by 1/1st Gurkha Rifles[1]

29th Infantry Brigade   *Brigadier H. C. Stockwell*
  2nd East Lancashire Regiment   *Brigadier G. E. R. Bastin*
  1st Royal Scots Fusiliers   (from 9.1.45)
  2nd Royal Welch Fusiliers

72nd Indian Infantry Brigade   *Brigadier A. R. Aslett*
  10th Gloucestershire Regiment
  9th Royal Sussex Regiment
  6th South Wales Borderers

---

[1] The three Indian Army battalions in 36th Division exchanged into 20th Indian Division in April 1945. See page 485.

LINE OF COMMUNICATION AREAS

LINE OF COMMUNICATION COMMAND
(formed 15.11.44)

Major-General G. W. Symes

202 L. of C. Area (Gauhati)   *Major-General R. P. L. Ranking*

    251 L. of C. Sub-Area
    252 L. of C. Sub-Area
    253 L. of C. Sub-Area
    256 L. of C. Sub-Area
    257 L. of C. Sub-Area

404 L. of C. Area (Chittagong)   *Brigadier T. R. Henry*
    451 L. of C. Sub-Area   *Brigadier M. L. Hayne*
    452 L. of C. Sub-Area   (from 7.1.45)
    453 L. of C. Sub-Area
    454 L. of C. Sub-Area
    455 L. of C. Sub-Area

505 DISTRICT (Shwebo, to Meiktila in May)
(formed 9.3.45)

Major-General A. H. J. Snelling

25th Gurkha Rifles
2nd Burma Regiment

253 L. of C. Sub-Area[1] (Shwebo, to Mandalay April 1945)

256 L. of C. Sub-Area[2] (Imphal)

455 L. of C. Sub-Area[3] (Magwe)
    1st Jammu and Kashmir Infantry, I.S.F.

551 L. of C. Sub-Area (Kalewa)
    1st Chin Rifles
    2nd Chin Rifles

552 L. of C. Sub-Area (Alon, to Myingyan in April)

553 L. of C. Sub-Area (Myitkyina)
    1st Kachin Rifles
    2nd Kachin Rifles

---

[1] Transferred from 202 L. of C. Area to Shwebo in February 1945.
[2] Transferred from 202 L. of C. Area in March 1945.
[3] Transferred from 404 L. of C. Area in May 1945.

APPENDIX 19

Maintenance by Air of 14th Army During Phases 2 and 3 of 'Extended Capital', January–March 1945

1. The main air bases used by Allied transport squadrons throughout the operation have been referred to in Chapter XVIII, Appendix 15 and Sketches 20 and 21. If the advance of 14th Army were to be carried out without check, forward airfields on which air supplies could be landed had to be established in central and southern Burma. As the advance continued, the forward airfields which became available consisted of the few which had been constructed by the Japanese and the pre-war airfields abandoned by the Allies during the withdrawal of 1942. Most of these were fair-weather.[1] On many, the Japanese had had time to carry out denial measures, and the army and corps engineers had to undertake considerable repair work. The engineers also built a large number of airstrips at suitable places on the axis of the advance of the formations concerned; at first these were often no more than earthen runways some 2,000 yards in length and 50 yards wide. So quickly were they built that on occasions they were brought into use within three days of work beginning on them.

2. Except in country which made construction of airfields unusually difficult, as in the Myittha valley, the airfields used formed a number of distinct groups in successive areas as the advance progressed. These groups were five airfields in the Kalemyo area, five in the Shwebo area, five in the Monywa area, eight around Mandalay, five in the vicinity of Pakokku and four around Meiktila. Excluding the large number of short airstrips built by troops for use by light aircraft, which were invaluable for the evacuation of casualties and for liaison and communication purposes, the transport squadrons at one time or another during 'Capital' used some fifty forward airfields. The tactical squadrons of 221 Group R.A.F. and some of those in close support of 14th Army from 224 group made use of several of these airfields during the advance. But, so as not to interfere with the steady flow of air supply, tactical squadrons did not normally operate from an airfield which was actually in use at the time by transport aircraft.

3. Maintenance by air involved the lift by transport aircraft from base airfields to the forward area of all requirements, including reinforcements, for the maintenance of the fighting formations and the evacuation of casualties and prisoners-of-war, etc. Airheads were established in the forward area so that transport aircraft could land with their loads, but supply-dropping (at the expense of the tonnage carried) was resorted to as operationally necessary. An airhead included all installations, depots and dumps established in an area controlled by the Forward Airfield Maintenance

---

[1] The only all-weather airfields were Shwebo, Monywa, Pakokku, Meiktila, Magwe, Toungoo and Myingyan.

Organization (F.A.M.O.) in charge of it. Forward maintenance areas (F.M.A.s) were established at or near airheads, but independent of them, by corps and divisions for handling their daily maintenance and holding reserve stocks. Each F.M.A. consisted of a small headquarters, assisted by labour and transport provided by the formation it was serving.

A Rear Airfield Maintenance Organization (R.A.M.O.) was established at each base airfield and was responsible for loading the aircraft with supplies and stores from stocks held at the airfield or obtained from nearby supply depots. Each R.A.M.O. was controlled by C.A.A.T.O., to which all demands were made by both corps within the tonnages allotted to them by 14th Army.[1] An F.A.M.O., comprising a headquarters and two control centres, was allotted to 14th Army Headquarters and to each corps. These units controlled the reception of stores, supplies and reinforcements into and distribution from the forward airheads used by the formation to which they were allotted.

From mid-January 1945, 130 tons was fixed as the daily allotment for the maintenance of each division and for corps troops. This total was made up as follows: supplies and rations 52, P.O.L. 33, ammunition 21, ordnance stores 14, engineer stores 3, and miscellaneous 7 tons. Each tank brigade was allotted 70 tons a day.

4. The air bases used during this period were:

Imphal Group	Kangla, No. 2 R.A.M.O.
	Imphal, No. 1 R.A.M.O.
	Tulihal, No. 6 R.A.M.O.
Chittagong Group	Chittagong, No. 7 R.A.M.O. (from Agartala, opening on the 2nd February).
	Hathazari, No. 5 R.A.M.O.
	Dohazari, No. 4 R.A.M.O. (from Comilla, opening on the 16th February).
Comilla	— No. 3 R.A.M.O. (This airfield was used for reinforcements only.)

5. *see overleaf*

---

[1] For details of functions of the R.A.M.O. see page 37.

5. The airfields used by IV and XXXIII Corps during the advance were:

Formation	Airhead	Date opened	Date closed	Narrative
IV Corps				The corps, consisting initially of 7th and 17th Divisions, 28th (E.A.) Brigade, the Lushai Brigade and 255th Tank Brigade, moved up the Myittha valley to the Irrawaddy near Pakokku. The crossing of the Irrawaddy was forced by 7th Division, and 17th Division and 255th Tank Brigade then advanced to and captured Meiktila. The corps was reinforced by 5th Division.
	Kan	16 Jan.	28 Feb. ⎫	Maintenance of IV Corps during its advance to the Irrawaddy.
	Tilin	31 Jan.	21 Feb. ⎬	
	Sinthe	10 Feb.	2 Apr. ⎫	Maintenance of IV Corps during the crossing of the Irrawaddy at Nyaungu and during the advance on Meiktila; the subsequent maintenance of 7th Division, 5th Division and corps troops. On the 7th April Myitche passed under control of XXXIII Corps. See Appendix 23.
	Myitche	18 Feb.	7 Apr. ⎬	
	Thabutkon	27 Feb.	3 Mar.	Used for the fly-in of 99th Brigade of 17th Division and the topping-up of 17th Division and 255th Tank Brigade before their final attack on Meiktila.
	Meiktila	4 Mar.	21 Mar.	Used for the fly-in of 9th Brigade of 5th Division and maintenance of 17th Division and 255th Tank Brigade during the defence of Meiktila. On 21st March the airfield could no longer be used for air landing owing to enemy action.
		1 Apr.	Onwards	Airfield reopened on the 1st April and thereafter used for maintenance of IV Corps. See Appendix 23.

Formation	Airhead	Date opened	Date closed	Narrative
XXXIII Corps	Taungtha	28 Mar.		Airfield used for maintenance of 5th Division (less one brigade flown to Meiktila) and corps troops on their way to Meiktila. It was handed over to XXXIII Corps on the 5th April. See Appendix 23.
				The corps, consisting of 20th, 2nd, 19th Divisions, 268th Brigade and 254th Tank Brigade, advanced on a broad front from the Chindwin (Kalewa to Tonhe and Thaungdut) to the Irrawaddy (Myinmu to Thabeikkyin) and forced crossings at Myinmu, Ngazun, Kyauk-myaung and Thabeikkyin. Each formation followed a separate route, but the axes of all formations except 20th Division had converged by the 18th January so that the corps (except for 20th Division) could be maintained from the 18th January to the 4th March from a corps F.M.A. formed at the Shwebo airhead.
Headquarters XXXIII Corps and corps troops	Yeu	10 Jan.	18 Jan.	A corps F.M.A. was established at Shwebo on the 18th January. Reserve stocks were built up at Shwebo so that the advance could be resumed. Stocking began on the 14th at Yeu and was continued at Shwebo from the 18th.
	Shwebo	18 Jan.	4 Mar.	
	Sadaung	11 Feb.	5 Apr.	A subsidiary corps medical centre was opened at Sadaung to support 2nd Division from 12th February. The main corps medical centre at Shwebo supported 19th and 20th Divisions.
	Ondaw	25 Feb.	5 Apr.	The airhead at Ondaw was opened to receive stocks of P.O.L., ammunition and engineer stores. On the 4th March maintenance for the corps, less 19th Division, was switched from Shwebo to Ondaw, which became the corps F.M.A. On the same date maintenance of 19th Division was switched from Shwebo to Singu.

Formation	Airhead	Date opened	Date closed	Narrative
20th Division	Budalin	22 Jan.	17 Feb.	This airhead was used until the division crossed the Irrawaddy.
	Allagappa	17 Feb.	12 Mar.	This airhead maintained the division in the bridgehead area south of the Irrawaddy at Myinmu.
	Ywabo	12 Mar.	20 Mar.	
	Chaunggwa	20 Mar.	26 Mar.	
	Dwehla	26 Mar.	9 Apr.	
2nd Division	Shwebo	18 Jan.	4 Mar. ⎫	This division was maintained from the corps F.M.A.s at Shwebo and Ondaw till the 12th March, by which time it had crossed the Irrawaddy and an airhead could be established south of the river.
	Ondaw	4 Mar.	12 Mar. ⎭	
	Ngazun	12 Mar.	20 Mar.	
	Tadau	20 Mar.	30 Mar.	On the 31st March 19th Division took over Tadau airfield from 2nd Division.
19th Division	Kawlin	25 Dec.	5 Jan.	
	Onbauk	12 Jan.	20 Jan.	
	Shwebo	20 Jan.	4 Mar.	Maintained from corps F.M.A.
	Singu	4 Mar.	17 Mar.	
	Mandalay (north)	17 Mar.	4 Apr.	
	Tadau	31 Mar.	6 Apr.	

APPENDIX 20

Deception Scheme 'Cloak', 25th January 1945

INFORMATION

1. The presence of IV Corps in the GANGAW VALLEY is believed to be still undetected by the Japanese, but as soon as the corps begins to emerge into the open country east of PAUK they will realize that we are a strong force and that we intend to cross the IRRAWADDY.

INTENTION

2. To continue to conceal from the Japanese for as long as possible the presence of the corps in the GANGAW VALLEY.

3. Subsequently to mislead the Japanese about the corps' crossing place over the IRRAWADDY and about the corps' objective east of the IRRAWADDY, at the same time misrepresenting to them the composition of the corps.

METHOD IN OUTLINE

4. (a) To continue, as long as possible, the methods at present being employed to conceal the composition of IV Corps and the presence of a corps in the GANGAW VALLEY.

  (b) To make a feint crossing at CHAUK, three or four days before our actual crossing elsewhere.

  (c) To simulate preparations for crossing the IRRAWADDY at PAKOKKU shortly before our actual crossing elsewhere.

  (d) To 'sell' YENANGYAUNG to the Japanese as the objective of IV Corps east of the IRRAWADDY.

METHOD IN DETAIL

Concealment of the Location and Composition of IV Corps

5. The present restrictions on the use of wireless will continue until relaxed by Corps H.Q.

6. 17th Division and 255th Tank Brigade will remain on wireless silence till deployed east of the IRRAWADDY.

7. No formation signs will be displayed on uniform, vehicles, noticeboards or elsewhere until permission to do so is given by Corps H.Q.—but see para. 9(a) below for special instructions for one brigade of 7th Indian Division.

The Feint Crossing at Chauk

8. As soon as possible after securing PAUK area 7th Indian Division will despatch one brigade with some artillery in support (28th (E.A.) Brigade

simulating 11th (E.A.) Division) down the YAW Chaung towards SEIK-PYU. During this advance, the brigade will 'sell' to the Japanese the bogus fact that it is a brigade of 11th (E.A.) Division and that the whole of this division is advancing by the same route. One section 'D' (from 11th (E.A.) Division) and 57th Company 'D' Force will be under command this brigade to assist in the deception. C.S.O.IV Corps is issuing separately details of W/T deception methods to be employed as part of this 'selling' of 11th (E.A.) Division.

9. Methods to be employed by this brigade for simulating the presence of large numbers:

(a) They will wear on their uniforms the sign of 11th (E.A.) Division. Corps H.Q. will arrange a supply of these.

(b) Movement wherever possible by day.

(c) Movement on a wide front, and widespread patrolling.

(d) Faked dust clouds, simulating the movement of large columns of transport or troops.

(e) Wherever contact is made with the enemy, the use of tactical deception devices to simulate considerable firepower and strength.

(f) The spreading of rumours that 20,000 E.A. troops are advancing down the YAW Chaung axis, and that airborne troops will be co-operating in advance of them in considerable strength.

10. On arrival at the IRRAWADDY, preparations will be made for a divisional crossing, as described in paras. 13 and 14 below.

11. At the appropriate moment this brigade will carry out a diversionary crossing over the IRRAWADDY. At least one company of infantry will be employed for this crossing. The deception units with the brigade will be able to assist in magnifying the strength of our force which lands on the far bank. This diversionary crossing will take place a few days before the real crossing by 7th Division elsewhere. To support the illusion that this diversionary crossing is the real thing, Corps H.Q. will arrange for dummy paratroops and other deception devices to be dropped from the air on the east side of the IRRAWADDY to assist this diversionary crossing.

12. Only negligible engineer assistance is likely to be available for this whole operation, since all available engineer resources will be required for the main crossing.

Spurious Preparations for Crossing at Pakokku

13. These preparations will be made by 7th Indian Division, who will send one brigade and engineers with river crossing stores into PAKOKKU itself. The activities of this brigade will conform as nearly as possible to those of a brigade which is, in fact, going to cross the river and will include:

(a) Reconnaissances for crossing places by suitable reconnaissance parties. In addition to reconnoitring the near bank, some of these parties will reconnoitre the far bank at a number of different places during darkness, making sure that their presence becomes known to the locals.

(b) Visits to selected crossing places by an officer wearing a red hat and red tabs.

(c) Inquiries from local inhabitants concerning speed of current, sandbanks, nature of far bank, time required for crossing, exits from the river opposite PAKOKKU, enemy strengths and dispositions opposite PAKOKKU.

(d) The 'losing' on the far side of a marked map, showing a few sketchy details of projected reconnaissances and Japanese positions. This map will be prepared at Corps H.Q.

(e) The collection of country boats from local boatmen—demands to be sufficient for the crossing of a whole division.

(f) Work on the approaches to the river bank.

(g) The establishing of dummy camps and dumps in the crossing area.

(h) Unloading bridging equipment from M.T. in the PAKOKKU area. If this can be arranged so that the local boatmen become aware of the activity, or even so that the Japanese hear the work in progress, the effect will be improved.

14. Throughout these preparations, efforts will be made to confuse and jitter the Japanese on the far bank by dropping deception devices from the air and floating them downstream on rafts and boats at night and by any other means by which these devices can be usefully used.

15. 51st Company 'D' Force will be under command 7th Indian Division to help carry out these various deception measures.

The 'Selling' of Yenangyaung as the IV Corp Objective

16. On arrival of 28th (E.A.) Brigade in the SEIKPYU area, a force of armoured cars and artillery will operate south from there along the west bank of the IRRAWADDY, to simulate a threat to YENANGYAUNG. This force will:

(a) Create a strong show of force wherever possible.

(b) Shoot up any Japanese positions or movement seen on the east bank of the IRRAWADDY.

(c) Publish amongst locals rumours of large forces due to arrive from the PAUK area to operate on west bank of the river.

(d) Make inquiries concerning roads, water and enemy dispositions on both banks of the IRRAWADDY as far south as YENANGYAUNG.

(e) Make inquiries regarding suitable landing areas for airborne forces in the same area.

17. The CHIN HILLS battalion moving on the general line TILIN–SAW–SIDOKTAYA PT 4886–NGAPE PT 7241, will also simulate a threat to YENANGYAUNG, by exaggerating their own strength and making similar inquiries about the area west of the IRRAWADDY as far south as MAGWE.

18. Corps H.Q. will arrange leaflet drops to indicate an interest in YENANGYAUNG.

19. An interest in YENANGYAUNG will also be 'sold' to the Japanese through certain reliable secret channels. Corps H.Q. is arranging this.

Wireless Deception

20. The question of wireless silence and of a bogus network representing 11th (E.A.) Division have already been dealt with (paras. 5, 6 and 8 above).

21. In addition Corps H.Q. will arrange for a few intentional mistakes to be made in our own wireless transmissions with the object of supporting the overall deception. Details will be worked out at Corps H.Q. and notified to those formations required to participate.

22. Wireless activity by 28th (E.A.) Brigade will show a considerable increase during the days immediately prior to the feint crossing at CHAUK. Details are being issued separately by C.S.O. IV Corps.

23. The armoured cars and artillery force will maintain a high level of wireless activity from the time of their arrival at SEIKPYU onwards.

Air Activity

24. Dropping of deception devices to jitter the Japanese will be carried out under arrangements to be made by Corps H.Q. and on request from 7th Division in support of bogus activity and the feint crossing.

25. Air reconnaissance, air photography and air attacks will be asked for by Corps H.Q. in areas away from our real crossing places and objectives, in order not to draw the Japanese attention to any particular area through undue air activity over it.

Date of Crossing the Irrawaddy

26. By other means arrangements are in hand to convey the impression to the Japanese that our crossing over the IRRAWADDY is going to occur one month later than we do, in fact, intend to cross.

SECURITY

27. The deception plan to be known by the code work CLOAK.

28. As far as possible everyone taking part in these deceptive activities should believe them to be genuine. Where the personnel involved are

bound to guess that their activities are not entirely genuine, they may be told confidentially—in order to obtain their wholehearted co-operation— that they are taking part in a deception.

29. Signal instructions with wide distributions will not be issued in connection with this scheme.

30. Acknowledge.

APPENDIX 21

Grouping of 14th Army for the Advance to Rangoon, March 1945

IV CORPS
5th Indian Division
17th Indian Division
19th Indian Division[1]

Armour:

255th Indian Tank Brigade
  plus 7th Cavalry (less one
  squadron) and 16th Cavalry

Artillery:

18th (S.P.) Field Regiment, R.A.
8th Medium Regiment, R.A.
52nd Heavy A.A. Regiment, R.A.
28th Light A.A. Regiment, R.A.
1st Survey Regiment, R.A.
  (less one battery)
B Flight 656 Air O.P. Squadron
One mobile pilot balloon unit
Two 7·2-inch howitzers
5th (Mahratta) Anti-Tank
  Regiment

Engineers:

H.Q. Commander 471 Army
Group
  12th Engineer Battalion, I.E.
  653rd Mechanical Equipment
    Company, I.E.
  One mechanical equipment
    platoon
  One bomb disposal platoon

H.Q. Commander R.E. Forward
  Airfield Engineers
  363rd Field Company, I.E.
  401st Field Company, I.E.
  24th Engineer Battalion, I.E.
  One mechanical equipment
    platoon

XXXIII CORPS
7th Indian Division
20th Indian Division
268th Indian Infantry Brigade

Armour:

254th Indian Tank Brigade
  plus 11th Cavalry and one
  squadron 7th Cavalry

Artillery:

2nd Indian Field Regiment
5th Indian Field Regiment
1st Medium Regiment, R.A.
134th Medium Regiment, R.A.
101st Heavy A.A. Regiment, R.A.
44th Light A.A. Regiment, R.A.
One battery 1st Survey Regiment,
  R.A.
1st Indian Survey Regiment, I.E.
A Flight 656 Air O.P. Squadron
One mobile forecast centre
Two mobile pilot balloon units
Four 7·2-inch howitzers
8th (Mahratta) Anti-Tank Regiment

Engineers:

H.Q. Commander 474 Army Group
  10th Engineer Battalion, I.E.
  652nd Mechanical Equipment
    Company
  One mechanical equipment
    platoon
  One bomb disposal platoon

H.Q. Commander R.E. Forward
  Airfield Engineers
  430th Field Company, I.E.
  431st Field Company, I.E.
  21st Engineer Battalion, I.E.
  One mechanical equipment
    platoon

---

[1] 19th Indian Division came under command of 14th Army between the 1st and 5th April, a brigade at a time, and was transferred to the command of IV Corps on the 5th.

IV CORPS
One Bailey Bridge platoon
One raft platoon
One folding boat equipment
platoon

Signals:

Two V.H.F./Carrier terminals
Two medium W.T. detachments
One cipher detachment

XXXIII CORPS
851st Indian Bridging Company,
less one raft platoon

Signals:

Two VHF/Carrier terminals
Two medium W.T. detachments

Attached:

Lushai Scouts
Two units of Small Operations
Group

APPENDIX 22

Air Deliveries in Long Tons to 14th Army and XV Corps, January–May 1945

14TH ARMY

Air Base	Imphal Group	Agartala	Comilla	Chittagong Group	Akyab	Ramree	Total	Percentage of Total	
								Landed	Dropped
First period of 4 weeks (2nd to 29th January 1945)									
R.A.M.O.s	Nos. 1, 2 & 6	No. 4	No. 3	Nos. 5 & 7	—	—			
14th Army .	501	4,678	772	—	—	—	5,951	100	—
IV Corps .	532	2,765	3,029	70	—	—	6,396	64	36
XXXIII Corps .	9,946	1,981	21	—	—	—	11,948	55	45
R.A.F. .	2,134	—	—	—	—	—	2,134	100	—
	13,113	9,424	3,822	70	—	—	26,429	70	30
Second period of 4 weeks (30th January to 26th February 1945)									
R.A.M.O.s	Nos. 1, 2 & 6	—	No. 3	Nos. 4, 5 & 7	—	—			
14th Army .	451	—	227	5,117	—	—	5,795	97	3
IV Corps .	4,038	—	403	7,425	—	—	11,866	69	31
XXXIII Corps .	8,018	—	361	10,144	—	—	18,523	93	7
R.A.F. .	5,767	—	—	—	—	—	5,767	100	—
	18,274	—	991	22,686	—	—	41,951	87	13

Third period of 4 weeks (27th February to 26th March 1945)

Air Base	Imphal Group	Agartala	Comilla	Chittagong Group	Akyab	Ramree	Total	Percentage of Total	
								Landed	Dropped
R.A.M.O.s	Nos. 1, 2 & 6	—	No.3	Nos. 4, 5 & 7	No. 1	—			
14th Army	1,567	—	—	8,252	—	—	9,819	97	3
IV Corps	3,965	—	—	9,915	1,083	—	14,963	78	22
XXXIII Corps	5,199	—	—	11,817	—	—	17,016	84	16
R.A.F.	1,833	—	—	3,499	—	—	5,332	100	—
	12,564	—	—	33,483	1,083	—	47,130	87	13

Fourth period of 4 weeks (27th March to 23rd April 1945)

Air Base	Imphal Group	Agartala	Comilla	Chittagong Group	Akyab	Ramree	Total	Percentage of Total	
								Landed	Dropped
R.A.M.O.s	Nos. 2 & 6	—	No. 3	Nos. 4, 5 & 7	No. 1	No. 2			
14th Army	2,827	—	—	10,410	591	—	13,828	92	8
IV Corps	1,381	—	—	7,258	8,689	—	17,328	84	16
XXXIII Corps	2,478	—	—	11,371	843	—	14,692	87	13
R.A.F.	775	—	—	3,314	77	—	4,166	100	—
	7,461	—	—	32,353	10,200	—	50,014	88	12

Fifth period of 4 weeks (24th April to 21st May 1945)

Air Base	Imphal Group	Agartala	Comilla	Chittagong Group	Akyab	Ramree	Total	Percentage of Total	
								Landed	Dropped
R.A.M.O.s	No. 6	—	No. 3	Nos. 2, 5 & 7	No. 1	No. 2			
14th Army . .	4,753	—	1,475	7,455	363	—	14,046	91	9
IV Corps . .	285	—	—	4,957	5,105	1,681	12,028	63	37
XXXIII Corps .	511	—	—	9,610	2,142	528	12,796	85	15
R.A.F. . .	354	—	—	5,413	69	—	5,836	100	—
	5,903	—	1,480	27,435	7,679	2,209	44,706	83	17
						Grand Total	210,230	84½	15½

Notes:

1. Comilla air base was used throughout the period for reinforcements.
2. 36th Division from N.C.A.C. and 19th Division were administered by 14th Army from the 31st March 1945.
3. The 14th Army totals include civil supplies, viz. 174 tons between 30th January and 26th February, 320 tons between 27th February and 26th March, 247 tons between 27th March and 23rd April and 241 tons between 24th April and 21st May.
4. No. 1 R.A.M.O. ceased operating at Imphal on the 7th March and reopened at Akyab on the 20th March.
5. No. 2 R.A.M.O. ceased operating at Imphal on the 24th March and reopened at Ramree on the 15th April.

XV CORPS

Air Base	Chittagong Group	Akyab	Ramree	Total	Percentage of Total Landed	Percentage of Total Dropped
First period of 4 weeks (2nd to 29th January 1945)						
R.A.M.O.s	Nos. 4, 5 & 7	—	—			
XV Corps .	2,442	—	—	2,442	½	99½
Second period of 4 weeks (30th January to 26th February 1945)						
R.A.M.O.s	Nos. 4, 5 & 7	—	—			
XV Corps . .	2,149	—	—	2,149	4	96
Third period of 4 weeks (27th February to 26th March 1945)						
R.A.M.O.s	Nos. 4, 5 & 7	—	—			
XV Corps . .	1,669	—	—	1,669	2½	97½
Fourth period of 4 weeks (27th March to 23rd April 1945)						
R.A.M.O.s	Nos. 4, 5 & 7	No. 1	No. 2			
XV Corps . .	89	31	280	400	13	87

Fifth period of 4 weeks (24th April to 21st May 1945)

Air Base	Chittagong Group	Akyab	Ramree	Total	Percentage of Total	
					Landed	Dropped
R.A.M.O.s	Nos. 4, 5 & 7	No. 1	No. 2			
XV Corps	3	309	529	841	4	96
			Grand Total	7,501	5	95

Notes:

1. As it became necessary to use more transport aircraft to supply 14th Army, the air supply to XV Corps had to be drastically reduced. For the ten weeks from 2nd January to 12th March the corps received an average of 85 tons a day. For the next five weeks (to 16th April) the average fell to 15 tons, but with the opening of the Ramree airstrip it became possible to increase deliveries up to 32 tons a day for the five weeks ending on 21st May.

2. The total deliveries by air to 14th Army and XV Corps over twenty weeks amounted to 217,731 long tons of supplies of all natures, or on average of about 1,555 tons a day.

APPENDIX 23

Maintenance of 14th Army During Phase 4 of 'Extended Capital', April–May 1945

1. The 14th Army plan for Phase 4 of 'Extended Capital'—the advance on Rangoon—was that:

   (a) IV Corps, with two fully mechanized divisions (5th and 17th) and a tank brigade, with a standard division (19th) following up and securing the line of communications, was to advance as rapidly as possible from Meiktila down the main road and rail to Rangoon.

   (b) XXXIII Corps, consisting of two standard divisions (7th and 20th), 268th Brigade and a tank brigade, was to move down the Irrawaddy River towards Rangoon.

Both corps were to be supplied mainly by air, but priority was to be given to the thrust by the motorized divisions of IV Corps, which were expected to move far more quickly than the standard divisions moving down the Irrawaddy.

2. IV Corps

The most difficult problem facing the administrative staff of 14th Army was how to maintain IV Corps (totalling altogether between 70,000 and 100,000 men and 8,250 vehicles) entirely by air during its advance over some 300 miles from Meiktila to Rangoon, in view of the fact that beyond Toungoo it would be outside the range of the Akyab air base and that the Ramree air base was not expected to be fully in operation until late in April.

An airlift had been allotted on the basis of 130 tons a day for each division and for corps troops, and 70 tons a day for a tank brigade, figures which could not be exceeded in any way. If for any reason air supply fell short or proved to be abortive on any single day, it could not be made up later on. The road transport at the disposal of IV Corps was two 30-cwt. and four 3-ton general purpose transport companies, and each division had one 3-ton company and one 15-cwt. company. Troops were to be maintained from forward airfields up to the maximum range of the available motor transport; outside that range, troops would have to be maintained by supply-dropping. Since this was wasteful, it was to be avoided as far as possible.

The normal sequence of events was to be:

   (a) The reconnaissance of a projected airhead by a party carried in a light aircraft, and then its construction.

   (b) The establishment of F.A.M.O. at the airhead (the size being determined by the role of the airfield).

   (c) The issue of supplies and stores to all troops within range of the available motor transport from the airhead, any surplus over daily maintenance being stocked as a reserve.

(d) Should the forward troops advance beyond the range of the available motor transport from the airhead, they would have to be maintained by reserves carried with them in their own transport, supplemented as necessary by supply-dropping until the next airfield on the line of advance was ready to receive transport aircraft.

(e) The opening of the next airfield.

This system was limited in its application by the following factors:

(i) Since the available air transport in S.E.A.C. was working at the highest possible rate, any maintenance lost on one day could not be made up on another.

(ii) With the exception of Meiktila and Toungoo, all the airfields which the corps could use during its advance were fair-weather and liable to become unserviceable in wet weather.

(iii) Owing to the tonnage which could be delivered daily being limited and to the short time that an airfield would be in use, it would not normally be possible to build up any appreciable reserves.

(iv) Since the available airlift was sufficient to supply only one division and a brigade by supply-dropping at any time, the rest of the corps had either to remain within the range of its motor transport from an airhead or to live on any reserves it had been able to put by.

(v) Owing to the need for changing loads and briefing pilots, a change from supply-dropping to air landing, or vice versa, could not be quickly undertaken. Changes from dropping to air landing had to be notified to C.A.A.T.O. by 4 p.m., and from air landing to dropping by noon, on the day previous to the desired delivery.

(vi) Reinforcements were held at Comilla only, and two aircraft a day were allotted to bring them forward. Since Meiktila was located beyond the maximum economic range of Dakotas operating from Comilla, the number of reinforcements which could be supplied to points farther south would be progressively reduced.

Despite its many drawbacks, the administrative plan drawn up on this basis proved in practice to be satisfactory, and supplies of ammunition and equipment for the various engagements during the advance were always adequate. To overcome delays caused by supply-dropping, forward troops had, however, often to be put on a reduced scale of rations since they had to carry the maximum number of days' subsistence in their own transport while between airheads. Towards the end of the advance heavy storms began earlier than usual in south Burma and almost all airfields south of Meiktila became unserviceable. The corps was then forced to subsist on supply-dropping at a net rate of 175 tons a day instead of the normal air-landed 460 tons a day. This meant that all troops had to be placed on half rations for some twenty-four days until the port of Rangoon could be opened for maintenance.

3. XXXIII Corps

The problem of maintaining XXXIII Corps in its advance down the Irrawaddy towards Prome offered less difficulty. Up to and including Magwe, the corps was within the economic range of transport aircraft operating from the Chittagong air base. An airlift of 460 tons a day, reduced to 410 tons after the 23rd April, had been allotted to the corps. The road system along the east bank of the Irrawaddy was good and there was adequate motor transport. Moreover, an I.W.T. company with a lift of 140 tons a day and a radius of 50 miles was available and there was a possibility that this lift could be increased during April. Petrol could also be floated down the river in rafts made up of drums. It was planned that, until an airhead could be opened at Magwe, corps headquarters, corps troops, 268th Brigade, and 2nd Division (until it was flown out) were to be supplied by road from the Taungtha airhead, and that 7th Division was to be supplied from Myitche by road and by I.W.T. to Yenangyaung and beyond this point by road. Supplies for 20th Division, moving south-west from Meiktila towards Magwe and Prome, were to be flown in to a succession of airstrips in a similar manner as IV Corps'. For any advance beyond Prome it would, however, be necessary for the corps to be allotted some of the airlift from the Akyab air base, since the forward troops would not only be beyond the range of motor transport from Magwe but also beyond the economic range of transport aircraft operating from the Chittagong air base.

4. The airfields used by IV and XXXIII corps during April and early May were:

Formation	Airhead	Date opened	Date closed	Narrative
IV Corps	Meiktila	1 Apr.	Remained in use throughout period	The corps, consisting of 5th, 17th and 19th Divisions and 255th Tank Brigade, was given the task of undertaking the advance in Phase 4 of 'Extended Capital' from Meiktila by road and rail to Rangoon. The 19th Division came under command on the 5th April, and was maintained from Meiktila from the 6th April. Dwehla and Kume airstrips were also used.
	Tatkon	20 Apr.	22 Apr.	Maintenance of 17th Division and corps troops and topping-up of 5th Division before action at Shwemyo Bluff.
	Lewe	23 Apr.	30 Apr.	Maintenance of 17th Division
	Toungoo	24 Apr.	Till end of period	Maintenance of 5th Division and corps troops, stocking of 17th Division for its advance on Pegu and maintenance of 19th Division from 26th April.
	Pyuntaza	30 Apr.	2 May	Maintenance of 5th and 17th Divisions.

Formation	Airhead	Date opened	Date closed	Narrative
IV Corps	Payagyi	2 May	Till end of period	Maintenance of 5th Division and corps troops and topping-up of 17th Division before action at Pegu.
	Zayatkwin	8 May	12 May	Supplementary to Payagyi.
	Rangoon (Mingaladon)	19 May	—	
XXXIII Corps	Taungtha	5 Apr.	4 May	During March it was decided that the corps, consisting of 7th and 20th Divisions, 268th Infantry Brigade and 254th Tank Brigade, would move south on the axis of the Irrawaddy. The corps F.M.A. was therefore moved from Ondaw to Taungtha when the airfield was taken over from IV Corps. Myitche, which was the airhead for 7th Division, was also taken over when the division came under command of XXXIII Corps. The airheads for the corps during its advance therefore were Taungtha and Myitche until Magwe was opened on the 4th May.
	Magwe	4 May	—	
20th Division	Kume	9 Apr.	15 Apr.	
	Meiktila	15 Apr.	23 Apr.	
	Natmauk	23 Apr.	29 Apr.	
	Taungdwingyi	29 Apr.	2 May	
	Ywataung	2 May	5 May	
	Prome	5 May	—	
2nd Division	Myingyan	31 Mar.	5 Apr.	
	Taungtha	5 Apr.	*	* Closed when division flown out to India.
7th Division	Myitche	7 Apr.	4 May	
	Magwe	4 May	—	

Notes:

1. Until the end of March the air bases used were those of the Imphal and Chittagong groups. As soon as the air base at Akyab was opened on the 20th March, it began, with the Chittagong group, to maintain 14th Army during its advance south of the line Magwe–Kyaukse. The transport squadrons operating from Imphal were reduced; see Appendix 15.

2. The Ramree air base began to operate on the 16th April (see Appendix 15, note [e]) but was not functioning fully by the time Rangoon had been reoccupied.

3. On the 23rd March Myingyan was occupied. It was then developed as an advanced base for the maintenance of 14th Army during the monsoon.

APPENDIX 24

14th Army's Estimate of the Supply Position from March to May 1945, and Actual Deliveries in Tons a Day

Month in 1945	14th Army's estimated daily requirements	A.L.F.S.E.A.'s forecast of 25/2/45 of daily air deliveries at 250 miles radius	14th Army's daily air deliveries adjusted to distances to be actually flown as estimated on 16/3/45	14th Army's re-estimate of 28/3/45 of daily air deliveries adjusted to allow for distance and percentage of dropping	14th Army's daily road deliveries as estimated on 16/3/45	14th Army's daily I.W.T. deliveries as estimated on 16/3/45	Total estimated daily deliveries	Estimated daily surplus or deficit	Actual average daily deliveries			
									Air[2]	Road	I.W.T.[3]	Total
	(a)	(b)	(c)	(d)	(e)	(f)	(d) + (e) + (f)					
March	2,428	1,860	1,792	1,792	207	255	2,254	−174	1,682	175	190	2,047
April	2,700	1,921	1,795	1,791	—	415	2,206	−494	1,789	3	458	2,250
1st–15th May[1]	2,890	2,075	1,918	1,755	—	575	2,330	−500	1,605[4]	—	660	2,265

[1] The monsoon was expected to begin on the 15th May.

[2] These figures are for the calendar month and cannot be compared accurately with those in Appendix 22 since actual tonnages delivered each day varied considerably.

[3] These figures are taken from Appendix 16.

[4] There were heavy pre-monsoon storms on the 29th April and between the 3rd and 11th May, which flooded airfields and roads. Since airfields could not be used, resort had to be made to supply-dropping direct to army formations and units, which reduced the tonnage delivered below the estimate.

APPENDIX 25

A—Tonnages Delivered to China Theatre
August 1944–June 1945

Month	By Air	By Road	P.O.L. by Pipeline	Total
August 1944	29,092	—	—	29,092
September	29,625	—	—	29,625
October	35,131	—	—	35,131
November	39,004	—	—	39,004
December	34,777	—	—	34,777
January 1945	46,482	—	—	46,482
February	42,469	1,111	—	43,580
March	48,944	1,509	—	50,453
April	46,478	4,198	439	51,115
May	51,462	8,435	5,530	65,427
June	58,219	6,985	5,187	70,391

Notes :
  1. The figures are all in short tons (2,000 lb.)
  2. The tonnage carried by air is the total carried by Air Transport Command, the Chinese National Aviation Corporation and aircraft of Eastern Air Command temporarily diverted for the purpose.

B.—Vehicles Delivered to China Theatre by Road
February–June 1945

Month	Vehicles	Trailers
February 1945	1,333	609
March	1,152	745
April	2,342	1,185
May	4,682	1,103
June	4,901	964

APPENDIX 26

The Supply of Petrol, Oil and Lubricants to 14th Army and 221 Group R.A.F., January–May 1945

Since the rapid advance of 14th Army from the Chindwin to Rangoon, and in particular from the Irrawaddy to Rangoon, depended on the mobility of armoured and mechanized formations, the supply of P.O.L. to the forward areas was a matter of extreme importance.

When 14th Army crossed the Chindwin in December 1944, it was entirely maintained along the northern line of communications from Dimapur. P.O.L. was at that time sent direct by rail from the tank farm at Chittagong (supplied by ocean-going tankers) to both Dimapur and Chandranathpur; from the latter it was pumped along the 4-inch pipeline to Dimapur, where a barrel- and container-filling plant had been installed.[1] The L. of C. Road Transport Column took it forward from Dimapur to the airfields on the Imphal plain, from where it could be delivered by the air transport squadrons operating from the Imphal air bases to forward airheads beyond the Chindwin,[2] or by road to the depot at Indainggyi for distribution to corps, army and L. of C. units as well as to airfields in the Kabaw Valley.

By the middle of February 1945, when the Irrawaddy crossings began, the air base at Agartala had been moved forward to the three airfields around Chittagong, all of which were within economic range of IV Corps' and most of XXXIII Corps' airheads. Daily maintenance of 14th Army's forward formations and of the squadrons of 221 Group R.A.F. deployed east of the Chindwin was then progressively transferred from the Imphal air base on the northern L. of C. to the Chittagong air base on the southern L. of C.[3] The 4-inch pipeline with a capacity of $3\frac{1}{2}$ million gallons a month had meanwhile been completed from Chittagong to the tank farm at Dimapur.[4] As before, the L. of C. Road Transport Column carried forward P.O.L. to the Imphal airfields and on to depots at Indainggyi and Kalewa, from which army and L. of C. units west of the Chindwin as well as the I.W.T. service (which had by this time begun to operate between Kalewa and Alon) were supplied.

On the 1st March the pipeline from Dimapur to Imphal, with a capacity of $3\frac{1}{2}$ million gallons a month, together with a tank farm and barrel- and container-filling organization, came into operation at Kamrol, just outside Imphal. The opening of this pipeline saved the road transport the task of carrying P.O.L. along the 134 miles from Dimapur to Imphal and therefore released more transport to operate forward to

---

[1] See Appendix 2. The pipeline from Chittagong to Akhaura, which was completed, was being used at this time to supply the airfields at Feni, Comilla and Agartala.
[2] Of the 130 tons a day airlift allotted to a division, 33 tons consisted of P.O.L.
[3] See Appendices 15 and 22.
[4] See Appendix 2.

Indainggyi and the I.W.T. port at Kalewa. At the same time a gravity pipeline was brought into operation between Kangpopki and the airfields around Imphal to supply them with aviation petrol.[1]

By the 26th March, when the I.W.T. service from Kalewa was extended from Alon to the newly established 14th Army maintenance centre at Myingyan, the new air base at Akyab had come into operation and transport aircraft squadrons had been moved forward to it from Imphal and Chittagong.[2] Thus during April all P.O.L. for 14th Army formations and those squadrons of 221 Group R.A.F. which were east of the Chindwin was flown in from Chittagong and Akyab on the southern L. of C.[3] On the northern L. of C., P.O.L. was being pumped direct from Chittagong to Imphal and carried forward by road transport to supply L. of C. units west of the Chindwin and engineering units on road construction, and to meet the needs of the I.W.T. service, build up a reserve for that service at Kalewa and enable it to build up the Burma Stockpile at Myingyan, which was to contain fifteen days' supply for 14th Army and 221 Group R.A.F.

By the end of May the Dimapur–Imphal pipeline had been extended over the hill section of the road between Palel and Moreh to a tank farm and filling organization. This again reduced the distance that the road transport had to carry P.O.L. products to Kalewa, thus releasing transport for other purposes. When Rangoon was reoccupied, a great deal of the original oil tankage installations were found intact. This enabled ocean-going tankers to begin to deliver P.O.L. direct to Rangoon, from where it could be distributed to 14th Army formations and units in southern Burma which were within convenient radius of Rangoon by road and rail. The importance of the northern L. of C. to Kalewa gradually diminished as the supply of P.O.L. from Rangoon to southern and central Burma was established, and on the 15th August 1945 the Chittagong–Tamu pipeline closed down.

---

[1] This pipeline was completed rather late. Although it was of value in supplying P.O.L. to the airfields, the airlift of P.O.L. to 14th Army and 221 Group R.A.F. had been shifted to air bases on the southern L. of C.

[2] See Appendix 15.

[3] P.O.L. was delivered from India Base by ship to Akyab in its barrels and containers in readiness to be flown into southern Burma within the economic range of the air base.

APPENDIX 27
Code Names Used in The Text

Allied

Alpha: Plan for concentrating Chinese troops for the defence of Kunming.

Argonaut: Conference in Malta and the Crimea, January–Febuary 1945.

Capital: Capture and consolidation of the general line Pakokku–Lashio–Mandalay and exploitation southwards towards Rangoon.

Character: Operation to raise guerillas and provide intelligence in the Kachin Hills.

Cloak: Deception plan for IV Corps' advance on Meiktila, January–February 1945.

Conclave: Deception operation in April 1945 to cover the left flank of 14th Army's advance on Rangoon.

Culverin:* Occupation of northern Sumatra.

Dracula: Amphibious and airborne operation for the capture of Rangoon.

Extended
Capital: 'Capital' plus the capture of Meiktila.

Nation: Operations with the A.F.O. and B.N.A. in Burma.

Octagon: The Second Quebec Conference, September 1944.

Python: War Office scheme for the repatriation of British troops with long service overseas.

Roger:* Occupation of Phuket Island.

Romulus: Operations to clear northern Arakan.

Stanza: Rehabilitation and opening of Rangoon port, and the establishment there of an advanced base for 14th Army's maintenance during the monsoon.

Talon: Capture of Akyab.

Japanese

ICHI-GO: Offensive in China, 1944.

SHO–1: Defence of the Philippines.

SHO–2*: Defence of Formosa and the Ryukyu Islands.

SHO–3*: Defence of Japan.

SHO–4*: Defence of the area north-east of Japan.

---

* These operations were not carried out.

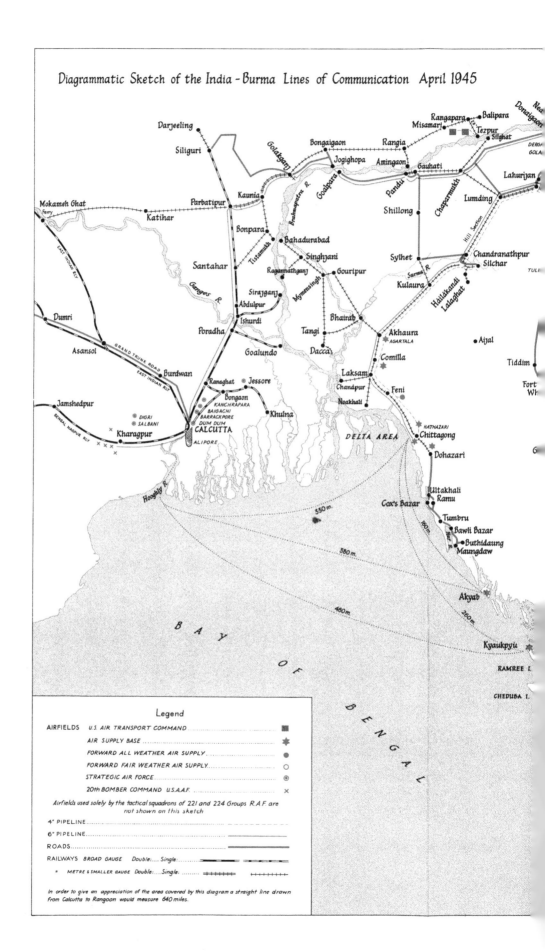

Diagrammatic Sketch of the India-Burma Lines of Communication April 1945

Legend

AIRFIELDS

U.S. AIR TRANSPORT COMMAND	■
AIR SUPPLY BASE	★
FORWARD ALL WEATHER AIR SUPPLY	●
FORWARD FAIR WEATHER AIR SUPPLY	○
STRATEGIC AIR FORCE	◉
20th BOMBER COMMAND U.S.A.A.F.	×

Airfields used solely by the tactical squadrons of 221 and 224 Groups R.A.F. are not shown on this sketch

4″ PIPELINE	
6″ PIPELINE	
ROADS	
RAILWAYS BROAD GAUGE Double:.... Single:.......	
″ METRE & SMALLER GAUGE Double:.... Single:..........	

In order to give an appreciation of the area covered by this diagram a straight line drawn from Calcutta to Rangoon would measure 640 miles.

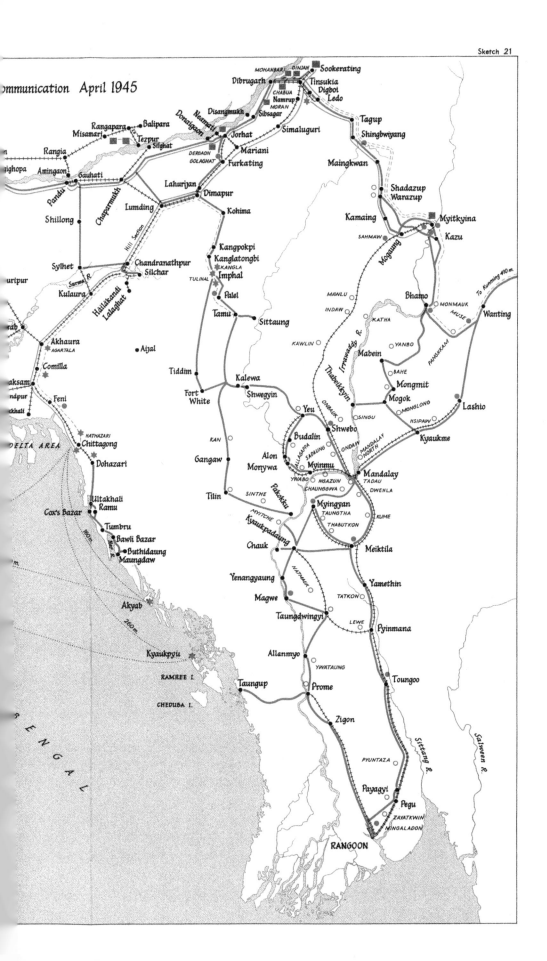

mmunication April 1945

Index

INDEX

Note: Formations and units of the British, Commonwealth and Indian Armies, and of the Burma and Colonial military forces, are indexed under 'Army'. British infantry battalions are in order of regimental seniority.

Abukuma, Japanese cruiser: 77, 78
Achilles, New Zealand cruiser: 212 fn. 3
Administration: *see* Air Supply, Communications *and* Maintenance
Agartala: airfield at, 38, 106, 200; move of air base from, 201–2
Airborne Operations: in 'Capital', 28, 102, 108, 149–50, (Wedemeyer thinks unnecessary) 125, (ruled out by withdrawal of training aircraft) 128–30, (not practicable before February) 155; in 'Dracula', 28, 102; Japanese preparations against, 59, 60, 377 fn. 2; in modified 'Dracula', 329, 330, 351, (launched) 394
Air Command, South-East Asia: 35, 204
Aircraft: needed, (for 'Capital') 4–5, (for 'Dracula') 5, 11 fn. 1, (for 'Capital'/'Dracula') 107 fn. 1; allotted to S.E.A.C., 12; inferior performance of Japanese, 132, 231, 232 fn. 1, 402; for evacuating casualties, 412–13
Aircraft, Transport: needed, (in Giffard's plan) 3, (for 'Capital'), 4–5, (for 'Dracula') 5, 11 fn. 2, 12, (for 'Capital'/'Dracula') 107 fn. 1, (for 'Extended Capital') 167, 200–1, (for modified 'Dracula') 329–30; allotted, (to S.E.A.C.) 12, 207, (to Pacific) 12; shortage of, (for Special Force) 29, (for 'Capital') 125, (for moving force south of Mandalay) 165; airfields for, 38, *now see* Airfields and Airstrips; availability of, (estimated) 105–6, 247, (actual) 201, 409; diversion and transfer of, to China, 125–31, 280–1, 315–20, 338–9, (Calcutta conference on) 129, (effect of, on Slim's plan) 164, (affects need to open Rangoon port) 399, (referred to) 410, 424, (summarized and commented on) 418–20; losses of, 179, 307, 309; possible move of 17th Division by, 180; economic range of, 200, 247, 248, 321, 323, 325, (referred to) 410, 411, 424; redeployment of, 200–2, (referred to) 410, (summarized) 424–6; working of, over sustained rates, 203–4, 317, 330, (referred to) 411, 412, 426; diverted from airborne training, 204; and maintenance of 36th Division and N.C.A.C., 316, 317 fn. 1, 326 fn. 1, 338; date for removal of, from S.E.A.C., 318–19, (referred to) 330, 356, 419; use of, to support rising in Burma, 337; squadrons of, in Eastern Air Command (December), 401; effect of possible Japanese attacks on, discussed, 402, 434; immunity of, by March, 403
Airfields and Airstrips:
in India and Burma:
needed, (in Giffard's plan) 3, (for 'Dracula')

Airfields and Airstrips—*cont.*
20, (for 'Capital') 103–4, 136 fn. 4, 149–50, 155, (for 'Extended Capital') 166, 168–9, 172, 181, 200–1, 241, 244–5, 247, 253 fn. 2, 267, (for advance on Rangoon) 297, 322, 324, 325, 366, 391, (for modified 'Dracula') 329–31 *passim*; on Northern front, 23, 38, (to be captured) 144, (construction of) 278, 320; in Bengal, 37–8, (too far back for 'Extended Capital') 200, 410, (referred to) 401; in Assam, 38, (referred to) 401; on Imphal plain, 38, (to be main base airfields for 'Capital') 106, (referred to) 247, (too far back for 'Extended Capital') 200, 410, 424; at Tiddim, 50; construction, development and capture of, 142, 151, 156, 157, 176 fn. 1, 177, 178, 180 fn. 2, 181 fn. 2, 183, 199, 253 fn. 2, 268, 271, 306, 356, 360, 362, 385, 386, 390 fns. 1 and 2, (of Akyab and Kyaukpu referred to) 410, 425–6; redeployment of, 200–2, (referred to) 253, 424–6; administration of, in advance to Rangoon, 326; to be constructed in Rangoon area, 331; engineers for, with advanced troops, 385; put out of action by the monsoon, 393, 399; Japanese failure to prevent establishment of, 434
in Pacific:
in Morotai, 65; in Peleliu, 65–6; in Ulithi Atoll, 66; in Bonins and Ryukyus (required), 69; in Leyte, 69, (capture and development of) 72,83–4; in Marianas, 89, 133, 404; in Iwojima, 235–6, 240
in China:
at Chengtu, 37 fn. 4, 71, 89 fn. 2, (closed) 132–3, 404; at Kweilin and Liuchow, 116, 121, (referred to) 122; at Chihkiang, 338
Air Forces: *see* Japanese Air Force, Royal Air Force, United States Army Air Force, etc.; *for combined Anglo/American air forces in S.E.A.C. see under* Air Forces, Allied
Air Forces, Allied: achievements of, by June 1944, 34; American reservation on integration of, 127, (British views on) 208; aims and tasks of (1944–45) 401; aircraft of, superior to Japanese, 402
Eastern Air Command: mentioned, 3, 35 fn. 1; airfields needed for, 20; at Calcutta, 34, 432; recommended formation of air supply staff section at, 35; deputy commander of, 36; controls Combat Cargo Task Force, 37; H.Q. A.L.F.S.E.A to be in close touch with, 114; prepares redeployment plan, 200, 201; authorized to exceed sustained rate, 204; allotted transport air-

Air Forces, Allied—*cont.*

Eastern Air Command—*cont.*

craft, 204; and 14th Army/221 Group plan, 242, 244, 245; jointly produces new administrative plan, 246–7; composition and strength of (December), 401; air supply formations in, 409

Combat Cargo Task Force: formation and task of, 37; composition of, 37 fn. 1, 409; on impracticability of airborne operations, 155; possibly to transport part of 17th Division, 180; representative of, at conference on IV Corps' plans, 182; 'teething troubles' of, 183; planned transport capabilities of, 248; maintains 221 Group, 311; aircraft to be transferred to, 316

Photographic Reconnaissance Force: 408–9

Strategic Air Force: proposed role of, in 'Capital', 4; airfields for, 37; units of, for transfer to China, 124–5, 403; in operations, (in Burma) 136, 219, 254, 404, (in S.E.A.) 213; priority of targets for, 403; strategic air offensive by, 403–5

3rd Tactical Air Force: airfields needed for, 3; formation and composition of, 34, 36 fn. 2; recommended establishment of air supply section at, 35; mentioned, 35 fn. 1; disbanded, 36; uses Chittagong airfield, 38 fn. 2; controls air transport for 14th Army, 42; submits joint plan for 'Capital', 101

Air Superiority, Allied: achieved in South-East Asia, 8, 29, 401; easily maintained, 402; advantages of, 403; air supply impossible without, 426–7

Air Supply: requirements for development of, 3; inadequate for 14th Army's requirements (August), 20; possible need for, 21; needed for Northern front, 21–2; problems of, reviewed, 35–6; organization for, altered, 36–7; mentioned in 'Capital' appreciation, 103–4; difficult conditions for, 107; Calcutta conference on, 129, (referred to) 164; development of airfields and strips for, 157, 172, 253 fn. 2; bases for, needed in Arakan, 167; tonnages available to IV and XXXIII Corps, 169, 326; effect on, of raid on Onbauk, 179; demands on, underestimated, 183; increased demands for, in 'Extended Capital', 200, 243, (examination of) 244; efforts to increase, 204, 339; reduction of, for XV Corps, 224, (referred to) 249, 317, 339, (effect on its operations of) 344, 345, (referred to) 351; from Akyab and Ramree, 246, 321–2; planned delivery of, in army/air plan, 247–8; shortfall in, 317, (methods to counteract) 323–4; Mountbatten reports on 14th Army's, 318; general policy for, in advance to Rangoon, 325–6; possible reduction in, if modified 'Dracula' launched, 330; limits XXXIII Corps' advance on Rangoon, 375; tonnages received by XV Corps and 14th Army, 409, 412; for 14th Army, summarized and discussed, 409–12, 424–6; air formations for, 409

For formations: 36th Division, 23, 41, 316, 383; XXXIII Corps, 42, 169, 182–3, 325–6,

Air Supply—*cont.*

375; 11th (E.A.) Division, 44, 156 fn. 2; 123rd Brigade, 46 and fn. 3; 5th Division, 48 and fn. 3; XV Corps, 136, (reduction in) 224, (referred to) 317, 339, (total tonnage received by) 409; 81st (W.A.) Division, 137, (for brigade of) 346; formations on Northern front, 145, 317 fn. 1, (referred to) 409; 19th Division, 176 fn. 1, 182; 2nd Division, 182; 20th Division, 182; 82nd (W.A.) Division, 218, 348; 17th Division, 269, 283; 255th Indian Tank Brigade, 283; 7th Division, 305 fn. 3, 374; IV Corps, 169, 325–6, 399 fn. 1; 22nd (E.A.) Brigade, 349

Air Transport: organization for, altered, 36–7; controlled by 3rd Tactical Air Force, 42; casualties and reinforcements moved by, 103, 412–13; tonnages to be carried by, for forward stocking, 105; postponement of 'Dracula' eases position of, 109; need for, in China, 124–5

Air Transport Command: *see under* United States Army Air Force

Akyab: proposed capture of, 1, 2; in Japanese defensive plans, 59, 60; capture of, 'Talon', (approved) 110, (aircraft for) 125, 130, (ordered) 136, (preparatory moves for) 137, (plans and forces for) 138–42, (maintenance during) 141 fn. 3, (carried out) 142, (exploitation of) 215, (referred to) 350; airfields needed south of, 136 fn. 4; Japanese forces in, 138, 215; Japanese evacuation of, 141–2, (discussed) 215, 425, 434; airfields on, (in operation) 142, (bring Toungoo within economic range) 200, (development of, as advanced base) 201–2, 219, 244–5, 247, (to maintain forces on Mandalay–Rangoon road) 322, 410, (Prome economic limit from) 375, (development of, referred to) 351, 410, 425–6; anchorages at, 142; development of port at, 203; air forces at, 214; 53rd Brigade to hold, 215; Japanese communications affected by loss of, 216; troops withdrawn to, 343, 346, 348; mentioned, 375; 'Dracula' convoys mounted from, 395; holds stores for Indian troops only, 411

Allanmyo: Japanese withdrawal from Arakan to, 349, 369, 377, 378, (disrupted) 374; Japanese plans for defence of, 357, 377, (failure of) 378, 379; 20th Division's advance to, 372, 374, 375; virtually undefended, 374; Stopford holds conferences at, 375, 380; cordon to be established on Allanmyo–Prome road, 375; mentioned, 377

Allied Land Forces, South-East Asia: and Intelligence organizations, 32–3; formation of, (recommended) 35–6, (proposed) 113–15, (carried out) 118, (commented on) 417–18; position of H.Q.s of, 114, 118, (commented on) 432; C.-in-C. of, 114–15, 118; composition of, 118; conference on air supply at Advanced H.Q., 129; receives, examines, approves and comments on Slim's plans, 164, 242, 244, 245, 254, 321, 323, 333; administrative problems for, 200, (referred to) 424, 425; prepares redeployment plan, 201; strength of (March), 202 fn. 3; tasks of,

Allied Land Forces, South-East Asia—*cont.*
241; 'Dracula' resources at disposal of, 241; produces fresh administrative plans, 246-9, (referred to) 411-12; issues instructions for capture of Rangoon, 249, 321; channel for submitting proposals to arm civil population, 251; to provide G.P.T. companies, 326; and modified 'Dracula', 328, 331-2; prepares 'Stanza' appreciation, 331; mentioned, 338; 82nd (W.A.) Division comes under, 349-50; deception plans of, 366-7; receives reports of Rangoon being evacuated, 395

Alon: I.W.T. service to, 166, 322, (tonnages delivered by) 409; L. of C. sub-area at, 327

'Alpha' Plan: *see* Wedemeyer

Alston-Roberts-West, Brigadier M.M.: 177, 363

Ameer, H. M. escort carrier: 219 fn. 3, 342

Amphibious Operations: Chiang Kai-shek on Allied failure to carry out, 117; launched against (Akyab), 142, (Myebon Peninsula) 216, (Ramree) 219-20, (Kangaw) 220-1, (Ruywa) 223, (Rangoon) 393-7; amphibious force to be formed for, 244; in Japanese estimate of British plans, 272; contemplated on formation of S.E.A.C., 431; lack of resources for, 432

An: mentioned, 217; proposed capture of, 223, 249, 343; information on forces in area of, 342; Japanese plans to defend, 343; operations towards, 344-9; *54th Division's* withdrawal from area of, 377-8

'Anakim' Operation: compared with 'Capital'/'Dracula', 416 fn. 2

Andaman Islands: responsibility for defence of, 54; in Japanese chain of defences, 58; possible Allied operation against, 109, 111; photographic reconnaissance of, 214; bombarded, 341, 393

Andaman Sea: fleet operations in, 341-2

An Pass: Japanese plans to hold, 215, (success of) 222; Japanese L. of C. through, 218; operations against, 223, 343, 347, 349, 374; Japanese withdrawal from, 347; kept under air observation, 406-7

Anti-Fascist Organization: organizing resistance movement, 33; Force 136 plans to operate with, 'Nation', 33, (progress of) 205; policy on arming members of, 250-1, 334; rises, 333-4, 337; attitude to be taken by Force 136 towards, 334-7; guerrilla operations of, 337

Antu: 270, 288, 295

Aoba Group: composition of, 188 fn. 2; its counter-attack task at Myinmu, 273 fn. 2; on the Irrawaddy, 284 fn. 1; at Myingyan with *214th Regiment*, 298

Arakan (Front): *see also* Air Supply, Communications *and* Maintenance (of XV Corps): proposed operations in, 1, 4 and fn. 1, 107, 110, 136-7, 138-9, 141-2, 200-1, 218-19, 249, (referred to) 341; defensive policy advocated in, 2; description of and forces in (August), 2 fn. 1; situation and dispositions in, (August) 6, 39, (October) 135, (May) 380; planning to begin for offensive/de-

Arakan (Front)—*cont.*
fensive in, 6; appreciations of possible Japanese action in, 9, 10; L.s of C. to, and their capacity, 18-20 *passim*; allotment of 'V' Force to, 31; Force 136 operations in, 33; 224 Group to support operations in, 36, 38; Combined Cargo Task Force to control air transport and supply for, 37; overrunning of dressing station in, referred to, 49; Japanese aims and dispositions in, (July) 56, 59, (November) 60, 138, (January) 215, (February) 343-4, (discussed) 350, 434; need for offensive action in, 109; change of operational policy in, 136; release of forces from, (for 'Capital' and 'Dracula') 136-7, 139, 214, 246 and fn. 4, (for modified 'Dracula') 328, 329, 346-9 *passim*; naval forces for operations in, 136, 138, 141, 216, 219, 220-1, 223; operations in, 137-8, 139-42, 215-24, 342-50, (affected by 'Dracula') 348, (discussed) 350-1; withdrawal of Japanese from, 56, 140-1, 304 fn. 4, 317, 343, 376, (plans to prevent) 343, 345, 347, 349, 374, (plans to help) 357, 369, 377-8, (discussed) 350-1, 380, (completed) 380; air supply bases in, (needed) 167, (achieved) 341; reserve stocks for 14th Army to be held on coast of, 202; appreciations of Japanese forces and intentions in, 217, 218, 223, 342-3, 349; Japanese defences constructed in, 217 fn. 3; Japanese L. of C. from, 218, (to be blocked) 374; possible amphibious operation from, 244; scope of operations in, reduced, 245-6, 345; XV Corps' casualties in, 350; justification of campaign in, 353; air operations in, 406-7; rivalry between Muslims and Buddhists in, 430-1

Arakan Beaches, Battle of the: 215-24, 342-50; assessed, 350-1; flexibility of tactics in, referred to, 428

Arakan Coastal Forces: proposed operations for, 136, 138 and fn. 3, 141-2; composition of, 136 fn. 5

Arakan Yomas: 2 fn. 1, 61, 135 fn. 1, 380

Argonaut Conference: agreement at, on allocation of American resources, 209, (referred to) 279, 317

Argonaut, H.M. cruiser: 212 fn. 3

Ariadne, H.M. minelayer: 69 fn. 4

Army: *1st Australian Army*: 70
11th Army Group: proposed operations for, 1-2, 107-8, (referred to) 149; shortage of British infantry in, 2, 26-7; forces available to, for operations, 3, 101-2; reinforcements needed for 'Dracula', 11 fn. 1; size of, to be maintained in India, 16; standardization of divisions in, 25-6, (effect of formation of airborne division on) 28, (commented on) 430; number of intelligence reports reaching, 32 fn. 3; its comments on army/air plan, mentioned, 106; Stilwell's refusal to serve under, referred to, 113; proposal to replace, 113, (referred to) 417; replaced by A.L.F.S.E.A., 118, (discussed) 417-18
14th Army: progress of its operations, (June) 2, (August) 6, (January) 179,

Army—*cont.*

14th Army—*cont.*

(February) 188–9, (March) 283; dispositions of, 2 fn. 1, 355–6; British units in, understrength, 2, 26–7; proposals for offensive by, 2–3; proposed role of, in 'Capital' and 'Dracula', 4–5; Cs.-in-C.'s views on operations by, 10; its Planning Staff mentioned, 11, 415; morale of, 12, 284, 313; maintenance of, 20–1, 150, 166, 172–3, 200, 203, 325, (redeployment plan necessary for) 200, (referred to) 214–15, (aircraft needed for) 200–1, 338–9, (from Akyab and Ramree) 246, (referred to) 410, (in army/air plans) 247–9, 321–3, (Mountbatten on) 317, 318, (general policy for, in advance to Rangoon) 325–6, (Rangoon to be advanced base for) 331, (tonnages delivered for) 409, 410, (summarized and commented on) 424–7; resumes administrative control of Imphal plain, 21; intelligence groups in, 31; 'P' Division officers to be attached to, 31; need for army/air co-operation on its front, 34; Headquarters of, (location of) 34, 254, 366, (mentioned) 125, 327, 332; forms joint H.Q. with 221 Group, 36, 114, 155; air transport for, 42; Japanese appreciations of plans of, 59, 186–7, 271–2, 272–3; effect of its operations, 60, 197; its appreciation and outline plan for 'Capital', 101–6; its views on 'Dracula', 101–3; transport aircraft available for, 105–6, (effect of diversion of, on operations) 131; boundary of, (with N.C.A.C.) 108 fn. 1, 168, (with XV Corps) 118 fn. 2, (with 505 District) 327; relieved of general administrative tasks, 114, 155; air supply for, (increase in demands of) 129, (inadequate) 204, (allocated more) 245, (shortfall in) 317, (possible reduction in) 330, (discussed) 410–12; proposed operations for, 149, 242, 249, 255, 324–5, (referred to) 321; XV Corps no longer under, 155; its information on Japanese dispositions, 157–8, 163–4, 171–2, 179–80, 267; problems of its concentration on Chindwin, 156; engineer tasks for, 166–7, 326, 362; its deception plans, 173–4, (success of) 266; representative of, at conference on IV Corps' plans, 181; air support for, 182, 253–4, 311–12, 366, 393, 404; strength of (March), 202, 284; new L. of C. for, 202; to be no change in plan for, 203; relieved of control of L. of C. Transport Column, 204; operations to assist, 218–19, 244; V.C.P.s with, 254 fn. 3; its general advance to Irrawaddy begins, 258; its views on Japanese fighting capabilities, 273, 284; effect on, of removal of Chinese formations and aircraft, 280, 316, 338–9; its practice in issuing amendments, 297 fn. 3; Japanese plan to contain it north of Meiktila, 298; 36th Division joins, 302 fn. 1, 316, 320, (referred to) 326 fn. 1; its losses (to end of March), 311; fly-out of formations of, 323, 325; re-

Army—*cont.*

14th Army—*cont.*

groups, 324, 355, 366; to take over rear F.M.A.s, 325; medical centres for, 325; signal tasks for, 325–6; forms L. of C. subareas, 327 and fn. 1; and modified 'Dracula', 328–9; to capture airfields for modified 'Dracula', 329–31 *passim*, (need for speed) 384–5; and control of Rangoon, 332; progress of (in relation to rising in Burma) 334–5, 337, (in relation to mounting of modified 'Dracula') 352; object of its operations, 357; possible attack on flank and communications of, 361; command of 19th Division transferred from, 361; responsible for airfield security, 362; effect of monsoon conditions on, 367; hopes to reach Rangoon first, 390–1; 26th Division comes under command of, 397; Chief Surgical Officer of, 398–9; total reinforcements flown in for, 413; its operations summarized and commented on, 420–30

Corps:

1st Australian: 70

IV: on Central front, 2 fn. 1; leaves Imphal-Kohima area, 40 fn. 2; its crossing at Nyaungu referred to, 60 fn. 1, 423; proposed operations for, 149–50, 154, 157–8, 165, 168, 172, 180, 242–3, 297, 324–5, (referred to) 421, 422; Headquarters become operational, 150; troops under command of, 150, 155 fn. 1; location of Headquarters, 150, 168, 173–4, 356, 388; engineer tasks for, 154, 169, 172–4 *passim*, 181; boundary of, with XXXIII Corps, 154, 168–9; method of its introduction to Yeu-Shwebo area, 155; its advance to Meiktila, (to be secret) 168, (regrouping of, and forces for) 168, 173, (limited distribution of orders for) 173, (referred to, in Retrospect) 421–3; airlift for, (allotted) 169, 326, (delivered) 399 fn. 1; dispositions of, (December) 171, (April) 355, 388–9; maintenance of, 172, 253 fn. 2, 323, 325, 399, (corps airhead for) 356, (referred to) 410; deception measures for concentration and advance of, scheme 'Cloak', 173–5, 181, (success of) 186, (referred to) 255; progress of operations of, (January) 179, (March) 273, 283, 296; plans for its advance to the Irrawaddy and Meiktila, 180–2, (being perfected) 255; air support for, 182, 253, 366; forms joint H.Q. with 221 Group, 253; V.C.P.s with, 254 fn. 3; given 5th Division, 255, 262, 282, 284; its bridgehead at Nyaungu, 256, (vehicle ferry in) 266 fn. 1, (referred to) 283, (Japanese hopes regarding effect of counter-attack on) 298, (referred to, in Retrospect) 423; its thrust to Meiktila begins, 263; success of its thrust across Irrawaddy, 266; its knowledge of Yamamoto's plans, 286, 304; *18th Division* operating in

Army—*cont.*
  IV Corps —*cont.*
    area of, 294; redeployment of, for advance on Rangoon, 309–10, 313, 324, 325; casualties of, (in Meiktila fighting) 311, (during Battle of Rangoon Road) 398; tank losses of, 311; establishment of F.M.A.s by, 325–6; restrictions on reinforcements and replacements for, 325; mentioned, 332; 19th Division to support, 356, 365; takes over command of 19th Division, 361; its estimation of Japanese strength, 363 fn. 2; XXXIII Corps' advance subsidiary to, 375; lays cordon in Sittang valley, 380; speed of its advance increasing, 381, (effect of) 386; delayed at Yamethin, 382; general concept of operations for (April), 383; learns of Japanese moving east of Sittang, 390; its operations summarized and referred to, 421–3, 429–30
  XV: on Arakan front, 2 fn. 1; L. of C. for, 19–20; forms joint H.Q. with 224 Group, 36, 135; air support for, 38, 135–6; dispositions of, (August) 39, (October) 135; allotted 'V' Force group, 43; comes directly under A.L.F.S.E.A., 118; its boundary with L. of C. Command, 118 fn. 2; forces earmarked for, 135; to release forces from Arakan, 136–7, 246, 249; air supply for, 136; F.M.A.s for, 140, 141 fn. 3; proposed operations for, 203, 218–9, 249, 344, 345, 348, (referred to) 341, 420, 425; takes 53rd Brigade under command, 216; progress of its operations (February), 224; withdrawal of air supply from, 224, 245, 249, 344, (effect of, on operations) 245–6, 344–5, (referred to) 317, 339, 342, 351, (summarized and commented on) 425–6; curtailment of its operations, 245–6, 344; maintenance of, by sea, 245–6; to direct and mount modified 'Dracula', 328, 350, 351; and control of Rangoon, 332; casualties in, 350; its operations discussed, 350–1; its operational career ends, 397; tonnages delivered to (January to May), 410
  XXXIII: on Central front, 2 fn. 1; dispositions of, (August) 6, 39–40, (December) 171, (April) 356; operations of, (in advance to Chindwin) 41–51, 150–4, (to Irrawaddy) 154–7, 175–6, 183, 273, (at Mandalay) 283, 288, 296, (at Kyaukse) 302–4 *passim*, (to Rangoon) 369–80; air support for, 41–2, 151, 182, 366; air supply and maintenance of, 42, 169, 172, 182–3, 253 fn. 2, (tonnages allotted for) 326, 375; proposed operations for, 42, 149–50, 157, 165, 168, 172–4 *passim*, 242, 288 fn. 1, 297–8, 302, 324–5, (referred to) 421–2; allotted 'V' Force group, 43; engineer forces for, 150–1 and fn. 1, (tasks of) 157, 168–9, 172–3, 362; location of its Headquarters, 150, 157;

Army—*cont.*
  XXXIII Corps—*cont.*
    information on Japanese forces opposing, 151; its boundary with IV Corps, 154, 168–9; losses of, (in monsoon campaign) 160, (in Battle of Mandalay) 311; its method of issuing orders, 173; its part in deception plans, 174–5; possible reduction in size of, 243; V.C.P.s with, 254 fn. 3; 7th Division passes to, 310; its administrative tasks, in advance to Rangoon, 325–6; restrictions on reinforcements and replacements for, 325; I.W.T. flotilla for, 326; takes over Myitche, 356; prepares for drive down Irrawaddy, 362; its advance on Rangoon limited by air supply, 375; general concept of operations of, 375; to establish cordon east of Irrawaddy, 380; 28th (E.A.) Brigade joins, 380
  XXXIV: formation and composition of, 252
  Divisions:
    2nd (British): organized for amphibious role, 25; brought up to strength, 26–7; in rest area, 40 fn. 2, 43, 150; moves forward, 156–7; relieves 11th (E.A.) Division, 160; proposed operations for, 165, 174, 177, 183–4, 242, 256, 288, 289, 294, 297, 302, 351–2, 362, (referred to) 423; in operations, (to Pyingaing) 171, 175, (to Kabo, Yeu, Shwebo) 177–9, (against Sagaing) 185, (at Saye) 258, (to establish Ngazun bridgehead) 262–3, (in Mandalay area) 292–3, 301; on half rations, 178; greatly dependent on air supply, 182; armour and artillery allotted to, 184 fn. 3, 362 fn. 4; progress of its operations, (February) 188, (March) 273, 283; tank losses of, 293; 19th Division to contact, 299; relieved of task at Mandalay, 300; its move to Myingyan area, 324, 356, (referred to) 355; fly-out of, to India, 325, 356, 362, 374; for modified 'Dracula', 328, 331, 351, 352, (its movement to concentration area) 331 fn. 2, (its dispatch delayed), 399; to command 268th Brigade, 363
    4th Indian: 8 fn. 1
    5th Indian: in operations, (on Tiddim road) 6, 39, 45, (at Manipur bridge) 46–9, (at Tiddim) 50, (at Kalemyo) 152–3, (at Meiktila) 310–11, (at Yamethin) 381–3, (to capture and consolidate Toungoo) 384–7, 389; proposed operations for, 42, 242, 255, 309–10, 383, 391; achievements of its engineers, 45, 48; commands Lushai Brigade, 45; maintenance of, (by air), 48–9, 50, 156, (to be through Rangoon) 399; its strength forward of Manipur River, 48 fn. 3; incidence of scrub typhus in, 49; trained nursing sisters with, 49; contacts 25th (E.A.) Brigade, 153; relieved at Kalemyo, 156; to be 14th Army reserve, 165; reorganized

Army—*cont.*
  5th Indian Division—*cont.*
    as mechanized division, 181 fn. 3, 255; Katamura concludes it has been withdrawn, 186; its move to Monywa, 262, 283, 286; under IV Corps, 284, 286; mentioned, 305; 1st Burma Regiment to join, 305 fn. 1; to link up with 17th Division, 308, 309; armour for, 310; arrives at Meiktila, 311; resumes command of 9th Brigade, 353, 383; concentrates as mobile reserve, 355; relieves 99th Brigade, 358; moves forward to take up pursuit, 361, 366; Japanese plans to attack, 364; task of, completed, 387; disarms *I.N.A.* division, 387 fn. 2; to be responsible for Pegu area, 398
  6th Indian: 8 fn. 1
  7th Indian: at Kohima, 40 fn. 2, 150, 171, 174; maintenance of, 129, 305 fn. 3, 374; under IV Corps, 149, 150, (in reserve) 171; engineer tasks for, 154, 174–5; not to be committed east of Chindwin, 155; possible fly-in of, to Northern front, 157; new commander for, 157 fn. 3; proposed operations for, 165, 173, 181, 242, 255–7 *passim*, 283, 310, 362, 374; forward concentration of, 174–5; troops under command of, 175; location of, (January) 179, (unknown to Japanese) 186, (April) 356, 366; forces opposing, 179; armour and artillery allotted to, 181, 269 fn. 2, 362 fn. 4, 369 fn. 2; advances to Irrawaddy, 182; progress of its operations, (January) 188, (March) 283; its deception plans, 256–7; in operations, (in Nyaungu bridgehead) 257–8, 263–6, 266–7, 269–70, (from bridgehead) 285–7, 305–6, (to Chauk and Seikpyu) 362, 365, 370–1, (in Yenangyaung area) 372–7, (to Shandatkyi) 380, (at Nyaungu referred to, in Retrospect) 423; air attack on, 266; situation in its sector (March) 284; reinforced, 286, 305 fn. 1, 364; regrouped, 304, 362–3; to be relieved of 17th Division's base, 310; passes to XXXIII Corps, 310, 324, 355 362 fn. 2; brigade of, to be waterborne, 362, 373
  8th Indian: 8 fn. 1
  10th Indian: 8 fn. 1
  11th (East African): operations of, in Kabaw Valley, 6, 39–40, 43–5, 153–4, 160; believed highly resistant to malaria, 40 fn. 1; proposed operations for, 40, 42; air supply for, 42, 44, 156 fn. 2; artillery for, 42 and fn. 5; ready to begin operations, 43; tank squadron for, 45; its speed of advance determines rate of road construction, 151; protection for its right flank, 156; withdrawn, 160; to be in 14th Army reserve, 165; its sign used in deception plans, 257
  17th Indian: mentioned, 40 fn. 2, 42, 46

Army—*cont.*
  17th Indian Division—*cont.*
    fn. 2; needed for 14th Army, 164; proposed operations for, 165, 242, 255, 309, 357–8, 391, 398; possible fly-in of, to Pakokku, 167; to reinforce IV Corps, 168; concentrates ready to move forward, 173 fn. 2; reorganized for motor and air transport, 180–1; Katamura concludes it has been withdrawn, 186; moves forward to cross Irrawaddy, 188–9, 257; its composition for strike on Meiktila, 255 and fn. 2; crosses Irrawaddy, 266, (referred to) 423; in operations, (to Meiktila) 267–8, (at Meiktila) 270–1, 286–8, 307–9, 310, 313, (at Pyawbwe) 358–61, (referred to) 381, 382, (to Pyinmana) 366, (to Pegu) 389–90, 391–3, (towards Rangoon) 397–8; on air supply, 269, 283; casualties in, 271, 288, 389 fn. 3; administrative echelons of, 285, 311; contact by 20th Division, (planned) 294, 302, (achieved) 303, 304; tank losses of, 308, 369 fn. 3; and possible link-up with 5th Division, 308; to be relieved, 310; dispositions of (April), 355; behind schedule, 360; to be reorganized for advance on Rangoon, 383; resumes lead in advance to Rangoon, 387, 389; links up with 26th Division, 398
  19th Indian: to be supplied by air, 129; move of, to Indaw, 130; in contact with 36th Division, 130 fn. 3, 145, 159, 171; in operations, (to Pinlebu and Banmauk) 145 fn. 2, 159–60, (to Monywa and Shwebo) 176–9, (in Kyaukmyaung area) 185–6, (to Mandalay) 258–60, (at Mandalay) 288–92, 299–301, (in Wundwin area) 366, 383, (in Toungoo area) 387–8, 388–9, 398, (referred to, in Retrospect) 422, 423; under command, (of IV Corps) 149, 361, (of XXXIII Corps) 168 fn. 3, 176, (of 14th Army) 324, 355; proposed operations for, 154–5, 157, 165, 174, 177, 183–4, 242, 255, 294, 297, 302, 324, 381, 383; engineer tasks for, 155, 160 fn. 1; to report on routes east of Chindwin, 155; moves forward to Tamu, 156; advances without artillery, 158–60; in contact with Japanese, 168; dispositions of, (December) 171, 176, (March) 288–9; supply-drops for, 176 fn. 1, 182; armour and artillery support for, 184 fn. 3, 258 fn. 3; Katamura's appreciation of, and plans against, 186–7; progress of operations of, (February) 188, (March) 273, 283; forces opposing, 259 fn. 1; regrouped, 300; contacted by 20th Division, 303; to relieve brigade of 20th Division, 304, 310; release of, for Meiktila battle, 316; to support IV Corps, 324, 356, 365, 366; to take over Kyaukse, 362; relieves part of 9th Brigade

Army—*cont.*
  Divisions—*cont.*
    20th Indian: near Imphal, 40 fn. 2; Tar-
      col column of, 43, 44; ready to advance,
      150; moves forward, 156–7; in opera-
      tions, (to Pyingaing) 160, (to Monywa)
      176–7, 184–5, (in Irrawaddy crossing)
      258, 260–2, (to Singaingmyo–Ava)
      292–4, 296, (to Wundwin) 302–4, (to
      Magwe) 365–6, 371–2, (at Allanmyo)
      375, 377, (at Prome) 379–80; disposi-
      tions of (December), 171, 175; proposed
      operations for, 174, 183–4, 242, 255,
      288, 294, 297, 302, 362, 374; on half
      rations, 174; dependence on air supply,
      182–3; armour and artillery support
      for, 184 fn. 3, 260, 362 fn. 4; Japanese
      formations identified in attacks against,
      262; progress of operations of, (March)
      273, 283, (April) 356, 366; contacts
      19th Division, 303; 5th Division con-
      tacts, 310; to concentrate for advance
      on Rangoon, 324, 355; relief of, at
      Kyaukse, 356; begins move on Magwe,
      365–6; exchanges battalions with 36th
      Division, 366 and fn. 1
    21st Indian: 28
    23rd Indian: 40 and fn. 2, 252, 328
    25th Indian: its dispositions in Arakan,
      (August) 39, (October) 135; proposed
      operations for, 136, 138, 141, 215, 217–
      18, 223, 343, 344; in operations, (in
      Buthidaung area), 137, (to Foul Point)
      139–41, (on Myebon Peninsula) 216,
      (at Kangaw) 220–2, (at Tamandu)
      344, 345; new maintenance arrange-
      ments for, 245–6; withdrawal of, 246
      and fn. 4, 346–8 *passim*; mentioned,
      252 fn. 3
    26th Indian: its dispositions in Arakan,
      (August) 39, (October) 135, 201, 215;
      proposed operations for, 136, 138–9,
      201, 215, 343, 345, 351; forward
      brigade of, to be relieved, 136; freed for
      operations on mainland, 224; mainten-
      ance of, 245; to be no further opera-
      tions for, in Arakan, 246; withdrawal
      of, 246 fn. 4, 345, 346, 347, 348; for
      modified 'Dracula', 246 fn. 4, 327, 328,
      330, 331, 332; new commander for, 351;
      issues orders for assault on Rangoon,
      352–3; in modified 'Dracula', 395–7;
      casualties in, 395; under command of
      14th Army, 397; links up with 17th
      Division, 398
    36th Indian (later British): in operations,
      (in railway corridor) 23, (at Pinbaw)
      40–1, (referred to) 44, (at Auktaw and
      Pinwe) 144–5, (to Kyaukme) 192, 194–6,
      275–8, 320, (referred to) 316, 318; air
      supply for, 23, 41, 316, 326 fn. 1, 338,
      383; organized for amphibious opera-
      tions, 25, (referred to) 430; deficiency
      of British infantry in, 26–7; allotted
      reinforcements, 28, 30 fn. 2; railway L.
      of C. for, (being developed) 41, (being
      attacked) 144; mentioned, 101; loca-

Army—*cont.*
  36th Division—*cont.*
      tion of (October), 143, (December) 148,
      171, (March) 273, (April) 366; re-
      designated British division, 143 fn. 4;
      casualties in, 145; contact with 19th
      Division, 130 fn. 3, 145, 154, 157–9
      passim, 171; proposed operations for,
      145, 158, 191, 383, (mentioned) 183;
      Mars Force contacts, 146; Japanese
      plans to delay, 272; widely dispersed,
      276–7; regroups, 278; decreasing opposi-
      tion to its advance, referred to, 294;
      moves to Mandalay area and comes
      under 14th Army, 302 fn. 1, 316, 320;
      fly-out of, to India, 325, 328, 388, 398;
      to operate Mandalay airhead, 326; for
      possible use in modified 'Dracula', 328;
      its area of responsibility, 361; relieves
      19th Division, 365, 383; exchanges
      battalions with 20th Division, 366 fn. 1;
      to be maintained by road, 383
    44th Indian Airborne: formation of, 28–
      30; proposed date of readiness of, 29,
      (postponed by withdrawal of transport
      aircraft) 129; battalion of, in modified
      'Dracula', 329; ready too late, 430
    44th Indian Armoured: 28
    81st (West African): proposed return of
      3rd (W.A.) Brigade to, 29–30; in
      corps reserve, 39; for Arakan front, 101;
      dispositions of (October), 135; proposed
      operations for, 136, 137, 218; opera-
      tions of, in Kaladan valley, 137–8, 140–
      2 *passim*, (believed effect of) 140; sup-
      plied by air, 137; withdrawal of, 203,
      217, 218, 246 fn. 4; forms part of
      XXXIV Corps, 252
    81st (W.A.) Reconnaissance Regiment:
      137
    82nd (West African): at Ranchi, 39; for
      Arakan front, 101, 135; proposed opera-
      tions for, 136, 138, 217, 218, 223, 343,
      344, 345, 348; to relieve brigade of 26th
      Division, 136; moves forward, 137;
      maintenance of, 138, 218, 245–6, 348;
      operations of, (to Thayettabin), 141,
      (to Dalet) 244, (to An) 345–7, (dis-
      cussed) 351; I.W.T. transport for, 218
      fn. 1; effect on, of cessation of air sup-
      ply, 345; to be withdrawn, 346, 347;
      under command of A.L.F.S.E.A., 349–
      50, 380; in monsoon quarters, 380
    82nd (W.A.) Reconnaissance Regi-
      ment: 224
  Brigades:
    1st (West African): in Arakan operations,
      139, 140, 224, 343–9 *passim*
    2nd (West African): in Arakan opera-
      tions, 137, 139–40, 222, 223, 343–9
      passim; air supply for, 346
    3 Commando: 40 fn. 2, 101, 135; pro-
      posed operations for, 136, 138–9, 141,
      215–16; release of, from Arakan, 136,
      246 fn. 4, 343; in operations, (on Mye-
      bon Peninsula) 216, (at Kangaw) 220–
      2; casualties in, 222 fn. 1; at Akyab,

Army—*cont.*

3 Commando Brigade—*cont.*
223 fn. 2; under XXXIV Corps, 252; possible use of, in modified 'Dracula', 328; referred to, in assessment of specialized formations, 430

3rd (West African): 27, 29, 30

4th (British): location of, 176; in operations, (in advance to Irrawaddy) 177–9, 185, (in Irrawaddy crossing) 262–3, (towards Mandalay) 293, 301, (in Mahlaing area) 306 fn. 4, 362; withdrawn to India, 333 fn. 1, 362

4th Indian: in operations, (in Arakan) 219, 220, 346, 347, 349, (in modified 'Dracula') 396; maintenance of, 246; troops under its command for Letpan operation, 346 fn. 2; relief of, for modified 'Dracula', 348, 349, 352

4th (West African): in Arakan operations, 140, 217 fn. 1, 222, 224, 343–6 *passim*, 349; under 81st (W.A.) Division, 217; returned to own division, 218; relieves 4th Indian Brigade, 349

5th (British): occupies Tamu, 40; rejoins 2nd Division, 43; in operations, (at Pyingaing) 175, (in Shwebo area) 177–9, 185, (in Irrawaddy crossing) 258, 262–3, (to Ava) 293, 301, (in Mount Popa area) 356, 371, (at Legyi) 363–4; at Myingyan, 310 fn. 2; withdrawn to India, 331 fn. 1, 374; to assist in capture of Chauk, 362

5th (West African): 137–8

6th (British): in operations, (to Irrawaddy) 160, 171, 175, 177, 179, (in Irrawaddy crossing) 262–3, (to Mandalay) 293, 301; withdrawn to India, 331 fn. 1, 362; mentioned, 399

6th (West African): 137, 140

9th Indian: in operations, (in advance to Chindwin) 45–6, 49, 153, (in Meiktila area) 307–9 *passim*, 361, 383, (in advance to Rangoon) 386, 390; its casualties in 1944 monsoon campaign, 46 fn. 1; fly-in of, (to Meiktila) 262, 283, 284 fn. 2, 306–7, (to Shwegyin–Waw area) 390; mentioned, 311, 391; rejoins 5th Division, 355, 383

14th Indian Air Landing: 28

14th (L.R.P.): 27–9 *passim*

16th (L.R.P.): 27, 30

21st (East African): in operations in Kabaw Valley, 43, 44–5, 153–4; air supply for, 44

22nd (East African): earmarked for XV Corps, 135; to be in corps reserve, 139; arrives in Arakan, 140; garrisons Ramree, 220, 224; maintenance of, 245, 246, 349; in operations in Arakan, 343, 344–7 *passim*, 349; arrives at Tamandu, 346; to join XXXIII Corps, 380

23rd (L.R.P.): 27, 30, 40 fn. 2

25th (East African): 43–5 *passim*, 153, 154

26th Indian: allotted to 36th Division, 28, 145; in operations, (in Shweli valley)

Army—*cont.*

26th Indian Brigade—*cont.*
192, 195, (at Myitson) 196, 275–7, (to Kyaukme) 320

26th (East African): in operations in Kabaw Valley, 43–5 *passim*, 153, 154; air supply for, 44

28th (East African): proposed operations for, 165, 173, 180, 242, 256; to come under IV Corps, 168; in corps reserve, 171; forward concentration of, 174–5; on Me Chaung, 179; at Tilin, 182; in operations, (to Seikpyu) 257, (referred to) 423, (at Letse) 266, 269, 284, 285, 304–5, 362; armour allotted to, 269 fn. 2; relief of, 269, 286, 305, 310, 356, 363, 365

29th (British): in operations, (at Pinbaw) 40, (to Auktaw) 144, 145, (to Mongmit) 192, 195, 196, 276–8 *passim*, (on Kalaw road) 383, 388, 389

32nd Indian: moves to Mawlaik, 156; in operations, (in advance to Irrawaddy) 160, 171, 175, 176, 184, (in Irrawaddy crossing) 260–2, (to Kyaukse) 292, 293, 302, 303–4, (at Taungdwingyi) 365–6, 371–2, 375, (in Prome area) 379; British battalion in, replaced, 366; to make for Rangoon, 375

33rd Indian: to practise for assault crossing of Irrawaddy, 180; at Pauk, 182; in operations, (in Irrawaddy crossing) 257, 266, (to Myingyan) 269–70, 285, (to Taungtha) 285, 286, 306, 310, (at Yenangyaung) 356, 363, 372–3, (at Kyaukpadaung) 364–5, (at Chauk) 370–1, (to Magwe) 374, 375; armour allotted to, 269 fn. 2; replacement of units in, 305 fn. 1; leaves Myingyan, 310 fn. 2, 356; casualties in, 373; tasks for, 374, 376

36th Indian: 219, 348, 395, 396

48th Indian: reorganized for move on Meiktila, 181; in Meiktila striking force, 255 fn. 2; crosses Irrawaddy, 266; in operations, (to Meiktila) 267–8, (at Meiktila) 270–1, 286–7, 307–9, (to Pyawbwe) 355, 358–60, 390, (at Pegu) 392, (towards Rangoon) 393, 397; loses tanks, 308; casualties in, 309 fn. 3, 359

50th Indian Tank: 135, 138

50th Parachute: to be released for training, 2; date of readiness of, 3, 102, 149, 164; to form part of 44th Indian Airborne Division, 28, 29–30; composition of, 30 fn. 1; being trained, 129; under IV Corps, 149; in modified 'Dracula', 351, 394; casualties in, 394

51st Indian: in operations, (in Mayu valley) 140, 141, (at Kangaw) 220, 221; to be withdrawn to Akyab, 343

53rd Indian: to be maintained by air, 138; in operations, (in Mayu valley) 139, 140, 141, (to Minbya) 215, 216, 218, (at Ruywa) 223, 344; under command of XV Corps, 216; to reinforce

Army—*cont.*

53rd Indian Brigade—*cont.*

25th Division, 218; sent forward to Myebon, 221

62nd Indian: proposed operations for, 154–5, 289, 292; in operations, (in advance to Irrawaddy) 155, 159, 177–8, 186, (to Chaungmagyi Chaung) 259, (to Maymyo) 291, 294, (in Mandalay area) 299, 300, 301; to relieve 98th Brigade, 289; at Singaingmyo, 303; ordered to Yamethin, 383

63rd Indian: reorganized for move on Meiktila, 181; crosses Irrawaddy, 266; air attacks on, 266; in operations, (to Meiktila) 267–8, (at Meiktila) 270, 286–8, 307–8, (at Pyawbwe) 358–9, (at Pegu) 389–90, 392; relieved at Meiktila, 355

64th Indian: battalion of, under 62nd Brigade, 154; proposed operations for, 155, 258, 289; moves to Sittaung, 155; in operations, (in advance to Irrawaddy) 155, 159, 177–9, 185, (to Mandalay) 259, (at Mandalay) 290, 291, 292, 299–300, (in Thazi area) 361, (at Hlaingdet) 383; contacts 36th Division, 159; at Kyaukmyaung, 186; composition of, for attack on Mandalay, 292 fn. 1; to Wundwin, 304; to move from Kalaw road to Meiktila, 383; to return to Kalaw road, 388–9

71st Indian: in Ramree operation, 219–20; moves to India and is recalled, 348; in modified 'Dracula', 395–7 *passim*

72nd (British): in operations, (in railway corridor) 40, (at Pinwe) 144–5, (to Myitson) 192, 195–6, 276–7, (at Mongmit) 278; casualties in, 145; reinforced, 278 fn. 1; flies to Mandalay, 320

74th Indian: in operations, (in advance to Akyab) 139–41 *passim*, (in capture of Akyab) 141, (on Myebon Peninsula) 216, 217–18, (at Kangaw) 220, 222, (at Tamandu) 345; maintained by sea, 139; at Ruywa, 344

77th (L.R.P.): 27, 29–30

77th Indian Parachute: 29, 30 fn. 1

80th Indian: moves to Kalemyo, 156; in operations, (in advance to Irrawaddy) 176–7, 184, 260–2, (to Kyaukse) 292–3, 302–4, (at Magwe) 371–2, (to Prome area) 375, 379–80; armour for, 371; casualties in, 372 fn. 1

89th Indian: proposed operations for, 180, 256; in operations, (in advance to Irrawaddy) 182, (in Irrawaddy crossing) 257, 266, (to Chauk) 269, 284–5, 356, 363, 370, 371, (at Yenangyaung) 372–3, (west of Irrawaddy) 375, 376–7, (at Yenanma) 379, (at Shandatkyi) 380

98th Indian: proposed operations for, 155; in operations, (in advance to Irrawaddy) 155, 178–9, 185, (against Kabwet) 186–7, (to Mandalay) 258–9, 288–9, (at Mandalay) 289–92, 299, 300, 301, (on Mawchi road) 388; moves

Army—*cont.*

98th Indian Brigade—*cont.*

to Sinlamaung, 159–60; composition of, for operations south of Mandalay, 292 fn. 1; ordered to Pyawbwe, 383

99th Indian: reorganized as air-transported brigade, 181; fly-in of, to Meiktila area, 182, 255, 267, 268; mentioned, 255 fn. 2; in operations, (to Meiktila) 270, (at Meiktila) 286, 307, 308, 310, (at Pyawbwe) 358–60, (at Pegu) 392; casualties in, 308 fn. 4, 359

100th Indian: in operations, (on Tamu-Sittaung road) 42–3, (in advance to Irrawaddy) 176, 184–5, (in Myinmu bridgehead) 260–2, 263, 292, (in advance to Kyaukse) 293, (in Wundwin area) 294, 303, (in Prome area) 375, 379, 380; battalion of, with 32nd Brigade, 156; at Khampat, 156–7; armour allotted to, 294; contacts 17th Division and is relieved by 64th Brigade, 304, 310

111th (L.R.P.): 27, 30

114th Indian: at Tonhe, 171; to capture Pakokku, 180, 182, 256; in operations, (to Pakokku) 174, 180, 182, 256, 257, 266, 269, (in Nyaungu bridgehead) 285, (in Letse area) 305, 356, 362, 363, (to Seikpyu) 365, 370–1, (in Salin area) 373, 374–5, (on Minbu–Ngape road) 376; air attacks on, 266

123rd Indian: in operations, (towards Tiddim) 46–7, 48, 49–50, (at Vital Corner) 152, (in advance to Meiktila) 306, 310, (at Yamethin) 381–2, 383, (at Shwemyo bluff) 384, (to Toungoo) 385–6, (at Pyu) 387; air supply for, 46; air support for, 50; under IV Corps, 286; casualties in, 382

161st Indian: in operations, (to Tiddim) 45–6, 47, 49, 50, (to Kalemyo) 152–3, (to Meiktila) 306, 310, (towards Toungoo) 382–3, 384, 385, (at Pyu) 386–7; under IV Corps, 286; reinforces 7th Division, 286, 305; reverts to 5th Division, 310; casualties in, 385, 387; air attack on, 386–7

254th Indian Tank: at Kanglatongbi, 40 fn. 2; squadron of, in Kabaw Valley, 45; in advance to Kalemyo, 150 fn. 1; proposed operations for, 165, 242; in advance to Irrawaddy, 174, 184; in advance to Prome, 374

255th Indian Tank: under IV Corps, 150, 168; proposed operations for, 165, 173, 242; forward concentration of, 174–5; regimental group of, allotted to 7th Division, 181; in Meiktila striking force, 255 fn. 2; in operations, (to Meiktila) 182, 267–8, (at Meiktila) 270–1, (at Pyawbwe) 381, (towards Pegu) 389 fn. 1, 392; on air supply, 283; tank losses in, 268, 271, 287, 308 and fn. 1, 311, 387, 389 fn. 3; administrative echelon of, 285, 311; concentrates

Army—*cont.*

255th Indian Tank Brigade—*cont.*
at Pegu, 398; to be supplied through Rangoon, 399

268th Indian: withdrawn to Imphal, 43; composition of, 44 fn. 1, 155 fn. 1, 374 fn. 1; proposed operations for, 44, 165, 174, 242, 302, 362, 363, 364, 374, 375; mentioned, 101; under IV Corps, 155 fn. 1; in operations, (in advance to Irrawaddy) 154, 155, 160, 171, 176, 258, 283, 293, 301, (in Mount Popa area) 365, 366, 371, 374, (west of Irrawaddy) 375–6, 377, 379; under XXXIII Corps, 168 fn. 3, 184, 363, 364, 374; at Myingyan, 356; takes over, (Kabo Weir) 177, (Sagaing salient) 262, (Kyaukpadaung) 370, (Taungdwingyi) 375; 2nd Division to contact, 294; proposed fly-out of, 325; artillery allotted to, 362 fn. 4; casualties in, 365

Lushai: proposed operations for, 42; allotted 'V' Force group, 43; in operations, (in advance to Irrawaddy) 45, 46, 48, 49, 152, 153, (at Gangaw) 171, 174, 175; mentioned, 101, 173, 180 fn. 1; in 14th Army reserve, 165, 175; to come under IV Corps, 168 fn. 3

Beach Groups:
41st Indian: 329 fn. 1, 351
45th Indian: 356

Royal Armoured Corps:
3rd Carabiniers: in operations, (towards Tiddim) 48, (in advance to Irrawaddy) 184 fns. 2 and 3, 185, (in Irrawaddy crossing) 263, (to Magwe) 362 fn. 4, (at Mount Popa) 363, (west of Irrawaddy) 373, 376, (to Prome) 375, 379; tank losses in, 263, 376

116th R.A.C.: mentioned, 255 fn. 2, 392; in operations, (in Irrawaddy crossing) 257 fn. 2, (from Nyaungu bridgehead) 269 fn. 2, 285, 306, (in advance to Rangoon) 381 fn. 3, 382; transfers to 5th Division, 310; tank losses in, 382

146th R.A.C.: 219 fn. 4, 346 fn. 2

150th R.A.C.: in operations, (in Irrawaddy crossing) 184, 258 fn. 3, (at Mandalay) 290 fn. 2, 292 fn. 1, (to Magwe) 362 fn. 4, 371–2; in Barcol, 303 fn. 2

2nd Reconnaissance Regiment: 177, 363

Indian Armoured Corps:
5th (Probyn's) Horse: in operations, (to Meiktila) 266 fn. 2, 268, 287 fn. 1, 288, 307, (at Pyawbwe) 359 fn. 1, (to Toungoo) 384, 385, (at Pyu) 387 fn. 1, (at Pegu) 390, 392

7th Light Cavalry: allotted to 20th Division, 184 fn. 3; one squadron allotted to 19th Division, 258 fn. 3; in operations, (to Mandalay) 259, 289 fn. 1, 291, 292 fn. 1, (in Myinmu bridgehead) 260, 261, (to Toungoo) 381 fn. 3, (in Pegu area) 389 fn. 1, 390, 392 fn. 2, (at Hlegu) 398; in Barcol, 303 fn. 2; passes to IV Corps, 324; one squad-

Army—*cont.*

7th Light Cavalry—*cont.*
ron of, in drive down Irrawaddy, 371 fn. 2

8th K. G. V's O. Light Cavalry: 324

9th (Royal Deccan) Horse: in operations, (at Meiktila) 266 fn. 2, 271, (at Pyawbwe) 358, 359, (at Pegu) 389 and fn. 1, 390, 392; tank losses in, 392

11th Cavalry (P.A.V.O): under IV Corps, 168; detachments of, to 19th and 20th Divisions, 184 fn. 3; in operations, (at Kabwet) 186 fn. 1, (to Magwe) 371 fn. 2, (to Prome) 375; proposed operations for, 242; in Barcol, 303 fn. 2

16th Light Cavalry: squadron of, (for 7th Division) 181, (reverts to 5th Division) 310; proposed operations for, 242; in Meiktila striking force, 255 fn. 2, 266 fn. 2; in operations, (at Meiktila) 268, 287 fn. 1, (at Pyawbwe) 359 fns. 1 and 3, (to Toungoo) 381 fn. 3, (to Pegu) 389 fn. 1, 392 fn. 2, (in Shwegyin area) 390, (at Hlegu) 398; detachment of, in Puffcol, 269 fn. 4

19th Lancers: 221, 346, 351

Royal Artillery:
4th Field Regiment: 48
8th Field Regiment: 346, 347
9th Field Regiment: 260 fn. 2
10th Field Regiment: 260 fn. 2, 363
18th (S.P.) Field Regiment: in Myinmu bridgehead, 260 fn. 2; in Barcol, 303 fn. 2; to pass to IV Corps, 324; in Toungoo operations, 381 fn. 3, 387 fn. 1; in advance to Pegu, 389 fn. 1
27th Field Regiment: 223 fn. 1
28th Field Regiment: 48
99th Field Regiment: 362 fn. 4
114th Field Regiment: 260 fn. 2
115th Field Regiment: 292 fn. 1
136th Field Regiment: 373
139th Field Regiment: 285, 306
160th Field Regiment: 219 fn. 4, 346 fn. 2
1st Medium Regiment: 42, 186 fn. 1, 260 fn. 2, 362 fn. 4
6th Medium Regiment: 223 fn. 1, 346 fn. 2, 347
134th Medium Regiment: 292 fn. 1, 300–1
24th Anti-Tank Regiment: 257 fn. 2
33rd Anti-Tank (Mortar) Regiment: 292 fn. 1
101st Heavy Anti-Aircraft Regiment: 260 fn. 2
44th Light Anti-Aircraft Battery: 362 fn. 4
59th (S.P.) Battery: 255 fn. 2, 359 fn. 1
239th Field Battery: 289 fn. 1
240th Field Battery: 186 fn. 1
366th Light Battery: 40

Indian Artillery: 138 fn. 2
1st Indian Field Regiment: 309
2nd Indian Field Regiment: 362 fn. 4
4th Indian Field Artillery: 292 fn. 1
24th Mountain Regiment: 48, 287 fn. 1, 390
1st Indian Anti-Tank Regiment: 346 fn. 2

Army—*cont.*
  Indian Artillery—*cont.*
    5th Mahratta Anti-Tank Regiment: 381
      fn. 3
    8th Mahratta Anti-Tank Regiment: 362
      fn. 4
  East African Artillery:
    302nd (E.A.) Field Artillery Regiment:
      43
  Royal Engineers: 347 fn. 1
    Headquarters:
      C.A.G.R.E. 14th Army: 362
      274th Army Group Engineers: 151 fn.
        1
      XXXIII Corps Troops Engineers: 151
        fn. 1
      D.C.E. 145: 151 fn. 1
      C.R.E.: 151 fn. 1
    General Reserve Engineer Force: 151
      fn. 1
  Indian Engineers:
    10th Battalion: 151 fn. 1
    15th Battalion: 41
    36th Field Squadron: 359 fn. 1, 387 fn. 1,
      389 fn. 1
    65th Field Company: 292 fn. 1
    67th Field Company: 151 fn. 1
    72nd Field Company: 346 fn. 2
    76th Field Company: 151 fn. 1
    322nd Field Park Company: 151 fn. 1
    361st Field Company: 151 fn. 1
    401st Field Squadron: 303 fn. 2
    459th Forward Airfield Engineers: 151
      fn. 1
  British Infantry:
    1st Queen's Royal Regiment: 305 fn. 1,
      372–3
    2nd Buffs: 196, 275, 276
    2nd King's Own Royal Regiment: 28
      fn. 2
    1st Lincolnshire Regiment: 398
    1st Devonshire Regiment: 262
    1st West Yorkshire Regiment: 271, 358
    2nd West Yorkshire Regiment: 309, 390
    The Green Howards: 271 fn. 1
    1st Royal Welch Fusiliers: 177
    2nd King's Own Scottish Borderers: 269,
      375, 376
    9th Gloucestershire Regiment: 276, 277
    2nd Worcestershire Regiment: 292 fn. 1
    7th Worcestershire Regiment: 178,
      262–3
    2nd East Lancashire Regiment: 144
    2nd Border Regiment: 260
    9th Border Regiment: 268, 287
    2nd Dorsetshire Regiment: 185, 263
    2nd South Lancashire Regiment: in
      assault crossing of Irrawaddy, 257–8,
      264; in Puffcol, 269 fn. 4, 305 fn. 2;
      at Letse, 305; at Seikpyu, 365
    2nd Welch Regiment: 186 fn. 3
    2nd Black Watch: 28 fn. 2
    6th Oxford and Buckinghamshire Light
      Infantry: 345
    1st Northamptonshire Regiment: in Irra-
      waddy crossing, 260–1; in Mount Popa
      operations, 366, 369, 371

36—TWAJ

Army—*cont.*
  British Infantry—*cont.*
    1st Royal Berkshire Regiment: 293
    2nd Royal Berkshire Regiment: in opera-
      tions, (at Kabwet) 186 fns. 1 and 2,
      (at Madaya) 289, (at Mandalay) 290
      fn. 2, 291
    4th The Queen's Own Royal West Kent
      Regiment: 385, 387
    7th York and Lancaster Regiment: 382,
      386
    9th York and Lancaster Regiment: 221
    1st Queen's Own Cameron Highlanders:
      262–3
    1 Commando: 221–2
    5 Commando: 221
  Indian Infantry:
    1st Punjab Regiment:
      1st Battalion: 47, 50, 152–3, 385
      2nd Battalion: 381, 382, 152 fn. 3
    2nd Punjab Regiment:
      3rd Battalion: 307, 309
      7th Battalion: in operations, (in ad-
        vance to Irrawaddy) 175, 176, 258,
        (at Myingyan) 306, (at Gwegyo)
        370, 371; proposed operations for,
        180; relieves 2nd South Lancashire,
        305 and fn. 2
    3rd Madras Regiment:
      1st Battalion: 305, 310 fn. 2, 371
      4th Battalion: 44 fn. 1, 155 fn. 1, 374
        fn. 1
    4th Bombay Grenadiers:
      3rd Battalion: 371, 372
      4th Battalion: 255 fn. 2, 359 fn. 1, 381
        fn. 3, 389 fn. 1, 392 fn. 2
    6th Rajputana Rifles:
      3rd Battalion: 186 fn. 3
    7th Rajput Regiment:
      4th Battalion: 385
      6th Battalion: 255 fn. 2, 268, 359 fn. 1,
        389 fn. 1
    8th Punjab Regiment:
      2nd Battalion: 276, 277
    9th Jat Regiment:
      3rd Battalion: 152, 381, 382
      5th Battalion: 396
    10th Baluch Regiment: 137 fn. 2
      5th Battalion: 178, 292 fn. 1
      7th Battalion: 359, 390, 393 fn. 1, 270
    11th Sikh Regiment:
      1st Battalion: 257, 258, 265, 376
      M.G. Battalion: 186 fn. 1, 292 fn. 1
    12th Frontier Force Regiment:
      4th Battalion: in operations, (at
        Meiktila) 270, (to Pyawbwe) 358,
        359 fn. 1, 360, (at Pegu) 392, 393 fn.
        1
      8th Battalion: in Mandalay operations,
        289, 290–2, 299
      9th Battalion: 304
      M.G. Battalion: 346 fn. 2
    13th Frontier Force Rifles:
      8th Battalion: 397
      14th Battalion: 185, 260, 261, 379
      M.G. Battalion: 219 fn. 4, 257 fn. 2
    14th Punjab Regiment:

Army—*cont.*
14th Punjab Regiment—*cont.*
4th Battalion: in operations, (at Saw) 182, (at Pakokku) 258, (at Letse) 269, 284, 285, 305, 365
7th Battalion: 48, 180 fn. 1
9th Battalion: 260–1, 371 fn. 2
15th Punjab Regiment: 186 fn. 3
1st Battalion: in operations at Mandalay, 289 fn. 1, 290, 291, 292 fn. 1, 299
4th Battalion: in operations, (in Irrawaddy crossing) 257 fn. 2, 264, (at Myingyan) 270 and fn. 1, 285, 306 and fn. 2, (at Chauk) 370, (at Yenangyaung) 372–3
6th Battalion: 287 fn. 1, 307
16th Punjab Regiment:
7th Battalion: 215, 216 fn. 2, 221
17th Dogra Regiment:
1st Battalion: 48, 381 fn. 3, 387 fn. 1
18th Royal Garhwal Rifles:
1st Battalion: 346 fn. 2, 396, 397
19th Hyderabad Regiment:
1st Battalion: 276
Assam Regiment:
1st Battalion: 44 fn. 1, 186 fns. 1 and 3
Sikh Light Infantry:
1st Battalion: 358
Chamar Regiment:
1st Battalion: 44 fn. 1, 155 fn. 1, 370 fn. 3, 374 fn. 1
Gurkha Rifles:
1st King George V's Own:
1st Battalion: 278 fn. 1, 366, 379
4th Battalion: in operations, (in Irrawaddy crossing) 257 fn. 2, (to Myingyan) 270, 285, 306, (at Chauk) 370, (at Yenangyaung) 372–3
2nd King Edward's Own: 345 fn. 2
3rd Queen Alexandra's Own:
1st Battalion: in operations, (at Meiktila) 307, (to Pyawbwe) 358, (to Pegu) 389 and fn. 1, 392, 393 fn. 1
4th Prince of Wales's Own:
4th Battalion: 289–91 *passim*, 292 fn. 1
5th Royal:
4th Battalion: 257–8, 374, 376
6th:
1st Battalion: 178, 186 fn. 3, 292 fn. 1
4th Battalion: 186 fn. 3
7th:
1st Battalion: in operations, (at Meiktila) 268, 270, 308, (to Pyawbwe) 358, (at Pegu) 393 fn. 1, (to Rangoon) 393, 397–8; links up with 26th Division, 398
8th:
1st Battalion: 397
4th Battalion: 305
10th:
1st Battalion: 359, 390, 393 fn. 1
4th Battalion: in operations, (in Pyingaing area) 160, 171, 175–7 *passim*, (in Irrawaddy crossing) 184–5, (at Talingon) 261, (with Barcol) 303 fn. 2, (in Prome area) 379
Assam Rifles: 31, 44 fn. 1

Army—*cont.*
Burma Army:
Burma Regiment:
1st Battalion: in operations, (in Irrawaddy crossing), 257 fn. 2, (at Taungtha) 270, 285–6, (in Shwegyin area) 390; sent to Nyaungu, 305,306; to join 5th Division, 305 and fn. 1
Burma Rifles: 250 fn. 2
Chin Hills Battalion: 175, 180, 256 fn. 3, 274
Nepalese Army:
Mahindra Dal Regiment: 44 fn. 1, 155 fn. 1, 371, 374 fn. 1
Kalibahadur Regiment: 44 fn. 1
Indian State Forces:
Jammu and Kashmir Infantry:
4th Battalion: 307
Tripura Rifles: 31
Chin Levies: 175, 180
Lushai Scouts: 175, 180, 256 fn. 3, 374, 375
Royal Army Service Corps: 37
Royal Indian Army Service Corps: 37
Elephant Company: 151 fn. 1
Indian Electrical Mechanical Engineers: 265
Line of Communication Formations:
Line of Communications Command: formation and composition of, 114, 118 and fn. 2; task of, in later phases of 'Extended Capital', 167; takes over L. of C. Transport Column, 204; proposed abolition of, 204; responsible for development of Akyab and Ramree, 219; and 'Stanza', 331
202 L. of C. Area: 118 fn. 2, 204, 327 fn. 1
404 L. of C. Area: 118 fn. 2, 204, 219 fn. 1
253 L. of C. Sub-Area: 326–7, 327 fn. 1
256 L. of C. Sub-Area: 204
451 L. of C. Sub-Area: 219 fn. 1
453 L. of C. Sub-Area: 219 fn. 1, 348
551 L. of C. Sub-Area: 326, 327 fn. 1
552 L. of C. Sub-Area: 327 and fn. 1
553 L. of C. Sub-Area: 327 fn. 1
505 District: proposed formation and tasks of, 204, 325; formation and composition of, 326–7; its boundary with 14th Army, 327; takes over, (administrative responsibility north of Irrawaddy) 356, (Ava ferry) 362
Headquarters No. 1 Area: 331, 332
Army/Air Co-operation: *see also* Visual Control Posts: reorganization of, 34–6; air O.P. squadron in, 150 fn. 1; technique of joint land/air attacks in Burma, 175 fn. 1; mobile balloon flight in, 260
Arunta, Australian destroyer: 69 fn. 4, 76 fn. 2, 94
Aslett, Brigadier A. R.: 40
Assault Ships: *see* Landing Craft
Atago, Japanese heavy cruiser: 74
Auchinleck, General Sir Claude: responsibilities of, 15; finds British infantry replacements, 26 7; and formation of Indian airborne division, 28; recom-

Auchinleck, General Sir Claude—*cont.*
mends disbandment of Special Force, 29; prepared to release G.H.Q. (I) reserve, 109; receives report from Leese, 204; raises XXXIV Corps, 252; his contention on standard divisions referred to, 430

Auktaw: attack on, 144–5

Aung San: 33, 333, 335–8 *passim*

Australia, Australian cruiser: 69 fn. 4, 72 fn. 1, 94–5

Australian Army : role of, in Pacific: 69–70

Ava: Irrawaddy to be crossed near, 256; operations towards, 263, 288, 292–3, 294; captured, 301; 19th Division to be responsible for area of, 302; ferry at, 362

Ayadaw: capture of, 176–7, 184; Japanese defended area at, 179

B. 24s (heavy bombers): in attacks on Iwojima, 90, 236, 237 fn. 2; mentioned, 125

B. 25s (medium bombers): 175, 254

B. 29s (heavy bombers): airfields for, (in India) 37, (in Iwojima) 240 fn. 1; raids by, (on Formosa) 70, 94, 95 fn. 3, (on Japan) 89–91, 131–2, (on Iwojima) 90, (on Luzon) 90 fn. 2, (in S.E.A.C.) 132, 404–5; superior to Japanese aircraft, 231–2; emergency landings by, on Iwojima, 240 fn. 2

Bain, Brigadier G. A.: 155, 178, 258 fn. 4

Baldwin, Air Marshal Sir John: 34

Bandon, Air Vice-Marshal the Earl of: commands 224 Group, 36; mentioned, 135, 405; appointed Joint Force Commander, 137 fn. 1; lands on Akyab, 142

Bangkok: railways to, (attacked) 403, 404, (photographic reconnaissance of) 408; air attacks on, 405

Banmauk: 19th and 36th Divisions make contact at, 145, 159

Barbey, Vice-Admiral D.C.: 94, 95 fn. 1

Barcol: 303, 304

Barlow, Lieut.-Colonel J. M.: 303

Bassein: 59, 60, 367, 407

Bastin, Brigadier G. E. R.: 195, 276, 277

Bastyan, Major-General E. M.: 245

Bawlake: Karen Levy operations in area of, 205, 332, 387 fn. 4; *15th Army* reaches area of, 387

Bawli Bazar: 19, 107, 138

Bayley, Lieut.-Colonel K.: 309

Beaufighters: 254, 406, 407

Beltang Lui: 49, 50

Bengal, Bay of: mentioned, 2 fn. 1; unlikelihood of Japanese fleet action in, 8; capture of Rangoon made practicable by Japanese weakness in, 9; British fleet being built up in, 9; Chiang Kai-shek on Allied failure to carry out operations in, 117; command of, regained, 214; East Indies Fleet safeguards, 341; air patrols over, 413

Beyts, Brigadier G. H. B.: 383

Bhamo: proposed capture of, 4, 51, 144; roads to, 4, 22–3, 41, 191; pipelines to, 18, 41, 123; Force 136 H.Q. near, 33; Japanese

Bhamo—*cont.*
plans to defend, 57, 144; *18th Division* in area of, 58; Chiang Kai-shek demands attack towards, 116; Chinese divisions to be withdrawn after capture of, 125; Allied troops in area of, 143, 145, 148; Japanese forces in area of, 143–4; capture of, 146–7; garrison of, 144, 146 fn. 2

Bhanbagta Gurung, Rifleman, V.C.: 345 fn. 2

Bhandari Ram, Sepoy, V.C.: 137 fn. 2

Bismarck Sea, U.S. escort carrier: 240

Black Prince, H.M. cruiser: 212 fn. 3

Blandy, Rear-Admiral W. H. P.: 236

Bogan, Rear-Admiral G. F.: 69 fn. 5, 74, 82

Bonin Islands: proposed operations against, 69–70, 91, *now see* Iwojima; attacked by B.29s, 90; in Japanese appreciation of American strategy, 226

Brain, Brigadier H. G. L.: 361, 390

British Pacific Fleet: mentioned, 94 fn. 3; formation and composition of, 118, 212; operations of, 212–13; leaves for Pacific, 212–13

Browning, Lieut.-General F. A. M.: becomes Chief of Staff, S.E.A.C., 119; visit of, to London, 201, 206–7

Bruce, Major-General C. Mc I. S.: 39, 135, 217 fn. 2

Bruce, Brigadier J.: 398

Budalin: airfield at, 172, 183, 253 fn. 2; captured, 176

Burauen: airfields at, 69, 83, 84 fn. 1, 86–7

Burma: *for rising in, see under* Force 136: alternative plans for operations in, 2–5, *now see* 'Capital' *and* 'Dracula'; Prime Minister's dislike of operations in, 6–7, 319; approved operations for, 12–13; operations for reconquest of, referred to, 18; Intelligence organizations and coverage in, 31–3; granted independence by Japan, 33; army/air cooperation for operations in, 34–6; airfields for support of offensive in, 37–8; object of operations in, 107, 241, 247, (referred to) 331; Allies ready to drive into, 51; Japanese plans and appreciations for, 56, 58–61, 357, (commented on) 433–5; effect on campaign in, (of withdrawal of Chinese troops and aircraft) 125, (of halting of Yunnan armies) 130, (of end of Salween campaign), 194; Wedemeyer's views on campaign in, 126; object of Slim's operations in, 164; effect of climate in, on operations and maintenance, 175, 176, 178, 183, 367, 373, 376, 387, 391, 393, 399; aircraft to supply civil population of, 201; Chiefs of Staff's views on operations in, 206–7; to be liberated at earliest date, 209; anti-submarine patrols off coast of, 213; policy on arming civil population of, 250–1; responsibility for security of, 279, 315; civilian refugees in, 293, 431; date for removal of American aircraft from, 319; decreasing Japanese air strength in, 401–3; discussion on role of Japanese air force in, 402; strategic air offensive in, 403; mapping of, 408–9; controversy between British and Americans on strategic policy in, 416; disappearance of

Burma—*cont.*
specialized formations for 1944-45 campaign in, 430; behaviour of civil population in, 430-1
Burma Intelligence Corps: 31
Burma National Army: raised, 33; prepares to fight Japanese, 33, 333-4; strength of, 33, 337; plans to operate with, ('Nation'), *see under* Force 136; mentioned, 335, 338, 395; rises, 337, 384 fn. 1, 388; unco-operative, 337; parties of, surrender, 387
Burma Road: proposed clearance of, 4; to form part of road link from Bengal to China, 4, 22; mentioned, 41, 320, 327; Japanese plans for offensive astride, 56-7; Allied forces on, quiescent, 57-8; effect of withdrawal of Chinese divisions on operations against, 131; operations to open, 147, 191, 193-5, (needed) 148; Japanese strength on, 194; opened, 194; to be secured, 241; Force 136 operations on, 249; responsibility for protection of, 279-81, 315, 318; Japanese losing interest in, 294; *56th Division* withdrawing south of, 320; under Allied control, 320
Burton, Brigadier G. W. S.: 267, 358, 392
Bush, Captain E. W.: 138 fn. 3, 219 fn. 2
Buthidaung: operations in area of, 137; captured, 139; I.W.T. craft assembled at, 138-9; XV Corps forward maintenance centre at, 140

California, American battleship: 94
Canberra, Australian heavy cruiser: 70
Canton: operations in area of, 54, 55, 116, 122; Americans to be prevented from securing bases in, 226
'Capital' Operation: submitted to C.O.S., 3-5; possible task for Special Force in, 4, 29, 165; resources needed for, 4-5, 107-10; discussions on, 6-12, 39, 106-10, (summarized and commented on) 415-17; Giffard's instructions on, 6; American views on, 11; approved by C.C.S., 12-13; maintenance of 14th Army during, 20, *now see under* Maintenance; possible airborne operations in, 28, 102, (referred to) 128; its first phase being anticipated, 39; directive for first two phases of, 107-8; 14th Army/3rd T.A.F. appreciation and plan for, 101-6; shortage of transport aircraft for, 125; effect of withdrawal of Chinese divisions and aircraft on, 126, 127, 129-31 *passim*; Wedemeyer's views on, 126; forces to be released from Arakan for, 136; airfields needed south of Akyab for, 136 fn. 4; progress of, 148; Slim's revised plan for, 164-7, *now see* 'Extended Capital'; last action in, 398; summarized, 420-1
Carton de Wiart, General Sir Adrian: 125 and fn. 1
Casualties: *see also* Sickness:
American: in 3rd Fleet, 93; in Iwojima, 238
British, Indian and African: in S.E.A.C. in first 6 months of 1944, 8-9; difficulty of

Casualties: British, Indian and African—*cont.*
evacuation of, from Kabaw Valley, 42, 44, 50; during 1944 monsoon, (in 9th Brigade) 46 fn. 1, (in XXXIII Corps) 160; planned evacuation of by air, (during 'Capital') 103, 106, 151, (from Arakan) 136, (during advance to Rangoon) 325, (R.A.F. squadron for) 409 fn. 4, 413, (method of) 412-13; at Pinwe, 145; in Irrawaddy crossings, 186 fn. 2, 263, 264; at Myitson, 196, 276, 277; at Kangaw, 222 fn. 1; in Myinmu bridgehead, 261 and fn. 1; in Nyaungu bridgehead, 268, 269; in Battle of Meiktila, 271, 288, 307, 308 fn. 4, 309 fn. 3, (total in IV Corps) 311; total in XXXIII Corps in Battle of Mandalay, 311; total in 14th Army to end of March, 311; in XV Corps in Arakan, 350; in advance to Rangoon, 359, 382, 385, 387, 389, (total in IV Corps) 398; in Battle of Irrawaddy, 365, 372 fn. 1, 373, 376; in modified 'Dracula', 394; total evacuated by air, 413
Japanese: on Tiddim road, 46 fn. 1; in China, 57, 58 fn. 1; on Northern front, 145, 147 fn, 1, 195, 227; in withdrawal to Irrawaddy, 177 fn. 1, 187; at Kangaw, 222 fn. 1; in Iwojima, 238; in Myinmu bridgehead, 261; in Nyaungu bridgehead, 265, 268, 285, 305 and fn. 4; in Battle of Meiktila, 268, 271 fn. 2, 287-8, 308 fns. 2 and 4, 309 fns. 1 and 3, (total) 313; in Mandalay area, 289, 301-2; in Kume area, 303; at Pyawbwe, 358 fn. 5, 359, 360, 361 fn. 1; in Battle of Rangoon Road, 382, 385, 386, 389 and fn. 3, 390, 391, 392 fn. 3, (total) 398; in Battle of Irrawaddy, 365, 372, 373, 374, 376, 380; in amphibious assault on Rangoon, 394
Cebu: *102nd Division* to defend, 68; battalions from, reinforce Leyte, 83 and fn. 1, 84
Celebes: responsibility for its defence, 54; Japanese forces in, 54 fn. 2, 69; carrier strikes on, 65; Japanese units moved from, 229, 233
Central Burma Stockpile: 104-5, 106, 202, 243, 244, 322, 324, 411
Central Front: *see also* Air Supply, Communications *and* Maintenance (during 'Capital' and 'Extended Capital'): directives for operations on, 1-2, 107-8; description of, and formations on, 2 fn. 1; proposed reinforcements for, from Arakan, 2; situation on, (August) 6, 39-40, (December) 171-2, (January) 179, (March) 283, (April) 355-6; planning for advance on, to begin, 6; maintenance of 14th Army on, 20-1; 'V' Force allotted to, 31; 221 Group responsible for close support on, 36; C.C.T.F. to control air transport and supply for, 37; airfields for support of, 38, 253-4; operations on, 41-50, 151-60, 175-82, 183-9, 253-73, 283-96, 297-313, 355-67, 369-80, 381-98; maintenance problems on, 102-6; Mountbatten's need to maintain momentum on, 130; estimated and actual Japanese dispositions on, 151-2, 157-8, 171-2, 179-80, 188,

Central Front—*cont.*

259 fn. 1, 262, 267; contact established with Northern front, 159; Mountbatten visits, 385

Ceylon: mentioned, 11, 119, 132, 135, 213, 327; 11th Army Group to provide forces for its defence, 107; aircraft based on, 214; East Indies Fleet based on, 341, 342; Headquarters in, 431

Ceylon, H.M. cruiser: 212 fn. 3, 393

Chambers, Major General H. M.: 351, 395 fn. 4, 396

Channer, Brigadier V. K. H.: 43

'Character' Operation: *see* Force 136

Chauk: 28th (E.A.) Brigade to threaten crossing opposite, 180, 256; operations to, from Nyaungu bridgehead, 181, 267, 269, 283, 284–5, 297–8; Japanese plans to hold, 267, 269, 285, 357, 363, 364; Japanese offensive from, 304–5, 306; operations to capture, 302, 324–5, 356, 362–6 *passim*, 370–1; mentioned, 327; topographical description of, 370; effect of its loss on Japanese plans, 378; air attacks on Chauk–Meiktila road, 406

Chaungmagyi Chaung: 19th Division's bridgehead on, 259, 283, 288; Japanese believed to be holding, 260

Cheduba Island: Japanese plans to hold, 56; proposed capture of, 109, 203, 215; occupation of, 219; not to be garrisoned, 220

Chengtu: American airfields at, 37 fn. 1, 71, 89 fn. 2, 131, (closed) 133, (Japanese learn of) 231

Chennault, Major-General C. L.: 22, 405

Chiang Kai-shek: and appointment of Stilwell as C.-in-C., 113, 115–16; and formation of A.L.F.S.E.A., 114; withdraws Yunnan armies, 116, 125, 194; receives message from Roosevelt, 116–17; asks for Stilwell's recall, 117, (referred to) 417; Wedemeyer becomes C.O.S. to, 117–18; his relationship with Wedemeyer, 123; and withdrawal of Chinese divisions from S.E.A.C., 124, 125, 128, 131, 278, (referred to) 157; decides Yunnan armies to halt at Wanting, 130 fn. 2; possibly issues secret instructions, 145 fn. 1, 275; and security of Burma Road, 280–1, 318; meets Mountbatten, 281; his views on operations in Burma, 281; issues instructions to N.C.A.C. troops, 317; Mountbatten's difficulties with, referred to, 418

Chief Civil Affairs Officer, Burma: 250, 251

Chief of Imperial General Staff: on need for specialist formations in airborne operations, 28; at Tolstoy Conference, 108 fn. 2; meets Mountbatten in Cairo, 109–10

Chiefs of Staff, American: offered and accept British naval unit for Pacific, 8–9, 12; their views on 'Capital' and 'Dracula', 11, (referred to) 416; allot aircraft, 12; issue directives, (for Pacific) 63, 68–9, (for long-range bombing of Japan) 89; decide priorities for C.B.I. Theatre, 22; agree with postponement of 'Dracula', 108; propose Stilwell as commander of Chinese armies, 113; divide C.B.I. Theatre, 117–18, (referred to) 417; propose Wheeler as Deputy Supreme Com-

Chiefs of Staff, American—*cont.*

mander, 118; and transfer of aircraft and formations to China, 124–7, 315, 317–19 *passim*; Wedemeyer reports to, 126; their proposed instructions to Wedemeyer, 126; their views on allocation of American resources to S.E.A.C., 127, 208–9, 315, 319; asked to urge limit on diversion to China, 131; agree to withdrawal of 20th Bomber Command, 133; and return of aircraft to S.E.A.C., 206–7; on S.E.A.C.'s responsibilities, 315

Chiefs of Staff, British: receive plans and appreciations from Mountbatten, 3, 10, 11, 106, 110, 252, 279, 316–18, 329, 335; require Mountbatten to come to London, 6; discuss operations in Burma and provision of forces, 6–9, 11, 108, (commented on) 415–17; decide role of British forces in Far East, 8; offer naval assistance for Pacific, 8–9; ask C.C.S. to approve 'Dracula', 9; at Octagon Conference, 11; recommend despatch of wheat to India, 16; and Special Force, 27, 29; decide to postpone 'Dracula', 108; approve 'Romulus' and 'Talon', 110; ask for plans for future operations, 110–11; and reorganization of S.E.A.C., 113–15 *passim*, (referred to) 417; agree with Mountbatten on aircraft for China, 125; and proposed instructions to Wedemeyer, 126–7; and withdrawal of formations to China, 126–7, 315–17, (referred to) 418; find transport aircraft for S.E.A.C., 201, 206–7, 329; and Browning's visit, 206; their views on allocation of American resources, 208; receive report from Leese, 316; not told of orders to Sultan, 317, 318; their views, (on 'Roger') 327, (on modified 'Dracula') 329–30; and rising in Burma, 336, 337

Chikuma, Japanese heavy cruiser: 81

China: policy towards, in Mountbatten's directives, 1, 13, (plans to implement) 3–4, (possible prejudice of) 107, 116, (undermined) 126; air link with, (to be maintained) 1, 13, 107, (to be protected by N.C.A.C.) 108, (importance of) 117, (safe) 123; supplies to, (policy on) 1, 4, 18, 22, 132–3, (airfields in India for) 37–8, (importance of) 117, (increasing) 123; road communications to, (development of) 1, 4, 13, 22–3, 41, 123, (Stilwell's views on) 5, (Japanese policy towards) 58, 433, 434, (not to be prejudiced) 107, (to be protected by N.C.A.C.) 108, 164, (operations to open) 116, 148, 191, (opened) 194, (American views on, in relation to strategy in Burma) 416; pipelines to, 4, 18, 22, 41, 123; policy of America towards, 22, 209, 315; American air forces in, 22, 37 fn. 4, 89 fn. 2, (operations of) 71, 94, 95 fn. 2, 131–3, (airfields of, destroyed) 122, (part of, withdrawn) 133, (Japanese to prevent build-up of) 228; Japanese aims in, 54, (*now see* 'Ichi-Go' Operation), 226, 228, (Wedemeyer's appreciation of) 123–4; suggested American landing on coast of, 63; airstrikes against coast of, 96; political situation in, 115, 123;

China—*cont.*
military situation in, 115, 126, (British views on) 130, 206–7, (its effect on S.E.A.C. operations) 157; Japanese units from, sent to Indo-China, 122, 229; transfer of aircraft and N.C.A.C. units to, 124–31, 164, 278–81, 315, 338–9, (effect of, on S.E.A.C.) 125–6, 129–31, 157, 164, 191, (C.O.S. views on) 206, (summarized and commented on) 418–20; Wedemeyer's plan 'Alpha' for offensive in, 124, 278–9 281; return of aircraft to S.E.A.C. from, 200–1, 207; decision on transfer of American resources to, 208–9; French troops escape to, 230; N.C.A.C. forces to be transferred in aircraft from, 280–1, 315, 317, 320

China–Burma–India Theatre: commanded by Stilwell, 3; priorities for, 22; American misuse of H.Q. in, 113; reorganization of, 117–18, (effect of, on allocation of resources) 208, (referred to) 417

China Sea: American fleet operations in, 91, 94, 95–6; Japanese plan to destroy invasion convoys in, 232

Chindits: *see* Special Force

Chindwin River: *for I.W.T. service on, see under* Communications: planned operations in valley of, 2, 4–5, 51, 108, 149; pursuit to and across, 6, 10, 40–2, 150, 153–6 *passim*, 160, 171; bridge over, at Kalewa, (planned) 20, 103–4, 156, (engineer force for) 151 fn. 1, (opened) 160, (replaced) 166 fn. 3, 199–200; Japanese withdrawal across, 43 and fn. 4, 56, 151, 157; possibility of 14th Army having to withdraw west of, 131; difficulty of 14th Army's concentration on, 150; movement of troops and armour east of, to be investigated, 154; 552 Sub-Area established in valley of, 327 fn. 1

Chinese Army: American re-equipment of, 22, 123, 132; Stilwell proposed as C.-in-C. of, 113; estimated effect of 'Ichi-Go' offensive on, 123; Wedemeyer's plan 'Alpha' for, 124, 278–9, 281; airlift needed for, 124–5; state of, 126; to undertake protection of Burma Road, 318

XI Army Group: in operations on Salween front, 147, 193–4; composition of 147 fn. 2; N.C.A.C. to link up with, 191; its reluctance to advance, 192; its poor security, 193; contacted by N.C.A.C., 194

Armies:

New First: to go into training camp, 40; composition of, 143; in operations on Northern front, 143, 146, 148, 191–4 *passim*; its reluctance to advance, 192–3, 275

2nd: 147

New Sixth: 40, 143, 145

6th: 147

53rd: 147

71st: 147

Divisions:

14th: withdrawal of, from N.C.A.C., 128, 129, 131, 145, 164, 191; on Northern front, 143

22nd: withdrawal of, from N.C.A.C., 124,

Chinese Army—*cont.*
22nd Division—*cont.*
126–9 *passim*, 131, 145 and fn. 1, 164, (effect of, on Sultan's plans) 191; in operations on Northern front, 143–5 *passim*; effect of its advance, 146; relieved, 192

30th: in operations on Northern front, 40, 143, 147, 148, 191, 192, 275

38th: withdrawal of, from N.C.A.C., 124, 126, 127, 128, 130, 131; in operations on Northern front, 143, 144, 146–7, 148, 191, 192, 275, 278, 320; effect of its advance, 146

50th: 128, 130; in operations on Northern front, 143, 144, 146, 148, 191, 192, 194–6 *passim*, 275, 320; doubtful co-operation of, 144–5

200th: 147

Infantry Regiments:
1st: 275, 320
65th: 145
66th: 145
90th: 192
112th: 146
113th: 146
114th: 146
148th: 144

Chinese/American Armies: on Northern front, 2 fn. 1; based on Myitkyina, 23; artillery units of, in attack on Pinbaw, 40; command of, 117, 118; withdrawal of, to China, 124–6 *passim*, 130–1, 145 fn. 1, 164, 278–81 *passim*, 315–17 *passim*, 338, (result of "Ichi-Go' offensive) 122; frequent failure of, to comply with orders, 145 fn. 1; reluctance of, to advance, 192–3; and protection of Burma Road, 279–80, 315; to be spearhead of offensive in China, 281; decreasing opposition to advance of, 294; instructions from Generalissimo to, 317–18

Chinese Yunnan Armies: proposed operations for, 3–5 *passim*, 191, (referred to) 51; operations of, 39, 41, 147–8, 193–5; withdrawal of, across Salween, (threatened) 116, 125, (ordered) 194, (effect of, on N.C.A.C.) 197, (effect of, on IV Corps' advance) 356; proposal for Stilwell to continue in command of, 117; their co-ordination with N.C.A.C., 118; A.L.F.S.E.A. to control their units in Burma, 118; effect of their halting at Wanting, 130; air supply for, 131; Japanese forces opposing, 144, 193; their slow advance, 147–8, 192; their Salween campaign assessed, 194; their numerical superiority, 197 fn. 1; in reorganized Chinese army, 281 fn. 1

Chiringa: road to, 19; airfield at, 38; XV Corps reserve at, 39, 139; 81st (W.A.) Division, (based on) 135, (to withdraw to) 218

Chitose, Japanese carrier: 81

Chittagong: airfields, and their protection and use, in area of, 4 fn. 1, 20, 38, 200–2, 247–8, 322, 375, 411, (referred to) 425, 426; L. of C. through, 15, 17, 19, 20, (by sea for forward divisions) 246; port of, (development of) 16, 17, (pipelines from) 16 fn. 1, 18,

Chittagong—*cont.*
(congestion at) 141 fn. 3, 246, (supplies through) 203; considered most worthwhile enemy objective, 101; as a base, (for 'Dracula') 102, (for assault on Ramree) 219, (for I.W.T. fleet) 245 fn. 2, (for 'Stanza') 331, (for 82nd (W.A.) Division) 346-7 *passim*

Chiyoda, Japanese carrier: 81

Chocolate Staircase: 49, 50

Chokai, Japanese heavy cruiser: 79

Christison, Lieut.-General A. F. P. (later Sir Philip): commands XV Corps, 39; mentioned, 135; plans, (to clear north Arakan and capture Akyab) 136, (referred to) 138, (to capture Ramree) 214, (to complete his task) 217, (to help 14th Army) 223, (to prevent Japanese reinforcing Irrawaddy front) 343, 346-7, (discussed) 351; appointed Joint Force Commander, 137 fn. 1; directs operations, 137, 217-18, 220, 223, 344; his appreciations on Japanese forces, 141, 222-3, 342-3; lands in Akyab, 142; insists on Akyab operation continuing, 142; knighted, 161; warned, (of possible extension of operations) 218, (of reduction in air supply) 224; flies to see Slim, 223; reorganizes to make best use of air supply, 343; receives instructions from A.L.F.S.E.A., 344; on necessity for I.W.T. reinforcements, 344-5; issues new directive, 348

Chungking: mentioned, 115, 121, 125 fn. 1; Wedemeyer's plans for defence of, 123-4; Japanese to abandon any operations against, 228; Mountbatten visits, 280, 281

Churchill, Rt. Hon. W. S.: and operations in Burma, 6-7, 11, 319, (referred to) 415-6; decides on role of British forces in Far East, 8; at Octagon Conference, 11, (approves directive for Mountbatten) 11, (his decision with Roosevelt) 116; asked to agree to disbandment of Special Force, 29; warns Mountbatten of postponement of 'Dracula', 108; meets Mountbatten in Cairo, 108, 109-10; at Tolstoy Conference, 108 fn. 1; his representative in Chungking, 125 fn. 1; at Argonaut Conference, 208-9; appeals to General Marshall, 319

Claudcol: in Pyawbwe operations, 358-60 *passim*

Climate: *see* Burma

'Cloak' Deception Scheme: *see* IV Corps

Cocos Islands: possible development of, 107

Collingwood, Brigadier R. G.: 257, 364 fn. 1; in operations, (in Irrawaddy crossing) 264, (at Myingyan and Taungtha) 270, 285

Combat Cargo Task Force: *see under* Air Forces, Allied

Combined Army Air Transport Organization: formation and function of, 37; reports on impracticibility of airborne operation, 155; 'teething troubles' of, 183

Combined Chiefs of Staff: issue directives to Mountbatten, (June 1944) 1, (referred to) 415, (September) 12-13, (February) 209; asked for decision on S.E.A.C. operations, 5, 9; decisions of, (at Sextant referred to) 8,

Combined Chiefs of Staff—*cont.*
(at Octagon) 12-13, 64, (at Argonaut) 209; and formation of A.L.F.S.E.A., 113-14; and instructions to Wedemeyer, 126; and transfer of resources to China, 127, 128, 131, 317, 338; Mountbatten anticipates approval of, 129; send instructions to Mountbatten, 281

Combined Fleet: *see under* Japanese Navy

Combined Operations: (in Arakan), discussed, 350

Combined Operations Pilotage Parties: role of, 30; in operations in Arakan, 138 fn. 3, 216

Comilla: Headquarters at, 34, 118; airfield at, 38, 106, 200, (squadron for evacuating casualties based on) 409 fn. 4; reinforcement camps to be at, 106; move of air base from, 201-2; method of evacuating casualties to hospitals at, 412-13

Communications: Giffard's requirements for developing, 3; Leese's plan for reorganizing, 204

Arakan: description and capacity of, 19-20; to be secured, 107; increasing importance of, 202, (referred to) 204, 425; opening of Taungup–Prome road, 219, 241, 243, 244

Assam and Eastern Bengal: development of, 16-17; capacity of (August), 17; estimated requirements and capacity of, for 1945, 18-19; 14th Army's maintenance to be switched from, 202

Central Front: required development of, (for 'Capital') 20-1, 102-5, 149-50, 154-5, (referred to) 424, (for 'Extended Capital') 166, 172-3, 248, 321; capacity of, by October, 21; to 5th Division, 48; reduction of troops on, 103; development of, 151, 156-7, 173 fns. 1 and 2, 174-5, 182-3, 199; engineering units for, 151 fn. 1; to be investigated east of Chindwin, 155; across Zibyu Taungdan, 158; effect on, of redeployment plan, 202-3; to Rangoon (rehabilitation of railways), 322, 324, 326; delay in clearing, to Myingyan, 323

Inland Water Transport: in Arakan, 19, 138, 139, 140, 218 fn. 1, (importance of) 245, 344-5, (size of) 245 fn. 2; on the Chindwin, (considered) 20-1, 103, (ordered) 149, (build-up of) 156, 199-200, 203, 244, (extension of, to Myingyan) 166, 322, (in army/air plan) 247-8, 249, (shortfall of deliveries by) 317, (target capacity of) 326, (tonnages delivered from Kalewa by) 409, (creation of, commented on) 426; on the Irrawaddy, 166, 322, 325, 326, (craft for) 325 fn. 4, (tonnages to be delivered by) 243, 325, 326, (more craft needed for) 322, 326, (possible shortfall of deliveries by) 324

Japanese (in Burma): plans and operations to cut, 5, 33, 39, 136, 217, 220, 223, 271, 296, 297, 324, 332, 333; information on, 33, 218; effect on, (of loss of Akyab) 216 fn. 1, (of loss of Meiktila) 273; air operations against, 311-12, 401, 403, 404, 406-7

Northern Front: development of, 22-3, 41;

Communications: Northern Front—*cont.*
  Mogaung railway to become 36th Division's L. of C., 41, (being raided) 144
'Conclave' Deception Scheme: 288 fn. 1, 367
Coryton, Air Marshal W. A.: 36, 203, 330
Cottrell-Hill, Brigadier R. C.: 219, 351 fn. 1
Cowan, Major-General D. T.: commands 17th Division, 257; in operations, (to Meiktila) 266, 267, (at Meiktila) 270, 271, 286, 288, 307, 310, (to Pyawbwe) 309, 355, 357, 359, 360, (to Pegu) 391–2, 393 fn. 1
Cox's Bazar: communications to, 19; covered by R.A.F. defence organization, 34; airfield at, 38; American squadrons operating from, 246
Crowther, Brigadier W. A.: 257, 372, 376
'Culverin' Operation: *see* Sumatra
Cumberland, H.M. cruiser: 342, 393

'D' Division: 30–1
53rd Deception Company: 362 fn. 4
Daingbon Chaung: 220, 221
Dakotas (transport aircraft): in support of operations in Burma, 42, 179, 268, 394, 407, 424; needed for modified 'Dracula', 329; in 3rd Combat Cargo Group, 409; evacuation of casualties by, 413
Dalet: operations towards, 224, 343–4; *21st Regiment* thought to be in area of, 342; occupied, 345; Japanese forces moving to, 348
Dalet Chaung: 222, 223; Japanese ferry and I.W.T. base on, destroyed, 223; operations towards, 224; Japanese forces on, 343–4; 4th (W.A.) Brigade to move down, 344
Davao: Japanese force to defend, 68; reinforcements sent to Leyte from, 83, 84
Davidson, Major-General H. C.: 37
Davies, Major-General H. L.: 39, 135 fn. 3, 252
Davison, Rear-Admiral R. E.: 69 fn. 5, 74
Dawson, Brigadier J. A.: 37
Deception Plans: of 14th Army, 173–4; of IV Corps, 174, 256–7; of A.L.F.S.E.A., 366–7
Denholm-Young, Brigadier E. J.: 46, 381
Denning, Major-General R. F. S.: 244; report of committee of, 244–5, (used as basis for fresh administrative plan) 247
Dimapur: operations to cover, 1–2; railhead at, 15, 17, 19; road to, 17; pipelines at, 18, 105; maintenance of 14th Army forward of, 20; extension of road from, to Kalewa, 20–1; L. of C. Transport Column working from, 21, 105, 322; deliveries by road forward of, 21; airfield at, 38
Dimoline, Brigadier W. A.: 257, 269 fn. 1
Dinjan: airfields in area of, 38 and fn. 5
Dinwiddie, Brigadier H. W.: in operations, (against Pakokku) 257, 269, (in Nyaungu bridgehead) 285, (towards Seikpyu) 363, 365, (on Minbu–Ngape road) 376
Disease: *see* Sickness
Dohazari: railhead at, 15, 19; L. of C. to Arakan from, 19; airfield at, 38, (economic range from) 200

Dolluang: operations at, 50, 152
Donbaik: proposed capture of, 136; occupied, 140
'Dracula' Operation: submitted to Chiefs of Staff, 3–4, 5; discussions on, and provision of forces for, 6–12, 101–3, 106–7, 108–10, (summarized and commented on) 415–17; American views on, 11; development of India base for, 11, (referred to) 18; Combined Chiefs of Staff approve, 12–13; airfields for (referred to), 20; provision of airborne formations for, 28; postponed, 108, (referred to) 416; forces to be released from Arakan for, 136; mounting base for, (to be secured) 139, (suggested reduction of work on) 166; resources for, (placed at A.L.F.-S.E.A.'s disposal) 241, (needed for future operations) 252; revival of, in modified form, 327–31, (commented on) 427–8; D-day for, 328–30 *passim*, 351–2; forces for, 328, 349; effect of launching of, (on future strategy) 328, 329, (on Arakan operations) 348; airfields for, 329, 330, (Mountbatten's concern over) 384–5, (captured) 386, 388; aircraft for, 329, 330; airborne operations in, 329–30, (referred to in Retrospect) 427; to have overriding priority, 330; plan for, 330, 351–2; air support for, 330, 388; shipping programme for, 331–2; intelligence for, 337; control of, 328, 350; directives for, 351–2; Assault Forces Commanders for, 351; to be carried out, if Rangoon not already captured, 352; XXXIII Corps' operations subsidiary to, 375; launched, 393–7, (discussed) 399; landing craft lost during, 395
Dufferin and Ava, 4th Marquis of: 301 fn. 2
DUKWS: needed for operations in Arakan, 110 fn. 4; in Arakan operations, 139; in support of XXXIII Corps, 173, 325 fn. 4; in Irrawaddy crossing, 260 fn. 3, 263
Dulag: airfield at, 69, 72, 84 fn. 1, 86
Dyer, Brigadier G. M.: 44, 154, 171, 375

'E' Group: 31
Eastern Air Command: *see under* Air Forces, Allied
Eastern Fleet: ceases to exist, 118, 212; to support assault on Akyab, 136; composition of, 211; operations of, 211–12
East Indies Fleet: formed, 118; composition of, 212; operations of, 341–2, 413; in modified 'Dracula', 352, 393–4
Elephant Point: airborne assault on, (examined) 241, 244, (planned) 329, 330, 352, (carried out) 394, (referred to) 428; mentioned, 399 fn. 3
Emperor, H.M. escort carrier: 342, 395 fn. 2
Empress, H.M. escort carrier: 342, 393
Europe: situation in, in relation to forces, (for 'Dracula') 7, 8, 11–12, 108, (for liberation of Burma) 209; Indian Army troops in, 15 fn. 2; effect of war in, on British infantry replacements for S.E.A.C., 26

Evans, Brigadier-General F. W.: 37
Evans, Major-General G. C.: commands, (5th Division) 39, (7th Division) 157 fn. 3; in pursuit to the Chindwin, 42, 46, 47; contracts typhoid, 48 fn. 2; to establish bridgehead, (over the Irrawaddy) 181, (at Nyaungu) 256; his deception plans, 256–7; in Irrawaddy crossing, 257; in Meiktila operations, 269, 284, 286, 304–5; in operations, (to capture Seikpyu and Chauk) 356, 362–5, 371, (to capture Yenangyaung) 372–3, (west of the Irrawaddy) 376, 379; confers with Stopford 375
'Extended Capital' Operation: *see also* Maintenance *and* Air Supply: plans for, 164–7, 242–3, (conditionally accepted) 254, (discussed) 421–3, 428; planning for fourth phase begins, 241

Feni: airfield at, 38, 106, 200
Ferries: across the Brahmaputra, 17; across the Chindwin, (at Thaungdut) 156, (at Tonhe) 159; at junction of Myittha and Manipur Rivers, 175; across the Irrawaddy, (at Kyauktalon) 185, 362, (at Ngazun) 263, (at Nyaungu) 266 fn. 1, 362, (at Ava) 362; across the Shweli, (at Myitson) 277, (at Shwegyin) 390
Festing, Major-General F. W.: commands 36th Division, 40; in operations, (at Pinbaw) 40–1, (at Pinwe) 144–5, (on the Shweli) 196, 275, 277, (towards Mongmit) 278, (to capture Kalaw) 388; asks that Chinese comply with orders, 144; warned of transfer to 14th Army, 320; responsible for Mandalay area, 361
Field Broadcasting Unit: 301 fn. 2
Findhorn, H.M. frigate: 213
Flamingo, H.M. sloop: 219, 223
Fleet Air Arm: India to maintain 30 squadrons of, 16
Flewett, Brigadier J. G.: 258, 290, 299, 361, 383
Force 136: tasks of, 30, 32; amalgamation of, with 'Z' Force, 32, 33 fn. 1; activities of, (in Arakan) 33, (on Northern front) 33–4, 192, (on Central front) 249; operations of, with A.F.O. and B.N.A., 'Nation', (planned) 33, (progress of) 205–6, 333–4, 337, (political implications of) 250–1, 335–7, (mentioned) 332, 407; provides information for air forces, 33, 408; operations of, with Karen Levies, 'Character', (planned) 205, (progress of) 249–50, (Slim's recommendations on) 332–3, (begin) 387 fn. 4, (mentioned) 407; and arming of A.F.O., 250–1, 334; to establish H.Q. alongside 14th Army, 333; directive for Jedburgh teams of, 334–5, 336–7; to provide intelligence for modified 'Dracula', 337; and exfiltration of Aung San, 338; in deception plan 'Conclave', 367; in modified 'Dracula', 394; air support for, 407–8
Forman, Brigadier J. F. R.: 219, 346

Formosa: British wish to participate in operations against, 8; mentioned, 22, 88; Japanese plans for defence of, 43–4, 66, 226, (referred to) 435; argument over capture of, 63, (referred to) 68; directive for its invasion never issued, 69; carrier strikes and bomber attacks on, 70, 94, 95, 132, (referred to) 88; effect of exaggerated Japanese claims in air battles over, 70–1, 88; aircraft from, for *4th Air Army*, 84; *1st Air Fleet* in, 97; build-up of garrison in, 227–8 *passim*; role of air forces in, 232
Fort Dufferin: description of, 290; operations against, 290–2, 299–301; Japanese forces in, 300
Fort White: mentioned, 20; operations towards, 49, 50, 152–3; enemy units in area of, 152
Forward Airfield Maintenance Organization: 106, 286
Foul Point: operations towards, 138, 140–1; attack on Akyab to be mounted from, 141; F.M.A. at, 141 fn. 3
Fowkes, Major-General C. C.: commands 11th (E.A.) Division, 39; task of, 42; assumes operational control, 43; in operations in Kabaw valley, 44, 153
Franklin, American light cruiser: 80 fn. 3
Fraser, Admiral Sir Bruce: 94 fn. 2, 118, 211, 212
Fuller, Major-General H. H.: 118, 247
Fullerton, Colonel R.: 398–9
Fuso, Japanese battleship, 74, 77

Galletly, Brigadier T. H. S.: 269 fn. 1, 284
Gambia, New Zealand cruiser: 212 fn. 3
Gambier Bay, American escort carrier: 79
Gangaw: Japanese plans to hold, 44, 56, 66; situation at (December), 171; attacked, 174–5; 7th Division in area of, 179
Gardiner, Lieut.-Colonel S.: 289 fn. 1
Garnons-Williams, Captain G. A.: 30
Garrod, Air Marshal Sir Guy: 119, 247
General Reserve Engineer Force: 151 fn. 1
German Navy:
U-boats of, in Indian Ocean, 213–14, (referred to) 413
Germany: progress of war against, in relation to forces, (for 'Dracula') 7, 8, 11, 108, (for liberation of Burma) 209; Japanese aims to mediate between U.S.S.R. and, 54, (failure of) 432–3; invasion of Formosa contingent on defeat of, 69
Gerty, Brigadier B. C. H.: 215, 223
Gian Singh, Naik, V.C.: 270 fn. 1
Gibbons, Brigadier H.: 217
Giffard, General Sir George: receives directive from Mountbatten, 1–2; his proposals for implementing directive, 2–3; confers with Mountbatten, 3; issues instructions, (to Slim) 6, 149, (to Stratemeyer) 6, (to Christison) 136; his views on operations in Burma, 10, (referred to) 417; told of C.O.S.'s wishes on 'Capital' and 'Dracula', 11; recommends standardization of infantry divi-

Giffard, General Sir George—*cont.*
sions, 25, (referred to) 430; and formation of Indian airborne division, 28; confers with Slim, 42, (his instructions following on this referred to) 416; comments on joint army/ air plan, 101; advocates operations in Arakan, 109, 136; replacement of, 113–14, 118, (referred to) 417; his refusal to move to Ceylon referred to, 431–2

Godavari, R.I.N. sloop: 213

Godusara: 135, 137

Gokteik Gorge: viaduct over, destroyed, 320

Goppe Bazar: 39, 135

Gracey, Major-General D. D.: commands 20th Division, 171; in advance to Monywa, 176; in Irrawaddy crossing, 258, 260; in operations to Kyaukse, 288, 292, 356; in Meiktila operations, 294, 303; in drive down Irrawaddy, 362, 371, 375; confers with Stopford, 375

Greeves, Brigadier S.: 176, 260, 262, 302 fn. 3

Grimshaw, Brigadier E. H.: 382–3, 385

Gwa: mentioned, 32; *55th Division* to hold area of, 60; Allied estimate of Japanese strength in area of, 218; proposed operations at, 349

Gwegyo: proposed capture of, 364; Japanese plan to defend, 364; occupied, 370; mentioned, 371, 372

Halmaheras: 64–5

Hankow: 54, 55, 115

Halsey, Vice-Admiral W. F.: proposes seizure of Leyte, 64; in assault on Palaus, 65–6; in invasion of Leyte, 69, 84; in battle for Leyte Gulf, 74–6, 78, 81–2; attacks reinforcement convoys, 84–5; operations of, during Luzon invasion, 95–6; achievement of, 96

Haraden, American destroyer: 92

Hardy, Brigadier G. R.: 135

Hastings Harbour: 109, 342

Hathazari: airfield at, 38, 106, (economic range from) 200

Hedley, Brigadier R. C. O.: 267, 358, 392

Hendricks, Brigadier N. C.: 43, 153

Hengyang: 54, 55, 116

Henzada: mentioned, 32; proposed operations towards, 165, 166, 168; estimate of Japanese forces in area of, 218

Hill, Captain D. C.: 216

Hinoki, Japanese destroyer: 95 fn. 1

Hirst, Brigadier J. E.: 139, 216

Hlaingdet: 313, 361, 383

Hlegu: last action in 'Capital' fought at, 398

Holmes, Colonel R. J.: 21

Honda, Lieut.-General M.: commands *33rd Army*, 56; receives orders, (from Kawabe) 56, (from Kimura) 59, 296, 357; discontinues offensive, 57; redisposes forces, 58; directs operations on Salween front, 146, 147, 193, 195; critical position of, 194; achievement of, 197; at *Burma Area Army* conference, 272; in Meiktila counter-offensive, 296, 312–13; forces under his control, 298; discussion on Kimura's orders to, 357;

Honda, Lieut.-General M.—*cont.*
escapes, 360, 385; orders evacuation of Pyawbwe, 360, (discussed) 383; his hopes of reforming army and offering battle unavailing, 381; decides to withdraw to Pyinmana, 383–4; loses touch with *49th Division*, 384 fn. 1; his troops out of his control, 387; orders withdrawal to the Sittang, 388

Hong Kong: air strikes against, 96

Honshu: formations for defence of, 228 fn. 2; fast carrier attacks on, 237

Hopin: 36th Division concentrates in area of, 41; 50th Chinese Division at, 143

Houston, American heavy cruiser: 70

Howe, H.M. battleship: 211, 212

Hparybin: fighting at, 139, 140; Japanese withdraw from, 141

Hsenwi: proposed capture of, 4; slow progress towards, 148; Force 136 operations in area of, 192; Japanese forces at, 193, 195; operations towards, 194; captured, 275

Hsipaw: proposed operations in area of, 4; operations towards, 194, 275; Chinese not to advance beyond, 280, 317; entered, 320

Htinzin: 43, 44, 156

Htizwe: advance of 82nd (W.A.) Division to, 138, 140, 141

Hunan Province: Japanese reach boundary of, 55; American airfields in, destroyed, 122; Chinese proposals for recapture of, 281

Hunter, H.M. escort carrier: 395 fn. 2

Hurley, Major-General P. J.: 115, 117

Hurricane Fighter-Bombers: in operations in Burma, 175, 184, 186, 362, 406

Hutchinson, Brigadier H. P. L.: 395, 396

Hutton, Brigadier R. A.: 221

Hyuga, Japanese battleship: 95

'*Ichi-Go*' Operation: aim of, 54; progress of, 54–5, 116 (referred to) 113, 115; resumed, 121–2; results of, 122–3

Illustrious, H.M. fleet carrier: 211, 212

Imperial General Headquarters: confer with new Cabinet, 53; issue new strategic directive, 53–4, (referred to) 435; expect Philippines to be next American objective, 54, (referred to) 435; revise agreement on Southern Region defence, 54; make changes in Burma Higher Command, 58; consider withdrawal from Burma, 58, (commented on) 433, 434–5; issue new directive to *Southern Army*, 58, (referred to) 433; reinforce Palaus, 65; issue orders, (on 'SHO-1') 67, 70–1, (referred to) 73, 435, (to *5th Fleet*) 71; have no intention of taking Kunming, 124; their reaction to carrier-borne raids on Japan, 237; reconsider and plan general strategy and home defence, 225–33 *passim*, (referred to) 435–6; their appreciation of American strategy, 225–6; their views on situation in Southern Region, 229, 233–4; order Indo-China to be put under military control, 230; plan air operation to destroy invasion convoys, 232;

Imperial General Headquarters—cont.
mentioned, 365 fn. 1; situation facing (August), 432–3

Imphal: Japanese to be cleared from area of, 1–2; operational situation in area of, 2, 6; Slim sets up tactical H.Q. at, 2; enough forces to meet possible offensive against, 9–10; L. of C. Road Transport organization operating to and forward of, 21; size of force to be maintained forward of, 21; covered by R.A.F. defence organization, 34; airfield at, 38, 106, (squadron based on) 253; troops in area of, 40 and fn. 2, 150, 171; road to, from Tiddim, disintegrates, 48; pipeline to, 105, 149; IV Corps' Advanced H.Q. at, 150; knighting ceremony at, 161; need for all-weather communications from, 166

Imphal, Battle of: importance of, 1; mentioned, 2, 102 fn. 1, 215 fn. 2, 273 fn. 3; repair of communications after, 21; lack of information during, 32; exploitation of, complete, 41; Japanese reinforcements during, 41 fn. 3, 151 fn. 3, 267 fn. 3; Japanese ordered to abandon, 56; Japanese rearguards to cover removal of stores for, 151–2; British commanders knighted for services in, 161

Imphal Force: 44, 155 fn. 1

Imphal Plain: cleared, 6, 39; airfields on, (referred to) 20, (named) 38, (for 'Capital') 103, 106, (too far back for 'Extended Capital') 200, 410, 424, (move of transport aircraft from) 201, (in army/air administrative plans) 247, 248, 322; 14th Army resumes administrative control of, 21

Imphal Road: communications to be established on, 1; reopened, 2, (referred to) 21; dependence of 14th Army on, 20; planned extension of, to Kalewa, 20–1; capacity of, 21

Inbaung: airstrip to be built at, 157

Indainggale: airstrips to be built at, 157

Indainggyi: L. of C. Road Transport organization to operate to, 21, 105; development of stockpile at, 103–5, 199; Japanese troops holding, 152; operations against, 153–4; road reaches, 156; airfields to be developed near, 157; H.Q. 14th Army moves from, 254; tonnages carried by road to, 409 fn. 3

Indaw: *53rd Division* in area of, 44; proposed capture of, 51, 108, 144; in Japanese withdrawal, 56; 19th Division moving to, 130; operations towards, 144; capture of, 145, (effect of) 148; 36th Division in area of, 148, (19th Division to contact) 157, 158; situation in area of (December), 148; movement of troops and armour to, to be investigated, 154; *53rd Division* thought to be covering, 158

Indaw (Oil): 154, 160

Indefatigable, H.M. fleet carrier: 212

India: development of, as a base, (for 'Dracula') 11, (for S.E.A.C.) 15–17; size of army of, 15 and fn. 2; economic situation in, 15–16; forces to be maintained in, 16; development and capacity of north-eastern Ls. of C. in, 16–19; standardization of infantry divisions in, 25–6; shortage of British infantry replacements in, 26–7; clandestine and para-military formations in, 30–1; airfield expansion programme in, 37–8; N.C.A.C. to be responsible for security of Assam in, 108; administrative tasks of, referred to, 425; refugee organization in, 431

India—cont.

India–Burma Theatre: Sultan takes command of, 117–18; decision on American resources deployed in, 208–9, (referred to) 279

India Command: deficit of arms in, 26–7; to find air-landing brigade, 28; and formation of Indian airborne division, 28; shares control of 'E' Group, 31

India, General Headquarters: mentioned, 25; its reserve, (2nd Division in) 27, (use of) 109, 252; Intelligence Director of, 30; responsibility of, regarding 'Dracula', 331

Indianapolis, American cruiser: 263 fn. 4

Indian National Army: *1st Division* of, (disintegrates) 41, (to withdraw into Burma) 56, (surrenders) 387, (composition of) 387 fn. 2; units of, (in *15th Army*) 59, 284, (in Nyaungu–Pagan area) 60, 188, 266, 305, (in Mount Popa area) 304, (at Legyi) 363 and fn. 4; surrenders by, 265, 371, 375, 379, 386, 387; deserting, 333; *2nd Division* of, 363 fn. 2, 364; prisoners of, taken, 365, 372, 386

Indian Ocean: Japanese to maintain existing position in, 54; diversionary operations in, 211–12; enemy submarine activity in, 213–14; command of, regained, 214, (effect of) 341; air reconnaissance over, 413; immunity of Allied shipping in, 413

Indin: 139

Indo-China: carrier aircraft sweeps over coast of, 95–6; Japanese reinforcements for, 122, 188, 229, 360 fn. 2; *Southern Army* to hold, 226, 229; garrison in, 229; *Southern Army* assumes control of, 229–30; airfields in, attacked, 403

Indomitable, H.M. fleet carrier: 211, 212

Inland Water Transport; *see under* Communications

Inoue, Lieut.-General S.: 65

Intelligence: *see also* Force 136, 'V' Force, 'Z' Force, etc.: Slim's criticism of organizations for, 32; decisions on how to improve, 32–3; photographic reconnaissance for, 408

Inter-Service Liaison Department: 30, 33

Irrawaddy River: *for I.W.T. service on, see under* Communications: mentioned, 32, 143, 144, 145; in Japanese defensive plans, 56, 58–61 *passim*, 186, (referred to) 215; reported Japanese withdrawal across, 163; establishment of bridgeheads on, (at Pakokku) 165, 168, 172, (at Thabeikkyin) 174, 178–9, 180, 181, 184, 188–9; plans for crossing of, 255–7, (discussed) 422–3; crossing of, 258–66, (effect of, on Japanese plans) 272, (discussed) 429–30; XXXIII Corps to advance down, 297, 324–5, 356, 362, (I.W.T. for) 326; enemy strength west of, increasing, 304; maintenance of force operating down, 322; B.N.A. in delta of,

Irrawaddy River—*cont.*
337; Japanese reinforcements sent to, from Arakan, 342-3, 347, 357, 377, (air operations to prevent) 407; Battle of the, 362-80; Japanese plans for withdrawal down, 364-5, 369, 374; R.A.F. deployment down, 366; Japanese plans to cross, 377-9, (XXXIII Corps to stop) 380; Japanese craft on, attacked, 407

Ise, Japanese battleship: 95
Ito, Haruo: 396
Iwabachi, Rear-Admiral S.: 99
Iwojima: airfields on, 90, 235, 236, 238, 240; invasion of, (proposed) 91, 92, (forces for) 236, (carried out) 237-8, (American casualties in) 238; description and importance of, 235; garrison on, 236, (casualties in) 238; pre-invasion bombing of, 236; Japanese failure to attack shipping off, 240, (referred to) 436; effect of its loss, on Japan, 436

Japan: object of Allies in war against, 12; grants independence to Burma, 33; air attacks on, 53, 89-91, 132, 236-7, (effect of) 225, 232, 237, (referred to) 235, 240; new Cabinet formed in, 53, (referred to) 435, (resigns) 436; Supreme War Direction Council in, 53, 54; strategic situation of, (July-August) 53-4, (January) 225-7, (referred to) 432-3, 435-6; its communications with Southern Region, 53, 63; defence plans of, 54, 226-8, 230-3, (referred to) 66, (return of aircraft for, referred to) 401-2; economic situation of, 63-4, 225; mentioned, 82; *Combined Fleet's* carriers based on, 87; fails to appreciate true effect of 'Ichi-Go' offensive, 122-3; Wedemeyer's appreciation of its intentions, 123-4; importance of Iwojima to, 235; desperate position of (April), 436
Japanese Air Force: situation of, in Burma (June 1944), 34; apparent weakness of, in Philippines, 64; its role in defence of Philippines, 66-7, (assessed) 188; attacks by, (in Pacific) 70, 90, 92-4 *passim*, 238-9, (in China) 132, (in Burma) 142, 179, 220, 266, 382, 386-7, (on Eastern Fleet) 211-12; effect of its exaggerated claims on 'SHO 1' operation, 70-1, (referred to) 88; gains control over Leyte, 84; losses of, (claimed) 93 fn. 2, 96, 237, 350, (actual) 212, 342; its strength in Luzon, 97; performance of its aircraft, 132, 231, 232 fn. 1, 402; reorganization, build-up and role of, in Japan, 230-3; its decline in Burma, 402-3
Air Armies:
    1st: 230-1, 232
    3rd: 233, 401-2
    4th: role of, (in 'SHO-1') 67, 73, (in defence of Luzon) 97; composition of, and reinforcements for, 68; reinforced, 68, 84, 86; in operations in Leyte, 86; its airmen converted to infantry, 97
    5th: 55, 132 fn. 3, 232
    6th: 232, 237

Japanese Air Force—*cont.*
Air Divisions:
    2nd: 68, 74 fn. 1, 233
    4th: 68, 233
    5th: transferred to Indo-China, 188, (referred to) 402, 403; forced to operate from airfields in Siam, 188 fn. 2, (referred to) 403; strength of, in Burma, 401-2; its role and operations discussed, 402, 434; its airfields attacked, 403
    7th: 68, 233, 401
    9th: 233, 401
Air Brigade:
    4th: 188 fn. 2
Air Regiments:
    8th: 188 fn. 2
    64th: 188 fn. 2
    81st: 188 fn. 2
1st Airborne Group: 233
2nd Raiding Group: 86
30th Fighter Group: 67, 68, 233
Japanese Army: role of, in supreme direction of war, 53; views of Chief of Army of, 54; its responsibilities in Southern Region, 54; expansion of, 226-7
China Expeditionary Force: reorganization of, 55; issues orders for 'Ichi-Go' offensive, 121-2; new task for, and expansion of, 228; assistance for, 229
Armies:
    Kwantung: 227
    Southern: receives directives, 53-4, 58, 229, (referred to) 433; to defend Philippines, 67-8; ordered to hold Leyte, 71; passes order to Yamashita, 86, (referred to) 435; reinforces and secures Indo-China, 188, 229-30; to send air units to Japan, 233; orders defence of southern Burma, 357
Area Armies:
    Burma: orders withdrawal from Imphal, 56; Kimura succeeds Kawabe as commander of, 58; receives new directive, 58, (referred to) 433; task of its reserve, 59, 193, 271; 'Ichi-Go' offensive relieves pressure on, 122; approves Katamura's plans, 187, 272, (and reinforces him) 295; to send *2nd Division* to Indo-China, 229; effect of loss of Meiktila on, 263, 271; holds conferences at Meiktila, 272-3, (referred to) 295; destruction of, 313, 355-6, 369; its abortive plans to defend south Burma, 357, (criticized by Japanese) 357, (referred to) 377; its evacuation of Rangoon, 370, 378; loss of wireless touch with, 378; loss of control by, 386, (referred to) 426; its orders to *15th Army*, 387-8; air attacks on its H.Q., 405; its operations discussed, 420-3, 426
    6th: 55 and fn. 2, 121, 122
    14th: to defend Philippines, 67-8, (its inability, referred to) 225, 435; strength and dispositions of, 68 and fn. 2; to deploy maximum strength on Leyte, 71; does not control *4th Air Army*, 86 fn. 1; effect on, of attempt to hold Leyte, 96;

Japanese Army—*cont.*

14th Area Army—*cont.*

left without air support, 97; infantry reinforcements for, 233

Armies:

11th: 55, 121-2

15th: its defeat being exploited, 11; ordered to withdraw from Imphal, 56, (progress of withdrawal) 171-2; composition and strength of, 56, 59 and fn. 4, (March) 284, (Japanese report on) 298; change in command of, 58; proposed operations for, 59-60, 186, 188, (referred to) 343 fn. 3; mentioned, 143, 273, 380; effect of pressure on, 160; its counter-attack on Irrawaddy bridgeheads fails, 186-7; operations in Arakan to protect rear of, 215; cut off from its base, 263; effect of Slim's strategy on, (at Nyaungu) 266, (at Mandalay and Meiktila) 271-3, 295; in Meiktila operations, 294-6, (fear of its collapse) 296, (breakdown of communications of) 296 and fn. 1, 303; in Mandalay operations, (regroups) 298, (defends) 301, (its escape routes threatened) 302-3, (Honda helps its withdrawal) 312-13, 357, (its casualties) 313; its withdrawal down Sittang valley, 387-8; its operations summarized, 415, 420-3, 429

20th: 55 and fn. 2

23rd: 55 and fn. 2, 121-2

28th: tasks of, 56, 59, 60-1, 187, 188, 273, 298, 343 fn. 1, 357, 377, (jeopardized) 378, (to defend Rangoon) 391; issues orders, (to *54th Division*) 138, 343, (referred to) 434, (to *Sakura Detachment*) 141, (to Yamamoto) 364; to be contained by XV Corps in Arakan, 218; in Irrawaddy operations, 266-7, 272, 273 fn. 3, 355; mentioned, 284; its aims in Arakan discussed, 350; thought to be in Rangoon–Pegu area, 352; its plans and operations in Pegu Yomas, 369-70, 378, 380; its operations commented on, 422

29th: 54 fn. 2, 229

33rd: tasks of, 56, 59, 273, 357, 388, (criticized by Japanese) 357; composition and strength of, 56, 273, 357; in operations, (in Lungling area) 116 fn. 2, 144, (at Namhkam) 146, 187, 191, (on the Shweli) 193, (to Namhpakka) 194-5, 197, (to cover *15th Army's* flank) 273; cut off from its base, 272; to reinforce *15th Army*, 272; to recapture Meiktila, 296, (its plans) 298, (fails) 312, (referred to) 320, 355, 364; its operations to help *15th Army* withdraw, 312-13; casualties in, 313; its communications cut, 358 fn. 5, 359-60, 360 fn. 3; its H.Q. surrounded, 359, 385; shattered, 360, 381, (referred to) 375, 385, 386; plans to prevent it contacting *28th Army*, 380; in full retreat, 381, 383-4, 387; reassembles near Toungoo, 387; resumes retreat to Sittang estuary, 388,

Japanese Army—*cont.*

33rd Army—*cont.*

390; air support for, commented on, 402

34th: 55 and fn. 2

35th: role of, in Philippines, 68, (changed) 71; composition of, 68 fn. 2; mentioned, 83; greatly outnumbered, 85; receives orders from Yamashita, 86

Divisions:

1st: ordered to Philippines, 67, 68 fn. 2; sent to Leyte, 83 fn. 2, 84; in Leyte fighting, 86; in Japan, 227 fn. 1

2nd: allocation of, 56-9, 187, 229, 298, 360 fn. 2; casualties in, 58; in operations on Salween front, 57, 144; proposed operations for, (on Irrawaddy) 60, (in central Burma) 144; reported, (at Pyinmana) 163, (at Meiktila) 179, (in Myinmu area) 262

2nd Armoured: 68 fn. 2, 97 fn. 2, 227 fn. 1

3rd: 55 fn. 2, 122

4th: 158, 229, 267, 285

8th: 68 fn. 2, 97 fn. 2, 227 fn. 1

10th: 97 fn. 2, 227 fn. 1, 228

13th: 55 fn. 2, 121, 122

14th: 65, 227 fn. 1

15th: withdraws across Chindwin, 41, 43, 56, 151; tasks of, 44, 59-60, 187, 188, 294; estimated strength of, 59 fn. 4; withdraws to Irrawaddy, 145 fn. 2, 176; Allied information on, 151, 157, 163, 171, 178, 179, 180, 259 fn. 1, 267, 289 and fn. 2; in operations, (against Irrawaddy bridgeheads) 187, 188, (at Mandalay) 298, 301, 302, (on Mawchi road) 387-8; mentioned, 179, 273 fn. 2, 300; depleted state of, (January) 187, 284, (March) 301; referred to, 422

16th: 68 and fn. 2, 83, 86, 87

18th: in operations on Salween front, 56-8 *passim*, 60, 146 fn. 1; new commander for, 58; proposed operations for, 59, 60, 146, 273, 275, 260, 272; location of (September), 144, 193; Allied information on, 163, (confirmed) 195; Katamura asks for, 187; mentioned, 195, 273 fn. 2; withdraws to Mandalay, 277 fn. 2; in counter-offensive at Meiktila, 294-5, 298, 303, 307 fn. 1, 309 fn. 1, 312; Honda's estimate of state of, 312; withdraws, (from Meiktila) 313, (to Shwemyo) 360, 382 fn. 2, 383; casualties in, 313; its strength at Pyawbwe, 361; probably in fighting at Yamethin, 382 fn. 2; to withdraw to Pyinmana, 384; begins general retreat, 385; reassembles near Toungoo, 387

19th: 97 fn. 2

21st: 122, 229

22nd: 55 fn. 2, 122, 229

23rd: 67, 97 fn. 2, 227 fn. 1

26th: 68 fn. 2; sent to Leyte, 83 and fn. 2, 84; in Leyte fighting, 86-7

27th: 55 fn. 2, 227 fn. 1

30th: 68 and fn. 2, 83 fns. 1 and 3

Japanese Army—*cont.*

31st: withdraws across Chindwin, 41, 43, 44, 56, 151; proposed operations for, 59, 60, 187; strength of, 59 fn. 4, 284; information on, 151, 157–8, 163, 172, 179, 262, 267, 303; withdraws to Irrawaddy, 176, 187, 188, (discussed) 422; mentioned, 177 fn. 1, 178, 215 fn. 2, 259 fn. 1, 273 fn. 1, 284 fn. 1

33rd: in withdrawal from Imphal, 41, 44, 50 fn. 1, 56; strength of, 59 fn. 2, 284; proposed operations for, 60, 151–2,187; information on, 151, 157, 163, 172, 177 fn. 1, 179, 262, 267, 268 fn. 2, 303; in operations, (on Irrawaddy) 188, (referred to) 422, (at Myingyan) 298, 302, 306 fn. 4; mentioned, 273 fn. 2, 284 fn. 1, 295, 313

37th: 55 fn. 2, 121, 229

40th: 55 fn. 2, 121

49th: mentioned, 56, 57, 58, 59, 144, 193, 195, 267, 271, 361, 377; in reserve, 59, 165, 284 fn. 1; proposed operations for, 60, 360; Allied information on, 163; to attack Meiktila, 295; in Meiktila counter-offensive, 295–6, 298, 307 fn. 1, 312, 313; Honda's estimate of its state, 312; withdrawn to Yamethin, 313; casualties in, 313, 358 fn. 5; withdraws to Toungoo, 358 fn. 5; out of touch with *33rd Army*, 358 fn. 5, 360 fn. 2, 384 and fn. 2; identified, 359; reassembles near Toungoo, 387

53rd: in operations, (on Northern front) 44, 143–4, (against Irrawaddy bridgeheads) 187, (in Meiktila counter-offensive) 298, 312, 313; transferred to *15th Army*, 56; mentioned, 57 fn. 2, 259 fn. 1, 273 fn. 2, 284 fn. 1, 295; proposed operations for, 56, 59, 60, 294, 360; strength of, (estimated) 59 fn. 4, (at Pyawbwe) 361; dispositions of, 143–4, 188, (referred to) 422, (Allied estimate of) 143, 158, 163, 171, 179, 267; withdraws across Irrawaddy, 145 fn. 2, 171; suffers severe casualties, 187; to move to Kyaukse area, 187; reinforced, 188 fn. 2; battalions of, identified, 262, 359; ordered to Myotha, 267 fn. 2; in withdrawal down Rangoon road, 383–5, 387; in withdrawal to Sittang, 390

54th: proposed operations for, 56, 59, 60, 369, 377; mentioned, 58, 218, 364, 374; to form *Matsu Detachment*, 138; its infantry group mentioned, 138 fn. 1, 343; its dispositions in Arakan, 215, 343–4; Allied intentions against, 217, 218, 345, 380, (discussed) 350–1; Allied information on, and estimation of, 218, 222–3, 342; to move to Irrawaddy, 357; its withdrawal from Arakan, 377–9; in operations on Irrawaddy, 380; its effect on operations on Central front, commented on, 426 fn. 2

55th: proposed operations for, 56, 59, 60; its estimated dispositions, 136, 218, 342; mentioned, 141, 273 fn. 3, 284 fn.

Japanese Army—*cont.*

55th Division—*cont.*

1, 377; proposed operations against, 218, 345, (discussed) 350; elements of, in Pegu Yomas, 380; in Battle of Rangoon Road, 384, 386, 388; its effect on operations on Central front, commented on, 426 fn. 2

56th: proposed operations for, 56, 59, 273, 298, 357, (one battalion of) 146; in operations on Salween front, 56–8, 147, 193, 195, 196, 275; composition of, 57 fn. 2; strength of, (July) 57 fn. 2, (February) 195 fn. 2; casualties in, 58, 195; dispositions of, (September) 144, (February) 195; its critical position, 195; suggested as reinforcement for *15th Army*, 272; withdraws south of Burma Road, 320; left free to harass IV Corps, 356, (referred to) 361; to withdraw to Moulmein, 388

58th: 55 fn. 2, 121

100th: 68 and fn. 2

102nd: task of, 68 and fn. 2; sent to Leyte, 83 fns. 1 and 3, 85; in Leyte fighting, 86

103rd: 68 fn. 2, 97 fn. 2

104th: 55 fn. 2, 122 fns. 1 and 2

105th: 68 fn. 2, 97 fn. 2

Brigades:

2nd Mixed: 236 fn. 2

24th Independent Mixed: 391

68th Independent Mixed: 83 fn. 2, 85

72nd Independent Mixed: tasks for, 59, 60, 273, 304, 357, 364, 369, 374, 377; location of, 188, 285; units incorporated in, 267 fn. 3; mentioned, 273 fn. 3, 379 fn. 1; available to *15th Army*, 284 fn. 1; Allied estimate of its strength, 363 fn. 2; regrouped, 364; new commander for, 365; Japanese dissatisfaction with its conduct at Yenangyaung, 373; disintegrates, 378; crosses Irrawaddy, 378, 380 fn. 1

187th Battalion: 304

188th Battalion: 285, 304, 305

542nd Battalion: 267 fn. 3, 304, 305 and fn. 4, 379 fn. 1

543rd Battalion: 267 fn. 3, 304, 379 fn. 1

105th Independent Mixed: 391

Armour:

14th Tank Regiment: 60, 295, 391

14th Anti-Tank Battalion: 344

Artillery:

18th Mountain Artillery Regiment: 295, 309 fn. 1

33rd Mountain Artillery Regiment: 306 fn. 1

49th Artillery Regiment: 308

54th Artillery Regiment: 344

55th Mountain Artillery Regiment: 384 fn. 1

Engineers:

53rd Engineer Regiment: 259 fn. 1

55th Engineer Regiment: 384 fn. 1

Japanese Army—*cont.*
55th Signal and Transport Regiments: 384 fn. 1
Infantry Regiments and Battalions:
2nd Divisional Reconnaissance: 146 fn. 2
4th: 188 fn. 2, 193, 195, 360 fn. 2
5th: 85
16th: 188 fn. 2, 284 fn. 1, 298
  I Battalion: 261
  II Battalion: 146 fn. 2, 188 fn. 2, 268, 361
  III Battalion: 261
29th: II Battalion, 57 fn. 2
49th Reconnaissance: 358 fn. 5
51st: identified west of Chindwin, 158, 159 fn. 2, 178; in operations at Kabwet, 179, 187
  II Battalion: 41 fn. 3, 300
54th Reconnaissance: in withdrawal from Arakan, 223, 343, 349 fn. 1, 378, 379
55th: in operations, (at Namhkam) 146, (at Wundwin) 295, (at Meiktila) 309 fn. 1; returned to *18th Division*, 195; strength of (February), 195 fn. 2; casualties in, 309 fn. 3
55th Reconnaissance: 135 fn. 1, 138, 377 fn. 1, 386 fn. 2
56th: 295, 308 fn. 2
58th: 177 fn. 2, 259 fn. 1, 267
60th: identified, 178; in Mandalay operations, 289 fn. 2, 300, 301
  I Battalion: 41 fn. 3
61st: in Imphal offensive, 41 fn. 3; in withdrawal from Imphal, 43 fn. 5; in operations, (in Kabaw Valley) 151, (in Chauk area) 285; believed to be at Sagaing, 158; incorporated in 72nd I.M.B., 267 fn. 3
  I Battalion: 285, 305
67th: 158, 289
  I Battalion: 41 fn. 3, 151, 159 fn. 2
  III Battalion: 159 fn. 2
77th: 85
106th: 308 and fn. 3
  I Battalion: 358 fn. 5
  II Battalion: 309 fn. 1
  III Battalion: 358 fn. 5
111th: in operations in Arakan, 138 fn. 1, 141, 215, 223, 343–4, 349 fn. 1; in withdrawal from Arakan, 378
  I Battalion: in Arakan, 138, 141, 344; in withdrawal from Arakan, 378, 379
  II Battalion: in Arakan, 138 fn. 1, 344, 349 fn. 1; in withdrawal from Arakan, 377–8, 379
  III Battalion: in Arakan, 344, 349 fn. 1; in withdrawal from Arakan, 378–9
112th: to attack Pakokku, 273; mentioned, 284 fn. 1; in operations in Mount Popa area, 304, 363 fn. 2, 364; effect of its operations on Central front commented on, 426 fn. 2
  I Battalion: 369
  II Battalion: 135 fn. 1, 369
  III Battalion: 384 fn. 1
113th: 57 fn. 2, 195, 196

Japanese Army—*cont.*
Infantry Regiments and Battalions—*cont.*
114th: 195, 277 fn. 2, 298
119th: in operations, (on Northern front) 144, (at Meiktila) 295, 298, 309 fns. 1 and 3
  I Battalion: 57 fn. 2, 259 fn. 1
121st: tasks for, 215, 343, 377, 378; Allied information on, 218, 223, 342, 349; Allied intentions against, 349; mentioned, 379 fn. 1
  II Battalion: on Ramree, 215 fn. 3, 219; mentioned, 349, 379 fn. 1; in withdrawal from Arakan, 378; near Allanmyo, 379
124th: 177 fn. 1
  I Battalion: 177 fn. 2
  III Battalion: 177 fn. 2
128th: 259 fn. 1, 390
143rd:
  I Battalion: 135 fn. 1, 377 fn. 2, 379
  II Battalion: 135 fn. 1
144th: 384 fn. 1, 386 and fn. 1, 388
  I Battalion: 386 fn. 1
  II Battalion: 386 fn. 1
  III Battalion: 135 fn. 1, 386 fn. 1
146th: 57, 195
  I Battalion: 57 fn. 2
148th: 57 fn. 2, 193
151st: 32 fn. 1, 41 fn. 3, 144, 151
153rd: tasks for, 59 and fn. 2, 364; Allied information on, 179, 267, 363 fn. 2; in operations, (at Letse) 257 fn. 3, (in Nyaungu bridgehead) 304, 305, (at Seikpyu) 365; mentioned, 284 fn. 1, 298, 384 fn. 2; withdraws to Thayetmyo, 378–9
  II Battalion: 266, 377
  III Battalion: 377
154th: Allied information on, 141, 233, 363 fn. 2; in operations, (in Arakan) 215, 222, 349 fn. 1, (on Irrawaddy front) 364, 365 fn. 1, (in withdrawal from Arakan) 378; to move to Irrawaddy, 343; effect of its operations on Central front commented on, 426 fn. 2
  I Battalion: in operations, (on Irrawaddy) 304 fn. 4, 363 fn. 4, (in Arakan) 343, 349 fn. 1
  II Battalion: 41 fn. 3, 151; in operations, (on Irrawaddy) 304 fn. 4, 363 fn. 4, (in Arakan) 343, 349 fn. 1
  III Battalion: in Irrawaddy operations, 138 fn. 1; in withdrawal from Arakan, 378, 379
168th: in operations, (on Salween front) 57, 58, (at Meiktila) 271; tasks for, 59, (of one battalion) 146; location of (September), 144, 193; placed under *56th Division*, 193; (returned) 195; strength of (February), 195 fn. 2
213th: at Mawlaik, 43–4, 152; at Myingyan, 188; Allied information on, 172, 267
  I Battalion: 41 fn. 3
  II Battalion: 48 fn. 1, 152

Japanese Army—*cont.*
213th Infantry Regiment—*cont.*
III Battalion: 176 fn. 2
214th: location of, 48 fn. 1, 152; at
Pakokku, 188, 258, 267; in Meiktila
counter-offensive, 295, 312; mentioned,
298
I Battalion: 182, 306 fn. 1
214th Regimental Gun Company: 268
215th: at Tongzang, 48 fn. 1, 151; at
Indainggyi, 152; to Madaya, 187, 188
and fn. 4; Allied information on, 179,
267; strength of, 188 fn. 4, 261; identified at Kyigon, 261; in Meiktila operations, 268; reinforces Myingyan, 306
fn. 1
Japanese Army in Burma: Allied plans for
destruction of, 2, 4, 5, 150, 157, 160, 164–5,
168, 324, 398; known or believed dispositions of, 6, 11–12, 41, 47–50 *passim*, 157–8,
163–4, 168, 171–2, 179–80, 183, 196, 259
fn. 1, 262, 271, 304, 349, 355; its losses in
tanks, guns etc., 46 fn. 1, 261, 271 fn. 2, 285,
287, 302, 303, 305, 308 and fn. 2, 309 fn. 3,
313, 346, 358 fn. 5, 359, 360, 361 and fn. 1,
365, 371, 372, 373, 382, 389 and fn. 3, 392
fn. 3, (total in Battle of Rangoon Road)
398; expected resistance by, (in Arakan)
136, (at Meiktila) 273; suicide tactics of,
185, 263, 268, 379, 389 fn. 2; forced to conform to Slim's strategy, 189, 271–3, (commented on) 429–30; suspected ruse of, 196
and fn. 2; takes reprisals in Karen Hills, 250
and fn. 1; its necessity to hold Meiktila,
298; its artillery, (handled boldly) 308,
(misused) 387, (commented on) 429; engineer skill of, 312; evacuates Rangoon,
390, 394–6 *passim*; air operations against its
L. of C., 405, 407; attitude of Burmese to,
430–1
Japanese Army in China: *for operations of, see*
'Ichi-Go' Operation: its administrative
difficulties, 55; areas controlled by, 115;
effect of poor communications on, 121–2;
progress of, 126; Mountbatten's views on
intentions of, 130; Chinese numerically
superior to, 197 fn. 1; task of (January), 226;
its abortive offensive towards Chihkiang,
338 and fn. 3
Japanese Navy: unlikely to attack in Bay of
Bengal, 8, 9; role of, in supreme direction of
war, 53; views of Chief of Naval General
Staff of, 54; its responsibility in Southern
Region, 54; submarine activities of, 81, 84,
213, 240; claimed losses of, 96; personnel of,
(in Luzon) 97, (on Iwojima) 236 fn. 2;
attacks by suicide craft of, 97–8; orders submarines to Pacific, 213; forms fighter groups
for home defence, 231; misses opportunity
at Iwojima, 240;
Combined Fleet: its proposed strategy in
defence of Philippines, 67, (assessed)
87–8; alerted, 73; operations of, 73–
83, 92–3, (referred to) 435; its Headquarters mentioned, 79, 80; attacks on,
95–6
South-West Area Fleet: 73, 97

Japanese Navy—*cont.*
Centre Force: composition of, 73; in battle
for Leyte Gulf, 73–82 *passim*
Northern Force: composition of, 67, 74; its
role in 'SHO-1', 67; operations of, 74–6,
81–2; strength left in, (of aircraft) 75, 76,
(of ships) 81
Southern Force: composition of, 73; in
battle for Leyte Gulf, 73–4, 76–7; sole
survivor of, 78
1st Striking Force: 67, 73, *now see* Centre
Force *and* Southern Force
2nd Striking Force: in battle for Leyte Gulf,
74, 76–8
3rd Carrier Squadron: 71
4th Carrier Squadron: 71
5th Fleet: 71, 73
16th Cruiser Squadron: 71, 73, 74 fn. 1
21st Cruiser Squadron: 71, 73, 74 fn. 1
31st Special Naval Base Force: 99
Japanese Naval Air Force: weakness of, 67;
strength of, in Luzon, 97; fighter groups of,
formed, 231; its role in home defence, 232;
estimated strength of its aircraft by March,
233
1st Air Fleet: 67, 73, 97, 232
2nd Air Fleet: 67, 71, 73, 74, 97
3rd Air Fleet: 232
5th Air Fleet: 232
10th Air Fleet: 232
302nd Fighter Group: 231
332nd Fighter Group: 231
352nd Fighter Group: 231
Java: submarine activities off, 213; *7th Air
Division* in, 401
Jennings, Brigadier M. B.: 196, 275
Jerrard, Brigadier C. I.: commands 98th
Brigade, 155; in operations, (at Kabwet)
178, (to Kyaukmyaung–Singu area) 259, (at
Mandalay) 289–91 *passim*, 299, (to Pyawbwe) 383, (on Mawchi road) 388
Johnstone, Brigadier R. J.: 135, 346
Joint Force Commanders: appointed, 136–7;
issue directives, (for 'Romulus') 138–9, (for
earlier capture of Akyab) 141–2, (for capture of Ramree and exploitation) 215–16,
(for attack on An) 343, (for modified operations) 345–6, (for new operations) 347, (for
modified 'Dracula') 351–2; their H.Q.
mentioned, 140, 396; prepare plans, (for
Arakan) 141, 204, (for modified 'Dracula')
329, 330, 332; conferences of, 217, 219 fn. 4;
lack of precedent for, 350; aims and achievements of, discussed, 350–1
Joint Planning Staff, London: 10
Joint Planning Staff, S.E.A.C.: their plan for
amphibious attack on Rangoon, 241–2, 243–
4, (referred to) 427; put forward proposals for
future strategy, 252; to examine possibility of
mounting modified 'Dracula', 327; report of
their Directors of Plans, 328
Joint Staff Mission, Washington: 8, 319 fn.
2
Jorhat: airfield at, 38 fn. 5, 283, 284 fn. 2
Judge, Lieutenant Karamjeet Singh, V.C.:
306
Jumna, R.I.N. sloop: 216, 221, 223

Kabaw Valley: progress of operations in (August), 6; development of road down, 20, 44, 102–4 *passim*, 150, 156, 166, 199, (referred to) 424; proposed operations in, 40, 42, 101, 150; danger from malaria in, 40 fn. 1, 103; operations in, 43–5, 153–4, 160, (effect of weather on) 44, 45; R.A.F. operations in, 50; development of airfields in, 103, 104, 150, 157, 199; engineer force for work in, 151 fn. 1; Japanese dispositions in (November), 152; XXXIII Corps moves down, 156; 551 Sub-Area administers, 327 fn. 1

Kabo Weir: 172, 174, 177

Kabwet: operations against, 178, 179,185–6; Japanese defended area at, 180; Japanese force holding, 187

Kachin Levies: 33–4, 192, 277, 320

Kaing: development of road from, 173 and fn. 1, 183

Kaladan River: in Japanese defensive plans, 60; firm bases to be established east of, 215

Kaladan Valley: enemy penetration into, to be prevented, 4 fn. 1; detachment watching track from, 135; enemy forces in, 135 fn. 1, (estimated) 142, (Allied information on) 218; advance of 81st (W.A.) Division down, 137, 140, (effect of, on Japanese) 138, 140; proposed operations in, 138, 139, 216–17; move of Japanese forces to, 140–1; situation in (January), 142; *Matsu Detachment* to act as covering force in, 215

Kalapanzin Valley: operations in, 136, 137, 140

Kalaw: *Burma Area Army* conference at, 272; Honda arrives at, 298; Japanese efforts to keep open escape route to, 361; operations on Thazi–Kalaw road, 366, 383, 398; operations to capture, 388–9

Kalemyo: proposed capture of, 4, 10, 42, 101, 107, 149, (administrative preparation needed for) 103; advance on, 39, 49–50, 152–3; Japanese forces in area of, 48 fn. 1, 151; airfields at, (needed) 103–4, 106, 157, (squadrons based on) 253–4; development of roads through, 150, 169, 172, 174–5; 80th Brigade at, 156, 171

Kalewa: proposed capture of, 4, 11, 101, 102, 108, 149, (administrative preparation needed for) 103; proposed pipeline to, 18; development of communications through, 20–1, 103, 149, 166, 169, 199, 244, 247, (engineer force for) 151 fn. 1, (referred to) 424; I.W.T. service at, 20–1, 166, 199–200, 247–8, 322, 325, 326, (tonnages delivered by) 317, 409, (referred to) 424; in Japanese defensive plans, 56; airfield at, (needed) 103–4, (possible location of R.A.F. at) 249; stockpiles to be built forward of, 149; bridge over Chindwin at, (planned) 20, 103–4, 156, (engineer force for) 151 fn. 1, (opened) 160, (replaced) 166 fn. 3, 199–200; capture of, 153–4; operations on Kalewa–Yeu road, 160; boat-building factory at, 199; L. of C. Transport Column working to, 322, (tonnages delivered by) 409 fn. 3; L. of C. Sub-Area at, 326; mentioned, 420

Kama: Japanese bridgehead at, 379, 380

Kamaing: 2 fn. 1, 22, 40, 57, 113

Kamikaze Aircraft: first attacks by, 80; origin of name, 80 fn. 2; attack American shipping 84, 85, 92–7 *passim*, 240; increased danger from, referred to, 91; counter-measures against, 93; their numbers to be increased, 232

Kamikaze Special Attack Force: 80

Kan: airstrip at, 172 fn. 1, 180 fn. 2, 182, 253 fn. 2; IV Corps concentration area at, 174–5; 7th Division secretly concentrated in area of, 179; 17th Division moves to, 257; IV Corps H.Q. moves from, to Myitche, 271

Kandaung: operations at, 287, 296, 358

Kandy: Supreme Headquarters at, 11, (discussed) 431–2; A.L.F.S.E.A. Headquarters at, 114, 118, (referred to) 432; mentioned, 328; distances by air from, to Delhi and Calcutta, 431 and fn. 2

Kangaw: Japanese plans for defence of, 215; proposed capture of, 216–18 *passim*; Japanese defences at, 217 fn. 3; amphibious assault on, 218, 220–1; to be kept clear, 343; battle at, commented on, 350–1

Kanhla: Japanese unit at, 188; fighting at, 257–8

Kanjo Force: in operations in Mount Popa–Yenangyaung area, 273, 284 fn. 1, 364, 369, 377, 378; formation of, 273 fn. 3; Allied information on, 304, 363 fn. 2

Kantetsu Group: 364, 369, 377, 378

Karen Hills: 205, 250 fn. 2, 333, 387

Karen Levies: plans to raise, 205, (progress of) 250; raised during 1942, 250 fn. 2; Slim's proposals for operations by, 332–3; operations of, 387 fn. 4

Kashii, Japanese light cruiser: 96

Katamura, Lieut.-General S.: commands *15th Army*, 58; tasks of, (September) 59, (at Mandalay) 298; his appreciations and plans, (November) 59–60, (January) 186–7, 271–2, (dispositions resulting from) 188, (March) 294–5; Honda to take over from, at Meiktila, 296; forces under his control for Meiktila counter-offensive, 298; orders withdrawal from Mandalay, 301

Katha: mentioned, 3; capture of, 144–5, (referred to) 148; Mars Force contacts 36th Division near, 146; 36th Division in area of, 148, possible enemy force covering, 158

Katsu Force: task for, 59; composition of, 59 fn. 2; in operations, (in counter-attack at Seikpyu) 257, (at Nyaungu) 266, (to counter-attack Pakokku) 273, (at Seikpyu) 364–5, (under Miyazaki) 377, 379, (in Yamoto offensive) 304; Allied information on, 267, 363 fn. 2; mentioned, 284 fn. 1; to withdraw to Thayetmyo, 378–9

Kawabe, Lieut.-General M.: 56, 58

Kedah, H.M. depot ship: 136 fn. 5

Kemapyu: 387 and fn. 4, 388

Kennedy Peak: held by *214th Regiment*, 48 fn. 1, 152; operations towards, 49, 50, 152

Kenya, H.M. cruiser: 342

Kharagpur: 20th Bomber Command airfields

Kharagpur—*cont.*
  at, 37, 131–3 *passim*, 404, (Japanese learn of)
    231
Khedive, H.M. escort carrier: 342, 395 fn. 2
Kimura, Lieut.-General H.: commands *Burma
    Area Army*, 58 and fn. 2; his instructions from
    Imperial General Headquarters, 58, (commented
    on) 433; his appreciations and plan for de-
    fence of Burma, 58–9, (referred to) 145 fn. 2,
    (referred to and commented on) 421, 433–
    4; Slim's appreciation of his intentions, 163;
    orders *2nd Division* to Meiktila, 187; possible
    reserve for, 193; his fears for *15th Army* at
    Meiktila, 296; his orders to Honda, 296,
    298, (Japanese criticism of) 357; plans of,
    (to recapture Meiktila) 296, 298, (to defend
    south Burma) 357, (to defend Rangoon to
    the last) 370, 391 fn. 2; and Sakurai's plans,
    370; orders *15th Army* to cover withdrawal
    of *33rd Army*, 387–8; his description of
    Slim's thrust to Meiktila, 429
Kindaunggyi: F.M.A. at, 347, 348
King, Admiral E. J.: 63, 68
Kingcol: 305 fn. 2, 363, 364
King George V, H.M. battleship: 212
Kinkaid, Vice-Admiral T. C.: commands U.S.
    7th Fleet, 69; in invasion of Leyte, 71, 84; in
    battle for Leyte Gulf, 76, 78, 81–2; in in-
    vasion of Luzon, 94, 95
Kinu, Japanese light cruiser: 84
Kiso, Japanese light cruiser: 85
Kistna, R.I.N. sloop: 219
Knowland, Lieutenant G. A., V.C.: 222 fn. 1
Koba Force: moves from Arakan to Irrawaddy
    front, 304 fn. 4; in operations, (in Irra-
    waddy valley) 343, 363 fn. 4, 364, (as rear-
    rearguard to *54th Division*) 378–9; Allied in-
    formation on, 363 fn. 2
Koba, Major-General T.: in operations in
    Kaladan valley, 138, 141; orders evacuation
    of Akyab, 141; mentioned, 365 fn. 1; com-
    mands rearguard for *54th Division*, 378, (at
    Shandatkyi) 379–80
Kohima: Japanese to be cleared from area of,
    1–2; tonnages carried from, 21 fn. 2; troops
    in area of, 40 and fn. 2, 150, 171
Kohima, Battle of: importance of, 1; primary
    administrative task after, 21; lack of infor-
    mation during, 32; British commanders
    knighted for services in, 161; mentioned,
    215 fn. 2
Koiso, General K.: forms joint Cabinet, 53,
    (referred to) 435; resigns, 436
Korea: mentioned, 56; to be prepared to with-
    stand invasion, 226; build-up of garrison in,
    227, 228 fn. 2
Kra Isthmus: proposed operations against,
    109–11 *passim*, 252; railway across, attacked,
    404
Krueger, Lieut.-General W.: 69, 83, 87, 94, 98
Kumano, Japanese heavy cruiser: 85
Kumbhirgram: airfield at, 38, (aircraft based
    on) 42, 254
Kume: *18th Division* to move to, 295; opera-
    tions at, 303, 356; Japanese rallying-point,
    303, 355; brigade of 36th Division at, 366
Kunming: proposed pipeline to, 4, 18, 123;

Kunming—*cont.*
  construction of road to, 22; possible menace
    to, 116–17, 123, 124; Wedemeyer's plans for
    defence of, 124, 126, 128, (referred to) 157;
    convoy reaches, 194
Kunomura, Major-General M.: 58
Kuribayashi, Lieut.-General T. : 235
Kurile Islands: 53, 66, 228 fns. 1 and 2
Kurita, Vice-Admiral T.: in battle for Leyte
    Gulf, 73–82 *passim*
Kwangsi Province: Japanese operations in,
    55, 122; Chinese propose to recapture, 281
Kweichow Province: Japanese operations in,
    122, 126, (effect of) 122–3
Kweilin: Japanese operations against, 54, 55,
    116, 121; captured, 122
Kyaukme: proposed capture of, 191, 194, 242,
    249, 273, 275, (referred to) 302 fn. 1; 36th
    Division moves to, 316, 320; Chinese troops
    to contact 36th Division at, 318; mentioned,
    317
Kyaukmyaung: mentioned, 60; bridgehead
    at, (established) 178, 184, (fighting in) 185–
    6, 187–8, 258, (break-out from) 255, 258–9,
    (referred to) 423, (effect of, on *33rd Army's*
    communications) 194
Kyaukpadaung: proposed capture of, 181,
    324; mentioned, 256; operations towards,
    269, 283, 285; capture of, 362–5 *passim*,
    (referred to) 370; Japanese force in area
    of, 363 fn. 4; operations on road from, 366,
    370
Kyaukpyu: mentioned, 56, 348; port at, to be
    developed, 203; occupied, 219; L. of C.
    sub-area responsible for, 219 fn. 1; size of
    I.W.T. fleet operating to, 245 fn. 2; 82nd
    (W.A) Division not to be maintained from,
    245–6; development of air base at, accele-
    rated, 245–6, (referred to) 247, 410, 425–6;
    forces to be maintained from, 246, (referred
    to) 410; mounting base, (for modified
    'Dracula') 331–2, 351, 395, (for 'Stanza')
    399–400
Kyaukse: in Japanese defensive plans, 60, 187;
    proposed capture of, 184, 242, 297; F.M.A.
    to be established at, 242; operations towards,
    260, 288, 292, 294; Japanese formation in
    area of, 298; capture of, 302–4; escape route
    for Japanese at, 302–3, 355; mopping-up
    operations in area of, 356, 362
Kyauktalon: in Japanese appreciation of
    Allied plans, 59; in Japanese defensive
    plans, 60; ferry at, 185, 362; mentioned, 293
Kyauktan: 352, 353, 395, 396
Kyigon (Irrawaddy): Japanese forces in area
    of, 188; bridgehead at, 260–2 *passim*
Kyigon (Kabaw Valley): 172
Kyigon (Meiktila): 286, 307, 309
Kywiguseik: mentioned, 217; to be captured,
    218; operations towards, 220, 222, 224 fn. 1,
    343

Lahu Levies: 192
Lameng: mentioned, 4; Chinese offensive

Lameng—*cont.*
 against, 41, 56–7, (referred to) 144; Japanese casualties at, 57, 58 fn. 1
Landing Craft and Assault Shipping: required, (for 'Dracula') 11 fn. 1, (for capture of Akyab) 110 fn. 2, (for operations against Kra Isthmus) 110 fn. 3; to be sent to S.E.A.C., 111; in Arakan operations, 139 and fn. 1, 141, 142, 216, 220–1, (insufficient for landing at An River) 223; for Irrawaddy crossing, 260 fn. 3, 262–3; in 'Roger' force, 329 fn. 1; in modified 'Dracula', 352, 395; losses in, 395, 399 fn. 3
Langley, American fleet carrier: 96
Lashio: proposed capture of, 3, 4, 11, 101, 191, 194, 196, 249, (effect of withdrawal of Chinese divisions on) 164; in Japanese defensive plans, 59; Force 136 group in area of, 192; Japanese forces at, 195; N.C.A.C. responsible for area from, to Chinese border, 197; occupied, 278; Chinese not to advance beyond, 280, 281, 317; mentioned, 320
Lauder, Brigadier I. C. A.: 395, 396
Ledo: railhead at, 15, 19; road to, 17; mentioned, 23 fn. 1; covered by U.S.A.A.F. defence arrangement, 34; airfield at, 38
Ledo Road: mentioned, 17, 38, 193; pipeline along, 18, 41; progress of, 22–3, 41, 191, 194 fn. 2, (operations needed to assist) 148; maintenance along, 22, 139, 409; altered American policy towards, 22; to be secured, 241
Leese, Lieut.-General Sir Oliver: recommends disbandment of Special Force, 29; appointed C.-in-C. A.L.F.S.E.A., 114–15, 118, (commented on) 417–18; receives directive from Mountbatten, 203; confers, (with Mountbatten) 201, 203, 247, 317, 327, 330, (with Slim) 157, 254, 316, 327; issues orders, (to Slim) 157, 249, (to XV Corps) 218–19, 249, (to N.C.A.C.) 249, (on occupation of Rangoon) 332, (to Joint Force Commanders) 352; and occupation of Ramree, 200, 215; and maintenance of 14th Army, 200–1; plans new L. of C. organization, 204, 326–7; decides to extend Arakan operations, 218–19; reduces XV Corps' air supply, 224, 245, (referred to) 425–6; and modified 'Dracula', 241, 327–30, (commented on) 427–8; received plans, (from Slim) 242, 332–3, (from Christison) 344; and administrative plans, 245, 247; and arming of A.F.O., 250–1, 334, (referred to) 335; and operation against Phuket Island, 252, 327–8; and withdrawal of forces and aircraft to China, 280–1, 316, 339; orders opening of Rangoon port to be accelerated, 399–400; location of his H.Q. commented on, 432
Legyi: action at, 363–4; Japanese plans to attack from, 364
Leigh-Mallory, Air Chief Marshal Sir Trafford: 118–19
LeMay, Major-General C. E.: 37
Lethbridge, Brigadier J. S.: 44, 164
Letmauk: operations towards, 224, 344–6 *passim*; proposed Japanese operations at,

Letmauk—*cont.*
 343; Japanese forces at, 344; operations in area of, 347, 348–9
Letpan: beachhead at, 343, 345, 346; orders to 22nd (E.A.) Brigade in regard to, 344, 347; Stockwell takes over at, 349
Letse: operations at, 257, 266, 269, 283–5 *passim*, 362, 365, 366; Japanese counterattack at, 304–6 *passim*, (referred to) 426 fn. 2; area reinforced, 305–6; mentioned, 355; relief of African brigade at, 356, 363; Japanese forces leave, 363 fn. 4, 364
Lewe: airhead at, 325, 385; 9th Brigade flown forward from, 390
Lexington, American carrier: 84
Leyte: proposed capture of, 63–4, 66; Japanese forces for defence of, 68, (referred to) 435; description of, 69; airfields on, 69, (captured) 83, (attacked) 86–7; American forces for invasion of, 69; Japanese decision to fight main battle on, 71, (assessed) 88, (effect of, on defence of Luzon) 96; capture of, 71–2, 83–7, (diversionary raid in Indian Ocean during) 211, (referred to) 225, 229; Japanese reinforcements for, 83–5, (referred to) 74 fn. 1
Leyte Gulf: mentioned, 68, 87, 91, 92; American invasion force enters, 71; Japanese plans for engaging American fleet in, 73–4; battle for, 74–83, (naval losses in) 82–3, (referred to) 95, 225; fleet assembly area for Luzon invasion, 94
Liberators (B.24 bombers): mentioned, 66; in operations, (in Pacific) 82, (in South-East Asia) 213, 214, 341–2, 404, 408, 413, (in Burma) 219, 254, 394
Lindsell, Lieut.-General Sir Wilfred: 15, 18, 19
Lines of Communications: *see* Communications
Line of Communications Command: *see under* Army, Line of Communication Formations
Line of Communication Road Transport Organization: 21, 105, 151
Line of Communication Transport Column: its radius of action extended, 199, 322; taken over by L. of C. Command, 204; tonnages, (to be carried by) 248–9, (delivered by) 199 fn. 2, 409 fn. 3
Lingayen Gulf: 91, 93, 94, 98
Liuchow: Japanese operations against, 54, 55, 116, 121–2
Loftus-Tottenham, Major-General F. J.: 135, 137, 217
Loi-kaw: Karen Levy operations in area of, 205, 332, 387 fn. 4; in Japanese defensive plans, 357
Loilem: Force 136 operations in area of, 192; proposed capture of, 242, 247, (becomes deception scheme) 288 fn. 1, 367
Lomax, Major-General C. E. N.: commands 26th Division, 39; mentioned, 135; in operations in Arakan, 219, 220, 345; appointed Joint Assault Commander, 219 fn. 2; relinquishes command, 349, 351; new appointment for, 351 fn. 2
London, H.M. cruiser: 342

Long-Range Penetration Forces: *see* Special Force

Louisville, American cruiser: 94

Lumsden, Lieut.-General H.: 94 fn. 3

Lungling: Chinese offensive against, 41, 56–7, 147; Japanese counter-offensive from, 57–8, (referred to) 116, (failure of, referred to) 144; situation round (September), 144; Chinese numerical superiority at, 197 fn. 1

Luzon: dispute over capture of, 63, 68; role of, in Japanese defence plans, 68, (altered) 71, (effect of alteration in) 86, 88; proposed invasion of, 68–9, (postponed) 92; carrier attacks on, 70, 84–5, 93, 95; Japanese air force in, (reinforced) 73, 84, (attacks 3rd Fleet) 74–5; reinforcements sent to Leyte from, 83, (effect of) 435; invasion of, 93–5, 97–9, (referred to) 225; Japanese plan for defence of, and forces in, 96–7; *Southern Army* to hold, 229

Lyons, Colonel: 398

MacArthur, General D.: possible British naval force to serve under, 9; his views on Pacific strategy, 63, (referred to) 68; directives for, 63–4, 68–9; plans of, 64–5, 69, 91–2; his line of advance converges with Nimitz's, 66; his forces for invasion of Leyte, 69; asks Halsey's help, 84; in Luzon operation, 98, 99

McCain, Vice-Admiral J. S.: commands fast carrier group, 69 fn. 5; in battle for Leyte Gulf, 74, 76, 81–2

Mackenzie, Brigadier D.A.L.: 156, 176, 260, 365 fn. 3

Macnab, Brigadier J. F.: 43, 153

Madaya: Japanese plans to defend, 59–60, 294; *53rd Division* to assemble at, 187; operations towards, 260, 288, 289; mentioned, 283

Maddox, American picket destroyer: 96

Magwe: proposed capture of, 242, 297, 298, 302, 324, 325; airhead to be at, 322, 325, (R.A.F. wing to move to) 366; medical centre to be at, 325; intended concentration of *54th Division* at, 357; capture of, 362, 366, 371–2, (effect of, on Japanese plans) 377; 33rd Brigade moves to, 374, 375, 376

Mahlaing: mentioned, 182, 356; to be captured, 267; operations on road to, 287, 307–8; Japanese force covering road to, 295; occupied, 310; area to be mopped up, 362

Mainprise-King, Lieut.-Colonel T.: 305 fn. 2

Maintenance:
during 'Capital': preparations needed for, 20–2, 102–6, 149, 150, (progress of) 199–200; Mountbatten reports to C.O.S. on, 106–7; stockpiling for, 103–5, 129, 149, 199; transport aircraft available for, 105–6, (overall deficiency of) 125, (effect of diversion of) 129–31; main base airfields for, 106; discussed, 424
during 'Extended Capital': preparations needed for, 166–7, 172–3, 325; stockpiling

Maintenance—*cont.*
for, 166, 202, 243, 248–9, 322, 324; extra resources needed for, 166–7, 243; difficulties of, 182–3; redeployment of air bases and aircraft for, 167, 200, 201–2, 214–15, 244–5, 253, (administrative difficulty of) 202; transport aircraft needed for, 167, 200–1, (effect of withdrawal of, referred to) 410; development of ports for, 203; for Phase IV, (in Slim's plan) 243, (Denning Committee report on) 244–5, (A.L.F.S.E.A.'s examination of) 245–6, (new army/air plan for) 246–9; shortfall in lift for, 317, 322, (measures to counteract) 323–4; Mountbatten reports to C.O.S. on, 318; Slim's new plan for, up to capture of Rangoon, 321–3, 325–6, (effect of operational situation on) 323–4; XXXIII Corps' advance on Rangoon limited by difficulties of, 375; airhead at Toungoo needed for, 381; summarized and discussed, 409–12, 424–7; tonnages delivered for, (by air) 409, 410, (by road) 409 and fn. 3
of formations, (other than by air supply): IV Corps, 253 fn. 2, 323–4, (difficulties of) 399; XV Corps, 20, 138, 139, 141 fn. 3, 203, 218 fn. 1, 245–6, 348, (tonnages delivered to) 409; XXXIII Corps, 183, 184, 253 fn. 2, 325; 5th Division, 156; 7th Division, 305 fn. 3; 19th Division, 176 fn. 1; 20th Division, 176
on Northern front: 21–2; along the Ledo Road, 131, 409; shortfall in, 317 fn. 1; method of, to enable release of squadron, 338–9
during 1945 monsoon: *see under* Rangoon, 'Stanza'
for modified 'Dracula': 352

Maintenance Bases (India): Nos. 1–4 Reserve Bases, 16 fn. 3; Nos. 4 and 5 Advanced Base Supply Depots, 202

Makino, Lieut.-General S.: 68

Malacca Strait: to be opened, 209; submarine activity in, 213; mine-laying in, 214

Malaria: *see under* Sickness

Malaya: plans to be prepared, (for its recapture) 8, (for thrust down) 244; directive for reoccupation of, 13, 209; Japanese forces in, 54 fn. 2; proposed amphibious operation against, 110, (delayed) 329; air activity over, 214; *Southern Army* to hold, 226, 229; air supply for Force 136 in, 407

Manchuria: 53, 55, 67, 68, 132; forces withdrawn from, and raised in, 227–8

Mandalay: Slim begins to plan for its capture, 2; proposed capture of, 4, 7, 10, 11, 101, 149, 150, (in 'Extended Capital') 165–6, 168, 174, 177, 179, 183–4, 242–3, 255, 297; in Japanese defensive plans, 59, 146, 187, 271–3, 301; chance of destroying Japanese north of, lessened, 130; Slim's intention to bring Japanese to battle in Shwebo–Mandalay plain, 150, (south of) 164–5; reports of Japanese withdrawal south of, 163–4; *33rd Army's* communications to, threatened, 193; progress of operations towards, 206,

Mandalay—*cont.*
258–9, 273, 283, (Leese on) 247, 249; Japanese armies at, to be destroyed, 249; air support, (for assault on) 254, (during battle for) 311–12, 404; deception plans for move on, 255, 263, (success of) 266; Japanese dispositions in area of, 267, 298; roads from, blocked, 270; *18th Division* withdraws to, 272, 277 fn. 2; Japanese estimation of Allied intentions against, 272; Chiang Kai-shek advises Mountbatten to halt at, 281; plans to envelop, from north and south, 283; Battle of, 288–92, 299–301, (change of pattern in) 293–4, (Japanese losing interest in) 294, (XXXIII Corps losses in) 311; Japanese plan to hold, 298; Japanese withdrawal from, 301, 357, 361; Mountbatten on battle for, 317; move of 36th Division to, 320, 356; railway from, 322, 326; reduction in supplies for forces in area of, 323; area to be made secure, 324; civil telegraphic system to be reestablished to, 326; administration of airhead at, 326; 253 Sub-Area to administer, 327 fn. 1; mentioned, 410; size of population of, 431 fn. 1
Mandalay Hill: fighting on, 289–91 *passim*; mentioned, 299
Mangshih: 57, 144, 147
Manila: bombed, 84; to be open town, 97, 99; captured, 98–9
Manipur River: 5th Division crosses, 46–8, 49
Manpower: shortage of, in India and S.E.A.C., 26–7, (worsened by reduction in 'Python' qualifying period) 27, 325, (in relation to break-up of Special Force) 29, (hampers formation of airborne division) 29; shortage of, in Japan, 226–7, 228 fn. 2
Mansergh, Major-General R.: tasks for, 309–10; in operations, (at Meiktila) 310, (in advance on Rangoon) 355, 381, 384; appointed commander of 5th Division, 310 fn. 1
Marianas: effect of its capture, (on Japanese strategical position) 53, 66, (on preparations for 'SHO-1') 88; mentioned, 63, 66, 235; air force and air bases on, 89–91 *passim*, 133, 235, 236, 404
Marindin, Brigadier P. C.: 45, 171
Marshall, General G. C.: 319
Mars Task Force: on Northern front, 143; mentioned, 145, 148; in operations 191, 192, 194–5; in rest area, 275; withdrawn to China, 278–81 *passim*, 315–17 *passim*
Martaban, Gulf of: fleet operations in, 394
Martin, Rear-Admiral B. C. S.: 137 fn. 1, 142, 351, 352
Matsuda, Rear-Admiral C.: 75, 81
Matsu Detachment: formation, composition and tasks of, 138 and fn. 1, 215; in operations in Arakan, 141, 222; Allied plans against, 216–17, 218, (discussed) 350–1
Matsui, Major-General H.: 391
Matsuyama, Lieut.-General S.: in operations on Salween front, 147, 193–4, 195
Maungdaw: positions covering, to be maintained, 1, 4 fn. 1; communications to, 19; advanced base at, 21, 139 fn. 1, 246, (Foul

Maungdaw—*cont.*
Point stocked from) 141; consolidated, 39; mentioned, 107; 25th Division based on, 135; operations in area of, 137; move of I.W.T. craft from, 138, 139
Mawchi: operations in area of, 387 and fn. 4, 388–9, 398
Mawlaik: in Japanese defensive plans, 44, 56, 152; operations towards, 44–5; Japanese evacuate, 153; 32nd Brigade crosses Chindwin at, 156, 160
Maya, Japanese heavy cruiser: 74
Maymyo: proposed capture of, 4, 101, 242; Katamura fears airborne attack on, 59; Force 136 group near, 249; XXXIII Corps to cut road at, 273, 289; captured, 291; advance on, mentioned, 294; mentioned, 297, 324; 62nd Brigade to move towards Mandalay from, 299; 253 Sub-Area to administer, 327 fn. 1
Mayu Peninsula: *Sakura Detachment* to hold front on, 138; operations on, 138, 141, (cease) 142; hopes of it being cleared by end of December, 140
Mayu Range: mentioned, 135 fn. 1; operations on, 137–9 *passim*
Mayu River: mentioned, 135 fn. 1; operations on, 138–9, 141
Mayu Valley: Japanese evacuating, 140
Meiktila: Stilwell's proposals for operations towards, 3; in Japanese defensive plans, 59–60, 187–8, 272–3; proposed capture of, 165, 167, 168, 179, 180–1, 242–3, 255, 297; airfield at, (needed) 166, (captured) 271, (fighting at) 296, 306–7, 308–9, (reopened) 311, (administration of) 326, (developed as airhead) 356, (909 Wing at) 366; elements of *2nd Division* thought to be at, 179; state of Japanese defences at, 186, 188; Slim's hopes for thrust to, 255, 256, (commented on) 423, 429; Battle of, 256, 266–9, 283–8, 294–6, 304, 306–11, (change of pattern in) 293–4, (IV Corps casualties in) 311, (air support during) 311–12, 404; thrust to, 263, 267–8; capture of, 270–1, (effect of, on Japanese plans) 273, 295, (referred to) 427; Japanese garrison at, 271; Japanese conference at, 272; F.M.A. at, 286, 325; fly-in of 9th Brigade to, 284 fn. 2, 306–7; Japanese plans for defence and recapture of, 294–6, 298, 312–13, (failure of, referred to) 335; communications from, to Rangoon, 297, 324, 326; Japanese forces in area of, 298, (escape route for) 302, 361; 19th Division to move to, 302; reduction in supplies for forces in area of, 323; road and railway to Rangoon to be secured from, 324; medical centre at, 325; civil telegraph system from, to be restored, 325–6; 17th Division advances from, 358; R.A.F. group H.Q. to be set up at, 366; 5th Division moves south from, 381; 36th Division to be maintained from, 383; Mountbatten visits Messervy at, 385; Japanese convoys from, attacked, 406
Messervy, Lieut.-General F. W.: to command IV Corps, 157; receives instructions from Slim, 157–8, 168–9, 180, 297, 372; his

Messervy, Lieut.-General F. W.—*cont.*
character as a leader, 159; his dispositions, (December) 171, (March) 283; his plans and orders, (for advance to Irrawaddy) 173, 174, 180, (for advance to Meiktila) 180–1, (for Irrawaddy crossing) 256, 266, (referred to) 304, (for redeployment of IV Corps) 309–10, (for capture of Rangoon) 243, 391; his part in operations, 253, 271, 286, 357, 358, 381, 390, 398; flies to see Cowan, 270 fn. 3; given 5th Division, 284, 286; visited by Mountbatten, 385; his description of flight with Slim to Rangoon, 398–9; asks for troops to be supplied through Rangoon, 399

Middle East: troops from, to be moved to Far East, 8; possible provision of parachute brigade from, 28, (referred to) 102; transfer of aircraft from, to S.E.A.C., 207

Minbu: Japanese forces to move to, 343; operations in area of, 374–8 *passim*; air observation of track to, 406–7

Mindanao: 63, 64, 65, 68, 69, 99

Mindawgan Lake: fighting in area of, 287, 288, 308, 310; Japanese forces in area of, 295

Mindoro: capture of, 91–3, (referred to) 225

Mingaladon: airfield at, 366, 396, 397

Mitchell Bomber Aircraft: mentioned, 182, 254, 408; in operations in Burma, 186, 219, 299, 406

Mitscher, Vice-Admiral M. A.: commands fast carrier groups, 69; in battle for Leyte Gulf, 76, 81–2; in other operations, 236, 237, 240

Miyazaki, Lieut.-General S.: his aims and dispositions in Arakan, 215, 343–4, (referred to) 434; in operations, (in Arakan) 222, 346, (referred to) 351, (in withdrawal from Arakan) 369, 377–8, (to secure bridgehead on Irrawaddy) 378–9; his skill commented on, 345

Mogami, Japanese heavy cruiser: 77

Mogaung: capture and development of, 2, 6; mentioned, 4, 23 fn. 1, 32; views on security of, 9–10; road to, 22–3; airfields at, 38; situation at (August), 40; development of railway south of, 41; 22nd Chinese Division near, 143

Mogok: proposed capture of, 4, 11, 108; operations towards, 145, 177, 183, 191, 196, 278; occupied, 320

Momi, Japanese destroyer: 95 fn. 1

Monglong Range: 59, 187, 273

Mongmit: proposed capture of, 4, 108, 164, 191; Japanese plans to hold, 59, 60, 272; Honda expects Allied advance on, 146; Japanese forces at, 193, 277 fn. 2; operations towards, 195–6, 275–6, (referred to) 284; captured, 278; *18th Division* on move to Meiktila from, 295; airstrip at, 320

Monywa: possible establishment of I.W.T. service in, 21; in Japanese defensive plans, 60; proposed capture of, 149, 157, 165–6, 168, 172; Japanese forces believed in area of, 158, 163, 171, 179; operations towards, 174, 176–7; captured, 184; tonnages delivered to, (proposed) 243, (by road) 409

Monywa—*cont.*
fn. 3; 14th Army/221 Group H.Q. at, 254; 5th Division moves to, 262, 283, 286; conference at, 317, 327, (referred to) 339; mentioned, 332; Mountbatten visits Slim at, 385

Moody, Rear-Admiral C.: 211

Morale: of 14th Army, 12, 284, 313; of Japanese, 284, 298; of 82nd (W.A.) Division, 345

Moreh: 43, 44, 151, 155, 156

Morotai Island: 64, 65, 67, 76, 82, 225

Morris, Brigadier J. R.: in operations, (to Chindwin) 154, (in advance to Irrawaddy) 178, (to Mandalay) 259, (at Mandalay) 299, 301; 383 fn. 4

Morshead, Lieut.-General Sir Leslie: 70

Mosquito Light Bombers: mentioned, 42, 254, 366, 396, 408; in operations, (in Burma) 184, 407, (in South-East Asia) 214

Moulmein: proposed Levy operations in area of, 333; *H.Q. Burma Area Army* moves to, 378; *15th Army* and *56th Division* to withdraw to, 388; British P.O.W.s on way to, 390; convoy to, sunk 394; mine-laying off, 403; railway through, bombed, 404

Mountbatten, Admiral the Lord Louis: C.C.S. directives for, (June) 1, (referred to) 3, 8, (September) 12–13, (February) 209, (enables future strategy to be considered) 252; issues directives, (June) 1, (referred to) 6, 416, (October) 107–8, (November) 136–7, (referred to) 419, (February) 241, (April) 352; confers, (with Slim) 2, (with Cs.-in-C.) 3, 106, 108–9, 140, 247, 252, 328, 330, 338, (with Joint Force Commanders) 217, (with Chiang Kai-shek) 281; receives plans and recommendations from Giffard, 2, 136; submits plans to C.O.S., 3, 109–10, 252, 329, (referred to) 415; his views, discussions and orders on operations in Burma, 3–5, 6–7, 9–12, 106–7, 108–10, 125–6, 129–31, 140, 201, 203, 241, 244, 247, 279–80, 316–18, 327–32, 352, (referred to) 415–17, 418–19, 425, 427–8; visits London, 6; asks for directive for future strategy, 13, 201; agrees to standardization of infantry divisions, 25; and shortage of British infantry, 26–7; and formation of Indian airborne division, 28–9; recommends disbandment of Special Force, 29; and Intelligence organizations, 30, 31, 33; and army/air co-operation, 34; meets P.M. and C.I.G.S. in Cairo, 108, 109–10; proposes reorganization of command, 113–14, (discussed) 417–18; to be consulted on co-ordination of N.C.A.C. with Yunnan armies, 118; and release of aircraft to China, 125, 128–31, 316–18, 338–9, (discussed) 418–19; and withdrawal of formations to China, 125–6, 128, 130–1, 278–81, 316, (referred to) 418–19; his views on Wedemeyer's directives, 126–8, 316–17; does not control certain American air units, 127; acquires more transport aircraft, 201, 206–7, (referred to) 418, 424; orders transport aircraft to be worked above sustained rates, 203, 317; approves L. of C. reorganization, 204; his directive on integration of air forces re-

Mountbatten, Admiral the Lord Louis—*cont.*
ferred to, 208; decides on target for Eastern
Fleet, 211; strengthens naval force for Ramree operation, 219 fn. 3; and modified
'Dracula', 244, 327-32, 352, (referred to)
427-8; tours fronts, 247; his views on arming
of A.F.O. and rising in Burma, 251, 334-6;
decides on future strategy, 252; asks Auchinleck to form new corps H.Q., 252; and
security of Burma Road, 279-80, 316, 318;
at Monywa conference, 317, 327; asks for,
and receives assurance on American aircraft,
318-20, (referred to) 356, 418; orders plan
for rehabilitation of Rangoon port, 331;
and 'exfiltration' of Aung San, 338;
approves fleet operations, 341; visits Slim
and Messervy, 385; orders no more attacks
on Singapore and Penang, 405; his relationship with China Theatre discussed,
418; his qualities as a leader, 420; his decision to make Kandy his H.Q. discussed,
431-2

Mount Popa: operations towards, 269, 285,
363-6, 369, 371; enemy forces in area of,
273 fn. 3, 304, 355, 357, (estimated) 364;
mopped up, 374; effect of loss of, on Japanese plans, 377, 378; Japanese defence of,
commented on, 426 fn. 2

Mowdok: 39, 42, 135

Mu River: mentioned, 154, 174, 262; possible
Japanese force in valley of, 158; Japanese
posts on, 177; 20th and 2nd Divisions make
contact at bridge over, 185; 2nd Division at
mouth of, 258

Musashi, Japanese battleship: 75

Mutaguchi, Lieut.-General R.: 56, 58

Myebon (and Peninsula): in Japanese defensive
plans, 61, 215; operations in area of, 136,
139, 216-18 *passim*, 221

Myinba: operations in area of, 138, 215-18
passim, 221

Myingyan: in Japanese defensive plans, 59-
60; proposed capture of, 165, 168, 283, 297;
advanced army base at, 166, 199, 242, 243,
247, 248, 267, 321-2, 325, 326, (opening of,
delayed) 323, (effect of delay referred to)
411, 427, (being developed) 356, (security
of airfield in) 362, (tonnages delivered to)
409 and fn. 3; Japanese forces at, 179, 188,
267, 298, 306 fn. 1, (intercepted in withdrawal from) 362 fn. 3; Japanese defences
at, 186, (under attack) 296; to be responsibility of 28th Army, 187; capture of, 269-70,
285, 286, 306, (effect of delay in) 297, 323;
Japanese decision to counter-attack from,
272-3; road to, blocked, 293; 2nd Division
to move to area of, 297, 310 fn. 2, 362;
operations on Myingyan-Taungtha road,
310; 1/3rd Madras takes over, 310 fn. 2;
R.A.F. wings at, 393

Myinmu: in Japanese defensive plans, 59-60,
187; Japanese defended area at, 179, 267;
bridgehead at, 184, 255, 260-2, 283, 292,
(Japanese identified in attacks against) 262,
(effect of, on Japanese) 272, 423, (Japanese
decide to counter-attack) 273; mentioned,
185

Myitche: mentioned, 188; airhead and F.M.A,
at, 253 fn. 2, 304, 305 fn. 3, 325, 326, 356,
362; 7th Division to cross Irrawaddy near,
256; found clear, 258; H.Q. 17th Division
moves to, 271; Japanese offensive towards,
286, 304, 305, (failure of, referred to) 355

Myitkyina: development of area of, 2, 6, 13,
18, 22-3, 38, 41; capture of, 2, 6, (effect of)
8, (referred to) 39, 40; proposed operations
from, 3, 4; views on course of operations in
area of, 9-10; airfields at, 23, 38 and fn. 5,
(mentioned) 130; mentioned, 33, 143;
situation round (August), 40; Allied forces
at, inactive, 57-8; 553 Sub-Area at, 327 fn.
1

Myitnge River: operations to cross, 283, 288,
289, 292, 293, 300-2 *passim*; Japanese withdraw across, 294, 301, 302

Myitson: 18th Division at, 163, 272; operations
towards, 187, 192, 196; bridgehead at, 196,
275-6, (fighting at) 277-8; ferry in operation at, 277

Myittha Gorge: to be blocked, 153; captured,
154; road through, to be repaired, 156;
difficulty in passing bridge material through,
160

Myittha River: crossings over, to be captured,
42; ferry established on, 175

Myittha Valley: to be reconnoitred, 49;
Japanese retreat to be blocked in, 153; IV
Corps' advance up, 165, (deception during)
174-5, (success of deception during) 266;
flooded, 175; Japanese forces in, 179, 180;
551 Sub-Area in, 327 fn. 1

Myohaung: in Japanese defensive plans, 56;
operations towards, 136, 137, 138, 140, 216;
Japanese forces in area of, 141, 142; occupied, 217; area to be mopped up, 218

Myoko, Japanese heavy cruiser: 75

Myotha: 267 fn. 2, 288, 293, 302, 322

Naba: operations at, 144, 145; 19th and 36th
Divisions to link up in area of, 157

Nachi, Japanese heavy cruiser: 77, 84

Naf River: 19, 141, 219

Naganuma Group: 295

Naka, Lieut.-General E.: commands 18th
Division, 58; commands Meiktila counter-
offensive, 294-6

Namhkam: proposed capture of, 4, 108, 144,
191; Japanese plans for defence of, and
forces at, 57, 144, 146, 147, 193; operations towards, 146-8 *passim*, 192; captured,
193-4

Namhpakka: mentioned, 191, 278; Japanese
forces in area of, 193, 194; operations in
area of, 194-5; Japanese withdraw from,
195, 275

Nammeik Chaung: bridgehead on, 276-7;
72nd Brigade to move up, 278

Napier, H.M. destroyer: 138 fn. 3, 216, 219

Narbada, R.I.N. sloop: 216, 220-1, 223

Nashville, American light cruiser: 92

'Nation' Operation: *see* Force 136

Natmauk: 20th Division moves through, 302, 362, 365, 371, (effect of, on Japanese communications) 377

Nepal, H.M. destroyer: 138 fn. 3

Newcastle, H.M. cruiser: 142

Newfoundland, H.M. cruiser: 212 fn. 3

New Guinea: mentioned, 63, 65, 66, 69, 78; Australians assume responsibility for, 70

New Jersey, American battleship: 82

New Mexico, American battleship: 94 and fn. 3

Ngakyedauk Pass: 135, 140; Christison knighted for service in Battle of, 161

Ngazun: 2nd Division's bridgehead at, 262–3, (referred to) 283

Nicholson, Major-General C. G. G.: commands 2nd Division, 171; in operations, (to Shwebo) 177, (to cross Irrawaddy) 258, (south of Mandalay) 288, 293, (to Kyaukpadaung) 362; regroups 2nd Division, 179; considers plans, 183–4

Nicobar Islands: responsibility for defence of, 54; fleet attacks on, 211–12, 393–4; photographic reconnaissance of, 214; shipping sunk off, 342

Nigeria, H.M. cruiser: 142

Nimitz, Admiral C.: directives for, 63, 68–9; his views on Pacific strategy, 63; his plans, 64, 91; his line of advance converges with MacArthur's, 66; to retain control of 3rd Fleet, 69; asks where Task Force 34 is, 82; neutralizes Japanese airfields, 90; Power flies to see, 212; appoints commander for Iwojima, 236; mentioned, 435

Nishimura, Vice-Admiral S.: in battle for Leyte Gulf, 73–4, 76–7; drowned, 77; losses in his force, 78

Norman, H.M. destroyer: 219 fn. 3

Northern Air Sector Force: *see under* United States Army Air Force

Northern Combat Area Command: under direct command of Supreme Headquarters, 1, 35 fn. 1, 113, (referred to) 417; proposed operations for, 2, 3, 4–5, 101, 108, 249; situation in, (June) 2, (August) 6, (October) 51, (December) 148, (February) 196; views of Cs.-in.-C. on operations by, 10, (referred to) 416; allotted 'V' Force group, 31; need for army/air co-operation in, 34; its boundary with 14th Army, 108 fn. 1, 168; Stilwell replaced in command of, 118; Wedemeyer to effect co-ordination of, with Yunan armies, 118; to come under A.L.F.S.E.A., 118; effect of 'Ichi-Go' offensive on, 122–3; withdrawal of Chinese divisions from, 124–6 *passim*, (effect of, on its operations) 126, 164, 191, 279, (referred to) 157, 281, 418–19, (aircraft for) 315, 318, 320; composition of (October), 143; its estimation of Japanese dispositions, 143, 163; Chinese failure to comply with orders from, 145 fn. 1; Slim's forces to link up with, 157; to co-operate with advance on Central front, 168; new area of responsibility for, 197; effect of withdrawal of Mars Force on, 279; and security of Burma Road, 279–80, 315; transport aircraft supporting, 280, 317, 318, (diversion of) 338–9; Chiang Kai-shek's

Northern Combat Area Command—*cont.* views on operations of, 281; significance of decreasing enemy resistance to, 294; 36th Division transferred from, 302 fn. 1, 316, 320; Leese's views on operations in, 316; Japanese forces being drawn from its front, 316; Chiang Kai-shek's instructions to Chinese divisions in, 317–18; effect of rundown of, on advance to Rangoon, 356; maintenance of, referred to, 409

Northern Front: *see also* Air Supply, Communications *and* Maintenance: proposed operations on, 2, 4–5; extent of, and troops on, 2 fn. 1; situation on, (August) 6, 40–1, (October) 143, (December) 148, (February–March) 275; maintenance of forces on, 22; 'V' Force group allotted to, 31; Force 136 operations on, 33–4, 192; air support for, 35 fn. 1, 36–7; operations on, 40–1, 144–7, 192–6, 275–8, 320; transport aircraft allotted to, 105; withdrawal of Chinese divisions from, 124–6 *passim*, 128, 338; air supply for, 129, 131; insufficient aircraft to fly division to, 130; Japanese dispositions on, (estimated) 143–4, (actual) 193; operations on Central front to assist, 158; contact established with Central front, 159; decreasing enemy opposition on, 294, 320; Japanese withdraw troops from, 317; general air operations on, 407

Noshiro, Japanese light cruiser: 82

Nursing Sisters: volunteer for duties in forward areas, 49

Nyaunglebin: proposed capture of, 165–6, 168; airhead and F.M.A. to be at, 325; airfield at, 366; operations in area of, 390

Nyaungu: in Japanese defensive plans, 60 and fn. 1; bridgehead at, 60 fn. 1, 181, 255, 263–6, 283, (operations in) 269, 285, 304–6, (effect of, on Japanese plans) 272, (situation in) 284–5, (effect of, referred to) 423; Japanese force in area of, 188; difficulties of crossing Irrawaddy at, 256; vehicle ferry at, 266 fn. 1, 362; proposed Japanese offensive against, 286, 298, 304, 305, (failure of, referred to) 355; increasing enemy pressure on, 294; 2nd Division to move to area of, 297; units to move to, 305, 356, 363; airfield at, 362

Octagon Conference: line to be taken by British at, 11; decisions taken at, 12–13, 64, (referred to) 116, 416

Office of Strategic Services: 30, 34, 367

Office of War Information: 30

Ohara, Major-General K.: 365, 369, 377

Oil: effect of shortage of, (on movements of *Combined Fleet*) 66, 67, 87–8, 435, (on Japanese industry) 225; to be sent to Japan, from Southern Region, 229

Okamura, General Y.: 55, 121–2

Okinawa: carrier strikes on, 70, 95, 240; proposed capture of, 91–2; formation from, to reinforce Formosa, 228; to be held at all costs, 229; attack on, imminent, 436

Okochi, Vice-Admiral D.: 97, 99

Oldenorf, Rear-Admiral J. B.: in invasion of Leyte, 71–2; in battle for Leyte Gulf, 76–7, 78; in invasion of Luzon, 94–5

Oliver, Commodore G. N.: 352, 395 fn. 2

Ommaney Bay, American escort carrier: 94

Onbauk: airfield at, 172, 177, (captured) 178, (Japanese air attack on) 179, (brought into use) 183, (squadrons based on) 253, (air attack on, discussed) 402, 434; 19th Division's firm base at, 179

Ondaw: mentioned, 185, 258; airhead at, 253 fn. 2, 326

Onishi, Vice-Admiral T.: 80

Oriental Mission: 250 fn. 2

Ormoc: mentioned, 69, 86; to be attacked, 83; Japanese bring in reinforcements through, 84–5; capture of, 87, (landing for, referred to) 91

Osaka: raids on, 89, 231

Oyin: fighting at, 267–8

Ozawa, Admiral J.: 171; in battle for Leyte Gulf, 74–6 *passim*, 78, 81, 82

'P' Division: 30–3 *passim*

Pacific Ocean: support of operations in, from China, 1, 22; British naval force for, 8–9, 12, (arrival of) 213; main theatre of war against Japan in, 8; acceleration of American advance in, (referred to) 8, (effect of) 12, 22, 88; American strategy in, 63, 70, (Japanese appreciation of) 225–6; Japanese submarines concentrate in, 213

Padan: fighting round, 376–9 *passim*

Padang: fleet attacks on, 211, 342

Pagan: *I.N.A.* regiment in area of, 188, 266; F.M.A. to be established at, 242; subsidiary crossing at, 256–8 *passim*, 265

Pakokku: proposed capture of, 4, 11, 101, 165–6, 168; in Japanese defensive plans, 59, 60; Japanese troop movements to, 163, 171, 179; road to, 169, 172; operations to, and capture of, 173, 180, 181, 182, 256–8 *passim*, 266, 269; Japanese forces at, 186, 188, 267; proposed Japanese offensive against, 273; mentioned, 410

Palau Islands: capture of, 63–6 *passim*, (effect of, on Japanese plans) 67

Palel: transport to, 21, (referred to) 105; airfield at, 38, (9th Brigade flown to Meiktila from) 262, 284 fn. 2, 306; development of Palel–Tamu road, 104, 151; supply dump at, 105

Para-Military Formations: *see* Force 136, 'V' Force *etc.*

Park, Air Chief Marshal Sir Keith: 119, 247, 317

Parkash Singh, Jemadar, V.C.: 261 fn. 1

Pathfinder, H.M. destroyer: 219 fn. 3

Pauk: capture of, 180–2 *passim*; corps airhead established near, 181 and fn. 2; 7th Division's firm base at, 257

Payagyi: operations at, 389–92 *passim*

Pearce, Major-General C. F. B.: 250

Pegu: proposed exploitation to, in 'Dracula', 5, (effect of) 9; proposed operations against communications from, 205, 206, 333; railway attacked, 312, 404; B.N.A. fighting at, 337; Allied estimate of troops in area of, 352; capture of, 387, 389–92; Japanese garrison in, 391; advance towards Rangoon from, 397; 5th Division to be responsible for area of, 398

Pegu River: 390–3 *passim*, 395, 397

Pegu Yomas: mentioned, 165; Japanese withdrawal into, 370, 378–9, 380; both ends of route across, secured, 372; Japanese to be prevented from escaping, (into) 376, 380, (from) 398

Peirse, Air Chief Marshal Sir Richard: 1, 118; his refusal to move to Kandy commented on, 431–2

Penang: submarine activity off, 213; harbour mined, 213, 404; photographic reconnaissance of area, 342; no more attacks to be made on, 405

Pert, Brigadier C. E.: 267, 358, 389, 392

Pescadores: 73, 76, 94, 96

Philippine Islands: *for operations in, see* Leyte, Luzon *etc.*: American aircraft allotted for capture of, 12; Japanese plans for defence of, 'SHO-I', 53–4, 66–8, (changed) 70–1, (assessed) 87–8, (failure of, referred to) 225, 435; American plans for operations against, 63–4, 68–9; description of, 69; fast carrier forces in vicinity of, 84; progress of American operations against (March), 99, 225; Japanese units, (sent to) 227 fn. 1, 228, (removed from) 233

Philippine Sea, Battle of the: effect of Japanese losses incurred in, 53, 66, 67, 88, (referred to) 435

Phoebe, H.M. cruiser: 142, 216, 219, 352

Photographic Reconnaissance Force: *see under* Air Forces, Allied

Phuket Island: midget submarine raid on, 213; proposed capture of, 'Roger' Operation, 252, (C.O.S.' views on) 327, (diversion of force for, to modified 'Dracula') 328, 329; photographic reconnaissance of, 342

Pindale: operations in area of, 288, 295, 303, 306 fn. 4, 307

Pingka: Chinese offensive against, 41, 56–7

Pinlebu: mentioned, 44; operations towards, 130, 145 fn. 2, 154, 155, 158; captured, 159

Pinwe: operations to capture, 143–5 *passim*

Pipelines: development of, (to Myitkyina area) 2, 18, 41, (to China) 4, 18, 22, 41, (in Assam and Eastern Bengal) 16 fn. 4, 17–18, 19, (to Imphal) 105, 149

Playfair, Major-General I.S.O.: 243

Pleasance, Group Captain H.: 351

Poland, Commodore A. L.: 394

Political Warfare Section: 30

Poole, Brigadier R. G. C.: 48 fn. 2, 383 fn. 1

Porpoise, H.M. submarine: 213

Port Blair: bombarded, 393; mine-laying off, 403

Port Dickson: proposed operations against, 252; photographic reconnaissance of area of, 342

Port Swettenham: proposed operations against, 252; photographic reconnaissance of area of, 342
Power, Vice-Admiral Sir Arthur: becomes C.-in-C. East Indies Fleet, 118, 212; raids Nicobars, 211–12; selects targets for fleet, 212; on modified 'Dracula' 328–9; in operations in Andaman Sea, 341
Pownall, Lieut.-General Sir Henry: 113, 119
Princeton, American light carrier: 74
Prisoners-of-War: Japanese, 261, 271 fn. 2, 289, 302, 361 fn. 1, 365, 372, 376, 389, 390, (information from) 289 and fn. 2, 300; _I.N.A._, 365, 386; Allied, (reported near Pegu) 390, (in Rangoon) 396, 397, 405
Prome: in Japanese defensive plans, 56, 215; _55th Division_ responsible for area of, 60, 141; Taungup–Prome road, (proposed opening of) 203, 219, 241, 249, 344, 348, 349, (tonnages to be sent along) 243, (opening of, abandoned) 244, 345, (air attacks on) 407; Japanese plans to hold, 215, 343, 357, (affected by loss of Yenangyaung) 374, 377, (abandoned) 378; proposed capture of town and airfield, 242, 297, 298, 324, 325, 331, 372; capture of, 374, 375, 379; delivery of air supplies to, 375; cordon on Allanmyo–Prome road, 375, (referred to) 380
Puffcol: 269, 285, 305 fn. 2
Pugh, Lieut.-Colonel (later A/Brigadier) L.H.O.: commands, (Puffcol) 269 fn. 4, (33rd Brigade) 364 fn. 1; in operations, (at Kyaukpadaung) 364, (at Gwegyo) 370, (at Yenangyaung) 372, (west of Irrawaddy) 376
Pyawbwe: _2nd Division_ to move to, 59; operations towards, 271, 287; to be captured, 297, 324; Japanese attacks on Meiktila from, 307, 312; area to be cleared, 309, 310; _18th Division_ withdraws to, 313; _17th Division_ ready to attack, 313; action at, 355, 357–60, (effect of, on Japanese) 360, 369; Japanese plans to hold, 355, 357, 386, (in vain) 381; Japanese casualties at, 360; delay in capture of, 360 and fn. 1; mentioned, 382, 383
Pyinbin: operations at, 267–9 _passim_, 363–4
Pyingaing: operations at, 160, 171–2, 175, 177
Pyinma Chaung: 269, 285, 304, 370
Pyinmana: Japanese forces believed to be south of, 163; mentioned, 205; Force 136 'Nation' operations near, 206, 249, 333, 337; airhead and F.M.A. to be at, 325, (mentioned) 385; withdrawal of _15th_ and _33rd Armies_ by way of, 357; capture of, 366, 384, 385, (referred to) 375; Honda withdraws to, 384, (his H.Q. attacked at) 385; _144th Regiment_ at, 384 fn. 1, 388; air attack on convoy south of, 406
'Python' Repatriation Scheme: effect of reduced qualifying period for, 27, (referred to) 29, 325
Pyu: Force 136 team near, 334, 337; capture and consolidation of, 381, 383, 386–7, 389; _17th Division_ to move to, 398

Queen Elizabeth, H.M. battleship: 211, 212, 219, 342, 393
Queen Mary, S.S.: 11

Raider, H.M. destroyer: 219 fn. 3
Railways: congested state of, in India, 15–16; in Assam and Eastern Bengal, 17, 19; on Northern front, 41; to Rangoon, 248, 297, 322, 324, 326, (jeep trains on) 323
Ramree Island: held by Japanese as outpost, 56, 59, 215; airfield and advanced base on, required, 200, 201, 214–15, 219, 244, 245, 247, (referred to) 351, 410, 425; development of port on, 203; occupation of, 203, 214–15, 219–20, (referred to) 350; Japanese detachment on, 215, (Allied information on) 218, (withdraws) 220; 26th Division concentrates on, for modified 'Dracula', 345, 348, 349; units for defence of, 348; air supply for XV Corps from, 348, 349
Ram Sarup Singh, Acting Subadar, V.C.: 152 fn. 3
Rangoon: _for amphibious operation against, see_ 'Dracula': resistance movement in, 33; Japanese air base at, 34, (attacked) 403; in Japanese defensive plans, 59, 60; communications to, 165, 297, 324; air bases to maintain drive on, 200, 381; to be captured before monsoon, 203, 241, 247, 249, 297, 324, 330, (administratively necessary) 242; its capture in relation to future strategy, 252; Japanese views on Allied drive to, 272; Japanese communications to, (cut) 273, 296, (air attacks on) 311–12; its capture in relation to removal of American resources, 279, 280, 315, 318, 319; administrative plans to support drive on, 321–3, 325–6; plan to reopen port and establish advanced base at, 'Stanza', 331–2, 399–400; Japanese reinforcements to be prevented from reaching, 333; estimated size of garrison in, 352; airfield at, 366; Kimura proposes to defend it to last, 370, 391 fn. 2; Japanese evacuation of, 378, 390–1, 394–6 _passim_; its capture referred to, 379 and fn. 2; Messervy's plan for capture of, 391; Allied P.O.W.s in, 395–7 _passim_; state of, on recapture, 397; air attacks on, 405
Rangoon Defence Force: 391
Rangoon Road: Battle of the, 355–98, (Pyawbwe only large action in) 360, (Allied and Japanese losses in) 398; R.A.F. deployment down, 366; _55th Division_ moves to, 384 fn. 1
Rapid, H.M. destroyer: 219, 341 fn. 4
Rawlings, Vice-Admiral Sir Bernard: 212
Raymond, Lieutenant C., V.C.: 347 fn. 1
Read, Rear-Admiral A. D.: 142
Rear Airfield Maintenance Organization: 37, 106, 202 fn. 1
Rees, Major-General T. W.: in operations, (in advance to Irrawaddy) 154, 158–60 _passim_, 171, (in Shwebo area) 177–9, (at Mandalay) 258, 259, 288–92, 299–300, 301, (in advance on Rangoon) 361, 383; his character as a leader, 159; considers plans, 183–4

Reno, American light cruiser: 80 fn. 3, 84

Renown, H.M. battle cruiser: 211, 212

Repatriation: *see* 'Python' Repatriation Scheme

Richelieu, Free French battleship: 211, 342, 393

Ricketts, Brigadier A. H. G.: 140, 217

Roberts, Lieut.-General O. L.: 252 fn. 3

Rodham, Brigadier C. H. B.: in operations, (to Monywa) 176, (in Irrawaddy crossing) 260, (to Wundwin) 294, (to Prome) 375, 379

'Roger' Operation: *see* Phuket Island

'Romulus' Operation: approved, 110; Wedemeyer's views on, 126; and diversion of aircraft, 127, 129, 130; ordered, 136; plan for, and operations, 137–42; to be exploited, 215; referred to, 425

Roosevelt, President F. D.: approves directive for Mountbatten, 13; his dispute with Chiang Kai-shek, 115–17; recalls Stilwell, 117; at Argonaut Conference, 208–9

Royal Air Force: size of, to be maintained by India, 16; reorganized for army/air co-operation, 34–6; in tactical support of operations in Burma, 45, 50, 152, 175, 184–6 *passim*, 216, 270, 287, 292, 293, 310, 358, 360, 362, 363, 371, 386, 389; transport aircraft of, 105 fn. 2, 128–30 *passim*, 136, (sustained rates for) 204 fn. 1, (reinforced) 207; to support, ('Talon') 138–9, (XXXIII Corps) 151; mines Rangoon River, 352; redeploys for advance on Rangoon, 366; and A.L.F.-S.E.A. deception plans, 367; danger of monsoon conditions for, 367; strength of, in Eastern Air Command, 401; support by, discussed, 429

Air Headquarters, Bengal: 36

Headquarters R.A.F. Bengal/Burma: 36

221 Group: reorganization and responsibilities of, 35, 36, 41; joint H.Q. with 14th Army, 36, 114, 155, 254, 325, 366; airfields for, 38; strength of (September), 41–2; in operations, (in Kabaw Valley) 153–4, (at Fort Dufferin) 299, 300, (during Mandalay and Meiktila battles) 311–12, (generally) 405; mentioned, 155, 181–2, 401 fn. 3; freed of support of IV Corps, 181; prepares joint plan with 14th Army, 242; forward deployment of, (January) 253–4, (April) 366; reinforced, 254; maintenance of, 321, (reduction in tonnages for) 323; to support modified 'Dracula', 331

222 Group: 214, 342, 413

224 Group: 34; reorganization of, recommended, 35; its joint H.Q. with XV Corps, 36, 135; responsible for support on Arakan front, 36, 135–6, 405; airfields for, 38; 12th Bombardment Group available to, 136; to support Akyab operation, 142; in operations in Arakan, 219, 221, 223, (its losses) 350; to assist 221 Group, 254, 311; supports modified 'Dracula' 331, 395; in general description of air operations, 405, 407, 408

225 Group: 214, 413

231 Group: 404

Royal Air Force—*cont.*

177 (Transport) Wing: 37 fn. 1

905 Wing: 254

906 Wing: 253, 366, 388, 393

907 Wing: 253, 366

908 Wing: 249, 254, 312, 366, 393

909 Wing: 253, 366, 388

910 Wing: 249, 254, 366, 388, 393

20 Squadron: 261

110 Squadron: 395

357 (Special Duties) Squadron: 408

IV Corps Communication Flight: 388

Royal Air Force Regiment: 388

Royal Australian Navy: 65, 69 fn. 4

Royal Canadian Air Force: transport squadrons of, in Eastern Air Command, 105 fn. 2, 409, 410; jumpmasters from, 394 fn. 2

Royal Indian Navy:
55th Flotilla: 136 fn. 5
56th Flotilla: 136 fn. 5
59th (Burma) Flotilla: 136 fn. 5

Royalist, H.M. cruiser: 395 fn. 2

Royal Marines: 215, 219
42 R.M. Commando: 221, 222
44 R.M. Commando: 221, 223

Royal Navy: ships of, with American Pacific Fleet, 70 fn. 4; in support of Arakan operations, 139, 216, 219, (referred to) 350; helps to increase I.W.T. fleet in Arakan, 245; to simulate assault on Bassein, 367
1st Battle Squadron: 212
21st Assault Carrier Squadron: 352
4th Submarine Flotilla: 213
8th Submarine Flotilla: 213

Ruywa: beachhead at, 223, 343, (operations from) 344; in maintenance plan, 246; enemy force at, 342

Rylands, Captain J.: 136

Ryukyu Islands: Japanese plans to defend, 53–4, 226, 228, (referred to) 435; American plans to capture, 68–9, 91; mentioned, 70, 71, 73; carrier strikes on, 94, 96; Japanese formations sent to, 227 fn. 1

Sagaing: enemy defended area round, 60, 179, 183, 185, 188, 283; Japanese forces in area of, 158, 179, 267; operations in area of, 183–5 *passim*, 256, 301, 302; possibility of Japanese counter-attack from, 262; Japanese decide to counter-attack from, 272–3; capture of Ava bridge from, 293; L. of C. Transport Column to work to, 322

Saigon: army units in, 229; Japanese take control of, 230; B.29 raids on, 405

St. Lo, American escort carrier: 81

Saipan: 53, 85, 89, 90

Sakuma, Colonel T.: 298

Sakuma Force: 295, 298, 312

Sakura Detachment: proposed operations for, 56, 60, 138; composition of, 56 fn. 5; in operations in Arakan, 135 and fn. 1, 140; ordered to withdraw to Prome, 141; Allied information on, 218

Sakurai, Lieut.-General S.: orders to, 56, 59,

Sakurai, Lieut.-General S.—*cont.*
298; plans and orders of, (to *55th Division*) 56, (for holding *28th Army* front) 60–1, (discussed) 434, (for holding Yenengyaung area) 364, (for withdrawal from Arakan) 369, 377, (jeopardized) 378; visits Kimura, 370; decides to move into Pegu Yomas, 378; cannot help *54th Division* to cross Irrawaddy, 380

Sakurai, Major-General T.: 56 fn. 5, 141

Salin: Japanese plans to hold area of, 364, 369, 378; operations towards, 369, 371, 373–4; 114th Brigade to operate south from, 376

Salomons, Brigadier J. A.: 45, 306, 309 fn. 2

Salween Front: situation on, (August) 39, (September) 41, 116; *33rd Army* to be prepared to take offensive on, 56; operations on, 56–8, 147–8, 192–4; withdrawal of Yunnan armies from, 116, 125, 194; Japanese dispositions on (January), 193; campaign on, assessed, 194

San Bernardino Strait: naval operations in, 73–82 *passim*; mentioned, 85

Saratoga, American fleet carrier: 240

Saunders, Wing Commander A. E.: 395–6

Saw: covering operations at, 269, 283, 284, 356; mentioned, 327

Saye: operations at, 185, 256, 262

Scoones, Lieut.-General G. A. P. (later Sir Geoffry): prepares plans for capture of Yeu, 149; receives orders, (to cross Chindwin) 154, (for land advance to Yeu–Shwebo) 155; issues orders to 19th Division, 154; new appointment for, 157 and fn. 3; knighted, 161

Scott, Brigadier A. G. O'C.: 139, 215 fn. 4

Seagrim, Major H. P.: 250 fn. 2

Sea Reconnaissance Unit: 186 fn. 1, 260, 264

Seikpyu: simulated crossing at, 180, 256, 257, (referred to) 423; operations towards, 181, 182, 362, 363, 365, 370; mentioned, 269; proposed advance to, 297–8, 325; Japanese plans to hold, and forces at, 304, 357, 364; Japanese withdraw from Chauk to, 371; *Katsu Force* to withdraw from, 378

Sextant Conference: 8

Shah, H.M. escort carrier: 393

Shandatkyi: operations in area of, 376, 377, 379

Shan Levies: 192

Shan States: proposed operations in, 165, 242, 244; Force 136 operations in, 192; threat from *56th Division* in, 356, 361; air attacks on Japanese lines of retreat in, 407

Sherman, Rear-Admiral F. C.: 69 fn. 5, 74, 75

Sher Shah, Lance-Naik, V.C.: 216 fn. 2

Shima, Vice-Admiral K.: commands *5th Fleet*, 71; in battle for Leyte Gulf, 73–4, 77–8

Shin-i Force: 377 and fn. 2

Shipping: effect of India's shortage of, 15–16; Japanese losses in, 84–5, 95–6, 213, 237, 341–2, 394; local, in Arakan, 139 and fn. 1, 245 fn. 2; handled by Manila, 99; British losses in, in Indian Ocean, 213; severe Japanese shortage of, 225, 433; to be attacked by Strategic Air Force, 403; Japanese, forced to move by night in S.E.A.C., 413

'SHO-1' Operation: preparations for, begun, 53–4; plan of, 66–8; put into effect, 70–1, 73–83; effect of its failure on defence of Leyte, 86; assessment of, 87–8; its failure referred to, 225

'SHO-2, 3 and 4' Operations: 54

Shropshire, Australian cruiser: 69 fn. 4, 76 fn. 2

Shwebo: proposed capture of, 3, 11, 101, 102, 108, 149, 150, 155, 157, 165–6, 168, 172, 174; in Japanese defensive plans, 60; airfield at, (needed) 103–4, 166, 172, (opened) 183, 253 fn. 2; stockpiling at, 104–5, 199; Japanese forces believed in area of, 151, 163; development of road to, 166, 169; capture of, 177–8; air attack on, 179; suspected Japanese attack towards, abandoned, 267

Shwegu: operations in area of, 144–6 *passim*

Shwegyin: operations in area of, 160, 163, 171, 390; improvement of road through, 172, 173, 183, 199

Shweli River: 36th Division to clear crossings of, 145; Japanese force estimated to be on, 163; operations on, 187, 191–3 *passim*, 195–6; 36th Division crosses, 275–7; ferry on, 277; bridged, 278

Shwemyo: Japanese withdrawal to, 360, 381, 383–4; fighting at, 384

Shwemyo Gorge: 357

Siam: airfields in, (Japanese forced to use) 34, 188 fn. 2, (attacked) 403; *Southern Army* to hold, 226, 229; army in, reinforced, 229; French troops retreat to border of, 230; mentioned, 333; air attacks on Japanese lines of retreat to, 407; air supply for Force 136 in, 407

Sickness: wastage from, in S.E.A.C., 9, 26; losses from, (in 9th Brigade) 46 fn. 1, (in 5th Division) 49, (in XXXIII Corps) 160, (in IV and XXXIII Corps to end of March) 311; scrub typhus, 46 fn. 1, 49; malaria, (endemic in Kabaw Valley) 40 fn. 1, 103, (believed high resistance of 11th (E.A.) Division to) 40 fn. 1; in advance to Rangoon, 367

Siliguri: railhead at, 17; road link to China from, 22

Singaingmyo: operations in area of, 288, 292–3, 302, 303

Singapore: ships of *Combined Fleet* at, 67, 73, 74, 87–8, 95 fn. 4; air attacks on, 132, 404–5, (to be stopped) 405; mine-laying in area of, 214; Japanese division sent to, 229; proposed capture of, 252, (delayed) 329; railway to Bangkok from, (attacked) 404, (photographed) 408; Japanese air units at, 404–5

Singu (Chauk): Japanese withdraw to, 269; Japanese abortive attack north of, 305; fighting at, 355–6, 370

Singu (Kyaukpadaung): Japanese expect crossing at, 59; Japanese plans to reinforce, 60; 19th Division to leave brigade at, 183; to be captured, 255; operations towards, 258, 259; Japanese withdraw from, 301

Sinthe: IV Corps airhead at, 181, 253 fn. 2; squadrons located at, 253, 366; proposed Japanese offensive to capture, 286; airfield at, 362

Sinthe Chaung: Japanese plans to hold, 360, 381; operations in area of, 383–4

Sittang River: Japanese driven across, 355; Japanese withdraw to estuary of, 388–90 *passim*; operations on, 390; Japanese from Pegu Yomas to be prevented from escaping to, 398; air attack on convoy at, 406

Sittang Valley: Japanese reinforcements to be prevented from reaching, 333; Japanese plans, and forces, in, 357; communications to Irrawaddy from, 371; IV Corps cordon in, 380

Sittaung: possible development of I.W.T. service from, 20; development of roads to, 20, 103, 154; operations to, 40, 42–3; Japanese cross Chindwin at, 43; 268th Brigade to watch crossings in area of, 44; 62nd Brigade crosses Chindwin at, 154, 155

Si-u: mentioned, 130; operations in area of, 145, 148, 191, 192, 195, 196

Slim, Lieut.-General W. J. (later Sir William): discusses resumption of offensive with Giffard and with Mountbatten, 2; opens tactical H.Q. at Imphal, 2; receives orders, (from Giffard) 6, 11, 149, (from Leese) 157, 249; gives tentative tasks to Special Force, 29; his dissatisfaction with Intelligence organizations, 32; issues instructions, (for advance to Chindwin) 42, 149–50, (to cross Chindwin) 154, (on capture of Yeu-Shwebo) 155, 157, (for IV Corps to contact N.C.A.C. and take risks) 157–8, (for capture of Mandalay) 168, (for capture of Meiktila) 180, (for capture of Rangoon) 297–8, 324–5, (referred to) 355, (for operations to help modified 'Dracula') 372, 375; asks for airfields south of Akyab, 136 fn. 4; confers, (with Leese) 157, 254, 316, 327, (with Christison) 223, (with Cowan and Messervy at Meiktila) 270 fn. 3, (with Mountbatten) 317; appreciation of, (by Rees and Messervy) 159, (his ability as a commander) 428, 429; decides change of plan necessary, 160, (and informs Leese) 163–4; knighted, 161; his estimation of his opponents' intentions, 163, 420 and fn. 3; his plan for 'Extended Capital', 164–7, 242–3, (examined) 243–5, (administrative modification called for in) 247, (revised) 321–3, (referred to) 411–12, (summarized and discussed) 421–3; his deception measures, 173–4, 255, 263, (discussed) 423; warns of possible counter-offensive, 183, (and places reserve at Monywa to meet it) 262, 283; achieves complete initiative, 189, 284; and Karen Levy operations, 204–5, 332–3, 387 fn. 4; his plans, (for Irrawaddy crossings and capture of Mandalay and Meiktila) 255–6, (for advance on Rangoon) 297, 324, (reviewed) 420–4 *passim*; orders general advance across Irrawaddy, 258; Japanese conform to his moves, 271–2, 294–6; forces at his disposal (March), 284; reinforces IV Corps with 5th Division, 284, 286; recommends amphibious attack on Rangoon, 327, (referred to) 400, (commented on) 427; to capture airfields for modified 'Dracula', 329; his

Slim, Lieut.-General W. J.—*cont.*
views on rising in Burma, 334, (referred to) 335; and Aung San, 337–8; arranges release of 20th Division, 365; his orders to 36th Division on Kalaw road, 383, 388; urged by Mountbatten to speed advance on Rangoon, 385; his aircraft hit by A.A. fire, 398–9; his part in operations referred to, summarized and discussed, 416, 418, 420–3, 427, 428, 429

Small Operations Group: tasks and composition of, 30; in operations in Burma, 216, 285, 373

Smeeton, Lieut.-Colonel M. R.: 387 fn. 1

Smith, Wing-Commander H.: 219 fn. 2

Smith, Brigadier W. G.: 177

Snelling, Major-General A. J. H.: 326

Somerville, Admiral Sir James: 1, 118, 211

South African Navy:
49th Flotilla: 136 fn. 5

South-East Asia Command: decisive battles of war in, 1; operations in to be dictated by forces in, or allotted to, 1; sufficient forces in, for 'Capital', 4; 'Dracula' not within resources available to, 5, 11; casualties and sickness in, 8–9; maintenance of, by India, 15–16; ample capacity of Ls. of C. for, 19; standardization of infantry divisions in, 25–6; deficit of British manpower in, 26–7, (referred to) 325; and Indian airborne division, 28, 30 fn. 1; superiority of army in, proved, 29; disbanded battalions at disposal of, 30; clandestine and para-military formations in, 30–1; progress of its forces in Burma (August), 39; its broad mission, 107; to undertake alternative operations before 1945 monsoon, 110; reorganization of, 113–18 *passim*, (commented on) 417–18; new appointments in, 118–19; possible undermining of Allied strategy in, 126; use of American resources assigned to, 127, 208, (Argonaut decision on) 208–9; posed administrative problems, 200; receives transport aircraft, 207; future strategy for, 252; and responsibility for Burma and Burma Road, 315; strategic air offensive in, 403–5; tactical air forces in, 405; importance of photographic reconnaissance in, 408

South-East Asia Command Headquarters: N.C.A.C. under direct command of, 1, (referred to) 35 fn. 1, 113, 417; conferences at, 31, 243–4; Slim's complaint to, 32; approves recommendations of Whitworth-Jones' committee, 361; H.Q. A.L.F.S.E.A. to be alongside, 118, (referred to) 432; issues alarming meteorological report, 142; to examine amphibious operation, 241; establishment of, in Kandy discussed, 431–2

Southern Region: state of communications to Japan from, 53, 63, 433, 435; almost isolated, 225; areas vital to security of, 229; air units sent to Japan from, 233; subservience of, to Pacific, 433

Special Boats Section: 30, 264

Special Force: deficit of British manpower in, 2, 26–7; planned date of readiness of, 3; its possible use in operations, 4, 29, 165; its disbandment and allocation of units, 27–30,

Special Force—*cont.*
252; its incursions into Burma mentioned, 33, 144; 36th Division takes over animals from, 40 fn. 4; mentioned, 101; referred to, in assessment of specialized formations, 430
Special Operations Executive: 30, *now see* Force 136
Sprague, Rear-Admiral C. A. F.: 78, 79
Sprague, Rear-Admiral T. L.: 78
Spruance, Vice-Admiral R. A.: 96, 236 and fn. 4
Stalker, H.M. escort carrier: 395 fn. 2
'Stanza' Operation: *see* Rangoon
Stiletto Force: 259, 288–9
Stilwell, Lieut.-General (later General) J. W.: directives for, 1–2, 107–8, (referred to) 143, 416; submits plan, 3; his views on operations in Burma, 5, 10, (referred to) 417; progress of his forces (August), 6; deputizes for Mountbatten, 6; receives orders from American C.O.S., 22; controls 10th U.S.A.A.F., 35 fn. 1; issues orders to Chinese, 40; agrees to further advance by 36th Division, 40–1; hopes to contact Yunnan armies, 41; effect of his position on S.E.A.C. organization, 113, (referred to) 417; proposed as commander of Chinese armies, 113, 115–17; promoted General, 115; reports on situation in China, 116; recalled, 117, (referred to) 417; his appointment in China compared with Wedemeyer's, 123; plans of, 143–4
Stockwell, Brigadier (later Major-General) H. C.: in attack on Pinbaw, 40; commands 82nd (W.A.) Division, 195 fn. 3, 217; in operations in Arakan, 343–9 *passim*
Stopford, Lieut.-General M. G. N. (later Sir Montagu): commands XXXIII Corps, 39; issues orders, (for advance to Chindwin) 42, (for advance to Yeu) 149, (to airfield engineers) 157, (for capture of Mandalay) 177, (for drive down Irrawaddy) 362, 374; orders abandonment of Tiddim road, 48; completes forward concentration of corps, 156; knighted, 161; receives instructions, (for 'Extended Capital') 168–9, (for advance on Rangoon) 297, 375, (about modified 'Dracula') 372; mentioned, 171; resumes advance, 174; plans capture of Mandalay, 183–4, (referred to) 288; confers with Slim, 168, 184, 297; directs operations, (on Shwebo) 178, (on Mandalay) 283, 288, 289, (on Meiktila) 294, (on Yenangyaung) 373, (on Rangoon) 375–6, (to block routes to Pegu Yomas) 380; regroups corps, 302; allots corps armour and artillery, 362; reinforces 7th Division, 364
Stratagem, H.M. submarine: 213
Strategic Air Force: *see under* Air Forces, Allied
Stratemeyer, Major-General G. E.: confers, (with Mountbatten) 3, 203, 247, 317, 330, (with Leese) 316, 327; receives instructions from Giffard, 6; mentioned, 34; and release of aircraft to China, 125; Wedemeyer's proposals on reciprocal consultation with, 128; and 'Dracula' 330; his loyalty to Mountbatten, 420

Sturdee, Lieut.-General V. A. H.: 70
Stump, Rear-Admiral F. B.: 78, 79
Suffolk, H.M. cruiser: 393
Sultan, Lieut.-General D. I.: confers, (with Mountbatten) 3, 128, 247, 317, (with Leese) 316, 327; and control of air ferry route, 117; takes command of India–Burma Theatre and N.C.A.C., 117–18, (referred to) 417; Wedemeyer reports to, 126; and proposed directive for Wedemeyer, 126, 127; Wedemeyer's proposals on reciprocal consultation with, 127–8; and transfer of aircraft and divisions to China, 128, 279–81 *passim*, 315–17 *passim*, 338–9; in operations on Northern front, 130, 144–8 *passim*, 191, 192, 197; directed to release Chinese divisions, 145; instructions possibly given without his knowledge, 275; receives orders from Leese, 316; his loyalty to Mountbatten, 420
Sumatra: possible operation against, 'Culverin', 6–7, 8; Mountbatten asks for directive for, 13; Japanese chain of defences through, 58; air attacks on, 132; fleet attacks on, and operations off, 211–13, 342; photographic reconnaissance of, 214; *Southern Army* to hold, 226, 229; Japanese units transferred from, 229, 233; Japanese air division in, 401
Sun Li-jen, General: 192
Supreme War Direction Council (Tokyo): 53, 54
Surigao Strait: 73, 76–7, 78, 94
Suzuki, Lieut.-General S.: plans of, 68, 83; in battle for Leyte, 86–7
Swiftsure, H.M. cruiser: 212 fn. 3
Swynnerton, Brigadier C. R. A.: 139
Symes, Major-General G. W.: 118
Syriam: proposed capture of, 352, 353; captured, 395–6

Tacloban: airfield at, 69, 72, 79, 80, 84 fn. 1, 86
Takao, Japanese heavy cruiser: 74
Talingon: 261, 262
'Talon' Operation: *see under* Akyab
Tama, Japanese light cruiser: 81
Tamandu: in Japanese defensive plans, 56; Japanese forces in area of, 215, 344; *Matsu Detachment* withdraws to, 222; naval and air attacks on, 223; F.M.A. at, 246, 343–5 *passim*, 347, 348; capture of, 343–5; operations in area of, 345, 346, 348–9; 82nd (W.A.) Division responsible for area of, 346, 348
Tamu: occupied, 6, 40, (referred to) 39, 43; pipeline to be extended to, 18; development of communications through, 20, 102, 103–5, 149–50, 151, 154–5, 199, 244, 247, (engineer force for) 150–1 and fn. 1; deliveries to, 21 and fn. 3; airfield at, 38, 104, 151; operations on Tamu road, 39–40, 41–3; *Yamamoto Detachment* on Tamu road, 41; floods cut communications beyond, 44, 45; armour and artillery assembling at, 150

Tanaka, Lieut.-General N.: 44, 50 fn. 1, 151–2

Tanaka, Lieut.-General S.: 58, 272, 312

Tanlwe Chaung: operations on, 345–9 *passim*

Tarcol: 43, 44

Tarver, Lieut.-Colonel (later Brigadier) G. L.: 43, 268, 286, 358 fn. 1

Taukkyan: airstrip at, 156, 157, 254; maintenance south of, 172

Taung Bazar: 39, 135, 137

Taungdwingyi: 371, 374, 375, 385, 406

Taungtha: operations to, in advance to Meiktila, 265, 266, 268, 269; Japanese forces at, 267, 294, 298, (withdraw) 313 fn. 1; operations to reopen road to Meiktila at, 269–70, 283, 285, 305; operations from Meiktila towards, 308–10 *passim*; IV Corps to clear area of, 324; mentioned, 356, 363, 365; airfield at, 362; 268th Brigade responsible for, 362–3

Taungup: Japanese plans to hold, 56, 60, 215, 343; bridgehead to be established at, 203, 219, 249, 344; Allied information on forces in area of, 218, 223, 342; operations towards, 220, 223, 343, 344, 346–9 *passim*; Taungup-Prome road, (to be opened) 241, (tonnages to be delivered along) 243, (to be abandoned) 244, (operations on) 379, (air attacks on) 406–7; road to Tamandu from, to be cut, 345; firm base to be established at, 349; Japanese withdrawal from area of, 349, 377; 82nd (W.A.) Division in monsoon quarters at, 380

Taunton, Brigadier D. E.: 302 fn. 3, 371, 375

Tavoy: fleet operations in vicinity of, 341; mine-laying off, 403

Tengchung: mentioned, 4, 39; Chinese offensive against, 41, 56–7, (referred to) 144; Japanese casualties at, 57, 58 fn. 1

'Ten-Go' Operation: 232

Terauchi, Field-Marshal Count H.: directives for, 58, 229; recommends that 'SHO-1' begin, 67; orders priority to be given to Luzon, 68; his orders to *14th Area Army*, 71; adheres to his plan, 86; his orders to *Burma Area Army*, 229

Thabeikkyin: proposed capture of, 107, 108; bridgehead at, 174, 178–9, 184, 185, (effect of, on Japanese) 186, 194, (Japanese forces in fighting at) 187–8; mentioned, 259, 301

Thabutkon: airfield at, 267, 268, 271, (fly-in of 99th Brigade to) 268, 270; effect of its loss on Japanese plans, 295

Thakin Soe: 33

Tharrawaddy: Force 136 teams dropped near, 205, 337; proposed capture of, 374

Thayetmyo: operations in area of, 374, 375, 377; Japanese withdrawal to, 376–9 *passim*

Thayettabin: 140, 141, 142, 217

Thazi: airstrip at, 157, 254; proposed capture of, 165, 242; Force 136 operations in area of, 192; operations to, 267, 271, 287, 355, 358; mentioned, 283, 310; communications through, (to be cut) 297, 324, (attacked) 312, (estimated capacity of) 322–3, (to be developed) 326; proposals for occupation of, 302, 309, 310; Japanese plans to hold, 312, 357; mopping-up at, 361, 366, 383;

Thazi—*cont.*
deception operation in area of, 367; operations along Thazi–Kalaw road, 398

Thedaw: airstrip at, 271, 287, 303

Thimayya, Brigadier K. S.: 395 fn. 3

Thunderbolt Fighter-Bombers: mentioned, 41, 42, 182, 253, 254, 366; in operations in Burma, 175, 184, 186, 219, 299, 362

Ticonderoga, American fleet carrier: 96

Tiddim: road to, 20, (operations on) 6, 39, 42, 45–6, (Japanese forces on) 41, (proposed operations on) 101; Japanese withdraw to, 48; Japanese in area of, 48 fn. 1, 50 fn. 1; supporting arms for 5th Division's advance on, 48; airstrip at, 48, 50; capture of, 49–50; advance beyond, 152–3

Tigyaing: 145, 163, 171

Tilin: airfield at, 172 fn. 1, 182, 253 fn. 2; capture of, 180, 182; mentioned, 256 fn. 3

Tinma: 137–8, 140

Todd, Brigadier G. H. N.: 135

Tojo, General H.: his government falls, 53, (referred to) 435

Tokyo: Doolittle raid on, referred to, 53, 89, 230; mentioned, 53 fn. 2, 54, 58 fn. 2, 235; B.29 raids on, 89–91 *passim*, (referred to) 231–2; fast carrier raids on, 237

Tomcol: 266, 267

Tongzang: operations to, 46–9 *passim*, 151–2

Tonhe: development of communications through, 154, 155, 158; ferry at, 155, 158–9; 114th Brigade at, 171

Toungoo: Force 136, Karen Levy and A.F.O. operations in area of, 205, 332–3, 337, 387 fn. 4; in Japanese appreciation of Allied plans, 272; airfield and airhead at, 322, 325, 366, 381, (needed for modified 'Dracula') 330, 331, 384–5, (captured) 386, (aircraft fly into) 388, (units for defence of) 388–9, (flooded) 393; economic radius from Akyab, 321; communications to, to be secured, 324; medical centre to be at, 325; telegraph system to be re-established from, 325; Kimura's plans to hold, 357; Japanese forces reassemble near, 358 fn. 5, 387–8; operations to, 372, 381, 384–6; *55th Division* to have defended, 384 fn. 2, 388; IV Corps H.Q. at, 388; operations on Toungoo-Mawchi road, 388–9, 398

Toyoda, Admiral S.: his plan for defence of Philippines, 'SHO-1', 67, (assessed) 88; orders aircraft to undertake 'SHO-1', 71; effect of his not checking pilots' reports, 71; aims and orders of, 73–4; mentioned, 75, 78; sends force to Mindoro, 92

Trincomalee: base for fleet at, 212, 219 fn. 3, 342, 393, 394

Tromp, Dutch cruiser: 393

Tulihal: airfield at, 38, 42, 106, 326 fn. 1

Turner, Rear-Admiral R. K.: 236, 238

U-Boats: *see* German Navy

Uga, Colonel T.: 308 fn. 1, 358

Ulithi Atoll: capture of, 64, 66; used as fleet base, 74, 76, 84, 93, 95, 96, 240

Umrao Singh, Havildar, V.C.: 138 fn. 2
United States Army: railway troops of, in India, 17; command of, in China, 115, 123; maintained in China by Air Transport Command, 131
Central Pacific Forces: 63, 66
South-West Pacific Forces: 63, 66
Armies:
6th: 69, 83–4, 85, 94
8th: 98
Corps:
I: 94 and fn. 1, 95, 98
5th Amphibious: 236
X: 69, 72, 83, 86, 87
XI: 98
XIV: 94 and fn. 1, 95, 97–8
XXIV: 64, 69, 72, 83, 87
Divisions:
1st Cavalry: 72, 94 fn. 1, 98
1st Marine: 65
3rd Marine: 236
4th Marine: 236
5th Marine: 236
6th: 94 fn. 1
7th: 72
11th Airborne: 98, 99
24th: 72
31st: 65
32nd: 94 fn. 1, 98
37th: 94 fn. 1
38th: 98 fn. 2
40th: 94 fn. 1
43rd: 94 fn. 1
77th: 87
81st: 66
96th: 72
Regiments:
21st: 71–2
475th: in operations on Northern front, 145–6, 148; withdrawal of, to China, 279, 281, 316
34th Regimental Combat Team: 98 fn. 2
United States Army Air Force: squadrons of, in support of XXXIII Corps, 151; value of Iwojima to, 240; sustained rates for its transport aircraft, 204 fn. 1; squadrons of, in Eastern Air Command, 401
Air Transport Command: airfields for, 38; tasks of, 38, 131; staging post for, 41; increased tonnage carried by, 123; to transfer Chinese divisions to China, 126, 127, 315, 317; not under Mountbatten's control, 127
Northern Air Sector Force: 34, 35 fn. 1
5th: operations of, 65, 69, 84, 91, 92; airfields for, in Leyte, 72, 83–4, 85, (difficulty in establishing, referred to) 91
7th: 90, 236, 240
10th: Force 136 information useful to, 33, 192; responsible for air support on Northern front, 35 fn. 1, 36–7, 143, 409; airfields for, 38; operations of, (against Pinbaw) 40, (against Bhamo) 146; and maintenance of 36th Division, 41, 316, 326 fn. 1, 338; right of Americans to re-assign units of, 127; moves Chinese divisions, 130; possible emergency source

United States Army Air Force—*cont.*
10th U.S.A.A.F.—*cont.*
of aircraft for 'Capital', 131; withdrawal of, to China, 338; to fly at maximum rates, 338–9; general operations of its tactical squadrons, 407
14th: supplies for, 22, 133, 403; appreciation of Japanese intentions against, 124; right of Americans to re-assign units to, 127; aircraft needed to support its offensive, 130–1; supports attack on Lungling, 147; offensive against its airfields, 338
20th: 89 fn. 2
20th Bomber Command: airfields for, 37 and fn. 1; operations of, 70, 94, 95 fn. 3, 131–2, 404–5, (referred to) 231; composition of, 89 fn. 2; not under Mountbatten's control, 127; withdrawn from China, 132–3, 404; transferred to Marianas, 405
21st Bomber Command: base for, and composition of, 89 and fn. 2; bombs Japan, 89–91, (referred to) 231–2; takes over squadrons of 20th Bomber Command, 405
1st Air Commando Group: 37 fn. 1, 180, 246 fn. 2, 268, 403
1st Combat Cargo Group: 37 fn. 1, 105 fn. 2, 338
No. 1 Air Commando: 5, 105 fn. 2; to support IV Corps, 182, 253; in modified 'Dracula', 394
2nd Combat Cargo Group: 105 fn. 2
No. 2 Air Commando: 105 fn. 2; to support IV Corps, 182, 253
3rd Combat Cargo Group: 105 fn. 2, 338, 409
4th Combat Cargo Group: 37 fn. 1, 128, 129, 338
7th Heavy Bombardment Group: 125, 127, 130, 403
12th Bombardment Group: 136, 254, 404
58th Wing: 89 fn. 2
73rd Wing: 89 and fn. 2
313th Wing: 89 and fn. 2
314th Wing: 89 and fn. 2
166th Liaison Squadron: 388
317 Troop Carrier Squadron: 394
319 Troop Carrier Squadron: 394
United States Navy: submarine operations in Pacific, 74, 81, 92, 213, (effect of, on Japan's economy) 63
Fleets:
Pacific: 63
3rd: operations of, 64, 65, 70, 74–6, 78, 81–3, 84–5, 92, 93–6; to support Leyte invasion, 69; effect of reported huge losses of, on 'SHO-1' operation, 70–1; to be lured northwards, 74; *Kamikaze* attacks on, 84–5, 96, (reorganized against) 93; to make incursion into China Sea, 91; redesignated 5th Fleet, 96; achievements of, 96
5th: 65, 96, 236–40 *passim*
7th: operations of, 65, 71–2, 76–9, 94–5; to take part, (in Leyte invasion) 69, (in Luzon invasion) 94; Commonwealth ships in, 69 fn. 4; *Kamikaze* attacks on,

United States Navy—*cont.*
7th Fleet—*cont.*
  80–1, 87, 92–3, 94–5; 3rd Fleet helps, 82; suicide craft attacks on, 97–8
Joint Expeditionary Force: 236
3rd Amphibious Force: 65, 69
7th Amphibious Force: 64
Task Force 34: 75, 78, 81, 82
Unryu, Japanese aircraft carrier: 92
U.S.S.R.: Japanese aims towards, 54, 226, (failure of) 432; Japanese anxieties over attitude of, 225

'V' Force: organization and tasks of, 31–2; allotment of, 43; with Imphal Force, 44 fn. 1; report from, 348; inhabitants give information to, 431
Valiant, H.M. battleship: 211 fn. 2
Vian, Rear-Admiral Sir Philip: 212
Victoria Crosses: gained:
  in Arakan, 137 fn. 2, 138 fn. 2, 216 fn. 2, 222 fn. 1, 345 fn. 2, 347 fn. 1
  in Kennedy Peak–Fort White area, 152 fn. 3
  in Myinmu bridgehead, 261 fn. 1
  in advance on Myingyan, 270 fn. 1
  at Meiktila, 271 fn. 1, 270 fn. 3
  at Myingyan, 306
Victoria Point: possible operations against area of, 109; bombarded, 393; railway to, attacked, 404
Victorious, H.M. fleet carrier: 211, 212
Vincent, Air Vice-Marshal S. F.: 36, 405
Visual Control Posts: description of, 254 and fn. 3; in operations in Burma, 257 fn. 2, 264, 287, 303 fn. 2, 381 fn. 3, 387 fn. 1, 394, 405
Vital Corner: 50, 152

Walker, Vice-Admiral H. T. C.: 342, 393
Wangjing: airfield at, 38, 254
Wanting: proposed pipeline and road via, 18, 22, 41; Yunnan armies to halt at, 130 and fn. 2; Japanese forces at, 144, 193; operations towards, 147–8, 192–4, (new plan for) 191
Warazup: Ledo Road reaches, 22; extension of road forward of, 23; airfield at, 38
War Cabinet: on political implications of supporting rising in Burma, 336–7
War Office: unable to maintain infantry reinforcement pool in S.E.A.C., 26–7; decide to reduce 'Python' qualifying period, 27; and formation of Indian airborne division, 28; agree to disbandment of Special Force, 29
Warramunga, Australian destroyer: 69 fn. 4, 72 fn. 1
Warren, Brigadier (later Major-General) D. F. W.: 45; commands 5th Division, 48; in advance to Tiddim, 49, 50; killed, 310 fn. 1
Wastage: *see also* Casualties *and* Sickness: in S.E.A.C., (in first 6 months) 8–9, (in first half of 1944) 26; in Special Force, 29

Wavell, Field-Marshal Earl: 161, 416 fn. 2
Waw: 389, 390; Japanese troops in area of, 391
Wedemeyer, Lieut.-General A. C.: 9; replaces Stilwell in China, 117–18, 121, (commented on) 417–18; his assignment compared with Stilwell's, 123; his appreciation of Japanese intentions, 123–4; his plan 'Alpha', 124, (referred to) 278, 280; his requests for Chinese divisions and aircraft from S.E.A.C., 124–5, 128, 278–80, 281, 338, (Mountbatten's views on) 130–1, 279–80, (summarized and commented on) 418–20; aircraft released to, 125, 129–31 *passim*; reports to American C.O.S., 126, 128; his recommendations on orders to Mountbatten, 126; proposed instructions for, 126–8, 315, 317; his proposals for reciprocal information between S.E.A.C. and China, 127–8; recommends withdrawal of 20th Bomber Command, 132; protests to Chiang Kai-shek, 147–8; asks Chinese to resume advance, 192; returns aircraft to S.E.A.C., 207; mentioned, 331
Welaung: mentioned, 182, 326, 363; operations in area of, 267–9 *passim*, 285
Westcol: role of, in 7th Division's deception plans, 256; formation of, 256 fn. 3; operations of, 284, 356, 362, 374
Western, Brigadier E. W. D.: 139, 347 fn. 2
Weston, Lieutenant W. B., V.C.: 271 fn. 1
Wheeler, Lieut.-General R. A.: 18, 118, 247
Whitworth-Jones, Air Vice-Marshal J.: report of his committee, 34–6
Wilkinson, Vice-Admiral T.: 94, 97
Wilson, Field-Marshal Sir Henry Maitland: 319
Wilson-Brand, Brigadier A. T.: 347 fn. 2
Wood, Brigadier (later Major-General) G. N.: B.G.S. XXXIII Corps, 44; commands 25th Division, 135; in operations in Arakan, 140, 215–18 *passim*, 220, 222, 223, 344, 346
Woodford, Brigadier E. C. J.: 365, 371, 375
Woodhouse, Brigadier L. J.: 331
Woolner, Major-General C. G.: 39, 135 fn. 4
Wright, Brigadier M. V.: 358
Wundwin: operations in area of, 287, 296, 302–4 *passim*, 310, 366, 383; area to be cleared, 294, 297, 324; Japanese units, (sent to) 295, (withdrawing to) 306 fn. 4; road to, during Meiktila operations, 307, 308; *15th Army* withdrawing east of, 312; *20th Division* concentrates in area of, 362, 366
Wuntho: *15th Division* believed in area of, 151, 163; report on road to, called for, 154; proposed capture of, to isolate Japanese, 158; *19th Division* in area of, 171

Yamamoto Detachment: 41, 43
Yamamoto, Major-General T.: 273 fn. 3; IV Corps' knowledge of offensive by, 286, 304; his offensive ends, 305; to defend Yenangyaung, 364; promoted and posted to Tokyo, 365 fn. 1

Yamashiro, Japanese battleship: 77

Yamashita, Lieut.-General T.: commands *14th Area Army*, 68; protests over change of orders, 71, (referred to) 435; his orders on defence of Leyte, 83, 86, 87; wishes to suspend reinforcement of Leyte, 86, (referred to) 88, 435; cannot spare troops for Mindoro, 92; plans of, for defence of Luzon, 96–7; declares Manila open town, 97, (referred to) 99; orders withdrawal from Manila, 99

Yamoto, Japanese battleship: 74, 75

Yamazaki, Colonel: 146, 147

Yamazaki Force: 146, 147 and fn. 1, 193

Yamethin: Force 136 operations near, 249; *49th Division* to withdraw to, 313; 'Character' to begin when 14th Army reaches, 333; Honda escapes to, 360; fighting at, 382–4

Yanaung: operations in area of, during action at Pyawbwe, 313, 357–9 *passim*, 383

Yangtze River: 55, 226, 228, 405

Yazagyo: operations towards, 44–5, 150; road from Tamu reaches, 151; airstrip at, 156, 157; 2nd Division concentrates at, 156–7; tonnages delivered by road to, 409 fn. 3

Yenangyaung: oilfields vital to *Burma Area Army*, 58; Japanese plans and forces for defence of, 59, 60, 188, 295, 357, 364, 369, 372, (IV Corps' estimation of) 267; mentioned, 167, 256; deception threat to be made on, 180, 181; proposed capture of, 242, 298, 325, 356, 363, 371, (capture of Kyaukpadaung prerequisite to) 364; proposed Japanese counter-offensive from, 273, 298; F.M.A. to be established at, 325; effect of capture of, on Japanese plans, 357, 374, 377,

Yenangyaung—*cont.*
378; 7th Division closing in on, 366, 370; terrain at, 372; capture of, 372–3; 33rd Brigade at, 375

Yenanma: operations in area of, 376–9 *passim*

Yeu: proposed capture of, 3, 4, 101, 102, 107, 108, 149, 157–8, 168, 172, 174, (Slim's views on) 149–50, 155, 160, 163; development of communications to, 20, 101, 104, 149, 169, 172; Japanese rearguard withdraws on, 43 fn. 5; airfields, (required in area of) 103–4, 106, 172, (captured) 177, (opened) 183; operations on Yeu road, 160, 163, 171, 172; Japanese units at, 177 fn. 2; tonnages carried by road to, 409 fn. 3

Yindaw: action at, 287; capture of, 358–9

Yonai, Admiral M.: forms joint Cabinet, 53, (referred to) 435

Yoshida, Colonel: 271

Yoshida, Major-General G.: 58

Yunnan Armies: *see* Chinese Yunnan Armies

'Z' Force: tasks of, 30; Slim proposes expansion of, 32; amalgamation of, with Force 136, 32, 33 fn. 1

Zayetkon: 17th Division sweeps to, 287; 20th Division moves through, 362, 365, 366, 371

Zia-ud-Din, Captain: 47

Zibyu Taungdan: Japanese forces defending, 44, 56, 151, 157; description of, 158

Zuiho, Japanese carrier: 81

Zuikaku, Japanese carrier: 81

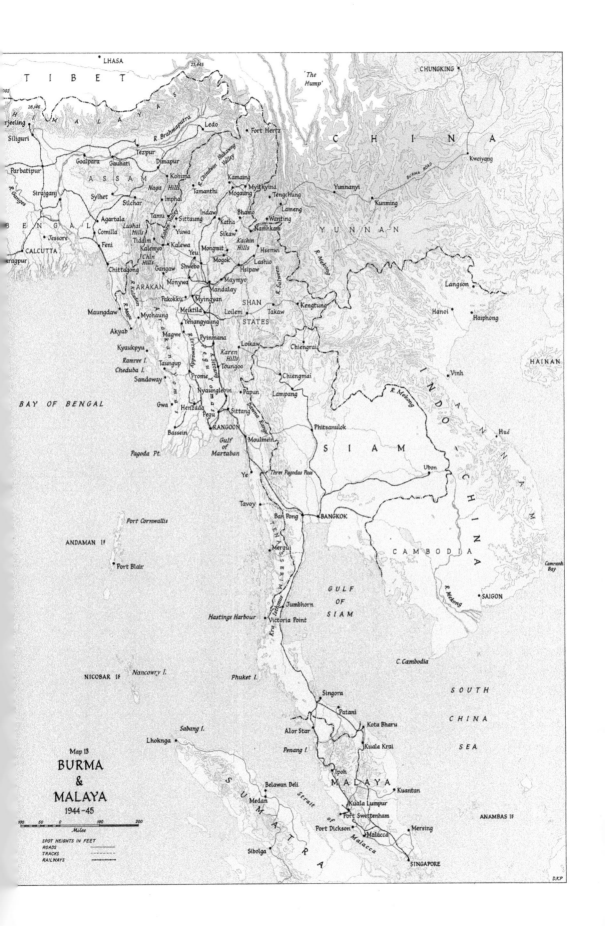

LHASA

TIBET

CHUNGKING

'The
Hump'

CHINA

28,146

25,445

Siliguri

Darjeeling

HIMALAYA

R. Brahmaputra

Ledo

Fort Hertz

Kweiyang

Parbatipur

ASSAM

Tezpur

Dimapur

Goalpara

Gauhati

Kohima

Kamaing

BURMA ROAD

R. Chindwin

Hukawng
Valley

Myitkyina

Mogaung

Tengchung

Yunnanyi

Kunming

Sirajganj

Sylhet

Silchar

Imphal

Naga Hills

Tamanthi

Indaw

Bhamo

Lameng

Wanting

Yuwa

Katha

Sikaw

Namkham

Kachin
Hills

Hsenwi

R. Salween

R. Mekong

YUNNAN

Agartala

Comilla

Feni

Tamu

Sittaung

Lushai
Hills

Tiddim

Kalemyo

Kalewa

Mongmit

Yeu

Kachin
Hills

Lashio

BENGAL

CALCUTTA

Jessore

ragpur

Chittagong

Chin
Hills

Gangaw

Shwebo

Hsipaw

Langson

Monywa

Mandalay

Maymyo

ARAKAN

Pakokku

Myingyan

SHAN

Loilem

Takaw

Kengtung

Hanoi

Haiphong

Maungdaw

Myohaung

Meiktila

STATES

Yenangyaung

Akyab

Magwe

Pyinmana

Loikaw

Chiengrai

HAINAN

Kyaukpyu

Taungup

Prome

Karen
Hills

Toungoo

Chiengmai

Vinh

Ramree I.

Cheduba I.

Sandoway

Nyaunglebin

Papun

Lampang

R. Mekong

BAY OF BENGAL

Gwa

Henzada

Pegu

Sittang

RANGOON

Phitsanulok

SIAM

Hué

Bassein

Gulf
of
Martaban

Moulmein

Pagoda Pt.

Ye

Three Pagodas Pass

Ubon

INDO-CHINA

Tavoy

Ban Pong

BANGKOK

CAMBODIA

Camranh
Bay

Port Cornwallis

ANDAMAN Is

Mergui

R. Mekong

SAIGON

Port Blair

TENASSERIM

GULF
OF
SIAM

C. Cambodia

NICOBAR Is

Nancowry I.

Phuket I.

Jumbhorn

Hastings Harbour

Kra Isthmus

Victoria Point

Singora

SOUTH

Sabang I.

Patani

Kota Bharu

CHINA

Lhoknga

Alor Star

Kuala Krai

SEA

Penang I.

Ipoh

BURMA
&
MALAYA

Belawan Deli

MALAYA

Kuantan

ANAMBAS Is

1944-45

Medan

Kuala Lumpur

Port Swettenham

SUMATRA

Strait

Port Dickson

Mersing

of

Malacca

Malacca

Sibolga

SINGAPORE

Map 13

100 50 0   100   200
Miles

SPOT HEIGHTS IN FEET
ROADS
TRACKS
RAILWAYS

D.K.P

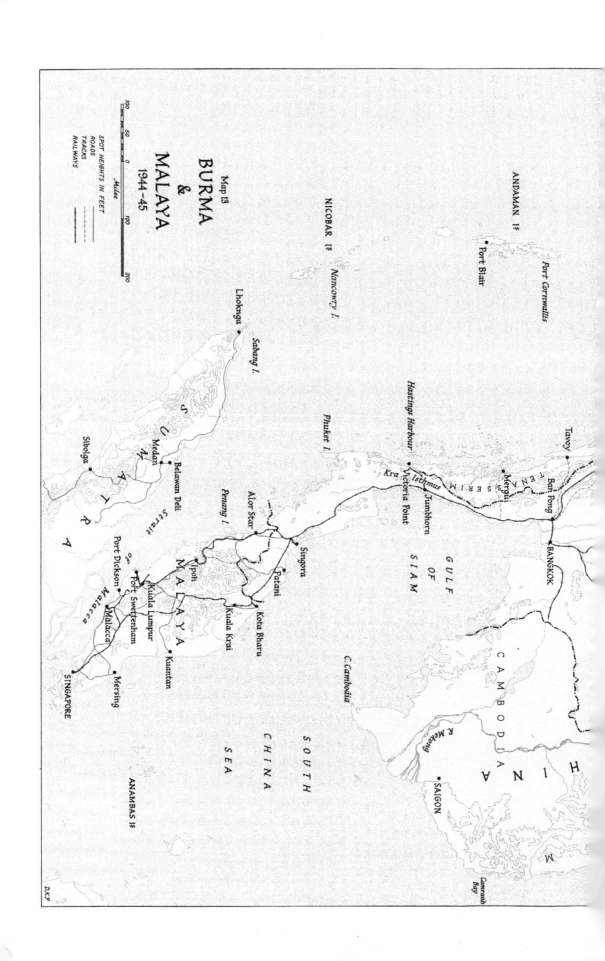

Map 13
BURMA
&
MALAYA
1944–45

SPOT HEIGHTS IN FEET
ROADS
TRACKS
RAILWAYS

Miles
100   50   0   100   200

ANDAMAN IS

Port Cornwallis

Port Blair

NICOBAR IS

Nancowry I.

Tavoy

Mergui

Ban Pong

BANGKOK

TENASSERIM

Hastings Harbour

Kra Isthmus

Victoria Point

Jumbhorn

GULF
OF
SIAM

C. Cambodia

R. Mekong

CAMBODIA

CHINA

SAIGON

Camranh
Bay

Phuket I.

Lhoknga

Sabang I.

Medan

Belawan Deli

Sibolga

SUMATRA

Penang I.

Alor Star

Malacca Strait

Port Dickson

Port Swettenham

Kuala Lumpur

Malacca

MALAYA

Ipoh

Singora

Patani

Kota Bharu

Kuala Krai

Kuantan

Mersing

SINGAPORE

SOUTH
CHINA
SEA

ANAMBAS IS

D.K.P

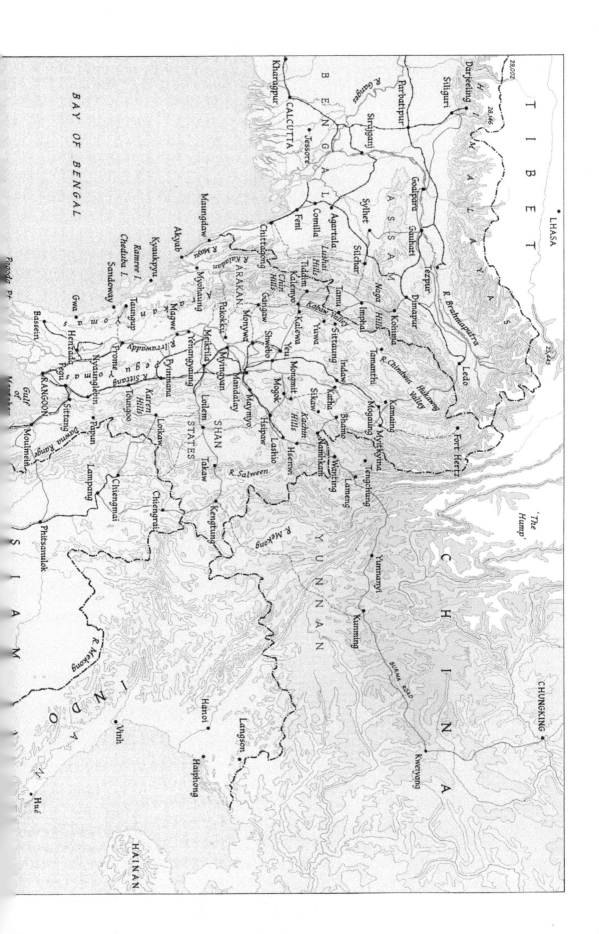

Lightning Source UK Ltd.
Milton Keynes UK
UKHW051150151220
374883UK00004B/28